New
TEPS
MASTER900

New TEPS MASTER 900

저자 | 죠셉킴
초판 1쇄 발행 | 2009년 9월 21일
초판 4쇄 발행 | 2015년 3월 10일

발행인 | 박효상
총괄이사 | 이종선
기획·편집 | 박운희, 박혜민
디자인 | 손정수
마케팅 | 이태호, 이전희
디지털콘탠츠 | 이지호
관리 | 김태옥

Special Staff
표지 | 장선숙
내지 | 연디자인
편집 | 강윤혜
조판 | 연디자인

출판등록 | 제10-1835호
발행처 | 사람in
주소 | 121-839 서울시 마포구 양화로11길 14-10(서교동) 4F
전화 | 02) 338-3555(代)   팩스 | 02) 338-3545
e-mail | saramin@netsgo.com
Homepage | www.saramin.com

:: 책값은 뒤표지에 있습니다.
:: 파본은 바꾸어 드립니다.

ⓒ죠셉킴 2009

ISBN 978-89-6049-138-0 18740
       978-89-6049-135-9 (세트)

사람이 중심이 되는 세상, 세상과 소통하는 책 **사람in**

New
TEPS
MASTER900 죠셉킴
TEPS 목표 점수 올리기 프로젝트 650 · 750 · 900

사람in
saram
in.com

머리말

본 교재는 대한민국 대표 영어시험 TEPS에서 900점 이상을 목표로 하는 Advanced level students를 위해 만든 실전 종합서로서 기출 유형에 맞춘 문제들과 강의 노하우 전수를 통해 중고급 레벨의 학습자가 원하는 고득점을 가장 빠른 시간 안에 얻는 훈련을 할 수 있도록 기획되었습니다.

TEPS 공부를 이미 시작하셨거나 여러 번 시험을 보았는데 점수가 800점 이하이신 분, 각종 특목고나 대학에 특차 입학을 준비하는 중고생들, 의치학 대학원(DEET나 MEET)을 준비하시는 분, 신대원(장로회신학대학교, 총신대학교)를 준비하시는 분, 그리고 미국식 실용영어의 전체적인 감각을 키워서 다양한 영어 매체들을 자유롭게 접하고 싶으신 분들이 계시다면 바로 이 책이 적격이라고 자부합니다.

청해 파트는 엄선된 기출 유형의 문제들을 가지고 최근 TEPS 유형에 맞추어 TEPS 청해문제들의 다양한 유형과 해법을 정리합니다. 또한 TEPS 출제자들의 심리를 파악하여 다양한 발음과 선택지의 오답 배치 유형 등을 다양하게 섭렵할 수 있도록 문제를 선별하였습니다. 역대 기출 문제 변형과 온라인, 오프라인에서 최고로 엄선된 자료로만 100% 구성하여 최대한 많은 문제를 유형별·토픽별로 접하며 실전 감각을 높이 도록 구성했습니다.

문법 파트의 경우 단순히 문제만 나열한 것이 아니라 최신 출제 경향에 맞게 Chapter를 정리하여 기출 포인트를 먼저 정리해서 각 단원별 핵심 사항을 파악한 후 Actual Test 문제들을 통해 풍부하고도 자세한 실전문제 풀이 연습을 하실 수 있도록 했습니다. 문법 실력이 조금 약하신 분들도 모두 무난하게 소화하실 수 있게 구성되었습니다.

어휘 파트는 주제별, 유형별로 정리된 실전문제들을 풀어보며 정리할 수 있도록 하였습니다. 또한 자세한 해설을 통해 이해를 도왔습니다. 어휘 고득점을 목표로 하는 분들은 이 문제들을 통해 가장 빠른 시간 안에 만점을 얻으실 수 있습니다.

TEPS 준비생들이 가장 부담스러워하는 독해 파트의 경우 먼저 저자의 실전 노하우가 녹아있는 해설과 Example 문제들을 통해 먼저 워밍업을 하신 후 미니 테스트 형식으로 구성된 Actual Test들을 통해 TEPS 독해 전략인 속독과 다독의 해법을 자연스럽게 익힐 수 있도록 도왔습니다.

아무쪼록 본 교재와 함께 원하시는 TEPS 900점의 꿈을 이루시길 기원합니다.

서초동에서

Joseph Kim

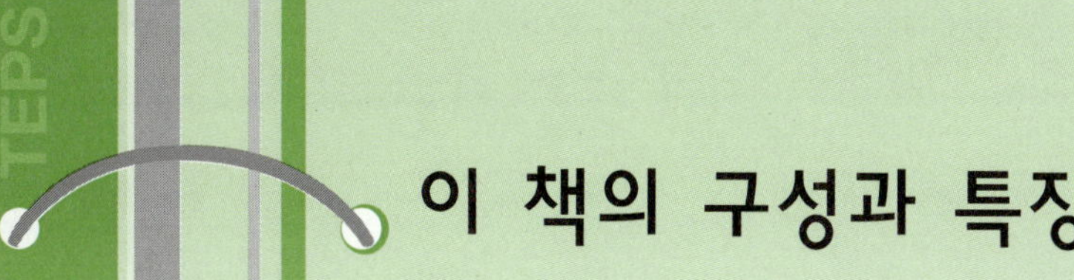

이 책의 구성과 특징

900점 완전 공략을 위한 New TEPS MASTER 900

이 책은 TEPS 목표 점수 올리기 프로젝트 〈New TEPS MASTER〉 시리즈 중 900점 공략을 위한 책입니다.

대한민국 TEPS 최고 강사의 점수대별 전략서

대한민국 TEPS 최고 강사 죠셉킴 선생님이 TEPS 관리위원회에서 출제한 10년간의 정기시험을 철저히 분석, 최신 경향에 꼭 맞춘 문제만을 수록하여 만든 문제풀이 중심의 점수대별 전략서입니다.

영역별 만점을 위한 900점대 고수들의 학습법 소개

TEPS의 영역별 구성 및 최신 출제 경향은 물론, TEPS 900점을 목표로 하고 있는 중급 학습자를 위한 '900점대 고수들의 학습법'을 수록하여 각 영역별로 만점을 얻기 위한 비법을 소개하였습니다.

4대 영역을 한 권에 아우르는 문제집

TEPS 4대 영역을 한 권에 끝낼 수 있어 학습하시기에 편리합니다. 최신 출제 경향에 맞추어 업그레이드된 문제를 풀며 학습자가 자연스럽고 효율적으로 TEPS 유형을 익힐 수 있도록 구성하였습니다.

900점 공략을 위해 실전 감각 최대화

TEPS 900점 공략을 위해 문제 형태별로 요점을 간단히 정리하고, 해당 실전 문제를 푸는 데에 집중함으로써 실전 감각을 최대한 키울 수 있도록 하였습니다.

스스로 학습을 돕는 스마트 해설

TEPS 고급 학습자들을 위해 900점 획득이라는 목표에 맞추어 수험자 입장에서 출제자의 의도를 보다 쉽고 정확히 파악할 수 있도록 상세하고 친절한 해설을 실었습니다.

※ 수록된 CD의 음원은 사람in 홈페이지(www.saramin.com)에서 MP3 파일로 다운로드 받으실 수 있습니다.

목차

Vocabulary

Reading Comprehension

New TEPS MASTER 900

Introduction

TEPS는 어떤 시험인가요?

1. TEPS란 어떤 시험인가요?

TEPS는 Test of English Proficiency developed by Seoul National University의 약자로 서울대학교가 주관하고 시행하는 새로운 영어 능력 검정 시험입니다. TEPS는 국내외 여러 대학에 종사하는 최고 수준의 영어 관련 전문가 100여 명에 가까운 인원이 출제하고 세계의 권위자로 구성된 자문 위원회에서 검토하는 시험입니다.

2. 어떤 곳에서 TEPS 점수를 요구하나요?

각종 고시를 비롯하여 많은 대기업과 공사의 취업 자격 시험으로 활용될 뿐만 아니라 대부분의 정부 기관과 군 기관에 의해서 인사 제도와 해외 파견 자격을 검정하는 시험으로 활용되고 있습니다. 최근에는 대학과 기업체, 정부 기관 중심으로 TEPS의 활용도가 크게 증가했습니다. 그러므로 다수의 응시자가 입시, 입사 지원, 고시 준비 등 특정한 목적을 위해서 응시하고 있습니다.

3. TEPS 문제는 어떻게 출제되나요?

한국인에게 맞는 시험인 TEPS는 영어 교육과 검정 분야에서 풍부한 경험을 갖고 있는 전문 출제자들이 영어와 한국어의 대조 분석과 오류 분석 이론에 근거하여 출제함으로써 한국인들이 특히 많이 범하는 영어의 실수를 정확히 짚어줍니다.

4. 일 년에 몇 번 정도 시험을 볼 수 있나요?

일 년에 12번 매월 첫째 일요일이나 토요일에 시행되고 있습니다. 자세한 내용과 변경 사항은 TEPS 관리 위원회 홈페이지(http://www.teps.or.kr)를 보시면 알 수 있습니다.

5. 주로 어떤 문제가 출제됩니까?

실용 영어 능력 시험 TEPS는 현장 영어 구사 능력을 중점적으로 테스트하기 위해 실제 생활에서 일어날 수 있거나 자주 접할 수 있는 상황 위주로 출제됩니다. 일상적인 대화는 물론 일상적으로 접할 수 있는 신문, 방송, 잡지, 서신, 광고, 전화 메시지 등이 모두 출제 범주에 포함됩니다.

6. TEPS의 시험 시간은 얼마나 되나요?

시행 초기에는 총 2시간 40분이었지만 2001년 2월 제13회 정기 시험부터 영역별 수험 시간 단축이 적용되어 현재는 2시간 20분이 소요됩니다. 청취, 문법, 어휘, 독해 총 4개 영역으로 나누어 청취 60문항 55분, 문법 50문항 25분, 어휘 50문항 15분, 독해 40문항 45분으로 구성됩니다.

7. 시험 점수는 얼마 후에 알게 되나요?

정기 시험의 성적은 시험일로부터 15일 이후 ARS(060-700-2884)나 TEPS 홈페이지
(http://www.teps.or.kr)에서 확인이 가능합니다. 정기 시험 성적표는 시험일로부터 대략 30일 안
에 우편으로 발송되고 특별 시험 성적표는 시험일로부터 7일 이내에 해당 기관이나 단체로 통보됩니다.

8. 각 레벨 중 가장 많은 분포를 보이는 레벨은 어떤 것인가요?

급수별 인원을 분석해보면 전체 80%의 응시자가 2급과 3급 사이 즉 2^+급, 2급, 3^+급, 3급에 집중되
어 있습니다. 그 중 2^+급을 제외한 2급과 3^+급, 3급의 응시생 비율은 세 레벨 모두 전체 수험자의 20%
정도로 비슷합니다.

9. TEPS 자격증은 어떤 것인가요?

2004년에 TEPS는 민간 자격 국가 공인을 취득하였습니다. TEPS 1^+급, 1급, 2^+급, 2급에 해당하는
응시자는 국가에서 인정하는 공인 증서를 발급 받을 수 있습니다.

10. TEPS와 TOEIC, TOEFL의 차이점은 무엇인가요?

TOEIC이나 TOEFL은 비즈니스나 대학원 진학을 위한 특정한 목적으로 만들어져 비즈니스 영어나
학문적인 영어가 주를 이룹니다. 그러나 TEPS는 실제 의사 소통 능력을 측정하기 위한 시험이라는
점에서 차이가 있습니다. TEPS 청취와 TOEIC 청취의 차이점은 상호 응대(interaction)를 다루는
비중입니다. TOEIC의 Part 1은 사진을 묘사하는 단순한 문제를 묻고 Part 2, 3에서 대화를 다루지
만 TEPS는 Part 1, 2, 3 모두 대화에 알맞은 응답을 고르는 문제입니다. 그 중에서 Part 3, 4는
TOEIC처럼 구체적인 정보를 묻는 문제가 아니라 전체적인 분위기, 대화의 주제, 대화를 근거로 추
론할 수 있는 것 등을 묻습니다. TOEIC은 Part 5, 6에서 대부분 문어체 문법과 어휘를 묻는 데 반해
TEPS는 구어체와 문어체로 구분해서 각각의 문법과 어휘를 묻습니다. TOEIC Part 7은 각 지문별
로 2~3개의 질문이 주어지고, TEPS는 한 지문 당 한 개의 문제만이 주어집니다. 또한 주제 찾기, 요
점 찾기, 전체 흐름에서 어색한 문장 찾기 등 문제 유형이 TOEIC과 다릅니다.

다른 시험과 구별되는 TEPS만의

1. 부분적인 학습이 가능한 시험이 아닙니다.

기존의 테스트는 시험 소재의 제한과 편협성으로 말미암아 수험자들이 영어 실력 향상에는 별로 관계 없는 찍기 요령이나 단편적인 시험 지식 습득에 그침으로써 교육적인 기능이 무시되는 경향이 있었지만, TEPS는 거의 모든 분야에서 다양한 소재를 바탕으로 출제되기 때문에 시험 준비를 하는 것이 바로 실력을 쌓는 것이라는 등식이 성립합니다.

2. 속도화 시험입니다.

암기 위주의 학습이나 시험 요령을 터득한 수험자가 고득점을 얻지 못하도록 속도화 시험을 도입하여 짧은 시간 안에 문제를 풀게 함으로써 완전히 숙달되지 않고는 풀기 어렵게 만들어 살아 있는 의사소통 능력을 평가할 수 있습니다.

3. 순수한 청해 능력을 측정합니다.

청해력 평가시 선택지까지 모두 들려줌으로써 순수한 청해력 평가를 꾀했으며 1지문 1문항 원칙을 지켜 기억 부담을 최소화했습니다. 또한 정상 속도로 선택지까지 들려줌으로써 순수한 청해력 평가뿐만 아니라 속도화 시험을 통해 영어 지식이 아닌 영어의 잠재 능력을 평가하여 진정한 영어 실력 판별이 가능토록 하였습니다. 청해 영역의 경우, 인쇄된 문제지가 주어지지 않음으로써 미리 문제를 보고 감을 잡는 요령이 통할 가능성을 방지하였으며, 독해 영역에서도 1지문 1문항 원칙을 지켜 한 문제의 답을 알면 나머지 문제의 답도 유추할 수 있는 가능성을 배제하였습니다.

4. 1지문 1문항 방식의 시험입니다.

1지문 1문항 방식의 시험은 지문을 이해하지 못했을 때 그 지문에서 출제된 여러 문제를 연속적으로 틀리게 되는 문제점을 보완한 것입니다. 문항 반응 이론을 적용할 경우, 낮은 난이도의 문제를 많이 틀린 수험자가 높은 난이도의 문제를 맞힐 경우, 실력에 관계없이 추측으로 우연히 맞추었을 가능성이 높다고 보고 감점 처리합니다. 또한 다양한 지문이 주어지기 때문에 지문의 배경 지식으로 인한 편파성을 극소화시킴으로써 점수의 타당성을 높일 수 있습니다.

5. 절대평가 시험입니다.

상대평가를 지향하는 다른 테스트들과는 달리 절대평가(Criterion-referenced Test)를 지향함으로써 수험 집단이나 제반 상황이 달라져도 개인의 시험 점수는 안정적으로 나타납니다.

특징은 어떤 것이 있습니까?

TOEIC, TOEFL과의 점수대 비교

TOEIC	TOEFL	TEPS
980	287 ~	951 ~
950 ~ 975	273 ~ 287	901 ~ 950
910 ~ 945	253 ~ 273	851 ~ 900
875 ~ 905	247 ~ 253	801 ~ 850
835 ~ 870	237 ~ 247	751 ~ 800
790 ~ 830	223 ~ 237	701 ~ 750
750 ~ 785	213 ~ 223	651 ~ 700
705 ~ 745	207 ~ 213	601 ~ 650
650 ~ 700	193 ~ 207	551 ~ 600
600 ~ 645	177 ~ 193	501 ~ 550
545 ~ 595	167 ~ 177	451 ~ 500
490 ~ 540	163 ~ 167	400 ~ 450

TEPS의 영역별 구성

TEPS는 청해, 문법, 어휘, 독해의 4개 영역에 걸쳐 총 200문항으로 구성되어 있으며 시험 시간은 140분입니다. 문항 반응 이론(IRT)에 따라 채점하기 때문에 전부 맞아도 990점이고 모두 틀려도 10점은 나옵니다.

영역	PART별 내용	문항 수	시간/배점
청 취 Listening Comprehension	Part Ⅰ: 문장 하나를 듣고 이어질 대화 고르기	15	55분/400점
	Part Ⅱ: 3문장의 대화를 듣고 이어질 대화 고르기	15	
	Part Ⅲ: 6-8문장의 대화를 듣고 이어질 대화 고르기	15	
	Part Ⅳ: 단문의 내용을 듣고 질문에 해당하는 답 고르기	15	
문 법 Grammar	Part Ⅰ: 대화문의 빈칸에 적절한 표현 고르기	20	25분/100점
	Part Ⅱ: 문장의 빈칸에 적절한 표현 고르기	20	
	Part Ⅲ: 대화문에서 어법상 틀리거나 어색한 부분 고르기	5	
	Part Ⅳ: 단문에서 어법상 틀리거나 어색한 부분 고르기	5	
어 휘 Vocabulary	Part Ⅰ: 대화문의 빈칸에 적절한 단어 고르기	25	15분/100점
	Part Ⅱ: 단문의 빈칸에 적절한 단어 고르기	25	
독 해 Reading Comprehension	Part Ⅰ: 지문을 읽고 질문의 빈칸에 들어갈 내용 고르기	16	45분/400점
	Part Ⅱ: 지문을 읽고 질문에 가장 적절한 답 고르기	21	
	Part Ⅲ: 지문을 읽고 문맥상 어색한 내용 고르기	3	
총계	13개 Parts	200	140분/990점*

* 총 배점은 산술상 1,000점이 나오나 실제로는 IRT(Item Response Theory)에 의하여 최고점이 990점, 최저점이 10점으로 조정됨.

TEPS의 등급 구성

등급	점수	영역	능력 검정 기준
1⁺급	901–990	전반	교양 있는 원어민에 버금가는 정도로 의사소통이 가능하고 전문 분야 업무에 대처할 수 있음
	361–400	청해	교양 있는 원어민에 버금가는 수준의 청해력
		독해	교양 있는 원어민에 버금가는 수준의 독해력
	91–100	문법	교양 있는 원어민에 버금가는 수준으로 내재화된 문법 능력
		어휘	교양 있는 원어민에 버금가는 수준으로 내재화된 어휘력
1급	801–900	전반	단기간 집중 교육을 받으면 대부분의 의사소통이 가능하고 전문 분야 업무에 별 무리 없이 대처할 수 있음
	321–360	청해	다양한 상황의 수준 높은 내용을 별 무리 없이 이해할 수 있는 정도의 청해력
		독해	다양한 소재의 수준 높은 내용을 별 무리 없이 이해할 수 있는 정도의 독해력
	81–90	문법	다양한 구문을 별 무리 없이 신속하게 이해할 수 있을 정도로 내재화된 문법 능력
		어휘	다양한 표현을 별 무리 없이 신속하게 이해할 수 있을 정도로 내재화된 어휘력
2⁺급	701–800	전반	단기간 집중 교육을 받으면 일반 분야 업무를 큰 어려움 없이 수행할 수 있음
	281–320	청해	일반적인 상황의 보통 수준의 내용을 별 무리 없이 이해하는 정도의 청해력
		독해	일반적인 소재의 보통 수준의 내용을 별 무리 없이 이해하는 정도의 독해력
	71–80	문법	일반적인 구문을 별 무리 없이 이해하는 정도의 문법 능력
		어휘	일반적인 표현을 별 무리 없이 이해하는 정도의 어휘력
2급	601–700	전반	중장기간 집중 교육을 받으면 일반 분야 업무를 큰 어려움 없이 수행할 수 있음
	241–280	청해	일반적인 상황의 보통 수준의 내용을 대체로 이해하는 정도의 청해력
		독해	일반적인 소재의 보통 수준의 내용을 대체로 이해하는 정도의 독해력
	61–70	문법	일반적인 구문을 대체로 이해하는 정도의 문법 능력
		어휘	일반적인 표현을 대체로 이해하는 정도의 어휘력
3⁺급	501–600	전반	중장기간 집중 교육을 받으면 한정된 분야의 업무를 큰 어려움 없이 수행할 수 있음
	201–240	청해	일반적인 상황의 보통 수준의 내용을 다소 이해하는 정도의 청해력
		독해	일반적인 소재의 보통 수준의 내용을 다소 이해하는 정도의 독해력
	51–60	문법	일반적인 구문에 대한 의미 파악이 어느 정도 가능한 문법 능력
		어휘	일반적인 표현에 대한 의미 파악이 어느 정도 가능한 어휘력
3급	401–500	전반	중장기간 집중 교육을 받으면 한정된 분야의 업무를 다소 미흡하지만 큰 지장은 없이 수행할 수 있음
	161–200	청해	일반적인 상황의 보통 수준의 내용을 이해하기 다소 어려운 정도의 청해력
		독해	일반적인 소재의 보통 수준의 내용을 이해하기 다소 어려운 정도의 독해력
	41–50	문법	일반적인 구문에 대한 신속한 의미 파악이 다소 어려운 정도의 문법 능력
		어휘	일반적인 표현에 대한 신속한 의미 파악이 다소 어려운 정도의 어휘력
4⁺급	301–400	전반	장기간의 집중 교육을 받으면 한정된 분야의 업무를 대체로 어렵게 수행할 수 있음
	201–300		
5⁺급	101–200	전반	단편적인 지식만을 갖추고 있어 의사소통이 거의 불가능함
	10–100		

900점대 고수들의 학습법

■ 청해 (Listening Comprehension)

1. 모의고사라고 해서 한 번 풀고 넘어가는 것이 아니라 풀어본 문제를 두세 번씩 다시 풀어본다.

TEPS 문제들은 유형이 다양하게 출제되고 문제를 푸는 행위 자체가 좋은 학습이 되기 때문에 한 번만 풀고 정답을 확인하기보다는 2회 이상 문제를 다시 풀어보는 것이 실제 시험장에서 청취력 향상에 도움이 될 뿐 아니라 의문문, 평서문, 대의 파악과 같은 TEPS 청해 문제의 각 유형을 숙지하고 Part별 시간 안배 연습을 하는 데에 상당한 도움이 될 수 있다.

2. Part 1, 2는 Dictation(받아쓰기)을 반드시 하자.

청해 Part 1, 2의 경우 크게 나누어 봤을 때 의문문과 평서문으로 분류할 수 있으며 문장의 첫 마디, 시제, 인칭, 동음이의어를 가지고 함정을 만든 오답을 배치하는 경우가 많으므로 각 문장을 듣고 받아쓰기를 통해 확실하게 대비할 수 있다. 청해 Part 1, 2에서 등장하는 모든 의문문과 평서문 표현은 영어를 모국어로 사용하는 사람들이 현장에서 늘 사용하는 생활 영어 및 구어체 관용 표현으로 구성되어 있으므로 이러한 표현을 소리 내서 통째로 암기해 익숙해지면 Part 3에 등장하는 대화에 대한 이해도도 상당히 좋아질 뿐만 아니라, 다양한 상황에 대한 표현을 익히게 되므로 우리나라 영어 학습자들이 취약한 미국 문화에 대한 이해도 상당히 향상된다.

3. Part 3, 4는 Shadowing(따라읽기)을 하며 질문이 무엇을 요구하는지를 파악하자.

Part 3, 4는 크게 봤을 때 대의 파악 유형과 세부 내용 파악 유형으로 나누어 볼 수 있는데, 이는 Part 1, 2와 달라서 두 번 들려주는데다가 Question이 등장하고 그 Question에 따라 집중해서 들어야 할 부분이 달라지므로 받아쓰기나 무작정 외우는 것보다는 shadowing(따라읽기)을 하면서 전체 문맥의 흐름과 질문에서 요구하는 점을 빠르게 파악하는 것이 중요하다. 들리지 않는데 무조건 듣기만 하지 말라는 외국어 습득 이론이 있다. 특히 Part 4처럼 내용이 많은 경우에는 더욱 그렇다. 긴 내용에 대한 '순간 독해력' 이 부족하기 때문에 지문의 내용을 절반도 이해하지 못하는 경우에는 반드시 대본을 빨리 읽는 '독해 훈련' 에 당분간 시간을 투자해야 한다. 이 과정에서 원어민 음성을 통해 끊어 읽기나 발음에 대해서도 숙달될 수 있기 때문이다.

▌문법 (Grammar)

1. 출제되는 부분이 정해져 있다.

문법의 경우 학원 수업 때 다룬 것이 항상 90% 가량 나오는 것을 확인할 수 있는데 평소에 공부할 때
도 항상 나오는 문법을 중점적으로 다루면 그것이 시험에 많이 출제된다. 시험에서 주로 많이 다루는
내용은 시제, 분사구문, 수동태, 문장의 형식, 조동사, 명사와 관사, 일치, 어순, 대명사인데 항상 출
제되는 시제, 조동사, 수동태, 준동사 부분은 중점적으로 공부하도록 한나. Part 4의 경우 그냥 독해
를 하지 말고 각각 선택지의 주어, 동사를 파악해서 수의 일치(주어와 동사의 단수/복수 일치), 시제
일치(각 선택지들 간의 시제 흐름 일치), 태의 일치(능동태/수동태)가 맞는지만 확인해도 상당수 문제
를 풀 수 있다.

2. 오답 노트를 만들자.

TEPS에서 문법 점수를 올리는 지름길은 오답 노트이다. 한 번 풀어본 문제라서 눈에는 익은데 정답
이 헷갈린다든지, 정답을 꼼꼼하게 확인해두지 않아서 공부할 때 틀렸던 문제를 실전에서 또다시 틀린
다면 고득점의 길은 멀어질 수 밖에 없다. 오답 노트야말로 실수를 줄여나가는 확실한 방법이다. 본 모
의고사를 본 후 틀린 문제만 따로 노트에 정리해서(문제와 답만 적기) 각 문제 옆에 그 문제에 해당하
는 Chapter를 표기해 둔다면 TEPS 문법이 항상 다루는 부분에서 출제된다는 사실을 깨닫게 될 것
이며, 본인이 어느 부분에서 취약한지도 파악이 될 것이다.

3. 뒤에서부터 풀자.

문법 Part의 경우 문제 푸는 순서도 중요하다. 필자는 수강생들에게 문법과 독해 섹션을 풀 때는 뒤쪽
문제부터 풀어 나가라고 권하곤 하는데, 실제로 그렇게 했을 때 점수가 생각 이상으로 잘 나오는 분들
을 많이 보았다. 문법 Part 4의 다섯 문제는 배점이 높으므로 반드시 모두 맞추어야 한다는 점을 명심
하자.

■ 어휘 (Vocabulary)

1. TEPS 어휘는 대부분 생활 영어이다.

어휘에서는 상당수 문제들이 LC section에 등장하는 informal한 영어 표현인데 informal한 표현이란 격의 없이 일반 구어체에서 빈번하게 사용되는 표현으로 저속한 표현과는 다른 개념이다. 문어체 표현과 관련해서는 기존의 다른 시험과 큰 차이를 나타내지 않고 있지만 요즘은 그리 많이 출제되고 있지는 않다. 어휘 영역에서는 쉬운 단어에 특히 주목할 필요가 있다. 우리는 익숙하다고 주의를 충분히 기울이지 않지만 실상은 정확한 쓰임을 몰라서 실수할 수 있는 단어들이 어휘 영역의 주요 출제 대상이 된다.

그리고 철자가 비슷한 단어나 모양이 비슷한 단어를 구별하는 문제도 매회 거의 빠지지 않고 출제되고 있다. 흔히 동의어라고 생각되지만 쓰임이 각각 다른 단어가 많이 있으므로 양적인 면에 너무 집착하지 말고 개별 단어의 정확한 쓰임을 의미 있는 문장을 통해 착실히 익혀두는 습관이 필요하다. 이때 가급적이면 예문이 풍부한 영영사전을 이용하는 것이 좋고, 이러한 실용 영어 능력에 추가하여 TOEFL 수준의 어휘력까지 보강한다면 TEPS 어휘 영역에서 큰 어려움은 없을 것이다. 개인적인 목적이 있다면 모르겠지만 몇 년이 가도 한 번 볼까 말까한 난해한 단어를 공부하는 데 더 이상 시간을 낭비하지 않는 것이 좋다. TEPS에서는 실제 영어에서 활용 빈도가 낮은 표현이나 구문은 출제를 꺼리는 경향이 있다는 점을 명심해두기 바란다.

2. 속도 감각을 가지고 빨리 풀어야 한다.

지금까지 TEPS 어휘 영역에서 출제된 단어의 수준은 기존의 다른 영어 시험과 비교할 때 결코 어렵다고 할 수는 없으나 기본적으로 속도 감각이 뒷받침되어야 좋은 점수를 얻을 수 있다. 신속한 문제해결 능력을 위해서는 정확한 표현이 내재화되어 있어야 하므로 쉬운 의미라고 하더라도 반복적으로 활용하는 습관이 중요하다.

▌독해 (Reading Comprehension)

1. 시간 배분에 따라 점수가 달라진다.

TEPS 독해는 수험자들이 가장 어려워하는 부분인데 이는 시간 배분을 제대로 못해서인 경우가 대부분이다. 한 문제에 너무 오랜 시간 머물지 않아야 하는데 초급자일수록 이것이 잘 지켜지지 않는다. 모의고사를 통해 평상시에 시간 배분 훈련을 해야 실전에서 다소 여유를 갖고 자신 있게 대처할 수 있다.

Part 1의 경우 다른 Part에 비해 비교적 배점이 낮으므로 한 문제당 평균 40초에서 50초를 넘기지 말고 풀고, Part 2의 경우 내용도 다양하게 나오는데다가 Question이 다양하게 등장하므로 한 문제당 1분에서 1분 30초 안에 풀어야 한다. 가장 배점이 높은 Part 3의 경우 문제당 2분에서 2분 30초를 잡는 것이 바람직하며 독해 문제를 푸는 순서는 Part 3 → Part 1 → Part 2 순으로 푸는 것이 효율적이고 특히 독해 점수가 300점 이하인 사람에게는 위의 순서가 가장 이상적이다.

2. 아는 만큼 읽힌다. 어휘력은 기본!

TEPS RC는 주로 비전문 학술문 위주로 출제되고 과학, 의학, 역사, 문학, 언어, 문화 전반에 걸쳐 다양하게 출제되므로 풍부한 어휘력이 TEPS RC 고득점을 좌우하는 요소라는 사실에는 이견이 없을 것이다. 어휘력 증진을 위한 여러 가지 방법이 있겠지만 가급적이면 주제별 어휘를 정리하고 영영사전을 통해 의미를 찾아보고 문징과 글을 이용해서 성확한 의미를 알아두어야 한다. 그리고 모의고사를 풀 때에는 지문의 전체를 보면서 주요 어휘들의 의미를 확실하게 익혀둠과 동시에 어법에 해당하는 요소들을 의식적으로 파악하는 훈련이 매우 중요하다.

독해력은 어휘력과 배경 지식이 전부라고 말할 수 있다. 따라서 특정 분야에 대한 어휘력이 약하거나 배경 지식이 부족한 경우라면 아무리 짧고 단순한 지문이 출제되어도 쉽게 문제를 해결할 수 없다. 이에 대한 대책으로는 문제를 풀고 난 후에 지문을 다시 한 번 읽으면서 어휘와 표현을 정리하는 것과 동시에 전체 내용에 대한 이해도를 높여야 한다. 그래서 고득점자들은 독해 Part를 공부할 때 문제 풀이로만 생각하지 않고, 반드시 지문을 2~3번 더 읽어 내용을 이해하면서 배경 지식을 쌓는 것과 동시에 어휘를 숙지하려고 노력한다.

New TEPS MASTER 900

Listening
Comprehension

Chapter 01

의문사가 있는 의문문 1

🔍 Focus 1 주제를 묻는 What 의문문

What 의문문은 정기 TEPS 시험 LC PART I, II에서 평균 3~4문제 정도 출제된다. What뿐만 아니라 의문사가 있는 5W1H 의문문은 의문사를 포함한 처음 두세 단어를 잘 듣는 것이 핵심이다. What이라고 해서 무조건 '무엇'이라는 뜻으로 생각하면 안 되는데, What으로 질문할 수 있는 범위가 워낙 다양하기 때문에 단순히 What만 듣고서는 정답을 고를 수 없기 때문이다. 질문으로 주어지는 문장 안에서 What과 연결되는 핵심 명사를 유의해서 들어야만 답을 잘 찾을 수 있다. 시험에 기출된 질문 유형으로는 What do you think of~?(의견), What made~?(이유), What kind of~?(종류), What should I do~?(방법), What's it like~?(상태) 등이 있다.

Sample 1

W: Do I always have to pick up after you?

M: What did I do wrong? My room is clean.

W: What are your books doing on the kitchen table?

M: ___________________________________

(a) That's where I left them.

(b) I wish you wouldn't put them there.

(c) You can pick me up after school.

(d) Oh, that. I was going to put them away.

Q Focus 2   직업, 직책, 신분을 묻는 Who 의문문

Who의 경우, 각 문장에서 주어인지 목적어인지에 따라 응답이 달라질 수 있으므로 주의해야 한다. 명심할 것은 대부분의 문제들이 Who를 주어로 배치시키므로 각 문장의 동사를 잘 들어야 한다는 것이다. Who가 묻는 것은 행위의 주체로 고정되어 있으므로 어떤 행위냐가 중요한데, 이에 대한 답변으로는 사람 이름이나 직책이 가장 기본적인 답변 유형이지만 가끔씩 단체, 친분 관계, 회사명으로 답하는 경우도 있다.

Sample 2

M: Who is supposed to host a send-off party for Roger?

W: ___________________________________

(a) No, you don't have to send them off.
(b) Janet sent off the invitations already.
(c) How about delivering it tomorrow?
(d) Patricia is, as far as I know.

Q Focus 3   날짜, 시간, 요일을 묻는 When 의문문

의문사 When으로 시작하는 문제의 경우, 시간을 나타내는 부사나 부사구를 잘 듣는 것이 요령이다. 문제를 풀기 전에 기본적으로 알아 두어야 할 것은 When 의문문의 경우 현재, 과거, 미래의 한 시점을 묻는 문제이며 역대 기출 문제들을 분석해 볼 때 미래 시점에 대한 질문의 출제율이 높은 편이다. 최근에는 시제를 틀리게 하거나 기간에 대한 답변으로 혼동을 유도하는 선택지가 눈에 띄게 많은 편이므로 동사를 주의해서 들어야 하며, 여러 유형의 오답을 철저히 분석하는 것이 필수 전략이다.

Sample 3

W: When does the concert in the park begin?

M: _________________________________

(a) No, I didn't go to the park last night.

(b) Yeah, this is a good place to park.

(c) It commences at 7:00 tonight.

(d) It began at 2 o'clock sharp in the afternoon.

Q Focus 4 장소를 묻는 Where 의문문

장소나 위치를 나타내려면 명사를 사용할 수밖에 없으므로 각 선택지의 명사를 주의해서 청취하는 것이 중요하다. 한 가지 참고할 것은 최근 들어서 When으로 시작하는 질문에 Where에 대한 답을 넣기도 하고, Where에 대한 선택지에 When에 대한 답변을 넣어서 혼동을 유발하는 문제가 있다는 것이다. When과 Where에 대한 오답 선택지에 유의하자.

Sample 4

M: Excuse me. How much is an airport user fee ticket?

W: It'll cost 20 dollars if you're local.

M: Alright. Where can I buy one?

W: _________________________________

(a) You'll need to show your boarding pass, sir.

(b) At any of the supermarkets.

(c) Let me get back to you on that tomorrow.

(d) At any of the information counters.

Actual Test

PART I   Choose the most appropriate response to the statement.

1. (a)   (b)   (c)   (d)
2. (a)   (b)   (c)   (d)
3. (a)   (b)   (c)   (d)

PART II   Choose the most appropriate response to complete the conversation.

4. (a)   (b)   (c)   (d)
5. (a)   (b)   (c)   (d)

PART III   Choose the option that best answers the question.

6. (a)   (b)   (c)   (d)

PART IV   Choose the option that best answers the question.

7. (a)   (b)   (c)   (d)

Actual Test **Script**

PART I Choose the most appropriate response to the statement.

1 W: This is between you and me only. Keep it to yourself.
M: _______________________________

(a) No thanks. You can have it.
(b) My lips are sealed.
(c) Thanks for helping.
(d) Thanks for the gift. I appreciate it.

2 W: What kind of toppings do you want on the pizza?
M: _______________________________

(a) I don't have any money at the moment.
(b) It's on the kitchen table.
(c) I'm pretty hungry, so get a big one.
(d) I'll fix it myself, thanks.

3 W: He was punished by Mrs. Walters for bullying the other students.
M: _______________________________

(a) Mrs. Walters likes to pick on other people.
(b) She's the sweetest teacher.
(c) Hopefully, he'll be nicer from now on.
(d) Don't make fun of me.

PART II Choose the most appropriate response to complete the conversation.

4 M: Slow down a little. The speed limit is 45 miles per hour.
W: Relax. That's how fast I'm going.
M: Make sure to check the rear-view mirror before changing lanes.
W: _______________________________

(a) Let me pull over and check the mirrors.
(b) There's no problem with the mirrors.
(c) Would you mind giving me some driving tips?
(d) Stop nagging. Will you please trust me to drive responsibly?

5 M: Is it too late to drop a course for this term?

W: It's possible. What were you thinking of?

M: I'm not happy with Global Financing. I'd like to switch to Philosophy instead.

W: ________________________________

(a) What's wrong with Philosophy all of a sudden?

(b) Okay. I guess you've decided to study something more interesting than profitable.

(c) You are qualified to graduate with honors.

(d) I wish I had talked to someone like you before I started university.

PART III Choose the option that best answers the question.

6 W: You made a very good choice, sir. The purse is selling like hot cakes.

M: Is that so? Well, my wife loves white-colored goods in any kind.

W: I think she has very good taste. Actually it was made by a top designer. Anything else I can get you, sir?

M: Actually, I've got to go. But my child needs to find a restroom.

W: Okay, that's about 50 meters away on the left. You'll see it right before the Food Court.

M: Thanks. She's been waiting to go for almost half an hour.

W: Oh, I'm sorry, sir. The girls' bathroom is on the first floor next to the information center.

Q. Which of the following is correct about the man's child?

(a) She has been waiting for over an hour.

(b) The woman mistook her gender.

(c) She is interested in the purse.

(d) She wants to go to the Food Court.

7 Are you a coffee fanatic? Is a cup of coffee your favorite part of dessert? Do you need more than just black, latte and cappuccino? If so, I have fantastic news for you. The Dairy Genie is just what you've been looking for. Simply follow one of the ten built-in recipes or use the custom setting for your own creations, and you are on your way to the perfect style of coffee, no matter what you are craving today.

Q. Which of the following is true of the Dairy Genie?

(a) Its price is lower than that of the competiton.

(b) It comes with a recipe for cappucino.

(c) It can be used to make unique flavors.

(d) It is available in a number of locations.

Memo 

Chapter

02 의문사가 있는 의문문 2

🔍 Focus 1 이유를 묻는 Why 의문문

각 질문의 상황에 맞는 원인이나 이유를 답으로 골라야 한다. 대표적인 질문 내용은 지각이나 논문을 늦게 낸 이유, 누가 화나거나 사이가 갈라진 이유, 연락을 하지 못한 이유 등이다. 우리가 흔히 알고 있는 의문문의 공식으로 본다면 Because로 시작하는 선택지가 답으로 나와야 하겠지만 TEPS 출제자들은 거꾸로 이것을 오답으로 이용하고 있다. 따라서 선택지가 Because로 시작하는 경우 일단 의심해 보고 의미가 통하는지 확인해야 한다. 또한 Why는 이유를 묻는 반면 Why don't you~?는 권유를 나타낸다는 것을 명심하고 혼동하지 않도록 한다.

Sample 1

W: Why don't you bring your girlfriend along?

M: _______________________________

(a) She would be thrilled at the idea.

(b) Because she didn't want to come.

(c) Oh, I had no idea.

(d) I thought it was fun.

🔍 Focus 2 여러 형태로 쓰이는 How 의문문

How로 시작하는 의문문은 질문에 따라 다양한 답이 나올 수 있으므로 문장의 첫마디를 들을 때 무엇을 의미하는 상황인지 재빨리 파악하는 것이 중요하다. 대표적인 질문 유형으로는 방법 외에도 How long(기간), How many(수), How much(양), How soon(시간), How often(빈도, 횟수), How do you like/find(소감, 평가), How come(이유), How would you like(제안) 등이 있으므로 모두 외우기로 하자.

Sample 2

W: This is a great restaurant. I enjoyed my meal.

M: I hope you saved room for dessert. They have the best cake in town.

W: How did you hear about this place?

M: ________________________

(a) I didn't hear anything.

(b) I just looked at the menu.

(c) You can have pie if you prefer.

(d) I read a review in the newspaper.

Sample 3

W: How did the steak you ate at the restaurant turn out?

M: ________________________

(a) It was very succulent.

(b) For 45 minutes.

(c) Three hundred and fifty degrees.

(d) In the oven.

Which로 시작하는 질문은 TEPS 시험에서 매달 출제되지는 않고 두세 달에 한 번 정도 출제된다. 다른 의문사에 비해 출제율이 그리 높지 않을 뿐더러 길 안내 같은 정보를 묻는 경우가 대부분이다. 그리고 Which는 대개 의문형용사로 등장해서 〈Which+명사~?〉형태로 출제된다. 이때 Which는 바로 뒤의 명사를 꾸며 주는데 이 명사가 정답을 결정하는 단서가 된다.

Sample 4

M: Aren't Russians real meat eaters?

W: Of course. We eat all kinds of meat dishes.

M: Which one do you like the best?

W: ________________________________

(a) There are more cattle ranches than you'd expect.

(b) Pork is cheaper than beef.

(c) Potatoes and cabbage.

(d) Sausage is everyone's favorite.

PART I Choose the most appropriate response to the statement.

1. (a) (b) (c) (d)
2. (a) (b) (c) (d)
3. (a) (b) (c) (d)

PART II Choose the most appropriate response to complete the conversation.

4. (a) (b) (c) (d)
5. (a) (b) (c) (d)

PART III Choose the option that best answers the question.

6. (a) (b) (c) (d)

PART IV Choose the option that best answers the question.

7. (a) (b) (c) (d)

Listening Comprehension

Grammar

Vocabulary

Reading Comprehension

Actual Test Script

 Choose the most appropriate response to the statement.

1　M: My brother and I had a big argument last night.
　　W: _______________________________

　　(a) It's about time!
　　(b) Who did you talk to?
　　(c) Hopefully, you guys will make up soon.
　　(d) I know, he always thinks highly of you.

2　W: The professor nearly bored me to death today.
　　M: _______________________________

　　(a) You seem much better now.
　　(b) You're right. He's not the most entertaining person.
　　(c) Did anyone try to help him?
　　(d) I enjoy his classes too.

3　M: I can't believe that you didn't remember our anniversary!
　　W: _______________________________

　　(a) I wish you would trust my judgement on these matters.
　　(b) Thank you so much for your kind words.
　　(c) I have a surprise that I've been saving for this moment.
　　(d) I swear that I will never make that mistake again.

PART II **Choose the most appropriate response to complete the conversation.**

4　W: It's nice and cool here these days.
　　M: Yeah. It's good that the air conditioner has finally been repaired.
　　W: What a relief! It was unbearable the other week.
　　M: _______________________________

　　(a) Sure, it'll be fixed in no time.
　　(b) I'm astonished that you noticed.
　　(c) Well, I'm still working on it.
　　(d) You're telling me! It was scorching.

5 W: Mark, you haven't finished cleaning your room.

    M: Sorry, Mom. I'll do it this afternoon.

    W: You need to get it done now, or you'll be grounded.

    M: _______________________________

    (a) My parents won't let me go out.

    (b) No, there's nothing on the ground.

    (c) I'll get right on it.

    (d) You'd better start cleaning now.

PART III Choose the option that best answers the question.

6 M: Doctor Brown, do you have a moment?

    W: Yes. How is the patient coming along?

    M: Not so well, I'm afraid. She's running a high temperature and her throat is swollen.

    W: Is there anything else unusual occurring?

    M: In fact, a skin rash has appeared on her arms and legs that seems quite irritated.

    W: That sounds peculiar. I'd like Dr. Bradshaw to take a look at her as well. After his feedback I'll make a decision for her treatment.

    Q. What is most likely to happen next?

    (a) The condition of the patient will continue to deteriorate.

    (b) The doctors will compare diagnoses before proceeding.

    (c) The illness will be misdiagnosed by the two doctors.

    (d) The sick person will be fully rehabilitatd.

7 Your diet can be an important factor in your risk of getting skin cancer, the most common form of cancer in the United States. The main culprit for skin cancer has long been thought to be ultraviolet light, leading people to avoid sunshine and apply sunscreen. But more recent research suggests that our nutritional intake, including fats, minerals, and vitamin B, should also be taken into consideration.

Q. What is the main idea of this talk?

(a) The relationship between ultraviolet light and cancer
(b) Ways to keep safe from the sun
(c) Cancer preventing activities
(d) How nutrition can reduce chances of skin cancer

Memo 

Chapter

03 의문사가 없는 의문문 1

🔍 Focus 1 간접의문문

Wh-의문사가 문장 중간에 등장하는 간접의문문은 TEPS 시험에서 출제율이 비교적 높은 편으로 매 시험 3~4문제 정도 출제된다. 간접의문문에 대한 답변은 의문사가 있는 의문문에 등장하는 5W1H의 답변과 동일하다고 보면 된다. 따라서 간접의문문의 중간에 들어가는 의문사를 잘 듣고 질문 의도를 간파하는 것이 필수이다. 첫마디가 Do you, Can you 등으로 시작하므로 정답에서 Yes/No로 답할 수 있다는 점에 유의한다.

Sample 1

M: I watched *Forest Gump* last night and it still gives me a great impression.

W: Yeah, that's one of my favorite films, too.

M: Do you know when the film was made?

W: ________________________________

(a) I am the biggest investor of the film.

(b) About a decade ago, I presume.

(c) I don't know because I've never watched the film.

(d) How come you didn't see the movie?

Q Focus 2 be동사, 조동사 의문문

TEPS 시험에서 be동사나 조동사로 시작하는 의문문은 의문사가 있는 의문문보다 난이도가 훨씬 높다. 출제율 또한 매우 높아 매달 정기 시험에서 평균 5~6문제 정도 출제되는데 조동사, 시제, 인칭에 대한 정보가 들어가 있는 문장의 첫 부분을 잘 들어야 한다. 뒤에 이어지는 목적어 이하 핵심 부분 역시 놓쳐서는 안 될 필수 요소이다. 최근 시험에서는 Yes/No 응답은 많지 않고, 그 대신 긍정이나 부정을 전제로 한 전혀 다른 말로 답변한 것이 정답인 경우가 많다.

Sample 2

M: Excuse me, do you mind if I borrow that magazine?

W: ______________________________

(a) Sure, go ahead.

(b) Yes, please. Go for it.

(c) No, you are not allowed to do that.

(d) Not at all, I'm done with it.

Q Focus 3 부가의문문

부가의문문은 우리말과 영어의 의사소통 방식의 차이 때문에 질문 문장이 부정문일 경우 학생들이 혼란을 겪기도 한다. 부가의문문에 강해지기 위해서는 동사를 중심으로 한 핵심어를 파악하는 훈련을 해야 하며, 선택지의 정답을 보고 질문과 답변의 관계에 적응하는 훈련을 하는 것이 필수이다. 명심할 점은 질문이 긍정문이든 부정문이든지 간에 긍정으로 대답할 경우 Yes, 부정으로 대답할 경우는 No이며 상당수 문제들에서 Yes/No는 생략되기도 한다는 것이다.

Sample 3

M: Mom, this is your license plate that you ordered, isn't it?

W: ______________________________

(a) Yup, but I expected this to arrive two days ago.

(b) These plates will match my dining room perfectly.

(c) This plate is chipped, and so is the cup.

(d) Yes, my new driver's license came in yesterday.

W: Excuse me, I'd like three tickets for my family.

M: OK, ma'am. I need your social ID, first.

W: Children under ten are admitted for free, aren't they?

M: _______________________________

(a) Yes, they have to pay as well.

(b) I am sorry they have to pay a discounted price.

(c) Our amusement park is the best place for children.

(d) OK, I'll talk to them tomorrow.

PART I   Choose the most appropriate response to the statement.

    1. (a)   (b)   (c)   (d)

    2. (a)   (b)   (c)   (d)

    3. (a)   (b)   (c)   (d)

PART II   Choose the most appropriate response to complete the conversation.

    4. (a)   (b)   (c)   (d)

    5. (a)   (b)   (c)   (d)

PART III   Choose the option that best answers the question.

    6. (a)   (b)   (c)   (d)

PART IV   Choose the option that best answers the question.

    7. (a)   (b)   (c)   (d)

Actual Test Script

PART I Choose the most appropriate response to the statement.

1 M: I want to apologize for running into you.
W: _______________________________

(a) I knew I might run into you here.
(b) You are more than welcome.
(c) That's alright.
(d) No need to be so angry.

2 W: How's the weather today?
M: _______________________________

(a) It doesn't matter whether it's good or not.
(b) The lights are off.
(c) It's supposed to be cloudy tomorrow.
(d) It's unbearable.

3 M: Let's review yesterday's lesson.
W: _______________________________

(a) The quiz took longer than expected.
(b) OK, time to go home.
(c) I know, you don't have to review my manuscript.
(d) Fine. After that we can go home.

PART II Choose the most appropriate response to complete the conversation.

4 M: You seem exhausted. Did you stay up having fun last night?
W: Far from that. I tried all night to make a CD for my friend, but ultimately failed.
M: Sometimes those programs take a while to figure out.
W: _______________________________

(a) Where is a good place to buy cheap CDs?
(b) I knew that technology was a bad idea.
(c) Could you give me some advice on getting it to work properly?
(d) I've pretty much figured out which CDs I like.

5 M: That's such a letdown that our student film was cancelled.

W: Why are you so upset?

M: Claire and I were excited about making this film. We had both co-written the script and invested a lot of time.

W: ________________________________

(a) That's what happens when you don't plan ahead properly.

(b) I'm sorry to hear that she treated you that way.

(c) You should do the right thing and let her know how you feel.

(d) Just try to appreciate the time you had with Claire.

PART III Choose the option that best answers the question.

6 W: Good afternoon. I'm Janet Wendell with the BBC. May I interview you briefly?

M: Sure. Go ahead.

W: Are you from a region affected by the tornado?

M: Yes. My house is in downtown Houston.

W: What effect has the recent tornado had on your housing condition?

M: My house has been flooded now for four days.

W: And so you were not able to stay in your home, I presume.

M: That's right. We were forced to move into one of the city shelters until the flooding subsides.

Q. Which of the following is correct according to the conversation?

(a) The woman's house was flooded during the tornado.

(b) The tornado caused the man to live in a government shelter.

(c) The man has been homeless for a week.

(d) The man can return to his house within four days.

7 Visitors to the island of Greenland may be surprised by what they see there. The island, located in the North Atlantic Ocean, is not very green at all. Even in the summer, most of it is buried beneath a layer of ice and snow. So why does this frosty place have such a seemingly incongruent name? In fact, Greenland may have been a spelling mistake. The island was once known as Gruntland, which refers to the shallow bays along the coast. It's possible that the name was recorded incorrectly by European visitors, thus leading to the confusion.

Q. According to the passage, why would visitors to the island be surprised?

(a) Because the name doesn't match what they see
(b) Because the island used to be called Gruntland
(c) Because there are not many visitors
(d) Because it is located very far from Europe

Memo 

Chapter 04

의문사가 없는 의문문 2

🔍 Focus 1 선택의문문

선택의문문이란 〈A or B?〉형태로 주어진 두 개의 선택 중 하나를 고르는 유형인데, 역대 TEPS 기출 유형을 분석해 보면 A나 B 중 하나로 대답하는 경우와 A, B가 아닌 제3의 선택 사항이나 다른 것이 오는 경우가 답이 될 가능성이 있다. 최근 문제들은 이전 문제들보다 비교적 평이하게 출제되므로 A나 B를 선택해서 대답할 때 의문문에서 사용된 단어가 상당수 그대로 사용된다. 다른 유형에서는 질문에 등장했던 단어나 어구가 선택지에 다시 나오는 경우 오답일 확률이 높지만 선택의문문 유형에서는 그렇지 않다는 점에 유의한다. 원칙적으로 선택의문문의 경우 답변을 Yes/No로 할 수 없다는 것도 유의하도록 하자.

Sample 1

W: Do you want to go to the movies or play soccer next Monday?
M: ________________________________

(a) Yes, I am free next Monday.
(b) Seeing a film is one of my favorites.
(c) I feel like watching a movie.
(d) Yes, I'd like to play hockey.

Sample 2

W: Chris, would you like to have dinner with me tonight?
M: That sounds great! Let's have something nice.
W: Which one would you like to have, beef or pork?
M: ________________________________

(a) Why do you suggest those?
(b) I'm fine with whichever you want.
(c) Thank you, I'll have fish.
(d) No, I don't like pork. It's got too much fat in it.

Q Focus 2 부정의문문

부정의문문이라는 질문 형태는 부정으로 시작하지만 긍정의 의미를 강조하는 의문문의 형태로서 상대방에게 무언가를 확인하거나 놀라움을 표시하고 싶을 때 사용한다. 매월 TEPS 정기 시험에서 1~2문제 가량 출제되는 편이며 질문이 긍정문이라고 생각하고 선택지에서 적절한 의미의 응답을 찾는 것이 정답을 고르는 요령이다.

Sample 3

W: Isn't there much faster way to go to the church?

M: ________________________________

(a) Nope, not that I know of.
(b) Yes, neither way is fast.
(c) Sure, Either direction is fine.
(d) Subway is the fastest means for many commuters.

Sample 4

M: I think you and Henry should talk to each other again.

W: No, I don't feel like seeing him.

M: But don't you think you should see him and have some conversation first?

W: ________________________________

(a) You and I don't have any chemistry.
(b) OK, I'll try to see my parents.
(c) Snap out of it, it's not the end of the world.
(d) No, doing it will be a waste of time.

1 **Are you with me?** 이해하겠니? 내 말이 무슨 말인지 알겠니?

2 **Can I take a rain check?** 다음으로 미룰 수 있을까요?

3 **Can you put me on the waiting list?** 대기자 명단에 올려 주시겠어요?

4 **Have we met before?** 우리 전에 본 적이 있던가요?

5 **Can't you overlook it just once?** 한 번만 그냥 넘어가 주시면 안 될까요?.

6 **When do you expect him?** 그 사람이 언제 올까요?

7 **While you're at it, can you get some water?** 너 가는[하는] 김에 물 좀 가져다 줄래?

8 **Whose side are you on?** (내 편인 줄 알았는데) 넌 누구 편이니?

9 **May I interrupt you?** 실례해도 될까요?

10 **Will you give me a lift/ride?** 나 차 좀 태워 줄래?

11 **Will you give/lend me a hand?** 나 좀 도와줄래?

12 **Would you care for a drink?** 음료수 좀 드시겠어요?

13 **How can I make it up to you?** 어떻게 하면 화가 풀어지겠니?

14 **How's your paper coming/getting/going along?** 보고서 어떻게 되어 가고 있어요?

15 **How do you like your new apartment?** 새 아파트 어때?

16 **How does it sound?** 어때?

17 **Don't you see?** 모르겠니?

18 **Does it work?** 그게 효과가 있을까?

19 **Can I count on it?** 그거 믿어도 돼요?

20 **Can I ask you a favor?** 부탁 하나 해도 될까요?

21 **How about seconds?** 더 드세요.

PART I   Choose the most appropriate response to the statement.

     1. (a)   (b)   (c)   (d)

     2. (a)   (b)   (c)   (d)

     3. (a)   (b)   (c)   (d)

PART II   Choose the most appropriate response to complete the conversation.

     4. (a)   (b)   (c)   (d)

     5. (a)   (b)   (c)   (d)

PART III   Choose the option that best answers the question.

     6. (a)   (b)   (c)   (d)

PART IV   Choose the option that best answers the question.

     7. (a)   (b)   (c)   (d)

Actual Test Script

1 W: My name is Linda. I'm the founder of this company. How do you do?

M: ________________________________

(a) Long time no see.

(b) I'm Jane. I've been fine.

(c) I'm Joe. Nice to meet you too.

(d) What's up, Linda?

2 M: What are your thoughts on capital punishment?

W: ________________________________

(a) You need to have enough capital to start business.

(b) It must be abolished, of course.

(c) I can't affirm anything on that topic.

(d) Action speaks louder than words.

3 M: What should I do? Sara is still mad at me.

W: ________________________________

(a) That is the least you could do for her.

(b) Did you bring her to the doctor?

(c) Take it easy. You guys will make up soon.

(d) I envy you. She loves you so much, huh?

PART II Choose the most appropriate response to complete the conversation.

4 W: What kind of visa are you here on?

M: It's F1. The student visa.

W: When that expires, what will you do?

M: ________________________________

(a) I can't tell you that information.

(b) I have to get a new credit card.

(c) I have to leave the country to renew it.

(d) I'm going to take a vacation somewhere.

5 W: I was hoping to find some inexpensive boat tickets to Japan.

    M: Our cheapest boat is an overnight boat between Busan and Fukuoka.

    W: I'd like to get there today if possible.

    M: _______________________________

(a) Why not? I've always wanted to go to Japan.

(b) Okay. There is a flight leaving this afternoon for Tokyo.

(c) There is an express ferry, but it's a bit pricier.

(d) I'm sorry. I'm working as fast as I can.

PART III Choose the option that best answers the question.

6 W: Thank God you arrived. It's almost our turn to show our designs. Where were you?

    M: My car broke down on the way here.

    W: Well, at least you could have taken a taxi or a bus.

    M: The problem was that there was no place for me to leave my car. So I had to wait for a tow truck to come and take it.

    W: Well, I'm glad you got here all right.

    M: Thanks. Let's hope that all my bad luck is finished.

    W: Right. Time to get to work. Give me the slide show disc you made.

    M: Oh, no! I've got some more bad news.

Q. What can be inferred from the conversation?

(a) The man didn't bring the disc.

(b) The man typically has good luck.

(c) The man isn't satisfied with his work.

(d) The man is going to be late again.

7 At 10 PM western time, Hurricane Lucy was located about 50 miles south of the Frazer Islands, moving north at 20 mph. Maximum winds near the center of the storm have increased to 70 mph. Lucy is expected to bring heavy rains, flash floods and dangerously strong winds. Hurricane warnings have been issued and residents have been advised to stay indoors. However, over the next few days, the storm is expected to lose intensity as it moves to a more eastern track.

Q. Which of the following is NOT true according to the weather report?

(a) Residents were told to evacuate the area.
(b) Heavy rain and high winds are expected.
(c) Hurricane Lucy will weaken in a few days.
(d) Sudden and severe floods are likely in some areas.

Memo 

Chapter 05

평서문

🔍 Focus 1 · 대화의 주제를 파악하라

평서문은 의문문과 달리 문장의 앞부분을 듣는 것은 별 의미가 없고 문장 전체의 의미와 상황을 파악하는 것이 관건이다. 따라서 문장 전체를 듣고 대화의 주제가 무엇인지 빠르게 파악하는 것이 고득점의 비결이다. 역대 기출된 평서문 유형으로는 인사, 소개, 축하, 감사, 제안, 불만, 의견 교환 및 정보 교류 등이 있다.

Sample 1

W: John, I can't believe you forgot my birthday.
M: I'm so sorry. It slipped my mind.
W: I'm disappointed in you. This is not the first time.
M: _______________________________

(a) Could you let the hem down, please?
(b) Don't try to have it your way.
(c) That's right. I slipped on the ice.
(d) You have every right to be angry.

🔍 Focus 2 · 관용 표현이 가장 많이 나오는 유형이다

관용 표현이란 그 문장을 구성하는 단어 하나하나가 갖는 직접적인 의미만으로는 그 뜻을 이해할 수 없는 어구들로 보통 영영사전이나 드라마, 시트콤 및 여러 실용 매체에서 다루는 표현을 말한다. 의문문보다 평서문에서 상당수 등장하므로 평소에 **TEPS** 교재 말고도 일반 파워 청취 교재나 회화 교재를 병행하는 공부 습관이 가장 효과적이다.

Sample 2

M: I'm sort of under the weather today.

W: _______________________________

(a) It'll be fine tomorrow.

(b) I know, the weather seems nice today.

(c) What's wrong? Didn't you sleep well?

(d) Today's weather forecast calls for clear skies.

🔍 **Focus 3** 정답은 정형화되어 있지 않다

TEPS LC 평서문의 경우 관용 표현도 많고 제시되는 상황 자체가 상당히 다양하므로 이런 상황에는 이런 것이 정답이라는 룰(rule)이 적용되기 힘든 유형이기도 하다. 따라서 질문 문장을 잘 듣고 그 질문과 제시된 선택지들을 하나하나 잘 비교해 가며 가장 어울리는 선택지를 답으로 골라야 한다. 특히 최근 시험에서는 한 번에 답을 파악해서 고르는 것보다는 답이 아닌 선택지들을 하나씩 지워 가며 최종적으로 정답이라고 판단되는 선택지를 고르는 소거법 유형의 문제 수가 증가하는 추세이므로 주어진 상황에 대한 그림을 머릿속에 재빠르게 그려 보는 연습이 필요하다.

Sample 3

M: Kelly, I'd like to hear about your blind date last night.

W: _______________________________

(a) Congratulations! Did you say yes?

(b) I am so glad to hear that.

(c) I know what you mean.

(d) I shouldn't have gone at all.

흔히 LC PART I, II의 질문은 의문문이든 평서문이든 그 문장이 하나씩 주어진다. 그러나 가끔 의문문과 평서문을 한꺼번에 나열한다든지, 의문문 두 개 또는 평서문 두 개를 한꺼번에 나열해 놓고 어느 문장에 집중해야 하는지를 묻는 문제도 상당수 등장한다. 특히 주의할 점은 평서문과 의문문 두 개를 한꺼번에 나열하는 경우에는 순서에 상관없이 평서문보다는 의문문 쪽에 비중을 두어 정답을 고르는 유형의 문제들이 상당히 많은 편이므로 특히 유의하도록 한다.

Sample 4

M: Honey, is lunch ready? I'm starving.

W: ___________________________

(a) And I'm Jill. Nice to meet you, too.

(b) Almost. Can you set the table?

(c) Oh, really? I am eating, then.

(d) Sorry, sir. We are closed today.

Actual Test

PART I   Choose the most appropriate response to the statement.

1. (a)   (b)   (c)   (d)

2. (a)   (b)   (c)   (d)

3. (a)   (b)   (c)   (d)

PART II   Choose the most appropriate response to complete the conversation.

4. (a)   (b)   (c)   (d)

5. (a)   (b)   (c)   (d)

PART III   Choose the option that best answers the question.

6. (a)   (b)   (c)   (d)

PART IV   Choose the option that best answers the question.

7. (a)   (b)   (c)   (d)

Actual Test **Script**

1 M: You must tell me what you did to make this soup so tasty.
W: ________________________________

(a) I used to try out all kinds of different diets.
(b) Don't add anything until I've tasted it.
(c) I enjoyed it as well.
(d) It was an instant mix packet.

2 W: I desperately hope that our business picks up soon.
M: ________________________________

(a) Once tourist season starts, it'll improve.
(b) Please try to stay out of my business.
(c) You are always burning the midnight oil.
(d) You should open up a store.

3 M: How long are we able to rent new releases?
W: ________________________________

(a) My friend Jack will be released from prison soon.
(b) They must be returned in two days.
(c) You cannot rent videos without payment.
(d) We don't have that much time.

4 W: I'm not going to try that sugar-contained orange juice.
M: How come? It's also got various nutrients and reasonably priced product.
W: The thing is I'm trying to avoid all sugar-based products from today.
M: ________________________________

(a) Well, I used to try out various sugar-based products.
(b) Well, there's no need to sugar coat the truth.
(c) Well, certain sugars are essential for getting energy.
(d) Well, now that you mention it, I'm hungry.

5 M: How come you never wear make-up anymore?

W: I thought you liked the natural look.

M: I do. But once in a while you could do something special.

W: ___________________________________

(a) I think you're special too.

(b) You can't take your eyes off from me, can you?

(c) Am I not exciting enough for you?

(d) Make-up is getting more and more expensive.

PART III Choose the option that best answers the question.

6 W: So tell me about the theater troupe you started.

M: Compared to what I had expected, it's not working out.

W: Why not?

M: There doesn't seem to be much chemistry between the actors.

W: Have you tried any games to get them to bond with each other?

M: No. Their personalities are very different from one another. They don't seem to want to be friends.

W: You should try some creative games that help them build trust and find some things in common.

M: Thanks for the tips. We'll see what happens.

Q. What can be inferred from the conversation?

(a) Good theatre requires chemistry among the actors.

(b) Having shared experiences can bring people closer.

(c) Creative games only work among similar personalities.

(d) People with different personalities from each other like engaging in creative games.

7 Is aerobics for infants becoming the next big exercise fad? While a growing trend of fitness courses for babies has convinced some parents to sign on, pediatricians like Dr. Strieser insist that such courses are little more than a waste of time and money. She explains that the muscular structure of babies is too underdeveloped to benefit from such activities. On the other hand, some docters insist that babies can get a head start on the fight against obesity by developing exercise habits at an early age.

Q. What can you conclude from the talk?

(a) People who exercised as babies are far healthier than those who didn't.
(b) Disputes remain in the medical field concerning obesity.
(c) Forcing infants to exercise borders on child abuse.
(d) There are pros and cons on the benefits of infant exercise.

Memo 

Chapter

06 대의 파악

🔍 Focus 1 첫 부분을 놓치지 마라

대의 파악 유형은 지문 앞부분에 정답의 단서가 들어 있거나 전체 내용을 근거로 답을 유추할 수 있는 경우가 대부분이다. 대체로 함정이 적은 유형이므로 질문이 묻는 핵심어만 지문을 두 번째 들을 때 재빠르게 뽑아낼 수 있으면 80% 이상 성공이라고 할 수 있다. 흔히들 첫 문장을 꼭 들어야 한다고 하는데, 역대 빈출된 General Questions 때문에 그런 말도 생겨난 것이다. General Questions는 주로 What is mainly taking place in the conversation?, What is the talk mainly about?, What is being advertised?, Who is the speaker?, Where is this conversation taking place? 등의 형태로 주어진다.

Sample 1

M: Would you like to go for a walk after dinner?
W: I'm rather tired. I think I'd prefer to watch a movie.
M: But a nice, leisurely stroll would help your food digest.
W: I suppose so. And the dog would probably appreciate it as well.
M: We can always watch a movie when we get back.
W: All right. That sounds good.

Q. What are the speakers talking about?

(a) Their after-dinner plans
(b) The benefits of exercise
(c) Their favorite movies
(d) Where they will take a walk

Q Focus 2 반복적으로 이어지는 관련 어구에 집중하라

PART Ⅲ, Ⅳ의 유형 상당수는 첫 문장에서 주제가 되는 도입이 이루어지고 중간 부분에서 이 주제를 뒷받침할 만한 구체적인 예들이 전개되다가 마지막 부분에서 주제를 다시 한 번 재진술하거나 재강조하는 식의 문제들이 많다. 그런데 어떤 문제는 앞부분에서 지문의 핵심이 정확히 밝혀지지 않고 대략적인 서론으로 시작하다가 중간 이하에서 본격적인 주제 제시가 이루어지는 경우도 있는데, 이런 경우에는 대화나 지문에 반복적으로 강조되는 관련 어구에 집중해야 한다. 그 관련 어구가 선택지에 등장하는 경우 정답인 경우가 많으므로 유의하기 바란다.

Sample 2

M: I've had a lot of dental pain recently.

W: Really? Have you been to see your dentist?

M: Yes. I had four cavities that needed to be treated.

W: Well, I hope you'll take better care of your teeth from now on.

M: Don't worry, I will.

W: Dental work is not only painful, it's also expensive.

Q. What is the main idea of the conversation?

(a) What needs to be done for dental health
(b) How often you need to brush your teeth
(c) Why oral care is important
(d) The price of dental care

Sample 3

A cold is caused by a virus of which there are over 200 varieties and is caught by breathing in the tiny infected droplets that are expelled when someone coughs and sneezes. Most adults can expect to have at least two or three colds a year. The link with cold weather arises because we tend to remain indoors during the winter months, in crowded situations, and it is therefore easier to catch the virus that is present in the air we inhale.

Q. What is the talk mainly about?

(a) Frequencies of colds
(b) The duration of a cold
(c) How one gets a cold
(d) Infectious germs

PART I   Choose the most appropriate response to the statement.

1. (a)   (b)   (c)   (d)
2. (a)   (b)   (c)   (d)
3. (a)   (b)   (c)   (d)

PART II   Choose the most appropriate response to complete the conversation.

4. (a)   (b)   (c)   (d)
5. (a)   (b)   (c)   (d)

PART III   Choose the option that best answers the question.

6. (a)   (b)   (c)   (d)

PART IV   Choose the option that best answers the question.

7. (a)   (b)   (c)   (d)

Listening Comprehension

Grammar

Vocabulary

Reading Comprehension

Actual Test Script

PART I Choose the most appropriate response to the statement.

1 W: Do you mind washing the dishes while I run a few errands?
M: _______________________________

(a) I'll go with you.
(b) Absolutely not. Glad to do it.
(c) Yes, I don't mind doing it.
(d) Do not run. You might get hurt.

2 W: Do you think the director made the right decision when he cast Andrew?
M: _______________________________

(a) I can't believe that you turned down the offer.
(b) I haven't really had time to sit down and think about it.
(c) Only time will tell, I suppose.
(d) It is really hard to decide between the two.

3 W: I was wondering if you had this pair of jeans in size 10.
M: _______________________________

(a) They look rather nice together, don't they?
(b) Yes, you can save by buying in bulk.
(c) I don't know offhand, but I'd be happy to check.
(d) Those aren't exactly what I had in mind.

PART II Choose the most appropriate response to complete the conversation.

4 W: I've got a coworker who will not stop bragging about his new car.
M: That sounds pretty annoying.
W: I've never met someone so materialistic.
M: _______________________________

(a) I wonder who his mechanic is.
(b) He should stay out of your personal life.
(c) His ego is quite healthy.
(d) Sounds like he's looking for attention.

5 M: Was the job interview a success?

W: Just the opposite. I bombed it.

M: Are you serious? What went wrong?

W: _______________________________

(a) He's going to hit the roof when he hears about this.

(b) I guess I came off too desperate.

(c) I'm afraid that he doesn't fully appreciate the problem.

(d) I was hired immediately.

PART III Choose the option that best answers the question.

6 M: Hey, Winnie. What's happening?

W: I wanted to ask if I could pitch for the upcoming game this weekend, coach.

M: Any special reason?

W: My family will be in town, so I wanted them to see me play.

M: You need to be careful with your arm. You don't want to hurt it any further.

W: It's been getting better. I think that it may be well enough to play.

M: Well, I'll let you start the game in the first inning, and we'll see how you do.

W: Thank you, coach. I promise I'll do a good job.

Q. What is correct according to the conversation?

(a) The woman needs medical help for her injury.

(b) The woman is asking for a chance to see her family.

(c) The woman lost the opportunity to play.

(d) The woman had a prior experience of injury while playing a game.

7   Many people believe that because herbal remedies are all-natural, there are few, if any, risks associated with them. This is definitely a myth. Although many herbal remedies are effective alternatives to over-the-counter drugs, they should still be used with caution. Just as with other drugs, many herbal remedies can radically affect the way the body functions and dosage instructions should be carefully followed. While it is true that many herbal remedies are less likely to have serious side effects, some can be dangerous or even deadly if used improperly.

Q. What is the main topic of the talk?

(a) Why herbal remedies are not very effective
(b) Reasons to avoid over-the-counter drugs
(c) The positive effects of herbs on the body
(d) The dangers of natural herbal remedies

Memo 

Chapter 07

세부 내용과 **추론**

🔍 **Focus 1** 질문의 요구 사항을 정확히 파악하라

일단 TEPS LC PART III, IV의 문제 중 correct 유형의 경우 어느 한두 문장에만 집중하기보다는 지문 전반에 걸친 내용과 세부적인 정보를 최대한 문제지에 받아 적으며 선택지 내용과 비교하여 정답을 고르는 것이 중요하다. 특히 세부 내용을 묻는 유형에서는 주어지는 질문을 잘못 들을 경우 지문 내용을 완전히 이해하고도 어이없게 정답은 못 고르는 상황이 발생할 수 있으므로 질문이 무엇을 요구하는지 정확히 파악하는 것이 관건이 된다. 또한 세부 내용 문제들은 Who(사람), Why(이유), When(시간) 등의 의문사를 이용하여 지문의 특정한 내용을 파악하는 능력을 물어보므로 5W1H에 근거해서 내용을 청취하는 연습이 필요하다.

Sample 1

W: I'll be stopping by the store on my way home. Do you need anything?

M: Yes, actually. Could you get some yogurt? We're all out.

W: Sure. What flavor do you want?

M: Peach, please.

W: All right. Do you want any ice cream?

M: No thanks, just the yogurt.

W: OK, see you later.

Q. What does the man ask the woman to buy for him?

(a) Peaches

(b) Unflavored yogurt

(c) Ice cream

(d) Peach yogurt

Focus 2 두 번째 들을 때 점수가 좌우된다

상황과 토픽에 관련된 주제가 여러 가지 등장하는 파트가 PART III, IV인데 그 중에서도 가장 쉽게 안 풀리는 부분이 바로 세부 유형이라 할 수 있다. 대의 파악 유형은 어느 특정 부분을 놓치더라도 전반적인 지문의 분위기로 정답을 고를 수 있는 반면, 세부 내용을 묻는 문제의 경우 질문에서 묻는 세부 내용을 놓칠 경우 정답을 고르기 힘들다. 따라서 첫 번째 들을 때에는 지문의 전체적인 내용을 파악하고 두 번째 들을 때에는 세부적인 내용 파악에 유의한다. 또한 대화나 담화 내용 중 금액, 연도, 수치, 나이 등은 정답을 고르는 데 있어 상당히 중요한 역할을 하는 경우가 많다. 영어를 잘하는 강사나 연구원조차도 시험 당일 어느 정도 긴장하는 상황에서 세부 내용 관련 문제를 모두 맞추기 위해서는 숫자들을 문제지에 재빠르게 필기해 놓는 습관이 필요하다.

Sample 2

Good afternoon, ladies and gentlemen. Welcome aboard Northwest Airlines 007 departing from Tom Bradely International Airport in Los Angeles and heading for Vancouver International Airport in Canada. I'm captain Kevin Williams in charge of this flight. As we can see, the weather in LA is very sunny with a little bit of wind from the southeast. As you are all aware, the flight time will be approximately seven hours, and we'll arrive in Vancouver at around eight o'clock in the evening. The local weather in Vancouver is nice and warm as well. In case of turbulence, please do not panic and remain seated with your seatbelt fastened. Thank you for flying with Northwest.

Q. Which is correct according to the announcement?

(a) The airplane will arrive at seven o'clock local time.

(b) The weather in Vancouver is overcast now.

(c) The airplane took off in LA at about one in the afternoon.

(d) You can use your laptop computer when the seatbelt sign is off.

추론 문제의 경우 LC 문제 중 배점이 가장 높다고 볼 수 있으며, 단순한 정보 파악 외에도 자신이 들은 내용을 전체적으로 정리하고 분석하여 들려주지 않은 내용을 추론해야 하므로 난이도가 가장 높은 유형이라 볼 수 있다. 추론 문제를 처음에 들을 때는 대화나 담화의 전체적인 주제를 파악하고, 두 번째 들을 때 좀 더 질문에 집중해서 들었던 내용을 기억하도록 한다. 중간 이하 부분에 의외로 힌트가 많다. 대의 파악 유형과 비교해 볼 때 추론 문제의 경우 첫 문장부터 중간 문장까지는 대다수가 서론인 반면, 중간 이하에 질문에서 원하는 힌트가 숨어 있는 경우가 있다. 정답을 고를 때도 각 선택지가 대화 내용과 무관한 내용인지 반대인지 일치하는지를 주의해서 살핀다. PART Ⅲ, Ⅳ는 지문에 한 번 나왔던 단어나 어구를 동일하게 반복하는 선택지보다는 지문에 있는 내용을 다른 단어나 어구로 바꾸어서 정답으로 등장시키는 경우가 특히 많은 파트이다.

Sample 3

W: Hello. How can I help you today?

M: I'd like some information on the telephone banking services offered by your bank.

W: Certainly. If you have an account with us, you can do all of your banking over the telephone, 24 hours a day.

M: How do I access my account?

W: Just call the bank, key in your access code and listen to the menu of options available.

M: That's great. What kind of things can I do?

W: You can check your balance, pay bills, order a statement or even transfer money to another account.

M: OK, but what do I do if I have any problems?

W: There's an automated answering machine and staff are available during business hours every day.

Q. What can be inferred from the conversation?

(a) The man has never visited the bank before.

(b) The man works at the bank.

(c) The man has never used telephone banking before.

(d) The woman is a good friend of the man.

Q Focus 4 어휘 실력이 판가름한다

TEPS 시험을 준비하는 수험자 입장에서는 들은 내용만으로 추측 가능한 선택지를 고르는 추론 유형이 세부 내용을 묻는 유형보다 훨씬 난해하게 느껴질 수 있다. 그러나 추론 역시 전체 내용을 이해한다면 큰 함정이 등장하지 않는 한 정답을 고르는 것은 그리 어렵지 않다고 볼 수 있다. 그리고 PART IV의 경우 전문적인 내용의 토픽이 추론 문제의 유형으로 주로 등장하는 반면, PART III의 경우에는 인사, 소개, 감정 교환, 건강, 학교 등 우리가 흔히 접할 수 있는 일상 생활 내용을 크게 벗어나지 않으므로 평소에 어휘 학습을 틈틈이 해둔 학생과 독해 지문을 많이 읽어본 학생에게는 절대 어려운 파트가 아니라고 할 수 있다.

Sample 4

The essential advice for purchasing a used car has always been "buyer beware." That advice still holds true, but over the past few years, the prices of new cars and light trucks have outpaced many consumers' incomes, sending demand for used cars up. While buying a used car is still filled with uncertainty, there are ways to increase your chances of making a satisfactory purchase.

Q. What can be inferred from the talk?

(a) Used cars are problematic for most buyers.

(b) Buying used cars is becoming more popular.

(c) Buying a used car is foolproof.

(d) Used cars are getting cheaper these days.

Essential Expressions for L/C

1 **Absolutely!** 물론이지! 당연하지!

2 **Beats me!** 모르겠어.

3 **Far from it.** 절대 그렇지 않아요.

4 **I'm all for that. / I support that idea.** 전적으로 찬성이야.

5 **It's a deal.** 좋아. (그렇게 하자.)

6 **You can say that again.** 동감이야. 네 말이 맞아.

7 **You don't say! / Really?** 정말이야?

8 **You have my word.** 내 말 믿어.

9 **You said it!** 암, 그렇고말고.

10 **You bet.** 틀림없어요. 물론이지요.

11 **No way! / Not on your life! / Over my dead body!** 절대 안돼!

12 **No sweat.** 괜찮아. 문제없어.

13 **Same here!** 나도 같은 것으로 할게. 나도 그래.

14 **Give it to me straight.** 솔직히 말해 봐.

15 **Put yourself in my shoe.** 너도 내 입장이 되어 봐.

16 **Save your breath.** 어때?

17 **Shake a leg!** 서둘러!

18 **Shame on you.** 창피한 줄 아세요.

19 **Good for you.** 잘됐네.

20 **Guess what!** (대화를 시작할 때) 있잖아. 맞혀 봐!

21 **I can't buy it.** 믿을 수 없어.

22 **Behave yourself.** 행동을 자제하세요. 얌전하게 굴어.

23 **Cut it out!** 그만해!

24 **Be punctual!** 시간 좀 지켜!

25 **Break it up.** 그만 좀 싸워.

Actual Test

PART I Choose the most appropriate response to the statement.

1. (a)   (b)   (c)   (d)

2. (a)   (b)   (c)   (d)

3. (a)   (b)   (c)   (d)

PART II Choose the most appropriate response to complete the conversation.

4. (a)   (b)   (c)   (d)

5. (a)   (b)   (c)   (d)

PART III Choose the option that best answers the question.

6. (a)   (b)   (c)   (d)

PART IV Choose the option that best answers the question.

7. (a)   (b)   (c)   (d)

Actual Test **Script**

PART I **Choose the most appropriate response to the statement.**

1 W: Guess what! Joseph got accepted into Princeton University.
    M: _______________________________

(a) I know. When are you going to hit the campaign trail for class president?
(b) Well done. I'm so proud of you.
(c) Well, I only browsed through the assignments.
(d) I knew he could make it.

2 M: Professor William, would it be possible for me to get an extension for my
      thesis?
    W: _______________________________

(a) Don't be so negative. It'll be fine.
(b) Our school board doesn't make any exceptions for students caught cheating.
(c) Only if you turn it in before the weekend.
(d) Yup. This is the time for some degree of expansion.

3 M: Jane, do you have time to pick up the materials for our project this afternoon?
    W: _______________________________

(a) Thanks, but I can't accept this.
(b) Sure, it's a quarter to three at the moment.
(c) I don't see why not.
(d) I know. He is so materialistic.

PART II **Choose the most appropriate response to complete the conversation.**

4 W: Matthew, have you delivered a box of vegetables to Green Garden this morning?
    M: Nope. Actually I was going to tell you. We'd better take orders from somewhere
      else.
    W: What makes you say that?
    M: _______________________________

(a) They are among the best businesses in our town.

(b) We had a great time last night. I think we really hit it off.

(c) They've been delinquent for over two months.

(d) They are quite happy with our service.

5 W: Do you know a good computer repair store?

M: JPU Broadband is a reputable computer business.

W: That's good to know. I hope they can fix my computer.

M: _______________________________

(a) Why don't you give it another shot?

(b) You won't be let down. They're cheap and reliable.

(c) I'm a skilled mechanic.

(d) I don't think they can. They are not that reputable.

PART III Choose the option that best answers the question.

6 W: A cold ice cream would really hit the spot right now.

M: There's a shop down the street where we can get some.

W: I wish I could, but I just found out that I'm lactose intolerant. That's why my stomach sometimes hurts.

M: I'm sure just a little bit of milk won't kill you.

W: No, my doctor said yesterday that I'd better not take any chances with my stomach until this weekend.

M: Then what about having soy desserts?

W: Oh, that sounds better.

Q. What can be inferred from the conversation?

(a) The woman will try a little ice cream.

(b) The man doesn't like soy desserts as much as ice cream.

(c) The woman cannot have any ice cream for a week.

(d) The woman has a low tolerance for pain.

7   Recent outbreaks of avian influenza has led to a dramatic drop in poultry purchases. However, eating chicken and other cooked meat provides very little risk of contracting the disease. While the majority of birds that are carriers of the virus are found in the wild, these non-domesticated birds rarely show any signs of illness. It is poultry grown on farms or in houses, on the other hand, that appears more highly susceptible to illness and death. Avoiding contact with potentially infected poultry is the most effective strategy for staying safe.

Q. What is correct according to the report?

(a) Chicken farmers are more at risk of infection than consumers.
(b) Birds in the wild are not exposed to the influenza virus.
(c) Experts are expecting a large outbreak of avian influenza.
(d) Cooking meat will not make it safe for consumption.

Memo

Chapter 08

광고와 공지

🔍 Focus 1 상품 광고

TEPS LC에 역대 기출된 내용으로는 가전 기기나 식품 같은 유형의 제품과 여행 상품이나 이벤트 같은 무형적 상품에 대한 광고가 주로 출제된다. 어떤 제품을 광고하는 것인지 제품의 특징이 무엇인지를 파악해야 한다. 구인이나 구직에 관한 광고도 최근 들어 자주 등장하는 편이며 광고 지문의 일반적인 진행 순서는 〈회사 소개 → 제품이나 서비스 소개 → 관련 세부 사항 → 구입이나 사용 방법, 연락하는 방법〉의 순서이다.

Sample 1

Congratulations! You have just purchased the highest quality chef's knife from Kitchen Aid. All of our knives are guaranteed for life. If you are unsatisfied, you can return it at any time for a full refund. Please take special care with your Kitchen Aid chef's knife. Do not leave your knives soaking in soapy water, as the sharpness of the blade may dull. Always dry your knife immediately after washing, and store in a safe place. Thank you for purchasing a Kitchen Aid product.

Q. Which is correct about Kitchen Aid knives according to the ad?

(a) They come with a lifetime guarantee.
(b) The blades should be left to soak.
(c) Knives should air dry after washing.
(d) They are inexpensive and of poor quality.

🔍 Focus 2 책, 인터넷 광고

다른 시험 못지않게 TEPS LC에서 자주 등장하는 내용이 책과 인터넷 광고인데 책 광고에서는 책의 주제와 제목이 상당한 힌트를 제공하며 그 책을 읽을 대상이 집중 조명되는 경우가 대부분이다. 인터넷의 경우는 상당수가 쇼핑 관련이고 offline shopping과의 가격 비교, 할인 금액, 웹사이트 주소 등이 결정적인 힌트를 제공하는 경우가 많다. 그러므로 문제를 들을 때는 제품의 종류, 특징, 가격, 할인 정도, 구매 시 혜택, 구입 가능 기간 등에 유의하여 청취하는 것이 중요하다.

Sample 2

Purchase your Explore Card today, and save tomorrow! With the Explore Card you will receive substantial savings and bonuses at a number of retailers. Look on our website at www.explorecard.com to see where you will save. Discounts range from 10-50% at respective retailers, including anything from hair salons to airlines. The Explore Card can be yours for only $49.99, and will never expire! Pick one up at any of the following locations.

Q. What is being advertised?

(a) A credit card program that rewards users
(b) A discount card with no expiration date
(c) A mileage card for frequent traveling
(d) A cashback card for retailers

안내문 및 공지의 경우 특정한 장소에 있는 사람들에게 전달하는 안내, 정보 및 지시 사항으로 주로 출제된다. 버스나 비행기, 열차 등의 대중교통 안내 방송과 기타 공공장소에서 손님이나 관람객에게 하는 안내 방송이 여기에 속한다. 안내문은 전개 방식에 익숙해져야 하는데 특히 청취할 때 지문의 초반 내용을 잘 듣는 것이 포인트이다. 또한 지문을 분석하고 중요한 내용을 정리해 보는 훈련도 필수이다. 문제를 풀 때 항상 질문의 내용과 지문에서 힌트가 나오는 위치를 확인하는 것 역시 핵심이다.

Sample 3

Attention, shoppers! We ask that at this time all customers please look inside their shopping bags and verify that you don't have the wrong bags. I repeat, please take a moment to check that you have not mistakenly taken someone else's bags. If you notice that you have done so, please report to the customer service desk on the main floor, immediately. Thank you for your attention, and thank you for shopping at Hillside Mall.

Q. Why is the announcement most likely being made?

(a) There is a shortage of shopping bags.

(b) Some merchandise has been stolen.

(c) A number of designer bags have gone missing.

(d) A customer has lost his or her shopping bags.

🔍 Focus 4 직장, 회의 관련 공지

직장, 회의 관련 공지의 경우 직원이나 회의 참석자들에게 회의 소집이나 회사 내부 및 외부 사정에 대한 알림, 그리고 회의 연기나 취소에 대한 공지 등이 출제되는 편인데, 공지의 전달자(Who is the speaker?)와 공지되는 장소(Where is this announcement heard?), 그리고 공지의 대상(Who is the intended audience for this announcement?), 공지의 목적(What is the announcement about?), 공지의 세부 사항(What is the reason of canceling the conference?) 등이 출제 대상이 된다.

Sample 4

In order to minimize the influence of the holidays on our productivity, we ask you to be aware of the following considerations. First, please be advised that it is next to impossible to accommodate every person's request for days off. Second, management will guarantee each employee only two of the holidays: Thanksgiving, Christmas or New Years. Third, priority will be given to employees who did not receive their preference last year.

Q. Which of the following is correct according to the announcement?

(a) Some employees will get first pick this year.

(b) The company will close on the holidays.

(c) Employees will not get paid for vacation.

(d) All employees will have three holidays off.

Essential Expressions for L/C

1 **Be my guest.** 사양하지 말고 하세요

2 **Break a leg!** 행운을 빌어!

3 **Come and get it.** 와서 드세요. 와서 가져가세요.

4 **Don't be such a stranger.** 가끔 들르세요.

5 **Don't boss me around.** 나한테 이래라저래라 하지 마.

6 **Don't get me wrong.** 오해하지 마.

7 **Don't let it get to you.** 너무 신경 쓰지 마.

8 **Don't let it get you down.** 너무 기운 빠져 있지 마.

9 **Hang in there!** (힘들어도) 참고 견뎌!

10 **Look who's here.** 이게 누구야! 만나서 반갑다.

11 **Make a way!** 길을 비켜 주세요.

12 **Pardon me for living.** 폐를 끼쳐 죄송합니다.

13 **Step on it!** 빨리 가주세요.

14 **Something came up.** 일이 좀 생겼어.

15 **I mean it.** 진짜야. 진심이야.

16 **I'll tell you what.** 좋은 수가 있어.

17 **I'm so flattered.** 과찬의 말씀이십니다.

18 **It's a good thing.** 다행이야.

19 **It's a bargain.** 싸게 잘 샀어.

20 **You are too much.** 당신 너무하는군요.

21 **You are so cheap.** 너 정말 치사하다.

22 **It serves you right.** 쌤통이다.

23 **It was a close call.** 큰일 날 뻔했어.

24 **You know better (then that).** 알 만한 사람이 왜 그래?

25 **You name it.** 말씀만 하세요.

26 **You say out of it.** 넌 끼어들지 마.

Actual Test

PART I   Choose the most appropriate response to the statement.

1. (a)   (b)   (c)   (d)

2. (a)   (b)   (c)   (d)

3. (a)   (b)   (c)   (d)

PART II   Choose the most appropriate response to complete the conversation.

4. (a)   (b)   (c)   (d)

5. (a)   (b)   (c)   (d)

PART III   Choose the option that best answers the question.

6. (a)   (b)   (c)   (d)

PART IV   Choose the option that best answers the question.

7. (a)   (b)   (c)   (d)

Actual Test Script

PART I Choose the most appropriate response to the statement.

1 M: Luke got a better offer at another company.
W: _________________________________

(a) You can't depend on anyone these days.
(b) I didn't expect him to be fired.
(c) He deserves that raise.
(d) He never misses a good opportunity.

2 W: I've never seen a more absurd movie!
M: _________________________________

(a) You're telling me.
(b) What is happening?
(c) Me, too. Let's watch it again.
(d) Then, don't go.

3 W: Could I borrow your cell phone for a second?
M: _________________________________

(a) Talk to me.
(b) Sounds great.
(c) By all means.
(d) Unfortunately, yes.

PART II Choose the most appropriate response to complete the conversation.

4 M: I want to sell my car.
W: Already? Didn't you buy it only two months ago?
M: Yes, but the engine keeps making strange sounds.
W: _________________________________

(a) Do what is best for your car.
(b) Sounds like a great deal to me.
(c) I had no problem with the sounds before.
(d) Why don't you explain this to your mechanic?

5 W: How did Nick like the project idea?

M: Truth is, he's less than enthusiastic.

W: You mean he didn't agree to it?

M: _______________________________

(a) Yes, he was quite adamant.

(b) No, he almost tore it up.

(c) Yes, he loved it completely.

(d) Yes, he missed you.

PART III Choose the option that best answers the question.

6 W: After being guided through the houses, I've narrowed it down to three.

M: What interests you the most?

W: The beachside house is my favorite, though on the pricy side.

M: That's because that house has the best location in town. The ocean view is gorgeous.

W: That may be so, but it seems to have been damaged by the weather. I noticed some chipped paint and rusty plumbing.

M: This is one of the hottest homes on the market. Perhaps we can find you a lot that matches your price range.

Q. What is the man's intention?

(a) To repaint the house for the woman

(b) To prevent the woman from buying the house

(c) To make a sale regardless of price

(d) To sell the house at the original price

7 I would like to express my gratitude for allowing me to speak at your university tonight. As you probably know, my name is Margaret Atwood, and I do consulting work with some of the top marketing firms in the country. As the economy opens up into a growing global market, the career opportunities for those with a marketing background will increase exponentially. Many graduates of business marketing become recruited right out of college into large corporations. In addition, the broad range of skills involved in the study of marketing means that graduates will be qualified to work in many other related fields.

Q. According to this talk, what are the job prospects like for graduates in marketing?

(a) Limited to a few specialized fields
(b) Will likely fluctuate due to globalization
(c) Pretty slim for the near future
(d) Very bright in the coming years

Memo 

Chapter
09   은행과 금융

🔍 Focus 1   계좌 개설 상황은 필수

은행 관련 문제 중 가장 많이 등장하는 것이 계좌 개설인데 고객(customer)용 표현과 은행원 (teller)용 표현으로 나누어서 암기하는 것이 좋다. 고객용 표현 중 가장 빈출되는 표현은 I'd like to open an account.(계좌를 개설하고 싶어요.), What kinds of accounts do you have?(어떤 종류의 예금이 있어요?), I want a savings account, please.(입출금 계좌를 개설하고 싶어요.), May I open a checking account?(당좌 계좌를 개설할 수 있나요?)이고, 은행원용 표현 중에서는 Please fill out this form.(이 서식 좀 기입해 주세요.), Do you have an account with us?(저희 은행에 계좌가 있으십니까?), Would you endorse it on the back?(뒷면에 이서해 주시겠습니까?), Your check was bounced.(손님 수표는 부도 수표입니다.) 등이 있다.

Sample 1

M: Excuse me, I'd like to open a savings account.

W: ___________________________

(a) Yes, you can cash the check here.
(b) Endorse this check, please.
(c) Why not? Here's my account.
(d) Sure, please fill out this application form.

🔍 **Focus 2** 송금, 이체

단순히 I'd like to send some money.(돈을 좀 송금하려고 하는데요.) 외에도 I'd like to remit some money to my son.(아들에게 돈을 좀 송금하고 싶어요.)라는 말도 나올 수 있고 Can I make a telegraphic transfer?(송금을 할 수 있나요?), Can I have direct billing?(자동이체 할 수 있나요?), Do I have access to the ATM?(현금 자동 지급기 쓸 수 있나요?) 등의 표현들이 많이 등장한다. 송금하기 전에는 잔액을 알아야 할 텐데 I'd like to know my balance.라는 문장이 등장할 경우 '저의 균형을 알고 싶어요.' 라고 해석하는 것이 아니라 '저의 예금 잔액을 알고 싶은데요.' 라고 해석해야 한다.

Sample 2

M: Hi, I'd like to remit some money to my son.

W: OK, sir. Do you have an account with us?

M: Yes. Can I have direct billing?

W: ________________________________

(a) Sure, what I need is your social security card and account number.

(b) Yes, we can directly take you home.

(c) Actually we need your account.

(d) How much did you pay for the car?

🔍 **Focus 3** 투자 관련

투자 관련 문제에서는 단연코 어휘 실력이 고득점을 좌우하는데 주택을 구입하는 상황이나 주식 관련 등이 등장할 수 있다. 참고로 주식(株式)이란 단어는 미국에서는 stock, 영국에서는 share 로 쓰이는데 현대 영어에서는 별 차이 없이 두 나라 사이에서 쓰이고 TEPS LC 시험에서도 두 단어 모두 번갈아가며 등장하는 것을 볼 수 있다. 기출 가능한 주식 관련 어휘로는 stock dividend(주식 배당), stock price(주식 시세), the face value of a stock(주식 액면가), stock subscription(주식 응모), stockbroker(주식 중매인), subscriber for shares(주식 청약인), transfer stocks(주식을 양도하다), deal in stocks/shares(주식을 매매하다) 등이 있다. 투자 관련 어휘로는 merger and acquisition(인수와 합병), capitally affiliated company(투자 관련 회사), capital(자본금), investor/financier(투자자), entrepreneur(실업가, 기업가) 등이 있다.

Sample 3

M: Wallace Corporation is interested in a merger. They could help us a lot.

W: Yes, they do have a lot of experience and depth.

M: We should definitely consider their offer very carefully.

W: _______________________________

(a) They have the same view with Wallace Corporation.

(b) I don't think we should take over their company.

(c) With all their assets, we can be the best in the market.

(d) No, I will contact them and arrange a meeting.

Focus 4 담보, 대출

Who are your references?라고 질문하는 경우 '당신의 참고인들은 누구신가요?' 라고 해석하는 경향이 있는데 이때 reference는 '신원보증인' 이라고 해석해야만 그 의미가 확실해져서 '당신의 신원보증인들은 누구입니까?' 라는 질문이 된다. 이보다 앞서 은행 직원이 대출을 신청하는 고객에게 물어보는 질문 중 Do you have any collateral?이라고 하면 '무슨 담보물이 있으십니까' 라는 의미가 되므로 확실히 기억해 두기 바란다.

Sample 4

W: Were you turned down on your loan request?

M: Yeah, I was really surprised, to be honest.

W: Do you know why the bank rejected your application?

M: _______________________________

(a) I think because I don't have a stable income.

(b) My expenses will no longer be covered.

(c) No, I only requested $50,000 in total.

(d) Yes, the hours are only 10 to 3 pm on weekdays.

Actual Test

PART I Choose the most appropriate response to the statement.

1. (a)   (b)   (c)   (d)
2. (a)   (b)   (c)   (d)
3. (a)   (b)   (c)   (d)

PART II Choose the most appropriate response to complete the conversation.

4. (a)   (b)   (c)   (d)
5. (a)   (b)   (c)   (d)

PART III Choose the option that best answers the question.

6. (a)   (b)   (c)   (d)

PART IV Choose the option that best answers the question.

7. (a)   (b)   (c)   (d)

Actual Test Script

PART I Choose the most appropriate response to the statement.

1 M: My eyes have been irritated and sore recently.
W: ________________________________

(a) I'm sorry that you believe so.
(b) Why don't you go see an oculist?
(c) What do you say to visiting obstetrician?
(d) I'm not pulling the wool over your eyes!

2 W: What's with the glum expression?
M: ________________________________

(a) I got mugged on my way here.
(b) I hope you feel better.
(c) I can't express how I feel.
(d) I had cosmetic surgery.

3 M: If you are free this weekend, I'd like to do something together.
W: ________________________________

(a) There must be a reason you didn't answer my phone call.
(b) Can I take you up on that some other time?
(c) I'm home all alone right now.
(d) Please hang on while I get dressed to go.

PART II Choose the most appropriate response to complete the conversation.

4 M: Is it true that you had hip replacement surgery?
W: That's right. I was in the hospital for almost a week.
M: That's awful. Was that covered by your insurance?
W: ________________________________

(a) No, that's a great deal.
(b) Yes, it will cost me an arm and a leg.
(c) No, it's going to hurt the pocketbook.
(d) Yes, it's very painful all over.

5 W: Thank you for calling Portland Industries. This is Janice speaking.

M: Good afternoon. I need to speak with Mr. Zinn.

W: Mr. Zinn has left the office for a business meeting.

M: _______________________________

(a) Would you tell him that I called?

(b) Our office is open all day.

(c) He'll be back around 1:30 pm.

(d) Is this Mr. Zinn speaking?

PART III Choose the option that best answers the question.

6 W: I can't decide what I want to see tonight.

M: Nothing heavy like the last one, I hope.

W: Have you seen this one? It looks pretty good to me.

M: A foreign film? You know that it's not easy for me to read the subtitles.

W: This is an award-winning film. It's supposed to be very romantic, as well.

M: Surely we can find something different. I can't enjoy the images if I'm reading text the whole time.

W: Fine. How about you just pick something?

M: Okay. A comedy would be good for a change.

Q. Which is correct according to the conversation?

(a) The man is not picky about movie genres.

(b) The man enjoys watching romantic films.

(c) The couple decided not to rent any movies tonight.

(d) The man wants to watch a film in his own language.

7   From sending letters to conducting research to download music, the Internet is replacing other mediums for more and more of our daily activities. New legislation has paved the way for people to use online contracts to conduct business transactions that, like their paper counterparts, are legally binding. People will be able to put their electronic signature on checks, wills, and house deeds with technology that authorizes that their identity is legitimate. While convenience is the biggest advantage of this new system, the potential for abuse has worried many security and consumer interest organizations.

Q. What is the main topic of the news report?

(a) A bill that restricts Internet contracts
(b) New technology for information security
(c) Legislation that legalizes electronic signatures
(d) A method for catching cyberthieves

Memo

Chapter 10

쇼핑과 교통

🔍 Focus 1 점원과 고객의 대화 차이

쇼핑 관련 대화는 서비스를 제공하는 사람과 서비스를 받는 사람의 대화를 주제로 가장 많이 설정한다. 따라서 선택지를 고를 때는 이 질문이 손님에 관한 것인지 점원에 관한 것인지를 정확히 감지해야 한다.

Sample 1

W: Your total comes to $15.46.

M: May I pay with a credit card?

W: I'm afraid not. This is a cash-only counter for 10 or fewer items.

M: I'm sorry I didn't know. But can't I just pay this once with my credit card?

W: Well, just this time, since there's no other customer behind you.

M: Thank you.

Q. What is the man going to do according to the conversation?

(a) Pay for his shopping in cash

(b) Go to another counter

(c) Pay with his credit card

(d) Talk to the manager

🔍 Focus 2 쇼핑 관련 어휘는 필수

쇼핑에서 우리 한국인들이 조심해야 하는 표현으로는 '와이셔츠' 를 Y-shirts라고 하지 않고 dress shirt라고 한다는 점, '둘러보는 것' 을 seeing이라고 하지 않고 browsing이라고 한다는 점 등이다. 특히 eye shopping이라는 말을 쓰는 경우 문자 그대로 눈을 구입한다는 의미가 되므로 상당히 엽기적인 뜻이 되어 버린다. 그러므로 window shopping이라고 한다는 점에 유의한다.

Sample 2

M: Can I exchange these pants? They're far too long.

W: ________________________________

(a) As long as you have a receipt.

(b) Sorry, we don't do tailoring here.

(c) Well, it will cost extra.

(d) Yes, they look a bit short on you.

옷 고르기, 물건 찾기, 계산하기 등 점원과 고객의 대화가 주인 쇼핑에서 빠지지 않고 출제될 수 있는 것이 바로 complaint 상황이다. 이 complaint 상황에는 반품(return), 교환(exchange), 환불(refund)이 포함되는데 보통 옷의 색깔, 사이즈, 스타일 등이 맞지 않아서 다른 것으로 바꿔 달라고 하거나 돈으로 전부 환불을 요구하는 케이스가 여기에 속한다.

Sample 3

W: Can I return these socks, please?

M: Certainly, ma'am. May I see your receipt?

W: Yes, here it is. And here are the socks.

M: Madam, these socks are dirty! You can only return clothes that are unworn.

W: Oh, I didn't know that.

Q. Why couldn't the woman get the refund?

(a) Because the socks had been worn

(b) Because she did not have a receipt

(c) Because she did not bring the socks

(d) Because the socks were bought elsewhere

Focus 4 길 안내 관련

매 시험 빠지지 않고 등장하는 길 안내(direction)는 특정 장소나 정류장 등 공공시설에 가는 방법뿐만 아니라 걸리는 시간, 거리 등을 묻는 경우로 선택지 정답이 대부분 동사원형으로 시작하는 경우가 일반적이다. 보통 질문할 때 Can you give me directions?, Could you show me the way?, Where can I find~?, Would you show me the way~? 등으로 시작하며 Just follow the nose.(그냥 앞으로 쭉 가세요.), It's a stone's throw away.(엎어지면 코 닿을 거리예요.) 등의 관용 표현도 종종 출제될 수 있으므로 유의하여 청취한다.

Sample 4

W: Excuse me. Can you direct me to the nearest post office?

M: You can buy stamps at the corner store if that's all you need.

W: No, I need to send a surprise package to my sister in Japan.

M: Oh, you'll have to go to the downtown post office to do that.

W: Could you tell me how to get there?

M: Certainly. Keep going down this street for two blocks. Look for North Street.

W: I'll hit North Street two blocks up. Which way do I turn?

M: Turn left on North Street. You can't miss it.

Q. What can be inferred from the conversation?

(a) The man doesn't know where the post office is.

(b) The woman's sister doesn't know about the package.

(c) Both the man and the woman are from out of town.

(d) The woman will probably go to the corner store.

비행기와 여행 관련 문제는 자주 출제되는 관련 어휘만 암기하면 어렵지 않게 문제를 풀 수 있는 토픽이다. aisle seat(통로 쪽 좌석), window seat(창가 쪽 좌석), personal effects(개인 소지품), customs(세관, 관세), scale(저울), vaccination(예방접종), carrousel(수화물 컨베이어) 등의 여행 관련 어구들은 반드시 외워 둔다.

Sample 5

W: Globe Travels. How may I direct your call?

M: Hi, I just have a question about cancellations.

W: Certainly. What would you like to know?

M: I have a flight booked to Vegas on Friday that I might have to cancel.

W: If you cancel with at least 24 hours' notice, there is no penalty.

M: And what if I cancel with less than a day's notice?

W: All cancellations less than 24 hours before departure incur a penalty.

M: Okay, that's good to know. I'll call back later.

Q. What is the man mainly doing?

(a) Canceling his flight reservation

(b) Reserving a seat for Vegas

(c) Checking the airline cancellation policy

(d) Requesting a refund on a reserved ticket

Actual Test

PART I Choose the most appropriate response to the statement.

1. (a) (b) (c) (d)
2. (a) (b) (c) (d)
3. (a) (b) (c) (d)

PART II Choose the most appropriate response to complete the conversation.

4. (a) (b) (c) (d)
5. (a) (b) (c) (d)

PART III Choose the option that best answers the question.

6. (a) (b) (c) (d)

PART IV Choose the option that best answers the question.

7. (a) (b) (c) (d)

Actual Test Script

PART I Choose the most appropriate response to the statement.

1 M: Don't you think we should ask Derrick Jensen to be master of ceremonies?
W: ________________________________

(a) I know. It won't be popular.

(b) Talking in front of groups is terrifying.

(c) He'll probably be interested in participating.

(d) There were lots of good speakers last time.

2 W: Whoa, careful! You almost hit that bicyclist.
M: ________________________________

(a) Oh, I wasn't paying attention.

(b) I prefer watching cars to bikes.

(c) No problem. I'm insured.

(d) I'm a much better driver than cyclist.

3 M: What do you say we ride bikes instead of drive?
W: ________________________________

(a) I don't have enough cash right now.

(b) I like my clothes this way.

(c) It's way too cold outside.

(d) Okay, here's the bus stop.

PART II Choose the most appropriate response to complete the conversation.

4 M: Traffic is getting worse and worse here.
W: I know. Even going outside has become dangerous for one's health.
M: I wonder if there is anything to be done.
W: ________________________________

(a) If gas were more affordable, that would help.

(b) Companies could reduce their electricity consumption.

(c) We could raise the price of cars.

(d) Taking public transportation is one solution.

5 M: Wanda, fancy running into you here!

    W: Ed, it's been such a long time. Is Elisabeth doing well?

    M: Things couldn't be better for her. In fact her first book was just published.

    W: ___________________________________

    (a) Is that so? Tell her congratulations from me.

    (b) I sure hope that things change for the better.

    (c) That bad luck won't last for long.

    (d) You really are too modest about it.

PART III Choose the option that best answers the question.

6 M: Okay, we'd better get going.

    W: Wait a second while I find my necklace.

    M: Why does this always happen? We are going to be late.

    W: Give me just a few more minutes.

    M: I've already been waiting for twenty minutes.

    W: Well, stop standing there and give me a hand looking.

    M: Look. They were in this drawer the whole time.

    W: That's not it. I'm talking about the one with diamonds.

    Q. What can be inferred from the conversation?

    (a) The couple will be on time to the party.

    (b) The man regrets giving her the necklace.

    (c) The woman was thinking of a certain necklace.

    (d) The woman typically leaves her necklace in the drawer.

7 One of the biggest concerns facing a college-bound student is getting accepted into their desired university. This admissions process can vary greatly between different countries, and understanding the differences can help students to decide the situation that fits them best. Take, for example, the difference between universities in Germany versus those in Sweden. While German universities have competitive admission standards and are, at times, quite exclusive, anyone who has completed secondary education can be admitted into Swedish universities.

Q. Which of the following most clearly distinguishes the German university system from that of Swedish universities?

(a) Academic level
(b) Citizenship
(c) The admissions policy
(d) An array of options

Memo 

Chapter

11 구직과 **직장**

Q Focus **1** 구직과 인터뷰

구직 상황은 상당히 자주 출제되는 토픽으로 이력서(resume) 넣기, 추천하기와 취직 부탁, 면접, 경력 말하기, 희망 부서와 급여 말하기, 면접 결과 확인 등으로 나뉠 수 있으며 우리에게 친숙하지 않은 표현도 있으므로 주의해야 한다. 예를 들어 I have a certificate of shorthand.라고 하면 '저는 짧은 손 증명서가 있어요.' 가 아니라 '저는 속기 자격증이 있습니다.' 라고 해석해야 한다.

Sample 1

M: Hi, there. Could I speak with you?

W: Certainly. What is it?

M: I was wondering if you spoke to your boss about an opening in your IT department.

W: Oh, dear. I forgot that I said I would do that.

M: Could you do it today?

W: Actually, my boss is away in Brazil for a month.

Q. What can be inferred from the conversation?

(a) The man is interested in a job.

(b) The woman is the man's boss.

(c) The man is thinking of retiring.

(d) The woman doesn't listen to the man.

Q Focus 2 사원끼리의 대화

사원끼리의 대화는 크게 분류했을 때 상사와의 갈등을 토로하고 그것에 대해 의견을 나누는 상황, 상대방이나 제3자가 승진했을 때 그것을 축하하는 상황, 자신의 문제를 같이 나누는 상황으로 볼 수 있다. 또한 서로의 부서에 대해 정보를 나누는 상황, 근무 조건에 대한 정보를 나누는 상황, 회사를 그만둘 것인가에 대해 의견을 나누는 상황 등도 있을 수 있다. 직장 쪽에서는 신입사원으로 입사한 상황, 새로운 부서로 전근하는(transfer) 상황, 진급(promotion)하는 상황, 직장을 그만두거나(resign) 고용인 본인의 잘못으로 해고되는(fired) 상황, 회사의 구조 조정(restructuring/downsizing) 등으로 정리 해고되는(laid off) 상황, 상사와의 갈등(conflict) 등 여러 가지로 나뉜다.

Sample 2

W: I didn't see you at the staff meeting at lunch.

M: ___________________________

(a) I know. I couldn't make it.
(b) I have some staffing concerns.
(c) Why don't I attend instead?
(d) Yes, I'll meet you for lunch.

Q Focus 3 직장 상사와의 갈등

보고서 제출(submit the report)로 상사와 갈등을 겪는다든지, 지각을 하는 상황, 초과 근무 때문에 다툰다든지, 상사의 성품(character) 때문에 갈등을 겪는 상황 등이 출제될 수 있다. I was under fire from the boss.(상사에게 혼났어.), I had words with my boss.(상사하고 말다툼을 했어요.), I don't get along with my immediate manager.(직속 상사와 잘 지내지 못해요.), Don't boss me around.(저에게 이래라저래라 하지 말아 주세요.) 등이 출제 가능한 관련 표현이다.

M: You don't look so good. Is your day going OK?

W: Not so good I'm afraid.

M: Do you want to talk about it?

W: Not really, but the boss really chewed me out earlier for being late with the spreadsheet.

M: When did he need it?

W: Last night, but it was so much work I needed a longer deadline.

M: So is it done or are you still on it?

Q. What are the speakers mainly talking about?

(a) The reason the woman is late to the office

(b) Why the woman is looking for another job

(c) The reason the woman is having a rough time

(d) Why the boss was angry at the woman

🔍 Focus 4 회의 관련 대화

회의 관련 대화에서는 conference나 meeting의 참석자끼리의 논쟁, 요구 사항, 제안과 평가 등이 출제 대상이 될 수 있다. 잘 나올 수 있는 표현으로는 How about starting from scratch?가 있는데, 이는 '긁는 것부터 시작하는 것이 어때요?' 라고 해석하는 것이 아니라 '처음으로 되돌아가는 것이 어때요?' 라고 해석한다. 또 What's the bottom line on your idea?라고 질문하면 bottom line을 '요점', '핵심' 으로 해석해서 '당신 아이디어의 핵심이 뭡니까?' 라고 해석한다는 것을 명심하자.

Sample 4

W: Would it be possible for us to postpone our meeting to next week?

M: Why? Is anything the matter?

W: Actually, I have yet to finish preparing a paper for the meeting.

M: _______________________________

(a) I'll talk with the manager about it later this afternoon.

(b) I promise I'll get it done by next weekend.

(c) That's easier said than done.

(d) I had words with my boss.

PART I Choose the most appropriate response to the statement.

1. (a)   (b)   (c)   (d)
2. (a)   (b)   (c)   (d)
3. (a)   (b)   (c)   (d)

PART II Choose the most appropriate response to complete the conversation.

4. (a)   (b)   (c)   (d)
5. (a)   (b)   (c)   (d)

PART III Choose the option that best answers the question.

6. (a)   (b)   (c)   (d)

PART IV Choose the option that best answers the question.

7. (a)   (b)   (c)   (d)

Actual Test **Script**

1 M: You went bungee jumping? How was that experience?
W: _______________________________

(a) I've done it a few times.
(b) I've heard that it's dangerous.
(c) It was both petrifying and exhilarating.
(d) It's going to be incredible.

2 M: What is taking so long to finish?
W: _______________________________

(a) I took all my equipment home.
(b) Take as much time as you need.
(c) This is not a long story.
(d) It's harder than I expected.

3 M: (*sneezing*) Excuse me.
W: _______________________________

(a) I'm sorry.
(b) Everything will be okay.
(c) What do you want?
(d) Bless you!

PART II Choose the most appropriate response to complete the conversation.

4 M: Hi, I'm Eric Schwartz.
W: I'm Jocelyn Graf. It's a pleasure meeting you.
M: Ms. Graf, how do you like to be addressed?
W: _______________________________

(a) I don't have a cell phone.
(b) Please call me after 4 pm.
(c) Just call me Jo.
(d) Indeed. Very nice to meet you.

5 M: I need to speak with you about something.

W: I'm overwhelmed with tasks right now.

M: It's just a quick question. I promise.

W: _______________________________

(a) Fine. Get to the point, though.

(b) How dare you question my judgement?

(c) Of course. It's worth it in the long run.

(d) Okay, start slowly from the beginning.

PART III Choose the option that best answers the question.

6 M: So, Phillip has been working with your project team?

W: Yes. What do you think about him?

M: He's a hard-working and decent person.

W: That's surprising to hear.

M: Seriously? Doesn't he fit in with your team?

W: Far from it. He's like oil in water.

Q. How is Phillip doing in his new project team?

(a) He is making lots of progress.

(b) He is praised for his diligence.

(c) He has impressed his supervisor.

(d) He is like a square peg in a round hole.

7 Authorities are still searching for the teenaged girl who went missing five days ago while vacationing in Hawaii. Search teams have been mobilized throughout the island, so far with no results. Investigators have suggested that foul play may be involved, but have yet to announce any suspects. The family is asking that anyone with any information of her whereabouts immediately contact the police. Tips can be given anonymously by calling 023-989-8763. Her hometown community is hoping for her wellbeing.

Q. Which is correct according to the recorded message?

(a) Police have apprehended suspects in the girl's disappearance.
(b) The missing girl is a Hawaii resident.
(c) The police are hoping to receive help from the public to find her.
(b) Authorities are confident that they will solve the case soon.

Memo

Chapter 12

전화와 우체국

🔍 Focus 1 전화로 다른 사람을 찾을 때

전화 통화 관련 문제는 난이도는 그리 높지 않지만 가끔씩 시제와 인칭을 혼동시키는 함정이 등장하고 출제율이 상당히 높은 토픽이므로 절대 소홀히 공부해서는 안 되는 파트라고 할 수 있다. 다른 사람을 찾을 때의 표현도 그렇지만, 다른 전화 통화 관련 표현도 대부분 한 가지 상황에도 다양한 표현이 등장할 수 있으므로 표현들을 한꺼번에 외워 두는 것이 현명한 공부법일 것이다. 상대방을 찾는 표현은 May I speak to~?, Is ~ in?, Is ~ available?, I'm trying to reach~. 등 여러 가지가 있다.

Sample 1

W: Hello, this is Patricia White calling. I would like to speak with Mr. Tyre.

M: ___________________________

(a) I've wanted to see you.
(b) Please sign your name here.
(c) May I ask what this is regarding?
(d) Why don't you give him a call?

🔍 Focus 2 찾는 사람이 있을 때와 부재중일 때

전화로 사람을 찾을 때는 두 가지 상황이 연출될 수 있다. 그 중 첫 번째는 찾는 이가 자리에 있어서 그 사람 본인이 받든지 다른 사람이 연결해 주는 상황이다. 이런 경우 전화 연결을 해줄 테니 기다리라든지(I'll put you through.) 내가 그 사람이라는(Speaking, who's calling?) 표현을 쓴다. Please hold on.(기다려 주십시오.), You are wanted on the phone.(당신 전화예요.), There's a call for you.(전화 왔어요.) 등이 유용한 출제 예상 표현들이다. 두 번째 상황은 찾는 사람이 잠깐 화장실에 갔다든지 복사하는 중이라든지 하는 이유로 부재중이니까(She's stepped out.) 잠시 기다리거나 1~5분 후에 다시 전화하라는 상황, 찾는 사람이 식사하러 갔다든지(He's gone for lunch.) 퇴근했으니(He's gone for the day.) 나중에 다시 전화하라고 하는 상황이다.

Sample 2

M: May I please speak to Joss? It's Daniel calling.

W: _______________________________

(a) Sorry, she's in the shower.

(b) You'll have to call her.

(c) Please leave a message.

(d) No, Danielle's not here.

🔍 Focus 3 통화 중, 혼선

우리가 흔히 알고 있는 The line is busy. 외에도 The line is engaged.로 표현되는 '통화 중'은 가끔 The line is occupied.라고 표현될 때도 있다. 참고할 것은 통화 중이라고 할 때는 내 전화선은 상관없고 전화 건 사람이 찾는 사람의 line만 가지고 얘기하는 것이므로 항상 단수 동사를 써서 표현하는 반면, The lines are messed up.이나 The lines are crossed.로 표현되는 혼선의 경우는 적어도 두 전화선 간의 혼선을 말하므로 동사를 항상 복수로 표현하는 것이 원칙이다.

Sample 3

Thank you for calling the Mammoth Medical Center. All of the nurses are currently busy. If you are experiencing a medical emergency, please hang up and dial 911. If you would like to make an appointment for immunizations, please dial 1. If you would like to speak with a nurse about a health concern, please stay on the line and a nurse will be with you as soon as possible.

Q. What can be inferred from the message?

(a) The office is presently closed.

(b) The phone line is for emergencies only.

(c) For immunization appointments, stay on the line.

(d) The nurses are currently occupied with other patients.

○ Focus **4** 우체국 관련

우체국 관련 문제는 어휘가 필수적인데 국제우편(international/overseas mail), 선박우편(surface mail), 등기우편(registered mail), 속달우편(express mail), 소포우편(parcel post), 우편번호(zip code), 우편요금(postage) 등이 자주 등장한다. 우체국 역시 레스토랑이나 호텔처럼 서비스를 제공하는 우체국 직원과 서비스를 받는 손님과의 화자 혼동을 함정으로 하는 경우가 가끔 있으므로 주의하도록 한다.

Sample 4

W: Hi, I need to send this to Canada.

M: Is your shipping label filled out?

W: Yes, here it is.

M: OK. Do you want to send this by regular mail or express mail?

W: I think ground would be fine. It's not urgent.

M: Anything liquid, perishable or fragile?

W: No, but it does have some valuables inside.

M: Then I suggest you insure it.

Q. Which is correct according to the dialogue?

(a) The man recommends insuring the package.

(b) The woman wants to send it by express mail.

(c) The man advises to send it by regular mail.

(d) The woman has not filled out the shipping label.

PART I Choose the most appropriate response to the statement.

1. (a) (b) (c) (d)
2. (a) (b) (c) (d)
3. (a) (b) (c) (d)

PART II Choose the most appropriate response to complete the conversation.

4. (a) (b) (c) (d)
5. (a) (b) (c) (d)

PART III Choose the option that best answers the question.

6. (a) (b) (c) (d)

PART IV Choose the option that best answers the question.

7. (a) (b) (c) (d)

Listening Comprehension

Grammar

Vocabulary

Reading Comprehension

Actual Test **Script**

PART I Choose the most appropriate response to the statement.

1 M: Good morning, Betty. What's cooking?
W: _______________________________

(a) I'm going right now.
(b) Some instant noodles.
(c) Not much. How about you?
(d) She doesn't know.

2 M: Are the chances good that I'll get that promotion?
W: _______________________________

(a) Yes, you should take a well-deserved break.
(b) No, it's not necessary to renew the contract.
(c) No, I don't engage in gambling.
(d) Yes, I'd say it's a possibility.

3 M: I think I may have caught a bug from my kids.
W: _______________________________

(a) Aren't you proud to have such brave kids?
(b) You should be careful. Insects can be dangerous.
(c) Go ahead and stay home. Relax for the day.
(d) I love playing catch with my children, too.

PART II Choose the most appropriate response to complete the conversation.

4 W: It's about time you got here. I'd almost given up on waiting.
M: It wasn't my fault. I got a flat tire and had to replace it.
W: In a situation like that, you should have at least given me a call to let me know.
M: _______________________________

(a) Well, I can't change tires so well.
(b) I'll do that if it ever happens again.
(c) I won't worry much about that.
(d) Okay. I'll call you as soon as possible.

5 M: Have you heard about the mobile phone company that is offering free telephone
service for calls between family members?

W: No, I haven't. That could really save me a lot of money. Most of my phone bills
are from chats I have with my parents.

M: I'm a little skeptical. I think a deal as good as that must have a catch somewhere.

W: ________________________________

(a) I'm going to call my mom right now.

(b) The cost of calling long distance is enormous.

(c) I don't think that my family would like that service.

(d) It's important to know the details before signing up.

PART III Choose the option that best answers the question.

6 W: John, what a pleasant surprise!

M: Hi, Rachel. I spoke with Katie the other day and she mentioned that we should
get together sometime for drinks.

W: Great. How soon are we talking?

M: Is this Friday too short a notice?

W: No, Friday's good for me. What about dinner?

M: Katie volunteered to grill up something tasty at her place.

W: That sounds like fun. I'll bring the wine.

M: Okay. So it's this Friday at Katie's place.

W: I look forward to it. It's been a long time since I saw you guys.

M: Yeah, too long. Well, I'll see you Friday.

Q. Which is correct according to the dialogue?

(a) John and Rachel scheduled a date on Friday.

(b) Katie made reservations for dinner.

(c) Rachel will provide the wine.

(d) The three friends often meet.

7 Controversy has been brewing among California teachers over how to best teach English to non-native speaking students. Proponents of intensive ESL claim it is necessary in order to raise students' English levels to the degree where they could rapidly assimilate into a native speakers' classroom. Some teachers, however, believe that bilingual instruction will benefit children more. By teaching core lessons in their native language, while simultaneously providing English instruction, teachers believe that the sometimes traumatic adjustment to a new culture will be slower, but smoother.

Q. Which is correct according to the passage?

(a) Because it is the quickest method, instructers prefer intensive ESL instruction.

(b) Learning English is optional, and not emphasized in the bilingual method.

(c) Because it eases their transition into a new culture, the bilingual method is superior.

(d) Intensive ESL is designed to accelerate children's acclimation into classes with native speaking peers.

Memo 

Chapter 13

호텔과 레스토랑

Q Focus 1 예약에 대해 묻는 문제가 상당수

호텔과 레스토랑 관련 문제에서 어느 시험을 막론하고 가장 많이 등장하는 단어는 reservation(예약)이다. How large is your party?라고 하면 '당신의 파티는 얼마나 크냐?'가 아니라 '일행이 몇 명입니까?'로 봐야 한다는 것에 유의한다. 그리고 예약 관련 문제이므로 금액이나 시간 같은 숫자를 주의해서 청취하기 바란다.

Sample 1

W: I need a reservation for a double room in June. We're with the Russell wedding party.

M: Okay, we have a discounted rate arranged for that group.

W: Oh, wonderful. What is the rate then?

M: Will you be staying Friday to Sunday?

W: Yes, Friday and Saturday night at the hotel.

M: The discounted weekend rate for those dates will be $345.00.

Q. What is mainly taking place in the conversation?

(a) The man is planning a wedding.

(b) The woman is canceling a reservation.

(c) The speakers are discussing hotel rates.

(d) The man is asking the woman out on a date.

🔍 Focus 2 호텔 관련 기본 어휘

호텔 관련 문제는 기출 경향을 볼 때 숙박 기간과 원하는 방의 스타일 및 개수, 숙박 요금, 방이 없을 때의 상황, 예약 확인과 변경 · 취소, hotel이나 resort의 시설 물어보기, 귀중품 보관 및 체크아웃 등으로 나눌 수 있는데 관련 어휘를 철저히 정리하는 것이 중요하다. vacancy(빈방), rate(숙박 요금), valuables(귀중품), wake-up call(기상 전화 서비스), locked out of the room(방에 열쇠를 두고 나옴), booked up(빈방 없음), porter/concierge(짐꾼), laundry(세탁물 서비스) 등이 최근 출제되는 필수 어휘이다.

Sample 2

M: Does this hotel offer room service?

W: ________________________________

(a) We do, from 8 am-5 pm.

(b) It should be there promptly.

(c) We do have a full-service gym.

(d) No, our rooms are all booked.

🔍 Focus 3 레스토랑 관련 기본 어휘

This is on me.라고 하면 '이건 제가 내겠습니다.' 라는 의미이며, 만일 레스토랑 waiter가 This wine is on the house.라고 하면 '이 와인은 house가 내는 것입니다.' 라는 의미로 여기서 house는 레스토랑을 뜻한다. 그러므로 '이 와인은 서비스입니다.' 라고 하면 100% 완벽한 해석이다. 최근 들어 학생들이 의외로 모르는 부분을 발견했는데 Let's go Dutch.와 Let's go fifty-fifty.의 의미 차이이다. 전자는 네덜란드에 가자는 것이 아니라 '각자 부담하자.' 는 의미이고 후자의 경우는 '비용 나온 것을 반반씩 부담하자.' 이다. 특히 전자를 Let's do Dutch pay.라고 하는 학생이 있는 것 같은데 어법상 그렇게는 쓰지 않는다. go Dutch를 '비용을 각자 부담하다' 라는 의미로 외우도록 하자.

W: Dinner was so wonderful. Thank you so much.

M: You are more than welcome and it's on me.

W: No, let's go Dutch.

M: _______________________________

(a) No, let's go fifty-fifty.

(b) Here you are. Keep the change.

(c) How would you like it?

(d) Yes, of course. I especially like to go to Amsterdam.

Q Focus 4 화자 파악이 관건

쇼핑에서도 다루었듯이 호텔, 레스토랑에서도 서비스를 제공하는 화자(waiter, waitress, front office clerk, porter, etc.)와 서비스를 제공받는 화자(customer)의 관계 파악이 관건이 된다. 특히 격식을 갖춘 표현이 주를 이루므로 문장의 첫마디가 조동사와 과거형으로 쓰인 것들이 많음을 명심한다. Are you being served/helped/waited on?(주문하시겠습니까?) 또는 Would you mind filling this out?(서류 양식을 작성해 주시겠습니까?) 등 빈출되는 표현에 유의하자.

Sample 4

W: Brad's auto repair shop. How can I help you today?

M: I need to schedule an appointment for my car.

W: OK, what do you need done?

M: _______________________________

(a) I prefer to drive a truck.

(b) Two o'clock tomorrow sounds good.

(c) It's due for an oil change.

(d) Your car is ready to pick up.

Actual Test

PART I Choose the most appropriate response to the statement.

1. (a)   (b)   (c)   (d)
2. (a)   (b)   (c)   (d)
3. (a)   (b)   (c)   (d)

PART II Choose the most appropriate response to complete the conversation.

4. (a)   (b)   (c)   (d)
5. (a)   (b)   (c)   (d)

PART III Choose the option that best answers the question.

6. (a)   (b)   (c)   (d)

PART IV Choose the option that best answers the question.

7. (a)   (b)   (c)   (d)

Actual Test Script

PART I Choose the most appropriate response to the statement.

1 M: Get over it. Being teased by some bullies isn't such a big deal.

W: _______________________________

(a) That's a bad deal.

(b) You shouldn't pick on people.

(c) Do you have a problem with it?

(d) Oh, yeah? Try walking in my shoes.

2 M: I wish I hadn't lied to Fara.

W: _______________________________

(a) You should get up right now.

(b) Why did you tell her the truth?

(c) I thought you were better than that.

(d) I thought you'd make a good couple.

3 M: Why didn't I get a wedding invitation?

W: _______________________________

(a) Invite whoever you want to come.

(b) We changed our honeymoon destination.

(c) Perhaps it got lost in the mail.

(d) Glad you could make it.

PART II Choose the most appropriate response to complete the conversation.

4 M: I'm having back problems again.

W: Have you gotten a doctor to look at it?

M: I did. She recommended an expensive surgery.

W: _______________________________

(a) Surgery techniques have advanced recently.

(b) I doubt those problems will come back again.

(c) I'll be happy to help if money is a concern.

(d) I hurt it while playing basketball.

5 M: When did you decide to leave?

W: I made up my mind last month. I'm moving to Oregon.

M: What's your reason for leaving Los Angeles?

W: _________________________________

(a) We want to live closer to nature.

(b) I can see why you would want to leave.

(c) We have family we want to visit.

(d) I'm planning a camping trip over there.

PART III Choose the option that best answers the question.

6 M: Would you like to add a box of candy for just one dollar more?

W: No, thanks. I'll just take the two movies, please.

M: All right, then. Your total is going to be $21.78.

W: You can't be serious. Is it really that expensive to rent two videos?

M: Well, the cost of the two movies is $8.00, but you have $10 in late fees, plus tax.

W: Oh, yeah. I forgot about those. Is there any way you could take those off since I come here so often?

M: Sometimes the manager will erase late fees for regulars, but she's not in right now.

W: Oh, well, in that case, I'll just go ahead and get these anyway, I guess.

Q. What does the woman want?

(a) To get a deal on movie snacks

(b) To get her late fees taken off her total

(c) To sign up for a movie rental membership

(d) To buy movies for a lower price

7 Your susceptibility to heart disease is dramatically different depending on which gender you are. In the case of women, problems with family members or relationships may cause an emotion-based stress that, compared with physical stress, has more chance of inciting a heart attack. Studies of men show a situation completely reverse. Scientists theorize that men and women's bodies respond differently to different types of stress, with women exhibiting increased heart activity from emotional triggers while men's heart rate sees its biggest increase during physical exertion.

Q. Which is correct according to the passage?

(a) Women have less chance of experiencing a heart attack.
(b) Women are especially susceptible to heart problems when working hard.
(c) Men experience more adverse impact from physical stresses than women.
(d) There is little difference between the response of different genders to emotional problems.

Memo 

Chapter 14

날씨와 기상

🔍 Focus 1 날씨 문제는 결국 어휘 문제

날씨와 기상에서는 뭐니 뭐니 해도 어휘가 생명이라고 할 수 있는데 storming은 '폭풍우' 로, drizzling은 '이슬비' 라는 의미로 쓰인다. It's a snowstorm.이라고 하면 '눈보라가 휘날린다.' 는 뜻인 반면 It's sleeting.이라고 하면 '진눈깨비가 내린다.' 는 의미로 해석할 수 있다. 덥다는 표현 하나도 It's boiling hot.(삶는 듯한 더위예요.), It's sweltering hot.(푹푹 찌네요.), What a sizzler!(정말 푹푹 찌는군요!) 등 상당히 다양한 표현들이 응용되어 출제되므로 우리말 하나에도 되도록이면 여러 가지 표현을 같이 그룹으로 외워 두는 습관이 필수적으로 요구된다.

Sample 1

M: What a sizzler! It's boiling outside.

W: I know. Looks like another scorcher today.

M: I hope we are going to have some rain today.

W: ________________________________

(a) How did you know that we are going to have a shower?

(b) Actually I heard that we will have some showering today.

(c) It will clear up in the afternoon.

(d) It seems to be overcast today.

Q Focus **2** 오늘의 날씨? 내일의 날씨?

날씨 문제도 시제와 상당히 밀접하게 연관되어 출제된다는 점에 유의하자. 대화에 등장하는 날씨가 오늘 날씨인지, 내일 날씨인지, 아니면 다음 주 날씨인지 순간적으로 잘 포착하고 선택지를 고를 때도 질문의 시제가 무엇이었는지 잘 파악하여 내용은 맞는데 시제가 틀려서 오답을 고르는 일이 없도록 주의하자.

Sample 2

M: Have you seen the weather out there?

W: No, I've been inside all day.

M: You're not missing anything. It's gray and rainy.

W: ______________________________

(a) Actually we could use a good shower.

(b) It's too hot in July.

(c) Aren't there any windows?

(d) I've never been there before.

Q Focus **3** PART IV에 등장하는 기상 보도문

LC PART IV에서 등장하는 기상 보도문의 경우에는 AP 5분 뉴스나 AFN 방송을 꾸준히 청취하는 것이 좋다. Today's weather forecast calls for clear skies~라고 하면 자칫 '오늘 일기예보는 화창한 날을 부른다.' 라고 엉터리 해석을 할 수 있으나 call for라는 이어동사가 '예측하다, 예보하다' 라는 뜻이란 것을 안다면 '오늘 일기예보는 화창한 날이 될 것을 예보[예측]해 드립니다.' 라는 제대로 된 해석을 할 수 있다. 기상 보도문은 항상 시험 때마다 나왔던 말과 잘 쓰는 전문 어구들을 반복한다는 점을 명심하자.

Today's weather forecast calls for a serious strong tornado strike. The experts are currently chasing the tornado off the south coast of Pennsylvania. Winds are estimated up to 75 miles per hour and we are expecting a heavy shower. If you are a resident of a coastal area, it is strongly urged that you move inland immediately because this tornado is changing its position quite quickly and devastating any area it strikes. Local police are on their way to assist the evacuation. Please pay attention to their instructions.

Q. Which of the following is correct according to the weather forecast?

(a) The storm is unlikely to change its direction.
(b) People in coastal areas are being asked to leave their hometown due to the tornado.
(c) Police desperately need volunteers to assist the evacuation.
(d) The weatherman says there's no point in tracking the storm.

Sample 4

The forecast for Paris today is partly cloudy with a chance of rain overnight. Highs should reach the low 70s with the low dipping down to around 53. Tomorrow is the best chance we'll have at some sunshine. Expect rain and lower temperatures in the upper 60s and low 70s all weekend through Monday. Sunny skies return next Tuesday, and the weather should stay clear throughout the week.

Q. What will the weather be like tomorrow?

(a) Partly cloudy
(b) Rainy
(c) Sunny
(d) Cold

Actual Test

PART I Choose the most appropriate response to the statement.

    1. (a)   (b)   (c)   (d)

    2. (a)   (b)   (c)   (d)

    3. (a)   (b)   (c)   (d)

PART II Choose the most appropriate response to complete the conversation.

    4. (a)   (b)   (c)   (d)

    5. (a)   (b)   (c)   (d)

PART III Choose the option that best answers the question.

    6. (a)   (b)   (c)   (d)

PART IV Choose the option that best answers the question.

    7. (a)   (b)   (c)   (d)

Actual Test **Script**

1   W: You've been skipping dinner a lot recently.
M: ______________________________

(a) I know. I'm quite proud of myself.
(b) Okay. I'll stop bothering you from now on.
(c) Yes, I'll go on a diet starting tomorrow.
(d) I'm sorry, but my stomach has been acting up.

2   M: You just cut in line in front of that man.
W: ______________________________

(a) It's okay. I can wait.
(b) I'm cutting down on fat.
(c) I didn't realize that.
(d) Why is he in a rush?

3   M: Apparently, your film is making quite a buzz. I'm so proud of you.
W: ______________________________

(a) Look for it at a theatre near you.
(b) Trust me. The book is infinitely better.
(c) I'm confident that my audition will go well.
(d) I appreciate it. But I can't take responsibility for its success.

4   W: I've decided to join the circus. I hope you accept my decision.
M: Are you crazy? You can't make a career out of that.
W: Nonetheless, I've made up my mind.
M: ______________________________

(a) I knew I raised you to make good decisions!
(b) You're going to drive me to an early grave!
(c) Well, then. Let's celebrate!
(d) The apple doesn't fall far from the tree!

5 W: That was a mistake to buy so many lottery tickets.

M: Yeah. Sorry to say it, but you've got gambling issues.

W: You should have talked to me out of it.

M: ________________________________

(a) I doubt anything I said would have made a difference.

(b) I figured you had enough money, anyways.

(c) You don't need any more lottery tickets.

(d) You should give yourself a limit to control your spending.

PART III **Choose the option that best answers the question.**

6 W: How's the work coming along?

M: The job's great. I really like how flexible it is.

W: So, you have no time constraints?

M: Not exactly.

W: Huh? What does that mean?

M: I have quota goals that must be completed each month.

W: I'd like a situation like that.

Q. What can be inferred from the conversation about the man's job?

(a) Completing the quota takes up extra time.

(b) He doesn't work more than his coworkers.

(c) His work total is calculated on a monthly basis.

(d) His quota is flexible depending on available time.

7   Two massive earthquakes rocked Japan on Monday night, killing eight people and injuring 800 in the city of Kashiwazaki alone. The island nation is in one of the most earthquake-prone areas of the globe, but the recent quakes were worse than most, destroying structures that are built to survive Japan's frequent tremors. Roads, houses, and other buildings crumbled. But the most troubling damage was caused by a fire at a nuclear power plant. Thankfully, tsunami warnings turned out to be false alarms.

Q. What can be inferred from the article?

(a) Japan is located on a fault line.
(b) A tidal wave occurred after the earthquake.
(c) The nuclear plant will be closed for good.
(d) Kashiwazaki is one of Japan's largest cities.

Memo

Chapter

15 과학과 뉴스

Q Focus 1 기술 과학

에너지 자원(energy resources), 발명(invention), 자동차 기술(automobile technology), 건축 기술(construction technology), 전기(electricity), 컴퓨터(computer), 디지털 혁명(digital revolution) 등 기술 과학 담화문이 PART IV에서 자주 출제된다. 시사적으로 유행하는 전문 용어들을 정리하는 것이 필수적이다.

Sample 1

At this point in time, it is indisputable that technology has changed the way that people interact with one another. Mobile phones, e-mail, messenger, and networking sites such as 'facebook' have made it easier for people to stay in touch throughout the day. The question, though, is whether technology has changed things for the better. While the ease and frequency of communication has increased, what about the quality? People are becoming more and more isolated in spite of easier means of communication.

Q. Which is correct according to the speaker?

(a) Technology has made communication more difficult.
(b) Increased communication does not mean better quality.
(c) People are less isolated than they were before the Internet.
(d) Technology has had no effect on the way in which people interact.

Q Focus 2 의료 과학

의료 과학과 불가분의 관계에 있는 토픽으로는 비만(obesity), 당뇨병(diabetes) 및 이 두 질병을 치료하는 치료법(therapy)과 장수(longevity)를 돕는 기술, 그리고 줄기세포 연구(stem cell research)나 인간 복제(human cloning)처럼 논란이 되는 이슈(controversial issue), 수술을 로봇이 대신해 주는 의학 기술(robotic technology) 등이 대표적인 예가 될 수 있다.

Sample 2

Last night, millions of viewers were on the edge of their seats to see who would take home the grand prize for the World's Most Charming Pet. The road leading to the big night was definitely a bumpy one, as thousands of dogs, cats, birds, snakes, and other creatures from all around the country—with the help of their human companions, of course—took part in contests to see who would make it to the finals and win the $1,000,000 cash prize. Viewers were encouraged to call in after each episode and vote for their favorite, whittling the contestants down to just three. For those of you who missed it, I won't give away the winner since channel 2 is re-airing the final show at 8 PM on Tuesday.

Q. Which is the purpose of the announcement?

(a) To announce the winner of the contest
(b) To tell viewers about a rebroadcast
(c) To inform viewers about a contest
(d) To advertise a new TV program

Q Focus 3 뉴스 보도문

TEPS LC PART IV에 등장하는 뉴스 보도문은 라디오에서 흔히 접하는 단순한 안내 방송이나 날씨, 그리고 특정한 내용을 다루는 뉴스로 구성되어 출제되는데 news, weather report, radio & TV broadcast, business report 등이 등장한다. news에는 자연재해나 범죄 관련 소식을 비롯한 다양한 소재들이 등장하므로 주제, 전달자의 신분·직업, 뉴스의 구체적인 내용, 상황에 대한 안내 등을 정확하게 파악하도록 한다.

For the second time this month a local fast food chain in Brandon has been robbed. For security reasons at this time, we are not allowed to show footage of the robbery, captured on the store's cameras. As far as we understand, a masked man walked into the store at 6:34 am, just minutes after opening, and held a gun to the girl working at the front register. All of the remaining employees were forced into the downstairs freezer, while the girl opened the safe. The robber must have been aware that the bank deposit would not be made until later in the morning, and walked away with over $6,000 in sales from the night before.

Q. Which statement is correct about the robber according to the news?

(a) He robbed the same fast food chain earlier in the month.
(b) He had some knowledge of the store's bank deposit system.
(c) He walked in wearing a mask but without a weapon.
(d) He was a frequent customer of this specific store.

Sample 4

Our top story tonight: James Wilson, the great plane hijacker, has been caught in Guam. He was arrested in a Guam tourist nightclub. He is being questioned at a local police headquarters, and he will probably be sent back to Chicago. In 2001, James was sentenced to seventeen years in prison for his part in the Great Plane Hijacking at Chicago International Airport. He escaped from the Illinois State Penitentiary in July. Since then he has been seen in ten different countries.

Q. Which of the following is true according to the above news?

(a) The plane hijacker has escaped from the police in Guam.
(b) The plane hijacker was arrested in Chicago.
(c) The plane hijacker has been seen in several countries.
(d) The plane hijacker was caught at the airport.

Actual Test

PART I   Choose the most appropriate response to the statement.

    1. (a)   (b)   (c)   (d)

    2. (a)   (b)   (c)   (d)

    3. (a)   (b)   (c)   (d)

PART II   Choose the most appropriate response to complete the conversation.

    4. (a)   (b)   (c)   (d)

    5. (a)   (b)   (c)   (d)

PART III   Choose the option that best answers the question.

    6. (a)   (b)   (c)   (d)

PART IV   Choose the option that best answers the question.

    7. (a)   (b)   (c)   (d)

PART I Choose the most appropriate response to the statement.

1 M: Those two are identical.

W: ________________________________

(a) They were born on the same day.

(b) As a matter of fact, they are never apart.

(c) Even I get confused telling who's who.

(d) They take after their father.

2 M: Do we get complimentary breakfast at this hotel?

W: ________________________________

(a) That was the best breakfast ever.

(b) For a small extra charge.

(c) From seven to ten in the morning.

(d) Our restaurant is located upstairs.

3 M: Doesn't your brother know a lot about gardening?

W: ________________________________

(a) He'll be home later this afternoon.

(b) You could say he's got a green thumb.

(c) He really loves fruits and vegetables.

(d) I seem to have a problem with pests.

PART II Choose the most appropriate response to complete the conversation.

4 W: What does this stereo cost?

M: It's $89.99. I dare you to find a cheaper deal!

W: I can get the same thing for 70 bucks at Mars Music.

M: ________________________________

(a) I'm sorry to hear that.

(b) Our money-back policy is for two weeks.

(c) If that's the case, we'll lower our price.

(d) I told you we were cheap!

5 M: What did you pay for your college tuition?

W: Just 500 dollars.

M: You're kidding, surely. Why was it so inexpensive?

W: _______________________________

(a) I got a scholarship to cover the rest.

(b) It was a prestigious university.

(c) I registered at the last minute.

(d) I always dreamed of going there.

PART III Choose the option that best answers the question.

6 M: Did you ride your bike here?

W: No, I took my car.

M: I heard on the radio that traffic was bad, huh?

W: Awful. People don't know how to drive in this weather. As a matter of fact,
I was hit by a car on the way here.

M: What? Is everything okay?

W: Yeah. The damage is just cosmetic.

Q. Which of the following is correct according to the dialogue?

(a) The woman thinks that other people drive poorly.

(b) The man was shocked that traffic was so bad.

(c) The woman's accident was not very serious.

(d) The weather caused the man to take his car to work.

7 Cases of Lyme disease have become more and more frequent in recent years. The source of the health hazard is the exploding population of deer, carriers of the disease. A century ago, deer were checked by hunting, natural predators, and less abundant food. Modern hunting restrictions combined with the buffet of shrubs and saplings that line residential lawns, have resulted in an ecological imbalance. Various strategies are attempting to combat this problem and decrease human exposure to Lyme disease.

Q. What can be inferred from the lecture?

(a) Development has led to higher rates of Lyme disease in deer populations.
(b) Some of the strategies likely involve reducing deer numbers.
(c) Suburban residents grow plants in order to attract deer.
(d) Lyme disease has killed off deer's natural predators.

Memo

New TEPS MASTER 900

Grammar

Chapter 01 동사의 활용

기출 POINT 1

문장 5형식은 종요소를 제외한 주요소에 의해 결정되므로 종요소는 빼고 생각하고, 종요소의 수식 관계를 정확히 이해해야 한다.

문장의 구성 요소
· 주요소: 주어, 동사, 목적어, 보어 (문장 5형식 결정 요소)
· 종요소: 수식어구 → 부사(구/절), 형용사(구/절), 관계사절 (제한적 용법)
　　　　　연결어구 → 접속사, 전치사
　　　　　독립어구 → 감탄사, 동격 어구, 삽입 어구, 호격어

기출 POINT 2

명사, 대명사, 부정사, 동명사는 모두 주어 · 목적어 · 보어가 될 수 있으나 형용사, 분사는 주어 · 목적어는 될 수 없고 보어가 됨을 명심해야 한다.

단, ⟨the + 형용사/분사⟩는 단수 명사, 복수 명사, 추상명사로 쓰이므로 주어, 목적어, 보어가 된다.

기출 POINT 3

등위절의 단어와 구는 같은 품사끼리 대구를 이루어야 한다.

등위절은 등위접속사(and, but, or, for)를 사용하여 단어-단어, 구-구, 절-절을 대등하게 연결하는데 이때 단어, 구는 같은 품사끼리 대구를 이루어야 한다.

기출 POINT 4

관계대명사가 이끄는 절은 주어나 목적어가 생략된 불완전한 절이다.

종속접속사가 이끄는 절 중 명사절과 부사절은 〈주어 + 동사〉가 반드시 있어야 하므로 문장 구성 요소를 모두 갖춘 완전한 절이지만, 관계대명사가 이끄는 절은 주어나 목적어가 생략된 불완전한 절임에 유의한다.

기출 POINT 5

문장의 빈칸에 주어와 동사를 넣는 문제가 자주 출제된다.

문장은 형태상 단문, 중문, 복문, 혼합문으로 분류되며 어느 문장이나 〈주어 + 동사〉가 포함되어 있는데, 각종 시험에서 주어나 〈주어 + 동사〉, 동사가 없는 문장의 빈칸에 주어, 동사를 넣는 문제가 자주 출제됨에 유의한다.

기출 POINT 6

다음에 소개하는 문장의 종류별 특징을 기억한다.

1. 평서문: 〈S + V〉의 어순

2. 의문문
 · Yes/No 의문문
 · 의문사가 있는 의문문
 · 선택의문문 → Which ~ ?
 · 부정의문문
 · 부가의문문

3. 명령문: 긍정 명령, 부정 명령, 간접 명령, 조건 명령

4. 감탄문: How로 시작하는 문장과 What으로 시작하는 문장이 있다.

기출 POINT 7

의문문이 다른 문장의 일부가 되는 간접의문문의 어순은 〈의문사 + 주어 + 동사〉이다.

동사가 believe, imagine, guess, say, suppose, think일 때는 의문사가 문두로 나가는 것에 유의한다.

Actual Test

PART I Choose the best answer for the blank.

1   A: What's up, Jack? You look pretty annoyed.

       B: Everyone's bothering me tonight. Now I hear someone ________________ on the door.

    (a) to knock   (b) knocked

    (c) knocking   (d) to have knocked

2   A: The soup ________________ funny.

       B: Really? I thought that I followed the recipe correctly.

    (a) tastes   (b) tasted

    (c) is tasting   (d) has tasted

3   A: John has gone for the day. Can I take a message?

       B: Yes, please. This is Andrew Perkins. Could you ________________ me back tomorrow, please?

    (a) have him call   (b) have his calling

    (c) have him called   (d) have his call

4   A: Have you ever been employed somewhere else, Jason?

       B: Of course, I used to ________________ at the Smithsonian Institution. Now I'm ________________ and spend most of my time travelling and watching my grandchildren.

    (a) working, retired   (b) working, retiring

    (c) work, retired   (d) work, retiring

5   A: Katherine, you didn't write to your dad for a while, did you?

       B: No, I feel sorry to him. Actually ________________ for a month.

    (a) I've been owed a letter him   (b) I've been owed a letter for him

    (c) I've owed him a letter   (d) I've owed him about a letter

6   A: Please get your daughter _________________ her medication regularly.

B: Don't worry. She will.

(a) take   (b) to take

(c) taking   (d) taken

7   A: Sam, did you hear? Mark had his nose _______________ in the fight.

B: Poor thing! I told him not to fight ever again.

(a) broke   (b) broken

(c) break   (d) breaking

8   A: How did you do on your final paper?

B: Great. I _______________ my mother to proofread it and she gave me some good tips.

(a) made   (b) had

(c) let   (d) got

9   A: Magie, I think you should ask the dietitian _______________ you the analysis of your diet.

B: Alright, I will.

(a) show   (b) to show

(c) showing   (d) shown

PART II Choose the best answer for the blank.

10 Exercising regularly and _____________ a healthy diet _____________ important strategies for preventing heart disease.

(a) eat − is   (b) eating − is

(c) eats − are   (d) eating − are

11 The students _________________ a graduation party at the restaurant.

(a) met their friends for

(b) met to their friends for

(c) are met their friends for

(d) are met their friends to

12 A massive group of fans _________________ to see the movie stars attend the film's premiere.

(a) to amass

(b) amassing

(c) amassed

(d) being amassed

13 The meal that you are eating now _________________ some vegetables from our rooftop garden.

(a) includes

(b) is included

(c) include

(d) are including

14 The teacher made the student _________________ his homework.

(a) finishing

(b) finished

(c) finish

(d) to finish

15 When I was walking down the 5th Avenue last night, I saw a detective _________________ a robber.

(a) chased

(b) to chase

(c) chasing

(d) have chased

16 This particular book _________________ 20 stories chosen by literary analysts.

(a) consists

(b) is consisted

(c) consists of

(d) is consisted of

PART III Identify the option that contains an awkward expression or an error in grammar.

17 (a) A: Thanks so much for fixing my computer. Let me to buy you dinner tonight.
(b) B: No, I don't want to take your money. Besides, I enjoy working on computers.
(c) A: Well, you really saved me a lot of time. Let me make it up to you.
(d) B: Okay, if you insist. But it wasn't a big deal, really.

18 (a) A: Good morning. You have reached to the John F. Kennedy Business School.
(b) B: Hi, I'm calling to find out how I can apply for your MBA program for the upcoming semester.
(c) A: First of all, you need to submit a completed application form with the registration fee.
(d) B: Alright. And I would like to ask you about your scholarship program.

19 (a) A: Professor William, I'd like you to come to my place for dinner next Monday.
(b) B: Oh, I'm sorry, but I will terribly busy the whole next week.
(c) A: What about next Friday, then?
(d) B: I'll try, but I can't promise anything.

PART IV Identify the option that contains an awkward expression or an error in grammar.

20 (a) New York City recently was implemented a smoking ban for all bars and restaurants throughout the metropolis. (b) Bar and nightclub owners are concerned that this new law will hurt their business. (c) The ban was the result of a long campaign by health activists and cancer prevention groups. (d) As a matter of fact, thousands of people die a year of lung cancer within the United States.

Chapter

02   동사의 시제

기출 POINT 1

시제 문제는 부사를 살핀다.

시제는 시간, 때를 표시하는 부사와 밀접한 관계가 있으므로 함께 쓰이는 부사의 확인이 문제 풀이의 핵심이다. 따라서 부사를 살핀다.

기출 POINT 2

완료 시제는 기간 개념이다.

1. 기본 시제(현재, 과거, 미래): 한 시점에 중심을 두며 기간 개념이 아니다.
2. 완료 시제(현재완료, 과거완료, 미래완료): 한 시점이 아닌, 어디에서 어디까지의 기간 개념이다.

기출 POINT 3

현재 시제의 용법을 정확히 이해한다.

1. 현재의 동작 · 상태 · 사실 · 습관, 불변의 진리
2. 미래 시제 대용: 〈현재 동사 + 미래 표시 부사구〉 → 가까운 미래

기출 POINT 4

시간 · 조건의 부사절에서는 현재 시제가 미래 시제를 대신함에 유의한다.

1. 시간의 부사절: after, till, until, when, while, as soon as, by the time
2. 조건의 부사절: if, if only, in case, on condition that, provided, supposing

기출 POINT 5

과거 시제의 용법을 정확히 이해한다.

1. 과거의 동작 · 상태 · 사실, 경험, 역사적 사실, 과거완료 대용
2. 과거 시제와 함께 사용하는 부사가 들어 있는 문장은 반드시 과거 시제를 사용한다.
   과거 시제와 함께 사용하는 부사: ago, yesterday, last year, at that time, just now, when

기출 POINT 6

진행형 시제(~중이다)는 진행형의 개념 파악이 중요하며 완료 진행형은 기간을 나타내는 부사구가 핵심이다.

1. 단순 진행형: 현재 진행, 과거 진행, 미래 진행
2. 완료 진행형: 현재완료 진행, 과거완료 진행, 미래완료 진행 → 〈완료 + 진행〉 의미
3. 진행형으로 쓰지 않는 동사: resemble, belong, see, taste, feel

기출 POINT 7

완료 시제는 출제 빈도가 높으므로 개념 이해와 용법을 숙지한다.

1. 현재완료 〈have/has + p.p.〉: 〈과거 → 현재〉의 완료, 경험, 계속, 결과
2. 과거완료 〈had + p.p.〉: 〈대과거 → 과거〉의 완료, 경험, 계속, 결과
3. 미래완료 〈will/shall + have + p.p.〉: 〈과거나 현재 → 미래〉의 완료, 경험, 계속, 결과

★ 주의: 완료형에는 기간 개념이 있으므로 문제를 읽고 기간 개념이 있으면 완료 시제를 선택한다.

기출 POINT 8

시제 일치의 적용을 받지 않는 표현에 유의한다.

역사적 사실은 항상 과거 시제를 쓰고 현재의 사실, 진리에는 현재 시제를 쓴다.

Actual Test

PART I **Choose the best answer for the blank.**

1 A: You know what? This classroom _______________ weird.
B: You're telling me. I should open the window right away.

(a) is smelling
(b) has smelled
(c) smells
(d) smelled

2 A: What did you think of Japan?
B: It was a fun place to visit, but it _______________ difficult for me to find food that fits my taste.

(a) have been
(b) is
(c) was
(d) has been

3 A: Battery-operated vehicles _______________ like hot cakes in the near future.
B: I totally agree with you.

(a) are selling
(b) were sold
(c) will sell
(d) will be sold

4 A: This book is very exciting. It gives me a good laugh.
B: What _______________ at the moment? Can I have a look as well?

(a) had you been reading
(b) are you reading
(c) will you read
(d) do you read

5 A: Does your daughter have a job?
B: Oh, yes. She _______________ since she graduated from high school.

(a) work
(b) will work
(c) is working
(d) has been working

6 A: I really enjoy running my stationery store.

B: When _________________ it?

(a) had you started (b) did you started

(c) have you started (d) did you start

7 A: Try to pick some berries while you're out in the woods.

B: If I _______________ any, I'll bring them home.

(a) find (b) found

(c) will find (d) had found

8 A: How long since you guys started this trip?

B: By tomorrow, we ________________ for five months straight.

(a) are travelled (b) have been travelling

(c) will be travelled (d) will have been travelling

9 A: Ever since I was helped out of poverty by a kind person, I __________ happy to return the favor to others in need.

B: I appreciate your generosity.

(a) were always (b) had always been

(c) am always (d) have always been

PART II Choose the best answer for the blank.

10 The game _______________ by the time he got home from work.

(a) will already finish (b) has already finished

(c) already finish (d) had already finished

11 Although slaves in America ________________ nearly two hundred years ago, many African-Americans still suffer from the legacy of institutionalized racism and discrimination.

(a) were emancipated
(b) emancipated
(c) to be emancipated
(d) had been emancipated

12 We ________________ no sign of Jerry since he drove to work yesterday morning.

(a) saw
(b) see
(c) have seen
(d) had seen

13 Scarcely ________________ taken a step outside when I started to sweat.

(a) had I
(b) I have
(c) have I
(d) I had

14 Ever since I got stuck in the hotel elevator, I ________________ claustrophobic.

(a) were always
(b) had always been
(c) am always
(d) have always been

15 From 1960s to 1970s, a great number of Korean mine workers and nurses ________________ to West Germany in order to solve German's workforce shortage as well as unemployment problems in South Korea.

(a) has been dispatched
(b) were dispatched
(c) have been dispatched
(d) were dispatching

PART III Identify the option that contains an awkward expression or an error in grammar.

16 (a) A: Did you talk to Jerry about our appointment?
(b) B: Sure, we've spoken early this afternoon.
(c) A: Did he say that he could make it?
(d) B: He will give me a ring tonight.

17 (a) A: Jerry, I want you to join us for a movie this weekend.

   (b) B: Sorry, I have to visit my friend in Finland.

   (c) A: Oh, really? That sounds like fun. Have a safe trip.

   (d) B: Thank you. I'll bring back some pictures when I will come back.

18 (a) A: Mom, my back has been hurting a lot recently, especially when I walk or bend over.

   (b) B: Actually back problems seem to run in our family, darling. Have you seen a doctor?

   (c) A: Not yet. But if it will get worse, I'll have no choice.

   (d) B: Please do that. These kinds of injuries can be permanent if not properly treated.

PART IV Identify the option that contains an awkward expression or an error in grammar.

19 (a) James had a bad habit to pull pranks on people. (b) Three weeks ago, he made a crank call to the police and reported a burglary in the neighborhood. (c) When he returned home, he found his own house is broken into. (d) After the incident, he never did it again.

20 (a) From ancient times to modernity, dominant establishments have used entertainment as a tool to exert authority and maintain power. (b) The Roman Empire's notorious carnivals focused Roman citizens' attention on spectacle while their empire crumbled. (c) In his novel *Brave New World*, Aldous Huxley envisioned a dystopia where inhabitants were distracted with shows and sedated with drugs so that they would willingly conform to the prevailing social order. (d) Renowned scholar Noam Chomsky noted the role that modern-day spectator sports play in instilling jingoistic attitudes and diverting people's passions away from true social issues.

Chapter 03 | 수동태

기출 POINT 1

목적어가 없으면 수동태를 만들 수 없다.

1, 2형식 문장은 수동태를 만들 수 없고 3, 4, 5형식 문장에서만 가능하므로 타동사가 목적어를 취하지 않는 경우에는 수동태가 되어야 한다. 특히 사물이 주어일 때 수동태가 되는 경우가 많음에 유의한다.

기출 POINT 2

타동사라고 모두 수동태로 쓸 수 있는 것은 아니다.

수동태로 쓰지 않는 타동사
1. 소유 동사: have, possess, belong, cost(비용이 들다)
2. 상태 동사: resemble, meet, reach, become, escape, lack
3. 사역동사: have → be asked to V
           let → be allowed to V

기출 POINT 3

능동태를 수동태로 바꿀 때 전치사는 by만 사용하는 것이 아님에 유의한다.

be filled with ~로 가득 차다	be covered with ~로 덮이다
be satisfied with ~에 만족하다	be pleased with ~에 기뻐하다
be devoted to ~에 전념하다	be surprised at ~에 놀라다
be astonished at ~에 놀라다	be frightened at ~에 놀라다
be exposed to ~에 노출되다	be expected to ~가 기대되다
be burnt to death 불타 죽다	be married to ~와 결혼하다

기출 POINT 4

수동태의 시제 변화는 기본적으로 숙지해야 한다.

1. 단순 시제: be + p.p.
2. 진행 시제: be + being + p.p.
3. 완료 시제: have + been + p.p.
4. 미래형 시제: will + be + p.p.

기출 POINT 5

4형식 문장은 수동태가 2가지 형태로 되는 것이 기본이지만 1가지만 되는 경우에 주의한다.

1. 직접목적어만 주어로 쓰는 경우 → 간접목적어를 주어로 한 수동태 불가
 · 형식: 직접목적어 + be + p.p. (+ 전치사) + 간접목적어 + by + 주어(목적격)
 · 동사: buy, write, read, get, sell, send

2. 간접목적어만 주어로 쓰는 경우 → 직접목적어를 주어로 한 수동태 불가
 · 형식: 간접목적어 + be + p.p. + 직접목적어 + by + 주어(목적격)
 · 동사: kiss, call, envy, save, spare, deny

기출 POINT 6

지각동사와 사역동사는 수동태가 되면 목적격 보어가 원형부정사에서 to부정사로 바뀜에 주의한다.

⟨have/get + 목적어 + p.p.⟩ 당하다, 피해를 입다

동사구의 수동태는 동사구 전체를 한 단어로 생각하여 수동태로 바꾸고, 전치사 뒤에 또 **by**를 써야 한다.
→「또 by 법칙」

· 「또 by 법칙」에 해당하는 동사구
  laugh at, run over, take care of, speak well/ill of, pay attention to

목적어가 명사절인 경우에는 2가지 형태의 수동태가 가능하다.

· They/People say/believe that S V (3형식)
→ It + be + p.p. + that S V
→ 명사절의 주어 + be + p.p. + to V
  ★ 주의: that절이 앞선 시제인 경우에는 〈to V〉 → 〈to have p.p.〉

e.g. Today's newspaper reports that Kevin Rudd have been selected as new Prime Minister
  of Australia.
  → It is reported that Kevin Rudd have been selected as new Prime Minister of Australia.
  → Kevin Rudd is reported to have been selected as new Prime Minister of Australia.

목적어로 취하는 능동 동명사와 수동 to부정사의 의미가 같은 타동사는 반드시 암기한다.

동사
need, want, require(필요로 하다), deserve(~할 만하다)

형식
〈타동사 + V-ing〉(능동 동명사) = 〈타동사 + to be p.p.〉(수동 to부정사)

동작 수동과 상태 수동은 의미 차이를 이해한다.

1. 동작 수동: ⟨get/become + p.p.⟩ ~하게 되다 → 동작이나 변화를 나타낸다.
2. 상태 수동: ⟨be/lie/remain/stand + p.p.⟩ ~되어 있다 → 상태를 나타낸다.

Actual Test

1 A: William, how has married life with your wife been so far?

B: Fantastic. We ________________ so many things about each other while living together.

(a) are learned

(b) have been learning

(c) had learned

(d) have learned

2 A: What did Warren Buffet say at the conference with regard to the government's budget problems?

B: He insisted that the wealthy ________________ more taxes.

(a) be made to pay

(b) be made to be paid

(c) make to pay

(d) be made to paying

3 A: Excuse me, but can my dog perform in the contest tonight?

B: I'm sorry. Only students ________________ the talent show.

(a) qualified to enter

(b) qualify to entering

(c) are qualified to enter

(d) are qualified to entering

4 A: Why were the police at your house yesterday?

B: My house ________________ while I was out shopping.

(a) was broken by a burglar

(b) broke into by a burglar

(c) was broken into a burglar

(d) was broken into by a burglar

5 A: Mrs. Kendrick, does your daughter Sophie still live alone?

B: No, she ________________ about five months ago.

(a) has married

(b) married

(c) gets married

(d) got married

6　A: Luke, your house looks quite old. Don't you think it needs _______________?

　　B: Well, actually I've been thinking of moving into somewhere.

　　(a) to remodel　　　　　　　　(b) remodel

　　(c) remodelling　　　　　　　　(d) to be remodelling

7　A: I want to hear your thoughts on my performance today.

　　B: I loved it. _______________

　　(a) I'm impressive.　　　　　　(b) It is impressed.

　　(c) Impress me.　　　　　　　(d) I'm impressed.

8　A: Would you mind feeding my pets for the weekend?

　　B: Don't worry. I'll make sure they will _______________.

　　(a) care of be taken　　　　　　(b) be taken care of

　　(c) take care of　　　　　　　(d) be taken care

9　A: Are these wild mushrooms edible?

　　B: Yes. According to this mushroom guidebook, they _______________ by natives
　　　　for thousands of years.

　　(a) eats　　　　　　　　　　(b) are eaten

　　(c) have eaten　　　　　　　　(d) have been eaten

10　A: Were the Anglo-Saxons the first settlers in Canada?

　　B: No. In fact, the Quebec region _______________ the French.

　　(a) was being first settled　　　(b) was first settled by

　　(c) first settled　　　　　　　(d) have first been settled by

11 Zoologists speculated _____________ from a rare genetic disorder.

(a) the elephant to die

(b) for the elephant to die

(c) that the elephant dying

(d) that the elephant died

12 During the interrogation the suspect _______________ the mastermind behind the robbery.

(a) persuades to reveal

(b) was persuaded to reveal

(c) persuaded by revealing

(d) was persuading to reveal

13 Up until recently, _______________ by many that technological progress would solve most of humanity's problems.

(a) it believes

(b) it was believed

(c) it had believed

(d) it is believing

14 President John Williams argued that it would be impossible for the students to meet tuition costs for the upcoming semester because government grants and other forms of financial aid ________________.

(a) has limited

(b) have limited

(c) was limited

(d) were limited

15 A former Pakistani ambassador ________________ to lead the convoy charged with negotiating for the release of the hostages.

(a) have been selected

(b) have been selecting

(c) has been selected

(d) was selecting

16 Measles is a common type of contagious disease that ________________ for three to four days, cause intense pain, and lead to death.

(a) can be lasted

(b) can last

(c) is able to last

(d) is lasted

PART III Identify the option that contains an awkward expression or an error in grammar.

17 (a) A: Maria, I've been heard that you are going to build your own house.

(b) B: That's right. But I'd like to meet some people with more experience who could help me.

(c) A: My old classmate is great at building the house.

(d) B: Oh, yeah? Could you introduce him to me sometime?

18 (a) A: So are you going to take that trip to Hawaii?

(b) B: Nope. My wife was said that we should save our money for something more important.

(c) A: You must be pretty disappointed, then.

(d) B: A little bit. But I guess she's right.

PART IV Identify the option that contains an awkward expression or an error in grammar.

19 (a) The Nobel Prizes founded by Swedish industrialist Alfred Nobel. (b) He grew wealthy from one of his most famous inventions, dynamite. (c) After seeing the destructive uses of dynamite, he became worried that his legacy would be one of death. (d) In his will, he dedicated his fortune to promoting science, literature, and peace.

20 (a) It took many brave and talented women to make the world willing to accept and judge writers based on their skills rather than their gender. (b) For too long, women expected to write only about subjects that were considered proper by society's standards, and even the best female writers were never considered equal to a male writer. (c) Nowadays, a celebrated female author who writes about any subject she chooses is not at all a rarity. (d) Of course, most female writers, even the successful ones, will tell you that there is much to be done in bringing more equality into their profession.

Chapter 04

수의 일치

기출 POINT 1

TEPS 시험에서 배점이 가장 높은 PART IV 문제를 풀 때는 각 선택지의 주어와 동사를 파악한 다음, 그 주어와 동사의 수 일치, 시제 일치, 그리고 태 일치를 확인한다.

기출 POINT 2

두 개 이상의 주어가 and로 연결된 경우에는 대부분 복수 취급하지만 불가분의 관계일 때는 단수 취급한다.

a needle and thread 실 꿴 바늘   a watch and chain 줄 달린 시계
brandy and water 물 탄 브랜디   slow and steady 느리지만 착실함
trial and error 시행착오   all work and no play 공부만 하고 놀지 않는 것

기출 POINT 3

수식 어구로 주어와 동사가 분리된 경우, 수식 어구는 일치와 관계없다.

〈주어 + 수식 어구 + 동사〉→ 주어에 수를 일치시켜야 한다.

기출 POINT **4**

주어에 every, each가 들어 있는 경우, 전체 문장을 3인칭 단수로 일치시킨다.

· 〈every/each + 단수 명사〉
· 〈every/each + A and B + 단수 동사〉 → 단수 취급 → 단수 대명사, 단수 소유격

기출 POINT **5**

상관접속사로 이어진 어구가 주어로 쓰인 경우, 수 일치에 주의한다.

〈either A or B〉 〈not A but B〉 〈neither A nor B〉 〈not only A but also B〉
→ 동사는 동사와 가까운 주어 B에 일치시킨다.

cf. 〈A as well as B〉는 A에 일치시킨다.

기출 POINT **6**

of 뒤에 오는 명사의 수에 따라 동사의 수를 일치시키는 경우에 주의한다.

형식
· ~ of + 복수 명사 + 복수 동사
· ~ of + 단수 명사 + 단수 동사

종류
· 〈분수 + of〉, most of, half of, part of
· the rest of, the bulk of, the majority of

다음에 소개하는 일치는 중요하므로 모두 암기한다.

---

1. many
- many + 복수 명사 → 복수 동사
- many a + 단수 명사 → 단수 동사

2. number of
- a number of + 복수 명사 → 복수 동사
- the number of + 복수 명사 → 단수 동사

3. 소유격
- 《(대)명사 + and + (대)명사》의 소유격 → 단수 취급 (공동 소유)
- 《(대)명사의 소유격 + and + (대)명사의 소유격》 → 복수 취급 (각자 소유)

4. There is/are: 이때 there는 유도부사로 주어가 동사 뒤에 온다.
- There/Here is + 단수 명사
- There/Here are + 복수 명사

5. 단수 취급의 예
- 병명, 나라명, 학문명, 놀이명, 운동명은 복수 형태일지라도 단수 취급한다.
- 시간, 거리, 가격, 무게의 복수 명사가 하나의 단위를 나타낼 때는 단수 취급한다.
- 부정대명사(every, no)가 주어인 경우 단수 동사로 받는다.

Actual Test

PART I Choose the best answer for the blank.

1 A: The horse that won many races ________________ white fur with black spots.
   B: I've never seen that horse before.

   (a) has
   (b) are
   (c) is
   (d) have

2 A: The same congressmen that voted for the war are now campaigning against it.
   B: That makes me wonder why nobody ________________ held accountable for their poor decisions.

   (a) am
   (b) are
   (c) be
   (d) is

3 A: How is the theater scene progressing?
   B: Slowly. Both students should have had ________________ scripts memorized last week.

   (a) her
   (b) your
   (c) their
   (d) his

4 A: What's the main difference between a crocodile and an alligator?
   B: Structurally, the crocodile ________________ the broad, powerful jaws that the alligator does.

   (a) does possess
   (b) do possess
   (c) doesn't possess
   (d) don't possess

5 A: I sincerely apologize for my mistake. I'd better quit my job.
   B: Don't take it too hard. Neither you, nor I, nor anyon else ________________ responsible for what happened.

   (a) are
   (b) am
   (c) is
   (d) be

6 A: There ______________ nothing left of the house by the time the firefighters
    arrived.
    B: That's a real shame!

    (a) were   (b) was
    (c) is   (d) have

7 A: Dad, would it be possible for me to get more allowances, please?
    B: Honey, I already gave you a lot. Two hundred dollars ______________ a lot of
    money when I was young.

    (a) were   (b) are
    (c) was   (d) is

8 A: Doesn't suspending the student seem a bit harsh of a punishment?
    B: Not at all. The teachers ______________ students repeatedly that smoking on
    campus would not be tolerated.

    (a) warn   (b) is warning
    (c) has warned   (d) have warned

PART II Choose the best answer for the blank.

9 The way that you handled the disgruntled customers ______________ very
professional.

    (a) had been   (b) were
    (c) was   (d) is

10 The lawyers chosen to represent Mrs. Stewart ______________ the top in their
field.

    (a) was being   (b) were being
    (c) is   (d) are

11 Every product made _________________ been subject to rigid tests for safety and durability.

(a) having

(b) had

(c) has

(d) have

12 The unemployment statistics released by the authorities _______________ really confusing.

(a) is

(b) are

(c) was being

(d) were being

13 The CEO, along with the board of directors, _________________ what steps would be best to take next.

(a) contemplate

(b) were contemplating

(c) are contemplating

(d) has contemplated

14 Being sedentary and _________________ the major factors in the current obesity epidemic.

(a) lack of healthy diet are

(b) lacking a healthy diet is

(c) lacking a healthy diet are

(d) having lack of healthy diets

15 The Korean Baseball Organization announced the final twenty four players to play in the WBC (World Baseball Classic) today, who _________________ from the original 50 candidates.

(a) were chosen

(b) has been chosen

(c) was chosen

(d) had chosen

16 Professor Anderson as well as his students _________________ how to use the new Internet system.

(a) learn

(b) is learning

(c) are learning

(d) have learned

17 People who dedicate their lives towards helping other people and improving the
state of the world _________________ be celebrated as much as movie stars or
sports athletes.

(a) deserves to (b) deserve to
(c) deserve (d) deserves

PART III Identify the option that contains an awkward expression or an error in
grammar.

18 (a) A: My girlfriend and her family will be coming to our town this weekend.
(b) B: Is she the one who write articles for USA Today?
(c) A: That's correct. Why don't you come over and meet her?
(d) B: Sorry but I can't. I've got a previous engagement this weekend

19 (a) A: The rumor has it that you went to America last summer.
(b) B: Yes, I did. I studied in an intensive language program.
(c) A: How was it? Were they very difficult?
(d) B: No, it was OK. I made friends from all around the world.

PART IV Identify the option that contains an awkward expression or an error in
grammar.

20 (a) A cow that escaped from its barn were given its freedom to live. (b) The cow
managed to unlock and open the barn door. (c) It later jumped over the fence and
swam across the river. (d) Impressed with the tenacity of the animal, the farmer
decided not to slaughter it.

Memo 

Chapter 05

부정사와 동명사

기출 POINT 1

to부정사의 명사적 용법

to부정사 (to V, to have p.p.)가 문장에서 명사와 같은 기능을 하며 주어, 목적어, 보어, 동격으로 쓰임에 유의한다.

1. 의미: ~하는 것
2. 타동사의 목적어 (3형식)
3. 가목적어(it) 진목적어(to부정사)
4. 〈의문사 + to부정사〉(3형식): know
5. 목적어로 to부정사를 취하는 전치사: except, but, save, about
6. 〈타동사 + 목적어 + to부정사〉(5형식)

기출 POINT 2

to부정사의 형용사적 용법

한정 용법
〈명사 + to V〉로 to부정사가 명사를 후치 수식한다. (~할)

서술 용법
1. 주격, 목적격 보어로 쓰임에 유의한다.
2. 〈be + to부정사〉: 예정, 의무, 가능, 운명, 의도를 나타낸다.

기출 POINT 3

to부정사의 부사적 용법

1. to부정사가 형용사, 동사, 부사를 수식하며 목적, 원인, 이유, 조건, 결과를 나타냄에 유의한다.
2. 목적 용법이 중요: ~하기 위하여(= in order to V)

기출 POINT 4

to부정사의 시제에 유의한다.

· 단순 부정사(to V): 본동사와 같은 시제나 미래 시제를 나타낸다.
· 완료 부정사(to have p.p): 본동사보다 앞선 시제를 나타냄에 유의한다.

기출 POINT 5

원형부정사를 사용하는 경우에 유의한다.

1. 지각동사, 사역동사의 목적격 보어에는 원형부정사가 쓰인다.
   단, help는 to부정사도 취한다: 〈help + O + (to) V〉(5형식)
   　　　　　　　　　　　　　　　　〈help + (to) V〉(3형식)

   cf. 〈get / cause / force / forbid + 목적어 + to부정사〉

2. 원형부정사를 취하는 관용 용법에 유의한다.
   · had better V
   · cannot help but V

기출 POINT 6

to부정사의 의미상 주어에 유의한다.

· 〈It is + 형용사 + for + 의미상 주어 + to V〉로 쓰는 형용사
   easy, difficult, natural, necessary, possible, impossible

· 〈It is + 형용사 + of + 의미상 주어 + to V〉로 쓰는 형용사: 사람의 성질, 성향을 표시하는 형용사
   foolish, clever, kind, nice, rude, stupid, silly, impudent

동명사 역시 개념 파악을 먼저 한다.

동명사(동사원형 -ing) = 동사의 성질 + 명사 역할
1. 목적어, 보어를 취한다. → 동사의 성질
2. 부사(구)의 수식을 받는다. → 동사의 성질
3. 동사의 목적어, 보어로 쓰인다. → 명사 역할

동명사의 시제에 유의한다.

· 단순 동명사(동사원형 -ing): 본동사와 동일 시제 또는 미래 시제일 때
· 완료 동명사(having p.p.): 본동사보다 앞선 과거 시제일 때

동명사의 관용 표현은 중요하므로 모두 암기한다.

There is no -ing ~은 불가능하다
be opposed to -ing ~에 반대하다
cannot help -ing ~할 수밖에 없다
make a point of -ing 반드시 ~하다
be worth -ing ~할 만한 가치가 있다
It is no use/good -ing ~해봤자 소용없다
be busy -ing ~로 바쁘다
come near -ing 거의 ~할 뻔하다
feel like -ing ~하고 싶다

on/upon -ing ~하자마자
in -ing ~할 때에는
look forward to -ing ~을 기대하다
of one's own -ing 자신이 직접 ~한
go -ing ~하러 가다
What do you say to -ing ~하는 게 어떻습니까?
It goes without saying that S V ~은 당연하다
not/never without -ing …하면 반드시 ~하다
be on the point of -ing 막 ~하려는 참이다

기출 POINT 10

3형식에서 to부정사만을 목적어로 취하는 동사에 주의한다.

wish, hope, decide, refuse, manage, pretend, plan

기출 POINT 11

3형식에서 동명사만을 목적어로 취하는 동사에 주의한다.

finish, avoid, quit, give up, consider, enjoy, anticipate

기출 POINT 12

to부정사와 동명사 양쪽을 목적어로 취하면서 의미가 다른 동사에 유의한다.

remember, forget, regret

· 목적어가 동명사인 경우: 과거 사실로 '~한 것, ~했던 것' (과거의 일)
· 목적어가 to부정사인 경우: 미래 사실로 '~할 것' (미래의 일)

PART I Choose the best answer for the blank.

1 A: Rachel, remember that you promised _________________ to your birthday party.
   B: Don't worry. I'll give you a call.

   (a) taking me out   (b) for taking out me
   (c) to take me out   (d) to take out me

2 A: I have to take the plane now, Jerry. It's time to say good-bye.
   B: Goodbye, Kathy. Have a great trip and don't forget _________________ hello to
      your parents for me.

   (a) to have said   (b) to say
   (c) saying   (d) having said

3 A: How about going to the movies after work?
   B: I'd _________________, but I have a previous appointment tonight.

   (a) love so   (b) love it
   (c) love   (d) love to

4 A: Charles came to visit me every day while I was sick at home.
   B: Really? That was very _________________.

   (a) thoughtful to him   (b) thoughtful for you
   (c) thoughtful of him   (d) thoughtful to you

5 A: I see you are trying on different clothes. Are you going to dress up for tonight?
   B: I'm having trouble figuring out _________________ to the dinner.

   (a) to wear what   (b) to what wear
   (c) what to wear   (d) what wear to

6 A: The due date for my dissertation is just next week, but I haven't done much work.

B: I bet you have no choice but ________________.

(a) asking for an extension (b) ask for an extension

(c) to ask for an extension (d) extension to be asked

7 A: Would you like to see *The Lord of the Ring* or *The Chronicles of Narnia*?

B: I can't decide ________________.

(a) to choose which (b) to which choose

(c) which to choose (d) which choose to

8 A: How do you know Kim?

B: I remember him ________________ in my TEPS class last year.

(a) being (b) to be

(c) be (d) it to be

PART II Choose the best answer for the blank.

9 My sister Jane still resents not ________________ invited to your wedding last week.

(a) be (b) to be

(c) having been (d) to have been

10 Excuse me. This cappuccino is not hot enough. It needs ________________.

(a) heat (b) heated

(c) heating (d) have heated

11 _________________ over details will only make you more frustrated.

(a) Obsessing

(b) Obsessed

(c) Obsess

(d) To have obsessed

12 My friend James was terribly ashamed of _________________ before his classmates.

(a) be made fun of

(b) being made fun of

(c) make fun of

(d) make of fun

13 Congratulations on your excellent performance. You seem _________________ the piano really hard last semester.

(a) to have practiced

(b) to practice

(c) practicing

(d) as if practicing

14 The man who robbed the bank was apprehended by the police just as he was about _________________ away the money.

(a) carry

(b) to carry

(c) carrying

(d) being carried

PART III Identify the option that contains an awkward expression or an error in grammar.

15 (a) A: I'm contemplating buying a car.

(b) B: What for? You are right down the street from work.

(c) A: But I may need it at some point.

(d) B: There's no point to have a vehicle if you don't really need it.

16 (a) A: How are you getting to work today?

(b) B: I was thinking of take my bike.

(c) A: Isn't it a little cold outside for that?

(d) B: Well, a little cold weather doesn't bother me.

17 (a) A: It turns out that my sister and I can't go to the play with you.

    (b) B: Really? Did something come up?

    (c) A: Yeah, she is feeling sick and I'm going to take her to the hospital.

    (d) B: Oh, no! I hope seeing her in better condition.

18 (a) A: Do you have any plans this afternoon?

    (b) B: I was thinking about going out to see a movie.

    (c) A: I'm a little low on cash. Would you mind rent a movie instead?

    (d) B: That could be fun, too.

PART IV Identify the option that contains an awkward expression or an error in grammar

19 (a) After the accident, Johnny began the long process of rehabilitation. (b) He exercised every day, working with his physical therapist. (c) Even though he couldn't walk at the time, he talked about hike up Mount Everest. (d) Eventually, Johnny made a full recovery and fulfilled his dream.

20 (a) People have different reasons for choosing to be vegetarians. (b) Some people believe that killing animals is inherently wrong. (c) Others objecting to the poor living conditions of animals in industrial farms. (d) Some people simply follow a diet that they believe is most healthy.

Chapter 06 | 조동사

기출 POINT 1

〈조동사 + 동사원형〉: 조동사 뒤에는 항상 동사원형이 오는 것에 유의한다.

기출 POINT 2

조동사의 기본적인 의미를 묻는 문제가 자주 출제되므로 조동사의 중요한 기본적인 의미는 반드시 숙지한다.

do
1. 대동사
2. 강조의 동사: 동사 앞에 사용
3. 부정문, 의문문에 사용

have
1. 현재완료: have/has + p.p.
2. 과거완료: had + p.p.

기출 POINT 3

can, could의 용법에 유의한다.

1. 가능, 능력(be able to)
2. 추측: 의문문, 부정문(과거형: cannot have p.p.)
3. 관용 표현: 〈cannot but + 동사원형〉〈cannot help -ing〉 ~하지 않을 수 없다

기출 POINT 4

must, have to의 용법에 유의한다.

1. 무조건적인 의무(~해야 한다) ↔ need not, don't have to
2. 강한 추측(~임에 틀림없다) ↔ cannot

기출 POINT 5

will, shall의 용법에 유의한다.

will
습성, 경향, 거부, 추측, 필연, 주어의 의지, 관용어구

shall
1. 긍정문: 말하는 사람의 의지 (2, 3인칭)
2. 의문문: 상대방의 의사를 물음 (1인칭: ~할까요?)

기출 POINT 6

would, should의 용법에 유의한다.

would
1. 과거의 불규칙적인 습관
2. would like to V ~하고 싶다
3. would rather A than B B보다 A하는 것이 더 낫다

should
1. 의무, 당연, 예언, 추측, 목적, 의도, 의외, 놀라움
2. 이성적, 감정적 판단의 형용사가 쓰인 that절에 사용
3. 제안, 충고, 요구, 주장 동사의 목적절에 사용 → (should) 동사원형

기출 POINT 7

〈조동사 + have + p.p.〉형은 반드시 암기한다.

1. 조동사의 현재형 + have + p.p.: 단정적 과거 추측
 · cannot have p.p. ~이었을 리가 없다
 · may have p.p. ~이었을런지도 모른다
 · must have p.p. ~이었음에 틀림없다

2. 조동사의 과거형 + have + p.p.: 단정이 아닌 과거와 반대 사실
 · should have p.p. (과거에) ~했어야 했는데 (하지 않아 유감이다)

PART I Choose the best answer for the blank.

1   A: What took you so long? I thought you were going to just drop her off and come straight home.

     B: Yes, I was going to, but she insisted that everyone ________________ stay for dinner.

  (a) should   (b) would

  (c) could   (d) might

2   A: Have you heard anything from Shelly recently?

     B: As a matter of fact, I ________________ her at the library yesterday.

  (a) have seen   (b) do see

  (c) did see   (d) had seen

3   A: You didn't mow the lawn like you said you would.

     B: Oops! I ________________ have forgotten about it.

  (a) must   (b) will

  (c) should   (d) do

4   A: Spencer is convinced that he will win the talent show.

     B: I'd be surprised if he ________________ The other competitors are quite talented.

  (a) did   (b) didn't

  (c) could   (d) won't

5   A: How did you learn to speak Russian so well?

     B: Actually, I ________________ in a store with many Russian people. They taught me a lot.

  (a) cannot have worked   (b) have been working

  (c) should have worked   (d) used to work

6 A: I don't feel much like cooking today.

B: Don't worry about it. I _______________ take care of it.

(a) will

(b) have

(c) am

(d) don't

7 A: He _______________ make an appearance at his ex-wife's wedding.

B: That would be a bad idea!

(a) need to

(b) needs not to

(c) need not

(d) doesn't have

8 A: Thomas was saying bad things about me again today.

B: You guys should stop fighting and _______________.

(a) to make it up

(b) making up

(c) made up

(d) make up

9 A: I feel blue today because I was late for work again.

B: I think you'd better _______________ earlier in the morning. Otherwise, you'll be sacked.

(a) getting up

(b) to get up

(c) gotten up

(d) get up

10 A: I wish that Mike didn't act so cold to me all the time.

B: Well, perhaps you _______________ have made those mean comments about him.

(a) must

(b) should

(c) shouldn't

(d) will

11 You _________________ to think more seriously about your future and stop spending all your time playing with friends.

   (a) might   (b) should

   (c) must   (d) need

12 Even though we are competitors, I _________________ respecting her for her perseverance and professionalism.

   (a) have to   (b) must avoid

   (c) can only   (d) cannot help

13 During my childhood I _________________ with my dad and learned a lot about the wildness.

   (a) am used to hunt   (b) used to hunt

   (c) am hunting   (d) will hunt

14 It is necessary that people in high governmental positions _________________ reveal all of their business connections to the public.

   (a) won't   (b) could

   (c) has to   (d) should

15 Many of us _________________ our inside feelings when we are seriously quarrelling with somebody.

   (a) cannot help but showing   (b) can help showing

   (c) cannot but to show   (d) cannot help showing

PART III Identify the option that contains an awkward expression or an error in grammar.

16 (a) A: Guess what. This week I've got three exams and two term papers are due.

(b) B: That's a huge amount of work. Are you going to be able to handle it?

(c) A: I don't know. This time I think I bit off more than I can chew.

(d) B: I said that you should not to overload yourself with too many classes.

17 (a) A: Are we low on gas?

(b) B: No, but I'm getting tired. I want to get some coffee here.

(c) A: If you are getting tired, then you would let me drive for a while.

(d) B: That's a good idea. Thanks.

18 (a) A: Oh, God! I got an F in Biology. This is impossible!

(b) B: Sorry to hear that. Does that mean you have to repeat the course?

(c) A: Unfortunately, yes. My mom's going to kill me.

(d) B: You must have listened to me when I urged you to spend time for the final.

PART IV Identify the option that contains an awkward expression or an error in grammar.

19 (a) We are looking for a qualified social worker to be based in Myrtle Beach. (b) Experience of working with young people is essential, and prior management experience is preferred. (c) The position's main duty consists of managing a caseload of young people. Other responsibilities will include the preparation of reports to meet national standards. (d) The applicants must understand that the minimum length of the position is able to last for five years.

20 (a) When you make an oral presentation before a large audience, it is very natural to feel nervous. (b) Therefore, you need to not avoid speaking in public because of nervousness. (c) As you gain more experience, you will find yourself becoming less apprehensive about your nervousness. (d) Then, when asked to speak before a group of people, your presentation will flow naturally and fluently.

Chapter 07

명사와 관사

기출 POINT 명사 1

TEPS 시험에서 명사 문제가 출제되면 가산명사인지 불가산명사인지부터 반드시 확인한다.
→ PART III, IV 에서 가산명사에 부정관사가 붙거나 복수형으로 되어 있으면 그것이 답이다.

가산명사 (countable noun)
1. 보통명사, 집합명사
2. 부정관사, 복수형 가능

불가산명사 (uncountable noun)
1. 고유명사, 추상명사, 물질명사
2. 부정관사를 붙일 수 없고, 복수형으로도 쓸 수 없음이 원칙

기출 POINT 명사 2

수 표시어와 양 표시어는 구별해서 사용한다.

1. 〈수 표시어 + 가산명사〉: few, a few, a large/great number of
2. 〈양 표시어 + 불가산명사〉: little, a little, a large amount of, a great deal of
3. some, any, no, a lot of, lots of, plenty of는 양쪽 수식어로 쓰임

기출 POINT 명사 3

집합적 물질명사는 출제 빈도가 높으므로 주의한다.

furniture 가구	baggage 수하물	clothing 의류	time 시간
mail 우편물	machinery 기계류	weaponry 무기류	poetry 시 작품
jewelry 보석류	money 돈	stationery 문구류	merchandise 상품
produce 농산물	rubbish 쓰레기	evidence 증거물	news 뉴스

1. 부정관사를 붙일 수 없고 복수형으로 쓸 수 없다.
2. 수 표시어(few, a few)로는 수식할 수 없으며 단수 동사로 받는다.

기출 POINT 관사 **1**

관사는 명사와 직접적인 관계가 있으므로 명사가 나오면 명사의 종류와 관사의 유무를 따져 본다.

1. 명사에 관사가 붙지 않는 경우: 불가산명사(물질명사, 추상명사, 고유명사)
2. 가산명사에는 관사, 한정사가 붙거나 복수형이 되어야 함

기출 POINT 관사 **2**

부정관사의 선택 문제는 철자가 아닌 발음에 의한 구별이다.

〈a + 자음 발음〉
e.g. a university, a uniform, a unique, a European, a hollow

〈an + 모음 발음〉
e.g. an honest, an hour, an heir, an office, an MP3, an MBA

기출 POINT 관사 **3**

부정관사의 위치는 중요하므로 반드시 암기한다.

· such/what/quite/rather/many + a/an + 형용사 + 명사
· so/as/too/how/however + 형용사 + a/an + 명사

기출 POINT 관사 **4**

부정관사의 용법을 기억한다.

1. per의 뜻: ~당, ~마다
   e.g. once a day, twice a minute, 5 dollars a yard
2. the same의 뜻
3. a certain의 뜻
4. 〈a/an + 고유명사〉: ~라는 사람
5. 종족대표: ~라는 것은
   · 〈a/an/the + 단수 명사〉→ 단수 동사
   · 복수 명사 → 복수 동사
6. a/an + 〈명사 and 명사〉 = 1명 → 단수 동사
   〈a/an + 명사〉 and 〈a/an + 명사〉 = 2명 → 복수 동사

정관사의 용법을 기억한다.

1. 서로 알고 있는 것
   e.g. Turn the light off, please.

2. 유일물
   e.g. the sun, the moon

3. 악기명, 발명품
   e.g. play the piano

4. 계량의 단위
   e.g. a dollar by the day(일당 1달러), by the pound(파운드당)

5. 명사가 형용사의 최상급, 서수로 한정될 때: the only/same/last/very + 명사

정관사의 특별 용법은 중요하므로 꼭 암기한다.

1. 〈the + 형용사/분사〉 = 복수 명사, 단수 명사, 추상명사
   e.g. the old = old people

2. 신체의 일부분 표시: 소유격을 사용하지 말 것
   e.g. He caught me by the hand.

3. 비교급에 the가 붙는 경우
 · the + 비교급 + of the two
 · the + 비교급 ~ , the + 비교급 …
 · the + 비교급 + for/because ~

기출 POINT 관사 **7**

고유명사에는 관사가 붙지 않는 것이 원칙이지만 고유명사에 정관사가 붙는 경우가 있으므로 주의한다.

1. 반도, 산맥, 공공건물, 관공서 건물의 이름이 지명을 딴 경우에는 무관사
    e.g. Seoul Station

2. 복수형 국가명, 강, 바다, 항만
    e.g. the United States, the Hudson, the Nile

3. 선박, 기차, 비행기, 신문, 잡지
    단, 책명이 인명인 경우는 무관사
    e.g. Hamlet

기출 POINT 관사 **8**

관사가 생략되는 경우가 있으므로 주의한다.

1. 가족 관계, 호격어 관계, 관직이 보어로 쓰인 경우

2. 〈명사 + as + S + V〉 양보 구문
    cf. a kind of + 명사

3. 교통, 통신 수단
    e.g. by taxi/bus/ship, by letter, by telegram
    cf. in a bus

4. 공공건물이 본래의 목적으로 쓰인 경우
    e.g. the church(교회) − church(예배)

Actual Test

1 A: Daddy, did you go fishing yesterday?
B: Sure, honey. I caught seven ________________.

(a) of fishes   (b) fish
(c) heads of fish   (d) fishes

2 A: James, how's your son's lawsuit going?
B: Well, he doesn't have much chance to win because ________________ to back up his claims.

(a) there is much evidence   (b) there is not much evidence
(c) there are many evidences   (d) there are not many evidences

3 A: How come you spent so much time in the city library last night?
B: I had to get some ________________ for my dissertation.

(a) knowledges   (b) facts
(c) advices   (d) informations

4 A: Britney's concert the other night wasn't a success, I think.
B: Well, I don't think so. There ________________.

(a) was a large audience   (b) was much audience
(c) were a lot of audiences   (d) were many audiences

5 A: What did you think of my grandmother's house?
B: It was amazing. I've never seen so ________________.

(a) many antique furniture   (b) many antique furnitures
(c) much antique furnitures   (d) much antique furniture

6 A: What do I need to become a plumber?

B: First, you must have _______________ and be properly trained.

(a) much equipments

(b) a lot of equipment

(c) many equipments

(d) a lot of equipments

7 A: Why do you look busy these days?

B: I've been helping _______________ with legal defense.

(a) the poor

(b) poors

(c) poor

(d) a poor

8 A: Why aren't you coming with us to the amusement park?

B: I don't want to spend _______________ waiting in line for rides.

(a) long time

(b) long times

(c) a much time

(d) a long time

9 A: I've prepared something special _______________ today.

B: I can't wait to eat.

(a) for breakfasts

(b) for the breakfast

(c) for a breakfast

(d) for breakfast

10 A: I'm looking for _______________ documents that I brought home from work.

B: I'll make sure to keep an eye out for them.

(a) a

(b) one

(c) the

(d) an

11 A: Excuse me. Is there _______________ fully-furnished studio for rent?

B: Sure, sir. Actually we have one available right now.

(a) a

(b) an

(c) one

(d) the

12 A: Would Ronald be a good person to babysit our kids for an evening?

B: Certainly! He is ________________. Your kids will definitely love him.

(a) a so sweet individual

(b) so a sweet individual

(c) a such sweet individual

(d) such a sweet individual

13 A: How would you like these traveler's checks, sir?

B: In ______________, please.

(a) fifty-dollar bills

(b) fifty-dollars bills

(c) fifty-dollar bill

(d) fifty-dollars bill

14 A: What does your boyfriend do?

B: He is ______________.

(a) a boxer and musician

(b) a boxer and a musician

(c) boxer and musician

(d) the boxer and musician

15 A: Frank wants to come to our housewarming party, but I've already invited 20 people and our place is too small.

B: Don't worry, honey. I'm sure we can make ______________ for one more.

(a) rooms

(b) room

(c) a room

(d) the rooms

PART II Choose the best answer for the blank.

16 I lent ______________ money to my coworker today.

(a) many

(b) several

(c) some

(d) a

17 You should research bank policies before opening both _________________.

(a) a savings account and a checking account

(b) a savings account and checking account

(c) a saving account and checking account

(d) saving account and checking account

18 His restaurant has _________________ that I recommend it to all of my friends.

(a) so a delicious food

(b) so delicious a food

(c) such delicious food

(d) such delicious a food

PART III Identify the option that contains an awkward expression or an error in grammar.

19 (a) A: You paid me for this month's rent, right?

(b) B: I gave you my share. Are we short of money?

(c) A: Only three quarters of the rent are accounted for.

(d) B: Alright. I'll talk to the other housemates about covering the rest.

PART IV Identify the option that contains an awkward expression or an error in grammar.

20 (a) The spectroscope were a popular form of entertainment during the late 19th century. (b) By arranging two pictures taken at different angles, the spectroscope produced the illusion of three dimensions. (c) Queen Victoria helped to popularize the hobby of stereo viewing in Britain. (d) The most commonly produced slides were travelogues showing far-off and exotic landscapes.

Chapter 08

형용사와 부사

기출 POINT 형용사 1

형용사의 기능을 제일 먼저 이해한다.

1. 한정적 용법: 명사 수식
2. 서술적 용법: 보어가 됨
 · 주격 보어(2형식)
 · 목적격 보어(5형식)

기출 POINT 형용사 2

형용사가 명사를 수식하는 경우는 중요하므로 그 예를 익힌다.

1. 두 개 이상의 형용사가 명사를 수식하는 경우
2. 형용사가 다른 요소와 결합하여 길어진 경우
3. 서술적 용법으로 쓰이는 형용사가 명사를 수식하는 경우

기출 POINT 형용사 3

한정적 용법으로만 쓰는 형용사와 서술적 용법으로만 쓰는 형용사는 모두 기억한다.

· 한정적 용법으로만 쓰는 형용사
  only, utter, upper, mere, wooden, former, woolen, elder, drunken, inner, live

· 서술적 용법으로만 쓰는 형용사
  alive, alone, aware, asleep, awake, afraid, unable, fond, drunk

기출 POINT 형용사 **4**

형용사를 보어로 취하는 불완전자동사에 유의한다.

feel, sound, seem, grow, appear: 보어로 부사를 사용하지 않도록 주의한다.

기출 POINT 형용사 **5**

의미상 혼동하기 쉬운 형용사는 사용에 주의한다.

respective 각각의, 각자의
respectful 공손한, 예의바른
respectable 존경할 만한, 상당한

considerate 동정심이 많은
considerable 상당한, 중요한

economical 경제적인, 절약되는
economic 경제의, 경제에 관한

healthy 건강한, 건강에 좋은
healthful 건강에 좋은

기출 POINT 형용사 **6**

many, much의 용법과 관용어구에 주의한다.

many
1. 가산명사와 사용
2. = a number of, a great/large number of
3. as many 같은 수의~
   like/as so many 같은 수의 ~처럼

much
1. 불가산명사와 사용
2. = a good deal of, a great deal/quantity of
3. as much 같은 양의~
   like/as so much 같은 양의 ~처럼

few, little의 용법에 주의한다.

few
- **few** 거의 없는 (부정적 의미)
- **a few** 약간 있는 (가산명사와 사용)

little
- **little** 거의 없는 (부정적 의미)
- **a little** 약간 있는 (양 표시, 불가산명사와 사용)

기출 POINT 형용사 **8**

〈수사 + 단위명사〉가 하이픈으로 연결되어 형용사적으로 쓰일 때는 단수 명사를 씀에 유의한다.

- 수사 - 단위명사 + 명사
e.g. a two-year-old boy (○)
a-two-years-old boy (×)

기출 POINT 부사 **1**

부사의 주된 기능은 수식이다.

동사, 형용사, 다른 부사, 문장 전체를 수식한다. 따라서 생략해도 문장이 성립하며 보어로 사용할 수 없다.

기출 POINT 부사 **2**

enough의 위치 문제는 중요하므로 반드시 기억한다.

1. 명사 수식 (형용사 용법): 전치, 후치 수식 모두 가능 → 〈enough + 명사〉, 〈명사 + enough〉
2. 동사, 형용사, 부사 수식 (부사 용법): 반드시 후치 수식 → 〈형용사/부사 + enough〉

기출 POINT 부사 3

두 가지 형태를 갖는 부사 중 의미가 서로 다른 경우에 주의한다.

late 늦게 − lately 최근에, 요즈음
high 높게 − highly 매우, 대단히
free 무료로 − freely 자유로이
hard 열심히 − hardly 거의 ~않다
direct 똑바로 − directly 즉시

deep 깊게 − deeply 매우
wide 넓게 − widely 널리
near 가까이 − nearly 거의
cheap 싸게 − cheaply 쉽게

기출 POINT 부사 4

빈도부사, 정도부사의 위치 문제는 출제 빈도가 높으므로 반드시 이해한다.

위치의 원칙
1. be동사 뒤
2. 일반동사, have동사 앞
3. 조동사와 본동사 사이, ⟨be + p.p.⟩ 사이

빈도부사
frequently, scarcely, ever, always, seldom, regularly, rarely, often, sometimes

정도부사
almost, greatly, nearly, wholly, mostly, hardly, deeply, generally, completely

1. 이어동사: ⟨동사 + 목적어(인칭대명사) + 부사⟩
   단, 목적어가 명사일 경우에는 부사가 목적어의 앞뒤 모두에 올 수 있다.

2. 왕래발착 동사 + ⟨장소 + 방법(빈도, 양태) + 시간⟩

의문부사는 **when**(언제), **where**(어디), **why**(왜), **how**(어떻게(수단, 방법))가 있으며 **how far**(거리), **how often**(횟수)을 묻는 것에 주의한다.

already, still, yet의 구별 문제는 정확한 이해가 필요하다.

already

1. 긍정문: 이미, 벌써(의문문에서 놀라움의 뜻을 나타냄)
2. ⟨already + 일반동사⟩
   ⟨be + already + p.p.⟩
   ⟨have + already + p.p.⟩(많이 쓰임)

yet

1. 부정문: 아직까지
2. 의문문: 이미
3. 긍정문: 아직도, 여전히

still

1. 긍정문, 부정문, 의문문: 아직(도), 여전히
2. ⟨still + 일반동사⟩
   ⟨still + 조동사의 부정형⟩(부정문)
   ⟨be동사 + still⟩

Actual Test

PART I Choose the best answer for the blank.

1 A: You are a reporter, right? Who do you normally interview?

B: Well, _________________—statesmen, sports stars, actors, to name but a few.

(a) Famous somebody   (b) Anybody famous

(c) Famous anybody   (d) Famous anyone

2 A: How was the art exhibit?

B: I thought it was _________________.

(a) interesting but special nothing enough

(b) enough interesting but nothing special

(c) interesting enough but nothing special

(d) enough interesting but special nothing

3 A: Please make sure that your children don't touch that machine.
It doesn't look _________________.

B: Thank you for your concern. I was just about to put it away.

(a) safely   (b) safe

(c) safer   (d) safety

4 A: Wouldn't it be nice to be young and energetic again?

B: Of course. But at that age we didn't care. _________________ not appreciate the gifts that they have.

(a) Young do   (b) Youth are

(c) The young do   (d) A young do

5 A: Where's Professor Fredrich?

B: Well, he actually told me this morning that he would go _________________.

(a) downtown   (b) to downtown

(c) toward downtown   (d) for downtown

6 The committee could never come to a consensus on the issue as _______________
members voted to tear the wall down and others voted to keep it in place.

(a) all (b) each
(c) some (d) any

7 Your mom doesn't think it's a good idea and I don't, _______________.

(a) also (b) either
(c) neither (d) so

8 Her grandfather had passed away _______________.

(a) many years before (b) many years ago
(c) many years since (d) many years from now

9 With the fire spreading quickly through the building, there was _______________
time to form a plan to evacuate the theatergoers.

(a) little (b) few
(c) any (d) less

10 People became upset that the taxes had gotten so _______________.

(a) cheap (b) expensive
(c) highly (d) high

11 The _______________ Johnson recalled fondly his memories from early
childhood.

(a) hundred-year-age old (b) hundred-years man
(c) hundred-years-old man (d) hundred-year-old man

12 Now that the House of Representatives is dominated by the Republicans, there will be newly-selected legislations that the Republicans were ________________ unable to pass.

(a) preliminary

(b) previously

(c) precise

(d) presently

13 Our newly built school building was nicely decorated with flamboyant scrollworks, ________________ the previous one torn down many years ago.

(a) very like

(b) much like

(c) very likely

(d) much likely

14 Doctors Without Borders currently have ________________ volunteering in Africa.

(a) four hundred medical staff

(b) four hundred medical staffs

(c) four hundreds medical staff

(d) four hundreds medical staffs

15 ________________ encourage their children to take risks and experiment.

(a) Do seldom parents

(b) Seldom do parents

(c) Do parents seldom

(d) Seldom parents do

16 I noticed that you have ________________ stamp collection.

(a) a quite impressive

(b) quite an impressive

(c) quite impressive

(d) the quite impressive

17 (a) A: Who did you have for your history teacher?
(b) B: Mrs. Sommers. I hated that class so much.
(c) A: Really? How come?
(d) B: She was cruel. She would punish us indiscriminate for no particular reason.

18 (a) A: It's time to leave. Miss Frazer, have you typed the letter?
(b) B: Not quite, sir. It can be done by this afternoon.
(c) A: Well, have you made my plane reservation for tomorrow yet?
(d) B: Sure, sir. I've made your flight reservation yet.

PART IV Identify the option that contains an awkward expression or an error in
grammar.

19 (a) Earthquakes were considered mysteriously acts of the gods up until recently.
(b) The discovery of plate tectonics led to an understanding of their origins. (c)
Now seismic technology can sense an oncoming tremor. (d) This has helped to
save lives, but it is not foolproof.

20 (a) For much of his life, Miguel Lopez didn't know about his younger brother. (b)
He had grown up thinking that he was the only child. (c) It was only after his
father's death that he was contacted by a stranger. (d) That stranger turned out to
be his brother, and they have remained closely since.

Memo 

Chapter 09

분사와 분사구문

기출 POINT 1

분사의 개념 파악을 먼저 한다.

1. 동사의 성질: 목적어, 보어, 부사(구)를 동반한다.
2. 형용사의 역할
 · (대)명사 수식
 · 주격 보어, 목적격 보어

기출 POINT 2

한정적 용법: 분사가 명사 앞뒤에서 명사를 직접 수식함에 유의한다.

 · 전치 수식: ⟨-ing/p.p. + 명사⟩
 · 후치 수식: 분사가 목적어, 보어, 부사를 동반한 경우 ⟨명사 + -ing/p.p.⟩

기출 POINT 3

서술적 용법에서는 주격 보어, 목적격 보어로 쓰임에 유의한다.

 · 목적어와 목적격 보어가 능동 관계 → 현재분사 사용(목적어로 주로 사람이 온다.)
 · 목적어와 목적격 보어가 수동 관계 → 과거분사 사용(목적어로 주로 사물이 온다.)

기출 POINT 4

· 현재분사: 진행형 (be + -ing)
· 과거분사: 완료형(have + p.p.), 수동태(be + p.p.)

기출 POINT 5

감정, 기분 표시 동사의 분사 용법은 정확히 이해한다.

용법

1. 주어가 사람인 경우: be동사 + 과거분사
   주어가 사물인 경우: be동사 + 현재분사

2. 사람을 수식하는 경우 과거분사를 쓴다.
   사물을 수식하는 경우에는 현재분사를 쓴다.

종류

excite, bore, amuse, surprise, please, embarrass, interest, annoy, bewilder, exhaust, satisfy, frighten

기출 POINT 6

분사구문은 출제율이 무척 높으므로 개념부터 정확히 이해한다.

분사구문은 〈접속사 + 주어 + 동사〉를 -ing나 p.p. 형태로 줄여 쓴 구로 시간, 조건, 이유, 양보, 부대상황(동시동작)의 의미를 가짐에 유의한다.

분사구문의 시제를 정확히 이해한다. (기준: 주절 동사)

1. 단순형: 주절 동사와 시제가 같을 때
2. 완료형: 주절 동사보다 한 시제 앞설 때
      현재 → 현재완료, 과거
      과거 → 과거완료

being, having been의 생략은 반드시 이해한다.

〈being/having been + 과거분사/형용사/명사〉 구문에서 being, having been은 생략 가능하다. 이때 분사구문의 시제가 주절과 같으면 being, 주절보다 한 시제 앞선 시제일 경우에는 having been이 생략되었다는 점에 유의해야 한다.

분사구문의 의미상 주어를 정확히 이해한다.

일반 분사구문
주절의 주어와 부사절의 주어가 일치 → 의미상 주어 생략

독립 분사구문
주절의 주어와 부사절의 주어가 불일치 → 의미상 주어를 표시해야 한다.
e.g. It being rainy, she didn't go out. (○)
     Being rainy, she didn't go out. (×)

Actual Test

PART I Choose the best answer for the blank.

1 A: Weren't you angry when your house caught on fire?

B: ________________ a mistake, there was nobody to blame.

(a) It being

(b) Being it

(c) It having been

(d) Having been it

2 A: Do you think that you can get the office ________________ in time for the report?

B: It will be difficult, but I'm confident that I can.

(a) organize

(b) to organize

(c) organized

(d) organizing

3 A: Are students allowed to grow their hair?

B: Traditionally, long hair ________________ at the school.

(a) frowns upon

(b) is frowning upon

(c) has frowned upon

(d) is frowned upon

4 A: Talk about what happened next.

B: Okay. ________________ the field, the coach argued with the referee.

(a) Walking onto

(b) Being walking onto

(c) Being walked

(d) Walk onto

5 A: What is Sarah doing right now?

B: ________________, she went outside to play with friends.

(a) Having cleaned her room

(b) To clean her room

(c) Her room having cleaned

(d) Her room cleaning

6 A: What do you appreciate most about working with the charity?

   B: That would be collaborating with my co-workers and ________________ animals.

   (a) to assist abusing   (b) assisting abused

   (c) to assist abused   (d) assisting to abuse

7 A: Were you serious about saying that this was our best president ever?

   B: No, I ________________ ironic.

   (a) am   (b) was being

   (c) was   (d) have been

8 A: The design looks great. What's next?

   B: Hurry up and get those samples ________________.

   (a) process   (b) processed

   (c) processing   (d) to process

9 A: Doing martial arts for a living must be exhausting.

   B: Once ________________, your body becomes used to the effort.

   (a) trained   (b) to train

   (c) training   (d) having trained

PART II Choose the best answer for the blank.

10 With only one senator voting against it, ________________.

   (a) the bill was passing 62-1   (b) the bill was defeated 62-1

   (c) the bill defeated 62-1   (d) the bill passed 62-1

11 Canada's trade deficit with Russia increased by four hundred percent, _______________ to the previous decade.

(a) comparing

(b) compared

(c) having been comparing

(d) having been compared

12 _______________ from a long day of hard labor, the construction worker collapsed onto his couch and turned on the television.

(a) Aching

(b) Being ached

(c) Ached

(d) Having been aching

13 _______________ by the press for her outfit before, the actress sought fashion advice for the upcoming awards ceremony.

(a) To be criticized

(b) Be criticized

(c) Having been criticized

(d) Being criticized

14 He stood in the doorway for a moment, _______________ what he had just heard.

(a) thinking about

(b) thinking

(c) thought about

(d) thought

15 Of the many major problems _______________ children today, environmental health will have the biggest impact on their quality of life.

(a) being confronted

(b) having confronted

(c) confronted

(d) confronting

16 _______________, she quickly wrote her thoughts down in her notebook.

(a) Inspiring the conversation

(b) Inspiring by the conversation

(c) Inspired the conversation

(d) Inspired by the conversation

17 There ______________ no means of escape, the man surrendered to the police.

(a) is

(b) has been

(c) being

(d) used to be

 Identify the option that contains an awkward expression or an error in grammar.

18 (a) A: We've had problems recently at the cafe.

(b) B: Really? What sort of problems?

(c) A: Giving away free drinks, the manager caught two employees.

(d) B: I guess that type of behavior shouldn't be tolerated.

PART IV **Identify the option that contains an awkward expression or an error in grammar.**

19 (a) Vanessa was busy for weeks preparing for her show. (b) She rehearsed three hours a day, every day of the week. (c) When she got tired from dancing, she would practice her singing. (d) Focusing exclusively on her show, neglecting her friends and family.

20 (a) The other day, the neighborhood association hosted a potluck dinner. (b) The purpose was to help build bonds among community members and discuss local issues. (c) Some of the issues had discussed included crime, rent increases, and the education system. (d) The potluck dinner was such a success that the attendees promised to have another one in the near future.

Memo 

Chapter 10

관계사

기출 POINT 1

관계대명사의 격을 정확히 정리한다.

1. 관계대명사절에 주어가 없으면 주격 관계대명사 → 〈선행사 + 관계대명사 + V〉
2. 관계대명사절에 목적어가 없으면 목적격 관계대명사 → 〈선행사 + S + V〉
3. 소유격 관계대명사 뒤에는 명사가 옴 → 〈whose + 명사〉, 〈of which the + 명사〉

기출 POINT 2

수를 확인한다. TEPS 시험에서는 수 일치 출제율이 높다.

주격 관계대명사인 경우 관계대명사절의 동사는 선행사의 인칭, 수와 일치해야 한다.

· 선행사가 단수 명사 → 단수 동사
· 선행사가 복수 명사 → 복수 동사

기출 POINT 3

관계부사는 선행사가 시간, 장소, 이유, 방법 중 무엇인지만 확인하면 된다.

· when: 선행사가 시간
· where: 선행사가 장소
· how: 선행사가 방법 (선행사와 how 중 하나만 사용하는 것에 주의)
· why: 선행사가 이유

기출 POINT 4

관계대명사 that을 쓰는 경우는 모두 암기한다.

선행사가 '사람과 동물', '사물'인 경우와 선행사에 다음과 같은 한정 어구가 있을 때는 that을 사용한다.

1. 서수, 최상급
2. 의문사(who, which)
3. the only/very/same/most/last
4. all, no, some, any, everything, something

that 앞에는 전치사를 쓸 수 없으며, 계속적 용법으로 사용 불가능하다.

기출 POINT 5

관계대명사 what은 관용 표현이 중요하다.

관계대명사 what은 선행사를 포함하고 있으므로 선행사와 함께 쓸 수 없으며 명사절을 이끈다.

- what we/you/they call, what is called 소위, 이른바
- what one is/used to be/was 현재[과거]의 인격
- what is + 비교급 더욱 ~한 것은
  what is + 최상급 가장 ~한 것은
- A is to B what/as C is to D A가 B에 대한 관계는 C가 D에 대한 관계와 같다

기출 POINT 6

복합관계대명사는 선행사를 포함하고 있으므로 선행사와 함께 사용할 수 없으며, 〈관계대명사-ever〉로 관계대명사를 포함하고 있어서 다른 관계대명사와 함께 사용할 수 없다.

e.g. Whatever may happen, you must go your own way.

6   A: Some people would describe those terrorists as freedom fighters.

B: _________________ you prefer to call them, they must be dealt with.

(a) Which   (b) However

(c) That   (d) Whatever

PART II Choose the best answer for the blank.

7   The sales agent decided to reduce the amount of travelling she did, _____________ was good news for her children who wanted to spend more time with her.

(a) that   (b) which

(c) what   (d) whose

8   We have plans to spend the summer in Romania, _________________ my grandmother have lived for 20 years.

(a) there   (b) which

(c) where   (d) when

9   _________________ you eat determines much about your appearance, including your weight, muscle mass, and skin condition.

(a) What   (b) Which

(c) As   (d) That

10 Go to our website to select _________________ you think deserves to be artist of the year.

(a) whomever   (b) whatever

(c) whichever   (d) whoever

11 Scientists have discovered a variety of plants ________________ useful for producing natural medicine.

    (a) which are   (b) are

    (c) which is   (d) is

12 Whenever I'm feeling down, there is one thing ________________ I like to do to lift my spirits.

    (a) in which   (b) who

    (c) what   (d) that

13 School authorities were still trying to determine the source of the contaminated food ________________ made a third of the dormitory sick with food poisoning.

    (a) who   (b) when

    (c) where   (d) that

14 It is a cunning and calculating person ________________ achieves power and prestige by becoming a politician.

    (a) where   (b) who

    (c) what   (d) when

15 Politicians, musicians, and prominent businessmen are among ________________ are promoting the use of solar energy.

    (a) the ones whose   (b) the ones those

    (c) the ones who   (d) the one that

16 Frida Castro is the candidate ________________ I believe is most qualified to head this committee.

    (a) whomever   (b) whom

    (c) which   (d) who

17 I just got a job painting houses, _______________ pays much better than mowing lawns.

   (a) why   (b) which

   (c) that   (d) what

PART III Identify the option that contains an awkward expression or an error in grammar.

18 (a) A: It's amazing that we are graduating. Time goes really fast.

   (b) B: You're telling me. Did you figure out which you're going to do after graduation?

   (c) A: Yup, I'm going to start my career at a legal consulting firm.

   (d) B: That's fantastic. Good luck with your job.

19 (a) A: One problem that I have I travel is eating spicy food.

   (b) B: What do you do if you eat something very spicy?

   (c) A: I drink as much water as I can to relieve the burn.

   (d) B: Surprisingly, water can spread the effect even more. It is more effective to eat bread or rice in order to absorb the spicy elements.

PART IV Identify the option that contains an awkward expression or an error in grammar.

20 (a) Dengue fever is occurring at a greater frequency among world travellers. (b) It is spread by the bite of mosquitoes who live in tropic and subtropic regions. (c) Symptoms can last as long as a week, and while painful, it is not fatal. (d) When travelling to a tropical region, be sure to use proper clothing, mosquito repellent, and netting in order to avoid this illness.

Chapter 11

어순과 도치, 강조, 삽입

기출 POINT 1

문제를 보고 무엇을 묻는 문제인지 출제 의도를 바로 알 수 있을 정도로 어순과 도치구문의 유형, 형태, 의미를 익힌다.

기출 POINT 2

도치는 도치되는 경우와 형태가 중요하다.

1. 조건절의 if를 생략하는 경우: 〈Were/Had/Should + S + V〉
2. 〈형용사/부사/무관사 명사 + as + S + V〉 비록 ~이지만
3. 〈So + V + S〉, 〈Neither + V + S〉
4. 유도부사가 문두에 오는 경우: There + V + S
5. 부정어구(부정부사)가 문두에 오는 경우: never, not, only, hardly

기출 POINT 3

부정은 부분부정, 전체부정, 준부정, 이중부정의 경우를 정확히 이해한다.

· 부분부정: 부정어(not/never) + all/every/always/quite/necessarily
· 전체부정: no/none/neither/never/not + any/either
· 준부정: little, few, seldom, hardly, rarely 등이 들어 있는 어구

기출 POINT **4**

강조는 강조하는 방법의 이해가 중요하다.

1. 동사의 강조: 강조의 조동사 do 사용
2. 대명사의 강조: 재귀대명사 사용
3. 강조구문: It is/was + 강조 어구 + that
4. 명사의 강조: the very 바로 그
5. 의문문의 강조: on earth, in the world, ever, whatever 도대체
6. 부정문의 강조: 부정어(not) + at all / in the least / whatever 결코 ~않다
7. 비교급, 최상급의 강조: much, far, by far

기출 POINT **5**

삽입의 경우는 관용구의 삽입을 암기한다.

as it were 말하자면
to be sure 확실히
so far as I know 내가 아는 한
if ever 있다손 치더라도

if you like 원한다면
that is to say 다시 말하면
if any 있다면, 있으면
as if S is/does 사실상

기출 POINT **6**

대부사의 용법도 출제되므로 반드시 알고 넘어가자.

· so: 선행한 긍정 의미의 문장 전체를 대신한다.
· not: 선행한 부정 의미의 문장 전체를 대신한다.

대명사의 용법도 중요하다.

· one = a + 명사
· it = the(한정사) + 명사
· none = no + 명사
· that = the + 단수 명사 + of
· those = the + 복수 명사 + of

TEPS에 자주 나오는 부가의문문은 다음과 같다.

· Let's ~(제안) → shall we?
· would rather ~ → wouldn't ~ ?
· had better ~ → hadn't ~ ?
· used to ~ → didn't ~ ?
· 직접 명령문 → will you?
· 권유의 명령문 → won't you?
· have to ~ → don't ~ ?
· ought to ~ → shouldn't ~ ?
· had to~ → didn't ~ ?

부정어(little, hardly)가 포함된 문장은 긍정의 부가의문문이 나온다.

PART I Choose the best answer for the blank.

1   A: I thought that the movie was a bit underwhelming.

B: _________________

(a) So did I.   (b) Neither did I.

(c) So was I.   (d) Neither was I.

2   A: Can I have a haircut?

B: No problem. How _________________?

(a) short a trim do you want   (b) do you want a short trim

(c) do you want a trim short   (d) a short trim do you want

3   A: _________________ such a funny show on television!

B: I can't wait to watch it.

(a) Never I've seen   (b) Have seen never I

(c) Never have I seen   (d) I've seen never

4   A: Could you lend me some money this month?

B: I'm sorry, but I _________________ the rent.

(a) hardly have enough to afford money

(b) have hardly money to afford enough

(c) have enough money hardly to afford

(d) hardly have enough money to afford

5   A: My parents want me to join the circus like my brother.

B: _________________ you have!

(a) How a unique family   (b) How uniquely a family

(c) What unique a family   (d) What a unique family

6 A: Hey, you see that guy in the yellow jacket? Could you introduce me to him?

B: I would, but I don't know ________________.

(a) who he is, neither (b) who is he

(c) who he is, either (d) he is whom

7 A: I take full responsibility for the accident and apologize sincerely.

B: Your honesty is refreshing. ________________ when they've made a mistake.

(a) Do people admit seldom (b) People do admit seldom

(c) Seldom do people admit (d) Seldom people do admit

8 A: After examining the body, coroners have determined the victim's time of death.

B: ________________

(a) When do they believe he died?

(b) When they believe did he die?

(c) When does he believe they died?

(d) When he died do they believe?

9 A: I wonder if Matilda is going to get a raise at her new job.

B: That depends on ________________ the potential she has to benefit the company.

(a) her boss to see whether (b) sees her boss whether or not

(c) whether not her boss (d) whether or not her boss sees

PART II Choose the best answer for the blank.

10 ________________ than the juice was spilled all over the kitchen floor.

(a) Had I finished mopping no sooner

(b) No sooner I had finished mopping

(c) I had finished mopping no sooner

(d) No sooner had I finished mopping

11 _______________ but also he installed a virus protection software for free.

(a) He did not fix my computer only

(b) Not only did he fix my computer

(c) Not only he fixed my computer

(d) He did fix not only my computer

12 _______________, she was unable to solve the teacher's riddle.

(a) Smart as she was   (b) Though smart she was

(c) As she was smart   (d) Smart since she was

13 Surprisingly, few historians recognize _______________ he was in the civil rights movement.

(a) how important figure   (b) how a important figure

(c) how important a figure   (d) how a figure important

14 Never _______________ so much of his personal time and energy into improving the livelihood of our residents.

(a) a mayor spent   (b) has a mayor spent

(c) a mayor has spent   (d) has a mayor spend

15 James Finnaker did not attend a single day of school, _______________ to send his own children to what he considers a governmental institution.

(a) he neither intends   (b) he does not intend

(c) nor does he intend   (d) nor he intends

16 No sooner _______________ than the students raced to the classroom door.

(a) had the bell rung   (b) the bell had rung

(c) rung had the bell   (d) had rung the bell

17 (a) A: You do seem like a talented person.
    (b) B: Well, I've been awarded numerous prizes for my writing and dancing abilities.
    (c) A: Look, we've been talking for almost completely about you tonight. Can we talk about something else?
    (d) B: Okay. Let's talk about you. What do you think of my new haircut?

18 (a) A: I haven't been able to prepare enough for this test.
    (b) B: Neither I have. Let's spend the night at the library.
    (c) A: If I don't get some rest, then I'll perform terribly during the test.
    (d) B: I'll buy you some coffee. We can help keep each other awake.

PART IV Identify the option that contains an awkward expression or an error in grammar.

19 (a) Earthworms are invaluable tools for any serious gardener. (b) This is due to the aeration created by the tunnels that they dig out. (c) Oxygen is then able to reach the roots of the plants, making them more healthy. (d) Not only they do add oxygen, but also nutrition by circulating organic matter such as dead leaves into the soil.

20 (a) More and more people are being exposed to unhealthy levels of mercury. (b) The main source of this exposure is the consumption of seafood. (c) Children and fetuses are at most risk of developing neurological disorders from too much mercury. (d) Symptoms of poisoning mercury may include impairment of speech, hearing, walking, and muscle weakness.

Memo 

Chapter 12

전치사

기출 POINT 1

〈전치사 + 명사 (상당 어구)〉는 부사구, 형용사구가 되며 전치사의 목적어가 인칭대명사인 경우에는 반드시 목적격을 사용한다.

기출 POINT 2

각각의 전치사가 갖는 용법과 의미를 묻는 문제가 자주 출제되므로 그 용법과 의미를 이해해야 하며 비슷한 뜻으로 쓰이는 전치사의 용법 차이에 유의한다.

기출 POINT 3

시간 전치사의 용법 차이는 출제율이 높다.

· at: 몇 시, 몇 분, 몇 초, 하루의 정오 · 새벽 · 밤, 시대의 전환기
  e.g. at seven, at noon

· on: 요일, 날짜, 특정일의 아침 · 저녁 · 밤
  e.g. on the morning of May

· in: 월, 년, 세기, 계절, 오전, 오후, 정한 시간
  e.g. in 2002, in the seventies

· for: for + 수사 + 시간 (명사) (일정한 기간) 동안
      How long ~ ?에 대한 대답

· during: 특정한 기간, 상태의 계속 기간
        When ~ ?에 대한 대답

· since: 과거에서 현재까지 계속을 표시.
      '~이래로 줄곧' 이라는 뜻으로 현재완료 시제와 많이 쓴다.

· from: till 또는 to와 함께 쓰며 과거의 출발점 표시(~부터 …까지)

기출 POINT 4

위치, 장소 전치사의 용법도 출제율이 높다.

· at: 한 지점, 주소 번지 표시(비교적 좁은 장소)

· in: 도시, 국가, 어느 지역 구역 안 표시(비교적 넓은 장소)

· on: 접촉해서 위(천장과 벽에 붙어 있는 물체에 사용)

· above: (비스듬히) 위
  below: (비스듬히) 아래
  beneath: (접촉해서) 아래에

· over: (수직으로) 위
  under: (수직으로) 아래
  by: 바로 옆에, ~ 를 끼고

· in front of: ~ 바로 앞에
  behind: ~ 바로 뒤에

· before: ~ 앞에(순서)
  after: ~ 뒤에(순서)

기출 POINT 5

수단, 도구 전치사의 용법은 기본적으로 암기한다.

· with: ~으로, ~을 사용하여(도구, 수단)

· by: ~에 의해(수동태: 행위자, 능동태: 수단, 방법)

· in: ~을 가지고(필기 도구, 미술 재료 등의 도구를 표시)
  e.g. write in ink

방향 전치사의 용법 차이에 유의한다.

· to: (목적지, 도착지)
· for: (방향과 목적지)

· from: ~에서(출발점)
· towards: ~쪽으로(목적지)

· up: (수직) 위로
· down: (수직) 아래로

· into: ~속으로
· out of: ~의 밖으로

· across: ~을 가로질러
· through: ~을 통과하여
· along: ~을 따라서

원인, 이유, 동기 전치사의 용법 차이에 유의한다.

· for: 동사 punish, blame, praise, 형용사 sorry, grateful, thankful 등과 사용

· of: 죽음의 원인이 병, 굶주림, 노령일 경우

· from: 죽음의 원인이 병이 아닐 경우(부상, 피로, 과로)

· through: mistake, neglect, fault, carelessness가 원인일 때

· out of: 동기를 나타냄(curiosity, fear, gratitude, friendship, necessity 등과 사용)

재료 전치사의 용법 차이에 유의한다.

· of: 재료의 형태가 제품에 남아 있는 경우(물리적 변화) → 형태는 변하나 성질은 변하지 않는다.

· from: 재료가 변하여 제품이 되는 경우(화학적 변화) → 형태, 성질이 변한다.

· into: 재료, 원료가 주어인 경우
   e.g. Grapes are made into wine.

Actual Test

PART I **Choose the best answer for the blank.**

1   A: Isn't it clear that dogs are more advanced animals than birds?
B: Though there are differences, I believe no species is inferior _______________
any other.

(a) in   (b) than
(c) to   (d) as

2   A: I wonder if it's supposed to rain _______________ Sunday.
B: I haven't heard any news about it.

(a) on   (b) for
(c) in   (d) at

3   A: How soon will the pizza get here?
B: If the pizza isn't delivered _______________ thirty minutes, then we will give
it to you for free.

(a) by   (b) at
(c) during   (d) in

4   A: I can't believe that Tim doesn't have a girlfriend. He is so handsome.
B: He may be good-looking, but he's always been poor _______________
expressing himself.

(a) for   (b) with
(c) at   (d) in

5   A: This week I leave _______________ the US.
B: We sure will miss you.

(a) with   (b) for
(c) to   (d) at

6 A: Why aren't you going home?

B: I'm going to complete this work. I'll have to stick around ________________ at
least an hour more.

(a) for (b) on

(c) until (d) at

7 A: I'd like to go to the museum ________________.

B: We had better not. The weather is not good today.

(a) in bike (b) by the bikes

(c) through bikes (d) by bike

8 A: We will have to reduce our workforce ________________ 30% this year.

B: I'd hate to be one of the people let go.

(a) with (b) from

(c) by (d) on

9 A: I'm so grateful to be back here living with my family.

B: So am I, grandpa. I'm only sorry I couldn't be here ________________ the day
that you got out of the hospital.

(a) on (b) at

(c) in (d) to

10 A: John, can you tell us the day when your uncle James moved out for good?

B: Sure, sir. I believe it was ________________ the morning of September 20,
2005.

(a) in (b) at

(c) on (d) to

PART II Choose the best answer for the blank.

11 I don't think it's very polite _________________ you to speak that way to your mother.

(a) with

(b) to

(c) of

(d) about

12 Kathy passionately loved the band, _________________ their lack of popularity among her friends.

(a) though

(b) unless

(c) because

(d) despite

13 Nobody has bought anything _________________.

(a) all day

(b) at all day

(c) on all day

(d) in all day

14 Luther Eldridge died _______ Atlanta _______ March 15, 1931 _______ midnight.

(a) at – by – on

(b) on – in – at

(c) in – on – at

(d) to – in – at

15 _________________ the large amount of star power and money invested into its production, *Water World* was a huge flop at the box office.

(a) Despite of

(b) Even if

(c) Although

(d) Despite

16 _________________ your persistence, our dream to create revolutionary media has come true.

(a) Even though

(b) According to

(c) But for

(d) Thanks to

17 (a) A: Sam, will you be available to join us at this weekend?
(b) B: I think so. But I have some writing to catch up on.
(c) A: I just want to grab a cup of coffee real quick.
(d) B: Sure. It could be nice to get out of the house for a change.

18 (a) A: How long are you going to be working in that paper?
(b) B: I'm not certain. It looks like it could take all day.
(c) A: Hurry up and finish, so we can go to that party.
(d) B: I'm doing it as fast as I can, but I don't think I'll make it.

PART IV Identify the option that contains an awkward expression or an error in grammar.

19 (a) Tammy's mother was famous as her delicious cookies. (b) The parents of Tammy's friends regularly asked for the recipe. (c) "It's a family secret," her mother would say. (d) The secret, however, was actually the bakery down the street.

20 (a) Christopher Reeve was paralyzed while a horse-riding accident. (b) He was unable to move both his arms and legs. (c) From that point on, he became a powerful advocate for investment in spinal cord injury research. (d) His valiant efforts did not, however, prevent him from passing away in 2004.

Memo 

Chapter 13 | 대명사

기출 POINT 1

문제에서 대명사가 나오면 그것이 가리키는 명사와 수, 성, 격이 일치하는지 반드시 확인한다.

기출 POINT 2

인칭대명사는 격의 사용에 주의한다.

1. 주어, 주격 보어 자리: 주격
2. 소유격 자리: 소유격
3. 목적어, 목적격 보어 자리: 목적격
4. it은 〈the/ 소유격 + 단수 명사〉를, one은 〈a/an + 단수 명사〉를 받는다.

기출 POINT 3

재귀대명사는 관용적 용법이 중요하므로 모두 암기한다.

by oneself 혼자서(= alone)
of itself 저절로(= spontaneously)
beside oneself 제정신이 아닌(= almost mad)
for oneself 혼자 힘으로(= without any other's help)
in itself 본래(= naturally)
to oneself 자기에게만, 독점하여

기출 POINT 4

소유대명사는 단독으로 사용할 수 있으나 소유격은 단독으로 사용할 수 없고 명사를 수식한다. 따라서 명사 앞에는 소유격을 사용해야 한다.

e.g. their book → theirs(소유대명사)

· 이중 소유격: 한정사(a, an, the) + 명사 + of + 소유대명사

기출 POINT 5

지시대명사의 핵심 포인트는 모두 암기한다.

1. ⟨that + of + 명사⟩: 앞에 나온 명사가 단수인 경우
   ⟨those + of + 명사⟩: 앞에 나온 명사가 복수인 경우

2. that: 전자(= the former, the one)
   this: 후자(= the latter, the other)

3. same: the와 함께 as, that과 상관적으로 사용한다.

기출 POINT 6

확인, 동의 표시의 대형태: 긍정적 동의와 부정적 동의를 정확히 이해한다.

1. ~도 역시 그렇다: 긍정적 동의
   · So + V + S: (다른 주어(사람)에 대하여) ~도 역시 그렇다(= also) → 도치
   · So + S + V: (같은 주어(사람)에 대하여) 정말로 그렇다(= certainly) → 정치

2. ~도 그렇지 않다: 부정적 동의
   · Neither/Nor + V + S
   · S + not + V ~ , either

3. too(역시) → 긍정문

부정대명사는 one, another, other의 관용구문을 모두 암기한다.

· one ~ , the other … : 하나는 ~, 또 하나는 …

· one thing ~ , another … : ~와 …는 별개이다

· other: 다른
 the other: (둘 중에) 다른 한쪽
 the others: 다른 사람들

· another + 단수 명사
 other + 복수 명사
 some other + 물질명사

· one – one's – one – oneself는 he – his – him – himself로 받는다.

some, any의 용법을 정확히 이해한다.

some
1. 긍정문
2. 의문문에 some을 쓰는 경우
 · 권유, 부탁의 경우
 · 긍정의 대답을 기대하는 경우

any
1. 의문문, 부정문, 조건문(if)
2. without, few가 들어 있는 문장은 any를 쓴다.

Actual Test

PART I Choose the best answer for the blank.

1 A: I'm looking for something special to give my girlfriend.

B: May I recommend one of these necklaces? ________________ of them was crafted by hand, giving a unique look and feel to every necklace.

(a) All   (b) Each

(c) Every   (d) Both

2 A: You've got an impressive garden here.

B: Most of the vegetables are growing well, but these ________________ here are struggling for some reason.

(a) ones   (b) one

(c) it   (d) thing

3 A: Please pass me a slice of pizza.

B: I can't because there's ________________ left.

(a) anything   (b) no one

(c) none   (d) some

4 A: How do you feel about this place?

B: I have to admit I like this house better than ________________ one.

(a) another   (b) other

(c) others   (d) the other

5 A: People are getting hungry. Should we all go out to a restaurant?

B: How about you and I go get some food while________________ keep working here?

(a) other   (b) another

(c) the others   (d) few

6　A: Would you rather live in Canada or the United States?

　　B: Well, Canada's healthcare system is more comprehensive than ______________.

　　(a) the US

　　(b) those of the US

　　(c) the one of the US

　　(d) that of the US

7　A: Did you have something to tell me?

　　B: Yes, Peter. I don't enjoy saying ________________, but you're fired.

　　(a) that

　　(b) these

　　(c) this

　　(d) those

8　A: It looks like somebody ate dad's burger.

　　B: Nobody had better have eaten ________________. I'm so hungry I could eat a horse.

　　(a) one

　　(b) mine

　　(c) myself

　　(d) the other

9　A: I want you to try this fruit smoothie that I invented.

　　B: Sure. ________________

　　(a) What does it taste like?

　　(b) What does it taste?

　　(c) How does it taste like?

　　(d) How is the taste like?

10　A: Are you more in the mood for Vietnamese or Cambodian food?

　　B: I guess it depends on ________________ is less expensive.

　　(a) that

　　(b) what

　　(c) which

　　(d) who

11　A: Hey, Eric. I'm calling to let you know that we found your cell phone.

　　B: Great! Do you think you could ________________ at my house sometime this week?

　　(a) drop off them

　　(b) drop them off

　　(c) drop off it

　　(d) drop it off

PART II Choose the best answer for the blank.

12 Measles is a common illness, with most children getting ________________ once
in their life.

    (a) those   (b) them

    (c) it   (d) one

13 No matter how individualistic we think we are, we cannot deny the
interdependence we have on ________________.

    (a) others   (b) anyone

    (c) another   (d) ones

14 I can't find ________________ the matter with her line of reasoning.

    (a) something   (b) anything

    (c) nothing   (d) something else

15 I'd like to offer you some advice on your problem, but I have ________________.

    (a) not   (b) any

    (c) neither   (d) none

16 The peaches here are much nicer than ________________.

    (a) that in the market   (b) those at the market

    (c) the market   (d) the market is

PART III Identify the option that contains an awkward expression or an error in grammar

17 (a) A: How does the meal taste like?
(b) B: Excellent. I had no idea you were such a talented chef.
(c) A: I enjoy cooking, but all I can do is improvise.
(d) B: Someday you'll have to show me how you do it.

18 (a) A: Julie, have you finished the book, *The Purpose Driven Life*?
(b) B: Not yet. Do you want me to give back it to you?
(c) A: Not right now. When you are finished with it, let me know.
(d) B: Sure thing. I will.

PART Ⅳ Identify the option that contains an awkward expression or an error in grammar.

19 (a) What would you do if yourself injured while trekking in the mountains. (b) Twenty-two year old Sara Parker was in that very situation. (c) Trapped on a cliff, she managed to tie a piece of clothing to a cable that alerted rescue workers to her location. (d) Her ingenuity probably saved her life.

20 (a) A massive recall of toys found to contain lead in the paint has sparked controversy throughout the industry. (b) Toy importers and retailers are scrutinizing their inventory to determine if any of whose products could pose a risk to children's health. (c) With Christmas shopping season looming ahead, parents have become especially concerned about the safety of the toys that their children play with. (d) China has been especially targeted by criticism, being the main producer of the controversial toy products.

Memo 

Chapter 14 | 비교

기출 POINT 1

원급, 비교급, 최상급의 개념을 정확히 이해한다.

· 원급: 서로 다른 2개를 대등한 수준에서 비교할 때 사용된다. (~한, ~하게)
· 비교급: 서로 다른 2개 중 우열을 비교할 때 사용된다. (보다 ~한[하게])
· 최상급: 서로 다른 3개 이상 중에서 가장 뛰어난 것을 비교할 때 사용된다. (가장 ~한[하게])

기출 POINT 2

문제에서 뒤에 than이 오면 앞에 -er/more/less가 와야 하고, 역으로 앞에 -er/more/less가 오면 뒤에 than이 와야 한다는 사실을 이해한다.

기출 POINT 3

원급과 비교급의 비교 형식을 정확히 이해한다.

· as + 원급 + as ~ ~만큼 …하다 (긍정)
· not + so/as + 원급 + as ~ ~만큼 …하지 못하다 (부정)
· -er/more + than ~ ~보다 더 …하다 (우등비교)
· less + 원급 + than ~ ~보다 덜 …하다 (열등비교)

기출 POINT **4**

비교급 비교에서 주의할 점은 다음과 같다.

1. 어미가 -ior인 라틴계 비교에는 than 대신 to를 사용한다.
   e.g. superior to

2. 〈배수사 + as ~ as〉, 〈배수사 + more/-er + than〉의 배수 표현에 유의한다.

3. 동일인, 동일물의 비교에는 more than 형식을 사용한다.

기출 POINT **5**

비교급의 빈출 사항을 반드시 이해한다.

· 〈the + 비교급 ~ the + 비교급 … 〉, 〈the + 비교급 + of the two〉
· 비교급 강조 어구로는 much, (by) far, even 등을 쓰고 very는 쓰지 못한다.
· 비교 대상은 문법상 같은 역할을 하는 것끼리 대구를 이뤄야 한다.

기출 POINT **6**

최상급의 형태는 매우 중요하므로 반드시 암기한다.

· the + 최상급 + of (+ all) + 복수 명사
· the + 최상급 + in + 단수 명사(장소, 범위, 분야)

기출 POINT **7**

원급의 관용 표현은 모두 암기한다.

· 〈as ~ as possible〉, 〈as ~ as one can〉 가능한 한 ~
· 〈as ~ as any + 명사〉, 〈as ~ as ever + 동사〉 어느 …에도 못지않게 ~한
· 〈not so much as + V〉 ~조차도 않다
· as good as ~ ~와 다름없는

비교급의 관용 표현은 모두 암기한다.

no more than 단지(= only)
not more than 기껏해야(= at most)
no better than ~와 다름없는

no less than ~만큼이나
not less than 적어도(= at least)

much/still more 한층 더 ~하다
much/still less 한층 더 ~하지 않다
more or less 다소

A is no more B than C is D A가 B가 아닌 것은 C가 D가 아닌 것과 같다

최상급의 관용 표현은 모두 암기한다.

at least 적어도
at first 처음에는

at most 많아야
at best 기껏해야

the most 가장 ~한
a most 매우
most 대부분의

Actual Test

PART I Choose the best answer for the blank.

1 A: Let's not buy these apples. For just a little more money we can get organic ones.

B: Why? Are organic apples ________________ that are treated with chemicals?

(a) more nutritious than them (b) not so nutritious as

(c) less nutritious than those (d) more nutritious than those

2 A: According to this psychological study, women were found to talk ________________ as did men.

B: They had to do scientific research to determine that?

(a) as much three times (b) three times as much

(c) as three times much (d) much as three times

3 A: Do you recommend nicotine patches as a method to quit smoking?

B: For me, chewing nicotine gum was ________________ using the patches.

(a) more effective than (b) more effective as

(c) as effective than (d) much effective than

4 A: What did you think of my standup comedy performance?

B: I thought you were ________________ talented as any comedian I have seen.

(a) as (b) very

(c) so (d) well

5 A: I think Michael W. Smith is one of the best-selling an ________________.

B: Absolutely. He has achieved considerable success in the mainstream music industry as well.

(a) more influential artists in contemporary Christian music

(b) most influential artist in contemporary Christian music

(c) most influential artists of contemporary Christian music

(d) most influential artists in contemporary Christian music

6   A: Should we invite Leroy and Shana to join us tonight?

      B: Of course. ________________

      (a) The more, the merry.   (b) The more, the merrier.

      (c) The more, the more merrier. (d) The more, the more merry.

7   A: Who is most likely to get first prize in the game show?

      B: Definitely Jean. She has more talent than ________________.

      (a) any other contestant   (b) any other contestants

      (c) all other contestant   (d) all the other contestant

8   A: What did you think of the new music editing software?

      B: The new version is inferior ________________ the original in terms of user-friendliness.

      (a) as   (b) to

      (c) than   (d) in

9   A: Could you comment on the speculation of Mr. Baker having a heart condition?

      B: There is nothing to be worried about. Mr. Baker is ________________ as ever.

      (a) as healthy   (b) most healthy

      (c) more healthy   (d) healthily

PART II Choose the best answer for the blank.

10 While both of the sequels were entertaining, the original film is ________________ of the entire trilogy.

      (a) the more impressive   (b) the most impressed

      (c) the most impressive   (d) the more impressed

11 The more you practice the language, _________________ it becomes to understand.

    (a) to be easier   (b) it gets easier

    (c) the easier   (d) it is easier

12 Prescription pills are _________________ as the advertisements portray them to be.

    (a) as effective rarely   (b) rarely as effective

    (c) as rarely effective   (d) effective as rarely

13 The vegetables in her garden grew _________________ the ones in mine.

    (a) twice as fast as   (b) as twice fast as

    (c) twice fast as   (d) as fast twice as

14 It is more effective to conduct research directly _________________ on second-hand references.

    (a) to rely   (b) than to rely

    (c) relying   (d) than relying

15 Magarette studies harder than _________________ in my class.

    (a) no other student   (b) no students

    (c) any other student   (d) all the students

PART III **Identify the option that contains an awkward expression or an error in grammar.**

16 (a) A: I'm so happy you came over and got to see my family.

    (b) B: All of your children are quite adorable.

    (c) A: Anna is a very clever girl, isn't she?

    (d) B: Yes, I think that she is smartest of the bunch.

17 (a) A: What do you think of Paul?

(b) B: Paul is nice, but he won't make much money as a carpenter.

(c) A: Frankly, money is lesser important to me than to other people.

(d) B: Well, I suppose that as long as you are happy money doesn't matter.

18 (a) A: There was a traffic jam on the highway.

(b) B: Did it cause you problems driving?

(c) A: It took us as twice long to get back!

(d) B: That must have been a boring ride.

PART Ⅳ Identify the option that contains an awkward expression or an error in grammar.

19 (a) Greetings are one of most significant social aspect of Arabic-speaking countries. (b) In Morocco, people begin by asking a series of questions about each other's health, family, and children. (c) Shaking hands is also necessary when meeting someone or when departing. (d) After shaking hands, it is common to place one's right hand on the heart as a sign of respect.

20 (a) Mom-and-pop shops are rapidly being eclipsed by giant superstores. (b) These megastores boast an endless array of goods. (c) Because of their economies of scale, they can also offer low prices than smaller stores. (d) Nonetheless, some people bemoan the loss of community that mom-and-pop shops brought to a neighborhood.

Memo 

Chapter 15 가정법

기출 POINT 1

가정법 현재는 요구, 주장, 제안 동사의 **that**절과 〈**It is** + 형용사 + **that**절〉이 매우 중요하다.

형식
· S + 동사 + that + S (+ should) + 동사원형
· It is + 형용사 + that + S (+ should) + 동사원형

동사
suggest, advise, move, insist, urge, demand, request, require, decide, recommend, desire, order

명사
suggestion, request, advice, recommendation, proposal

형용사
advisable, desirous, essential, imperative, important, required, strange, urgent, necessary, natural

기출 POINT 2

가정법 과거는 조건절과 귀결절의 형태에 주의한다.

· 조건절(if절): if + S + 과거 동사(be동사는 were)
· 귀결절(주절): S + would/should/could/might + 동사원형

기출 POINT 3

가정법 과거완료는 가정법 관련 기출율 1위이므로 반드시 암기한다.

· 조건절(if절): S + had + p.p.
· 귀결절(주절): S + would/should/could/might + have + p.p.

기출 POINT 4

혼합가정법은 조건절은 가정법 과거완료, 귀결절은 가정법 과거의 형태이다.

· 조건절(if절): S + had + p.p. → 가정법 과거완료
· 귀결절(주절): S + would/should/could/might + 동사원형 → 가정법 과거

기출 POINT 5

⟨It's (high/about) time + 주어 + 동사의 과거형(가정법 과거)⟩

be동사는 항상 were를 사용함에 주의한다.

기출 POINT 6

가정법 조건절의 if를 생략하면 ⟨(조)동사 + 주어⟩로 도치된다.

귀결절이 가정법 형태인지 반드시 살펴본다.

기출 POINT 7

다음 표현들도 출제될 확률이 높으므로 꼭 암기한다.

· If if were not for + 명사 ~이 없다면 → 가정법 과거
· If it had not been for + 명사 ~이 없었다면 → 가정법 과거완료
· 직설법 현재[과거], otherwise + 가정법 과거[과거완료] → 뒷부분이 가정법
· 가정법 과거[과거완료], but/except + 직설법 현재[과거] → 앞부분이 가정법
· as it were 말하자면

Actual Test

1 A: I don't have any good ideas for what to do.
B: If I _________________ that kind of free time, I'd take a trip somewhere.

(a) have (b) has
(c) had (d) will have

2 A: Did you say that the new employee is causing problems?
B: That's right. _________________ he would behave like this, I wouldn't have hired him.

(a) should I know (b) If I knew
(c) Had I known (d) If I would know

3 A: John made a fool of himself at Francine's wedding.
B: I can't believe he did that. _________________ there, I would have told him to be quiet.

(a) I had been (b) I was
(c) Had I been (d) Did I

4 A: I'm happy for you for finally getting yourself out of debt.
B: Well, _________________, I might have given up hope.

(a) were not it for your wise advice
(b) had it not been for your wise advice
(c) for it had not been your wise advice
(d) for it were not your wise advice

5 A: If they had been more prepared for an emergency situation, lots of victims _________________.
B: I know. That's a shame, isn't it?

(a) have saved (b) could have saved
(c) had been saved (d) could have been saved

6 A: I need to call my girlfriend. Can I use that phone?

B: I'd rather you ________________. It's out of service. Use this one.

(a) don't (b) didn't

(c) can't (d) needn't

7 A: Do you think I'd be more popular if I ________________ rich?

B: Probably. But many of your friendships would be superficial.

(a) be (b) is

(c) would be (d) were

8 A: I knew I should have brought the map with us.

B: I wish you ________________. Then we wouldn't be lost.

(a) had (b) were

(c) can (d) do

PART II Choose the best answer for the blank.

9 My secretary will contact you if he ________________ any further information.

(a) needed (b) needs

(c) will need (d) had needed

10 The government has asked that all New Zealand citizens living in Japan ________________ with their embassy.

(a) to register (b) registered

(c) register (d) be registered

11 The deadline for the project that you were working on was postponed, so it's not necessary that you ________________ it today.

(a) finish (b) finished

(c) had better finished (d) will finish

12 If I ________________ in that car accident, I would have never met your mother at
the hospital.

(a) hadn't been   (b) hasn't been
(c) wasn't   (d) shouldn't be

13 ________________ you not alerted me to the error in the report, it would have been
published including such an embarrassing flaw.

(a) Were   (b) Should
(c) If   (d) Had

14 I know that you've been busy with your new job, but I suggest you at least
________________ coffee with me once in a while.

(a) has   (b) would have
(c) have   (d) had

15 ________________ that plane, I would be dead now.

(a) Had I boarded   (b) Having boarded
(c) If I boarded   (d) If I should board

16 ________________ the house would increase that much in value, we would not
have sold it.

(a) Did we know   (b) If we have known
(c) Had we known   (d) If we would have known

PART III Identify the option that contains an awkward expression or an error in
grammar.

17 (a) A: Mike and I went canoeing and had a picnic on the river.
(b) B: That sounds so romantic.
(c) A: Then, we went to an outdoor music concert. It was fantastic.
(d) B: Wow. I sure wish my husband do things like that.

18 (a) A: Shouldn't you be studying for the big test tomorrow?

(b) B: Yeah, but it really helps me to study better after I've had a workout.

(c) A: Well, I hope you aren't just procrastinating.

(d) B: If I were you, I will stay out of other people's business.

PART IV Identify the option that contains an awkward expression or an error in grammar.

19 (a) There are many great reasons to drive less than we do. (b) One is that with less cars on the road, accidents will be reduced. (c) Should we abstain from driving, even temporarily, it would have had a significant impact on pollution levels. (d) By doing this, our lungs benefit and we save money on gas.

20 (a) How soon should you start saving for your child's college expenses? (b) Many parents have begun to save money for tuition even before their children are born. (c) Of all the parental duties, providing your child access to a good education is among the most important. (d) If you wanted to have children, you need to think carefully about how to afford this critical investment.

Chapter 16

접속사

기출 POINT 1

접속사는 〈S + V〉 형태를 갖추어 단어, 구, 절, 문장을 연결한다.

이에 반해 전치사는 〈S + V〉를 취하지 못하고 〈전치사 + 명사 (상당 어구)〉 형태로 부사구나 형용사구가 됨에 유의한다. 또한 접속사 없이는 한 문장에 술어 동사가 2개 있을 수 없음에 유의한다.

기출 POINT 2

접속사에서 가장 중요한 것은 대구법의 관계인데 등위접속사, 상관접속사로 연결되는 어구는 같은 역할을 하는 품사끼리 동일한 문법적 구조로 연결되어야 한다.

〈A, B, and C〉, 〈A and B〉, 〈A or B〉 형태의 문장이나 상관접속사가 사용된 문장이 나오면 동일한 품사끼리 연결되어 있는지 반드시 확인한다.

기출 POINT 3

등위접속사는 나열(and), 대조(but), 선택(or) 의미의 접속사를 문장의 논리에 맞게 선택하는 문제가 출제되므로 해석을 해본 후 문맥이 잘 통하는 것을 선택한다.

· 명령문 + and ~ …하라, 그러면 ~할 것이다
· 명령문 + or ~ …하라, 그렇지 않으면 ~할 것이다(= if ~ not)
· not A, but B A가 아니고 B이다

Actual Test

PART I **Choose the best answer for the blank.**

1   A: Will you still want to go to the lake ________________ the weather is bad?
     B: Good question.

   (a) as   (b) if
   (c) that   (d) with

2   A: What did you think of Gramsci's latest publication?
     B: It was such an inspiring read ________________ I read it twice.

   (a) as   (b) which
   (c) who   (d) that

3   A: Did you know about your husband's strange habits beforehand?
     B: No, it wasn't ________________ we moved in together that I grew aware of his
        problems.

   (a) until   (b) when
   (c) that   (d) how

4   A: Kyle must be excited about going to Disneyland this summer.
     B: Not especially. ________________ it was his idea, he doesn't seem particularly
        enthusiastic.
   (a) Even though   (b) Even then
   (c) Nevertheless   (d) Since

5   A: Your son was upsetting people in class today by making insulting jokes.
     B: Again? I really need to talk to him ________________ he won't continue saying
        mean things.
   (a) as to   (b) for that
   (c) in that   (d) so that

6 A: Those sketches are impressive. Jared has quite a talent.

B: He has the ability to draw with precise detail _______________ he is looking at.

(a) which (b) if

(c) that (d) what

7 A: Selah makes straight A's _______________ she doesn't study hard.

B: I know. I wish I knew her secret.

(a) even (b) even though

(c) if (d) as if

8 A: _______________ he wasn't chosen for the position really surprised me.

B: I guess some people have a different opinion than you do.

(a) That (b) Which

(c) What (d) Why

9 A: I don't think Dave will enjoy working in the garden very much.

B: He'll do it _______________ he likes it or not. That's his job.

(a) whether (b) when

(c) that (d) what

PART II Choose the best answer for the blank.

10 I have no interest in seeing that movie, _______________ do I want any of my children going out and watching it.

(a) or (b) nor

(c) neither (d) never

11 _______________ didn't even notify us of his plans was very disappointing.

(a) What he   (b) That he
(c) Because he   (d) He

12 _______________ I respect her opinion on and insight into many issues, I felt that she was making a flawed analysis on this one particular issue.

(a) Since   (b) As
(c) Until   (d) While

13 It was Bill Hicks _______________ joke about UFO's.

(a) whom I believe had told that
(b) who I believe had told that
(c) whom that had told I believe
(d) who had told that I believe

14 Hand in your final papers before the deadline, _______________ grade will be lowered by ten points.

(a) but   (b) though
(c) or   (d) unless

15 _______________ I'm a huge fan of Roman Polanski, I don't feel like watching a movie today.

(a) Although   (b) When
(c) Because   (d) Provided

16 It is considered rude to burp _______________ eating food around others.

(a) after   (b) only
(c) meanwhile   (d) while

17 (a) A: It's getting late. We should set up our tent soon.
(b) B: Yes, you're right. Look for a flat spot clear of vegetation.
(c) A: Do you think what animals might bother us tonight?
(d) B: As long as we don't leave any food outside the tent, we should be fine.

18 (a) A: Who do we know that speaks Spanish?
(b) B: Well, I think both Tom or Jeff can speak Spanish.
(c) A: Really? Do you think that they could help me with this paper?
(d) B: If one of them can't, I'm sure the other could help.

PART IV Identify the option that contains an awkward expression or an error in grammar.

19 (a) When we become highly stressed, a bodily reaction is triggered, called the "fight or flight" response. (b) This response is hard-wired into our brains, a biological reflex designed to protect us from danger. (c) By its very nature, the fight or flight system overrides our rational mind during moving us into "attack" mode. (d) Our fear becomes exaggerated and our thinking distorted, causing us to overreact to non-threatening circumstances.

20 (a) Frederick Douglass went from being a slave into being a renowned author, speaker, and activist. (b) During his childhood, he witnessed numerous atrocities conducted against slaves by their masters. (c) Once he escaped from slavery, he published a newspaper promoting abolition. (d) Eventually Douglass's dream was fulfilled what slavery was abolished in 1863.

Memo

Chapter 17

구어체 문장

기출 POINT 1

구어체 문장은 문맥 전체를 보고 의미를 판단한다.

구어체 문장은 문법을 위한 문법 문제가 아닌 실생활에서 자주 쓰이는 회화적인 표현을 주로 물어본다. 문장 구조의 일부만 보고 답을 추측하기보다는 문맥 전체를 보고 의미를 판단하여 가장 적절한 표현을 답으로 골라야 한다. 이를 위해서는 청해 학습을 할 때 따로 오답 노트를 만들어서 모르는 표현이나 어휘를 체계적으로 정리, 암기하는 습관을 키우는 것이 중요하다. 다른 시험보다 TEPS에서는 이러한 구어체 문장 출제율이 높다는 것을 명심한다.

Actual Test

PART I Choose the best answer for the blank.

1　A: Do you think you could give me a hand with this problem?
　　B: I do actually want to help you, but I have an appointment coming up soon.
　　　The truth is I should really get _______________.

(a) to go　　　　　　　　　　(b) go
(c) going　　　　　　　　　　(d) gone

2　A: What do you do to keep your trim figure?
　　B: I don't know. Good genes, perhaps? It seems to _______________ the family.

(a) run　　　　　　　　　　(b) run in
(c) run of　　　　　　　　　(d) run on

3　A: I would like to give some money to pay for that delicious dinner.
　　B: _______________ We invited you to dinner. This is our treat.

(a) Of course.　　　　　　　(b) Certainly.
(c) Certainly not .　　　　　(d) Sure.

4　A: Michael was voted best player of the year!
　　B: You _______________!

(a) say not　　　　　　　　(b) say it
(c) do say it　　　　　　　　(d) don't say

5　A: Can I possibly get a lift?
　　B: That depends on where _______________.

(a) you were heading　　　　(b) do you head
(c) you are headed　　　　　(d) do you head for

6 A: I must have a word with Jeremy.

B: He stepped outside for a moment, but I think he'll be ________________.

(a) back no time

(b) in no time back

(c) back in no time

(d) back in time

7 A: ________________ you didn't call me?

B: My phone battery died, so I came over instead.

(a) How come

(b) Why

(c) What if

(d) What made

8 A: What do you think of me without a beard?

B: ________________ difference!

(a) What

(b) How

(c) How a

(d) What a

9 A: Donnie's wedding is happening this weekend.

B: Speaking of ________________, I don't think I can make it.

(a) that

(b) any

(c) whom

(d) which

10 A: Guess what! I've got two free tickets to Hawaii.

B: Give me a break. You ________________!

(a) pulled my leg

(b) have pulled my leg

(c) will pull my leg

(d) are pulling my leg

11 A: Leo is coming into town in May.

B: I know. I can't ________________ him again.

(a) see to wait

(b) wait to see

(c) see waiting

(d) wait seeing

PART II Choose the best answer for the blank.

12 I've tried drinking things like tea and juice for breakfast, but nothing really _______________ early in the day like a hot cup of coffee.

(a) gets to me going   (b) gets me gone

(c) gets me to go   (d) gets me going

13 After I came back from boy scout camp, my father asked me to teach him some crafts, becoming, as _______________, my apprentice.

(a) he were   (b) it is

(c) it were   (d) he is

14 I signed up for a language class, but it's _______________ boring.

(a) a kind of   (b) kind of

(c) kind   (d) kinds of

15 _______________ the garden looks? I spent a long time tending it.

(a) Do you like how the way   (b) Are you like how the way

(c) How do you like the way   (d) How are you like the way

PART III Identify the option that contains an awkward expression or an error in grammar.

16 (a) A: You seem under the weather. Anything the matter?

(b) B: I was stood again yesterday by Evan.

(c) A: What? Did he apologize?

(d) B: No, I'm really angry now. I'm going to make him pay for this.

17 (a) A: I really love this house.

(b) B: I'm so happy to hear that.

(c) A: Mind if I check it up?

(d) B: Be my guest.

18 (a) A: I'm calling for Mr. Song.

(b) B: Spoken.

(c) A: Hello. This is Nora Lazar. Do you remember me?

(d) B: Yes, of course. What a surprise to hear from you!

19 (a) A: This is one of the most expensive cars on the market.

(b) B: I already see that.

(c) A: So how can you afford to buy that car?

(d) B: You're not going to believe this, but I won the lottery last week.

PART Ⅳ Identify the option that contains an awkward expression or an error in grammar.

20 (a) Are superheroes merely innocent entertainment, or do they represent role models that can influence young children? (b) The lack of positive female and nonwhite superheroes are a huge concern for some people. (c) Others believe that superheroes glorify violence and aggressiveness in children. (d) What negative effects do you think popular superheroes have on developing children?

Memo 

New TEPS MASTER 900

Vocabulary

Chapter 01 | 동사구 이디엄

구어체 표현을 많이 포함하는 동사구 이디엄은 대부분 PART I에서 출제되고 있으며 기본 동사의 여러 가지 뜻을 이해하는 학습법이 필수이다.

▌ 주요 어휘 모음

get out of ~에서 나가다

leave from ~에서 떠나다

hit the spot 말할 나위 없이 좋다, 만족스럽다

plead for mercy 선처를 구하다

make (both) ends meet 분수에 맞게 살다

keep *sb* posted ~에게 근황을 알리다

give *sb* a hand ~를 도와주다

make a scene 소란을 피우다

Keep your chin up! 힘내!

Snap out of it! 힘내!

Step on it! (택시 안에서) 빨리 좀 가주세요!

How is it/everything going? 어떻게 지내니?

keep track of ~에 대해 끊임없이 정보를 얻어내다

scratch the surface (연구 등에서) 수박 겉 핥기하다

beat around the bush 말을 돌리다, 요점을 피하다

talk back 말대답하다

hold one's horses 진정하다

give *sb* a ride/lift 차로 태워다 주다

take it to heart 심각하게 받아들이다

have second thought 재고하다

see *sb* ~를 사귀다

keep hanging 속 태우다

cut it short 간단히 말하다

play sick 꾀병 부리다

call in sick 전화로 병결을 알리다

behave oneself 행동을 조심하다

Actual Test **Preview**

- [ ] **Look who's talking.** 사돈 남 말 하네.
- [ ] **slip one's mind** 잊어버리다
- [ ] **spill** 엎지르다
- [ ] **slide** 미끄러지다
- [ ] **shift** 이동하다, 옮기다
- [ ] **make it** 성공하다
- [ ] **get it** 이해하다
- [ ] **get the hang of** ∼의 요령[방법]을 알다
- [ ] **be indebted to *sb* for *sth*** ∼에게 …의 빚을 지다, …한 것은 ∼덕택이다
- [ ] **stick by** ∼을 굳게 지키다…
- [ ] **wave/shake one's fist** (분노의 표시로) 주먹을 흔들다
- [ ] **ring a bell** 생각나게 하다, 귀에 익다
- [ ] **play it by ear** 임기응변으로 처리하다
- [ ] **do the trick** (약이) 잘 듣다, 효과가 있다

Actual Test

1 A: Why are you being so rude to me?

B: Look who's _______________. You're the one being inconsiderate!

(a) speaking   (b) saying

(c) telling   (d) talking

2 A: Hey, did you remember to take the dog to the vet?

B: Oops. I meant to do that. I guess it _______________ my mind.

(a) slipped   (b) spilt

(c) slid   (d) shifted

3 A: Did Javier _______________ it past the semi-finals?

B: Yeah, in fact he went all the way to the finals.

(a) score   (b) place

(c) make   (d) take

4 A: Why aren't you laughing at my joke?

B: I guess I don't really _______________ it.

(a) do   (b) have

(c) make   (d) get

5 A: You are telling me you still don't know how to work the washing machine.

B: It's taking me a while to get the _______________ of it.

(a) good   (b) tool

(c) way   (d) hang

6   A: Who was the most supportive person in your life during the trial?

B: I'm completely _______________ to my parents for sticking by my side.

(a) dependent   (b) helped

(c) indebted   (d) owned

7   A: Why is Mr. Cooper waving his _______________ at us?

B: I think he's still angry at me.

(a) nose   (b) head

(c) fist   (d) fingers

PART II   Choose the best answer for the blank.

8   I don't remember ever going there, but the name _______________ a bell.

(a) rings   (b) hits

(c) chimes   (d) dings

9   I have no idea what to expect from this meeting, so I'll just play it by _________.

(a) heart   (b) myself

(c) ear   (d) alone

10   If the pills that your doctor prescribes for you don't do the _____________, consider trying an alternative remedy.

(a) trick   (b) jobs

(c) cure   (d) work

Chapter

02 | 전치사구 이디엄

전치사구 이디엄 역시 구어체 표현이 주를 이룬다. 대부분 PART I에서 출제되고 있으며 전치사가 들어간 표현들을 덩어리로 암기하는 것이 필수적이다.

▌ 주요 어휘 모음

under the weather 몸이 좋지 않은, 기분이 언짢은

on the right track 옳은 방향으로

out of bounds 금지된

off base 불시에

pain in the neck 성가신[골치 아픈] 일[사람]

be between a rock and a hard place 어려운 상황에서 힘든 결정을 내려야 하는

be up a creek 곤경에 빠져

be on the ball 빠릿빠릿한

play by the book 규칙에 따라 행동하다

in the red 적자인

in the black 흑자인

in shape 건강한 상태의

out of shape 모양이 망가져, 몸이 쇠약하여

in hot water 어려움에 빠진, 곤경에 처해

off the top of one's head 당장은, 즉석에서

Actual Test **Preview**

- [ ] **get into shape** 몸을[몸매를] 다듬다, 몸을 단련하다
- [ ] **be out of town** (살고 있는) 집을[도시를] 떠나 있다
- [ ] **No can do.** (나로선) 불가능해. 그럴 수 없어.
- [ ] **keep one's chin up** 용기를 잃지 않다, 기운을 내다
- [ ] **up to here with** ~에 진절머리가 난, ~을 참을 수 없게 된
- [ ] **a screw loose** 나사가 풀림, 고장, 머리가 이상함
- [ ] **up to one's eyeballs** ~에 허덕여, ~에 파묻혀, ~때문에 정신없는
- [ ] **on one's own** 스스로, 혼자 힘으로, 독립하여
- [ ] **on/in one's behalf** ~를 대신하여[위하여]
- [ ] **at stake** 걸려[달려] 있는, 위태로운, 관련이 되어
- [ ] **out of shape** 모양이 엉망이 되어, (몸이) 쇠약하여
- [ ] **sanity** 제정신, 정신이 온전함
- [ ] **out of one's mind** 정신이 나간, 제정신이 아닌
- [ ] **over the counter** 처방전 없이
- [ ] **under the counter** (거래 따위를) 비밀리에, 암거래로
- [ ] **at one's wit's end** 어찌할 바를 몰라, 난처하여
- [ ] **on the spot** 그 자리에서, 현장에서, 즉석에서
- [ ] **be in the mood for/to** ~하고 싶은 마음이 들다

Actual Test

PART I Choose the best answer for the blank.

1 A: I need to get into _______________.
   B: Well, then, come to the gym with me sometime.

   (a) stress   (b) health
   (c) strong   (d) shape

2 A: Let's hang out sometime this weekend.
   B: No can do. All week I'm out of _______________.

   (a) town   (b) condition
   (c) time   (d) there

3 A: Do you want to grab a drink in a little bit?
   B: Sounds great, but I'm _______________ with stuff to do at the moment.

   (a) keeping my chin up   (b) had it up to here
   (c) a few screws loose   (d) up to my eyeballs

4 A: Is Brian still living at your place?
   B: No, he finally got a job and is living on his _______________ now.

   (a) own   (b) self
   (c) behalf   (d) room

5 A: I'm supposed to get vaccinated before travelling to Laos.
   B: You should make sure to do that. I mean, your well-being is at _______________.

   (a) sick   (b) stake
   (c) chance   (d) risky

6 A: Fran, you and Peter would make a cute couple. What do you say?

B: You must be out of your ______________. I have no interest in that guy.

(a) order   (b) shape

(c) sanity   (d) mind

7 A: Do I need to get a prescription for that medication?

B: I don't think so. I think you might be able to get it ______________ the counter.

(a) around   (b) under

(c) over   (d) inside

PART II Choose the best answer for the blank.

8 Mom is at her wit's ______________, preparing for Nina's upcoming wedding.

(a) gone   (b) end

(c) death   (d) loss

9 Clyde drove his car head-first into a tree and was pronounced dead on the

______________.

(a) dot   (b) second

(c) time   (d) spot

10 I must say I'm really more in the ______________ to be somewhere peaceful and quiet.

(a) urge   (b) mind

(c) mood   (d) moment

Chapter
03 | 문장으로 굳어져 쓰이는 이디엄

동사 중심의 아주 짧은 문장이 여기에 속한다. 동사의 의미를 파악하여 문제를 풀기보다는 대화의 상황과 문장 자체의 정형화된 표현에서 즉각적으로 답을 찾아야 하는 것이 특징이다. TEPS에서 중시되는 유형으로 대부분 PART I에서 출제된다.

▍주요 어휘 모음

rain cats and dogs 비가 억수같이 쏟아지다

Are you pulling my leg? 날 놀리는 거야?

trumped-up story 날조된 기사

flare up at ~에게 버럭 화를 내다

head over heels 거꾸로, 곤두박질쳐

head over heels in love 사랑에 푹 빠져

ace in the hole 비장의 무기

Be my guest. 좋을 대로 하세요.

be saved by the bell 간신히 곤경을 면하다

bite the bullet 고통을 참다, 싫은 일을 견디다

clean as a whistle 아주 깨끗한

make a mountain (out) of a molehill 사소한 문제를 크게 만들다

head and shoulders above ~보다 단연 뛰어나다

(from) head to toe/foot 머리에서 발끝까지, 완전히

sit on the fence 형세를 관망하다, 중립을 지키다

take *sth* at face value ~을 액면 그대로 받아들이다

give *(sb)* a dirty look ~를 기분 나쁘게 쳐다보다

have what it takes to ~을 하는 데 필요한 재능[자질, 돈]이 있다

jump to a conclusion 성급하게 결론 내리다

couch potato 하루종일 TV만 보는 게으름뱅이

dying to 몹시 ~하고 싶어 하는

get carried away 넋을 잃다, 열중하다

get an inkling of ~을 어렴풋이 알다, 눈치채다

Get real! 정신 차례!

go Dutch 비용을 각자 부담하다

Go ahead! (마음껏) 하세요!

goof off 농땡이 치다

hit below the belt 비겁한 행동을 하다

Break a leg! 힘내!

Actual Test Preview

- [ ] **What's with the long face?** 왜 그렇게 시무룩해?

- [ ] **have/get butterflies in one's stomach** (걱정으로) 가슴이 두근거리다, 안절부절 못하다

- [ ] **drink like a fish** 술을 많이[벌컥벌컥] 마시다, 술고래이다

- [ ] **get down to business** 본론으로 들어가다

- [ ] **in stock** 재고가 있는

- [ ] **from scratch** 아무것도 없는 상태에서, 아주 처음부터, 무(無)에서

- [ ] **What a rip-off!** 도둑질이나 마찬가지군요! 완전 바가지네!

- [ ] **Don't mention it.** 천만에요. 별말씀을요.

- [ ] **What's the occasion?** 오늘 무슨 날이에요?

- [ ] **catch** 알아듣다, 이해하다

- [ ] **as far as + 주어 + be동사 + concerned** ~에 관한 한

- [ ] **What's new?** 요즘 어때? 별일 없어?

- [ ] **Who's calling?** 전화 거신 분은 누구시죠?

- [ ] **You bet!** 물론이지!

- [ ] **I can't help it.** 어쩔 수 없어.

Actual Test

PART I Choose the best answer for the blank.

1 A: Veronica, what's with the _______________ face?

B: Nothing special. I sometimes get a little down during this time of year.

(a) odd
(b) long
(c) oval
(d) shallow

2 A: Feel confident about going on stage today?

B: I don't. I definitely have _______________ in my stomach.

(a) butterflies
(b) problems
(c) nerves
(d) insects

3 A: He sure had a lot of drinks at the bar last night.

B: Yeah, he can really drink like _______________.

(a) a pig
(b) a fish
(c) a cat
(d) a woman

4 A: Alright, we've wasted enough time with chitchat.

B: You're right. It's time we get down to _______________.

(a) office
(b) matter
(c) business
(d) talk

5 A: I'm looking for a jumbo-sized jar of hot sauce.

B: Actually, we don't have that in _______________ right now.

(a) order
(b) place
(c) sight
(d) stock

6 A: Did you buy a cake mix?

B: No, I was hoping to make it from _____________.

(a) ground   (b) bottom

(c) scratch   (d) basis

7 A: They wanted 30 dollars for washing my car.

B: What a _____________! It'd be much cheaper to do it yourself.

(a) deal   (b) run-off

(c) rip-off   (d) put-off

8 A: Thanks for helping with my homework.

B: Don't _____________ it.

(a) mention   (b) think

(c) suggest   (d) welcome

9 A: I'm inviting some people over for dinner tomorrow evening.

B: Really? What's the _____________?

(a) meaning   (b) occasion

(c) happening   (d) up

10 A: Turn right after you pass the bridge, and continue to the end of the road.

B: Whoops. I didn't _____________ that last part. Where do I turn again?

(a) got   (b) see

(c) catch   (d) find

11 A: I'm free anytime this week.

B: As far as I'm _____________, Wednesday would be the best time.

(a) pleased   (b) included

(c) concerned   (d) planned

12 A: What's ______________ at the workplace?

B: Well, we got a new supervisor last week.

(a) cool (b) neat
(c) new (d) fresh

13 A: Is Johnny available?

B: May I ask who's ______________, please?

(a) telling (b) calling
(c) asking (d) saying

14 A: Do you want to go fishing sometime?

B: You ______________! I know some great spots.

(a) catch (b) follow
(c) bet (d) say

15 A: Why did you get here so late? The food is already cold.

B: I couldn't ______________ it. Traffic was really bad today.

(a) resist (b) assist
(c) help (d) stop

Memo

Chapter 04

2어동사

settle in과 같이 〈동사 + 부사〉, 〈동사 + 전치사〉, 〈동사 + 부사 + 전치사〉의 형태로 원래 동사의 의미와 전혀 다른 새로운 의미를 만들어내는 2어동사는 구어체 어휘에 대한 수험자의 능력을 평가하는 것을 주목적으로 한다. 같은 동사라도 뒤에 붙는 부사에 따라 뜻이 크게 차이 나므로 평소 LC 공부를 할 때 등장하는 2어동사는 그때그때 암기하는 것이 중요하며 의미가 여러 개이므로 문장 단위로 암기하는 것이 효율적이다. 주로 PART I 에 등장한다.

▌주요 어휘 모음

attend to 돌보다, 주의하다

bawl out 마구 소리치다

bear down on 압박하다

beef up 강화하다

blow off (바람이) 불어 흩날리다

break down 파괴하다, 고장 나다

break into 침입하다

break away 도망치다, 이탈하다

break up 헤어지다, 부수다

call for 요구하다

cash in on ~을 이용하다

come across 우연히 만나다

count on 의지하다

call off 취소하다

get along with 사이좋게 지내다

come after 뒤쫓다

cut down on (양이나 금액을) 줄이다

cut off (전기, 가스, 수도 등을) 끊다

bring about 야기하다, 초래하다

come down with (전염)병에 걸리다

follow in *sb*'s footsteps ~의 뒤를 잇다

get hold of 연락을 취하다

get going 개시하다, 착수하다

hold back (감정 등을) 억누르다

inquire into 조사하다

idle away 빈둥거리며 보내다

interfere with 개입하다

iron out 문제를 해결하다

insist on 주장하다, 고집하다

keep away from 멀리하다

keep in touch with 연락을 유지하다

lay off 해고하다

let out (비밀을) 누설하다

let up (비가) 그치다

line up behind 단결하여 지지하다

make fun of 놀리다

make up for 보충하다

make out 이해하다

mess up 망치다

mix up 뒤섞다

name after ~의 이름을 따서 명명하다

nod off 졸다

pass on 전달하다

pile up 축적하다

pull out of 철수하다, 손을 떼다

pull over 차를 (길가에) 대다

queue up 줄 서다

ride out 이겨내다, 극복하다

rinse off 씻어내다

round off 완료하다

run after 뒤쫓다

run away from ~로부터 도망치다

run away with ~와 (눈이 맞아) 달아나다

save up 저축하다

see off 배웅하다

take place (사건 등이) 일어나다, 발생하다

take up 시작하다, 착수하다

wake up 깨다

stick to 집착하다, 고집하다

object to 반대하다

tag along 따라다니다

trudge along 터벅터벅 걷다

take out 데리고 나가다

put out (불을) 끄다

be tied to ~에 얽매이다, 구애받다

use up 다 써버리다

wipe off (부채 등을) 청산하다

write off 빚을 탕감하다

zip up 활력을 주다

- ☐ **sound off** (기상, 소등 따위의) 신호 나팔을 불다
- ☐ **go off** (자명종, 경보기 등이) 울리다
- ☐ **see through** (사람의 의중을) 간파하다, 꿰뚫어 보다
- ☐ **come through** 성공하다, 해내다
- ☐ **show up** (모임 등에) 나타나다, 나오다
- ☐ **account for** 설명하다, (~의) 비율을 차지하다
- ☐ **wrap up** (일, 회의 등을) 마무리 짓다, 끝내다
- ☐ **call off** 취소하다
- ☐ **let *sb* down** ~를 실망시키다
- ☐ **work out** (문제 등을) 해결하다, (일이) 잘되다, 잘 풀리다
- ☐ **figure out** 이해하다
- ☐ **run into** 우연히 만나다
- ☐ **get/have/catch hold of** 찾아내다, 이해하다, (전화로) 연락을 취하다
- ☐ **get through** 전화 연결이 되다
- ☐ **stick with** (일 따위를) 계속하다, (결심 등을) 지키다, 바뀌지 않다
- ☐ **get over** 극복하다, 이겨내다
- ☐ **skim through** 대충 훑어보다
- ☐ **focus on** ~에 집중하다
- ☐ **sit through** ~가 끝날 때까지 가만히 있다, ~을 끝까지 보다

Actual Test

PART I **Choose the best answer for the blank.**

1   A: Why didn't you meet me for breakfast?
     B: My alarm didn't ______________.

     (a) break up   (b) run up
     (c) sound off   (d) go off

2   A: Should I make reservations at the restaurant?
     B: No, you can just ______________ and be served immediately.

     (a) see through   (b) come through
     (c) walk up   (d) show up

3   A: How much of my final grade is this paper worth?
     B: It ______________ a fourth of your grade.

     (a) counts   (b) accounts for
     (c) takes   (d) explains

4   A: We've been talking about the same problem all night.
     B: You're right. Let's ______________ it up and call it a day.

     (a) add   (b) wrap
     (c) call   (d) draw

5   A: What happened to the football game that was scheduled for last night?
     B: It was ______________ due to rain.

     (a) cut off   (b) put down
     (c) called off   (d) kept down

6   A: I wish you had done what you said you were going to do.

     B: I'm sorry to _______________ you down.

     (a) turn   (b) mark

     (c) let   (d) calm

7   A: Relax. Things are going to _______________ in the end.

     B: I hope you are right.

     (a) work out   (b) make out

     (c) get over   (d) do over

8   A: I don't know why Steve would act that way.

     B: I can't _______________ sometimes, either.

     (a) take him away   (b) figure him out

     (c) sort him through   (d) follow him down

9   A: I _______________ your brother on campus the other day.

     B: Oh, yeah? I haven't seen him for a while.

     (a) came over   (b) ran into

     (c) got along with   (d) tried out with

10 A: Did you make a reservation yet?

     B: No. I tried calling the theatre, but I wasn't able to _______________.

     (a) keep track   (b) get hold of

     (c) get through   (d) keep up with

11 A: Have you guys started your exercise program?

     B: We started off diligently, but I doubt that everyone will _______________ it.

     (a) take over   (b) stick with

     (c) sniff at   (d) run over

12 A: Inez is upset that she didn't get the role in the movie.

B: I'm sure she'll _______________ it soon enough.

(a) break down (b) get over
(c) fall behind (d) turn into

PART II Choose the best answer for the blank.

13 I'd like you to _______________ this paper and tell me what you think.

(a) drive through (b) see through
(c) cut through (d) skim through

14 I suggest you _______________ on the reading assignments, and not worry as much about the lectures.

(a) focus (b) accompany
(c) venture (d) attend

15 Zach couldn't _______________ the entire show because he was feeling ill.

(a) lay through (b) sit through
(c) sit up (d) lay up

Chapter 05

혼동 어휘: 유사 의미

TEPS 어휘 영역은 단어 하나하나의 개별적인 의미보다는 문맥에 가장 적절한 정답 선택을 요구하는 것이 특징이다. 여기에 철저히 대비하려면 기본 단어를 꾸준히 연습하는 것도 중요하지만 우리말로는 별 차이가 없으나 그 쓰임새나 의미가 달라 혼동하기 쉬운 표현을 잘 정리해야 한다. 의미의 차이점뿐만 아니라 단어의 어울림 문제에도 대비할 수 있도록 철저히 준비해야 한다.

■ 주요 어휘 모음

revision 교정, 개정
edition (초판, 재판의) 판(版)
duplicate 복사

adopt 입양하다
sibling 형제, 자매
relative 친척

cub (사자, 곰 등의) 새끼
flock (양, 염소, 새 등의) 떼, 무리
school (물고기, 고래 등의) 떼, 무리
swarm (벌, 개미 등의) 떼, 무리

application 신청서, 지원서
postmark (우편의) 소인

conduct (연구, 조사 등을) 수행하다
deliver 연설하다, 공포하다

relationship 관계, 관련
chemistry (다른 사람과의) 공감대, 공통점
correlation 상관관계

delay 연기하다, 지연하다
remain 머무르다, 체류하다

turbulence 난류, 난기류, (사회적) 소란
commotion 동요, (정치, 사회적) 폭동
hassle 싸움, 말다툼

persuade 설득하다
usher 안내하다, 인도하다
urge 강요하다, 재촉하다

janitor 수위, 문지기
ranger 산림 감시원, 무장 순찰 대원
patron 보호자, 후원자, 지지자

advancement 승진, 출세
enhancement 상승, 향상, 증대
leap 급격한 증가, 도약

mediator 중재인, 조정자
adversary 적, 반대자

access 접근, 면회, (자료 등의) 이용
ride 태움, 타고 감
direction 방향, 방위
span 기간
extent 범위, 길이

gap 틈, 괴리

space 빈자리, 공간

position 위치, 위상

flat 균일한, 고정된

continuous 끊임 없는, 연속적인

serial 일련의

calculation 계산, 추측

intuition 직관(력)

cover (덮어) 감추다

protect 보호하다, 지키다

see (그냥 눈에 비치는 영상을) 보다

watch (주의를 집중해서 지속적으로) 보다

look (시선을 돌려서 의도적으로) 보다

negligent 게을리하는, 태만한, 부주의한

circumspect 신중한, 조심성 있는

irreverent 불손한, 무례한, 불경한

rub (물건이나 표면에 대고) 문지르다

apply (약, 연고 등을) 바르다

paste (종이 등을) 풀칠해서 붙이다

slim (보기 좋게) 날씬한

thin 매우 마른

pension 연금

grant (국가에서 지원하는) 보조금

distinction 구별, 차별

extinction 소멸, 폐지

impassioned 열정적인

impatient 성급한

industrial 산업의

industrious 근면한

successful 성공한

successive 계속적인

indelible (얼룩 등이) 지울 수 없는

indubitable 의심할 여지가 없는, 명백한

intimate 친밀한

intimidate 협박하다, 겁주다

sensitive 민감한

sensible 분별 있는

credible 믿을 만한, 신뢰할 수 있는

credulous 쉽게 믿는, 잘 속는

allude 암시하다, 시사하다

delude 현혹시키다, 속이다

relieve (통증을) 완화하다

ameliorate 개선하다, 개량하다

teach (일반적인 의미에서) 가르치다

educate (정식 교육기관에서) 교육을 받게 하다

instruct (특정 기술과 과목을) 체계적으로 가르치다

scatter (불규칙하게) 흩뿌리다

shatter 산산이 부수다

hire (특정직을 위해 사람을) 고용하다

recruit (신입 사원, 신병 등을) 모집하다

appoint (공직 등 중요한 직책에) 임명하다

turbulence 난류, 난기류, (사회적) 소란

commotion 동요, (정치, 사회적) 폭동

hassle 싸움, 말다툼

jam/pack 집어넣다, 쑤셔 넣다

cram 억지로 밀어 넣다, 벼락치기로 공부하다

Actual Test **Preview**

- [ ] **loan** 대출, 융자금

- [ ] **lease** 임대차 (계약)

- [ ] **congratulate** 축하하다, ~에게 축하의 말을 하다

- [ ] **celebrate** (특정한 날, 사건을) 축하하다, 즐겁게 놀다

- [ ] **collect** (우표, 표본 따위를) 수집하다

- [ ] **available** 이용할 수 있는, 이용 가능한

- [ ] **invest in** ~에 투자하다

- [ ] **be intent on** ~에 열중하다, 몰두하다, 빠져 있다

- [ ] **handle** 통제하다, 다루다, 취급하다

- [ ] **sense** (**that**절) 감지하다, 알아채다

- [ ] **boundary** 경계(선)(= border), 범위

- [ ] **barrier** 방벽, 장애물

- [ ] **margin** 여백, 가장자리(= edge)

- [ ] **territory** 영토, 영지

- [ ] **last name** 성(= family name)

- [ ] **dismiss** 해고하다

- [ ] **just the same** 똑같은, 마찬가지인

- [ ] **circuit** 순회, 우회로

- [ ] **detour** 우회 (도로)

- [ ] **discriminate against** 냉대하다, 차별하다

- [ ] **preliminary** 예비의

- [ ] **haphazard** 우연한, 계획성 없는. 아무렇게나 하는

- [ ] **superficial** 표면상의, 파상적인

- [ ] **compulsive** 강제적인, 억지의

- [ ] **clear sky** 맑은 하늘

Actual Test

PART I **Choose the best answer for the blank.**

1   A: I know you aren't that rich. How could you possibly afford that big house?

B: I got a sizable ______________ from my bank last month.

(a) investment   (b) credit

(c) loan   (d) lease

2   A: You know what? Barry got first prize in the talent show.

B: Wow! Why don't we go out and ______________?

(a) congratulate   (b) celebrate

(c) commend   (d) compliment

3   A: What a cool stamp! It looks rare.

B: How did you know? Do you ______________ stamps?

(a) gather   (b) choose

(c) pick   (d) collect

4   A: I'd like a window seat, please.

B: I'm sorry. I'm afraid no more window seats are ______________.

(a) accessible   (b) available

(c) possible   (d) preferable

5   A: If only I had ______________ in computer stocks long ago.

B: Had you done that, you would be very wealthy by now.

(a) preserved   (b) participated

(c) involved   (d) invested

Actual Test

6 A: I heard that you have some problems with your husband.

B: He is intent on ______________ all our family's money on his own.

(a) grasping　　　　　　　(b) shifting

(c) handling　　　　　　　(d) treating

7 A: The cats don't like the new house.

B: Maybe they ______________ that their environment has changed.

(a) remembered　　　　　　(b) reached

(c) sensed　　　　　　　　(d) smelled

8 A: How many bears live in this forest?

B: We can't know for sure. But there are an estimated 200 that reside within the park's ______________.

(a) boundaries　　　　　　(b) barriers

(c) margins　　　　　　　 (d) territories

9 A: Is Stephens your first name or ______________?

B: It's my family name. I'm Bob Stephens.

(a) Christian　　　　　　　(b) end

(c) last　　　　　　　　　(d) given

10 A: They shouldn't have ______________ the last coach.

B: I agree. The new one is much worse.

(a) retired　　　　　　　　(b) dismissed

(c) recruited　　　　　　　(d) dispatched

11 A: Dan is so funny.

B: That's not surprising. His father was just the ______________.

(a) like　　　　　　　　　(b) equal

(c) same　　　　　　　　 (d) similar

12 A: Interstate 35 is closed temporarily due to construction.

B: There must be a ______________ we can take.

(a) curb
(b) circuit
(c) detour
(d) driveway

PART II Choose the best answer for the blank.

13 The applicant felt she had been ______________ against because of her gender.

(a) discriminated
(b) distinguished
(c) classified
(d) recognized

14 While ______________ studies reveal that vitamin C-rich foods may benefit pregnant mothers, more research is needed.

(a) preliminary
(b) haphazard
(c) superficial
(d) compulsive

15 Mostly ______________ skies and cool temperatures are expected over the weekend.

(a) clear
(b) fresh
(c) high
(d) clean

Chapter 06

혼동 어휘: 유사 형태

형태가 비슷해서 혼동되는 어휘 문제는 선택지에 제시되는 4개의 단어 형태가 비슷하거나 그중 2개의 단어가 비슷하다. 그러므로 평소에 단어를 대충대충 공부한 수험생들이 낭패를 보기 쉬운 유형이기도 하다. 형태가 비슷한 단어들은 신문, 잡지, 학술문 등의 글에서 접하기 쉽기 때문에 문어체 형식의 단문을 제시하는 PART II에서 대부분 출제된다.

▌ 주요 어휘 모음

apparent 뚜렷한, 명백한
appendant 부가의, 부수적인

boost 부양하다, 증대시키다
boast 자랑하다, 큰소리치다

confident 확신하는
confidential 기밀의

complement 보충하는 것, 보완물
compliment 찬사, 칭찬
complaint 불평, 불만, 푸념

bare 벌거벗은, 노출된
blank 공백의, 텅 빈

expedite (작업 등을) 신속히 처리하다
exonerate 무죄임을 입증하다
exempt (의무, 책임 등을) 면제하다

alteration 변경, 수정
alternative 대안
alternate 교대하다, 교차하다

regretful 후회하는, 슬퍼하는
regrettable 유감스러운

classic 일류의, 권위 있는
classical 고전적인

affect 영향을 미치다
effect 실행하다, (변화 등을) 초래하다

amenable 순종하는, 잘 따르는
anemic 빈혈의, 생기 없는

comprehensible 이해할 수 있는, 알기 쉬운
comprehensive 이해력이 있는, 포괄적인

considerate 동정심[이해심]이 많은
considerable 상당한

economic 경제의
economical 알뜰한

healthful 건강에 좋은
healthy 건강한, 건강에 좋은

spacious 넓은, 거대한
specious 그럴듯한

splash (물을) 튀기다
sprinkle (액체 등을) 뿌리다

impersonate ~인 체하다, ~의 역을 하다
improvise (연주, 연설 등을) 즉흥적으로 하다
impregnate 임신시키다

consciousness 의식
conscience 양심
consolation 위안

confirm 확실히 하다
confer 수여하다, 협의하다

content 만족한
contend 다투다, 논쟁하다

collaborate 공동으로 일하다
corroborate (소신 등을) 입증하다

deficit 적자
deceit 사기

revoke 무효로 하다, 취소하다
rebuke 꾸짖다, 비난하다

urban 도시의
urbane 도시적인, 세련된

moderate 온건한, 적당한
modest 겸손한

inadvertent 부주의한, 경솔한
introverted 내성적인

observance (법 등의) 준수
observation 관찰

Actual Test **Preview**

- [ ] **company** 동석, 동행, 같이 있어 줌
- [ ] **accompaniment** 부속물, 딸린 것

- [ ] **splinter** 가시, (나무의) 쪼개진 조각
- [ ] **split** 쪼개다; 쪼개진[갈라진] 금[틈]
- [ ] **sprint** 전력 질주, 단거리 경주

- [ ] **foliage** (집합적) 잎, 무성한 잎, 군엽
- [ ] **florin** 플로린 은화
- [ ] **flotage** 부양, 부력

- [ ] **extension** (날짜의) 연기, 연장
- [ ] **expansion** 확장, 팽창

- [ ] **feat** 위업, 공적
- [ ] **feud** (두 집안 사이의 여러 대에 걸친) 불화

- [ ] **command attention** 남의 주의를 끌게 하다

- [ ] **equestrian** 기수(騎手)의, 승마의
- [ ] **enigmatic** 수수께끼 같은, 불가사의한
- [ ] **encyclopedic** 백과사전적인, 박식한

- [ ] **hotbed** 온상, 소굴

- [ ] **crash** 와르르 무너지다
- [ ] **crush** 으스러지다, 구겨지다

- [ ] **stature** 키, 신장
- [ ] **status** 지위, 신분
- [ ] **statute** 법령, 법규

- [ ] **aquatic** 물속에 사는, 물의
- [ ] **arctic** 북극의

- [ ] **transition** 이행, 전환, 변천
- [ ] **transit** 통행, 운송
- [ ] **transmission** 전달, 전송

- [ ] **shallow** 얕은
- [ ] **sheer** 완전한, 순전한

- [ ] **digress** (옆길로) 빗나가다, (주제에서) 벗어나다
- [ ] **distract** (주의, 마음 따위를) 딴 데로 돌리다

- [ ] **compile** 하나로 모으다, 편집하다, 편찬하다
- [ ] **combine** 결합하다, 연합하다

Actual Test

PART I Choose the best answer for the blank.

1 A: Thanks for the dinner. It was excellent.
B: I appreciate your ______________. Please come again.

(a) accompaniment
(b) circle
(c) association
(d) company

2 A: Ouch! There's a ______________ in my foot.
B: Let me find some tweezers to remove it with.

(a) splice
(b) split
(c) splinter
(d) sprint

3 A: What are your plans for the break?
B: I'm going to the woods to enjoy the autumn ______________.

(a) falling
(b) foliage
(c) florin
(d) flotage

4 A: What should I do if I can't finish the paper on time?
B: You have no option but to ask for a(an) ______________.

(a) extension
(b) expansion
(c) extinction
(d) expiration

PART II Choose the best answer for the blank.

5 Anyone who tries to take responsibility for such a big project will quickly find out that it is no small ______________.

(a) flea
(b) feat
(c) fee
(d) feud

6 Of the many commercials that we are exposed to daily, precious few will manage to ______________ our conscious attention.

(a) contend   (b) convert

(c) command   (d) convene

7 What turned Diana from a royal celebrity to a global icon was not her sense of fashion; but rather her ______________ personality.

(a) envious   (b) equestrian

(c) enigmatic   (d) encyclopedic

8 Much modern linguistic research is revealing that the Internet is a ______________ for language mutations.

(a) hotfoot   (b) hot line

(c) hot seat   (d) hotbed

9 Coming home from a long day at work, Mr. Hoffman ______________ on the sofa.

(a) crushed   (b) cracked

(c) crashed   (d) creaked

10 His strong voice and tall ______________ helped him to find leading role parts in Hollywood movies.

(a) station   (b) stature

(c) status   (d) statute

11 The Hawaiian coral reefs are home to an abundance of ______________ creatures.

(a) arctic   (b) aquatic

(c) continental   (d) terrestrial

12 If you intend to quit, notify two weeks in advance, thereby giving your employer time to find someone new for a smooth ______________.

(a) transit

(b) transition

(c) transmission

(d) transformation

13 To get to the other side of the stream, keep going for about 800 meters, where it should be ______________ enough to walk across.

(a) thin

(b) sheer

(c) narrow

(d) shallow

14 If a professor ______________ off the subject, it is not inappropriate to ask her to return to the topic.

(a) leaps

(b) misses

(c) distracts

(d) digresses

15 The Encyclopedia of Herbal Medicine was ______________ by experts from all over the world.

(a) conjoined

(b) compiled

(c) correlated

(d) combined

Chapter 07

우리말 간섭으로 생긴 오류

우리말과 영어가 1:1 대칭이 안 되기 때문에 잘못 사용하기 쉬운 단어가 이 유형에 속한다. 우리말의 '서명'에 해당하는 영어 단어로는 signature와 autograph가 있고 '모자'에 해당하는 단어로는 hat, cap, hood 등이 있다. 우리말로는 단어 하나이지만 영어로는 상황에 따라 적절한 어휘를 골라 써야 하며, 영어로 의사소통을 할 때는 이러한 어휘 때문에 의미 전달에 어려움이 생기거나 심한 경우 오해가 생기기도 한다. 이 유형은 PART I II에 골고루 출제된다.

▌ 주요 어휘 모음

(자동차) 핸들 handle → (steering) wheel

SF 영화 SF movie → sci-fi, science fiction

공중전화 박스 telephone box → phone booth

등 번호 back number → uniform/jersey number

롤러브레이드 rollerblade → in-line skate

일대일 man to man → one-to-one, one on one

비디오 카메라 video camera → camcorder

비치파라솔 beach parasol → beach umbrella

샤프 (연필) sharp pencil → mechanical pencil

써클, 동아리 circle → club, student group

썬크림 sunscreen lotion, sun block cream

아르바이트 arbeit → part-time job, moonlighting

아이쇼핑 eye shopping → window shopping

애프터서비스 after service → warrantee/after-sales service

에피소드 episode → memorable event, anecdote

오디오 기기 audio → stereo, audio system

오바이트 overeat → vomiting, throwing up, puke

오토바이 autobike → motorcycle, motorbike, bike

전자레인지 electronic range → microwave oven

컨닝 페이퍼 cunning paper → cheating sheet

휴대폰 hand phone → cellular/mobile phone

소개팅, 미팅 **meeting → blind date**

(춤) 블루스 **blues → slow dancing**

A/S 센터 **A/S center → repair shop**

가스레인지 **gas range → stove, oven**

개그맨 gagman → comedian

공책 note → notebook

교차로 rotary → intersection

껌 gum → chewing gum

나비넥타이 butterfly-tie → bow-tie

노처녀 old miss → old maid

데모 demo → demonstration

드라이버 driver → screw driver

등산 mountain climbing → hiking

만화 영화 animation → movie cartoon

매니큐어 manicure → nail polish

매직펜 magic pen → marker

멍든 눈 bruised eye → black eye

모닝콜 morning call → wake-up call

모래시계 sand clock → hourglass

무스탕 mustang → leather jacket

믹서기 mixer → blender

바바리 코트 trench coat, coat

백미러 back mirror → rear-view mirror

번호판 number plate → license plate

별장 villa

비닐백 vynyl bag → plastic bag

비디오 video → VCR

빌라 villa → tenement

펜치 pinch → pliers

사이다 cider → 7-Up, Sprite

샐러리맨 salaryman → salaried worker

설문지(앙케트) questionnaire

손전등 flash → flashlight

쇼핑백 shopping bag → paper bag

스탠드 stand → desk lamp

싸인 sign, signature → autograph

썬팅 sunting → window tinting

아이스커피 ice coffee → iced coffee

아파트 apart → apartment

엉덩이 hip → buttocks, butt

엑기스 extract, essence

역전승[패] come-from-behind win/lose

오픈카 open car → convertible car

올A all 'A' → straight 'A'

와이셔츠 Y-shirts → dress shirt

원샷 one shot → bottoms up

유모차 babe car → stroller

음반 record → album

인터폰 interphone → intercom

자동차 경적 Klaxon → car horn

자크 zack → zipper, flyer

재봉틀 sewing machine

재시험 re-exam → make-up test

점퍼 jumper → jacket

접착제 bond → glue

추리닝 training → sweat suit

커트라인 cutline → cut-off line/point

콘센트 consent → outlet, socket

클래식 음악 classic → classical music

파마 permanent wave, perm

파이팅 Fighting! → Go!, Way to go!

펑크 난 타이어 flat tire

포켓볼 pocketball → pool

프린트물 print → handout

플래카드 placard → banner

황금시간대 golden hour → prime time

형광펜 marker pen → highlighter

호치키스 Hotchkiss → stapler

화이트 whiteout, correction fluid

휘발유 oil → gas, gasoline

흘러간 노래 oldies but goodies

Actual Test Preview

- [ ] **vacancy** 빈방
- [ ] **free** 한가한
- [ ] **hood** 두건, 두건 모양의 모자
- [ ] **be pressed for** ~에 쫓기다
- [ ] **dissolve** 해산하다, 녹이다
- [ ] **dissolute** 무절제한, 방탕한
- [ ] **dissonant** 귀에 거슬리는, 불협화음의
- [ ] **dissident** 의견을 달리하는, 반체제의
- [ ] **collusion** 공모, 결탁
- [ ] **collision** 충돌
- [ ] **correlation** 상호 관련, 상관관계
- [ ] **counterfeit** 위조의, 가짜의; 모조품, 위폐
- [ ] **counterpart** 한 쌍의 한쪽, 등가물
- [ ] **counterstep** 대책
- [ ] **countenance** 용모, 표정
- [ ] **pour** 붓다, 따르다
- [ ] **prey** 먹이
- [ ] **signature** 서명
- [ ] **autograph** 유명인의 싸인

- [ ] **manuscript** 필사본
- [ ] **alternative** 대체의, 대안의
- [ ] **alterative** 점진적으로 체질을 바꾸는[개선하는]
- [ ] **altercate** (심하게) 말다툼하다, 언쟁하다
- [ ] **alliterate** ~에 두운을 쓰다
- [ ] **aggravate** 악화시키다
- [ ] **aggress** 공격하다
- [ ] **ingrate** 은혜를 모르는 사람, 배은망덕한 사람
- [ ] **dispose of** 처분하다
- [ ] **deposit** 예금하다, 맡기다
- [ ] **disburse** (돈, 경비를) 지불하다, 쓰다
- [ ] **defame** 비방하다, ~의 명예를 훼손하다, 모욕하다
- [ ] **inflame** ~에 불을 붙이다
- [ ] **deform** ~의 모양을 훼손하다, 불구로 만들다
- [ ] **inflate** 부풀리다, 팽창시키다
- [ ] **contrive** 연구하다, 고안하다, 시도하다
- [ ] **contingent** ~여하에 달린, ~에 따르는
- [ ] **contrite** 죄를 깊이 뉘우치는
- [ ] **contrastive** 대조적인

Actual Test

PART I **Choose the best answer for the blank.**

1 A: Do you have rooms available for tonight?
B: Sorry, we have no ______________.

(a) vacancies   (b) spaces
(c) places   (d) bookings

2 A: Do you think I can drop by for a chat tomorrow?
B: Sure, I'll be ______________ all afternoon.

(a) set   (b) free
(c) empty   (d) welcome

3 A: Have you seen my red sweatshirt?
B: The one with a ______________? It was in the laundry yesterday.

(a) lid   (b) hat
(c) hood   (d) cover

4 A: Can I speak with you for a second?
B: Yeah, but only for a moment. I'm ______________ for time.

(a) busy   (b) quick
(c) pulled   (d) pressed

5 A: Why is there no more reading club? Did it finish?
B: Yes, it was ______________ a few weeks earlier.

(a) dissolute   (b) dissolved
(c) dissident   (d) dissonant

6   A: Do you know the reason the judges are chosen randomly?

B: I guess it's a method to prevent ____________ between judges and the contestants.

(a) collision　　　　　　　　(b) conclusion

(c) collusion　　　　　　　　(d) correlation

7   A: Do you think this money could be ____________?

B: It looks real to me. Why don't you think it is genuine?

(a) counterpart　　　　　　　(b) counterstep

(c) countenance　　　　　　　(d) counterfeit

PART II Choose the best answer for the blank.

8   If you ____________ water on a hot pan, it will turn into steam.

(a) cover　　　　　　　　　　(b) pour

(c) sink　　　　　　　　　　　(d) roll

9   Not every spider makes webs to catch their ____________.

(a) cub　　　　　　　　　　　(b) goal

(c) breed　　　　　　　　　　(d) prey

10 People commonly end their letters with a(n) ____________.

(a) autograph　　　　　　　　(b) signature

(c) manuscript　　　　　　　　(d) autobiography

11 Some cancer patients seek traditional or ____________ therapies to deal with the painful side effects of hospital-based medicine.

(a) alterative　　　　　　　　(b) altercate

(c) alternative　　　　　　　　(d) alliterate

12 Do not use ointment on a bee sting as this may _____________ the swelling.

(a) aggress

(b) ingrate

(c) aggravate

(d) gratify

13 When I left college and joined the circus, I _____________ of all of my belongings.

(a) departed

(b) deposited

(c) disposed

(d) disbursed

14 The goal of the opposition party was to _____________ and attack the campaign's front-runner.

(a) defame

(b) inflame

(c) deform

(d) inflate

15 Serendipitous events rarely, if ever, occur in real life, but they are frequently _____________ in mainstream cinema.

(a) contrived

(b) contingent

(c) contrite

(d) contrastive

Chapter

08 | 동사 중심의 **연어**

연어란 항상 특정한 말과 함께 쓰이다시피 해서 굳어진 표현으로 영어로는 collocation이라고 한다. 영어에서 두 개 또는 그 이상의 단어가 흔히 붙어 쓰이거나 인접해 쓰이는 것은 일종의 연어로 간주할 수 있다. 연어는 그 안의 중심 단어를 기준으로 동사 중심의 연어, 형용사 중심의 연어, 명사 중심의 연어로 분류할 수 있다. 동사 중심의 연어에는 cover expense 같은 〈동사 + 목적어〉 구조와 (the) show runs ~ 같은 〈주어 + 동사〉 구조 두 가지가 있다. 동사 중심의 연어는 매 시험 3~4문항이 출제된다. 구어체 PART I과 문어체 PART II에서 골고루 출제된다.

▌ 주요 어휘 모음

deliver the address 연설을 하다

keep in mind 명심하다

take lessons 수업을 받다

lose pounds/weight 체중이 줄다

formulate a hypothesis 가설을 세우다

launch an attack 공격을 개시하다

make a remittance 송금하다

make a journey 여행을 하다

meet a demand 요구를 충족시키다

place an order 주문하다

prime the pump 경기 부양책을 쓰다

save one's face 체면을 지키다

make/place a call 전화를 걸다

fix dinner 저녁 식사를 준비하다

make a promise

make an appointment 약속을 잡다

exchange civilities 의례적인 인사를 주고받다

weigh the consequences 결과를 신중히 고려하다

make it 성공하다, 해내다

administer first aid 응급조치를 취하다

answer the door 문을 열어 주다

apply ointment 연고를 바르다

renew subscription 정기 구독을 갱신하다

reach a decision 해결이 되다, 결정되다

beat one's brains 머리를 짜내다

conclude a speech 연설을 마치다

bring a suit (against) 소송을 제기하다

cast a ballot 투표하다

claim damages 손해배상을 청구하다

commit a crime 죄를 짓다

catch a disease 병에 걸리다

draw a check 수표를 발행하다

strike a balance 균형을 맞추다

throw a party 파티를 열다

Actual Test **Preview**

- [ ] **book** (호텔방이나 표를) 예약하다
- [ ] **run errands** 용건, 볼일, 심부름
- [ ] **make out/issue/write a check to *sb*** ~앞으로 수표를 끊다[발행하다]
- [ ] **boost** 증대하다, 밀어올리다, 밀어주다
- [ ] **alleviate** 완화시키다, 경감하다
- [ ] **apply** (약 따위를) 바르다
- [ ] **turn nasty** 화내다, 난폭하게 굴다
- [ ] **impose A on B** A(세금, 형벌, 의무 등)를 B에게 부과하다
- [ ] **dismiss a charge** 고소를 기각하다
- [ ] **draw** (손님을) 끌다, 유인하다
- [ ] **raise a question** 문제를 제기하다
- [ ] **raise/make a point** 문제를 제기하다, 지적하다
- [ ] **hold/stage a demonstration** 시위를 하다
- [ ] **contain** 포함하다, 들어 있다
- [ ] **pump gas** 기름을 넣다, 주유하다

Actual Test

 Choose the best answer for the blank.

1 A: I'm taking a vacation to Italy next week.
B: This is the busiest part of the season. Have you ______________ a hotel room?

(a) planned
(b) booked
(c) hired
(d) owned

2 A: What're your plans for the morning?
B: I'm going to run some ______________ in town. Do you want me to pick up something for you?

(a) tasks
(b) errands
(c) jobs
(d) chores

3 A: Okay, and the total cost is $44.58.
B: Now, who do I ______________ this check out to?

(a) make
(b) get
(c) pay
(d) sign

4 A: We need to find a way to ______________ sales.
B: Why don't we purchase a promotional ad in a magazine?

(a) alleviate
(b) persuade
(c) boost
(d) extend

5 A: I heard I should ______________ moisturizer and sunblock even on a cloudy day.
B: That's right. That's because UV rays still contact your skin through the clouds.

(a) apply
(b) take
(c) stand
(d) hold

6 A: So, did you take back the blender?

  B: No, as soon as I told the cashier I wanted a refund, she _____________ nasty.

  (a) made   (b) played
  (c) turned   (d) lost

PART II **Choose the best answer for the blank.**

7 An Omaha law _____________ penal punishment on physicians who practice any form of unnecessary surgery.

  (a) deposes   (b) imposes
  (c) exposes   (d) reposes

8 The education minister will convene a panel to determine the advantages of _____________ uniforms on middle school students.

  (a) suggesting   (b) imposing
  (c) recommending   (d) wearing

9 The court surprisingly _____________ all charges and set the accused spy free.

  (a) dismissed   (b) tolerated
  (c) admired   (d) punished

10 The tourism department is working hard to _____________ foreign visitors to our country.

  (a) draw   (b) earn
  (c) subject   (d) employ

11 After the speech, the audience will have the chance to ______________ some
questions to our panel.

    (a) find   (b) raise

    (c) answer   (d) maintain

12 Mr. Gossim has raised quite a good ______________, which should be given more
consideration.

    (a) value   (b) sense

    (c) point   (d) respect

13 Activists ______________ a demonstration to raise awareness about political
corruption.

    (a) got   (b) took

    (c) held   (d) kept

14 This collection from The New Yorker ______________ illustrations from its
renowned political satirists.

    (a) leaves   (b) contains

    (c) totals   (d) prints

15 Most people in this country don't know where the gas they ______________ really
comes from.

    (a) pass   (b) push

    (c) pack   (d) pump

Memo 

Chapter 09

명사 중심의 **연어**

명사 중심의 연어는 그 구조에 따라 〈명사 + 명사〉(*e.g.* income tax), 〈명사 + 전치사 + 명사〉(*e.g.* treatment of disease), 〈형용사 + 명사〉(*e.g.* flat tire) 등으로 분류할 수 있다. 다른 유형의 연어보다 답을 고르기가 쉬운 편이다.

주요 어휘 모음

circulation desk 대출 창구	**nonaggression pact** 불가침 조약
booking arrangements 예약 준비	**population density** 인구 밀도
wedding arrangements 결혼 준비	**inferiority complex** 열등감
apartment complex 아파트 단지	**speed merchant** 속도광
ballot box 투표함	**current account balance** 경상수지
bull market (증권) 상승 시세, 강세 시장	**makeup exam** 추가 시험, 재시험
bear market (증권) 하락 시세, 약세 시장	**motion sickness** 멀미
charity fund 자선기금	**morning sickness** 입덧
credit sale 신용 판매	**price fluctuation** 가격 변동
fairy tale 동화	**shock therapy** 충격 요법
farewell party 송별회	**summit talk** 정상회담
instinctive response 본능적인 반응	**surprise attack** 기습 공격
illiteracy rate 문맹률	**transition period** 과도기
installment sale 할부 판매	**online/wire transfer** 온라인 송금
life expectancy 예상[평균] 수명	

Actual Test **Preview**

- [ ] **zero visibility** 시계 제로, 아무것도 안 보이는 상태
- [ ] **a crank call** 장난 전화
- [ ] **equivalent model** 동급 모델
- [ ] **thick hair** 숱이 많은 머리
- [ ] **bachelor party** 총각 파티
- [ ] **reception** 피로연
- [ ] **housewarming party** 집들이
- [ ] **farewell party** 송별회
- [ ] **baggage claim ticket** 수화물 보관표
- [ ] **vehicle registration** 차량 등록(증)
- [ ] **surface mail** (항공 우편을 제외한) 육상우편, 선박우편
- [ ] **rosy view** 낙관적인 전망
- [ ] **customs declaration** 세관 신고(서)
- [ ] **military code** 군법
- [ ] **international charity** 국제 자선 단체
- [ ] **plastic surgery** 성형수술
- [ ] **prolong life expectancy** 평균 수명을 연장하다
- [ ] **facelift** 안면 성형, 미용 성형
- [ ] **pink slip** 해고 통지서

Actual Test

1 A: What happened to the aircraft this morning?
B: The pilot attempted to make an emergency landing in _____________ visibility.

(a) none
(b) zero
(c) void
(d) nothing

2 A: Someone keeps making _____________ phone calls to me.
B: Why would someone want to bother you like that?

(a) crank
(b) trick
(c) fake
(d) joke

3 A: The model of the MP3 player you asked for is no longer produced.
B: Perhaps you know of an _____________ model?

(a) default
(b) equivalent
(c) delegate
(d) equal

4 A: I think I'm losing a lot of hair. I hope I'm not balding.
B: No way. You've still got _____________ hair.

(a) plenty
(b) heavy
(c) thick
(d) glossy

5 A: There's going to be a _____________ party for Bob a week before he gets married. Will you come?
B: Definitely. I'll be there.

(a) bachelor
(b) reception
(c) housewarming
(d) farewell

6 A: One of my pieces of luggage is missing!

B: Calm down. We can take care of it. Do you still have the baggage ____________ ticket?

(a) counter

(b) claim

(c) security

(d) declaration

7 A: What seems to be the problem, officer?

B: You were driving above the speed limit. Do you have your driver's license and vehicle _____________?

(a) order

(b) legislation

(c) ticket

(d) registration

8 A: I want to mail this package to Puerto Rico.

B: Is that going to be by airmail or _____________ mail?

(a) land

(b) shipping

(c) surface

(d) sea

9 A: I have hopes the high unemployment rate will go down.

B: I wish I shared that _____________ view, but the economic reality doesn't point in that direction.

(a) pink

(b) rosy

(c) high

(d) cool

10 A: Are you carrying any plants, fruits, or animals with you?

B: No, I'm not. This is my customs _____________.

(a) declaration

(b) proposition

(c) announcement

(d) testimony

11 A: Is that really Mary? She looks ten years younger.

    B: I know. Apparently, she's had a few _______________ recently.

   (a) C-sections   (b) jackpots

   (c) facelifts   (d) pink slips

PART II Choose the best answer for the blank.

12 Violations of _______________ code can result in being tried in a court-martial.

   (a) moral   (b) minor

   (c) civil   (d) military

13 She chose to assist those less fortunate than her by giving all the proceeds from her latest album to international _______________.

   (a) contributions   (b) chastities

   (c) corpus   (d) charities

14 More and more singers are having _______________ surgery to maintain their popularity.

   (a) aesthetic   (b) plastic

   (c) artistic   (d) heart

15 It is hoped that new medical research on nutrition will help _______________ life expectancy.

   (a) prolong   (b) repeat

   (c) postpone   (d) attach

Memo 

Chapter
10 고난도 어휘

일반적으로 신문이나 잡지에서 접하기 힘든 어휘가 이 유형에 속하며 입문, 기본반뿐만 아니라 정규, 실전반 수강생들도 가장 어려워하는 유형이다. TEPS 어휘 section은 실용적이면서도 학술적인 내용에 초점을 두고 있어 학술적인 성격이 강한 어휘도 등장한다. 하지만 최근 시험에서는 그 수가 점점 줄어들고 있으므로 너무 염려할 필요는 없는 파트라고도 볼 수 있다. PART II에서 주로 출제된다.

▌주요 어휘 모음

perk 임직원 혜택	**sojourn** (일시적인) 체류, 체재
turbulence (사회적) 소란	**apathy** 냉담, 무관심
distraction 주의 산만	**notoriety** 악명, 악평
derivative 파생적인	**repulsion** 반감, 증오
versatile 다재다능한	**antipathy** 반감, 혐오
smattering 얕은 지식	**commotion** 동요, 소요
glimmer 희미한 빛	**complacency** 자기만족
contentment 만족	**efficacy** 효능, 효험
deference 복종	**frugality** 절약, 검소
solicit 간청하다	**cornerstone** 기초, 초석
trespass 침입하다	**hindrance** 방해
loiter 빈둥거리다	**ferocity** 사나움, 잔인성
infidelity 불신, 부정	**lucidity** 명료
eyesore 눈에 거슬리는 것, 꼴불견	**docility** 온순
gimmick (요술쟁이, 약장수 등의) 비밀 장치, 속임수	**delinquency** (청소년) 범죄, 비행
divergence (의견 등의) 차이	**imposture** 사기, 협잡
condolence 조문, 애도	**contraband** 밀수, 밀매, 불법 거래
hideout 은신처, 피난처	**embezzlement** 횡령, 착복
whereabouts 소재, 행방	**ambiguous** 모호한
inertia 활발하지 않음, 무기력	**bland** 온화한, 순한, 지루한
hibernation 동면	**crouch** (몸을) 웅크리다

carcass (짐승의) 시체

drawback 결점, 문제점

frailty 약함, 약점

scarcity 부족, 기근

accomplice 공범

sleuth 형사, 탐정

backout 철회, 탈퇴

standstill 정지

equivalent 등가물, 상당하는 것

bereavement 사별

ignominy 불명예

masquerade 가면무도회

plight 곤경, 어려운 상태

proliferation 증식, 급증

quandary 당황, 곤경

quagmire 수렁, 궁지

ripple 파문, 파동

pinnacle 작은 뾰족탑, 정점

zenith 천정, (성공이나 명예 등의) 정점

flicker 깜박이다, 명멸하다

gleam 번쩍이다

glow 빛나다

deify 신성시하다

obstruct 방해하다

slander 중상하다, 명예를 훼손하다

forestall 앞서다

disclaim 권리를 포기하다

corroborate (소신이나 진술 등을) 확증하다

rear (물건 등을) 똑바로 세우다

dominate 지배하다

backfire 맞불을 놓다

spark 유발하다, 야기시키다

dribble (물방울 등이) 똑똑 떨어지다, 침을 흘리다

scribble 낙서하다

stricken (병에) 걸린, 고통받는

defraud (속여서) 빼앗다, 횡령하다

deactivate 비활성화시키다

sack 약탈하다

swap 교환하다

dissuade (설득하여) 단념시키다

quench (갈증 등을) 가시게 하다

nurture 양육하다, 교육하다

abstain 그만두다, 끊다, 삼가다

wane 작아지다, (권력, 명성 등이) 쇠하다

spawn (물고기, 개구리 등이) 알을 낳다, 산란하다

ordain (신, 운명 등이) 정하다, 운명 짓다

flaunt 과시하다

commensurate 액수[크기, 정도]가 알맞은, 적당한

commiserate 가엾게 여기다, 동정하다

susceptible 영향받기 쉬운, 감염되기 쉬운

exude 발산하다

amicable 우호적인, 평화적인

intact 손대지 않은

avaricious 탐욕스러운

crestfallen 풀이 죽은

skimpy 불충분한, 빈약한

hoarse 쉰 목소리의

bombastic 과장하는, 허풍 떠는

prosaic 산문적인, 단조로운, 지루한

clumsy 어색한, 서투른

creepy 오싹하는

barren 불임의, (땅이) 불모의, 메마른

ulterior (목적, 동기 등이) 감추어진, 이면의	**hiatus** (공간, 시간의) 틈
aberrant 정도에서 벗어난, 탈선적인	**veneration** 존경, 숭배
ancillary 부수적인	**fabricate** 날조하다
cumulative 누적되는, 점진적인	**berate** 호되게 꾸짖다
devout 독실한, 믿음이 깊은	**bolster** 보강하다
dubious 의심스러운	**defy** 무시하다, 거부하다
flagrant (거짓말, 실수 등이) 명백한	**embellish** 장식하다
heinous 극악한, 가증스러운	**gratuitous** 무료의
implacable 화해하기 힘든	**monogamy** 일부일처제
loquacious 수다스러운, 말이 많은	**polygamy** 일부다처제
luscious 달콤한, 감미로운	**hypochondriac** 건강염려증 환자
obscene 음란한	**ejaculate** 갑자기 외치다
pensive 생각에 잠긴	**flaunt** 과시하다
recalcitrant 완강히 반항하는	**adroit** 능숙한
restrained 삼가는	**aloof** 무관심한, 냉담한
slovenly 단정치 못한	**assiduous** 근면한, 끈기 있는
strenuous 굽히지 않는, 격렬한	**garbled** 왜곡된
subservient 비굴한, 아첨하는	**clandestine** 은밀한
unwavering 동요하지 않는, 확고한	**ephemeral** 덧없는
acquisition 획득	**hilarious** 유쾌한, 즐거운
espouse (주의 따위를) 받아들이다, 지지하다	**lenient** 관대한
insolvent 지급불능인	**lopsided** 한쪽으로 치우친
congeniality 친화성	**nonchalant** 냉담한, 무관심한
anatomy 해부학	**ticklish** 간지럼을 타는, 다루기 힘든
prodigy 비범한 사람, 천재	**salutary** 건전한, 유익한
disparage 얕보다, 험담하다	**resilient** 탄력 있는
eccentric 별난, 기이한	

Actual Test Preview

- [ ] **picky** 까다로운
- [ ] **lenient** 인자한, 관대한
- [ ] **humdrum** 평범한, 단조로운
- [ ] **virtuoso** (예술의) 대가, 거장, 명연주가
- [ ] **fiasco** 대실패
- [ ] **relic** 유적, 폐허
- [ ] **artifact** 가공품, 인공물
- [ ] **stimulant** 자극제
- [ ] **narcotics** 마취제, 마약, 최면제
- [ ] **devastate** 압도하다, 망연자실케 하다
- [ ] **hypnotize** 최면을 걸다
- [ ] **repress** 억제하다
- [ ] **placate** 달래다, 진정시키다
- [ ] **connotation** 암시, 함축적 의미
- [ ] **conjunction** 연합, 연결, 관련
- [ ] **conjecture** 짐작, 추측
- [ ] **configuration** (컴퓨터 시스템의) 환경 설정
- [ ] **foster** 촉진하다, 육성하다
- [ ] **hamper** 훼방 놓다, 방해하다
- [ ] **emulate** 경쟁하다, 본뜨다, 모방하다
- [ ] **mesmerize** 최면술을 걸다
- [ ] **unnerving** 맥 빠지게 하는, 낙담시키는
- [ ] **fussy** 야단법석인
- [ ] **endearing** 사랑스러운

- [ ] **solid** 견고한, 견실한
- [ ] **credulous** 쉽게 믿는, 잘 속는
- [ ] **crafty** 간교한, 교활한, 솜씨 있는
- [ ] **antidote** 해독제
- [ ] **anecdote** 일화, 기담, 비화
- [ ] **antithesis** 대조, 대립
- [ ] **anaesthetic** 마취제
- [ ] **grim** 어두운, 무서운, 섬뜩한
- [ ] **recur** 되풀이되다
- [ ] **incur** 초래하다
- [ ] **reverberate** (소리가) 울려 퍼지다
- [ ] **vaporize** 증발하다
- [ ] **discrimination** 차별 (대우), 구별
- [ ] **harassment** 괴롭히기, 희롱
- [ ] **distinction** 구별, 차이
- [ ] **philanthropic** 박애(주의)의, 인정 많은
- [ ] **pharmaceutical** 조제의, 제약의
- [ ] **phenomenal** 경이적인, 비상한
- [ ] **impeccable** 나무랄 데 없는, 흠이 없는
- [ ] **disconsolate** 절망적인, 불행한
- [ ] **gullible** 속기 쉬운, 잘 속는
- [ ] **unpredictable** 예측할 수 없는
- [ ] **impenetrable** 이해할 수 없는
- [ ] **unprecedented** 전례가 없는, 새로운

Actual Test

1 A: The boss is really _______________.
B: Yes, he sets very high standards for his employees.

(a) lenient   (b) picky
(c) upset   (d) humdrum

2 A: Do you know who Paganini was?
B: Of course! He was a renowned violin _______________.

(a) fiasco   (b) relic
(c) artifact   (d) virtuoso

3 A: Right before I go to sleep, I enjoy a cup of coffee and a smoke.
B: Seriously? _______________ like that wouldn't let me sleep.

(a) Stimulants   (b) Narcotics
(c) Minerals   (d) Medications

4 A: Too bad that your team lost the game. I know you were expecting a victory.
B: I can't believe how it turned out. I'm completely _______________!

(a) devastated   (b) hypnotized
(c) repressed   (d) placated

5 These phrases sound alike with respect to their meanings, but they have subtly
different _______________.

(a) conjunctions   (b) conjectures
(c) configurations   (d) connotations

6 Some people worry that the US government is starting to ______________ a policy of bilingualism, creating a scenario where English will be merely one among many competing languages in the country.

(a) hamper
(b) foster
(c) emulate
(d) mesmerize

7 It was so ______________ for us to lose a year's harvest because of a sudden harsh frost.

(a) fussy
(b) troublesome
(c) endearing
(d) unnerving

8 To convincingly back up your claims, ______________ information is critical.

(a) solid
(b) native
(c) credulous
(d) crafty

9 After eating a poison plant in the woods, Carl had to be treated with an ______________.

(a) anecdote
(b) antithesis
(c) antidote
(d) anaesthetic

10 Even more ______________ news arrived about the state of the war, bringing a cloud of despair over the population.

(a) grim
(b) bright
(c) promising
(d) serious

11 The kid related to his mom a strange dream that had ______________ throughout the week.

(a) recurred
(b) incurred
(c) reverberated
(d) vaporized

12 Our company has taken strong measures to prevent any kind of ______________ based on race, nationality, belief, or gender.

    (a) harassment   (b) enforcement

    (c) discrimination   (d) distinction

13 In addition to running his clinic, Larry enjoyed spending his free time on ______________ causes such as teaching underprivileged children.

    (a) phonetic   (b) pharmaceutical

    (c) phenomenal   (d) philanthropic

14 Unlike his disheveled twin brother, Andy took pains to look ______________ in his tailor-made suits.

    (a) impeccable   (b) disconsolate

    (c) gullible   (d) imperfect

15 The film will keep your eyes riveted to the screen with its totally ______________ plot.

    (a) impenetrable   (b) unpredictable

    (c) unprecedented   (d) unpronounceable

Memo 

New TEPS MASTER 900

Reading Comprehension

Chapter 01

빈칸 위치가 상단

빈칸의 위치가 지문 앞쪽, 즉 상단에 위치하면 문단의 주제와 관련된 내용이 정답이 될 확률이 높다. 글 전체의 흐름을 파악하는 것과 선택지에서 제시한 어구의 정확한 의미를 파악하는 것이 중요하다.

▌독해요령 1 선택지를 먼저 읽어 본다.

TEPS 독해 지문 중 상당수가 선택지에 힌트를 담고 있는 경우가 많다. 예를 들면, 선택지에 등장한 3개의 선택지가 비슷한 내용이고 나머지 1개가 이 3개의 선택지와 상반된 경우에는 정답일 확률이 높다.

▌독해요령 2 주제와 관련 있는 선택지를 고른다.

빈칸이 지문의 위쪽에 위치해 있다는 것은 대부분 주제문을 묻는 취지로 보면 된다. 따라서 일단 빈칸이 들어간 문장과 그다음 문장까지만 본 다음, 선택지를 보고 답을 찾을 수 있는 경우가 상당히 많으므로 지문 전체를 다 읽기 전에 답을 고르는 훈련을 하는 습관이 필수이다.

▌독해요령 3 전체 지문을 요약하는 어구를 고른다.

빈칸의 위치가 상단에 오는 유형 중에서 특히 처음 도입 부분부터 빈칸으로 시작하는 경우, 앞으로 나올 지문 전체의 내용을 함축한 단어나 어구를 묻는 경우가 많다.

Read the passage. Then choose the option that best completes the passage.

Many scientists now attribute ___________________ to factors other than the aging process. Indeed, few of us maintain perfect eyesight beyond middle age. Loss of vision is not inevitable, and there is no reason why the human eyes cannot maintain good vision beyond the age of 80. However, factors such as UV rays, pollution and nutritional deficiencies damage the eyes.

(a) the secrets of longevity
(b) one level of happiness
(c) age-related vision loss
(d) blindness at birth

어휘 attribute A to B A를 B의 탓으로 돌리다 **factor** 요인 **other than** ~을 제외하고 **maintain** 유지하다
eyesight 시력 **middle age** 중년 **loss** 손실 **inevitable** 피할 수 없는 **UV rays** 자외선
nutritional deficiency 영양 부족 **damage** 해를 끼치다

Actual Test

1   Individuals inflicted with Alzheimer's disease ultimately forget who they are. Researchers at a medical science company believe that they have found the enzyme that is the source of this serious illness. While a(n) ________________ solution is not forthcoming, this could signify a major step towards defeating one of the world's most devastating diseases.

(a) equivalent
(b) necessary
(c) eventual
(d) immediate

2   The protein-intensive Atkins diet could be harming the chances of weight-watching women to successfully reproduce. The Atkins diet promotes eating primarily meat, fish and egg while restricting carbohydrates such as bread, rice, pasta and starchy vegetables. Research shows that the embryos of rodents that had ingested mostly protein failed to survive womb implantation. These findings could be interpreted as a serious concern for women ________________.

(a) who worry about their weight
(b) who want to reproduce
(c) who consume too much meat
(d) who are unable to diet

3   Alcohol, a ubiquitous substance, has become increasingly dangerous to our social stability. It is extremely harmful to human relationships. It can destroy families and erode time-honored values. I have witnessed the awful abuse of women by intoxicated husbands. Despite this reality, I disagree with those who would outlaw alcohol. Were alcohol illegal, brewery workers would suffer. Anyone involved in the distribution of alcohol would lose their jobs. In addition, banning alcohol would only reinvigorate mafia groups who would seek methods to ______________ illegally.

(a) smuggle it
(b) abstain from it
(c) consume it
(d) organize it

PART II   Read the passage and the question. Then choose the option that best answers the question.

4   Although the technology that now permeates our modern lives can be seen as beneficial, there are some questionable aspects to it as well. For example, will interactive communication technology ultimately manipulate minds, eliminate privacy, or influence people to abandon family duties and human bonds? What long-term consequence will genetically modified foods have on our health? Sophisticated medical treatments can increase the lifespan of individuals, but can they improve the overall wellbeing and contentment of people? We can only wait and see.

Q. What is the best title for the passage?
(a) Interactive Media and Modern Dilemmas
(b) Human Health and Technology
(c) The Inevitable Power of Technological Progress
(d) The Pros and Cons of Evolving Technology

5   In Western societies today, it is expected of parents to instruct their children in basic ethics and provide them with a formal education. Apart from this, however, how an individual develops is largely believed to be based on genetic factors or on random coincidence. Contrary to this view is a growing body of research of the past decade suggesting that parents can contribute in many more areas to ensure their children become happy and successful members of society.

Q. Which of the following is the best title for the passage?

(a) Why Parents Should Do More
(b) The Proper Way to Raise Children
(c) The Parent-Child Bond
(d) Personality's Genetic Roots

6   It is important to make academic pursuits a high priority. However, it is equally important to spend some time doing something that you find fun and relaxing. Serious students often maintain that they don't have time to spend on anything but homework and school-related activities. They feel that a hobby might take away from their study time. However, what they fail to realize is that an activity that allows you to take a break from major responsibilities for a while may actually boost your performance in school. Taking time to relax and enjoy a hobby reduces stress and makes it easier to focus when it's time to settle into a study session.

Q. Which of the following best summarizes the above passage?

(a) Pursuing activities outside of school helps academic performance.
(b) Many students today have too many responsibilities.
(c) It is often difficult to find time to pursue a hobby.
(d) What you do in your free time can affect your grades.

7   Why should only wealthy celebrities have the opportunity to have lavish weddings? (a) Everyone should be able to tie the knot in style without having to spend a fortune! (b) My suggestion is to get ideas from celebrity weddings and carry out similar concepts focusing on innovation and cost efficiency. (c) Famous people have the big bucks to hire internationally renowned designers to make their wedding gowns. (d) Take it from me, there are infinite methods to imitate that glamorous movie star style without going broke.

Chapter 02

빈칸 위치가 **중간**

지문 중반부에 빈칸이 위치한 경우는 반드시 주제와 관련 있는 선택지가 정답이 되는 것은 아니므로 빈칸 주위의 문맥을 살펴서 문장의 가장 논리적인 흐름을 완성하는 선택지를 정답으로 고르면 된다.

▌독해요령 1 역접어 뒤에 빈칸이 이어지는 경우는 주제문을 완성하는 문제이다.

이런 유형은 글의 구조를 묻는 것이므로 주제문의 핵심 어구에 빈칸이 오는 경우가 많다. 지문의 도입부부터 빈칸까지의 내용과 상반되는 내용의 선택지를 고르면 정답이다.

▌독해요령 2 주제문 이후에 빈칸이 등장하는 경우는 주제문을 보충하는 내용이 답이다.

주제문이 주어진 다음, 그 주제문을 지지할 만한 문장에 빈칸을 만들어 정답을 묻는 유형이다. 일단 등장한 주제문에 나왔던 어구들과 관련 있는 말이 선택지에 정답으로 등장하는 경우가 많으므로 이에 유의하여 정답을 고른다.

▌독해요령 3 글의 논리적 흐름을 완성하는 유형은 빈칸 주위를 잘 살핀다.

빈칸이 지문 중간에 위치한 유형의 경우 글의 흐름을 완성하는 문제가 대부분이므로 빈칸을 기준으로 앞뒤로 이어지는 문장에 힌트가 대다수 등장한다. 결국 이 힌트들을 얼마나 잘 잡아낼 수 있느냐에 정답 여부가 달려 있다. 힌트들을 놓치지 않기 위해서는 문법을 통해 철저히 다진 문장 구조 지식과 어휘력이 관건이 된다. 더불어 빈칸의 앞뒤 문장이 인과 관계인지 역접인지 대조인지 순접인지 빠르게 파악하여 정답을 고르는 훈련이 필요하다.

Read the passage. Then choose the option that best completes the passage.

The long-held belief that schools favor boys is simply untrue. In fact, the opposite may be true. On most tests given in school, girls do better than boys. On average, boys _________________________________. Girls take more difficult classes and participate more in student government and honor clubs. In addition, boys get kicked out more often, and are less likely to go to college.

(a) are a year and a half behind their female peers in reading scores
(b) usually do better than girls in science and math
(c) don't typically get teachers' attention as much as girls do
(d) are more likely to cause trouble at school than girls

어휘 **long-held** 오랜 **favor** 선호하다 **student government** 학생회 **in addition** 게다가 **get kicked out** 쫓겨나다

Actual Test

1   Overpopulation is perhaps the most significant factor to our ecological crisis. Science and modern farming techniques have allowed a greater number of our species to survive childhood, reproduce and grow older than ever before. Simultaneously, we are extracting more of the planet's limited resources than our predecessors. There is a declining rate of population growth in some industrialized countries, but still the global reproduction rate is increasing, with many people still having difficulty being properly fed. If we are serious about preventing this dilemma, we must focus on ___________________.

(a) exploiting more resources
(b) curbing population growth
(c) reducing oil consumption
(d) mastering solar technology

2   Chocolate may conjure up ideas of sweet candy bars and syrupy milkshake, but the original chocolate was a dramatically different concoction. Cultivated for at least three millennia in Central America and Mexico, chocolate was originally used as a bitter-tasting beverage by the Aztec and Mayan people. While the widespread sweetened milk chocolate is considered largely unhealthy, dark chocolate, ___________________, has been found by doctors to lower blood pressure.

(a) by comparison
(b) after all
(c) with respect to
(d) consequentially

3 The region where I reside is in an endless cycle of violence, with two groups of people resenting each other. Existence is filled with stress and danger. I believe I should be able to live in my people's homeland. However, not everyone believes so, and some people vehemently try to keep us from getting back to our land. A week ago some close friends of mine were killed. They were sleeping in their home when a missile hit their house. Another friend was shot trying to cross the border. I am often disheartened to experience such atrocities inflicted upon people all around me. _________________, I am given hope by some indications that a resolution can be reached in the near future.

(a) On the other hand
(b) In conclusion
(c) Plus
(d) In addition

4 Mark Twain, who started his career writing comical verse, grew as a writer to produce dark chronicles of the vanities, hypocrisies and murderous acts of mankind. By the time he wrote *Huckleberry Finn*, his style combined rich humor, a strong plot and social criticism. Twain was gifted at utilizing colloquial speech and was successful at popularizing a unique American literature founded on American symbolism and language. Many of Twain's works have been suppressed throughout the years for a number of reasons. _____________________ *The Adventures of Huckleberry Finn* has been frequently restricted in American schools, not least for its frequent use of vulgar language that was in more prevalent use at the time the book was written.

(a) However
(b) Specifically
(c) Moreover
(d) Despite this

 Read the passage and the question. Then choose the option that best answers the question.

5 Students who wish to learn English by immersing themselves abroad had better realize that there is more to English-speaking countries than just the language. *The English Learner's Cultural Guide* is specifically designed to give students an insight into their country of study that goes beyond breaking down grammar. While the United States, South Africa, Australia, and Ireland all speak English, they do so within very different historical and cultural contexts. This book is designed to solve the problem caused when students of English are exposed to only one English-speaking culture, which leaves them ill-equipped when they find themselves in a real-world situation.

Q. Who is this book mainly intended for?

(a) English teachers in other countries
(b) English-learning exchange students
(c) Travellers on cultural tours
(d) Students preparing for their exams

6 Venus Flytraps can be challenging plants to grow. Due to their sensitivity to climate conditions, it is advised that you use a terrarium in which to grow them. Never give tap water to your Flytrap, as chlorine is poisonous to them. Instead, use bottled water or rain water. For potting mixture, try 60% peat moss and 40% sterilized sand. If you take good care of your Venus Flytrap, it can live up to 7 years and beyond.

Q. Which of the following is correct according to the passage?

(a) Rain water is harmful to Venus Flytraps.
(b) Venus Flytraps must be grown outdoors.
(c) Venus Flytraps need a carefully controlled environment.
(d) Venus Flytraps are good plants for beginner gardeners.

7   Throughout history, individuals and groups who stood up to their governments have often experienced great persecution. (a) The philosopher Bertrand Russell received such unfortunate treatment after criticizing both England as well as its military foes for their involvement in the first world war. (b) He never stopped trying to help those oppressed by society. (c) He was punished with a fine, later imprisoned, and subsequently fired from Cambridge University. (d) Russell encountered a very adverse environment in jail, but he still managed to author a book at the time.

Chapter 03 빈칸 위치가 하단

빈칸이 하단에 위치한 유형의 문제는 일단 지문 전체를 다 읽어야 하므로 다른 빈칸 유형보다 배점이 높다고 볼 수 있다.

▌독해요령 1 글 전체의 결론을 요약할 수 있는 선택지를 고른다.

세부적인 내용의 선택지가 정답이 되는 경우도 가끔 있으므로 주의해야겠지만, 세부적인 내용보다는 글 전체의 내용을 파악해야 정답을 고를 수 있는 유형이 대부분이므로 글의 결론에 해당되는 내용이 정답이 될 확률이 높다.

▌독해요령 2 역접 어구에 주의한다.

빈칸이 하단에 위치하더라도 빈칸 앞부분에 역접 어구가 등장하면 전체 글의 내용과 정반대의 선택지가 정답이므로 항상 역접 어구에 주의한다.

▌독해요령 3 문단 첫머리의 주제문을 재진술하는 선택지를 고른다.

빈칸이 하단에 나오는 유형의 상당수는 지문의 첫 부분에 등장한 주제문을 다시 한 번 재진술하는 경우가 많으므로 이 경우에는 지문 중간에 있는 부연 설명에는 너무 신경 쓰지 말고 첫 문장의 내용과 관련성이 큰 어구를 나타낸 선택지를 정답으로 고를 수 있어야 한다.

Read the passage. Then choose the option that best completes the passage.

John Dewey was an American theorist who believed that interaction was essential to learning. Dewey was an early proponent of the philosophy that people must link new experiences to old experiences in order to make sense of the new information. He advocated a radical reformation of public schools and continuity of experience. Learning only comes from personal experience, and this experience must ___________________________ in order for the new knowledge to have meaning.

(a) be built on past experiences
(b) relate to future goals
(c) contain spiritual significance
(d) be openly debated by peers

어휘 **theorist** 이론가 **interaction** 상호 작용 **proponent** 지지자, 옹호자 **philosophy** 철학 **link** 연결하다
make sense of 이해하다 **advocate** 옹호하다 **radical** 극단적인, 급진적인 **reformation** 개혁 **continuity** 연속성

Actual Test

PART I Read the passage. Then choose the option that best completes the passage.

1   The American inventor and businessman Thomas Alva Edison was responsible for the development of many devices that had profound effects on people around the world, including the phonograph and a long-lasting light bulb. He was one of the first inventors to put the principles of mass production into the invention process. ____________________, he is often credited with the founding of the first industrial research laboratory. Considered among the most prolific inventors ever, Edison received 1,093 US patents in his name.

(a) Regrettably

(b) Thus

(c) Nonetheless

(d) However

2   Dear Mr. Walker,

I am sending the resume of a personal friend of mine, James McDougal. He is experienced in the field of radio broadcasting. Over the years, he has often given me valuable media advice about my company. I am contacting you about this because James asked for potential client references and I figured this was the very least I could do in return for his past services to me. If you happen to know any businesses that ____________________, do not hesitate to connect them with James. I ask that you hang on to his resume for a while and keep in mind his radio broadcasting experience, in case his expertise would be of use.

Sincerely,

Eric A. Schmidt

Eric A. Schmidt

(a) could benefit from someone with his skills

(b) are interested in our products

(c) plan on starting your own company

(d) are considering filing for bankruptcy

3 Have you ever wanted to read a book incredibly fast? Professional speed reading courses provide students with a number of easy techniques that teach you how to better focus your attention. Motion naturally attracts the eye. The techniques of speed reading put that motion to work on the page. By sitting upright and holding the book with your left hand, your right hand can trace the words to set the pace of reading. If you do not have a firm grasp of vocabulary and grammar, then speed reading will not benefit you. Therefore, before you attempt to learn these methods, be sure that __________________.

(a) you are in the proper position
(b) read as many books as possible
(c) you are already a capable reader
(d) put the techniques into practice

4 People have pointed out that industrially manufactured milk is packed with chemicals, contributes to animal abuse, and is harmful to those with poor stomachs. Despite this, for the majority of individuals, __________________. As a good example, milk is a cheap and easy way to receive calcium. Everyone should have calcium for building healthy bones. In addition, milk is enriched with other nutrients that make it desirable for children. It has been well-documented that a balanced diet, including dairy, contributes to reducing the risk of heart disease. Moreover, some scientists suggest that milk could play a factor in preventing certain types of cancer.

(a) vitamins provide their daily calcium requirements
(b) milk is the only beverage option they are aware of
(c) drinking milk is something to be avoided if possible
(d) the advantages are judged to be greater than any disadvantages

5 Lucid dreaming happens when a person is aware that they are dreaming at the moment that they are in the dream. Unlike in most dream states, lucid dreamers are able to actively participate in and influence the dream environment. Depending on a person's degree of self-awareness within the dream, lucid dreams can be quite realistic. Lucid dreams are thought to happen in one of two ways. A DILD, or dream-initiated lucid dream, begins like a normal dream except the dreamer realizes that they are in a dream state. A WILD, or wake-initiated lucid dream, takes place when the dreamer transitions directly from being awake to dreaming without having technically gone to sleep.

Q. What is this passage mainly about?

(a) Abnormal dream experiences
(b) Pros and cons of DILD and WILD
(c) Techniques on how to have a lucid dream
(d) An explanation of lucid dreaming

6 Good news for grape farmers. A new study has validated the popular theory that moderate wine consumption lowers chances of developing heart disease. Scientists have concluded that, when contrasted with non-drinkers, light drinkers of wine are a third less likely to die of disease. Wine drinkers in general suffered considerably less occurrences of heart attacks. In fact, consumption of alcohol at all showed some benefit, the study found. However, the most dramatic results were displayed by those who primarily drank wine.

Q. What is the passage mainly about?

(a) Health benefits of wine
(b) Heart disease prevention
(c) Consequences of alcohol consumption
(d) The cause of wine's popularity

PART III Read the passage. Then identify the option that does NOT belong.

7   Like it or not, extreme sports are here to stay. (a) The younger generation seems more and more eager to endanger their livelihoods for the thrill of snowboarding, skateboarding, or kite surfing. (b) Basketball, too, has seen enormous growth in popularity globally, where it is replacing indigenous sports games as the number one pastime of youth. (c) Among the riskiest new sports is sky surfing, an activity where practitioners leap out of planes and use a board to manipulate their descent. (d) This extreme sport ranks up with skydiving and bungee jumping for its delivery of adrenaline rush excitement.

Chapter 04 | 연결사 넣기

빈칸에 들어갈 적절한 연결사를 고르는 문제는 TEPS 독해 파트 PART I의 마지막 부분인 15, 16번에 등장하는 유형으로 글의 구조나 문장과 문장 간의 논리적 흐름을 파악하는 것이 관건이다.

▌독해요령 1 글의 전체 구조와 흐름을 파악하며 읽는다.

빈칸 앞뒤의 전체적인 글의 흐름을 파악하고 역접, 인과, 부연 설명, 예시 등의 문단 구성 방식을 이해하며 지문을 읽는 연습을 해야 한다.

▌독해요령 2 연결 어구의 정확한 뜻을 알아둔다.

역접: but, however, in contrast, on the other hand, conversely

양보: while, although, despite, in spite of

예시: for example, for instance, to illustrate

부연: in other words, that is (to say), in fact

추가: besides, moreover, furthermore, in addition, what's more

유사: likewise, similarly, in the same way

결과: therefore, consequently, hence, thus, as a result, so, accordingly

Sample

Read the passage. Then choose the option that best completes the passage.

Hoping to give its young citizens an edge in a global economy, many governments have begun subsidizing early education programs. The expectation is that children who have this head start will ultimately learn more in shorter periods of time. ____________________, critics cite evidence to the contrary. Sweden is one such country that has state-sponsored preschool programs for infants as young as one. One might expect Swedish children to earn top marks on international standards tests, especially compared to their demographically identical neighbor, Finland (whose children do not attend school until age seven). Yet Finnish children consistently outperform their Swedish rivals.

(a) However
(b) For instance
(c) Therefore
(d) In general

어휘 **edge** 우위 **subsidize** 보조금을 지급하다 **head start** 유리한 출발 **ultimately** 궁극적으로 **critic** 비평가 **cite** 언급하다 **to the contrary** 그와 반대의, 그렇지 않다는 **state-sponsored** 국가가 지원하는 **infant** 영아 **compared to** ~와 비교해서 **demographically** 인구통계학적으로 **identical** 동일한 **consistently** 한결같이 **outperform** 보다 뛰어나다

Actual Test

1 A firewall is a computer device that monitors network traffic passing through it, and regulates access based on a set of rules. If a firewall is not adequately configured, it may serve little purpose. Many people, who do not understand how a firewall works, mistakenly choose the 'default' option during setup, ___________ ___________ significantly more probable.

(a) making the occurrence of spam mail
(b) causing total network protection to be
(c) making system and network problems
(d) making expensive equipment purchases

2 Students can easily grow disillusioned with their education when it does not seem relevant to their world. When learning becomes an abstraction, then many students lose the motivation to study. So conducting a curriculum that caters to the students' interests can transform learning from act of mere reception to one of dynamic engagement. According to various studies, students perform better in classes that give them the initiative to make academic decisions than those that ___________ ___________.

(a) force them to complete their homework
(b) rely on inefficient outdated textbooks
(c) put an emphasis on creativity
(d) make them simply passive spectators

3 I will readily admit that for me, the idea of having accomplished my goals in life gives me great pleasure. Don't you agree that a struggling writer who remained unknown most of his life would gladly welcome fame and fortune? Some people say with certainty that money can buy happiness. _________________, this is inevitably true. However, I do believe that the realization of our ambition is merely one of many factors in our quest for fulfillment. If it is made the sole object of focus in someone's life, then they are almost certain to be miserable.

(a) At the present moment
(b) After a certain point
(c) To some degree
(d) Even more

4 Any doctor will tell you that if you are at risk of getting heart disease, then it is important to _________________. Overweight individuals or people with a family history of heart disease are among those in the high risk category. This is a serious health problem across the globe, and without aggressive prevention measures, problems will only become more serious later down the road.

(a) limit physical activity
(b) live a carefree lifestyle
(c) exercise and eat healthily
(d) consider experimental treatment

5   Self-fulfilling prophecies are predictions that bring about the predicted results. In other words, a false prophecy that is able to influence enough people can lead them to react in ways that end up fulfilling the actually untrue prophecy. One commonly referred to example involves a financially sound bank whose customers hear that it is going bankrupt. Believing the rumor to be true, they rush to remove their money, ultimately bankrupting the formally solvent institution.

Q. What is the best title for the passage?

(a) How Expectations Can Become Real
(b) Prophecies of the Future Fulfilled
(c) The Dangers of Rumors on Banks
(d) How to Influence People's Actions

6   My friends and I took the most amazing trip to Mexico last summer. We loved everything about it: the spicy food, the ancient ruins and the gorgeous beaches. The part I will remember the most, however, was scuba diving in the Caribbean. I've never known such a freedom of movement and the excitement of discovering strange and beautiful sea creatures. I even caught lobsters with a net and later cooked them for dinner. That experience helped me to realize how many different worlds exist on this single planet.

Q. Which of the following is correct according to the passage?

(a) The writer went unaccompanied on her trip.
(b) The writer enjoyed the local cuisine.
(c) The writer bought lobsters for dinner.
(d) The writer is a frequent scuba diver.

7   In the 1870s, Alferd Packer, along with five other men, attempted to cross the Rocky Mountains after being warned to wait until spring. (a) Becoming lost and running out of supplies, the expedition member resorted to cannibalism. (b) It is generally held among anthropologists that cannibalism carries a special significance for its practitioners. (c) Alferd Packer was ultimately the only survivor of the trip and made it to a nearby camp. (d) Though he claimed that he acted in self-defense, few people believed him, and he was accused of murder and sent to prison.

Chapter

05 | 대의 파악

TEPS 독해 PART II의 대의 파악 유형은 주로 main idea, main topic, purpose 등을 고르라는 문제로 출제된다. 대의 파악 유형은 보통 단락의 처음이나 마지막 문장(재진술 또는 결론)에 요약되어 있는데, 기본적으로 가장 많은 문제들이 글의 상단에 key word를 배치하고 출제된다. 글의 전체적인 흐름을 파악해야 하며 출제자의 의도가 무엇인지 짚어 나가면서 문제를 푸는 것이 중요하다.

▌독해요령 1 글 도입부에 주제문이 등장하는 경우가 많다.

영어는 글 구조가 대부분 두괄식이기 때문에 글 첫머리에 문단 주제문(topic sentence)이 등장하는 경우가 많으므로 도입부를 주의 깊게 읽어 보면 쉽게 주제문을 찾을 수 있다.

▌독해요령 2 반복되는 key word에 주목한다.

지문에서 계속 반복되는 어구들이 주제어인 경우도 많다. 이것은 일부러 글쓴이가 의도했다기보다는 글을 쓰다 보면 글쓴이가 하고 싶은 말이 여러 형태의 비슷한 의미의 단어로 paraphrase되어서 반복 등장할 수밖에 없기 때문이다.

▌독해요령 3 역접 어구 뒤를 주목한다.

주제문처럼 보이는 문장이 지문 상단에 등장한다고 할지라도 but, however, nevertheless, although 등의 역접 어구가 중간에 등장하는 경우 그 역접 어구가 이끄는 절이 지문에서 정답을 고르는 데 상당히 중요한 역할을 하는 경우가 많다. 따라서 이 역접 어구가 이끄는 절은 각별히 주의하며 읽어야 한다.

▌독해요령 4 문단의 첫 문장과 마지막 문장이 일치하는 경우를 주목한다.

글의 주제나 대의를 파악할 때, 지문의 첫 문장에 등장했던 내용이 문단의 마지막 문장에 paraphrase 되거나 재진술(restatement)되어 글의 요지를 명백하게 보여 주는 경우가 많다.

▌독해요령 5 세부적인 내용의 선택지는 답이 아님에 주의한다.

주제문을 고르는 대의 파악 유형에서는 말 그대로 지문 전체를 아우를 수 있는 핵심 어구를 묻는다. 내용의 일부나 너무 포괄적인 것이 아닌, 전체 내용을 확실히 요약한 것을 정답으로 원하는 것이다. 따라서 선택지를 고를 때 지문에 등장했던 단어나 어구가 있다고 해서 생각 없이 정답으로 고르다가는 큰코다치는 경우가 많으므로 각별히 유의하기 바란다.

Sample

Read the passage and the question. Then choose the option that best answers the question.

In the late 1940s, radio advertising was a well-established industry when television made its debut. Based upon the successful format of the radio industry, television was deliberately developed as a commercial medium, and has since become the most effective and therefore most popular means of selling products. The regular commercial breaks, not your favorite shows that they interrupt, are the main reason any modern-day television networks exist. The programming is merely a method of grabbing the audience's attention and holding it so that viewers will stay in front of the television during commercial breaks. If a viewer changes the channel, he does not watch the advertisements, so the programs need to keep viewers glued to the set in anticipation.

Q. What is the passage mainly about?

(a) The development of television programs

(b) The best commercials shown on TV

(c) Television as a means for advertising

(d) The history of television networks

어휘 **well-established** 안정된, 정착된 **debut** 등장 **deliberately** 고의적으로, 신중하게 **commercial** 광고

medium 매체 **interrupt** 중단하다 **commercial break** 광고 방송에 의한 프로그램 중단 시간

programming 프로그램 편성 **merely** 단순히, 단지 **grab** 사로잡다, 붙잡아 두다 **viewer** 시청자

glue ~에 들러붙어 떨어지지 않다, ~에서 (눈을) 떼지 않다 **anticipation** 기대, 예상

Actual Test

1   Most modern-day executives get their MBA, or Master of Business Administration. This program was formed early in the 20th century as a method of building leadership skills for those who will take the reigns of big companies. When first devised, it consisted of two years of study where students become versed in business basics. These days, however, schools have altered their course format in order to accommodate a more diverse means of completing the coursework. _________________________ has led to a much higher number of students immersed in MBA programs.

(a) This school's construction
(b) Hiring so many instructors
(c) Providing this flexibility
(d) This latest funding source

2   Chinese documents refer to the herbal usage of Ma hwang, also known as Ephedra sinica, from as far back as 2700 BC. This plant is the origin of the modern drug ephedrine, which accounts for about 2% of the entire plant. The chinese herb, and later the extracted medicine, was used to treat a number of ailments, including asthma, allergic rhinitis, upper respiratory infection and colds. It was also used and sometimes abused as a stimulant. The chemical ephedrine had such a stimulating effect, that it was at times used recreationally and was blamed for ____________ _________________. Because of these negative effects, the United States Food and Drug Administration banned its use as a medicine or supplement.

(a) being an ineffective medicine
(b) helping people to lose weight
(c) causing heart attacks and addiction
(d) being available to children

3 Did you know that too much anxiety can ___________________? During moments of high stress, a substance known as cortisol is excreted in the brain. High levels of this substance appear to damage the region of the brain that handles basic memory tasks. The impairment of these hippocampus cells can lead an individual to experience memory problems, such as having difficulty remembering addresses and names.

(a) make us sick

(b) cause forgetfulness

(c) sap our determination

(d) distract us from tasks

4 One of the most dramatic revolutions in human society happened ten thousand years ago. The Neolithic Revolution was perhaps the prime catalyst towards _________________________. Wandering nomadic tribes discovered agriculture and formed societies that were settled and stable. The division of ownership over territory grew increasingly important, and economies based on trade created inequalities between those with and without land. In general, the reliance on a grain and vegetable diet allowed populations to expand greatly. The higher the population density got, the more vulnerable the society became to disease and famine.

(a) creating an agricultural global economy

(b) mastering nature with advancing technology

(c) a hierarchical organization of social structures

(d) oppressing neighboring nomadic tribes

5 Many company bosses make a point of being receptive to employee feedback. If a
worker wants to discuss an issue that affects the company, the employer is
supposed to be all ears. The concept of company leadership has begun to change,
however, and some employees want more than an occasionally available boss.
They seek to have a stake in the influential decisions that affect their workplace.
They want to be involved in how the offices are run and experience how their
contributions are realized and appreciated.

Q. How can we characterize new attitudes to the relationship between employers
and employees?

(a) Exploitative
(b) Horizontal
(c) Positive
(d) Cooperative

6 The belief that the United States is a place where hard-working people from all
over the world can come to realize their dreams has survived for centuries, despite
a mountain of evidence and experience to the contrary. While exceptional cases of
individuals from poor families working their way to economic or political success
are loudly touted as proof of the dream, the stories of the great majority of
immigrants, minorities, and impoverished people who call the country their home
are, for the most part, simply ignored.

Q. What is the main idea of this passage?

(a) America is no longer the land of opportunity that it used to be.
(b) Exceptional individuals will certainly succeed in the United States.
(c) Surprisingly, most people have a harder time succeeding in the US than
elsewhere.
(d) The idea that America is the land of opportunity is little more than a myth.

7   A Chinese legend says that the ancient empress Xi Ling-Shi discovered silk when a silkworm cocoon fell into her tea. (a) The Chinese were the first to cultivate silk and guarded the secret carefully. (b) The use of the Silk Road declined during the Middle Ages as sea routes grew more common. (c) The Chinese emperor threatened with death anyone who revealed the secret of silk. (d) According to stories, it was a Chinese monk who smuggled the silkworms to Europe inside a hollow stick.

Chapter 06 | 글의 목적, 제목 찾기

독해 PART II에서 글의 목적(purpose)을 물어보는 유형은 거의 대부분 편지나 공지 사항이 대부분으로 난이도가 그리 높진 않지만 시간 절약을 위해 충분한 연습이 필요하다. 제목 찾기 유형 역시 자주 출제되는데 지문 전체의 내용을 가장 잘 요약한 것으로 전체를 아우르는 내용의 선택지를 고르는 것이 관건이다.

▌독해요령 1 글의 목적을 묻는 문제는 지문의 종류와 용도를 먼저 파악한다.

글의 목적을 묻는 문제는 지문의 종류가 지시 사항인지 매뉴얼인지, 편지글인지, 공지 사항인지 지문의 종류와 성격을 먼저 파악하고 나서 글을 읽어 나가면 보다 쉽게 정답에 접근할 수 있다. 주의할 점은 글의 초반과 중반은 단순한 설명문 형식을 가장해서 진행되다가 마지막 부분에서 글쓴이의 저의가 드러나는 광고 글도 있으므로 각별히 주의할 필요가 있다.

▌독해요령 2 제목 찾기 문제에서 토픽의 범위가 너무 넓거나 좁은 선택지는 답에서 제외한다.

제목 찾기 문제 역시 대의를 파악하는 문제와 대동소이하지만 한 가지 주의할 점은 선택지가 굉장히 헷갈리는 경우가 자주 있다는 것이다. 이러한 경우는 토픽을 너무 넓고 포괄적으로 잡은 선택지나, 지문에 등장했지만 너무 세부적인 내용의 선택지를 답으로 고르지 않도록 주의해야 한다.

Sample

Read the passage and the question. Then choose the option that best answers the question.

Human beings have both an outer (conscious) and inner (subconscious) mind in which we think and behave, and both are equally important. Psychologist Carl Jung asserted this theory as the basis for all of his subsequent ideas. Since we function primarily in our conscious world, it follows that we attempt to use the same behavior patterns when it comes to solving our own personal and societal problems. Yet Jung's assumption was that to resolve conscious problems people need to focus on the subconscious realm. When we do not acknowledge our inner world, we deny an essential part of our being and of society.

Q. What is the best title for the passage?

(a) The Acquisition of Social Behavior
(b) The Psychology of Thinking
(c) The Importance of the Unconscious Mind
(d) Acknowledging Problems through the Subconscious

어휘 **conscious** 의식; 의식적인 **subconscious** 잠재의식; 잠재의식의 **psychologist** 심리학자 **assert** 주장하다
subsequent 그 이후의 **function** 기능을 하다 **primarily** 주로 **it follows that ~** 당연한 결과로서 ~이 되다
when it comes to ~에 관해서라면 **societal** 사회의 **assumption** 추정, 전제 **resolve** 해결하다 **realm** 영역
acknowledge 인정하다 **being** 존재 **acquisition** 습득 **unconscious** 무의식의 **acknowledge** 인정하다

Actual Test

PART I Read the passage. Then choose the option that best completes the passage.

1 Weddings that happen anywhere can be magical moments. Nonetheless, choosing the right venue is a difficult and important task. Before you make such a decision, you should figure out what sort of space best fits ______________________. For families with budget issues, even renting a hotel hall can be an unwelcome burden. If the couple has religious compatibility, a church is an elegant and inexpensive venue for the ceremony. Outdoor wedding, typically inexpensive if not free, can provide beautiful backgrounds for your special memories.

(a) your time constraints
(b) your financial circumstances
(c) your family arrangements
(d) your need for peace of mind

2 Do not expect sunblock to be a foolproof barrier to getting skin cancer. A number of doctors claim that sunscreens fail to offer complete defense from solar rays, and should not be relied upon so faithfully. These doctors recommend using clothing to shield your head and skin. "It's a common misbelief that by applying a dab of sunscreen, one is safe from solar radiation," says Dr. Brinner. ______________, the wiser method would be to combine the use of sunscreen while limiting overall exposure.

(a) Regardless
(b) In addition
(c) As a result
(d) Likewise

3 It is no secret to scientists that _____________________. What is news is that a pleasurable indulgence seems to have similar results. Red wine, legumes and other vegetable matter contain molecules that were recently found to show age-combating properties identical to the restriction of calories. This news is expected to aid researchers who are developing anti-aging medicine and treatment for related diseases.

(a) limiting caloric intake facilitates longevity
(b) a healthy diet may increase one's stamina
(c) genetic engineering could cause many problems
(d) medicinal properties exist within tasty beverages

4 The belief that children should have a low-fat diet akin to that of grownups is misguided if not dangerous. Very young children require a diet with fat to give energy and other vitamins necessary for their critical growth stage. While unhealthy products high in sugar and salt are inappropriate, the diet of children should be rich in variety and full of calories. Once they have grown a little older and their bodies are more developed, a parent may consider adjusting their diet more towards that of an adult, which _____________________.

(a) has less fat content
(b) is much more nutritious
(c) is more balanced
(d) contains iron

5   During my career in academia, I have made certain to engage within as many disciplines as I could. It has been a source of pride that I have created new spaces within departments for interdisciplinary discourse. My greatest hope and ambition lies within this university. I believe that together, we can create a unique and dynamic environment, one of innovation, activities, and discussions that push the boundaries of the departments. At the same time, we should be pragmatic and connected with society. I consider it a privilege to work with this faculty, and an honor to direct the university in its journey towards the future.

Q. What is this passage mainly about?

(a) An assessment of someone's past career
(b) A brochure for a school
(c) A fundraising presentation
(d) A speech by someone newly appointed

6   After the earlier AIDS epidemic drew international attention and prompted a massive mobilization of resources, the issue has become less and less in the public spotlight by the mainstream media. Governments as well, apart from making occasional lip service, have failed to rally a substantive investment into treatment or prevention. In developing countries, a mere 31% of the 9.7 million people who are in desperate need for life-saving drugs are in fact receiving them. Now, not merely in Africa, but all over the world, AIDS is spreading at alarming rates, leaving no demographic spared.

Q. Which of the following is the overall tone of the above passage?

(a) Neutral
(b) Cautionary
(c) Ambitious
(d) Scathing

 Read the passage. Then identify the option that does NOT belong.

7   A rash of attacks upon immigrants in a rural Appalachian town has struck fear in the local immigrant community. (a) A Mexican migrant was beaten unconscious by a gang of high schoolers as they shouted racial slurs and told his friend to get out of their town. (b) Many parents are complaining that their children lack proper after-school activities with which to occupy their free time. (c) Human rights groups have spoken out, demanding that legal action be taken as well as multi-cultural education in order to teach tolerance and diversity. (d) Racial violence such as this has been growing as Spanish-speaking migrants move to new areas in search of work.

Chapter 07

세부 내용 및 진위 파악

세부 파악과 진위 파악 유형은 TEPS 독해에서 가장 많이 출제되는 유형으로 고도의 집중력이 요구되며 시간이 많이 소요되어 수험생들이 가장 어려워하는 유형이다. 주로 지문에서 특정 정보를 찾으라는 문제나, 지문의 내용과 일치하거나 일치하지 않는 선택지를 고르는 유형이 대부분이다. 시관 관리상 지문을 두 번 세 번 읽지 않도록 평소에 지문을 읽으면서 기억력과 집중력을 기르도록 훈련하고, 다양한 문제를 접해서 오답 함정을 피하는 요령을 익혀야 한다.

▌독해요령 1 문제와 선택지를 먼저 읽어서 집중할 부분을 파악한다.

세부 내용 파악 유형은 글 내용의 일부만 묻기보다는 지문 전체를 범위로 삼아서 선택지가 해당 지문에 등장했던 사항인지 아닌지를 묻는 경우가 많다. 따라서 질문과 선택지를 먼저 읽어서 지문에서 무엇을 요구하는지 빠르게 파악하자.

▌독해요령 2 선택지에 등장하는 극단적인 단어와 표현은 오답 함정이다.

진위나 세부 내용 파악 유형의 문제에서 가장 흔하게 등장하는 오답 선택지는 all, only, always 등의 극단적인 단어나 표현이 들어간 경우가 많다. 따라서 이런 표현이 등장한 선택지는 가급적 답에서 제외시키는 것이 좋다.

▌독해요령 3 숫자는 항상 각별히 주의한다.

세부 내용 유형에서 절대 빠뜨려서는 안 되는 사항이 바로 숫자이다. 숫자 정보는 금액이나 시간, 나이, 연도, 통계 수치 등 여러 가지로 등장하는데, 선택지에서 지문과 다르게 제시하거나 반대로 제시하는 경우도 있으므로 각별히 유의하기 바란다.

▌독해요령 4 정답은 paraphrase되어 등장함에 유의한다.

세부 내용 파악과 진위 파악에서도 정답은 거의 대부분 paraphrase되어 등장하는 것이 원칙이다. 따라서 평소에 어휘 학습을 게을리하지 말아야 한다.

▌독해요령 5 주제와 관련 있는 선택지가 정답으로 등장하는 경우가 많다.

세부 내용이나 진위 파악에서도 주제와 관련 있는 선택지가 정답 선택지로 등장하는 경우가 상당히 많기 때문에 글의 대의 정도는 파악하고 문제 풀이에 접근하는 것이 바람직하다.

Sample

Read the passage. Then choose the option that best completes the passage.

Our young patients here at Southwick Children's Hospital deserve more when it comes to comfort, convenience and privacy. It is difficult to fit all of the medical equipment they need into their cubicles. For example, there is not enough room for wheelchairs. Parents of patients usually want to accompany their children in the hospital but do not have beds. Instead, they must sleep in recliners if they wish to room in, and there is no space for their bags. Our staff works very hard to make the ward comfortable and attractive, but upgrades are needed. For all these reasons, we hope you will consider our proposal for redevelopment in order to improve the facilities for our patients, their families, and our staff.

Q. Which of the following is correct according to the report?

(a) There are no funds to improve the facility.
(b) The hospital is in need of remodeling.
(c) The hospital wards do not accommodate parents.
(d) A new wing will be built especially for children.

어휘 **comfort** 위안, 위로 **convenience** 편리함 **privacy** 사생활 **cubicle** (칸막이가 된) 작은 침실 **wing** 부속 건물 **accompany** 동반하다, 함께하다 **recliner** 등받이가 뒤로 젖혀지는 의자 **ward** 병실, 병동 **redevelopment** 재개발 **accommodate** 수용하다, 숙박시키다

PART I Read the passage. Then choose the option that best completes the passage.

1   A health study released by two leading universities confirmed what many city planners have already suggested: ___________________. It seems that even a small park located in the center of a busy area can have profound health effects on residents. Besides making an area more aesthetically pleasing, the findings show that parks lead to an increase in exercise and a general reduction in stress among city dwellers. In addition, researchers involved in this study pointed out that increasing the number of green spaces in low-income neighborhoods may help to address health inequalities that exist between the rich and the poor. It seems that wealthier individuals who live in areas where greenery is prevalent are less at risk for certain diseases than poorer residents who tend to live in more densely populated areas with few green spaces.

(a) green spaces boost health
(b) city dwellers are often ill
(c) fewer parks are being built
(d) parks increase property value

2   When traditional medicine fails, or only provides a limited amount of relief, many patients look to alternative medicine for hope. However, medical experts warn patients to be wary of untested remedies that usually fail to live up to their promises. Often advertised on the Internet with few laws to stop them, alternative medicine companies make incredible claims that patients desperate for relief may be eager to try. These websites often promote cures for diseases doctors have deemed incurable, with personal testimonies replacing hard scientific facts and reliable clinical trials. Some alternative remedies, while ineffective, may only set the patient back a few dollars, while others may cost thousands of dollars and may actually worsen a condition. It is no wonder many experts are ___________________.

(a) willing to test these new cures
(b) discovering why these cures are popular
(c) suggesting alternative medicine to patients
(d) pushing for tighter regulations

3 There is a reason why many movies that were originally panned by critics and neglected by moviegoers during their run in theaters have ________________. Some films become what are known as "guilty pleasures." Although many movies have moments that may inspire unintentional laughter, guilty pleasures are movies so poorly made and so terribly acted, there is something endearingly humorous about them. The best of the worst often gain a cult following as movie lovers watch them, usually in the comfort of their own homes, with a gleeful sense of irony.

(a) become popular rentals as the years go by

(b) made many directors wary of new scripts

(c) led to an increase in the number of theatergoers

(d) caused some actors to lose their jobs

4 For those who call one of the world's population centers their home, city life can ________________. While tourists may find a teeming metropolis an exciting place to shop, dine, and experience cultural events, residents often find city life unpleasant. Residents of small towns often report that they feel a strong sense of community, but city dwellers may feel insignificant and lonely alongside so many millions of others. The pace of the city can also be stressful, as activity never seems to slow down, and residents are caught up in the rush of hurried crowds.

(a) take a significant toll

(b) be monotonous and repetitive

(c) build a sense of independence

(d) be an energizing experience

5 For most criminals, prison is a punishment that stifles successful integration into society as a responsible citizen. Rather than redeeming criminals, the prison system often makes them worse, especially in the case of non-violent offenders. After an inmate is released from a world where violence rules and every day is strictly regimented, he is asked to build a productive life. This task is impossible without some intervention during incarceration that examines and offers ways to counter criminal behavior. The vast majority of people believe that rehabilitation programs should have a place within the prison system. Many rehabilitation programs give inmates the emotional, professional, and sometimes, spiritual tools they need to enter society again and avoid another sentence.

Q. Which of the following is true according to the report?

(a) Rehabilitation is only effective for non-violent criminals.
(b) Rehabilitation programs take place during imprisonment.
(c) Many people believe rehabilitation should replace incarceration.
(d) Criminals are often given harsher sentences than necessary.

6 Clean water is necessary to the survival of all people, but in many communities, such a supply is a luxury. However, scientists are studying the properties of a common desert plant that may have filtration capabilities. The practice of using the mucilage from prickly pear cactuses has been around in Latin America for many hundreds of years. The gooey substance, which helps the plants store water, is boiled and the resultant liquid is dumped into contaminated drinking water. Floating particles settle to the bottom and clean water rises to the top. Scientists have also discovered that mucilage can clear away arsenic in 72 hours.

Q. Which of the following is true according to the article?

(a) Arsenic is often found in drinking water in Latin America.
(b) Cactus water is very popular in the Latin American market.
(c) A chemical in mucilage dissolves harmful particles.
(d) Using mucilage to filter water is an ancient practice.

7   Many job seekers walk into an interview with nothing more than a freshly pressed suit and a resume in hand. (a) However, experts insist that a successful job interview requires preparation of the part of the interviewee. (b) First, it is important that job seekers educate themselves as much as possible about the company they hope to work for, as this makes a good impression on the interviewer. (c) Many job seekers make the mistake of embellishing their accomplishments to seem more qualified. (d) Another good tip is to rehearse answers to common questions before the interview occurs to make sure they are strong.

Chapter
08 추론 문제

추론은 지문에는 등장하지 않는 내용이지만 유추해서 정답을 골라야 하는 문제로 상당히 많이 출제된다. 단순한 paraphrase가 아닌 지문 내용을 근거로 해서 다르게 표현한 문장이 등장하므로 평소에 어휘뿐만 아니라 다양한 글을 읽고 정보를 논리적으로 분석하는 훈련이 필요하다.

▌독해요령 1 철저하게 지문에 근거해서 추론한다.

지나친 상상이나 상식을 개입시키는 것은 오답으로 가는 지름길이다. 추론 문제는 지문의 주제나 지문에 언급된 세부 내용을 읽고 논리적인 결론을 내려야 하기 때문에 상식적으로 맞아 보이는 선택지라도 지문에 근거해서 추론이 불가능한 경우는 오답일 확률이 매우 높다.

▌독해요령 2 추론 문제 역시 주제 파악은 필수이다.

추론 문제 역시 주제와 관련된 선택지가 정답으로 등장하는 경우가 많기 때문에 글의 요지나 글쓴이의 태도, 어조를 파악할 필요가 있다. 저자가 어떤 태도(attitude)를 가지고 지문을 전개해 나갔는가는 정답을 고르는 데 상당히 결정적인 역할을 할 때가 많다.

▌독해요령 3 선택지를 먼저 읽어 본다.

보통 추론 관련 문제의 선택지에는 짧은 어구보다는 하나의 완벽한 문장 형태가 많이 등장한다. 그러므로 일단 선택지를 먼저 읽고 지문을 읽으면 보다 더 정확히 문맥을 파악할 수 있다.

Read the passage and the question. Then choose the option that best answers the question.

The disease known as Type I diabetes mellitus (DM-I) is on the rise in recent decades. This has prompted researchers to revise their understanding of what causes this disease. Increasing annually by 2.8% worldwide, the incidence is up four percent annually in the UK alone. Australia reports a jump of three percent more new cases each year. Historically, DM-I was thought to be genetic, but given the sudden rise in the diagnosis, experts say the cause must include environmental factors as well.

Q. What can be inferred from the passage?

(a) The incidence of Type I diabetes is declining in adults.

(b) More needs to be done to lower the mortality rate of DM-I in Britain.

(c) Australians may not be receiving the diabetes care they need.

(d) The cause-effect relationship of DM-I needs to be re-evaluated.

어휘 **diabetes mellitus** 진성 당뇨병 **incidence** (질병의) 발생 **genetic** 유전적인 **diagnosis** 진단

Actual Test

1 By allowing workers to ______________________, telecommuting has become more and more a popular alternative. They can begin work at their leisure. They can work at night and enjoy their free-time during the day. They don't have to waste so much time driving to work. Unlike their boxed-in colleagues, they can experience a beautiful day directly. On top of this, telecommuting provides time for mothers and fathers to spend with their loved ones.

(a) get to know their co-workers better
(b) be more productive in their house
(c) adjust their work schedule to fit their needs
(d) take however much time necessary to complete tasks

2 One of America's all-time most popular television shows, *The Simpsons* is a top-rated show known around the world. ______________________, the complex and sometimes mature topics that the show deals with are controversial at times, and to some people could even be considered offensive. There is little doubt that *The Simpsons* program has an influence on the youth population.

(a) And so
(b) However
(c) Therefore
(d) As a result

3   A necessary aspect of being a mammal, aggression is also a primal motivating factor among people. Aggressive behavior can be described as any action of an animal that intends to harm a target or to scare an enemy away. Gerald M. Joss characterizes aggression as any physical or verbal behavior meant to injure or kill. Aggressive behaviors vary greatly, ranging from physical acts with a clear agenda to non-physical acts with obscured motives. _____________________, an aggressive behavior may be harmful or beneficial, unintentional or overt, and violent or psychological.

(a) For example
(b) Primarily
(c) Rather
(d) Regardless

4   Architectural designs in the early 1900's United States, for the most part, followed the late 19th century style of fancy historical motifs. Skyscrapers built during that time often entailed finely crafted Gothic or Roman features. At this time of _____________________, a few maverick artists began a movement that shifted away towards the use of natural and united forms.

(a) intricate ornamentation
(b) organic forms
(c) clean and simple designs
(d) futuristic motifs

5   Fact is, no scientist has half the amount of curiosity that any random child between the ages of four months and four years possesses. Adults often misinterpret this heightened curiosity about everything as an inability to pay attention. Children have started their learning process by the time they are born, and have already amassed an incredible amount of information as they begin kindergarten, perhaps more than what they will subsequently learn as they age. Adults should support the powerful learning process of children by simultaneously appreciating and stimulating their curiosity.

Q. Which of the following is correct according to the passage?

(a) Children's innate curiosity is a form of scientific investigation.
(b) Children should begin school at a younger age.
(c) Children's lack of focus can often be traced to an excessive amount of curiosity.
(d) Letting children explore their strong curiosity would assist in learning.

6   Standing out from masses of other cover letters is a daunting challenge. If you learn some fundamental tips, you can increase your chances of getting noticed. For starters, you should have something special included in your resume. Using a literary quote tactfully could be useful. Showing a personal connection with the place where you wish to be employed could also work in your favor. Otherwise, it is perhaps most effective to utilize a unique format that contains a strong visual impact.

Q. Which of the following is the best title for the passage?

(a) Having an Attention Grabbing Resume
(b) Why Do I Need a Resume?
(c) Acing the Application Process
(d) Recommendations on Design Formats

7   A little-known but significant provision in a new education policy will force schools to assist the military by giving the name, address, and phone number of students to military recruiters. (a) The Pentagon claims the information aids in the search for potential soldiers who will serve their nation. (b) Parents, school officials, and other citizens are worried, however, and view the recruiting tactic as a dangerous exploitation of uninformed youth. (c) Military recruiters are connected directly to their headquarters at the Pentagon. (d) School systems that refuse to cooperate with the policy risk having their funding cut.

Chapter 09

기타 유형

지문의 출처, 글쓴이의 태도나 어조, 다음에 이어질 내용을 물어보는 유형이 간혹 출제된다. 대체로 난이도가 그리 높지 않지만 속독을 통해 시간을 절약할 필요가 있는 유형으로 문제 유형별로 정답을 빨리 찾는 연습을 많이 해둘 필요가 있다.

▌독해요령 1 분위기와 태도를 묻는 유형은 반복적인 키워드에 주목한다.

글쓴이의 태도나 어조를 물어보는 문제는 반복되는 키워드나 핵심어에 주목하면 의외로 쉽게 답을 구할 수 있다. 선택지와 지문에 등장한 부정적인 단어나 긍정적인 단어에 주목할 필요가 있다. 더불어 선택지에 등장하는 단어의 뜻을 몰라 답을 못 찾는 경우도 있으므로 academic(학구적인), descriptive(서술적인), legalistic(형식적인), narrative(이야기체의), idealistic(이상주의적인), skeptical(회의적인), liberal(자유분방한) 등 글의 분위기나 태도와 관련된 어휘들을 정리하도록 하자.

▌독해요령 2 다음에 이어질 내용을 묻는 문제는 지문 마지막 문장에 주목한다.

이 유형은 예외는 있지만 대부분 마지막 문장에 결정적인 단서를 주기 때문에 이것저것 생각할 필요 없이 일단 마지막 문장부터 점검할 필요가 있다. 마지막 문장을 통해 정답을 알 수 없는 경우는 지문 첫 문장이나 중반부를 참고해야 하겠지만 이런 경우는 언어 논리상 매우 드문 경우이다.

▌독해요령 3 지문의 출처를 묻는 유형은 글의 종류부터 파악한다.

지문의 출처가 어디인가를 묻는 유형으로 지문의 성격과 종류를 재빨리 간파하는 것이 관건이다. 과학 잡지, TV 광고, 학술 논문, 수필집, 신문 등 다양한 출처에서 추출한 지문이 등장할 수 있으므로 평소 다양한 종류의 글을 읽어 보는 훈련이 필요하다.

Read the passage and the question. Then choose the option that best answers the question.

Over the last one hundred years, the Earth's average temperature has increased about 1°F. There is still debate about the exact cause of global warming, but its effects are predictable. Climate changes will lead to an alteration in rainfall patterns and sea levels, which may, in turn, result in a range of impacts on humans and wildlife. Thankfully, there are several things you can do to help slow the rate of global warming.

Q. Which discussion is likely to immediately follow the passage?

(a) Worldwide efforts to reduce greenhouse gases
(b) Possible causes of global warming
(c) Steps one can take to reduce the temperature rise
(d) Ways to alter the impacts of global warming

어휘   **debate** 논쟁 **predictable** 예측할 수 있는 **alteration** 변화 **rainfall** 강수량 **in turn** 차례로, 이번에는

Actual Test

1 The gifted American, Samuel Morse, achieved more than most men could fulfill in one lifetime: he ___________________. As a young man, he attended Yale University to study art. Later he went to London, and found a very warm reception for his creative works. In London, his sculpture of Hercules won him a gold medal from the Adelphi Society of Arts, and the Royal Academy chose two of his paintings to be exhibited. Apart from these artistic achievements, Morse is primarily known for his work with the telegraph and his invention of the communication code that bears his name. On May 24, 1844, he strung a telegraph line from Washington, DC to Baltimore and communicated a message consisting of dots and dashes, the alphabet of Morse code.

(a) turned his artwork into breakthrough discoveries
(b) studied art and science while living in multiple countries
(c) gained renown in two very distant spheres of work
(d) experimented with technology in art

2 Dorothy Parker was a multi-talented writer, who rose to fame in early twentieth century America for her clever and satiric takes on society. She landed her first paying job as a writer in 1916, when she began working for a women's magazine. Nine years later, she was writing book reviews on a regular basis in The New Yorker. ___________________ her work at The New Yorker, she was a prolific poet and author of short stories where her cynical outlook on life was an ever-present theme.

(a) Besides
(b) Regarding
(c) However
(d) Rather than

3 Marriage-related laws in the US are dealt with on the state rather than federal level. Marriage regulations, therefore, _____________________. This absence of uniformity can be seen clearly in the recognition of gay marriage, which varies from state to state. In most states, only men and women are allowed to receive the benefits of a civil union. However, same-sex couples in the states of California and Vermont receive rights as a married couple, just like any other.

(a) are frequently found to be at odds with each other
(b) are better left decided at the top levels
(c) have little effect on people's actual relationships
(d) are too complicated to be properly enforced

4 The purpose of the Socialphil Center is to nurture one's ability to speak in public _____________________. Students who participate will receive self-assuredness, pronunciation tools, organization and the capacity to deliver a well written speech in a classroom environment and outside. In short, the center endeavors to provide students with a significant edge over others who remain inexperienced in communication training.

(a) while modeling the course on public school requirements
(b) that traditional schools do not typically address
(c) through constant repetition and oral drills
(d) by immersing students in social interaction scenarios

5 Fears of terrorism has greatly impacted international tourism. Detailed statistics are not yet clear, but the downward turn is undeniable. Rather than flying in a plane, people are choosing to drive or not to travel anywhere at all. The economic devastation this is having can be seen reflected in the unemployment rates for tourism-related jobs. Bad news of this kind is unlikely to reverse for the foreseeable future.

Q. What is the passage about?

(a) The roots of political violence
(b) Lack of opportunities for employment
(c) Slowing of global travel and its effects
(d) Rates of unemployment in tourism

6 The twister watch, which is in effect until 9 pm tonight, applies to Gloucester and Harriet counties. Strong lightening activity has been reported in the region, with one Springfield house so far being hit and two people injured from lightening blasts. The torrential downpour continues to follow the twister eastward across the state. So far, hundreds of households have reportedly lost power, with many more expected before the twister's damage is done. Residents are advised to stay inside for the duration of the storm.

Q. According to the passage, which of the following statements is correct?

(a) Loss of power has occurred in thousands of households.
(b) The twister is expected to hit Harriet county by 9 pm.
(c) Two individuals have been killed by lightening.
(d) The twister is heading in an eastern direction.

7   Since humans first took to the sea, the great blue depths have inspired legends of awe and terror. (a) A popular story of the seas features Davy Jones, the ill-tempered ruler of the world beneath the sea. (b) According to the legend, any object that falls into the ocean all the way to the floor is said to end up in Davy Jones's chest. (c) One would be hard-pressed to find a sailor keen on getting a glimpse of this chest. (d) Researchers have speculated that the name "Jonah," from the Old Testament character who was trapped inside of a whale, is related to the name "Jones."

Chapter 10

흐름 찾기

TEPS 독해 중 배점이 가장 높은 파트로 독해 문제를 풀 때 가장 먼저 푸는 것이 유리하다. 주로 글 전체의 흐름을 방해하거나 무관한 문장을 고르는 유형으로 ①주제(topic)가 불일치하는 것 ②시제가 안 맞는 것 ③어조(tone)가 안 맞는 것을 고르는 문제가 주로 출제된다. 전체적으로 세부적인 글인데 같은 토픽라도 너무 포괄적인 의미의 문장이 중간에 삽입되어 있거나, 반대로 토픽이 일치하더라도 포괄적인 내용을 이야기하다 갑자기 너무 세부적인 내용을 다루는 문장이 나왔다면 흐름상 어색한 것이므로 주의하여야 한다.

▌독해요령 1 항상 주제문인 첫 문장에 주목한다.

독해 PART III에서 두 번째 문장부터 선택지 (a)가 주어지므로 주제문은 무조건 첫 문장이다. 따라서 독해 PART III을 풀 때는 첫 문장을 무조건 주제문으로 간주하고 그다음에 이어지는 선택지 중 주제문과 맞지 않는 것을 골라야 한다.

▌독해요령 2 대명사와 지시대명사에 주목한다.

글의 흐름을 파악하는 문제 중에서 대명사나 지시대명사만 눈여겨 보아도 쉽게 답을 구할 수 있는 경우가 많다. 선택지에 등장한 지시대명사나 명사를 앞 문장에서 찾을 수 없다면 그 선택지가 답이 될 확률이 매우 높다.

▌독해요령 3 글의 구조를 파악한다.

일반적인(general) 내용이 진술되는 와중에 구체적인(specific) 진술이 등장하거나 그 반대인 경우엔 그 선택지가 정답이다. topic이 일치해서 정답이 잘 안 보이는 경우에는 글의 구조를 파악해보면 답이 나오는 경우가 많다.

Sample

Read the passage. Then identify the option that does NOT belong.

Seasonal Affective Disorder, or SAD, is a mood disorder that affects as much as 6% of the world's population. (a) Countries farther from the equator may have rates as high as 20%, leading to the hypothesis that the sun's rays are directly linked to emotional stability. (b) The sun plays a role in increasing vitamin D in the blood as well. (c) Also known as Winter Depression, SAD refers to the general depressive symptoms experienced during seasonally reduced hours of sunlight. (d) These may include fatigue, decreased appetite and irritability.

어휘 **equator** 적도 **hypothesis** 가설 **stability** 안정성 **depression** 우울증 **fatigue** 피로 **appetite** 식욕 **irritability** 과민성, 화를 잘 냄

Actual Test

1   Gold, similar to the paper money of today, has historically had certain advantages over other potential currencies. Specifically, _____________________. Since ancient times, when transportation was severely limited, the wide acceptance of gold meant that it could be melted down and used as a currency in far-reaching trade among people from disparate lands and cultures. Today, gold is valid in every country in the world, despite the predominance of paper money. Because people believe that it is worth something, it is still accepted as a respectable currency.

(a) it is useful for facilitating travel
(b) it maintains a reliable market rate
(c) it can be easily reshaped and standardized
(d) it is valued for its unmatched beauty

2   While there is no one source that can be held entirely responsible for the pollution of the ozone layer, _____________________ in some regions of the globe. Farmers in Brazil were given monetary incentive by the government to set fire to their land. The devastating drought of 1997 created widespread poverty. Desperate for loans, more and more farmers carried out such burnings. The massive fires put toxic smoke into the atmosphere and the smoke clouds that were created endangered the environment and nearby communities. Many villagers ended up sick from respiratory ailments caused by the smoke.

(a) the massive burning of forests exacerbated the problem
(b) humans are being singled out as the prime suspects
(c) pollution from car exhaust is known to contribute
(d) overconsumption in developed countries was a major factor

3 Studies have proven that communication takes up more time than any other social activity. Despite this, communication is an idea that can be hard for people to discuss or define. The term can encompass nonhuman activities. One could express the manner in which animals interact with one another as a form of communication. Likewise, electronic devices are commonly referred to as communicating. __________________, communication usually signifies human interactions. So, in a sense, communication is the way in which emotions and concepts are exchanged between one another.

(a) Naturally
(b) Simply
(c) However
(d) Rather

4 Oxford University has begun what is being described as the largest fundraising campaign in Europe's history with the aim of __________________. The school is currently shooting for an ambitious $2.5 billion in order to attract the world's top academics. More than 20,000 donors had pledged nearly 1 billion dollars already. Oxford sees itself as a world-class institution, but was unable to match the monetary strength of Ivy league schools.

(a) opening up a new global research institute
(b) improving its team with top-tier athletes
(c) catching up with its wealthy US rivals
(d) getting itself out of its financial difficulties

5   Whether you are contemplating the art of Paris, sampling exquisite cuisine in Thailand, or surfing the waves in Costa Rica, there is no excuse for you to miss this opportunity to receive special rates from Grant Hotels and Inns from now until October 30, 2009. Besides these discounted prices, certain locations offer special benefits including room upgrades, complimentary dinners, tours and welcome drinks. To get a list of participating hotels or to start planning your journey, get in touch with your travel agency.

Q. What is mainly advertised in the passage?

(a) Details for a global tour package
(b) A limited special offer by Grant Hotels and Inns
(c) Tips for comfortable travelling at Grant Hotels
(d) Cheap methods to explore Thailand

6   Ever since their invention, trains have held a special place in people's hearts, evoking numberless tales, myths, and movies. A certain romantic magic made trains different from other more common modes of travel and their environmental benignity is now being appreciated. They do not pollute, they are seldom affected by bad weather and don't give you jet lag. Airplanes are much more expensive, buses are less comfortable, and trains keep you tranquil with a view of slowing passing scenery. Few people would miss buses were they to disappear. Airports are rarely scenes of sentimental romance. Most people, however, will stop to watch and admire the sight of a train as it passes by.

Q. Which of the following is correct according to the passage?

(a) Trains have inspired various creative mediums.
(b) Planes are dangerous compared to train travel.
(c) Travel by plane is a romantic way to travel.
(d) Bus travel provides the best views at cheap rates.

7   It is the juxtaposition of the traditional and modern that makes Beijing most exciting to me. (a) There is no shortage of international food to find in Beijing, but traditional cuisine may be difficult for some visitors to stomach. (b) Mao Zedong's shining face can be seen overlooking stock traders fighting over international trade fluctuations. (c) While technology now permeates China, websites considered as critical of the government are blocked. (d) Beijing epitomizes and embraces these contradictions, unabashedly moving forward at a rapid pace.

TEPS 4대 영역을 한 권에 아우르는 점수대별 전략서

New
TEPS MASTER 900

Answer Book

New TEPS MASTER 900

정답 및 해설

Sample

1 **해석** W: 내가 항상 너를 따라 다니면서 뒷정리를 해야겠니?

M: 제가 뭘 잘못했는데요? 제 방은 깨끗해요.

W: 네 책들이 왜 부엌 탁자 위에 있는데?

M: ___________________

(a) 제가 거기에 뒀어요.

(b) 거기에다 놓지 않았으면 좋겠어요.

(c) 방과 후에 데리러 오면 돼요.

(d) 아, 그거요. 막 치우려던 참이었어요.

해설 여자가 어지르지 말라고 하면서 왜 책들을 부엌 탁자 위에 두었는지 묻고 있다. pick up after *sb*와 pick up *sb*를 혼동하지 않도록 주의한다.

어휘 pick up after *sb* ~의 뒷정리를 하다

pick up *sb* ~를 데리러 가다

put away 치우다

정답 (d)

2 **해석** M: 로저 송별 파티를 누가 주최하기로 되어 있나요?

W: ___________________

(a) 아니요, 그들을 배웅할 필요 없어요.

(b) 자넷이 이미 초대장을 보냈는데요.

(c) 내일 그것을 배달하면 어떨까요?

(d) 제가 알기로는 패트리샤입니다.

해설 파티를 여는 행위의 주체를 묻고 있으므로 행위의 주체를 밝히는 (d)가 정답이다. (a), (b)는 질문지에 등장한 send-off를 이용해서 혼동을 유발하는 오답 선택지이다. (c)는 send-off의 연상 어휘 deliver를 이용해서 오답을 유도하고 있다.

어휘 send-off party 송별회, 환송회

정답 (d)

3 **해석** W: 공원의 콘서트가 언제 시작하나요?

M: ___________________

(a) 아니요, 어젯밤 공원에 가지 않았어요.

(b) 예, 여기가 주차하기에 좋은 장소네요.

(c) 오늘 밤 7시에 시작합니다.

(d) 오늘 오후 2시에 정확히 시작했습니다.

해설 의문사 When으로 시작하여 콘서트가 언제 시작하는

지를 묻는 문제이다. 질문의 begin을 정답에서는 commences로 paraphrasing해서 표현한 것이 주목해야 할 점이다.

어휘 commence 시작하다

정답 (c)

4 **해석** M: 실례합니다. 공항 이용권이 얼마죠?

W: 내국인이시면 20달러입니다.

M: 좋아요. 어디서 살 수 있죠?

W: ___________________

(a) 탑승권을 보여 주셔야 할 겁니다, 고객님.

(b) 아무 슈퍼마켓에서나 구입하실 수 있습니다.

(c) 그 얘긴 내일 다시 합시다.

(d) 어느 안내 데스크에서나 구입 가능합니다.

해설 의문사 Where로 장소를 묻고 있으므로 (b)와 (d)가 답으로 가능하지만, 일반적으로 공항 이용권을 슈퍼마켓에서 팔 리가 만무하므로 (d)가 더 적절하다. (c)는 처음 만난 사람끼리 할 수 있는 말로서는 적절하지 않다.

어휘 airport user fee ticket 공항 이용권

local 내국인의

get back to 나중에 다시 이야기하다, 다시 연락하다

정답 (d)

Actual Test

1 **해석** W: 이건 너랑 나만 알고 있어야 해. 비밀 지켜.

M: ___________________

(a) 됐어. 너 가져.

(b) 비밀 지킬게.

(c) 도와줘서 고마워.

(d) 선물 고마워. 정말 고마워.

해설 keep *sth* to oneself는 '~을 비밀로 하다'라는 표현이다. 따라서 입을 봉하겠다는 My lips are sealed.라는 답변이 가장 자연스럽다. 그러므로 정답은 (b)이다.

어휘 keep *sth* to oneself ~을 비밀로 하다

seal (입을) 꼭 다물다, 봉하다

정답 (b)

2 **해석** W: 피자에 어떤 토핑을 올릴까?

M: ___________________

(a) 지금 돈이 하나도 없어.

(b) 그건 부엌 식탁 위에 있어.

(c) 난 배가 좀 고프니까 큰 걸로 할게.

(d) 내가 직접 올릴게. 고마워.

해설 fix는 식사나 음식 따위를 '준비하다, 만들다'의 의미를 지니고 있다. 어떤 토핑을 올려야 할지 고민하는 여자에게 남자가 직접 토핑을 올리겠다고 대답하는 (d)가 정답이다.

어휘 fix (음식을) 만들다, 준비하다

정답 (d)

3 **해석** W: 그 남자애는 다른 학생들을 괴롭혀서 월터 선생님한테 벌을 받았어.

M: _______________________

(a) 월터 선생님은 다른 사람들을 괴롭히는 걸 좋아해.

(b) 그녀는 가장 마음이 따뜻한 분이야.

(c) 제발 걔가 이제부터라도 말을 잘 들었으면 좋겠다.

(d) 나 놀리지 마.

해설 선택지에 열거된 답변들을 잘 해석해 보면 (c)가 문맥상 가장 자연스럽다는 것을 알 수 있다. (a)에서 pick on은 '괴롭히다'라는 뜻이다. 따라서 정답은 (c)이다.

어휘 bully 괴롭히다, 왕따 시키다

pick on *sb* 괴롭히다, 못살게 굴다

make fun of *sb* ~를 놀리다

정답 (c)

4 **해석** M: 속도 좀 낮춰. 제한 속도가 45마일(약 70km)이야.

W: 진정해. 딱 그 속도로 달리는 중이야.

M: 차선 바꾸기 전에 백미러 꼭 확인해.

W: _______________________

(a) 차를 길가에 대고 거울 좀 점검해 볼게.

(b) 거울에는 문제없어.

(c) 운전 요령 좀 알려 주면 안 될까?

(d) 잔소리 좀 그만해. 내가 책임지고 운전할 수 있도록 믿어 줄래?

해설 nag는 '성가시게 잔소리하다'라는 뜻을 나타낸다. 남자가 여자를 믿지 못하고 자꾸 잔소리하고 있는 상황이다. 따라서 여자의 응답은 잔소리 좀 그만하고 믿어 달라는 내용이어야 자연스럽다.

어휘 rear-view mirror 백미러

pull over 길가에 차를 세우다

nag 잔소리하다

정답 (d)

5. **해석** M: 이번 학기 과목 하나를 취소하기에는 너무 늦었나?

W: 가능해. 무슨 과목을 취소하려고?

M: 세계 금융 과목이 재미없어서. 대신 철학으로 바꾸고 싶어.

W: _______________________

(a) 갑자기 철학 과목에 무슨 문제라도 생겼어?

(b) 알았어. 실리적인 것보다는 흥미 있는 것을 공부하기로 결정한 모양이구나.

(c) 너는 우등으로 졸업할 자격을 갖추었어.

(d) 내가 대학에 들어오기 전에 너 같은 사람과 이야기를 했어야 했는데.

해설 drop a course는 '과목을 취소하다'라는 뜻이다. 문맥상 보기의 다른 대답들은 어색하고 남자가 철학 과목으로 수강 변경을 하는 것에 동의하는 내용인 (b)가 가장 적절하다.

어휘 drop a course 강좌[수강]를 취소하다

switch to ~로 변경하다, 바꾸다

all of a sudden 갑자기

profitable 돈 되는, 이익이 되는

graduate with honors 우등으로 졸업하다

정답 (b)

6 **해석** W: 손님, 아주 탁월한 선택을 하셨습니다. 이 지갑은 불티나게 팔리고 있는 제품입니다.

M: 그래요? 음, 제 아내는 흰색이면 뭐든 다 좋아해요.

W: 제 생각에 사모님 안목이 높으신 것 같아요. 사실 이 제품은 일류 디자이너의 작품이거든요. 추가로 다른 것들도 보여 드릴까요?

M: 실은 제가 가봐야 해서요. 근데 제 아이가 화장실에 가고 싶다네요.

W: 알겠습니다. 50미터 가셔서 왼편에 있습니다. 푸드 코트에 미처 못 가서 있어요.

M: 고마워요. 딸아이가 거의 30분이나 참고 있었거든요.

W: 어머, 죄송합니다, 손님. 여자 화장실은 1층 안내 센터 옆에 있습니다.

Q. 다음 중 남자의 딸에 대하여 옳은 것은 어느 것인가?

(a) 한 시간 이상 기다렸다.

(b) 여자는 딸의 성별을 착각했다.

(c) 지갑에 관심이 있다.

(d) 푸드 코트에 가고 싶어 한다.

해설 여직원은 아이가 남자라고 생각하여 남자 화장실을 안내하였으나, 남자 손님이 she라고 언급하자 다급히 1층에 있는 여자 화장실을 안내하였다. (a) 한 시간이 아니라 30분 정도 기다렸고, (c) 지갑에 관심 있는 사

람은 남자 손님이며, (d) 푸드 코트에 가고 싶어 하는
것이 아니라 남자 화장실의 위치가 푸드 코트 근처이
고, 아이가 가고 싶어 하는 곳은 화장실이다. 따라서
정답은 (b)이다.

어휘 sell like hot cakes 불티나게 팔리다
have a good taste 안목이 높다
gender 성별

정답 (b)

7 **해석** 당신은 커피광입니까? 한 잔의 커피를 가장 좋아하는
후식으로 꼽을 수 있습니까? 단순한 블랙, 라떼, 그리
고 카푸치노 이상의 무언가를 원하십니까? 만약 그렇
다면 아주 획기적인 소식이 있습니다. 데어리 지니가
바로 당신이 찾고 있던 것입니다. 내장된 10개의 조리
법 중 하나를 간단히 따라해 보시거나 사용자 설정을
이용해서 독창적으로 조리해 보세요. 그러면 당신이
오늘 무엇을 원하든지 간에 자신만의 완벽한 스타일의
커피를 창출할 수 있을 것입니다.
Q. 데어리 지니에 관하여 다음 중 어느 것이 옳은가?
(a) 가격이 경쟁사보다 낮다.
(b) 카푸치노 조리법이 딸려 있다.
(c) 독특한 맛을 만들기 위해 사용될 수 있다.
(d) 많은 구입처에서 구할 수 있다.

해설 선택지의 (a), (b), (d)에서 설명하는 가격, 카푸치노 조
리법, 구입처는 언급되지 않았다. 내용 중 the
custom setting for your own creations나 the
perfect style of coffee 같은 표현이 unique
flavors(독특한 맛)와 일맥상통한다. 따라서 정답은
(c)이다.

어휘 fanatic 광신자, 매니아
built-in 내장된
custom setting 사용자 설정
crave 원하다, 갈망하다
competition 경쟁사 제품
come with ~이 딸려 있다

정답 (c)

Sample

1 **해석** W: 여자 친구를 같이 데려오는 게 어때?
M: ______________________
(a) 그녀가 굉장히 좋아할 거야.
(b) 그녀가 오고 싶어 하지 않았기 때문이야.
(c) 이런, 몰랐어.
(d) 재미있었다고 생각했는데.

해설 Why don't you ~ ?로 제안을 하고 있다. 그녀가 굉
장히 좋아할 것이라고 맞장구치는 (a)가 가장 적절한
응답이 된다. 질문을 Why didn't you bring your
girlfriend with you?로 혼동하여 (b)로 대답하지 않
도록 주의하자.

어휘 bring *sb* along ~를 데리고 오다
be thrilled at ~에 전율을 느끼다, ~을 무척 반기다

정답 (a)

2 **해석** W: 참 좋은 식당이구나. 정말 맛있게 먹었어.
M: 디저트를 먹게 너무 배가 부르진 않으면 좋겠네.
이 동네에서 가장 맛있는 케이크를 팔거든.
W: 이 식당을 어떻게 알았니?
M: ______________________
(a) 아무것도 못 들었는데.
(b) 그냥 메뉴 봤어.
(c) 원하면 파이를 먹어도 돼.
(d) 신문에서 평을 읽었어.

해설 I hope you saved room for dessert.는 말 그대
로 디저트를 먹을 수 있게 위에 공간이 남아 있으면
좋겠다는 의미이다. 식당에서 종업원이 디저트를 먹겠
냐는 표현으로도 흔히 들을 수 있는 말이다.

어휘 room 공간, 여유
review (식당, 책, 영화 등에 대한) 평

정답 (d)

3 **해석** W: 그 식당 스테이크 어떠셨어요?
M: ______________________
(a) 육즙이 풍부하더군요.
(b) 45분 동안이요.
(c) 350도예요.
(d) 오븐에서요.

해설 의문사 How로 음식이 마음에 들었는지 묻고 있으므로
좋았다거나 나빴다거나 하는 응답이 가장 적절하다. turn

out의 의미를 알고 있어야 정확한 답을 고를 수 있다.

어휘 turn out ~임이 밝혀지다

　　　 succulent 즙[수분]이 많은

정답 (a)

4 해석 M: 러시아인들은 육류를 많이 먹지 않나요?

　　　 W: 물론이죠. 저희는 모든 종류의 육류 요리를 먹어요.

　　　 M: 어떤 육류 요리를 가장 좋아하나요?

　　　 W: ____________________

　　　 (a) 생각하시는 것보다 소 목장이 많아요.

　　　 (b) 돼지고기가 쇠고기보다 싸요.

　　　 (c) 감자랑 양배추요.

　　　 (d) 소시지는 누구나 좋아해요.

해설 많은 러시아 육류 요리 중에서 어떤 것을 좋아하느냐고 물었으므로 답변은 고기가 들어간 음식이 될 것이다.

어휘 meat eater 고기를 먹는 사람

　　　 cattle 소

　　　 ranch 목장, 방목장

　　　 cabbage 양배추

정답 (d)

Actual Test

1 해석 M: 나 형하고 어젯밤 대판 싸웠어.

　　　 W: ____________________

　　　 (a) 드디어!

　　　 (b) 누구랑 이야기했어?

　　　 (c) 곧 서로 화해하길 바랄게.

　　　 (d) 알아. 오빠는 항상 너를 높이 평가하잖아.

해설 make up은 '화해하다'라는 뜻으로 정답은 (c)이다. 참고로 (d)의 think highly of *sb*는 '~를 존경하다, 높이 평가하다'라는 뜻이다.

어휘 argument 말다툼

　　　 It's about time! 이제야! 드디어!

　　　 make up 화해하다

　　　 think highly of ~를 높이 평가하다, 존중하다

정답 (c)

2 해석 W: 교수님 때문에 오늘 지루해서 죽을 뻔했어.

　　　 M: ____________________

　　　 (a) 이제 훨씬 나아 보인다.

　　　 (b) 맞아. 그리 재미있는 분은 아니야.

　　　 (c) 그분 도와주려고 한 사람이 있었어?

　　　 (d) 나도 그분 수업 좋아해.

해설 bored to death는 '지루해서 죽을 것 같다'라는 의미이다. (a)와 (c)는 여자의 말과 관련 없는 대답이고, (d)는 여자의 말에 동의하는 응답이지만 내용이 정반대라서 틀렸다. 따라서 정답은 (b)이다.

어휘 bore *sb* to death ~를 엄청 지루하게 만들다

　　　 entertaining 재미있는

정답 (b)

3 해석 M: 당신이 우리 결혼기념일을 잊어버리다니 믿기지가 않아!

　　　 W: ____________________

　　　 (a) 이 문제들에 관해서는 내 판단을 믿어 주길 바라.

　　　 (b) 친절한 말씀 정말 고맙습니다.

　　　 (c) 이 순간을 위해 아껴 두었던 놀라운 소식이 있어.

　　　 (d) 다시는 그런 실수 없을 거라고 맹세할게.

해설 문맥상 anniversary는 '결혼기념일' 정도로 생각할 수 있다. 이에 대한 여자의 답변으로는 당연히 (d)가 자연스럽다.

어휘 anniversary 기념일

　　　 surprise 놀랄 만한 일[소식]

정답 (d)

4 해석 W: 요즘 여기는 엄청 시원하고 쾌적해.

　　　 M: 맞아. 드디어 에어컨이 고쳐져서 좋아.

　　　 W: 다행이야! 몇 주 전에는 참을 수 없었어.

　　　 M: ____________________

　　　 (a) 물론이지. 곧 수리될 거야.

　　　 (b) 눈치채다니 놀라워.

　　　 (c) 글쎄, 그거 아직 작업 중인데.

　　　 (d) 그러게! 엄청 더웠어.

해설 대화의 흐름상 여자의 말에 대한 남자의 반응으로는 동의하는 어조의 대답이어야 한다. scorching은 '타는 듯한, 무더운'이라는 뜻이다. 따라서 정답은 (d)이다.

어휘 nice and cool 상쾌하게 서늘한

　　　 What a relief! 다행이야!

　　　 unbearable 참을 수 없는

　　　 in no time 곧

　　　 You're telling me! 정말 그래! 네 말이 맞아!

　　　 scorching 몹시 더운, 타는 듯한

정답 (d)

5 해석　W: 마크, 아직 방 청소 안 했네.

M: 엄마, 죄송해요. 오후에 할게요.

W: 지금 해야 돼. 안 그러면 외출 금지다.

M: ＿＿＿＿＿＿＿＿＿＿＿＿

(a) 부모님이 외출을 못 하게 할 거예요.

(b) 아니요, 땅에 아무것도 없는걸요.

(c) 당장 할게요.

(d) 지금 청소하시는 게 나을 거예요.

해설　여기서 ground는 '벌로 외출을 금지시키다' 라는 뜻의 동사로 사용되었다. 대다수의 청소년들이 외출 금지를 두려워하므로 마크의 대답으로는 '당장 하겠다' 는 (c)의 답변이 가장 적합하다.

어휘　ground 외출 금지시키다

get right on *sth* 당장 ~하다

정답　(c)

6 해석　M: 브라운 박사님, 잠깐 시간 되세요?

W: 네. 환자의 상태는 어떤가요?

M: 유감스럽게도 별로 좋지 않아요. 열이 많이 나는데다가 목구멍이 부어 있어요.

W: 그 밖에 다른 이상 증세가 보였나요?

M: 사실 팔다리에 피부 발진이 나타났는데 염증이 심해 보였어요.

W: 이상하군요. 브래드쇼 박사님에게도 환자를 살펴보라고 부탁하고 싶네요. 그분의 답변을 들어 보고 나서 어떻게 치료할지 결정을 내리겠어요.

Q. 이후 발생할 일로 가장 적합한 것은 무엇인가?

(a) 환자의 상태가 계속 악화될 것이다.

(b) 의사들은 처치 전에 진단 결과를 비교할 것이다.

(c) 두 의사에 의해 병이 오진될 것이다.

(d) 환자는 완전히 회복될 것이다.

해설　대화의 마지막에서 브라운 박사는 브래드쇼 박사의 의견을 들어 보고 치료 방법을 결정하겠다고 하였으니 (b)의 상황이 벌어질 것으로 예상된다.

어휘　be running a temperature 열이 있는

swollen 부은

rash 발진, 뾰루지

irritated 염증이 난, 쓰라린

peculiar 이상한, 특이한

feedback 평가 정보, 의견

deteriorate 악화되다

diagnosis 진단

proceeding 처치, 처리

misdiagnose 오진하다

rehabilitate 회복시키다, 재활시키다

정답　(b)

7 해석　여러분의 식습관은 여러분이 미국에서 가장 흔한 형태의 암인 피부암에 걸리게 되는 주요인이 될 수 있습니다. 오랫동안 피부암의 주범은 자외선이라고 알려져 있어서 사람들은 햇빛을 피하고 자외선 차단제를 발랐습니다. 그러나 최근의 연구에 의하면 지방, 무기질, 비타민 B를 포함하는 양분 섭취 역시 고려되어야 한다고 합니다.

Q. 이 담화문의 주제는 무엇인가?

(a) 자외선과 암의 관계

(b) 태양으로부터 안전을 확보하는 방법

(c) 암 예방 활동

(d) 영양분이 어떻게 피부암 발생률을 줄일 수 있는가

해설　diet(식습관), nutritional intake(양분 섭취) 등의 중심어를 포착할 수 있어야 한다. 자외선 외에 양분 섭취가 피부암 발생에 영향을 준다고 했으므로 이와 가장 관련이 있는 (d)가 정답이 된다.

어휘　culprit 범인, (문제의) 원인

ultraviolet light 자외선

apply 바르다

nutrition 영양(소)

정답　(d)

Sample

1 **해석** M: 어젯밤에 〈포레스트 검프〉를 봤는데 아직도 여운이
많이 남네요.

W: 네, 저도 가장 좋아하는 영화들 중에 하나예요.

M: 그 영화가 언제 제작됐는지 아세요?

W: ＿＿＿＿＿＿＿＿＿＿＿＿

(a) 전 그 영화의 가장 큰 투자자입니다.

(b) 약 10년 전일 겁니다.

(c) 그 영화를 본 적이 없어서 잘 모르겠네요.

(d) 그 영화를 왜 안 보신 거죠?

해설 간접의문문은 의문사가 있는 문장 앞에 Do you
know를 써서 의문사가 있는 절의 어순을 의문문 어
순이 아닌 평서문 어순(의문사 + 주어 + 동사)으로 만
든 것을 말한다. When was the film made?라고
해도 되는데 Do you know를 넣어 헷갈리게 하는
것이다. 이때는 의문사 When에 초점을 두고 들어서
시간 정보가 나오는 것을 답으로 고르면 된다.

어휘 impression 인상

investor 투자자

presume 가정하다, 추정하다

how come 왜(= why)

정답 (b)

2 **해석** M: 실례합니다. 그 잡지 좀 빌려 보면 안 될까요?

W: ＿＿＿＿＿＿＿＿＿＿＿＿

(a) 안 돼요, 어서 하세요.

(b) 안 돼요, 시도해 보세요.

(c) 그럼요, 당신은 그렇게 하시면 안 돼요.

(d) 그럼요, 저는 다 봤어요.

해설 Do you mind로 시작되는 의문문은 응답에 주의해
야 한다. mind는 '꺼리다, 싫어하다'라는 의미이다.
그러므로 상대방에게 긍정적으로 허가할 땐 싫지 않다
고 하는 No, Not at all 등이 와야 하고, 싫다고 할
때는 Yes, Sure 등이 온다. (a)는 긍정의 Sure로 답
하지만 문맥상 부정이므로 뒤의 go ahead(어서 하세
요)와 같이 쓸 수 없다. 따라서 정답은 (d).

어휘 Go ahead. 먼저[어서] 하세요.

Go for it! 자, 해봐! 힘내!

정답 (d)

3 **해석** M: 엄마, 이거 엄마가 주문한 자동차 번호판 맞죠?

W: ＿＿＿＿＿＿＿＿＿＿＿＿

(a) 맞아. 그런데 이틀 전에 올 줄 알았는데.

(b) 이 접시들은 우리 집 식당에 완벽하게 어울릴 거야.

(c) 이 접시는 이가 빠졌네. 컵도 그렇고.

(d) 맞아. 내 새 자동차 면허증이 어제 왔어.

해설 부가의문문의 적절한 응답을 고르는 문제이다. 일반
의문문과 똑같이 응답하면 된다. 이 문제의 경우 어휘
지식이 문제 해결에 결정적인 역할을 한다. license
plate가 '자동차 번호판'이라는 걸 모르면 순발력 있
게 답을 고르기가 어렵다. (b)와 (c)는 plate의 '접시'
라는 의미로 혼동을 유발한다. (d)는 license로 혼동
을 일으키고 있다.

어휘 license plate 자동차 번호판

plate 접시

chip 깨지다, 이가 빠지다

정답 (a)

4 **해석** W: 실례합니다. 가족 입장권 3장 부탁합니다.

M: 네, 부인. 먼저 주민등록번호를 알려 주세요.

W: 10세 이하 어린이는 입장이 무료죠, 그렇지 않나요?

M: ＿＿＿＿＿＿＿＿＿＿＿＿

(a) 맞아요, 그들도 역시 돈을 내야 합니다.

(b) 죄송하지만 할인된 가격을 내야 합니다.

(c) 저희 놀이 공원은 아이들에게 가장 좋은 장소입니다.

(d) 좋아요, 내일 그들에게 말해 볼게요.

해설 여자가 10세 이하의 어린이는 공짜가 맞는지 묻고 있
으므로 공짜인지 아닌지 밝혀 주는 직접 응답이 오거
나, 선택지 (b)처럼 할인된 가격을 내야 한다는 간접
응답이 올 수 있다. (a) Yes(무료)라고 응답하고 나서
돈을 내야 한다고 말한 것은 모순이다. (c)와 (d)는 동
문서답이다.

어휘 admit 입장을 허락하다

as well 역시

discounted price 할인가

정답 (b)

Actual Test

1 **해석** M: 부딪쳐서 죄송합니다.

W: ＿＿＿＿＿＿＿＿＿＿＿＿

(a) 제가 당신을 여기서 만날 줄 알았어요.

(b) 천만의 말씀입니다.

(c) 괜찮아요.

(d) 그렇게 화낼 필요는 없어요.

해설 run into는 '충돌하다, 부딪치다' 라는 뜻의 숙어이다. 실수로 상대에게 부딪치고 사과하는 사람에 대한 응답으로는 '괜찮다.' 정도로 표현하는 것이 자연스럽다. (a)에서 run into는 '우연히 만나다' 라는 의미로 사용되었다. 따라서 정답은 (c)이다.

어휘 run into 우연히 만나다, 부딪치다(= bump into)
You are more than welcome. 천만에요.
(= You're welcome.의 강조. 감사에 대한 응답)

정답 (c)

---

2 **해석** W: 오늘 날씨 어때?

M: _________________

(a) 날씨가 좋든 나쁘든 상관없어.

(b) 불이 꺼져 있어.

(c) 내일은 날씨가 흐릴 거야.

(d) 참을 수 없어.

해설 여자는 오늘의 날씨를 묻고 있는데, (a)에서는 weather와 발음이 유사한 whether를 사용하여 혼동을 주고 있다. 가장 자연스러운 대답은 참을 수 없이 춥다[덥다]라는 의미를 내포하는 (d)가 되겠다.

어휘 unbearable 견딜 수 없는, 참기 어려운

정답 (d)

---

3 **해석** M: 어제 배운 단원을 복습합시다.

W: _________________

(a) 시험은 예상보다 시간이 오래 걸렸어요.

(b) 그래요. 집에 갈 시간이군요.

(c) 알아요. 제 원고를 검토하지 않으셔도 돼요.

(d) 좋아요. 그거 끝나면 집에 가도 되는 거죠.

해설 복습하자는 선생님의 제안에 대한 답변으로는 (d)가 가장 적합하다.

어휘 review 복습하다
quiz 간단한 시험
manuscript 원고

정답 (d)

---

4 **해석** M: 지쳐 보인다. 어제 밤새 놀았니?

W: 전혀 아니거든. 밤새도록 친구한테 줄 CD를 만들려고 했는데 결국 안 되었어.

M: 이따금 그런 프로그램은 이해하는 데 시간이 좀 걸려.

W: _________________

(a) 저렴한 CD를 살 수 있는 좋은 곳이 어디니?

(b) 기술이 좋은 게 아니라는 걸 난 알고 있었어.

(c) 올바로 작동시키는 방법에 대해 조언 좀 해줄래?

(d) 어떤 게 내가 좋아하는 CD인지 거의 구분할 수 있어.

해설 CD 만드느라 밤새 고생만 하고 실패했다는 여자의 말에 남자가 프로그램 작동법을 아는 듯한 대답을 하고 있으므로 이어지는 여자의 말은 (c)가 적절하다.

어휘 exhausted 지친
stay up 밤샘하다, 밤새 깨어 있다
far from ~이기는 커녕
ultimately 결국
figure out 이해하다, 판단하다

정답 (c)

---

5 **해석** M: 우리 학생 영화 제작이 취소되었다니 참 실망스러워.

W: 왜 그렇게 열 받아 있는 거니?

M: 클레어랑 내가 이 영화를 만드는 일로 신이 났었거든. 우리는 공동으로 대본을 썼고 많은 시간을 투자했어.

W: _________________

(a) 사전에 잘 준비하지 않으면 생기는 일이 바로 그런 거야.

(b) 걔가 너를 그렇게 대했다니 유감이군.

(c) 넌 바른 행동을 해야 해. 그러고 나서 걔한테 네 감정을 말해야 해.

(d) 그냥 클레어랑 함께했던 시간에 의의를 두는 수밖에.

해설 영화 제작의 취소로 좌절 상태에 빠져 있는 남자에게 할 수 있는 말은 위로의 말이다. 여기서는 문맥상 결과적으로 영화를 완성시키지는 못했으나 영화를 기획하면서 보낸 시간을 소중히 하라는 격려의 말이 가장 적절할 것이다. 따라서 정답은 (d)이다.

어휘 letdown 실망, 허탈감
appreciate 가치를 인정하다, 높이 평가하다

정답 (d)

---

6 **해석** W: 안녕하세요? 저는 BBC의 자넷 웬델입니다. 잠시 인터뷰를 해도 될까요?

M: 물론이죠. 그러세요.

W: 토네이도의 타격을 입은 지역 출신이신가요?

M: 네. 제 집은 휴스턴 시내에 있습니다.

W: 최근의 토네이도가 선생님의 주택 상태에 어떠한

영향을 주었나요?

M: 제 집은 현재 4일간 홍수에 잠겨 있습니다.

W: 그러면 제 생각에 선생님은 집에 들어갈 수 없으신 거군요.

M: 맞아요. 홍수가 해결될 때까지는 시에서 마련한 임시 거처로 이주하여 지내도록 된 상황이죠.

Q. 대화에 의하면 다음 중 어느 것이 옳은가?

(a) 여자의 집은 토네이도가 지나가면서 홍수에 잠겼다.

(b) 토네이도는 남자가 정부의 방공호에서 생활하도록 만들었다.

(c) 남자는 일주일간 부랑자 생활을 해왔다.

(d) 남자는 4일 안에 집으로 돌아갈 수 있다.

해설 홍수의 피해를 입은 것은 남자이므로 (a)는 적절치 않고, 남자는 4일간 집에 들어가지 못했으므로 (c)도 틀렸다. 남자가 집에 복귀하는 시점은 홍수가 해결되는 시점이므로 아직 불확실하다. 그러므로 (d)도 맞지 않는 내용이다. 토네이도로 인해 남자는 임시 거처에서 지내는 것이므로 (b)가 정답이다.

어휘 **flood** 물에 잠기게 하다, 홍수 지게 하다
shelter 피난처, 쉼터
flooding 홍수
subside 가라앉다, 진정되다, (홍수가) 빠지다

정답 (b)

7 해석 그린란드의 섬에 방문하는 사람들은 그곳의 광경을 보고 놀랄 것이다. 북대서양에 위치한 이 섬은 전혀 초록색을 띠고 있지 않다. 심지어 여름에도 섬의 대부분은 얼음과 눈에 묻혀 있다. 그러면 왜 이 순백의 땅이 겉보기에 어울리지 않는 그러한 이름을 갖게 된 것일까? 사실, 그린란드는 철자상의 실수로 그렇게 된 것인지도 모른다. 예전에 그 섬은 그런트란드(Gruntland)로 알려져 있었는데, 그것은 해안선을 따라 얕게 조성된 해변을 가리킨다. 그 이름이 유럽의 방문객들에 의해 잘못 기록되었을 가능성이 있고, 그래서 혼동을 가져온 것일 수 있다.

Q. 지문에 따르면 섬을 방문하는 사람들이 왜 놀라는가?

(a) 그들이 보는 광경과 섬의 이름이 어울리지 않기 때문에

(b) 그 섬이 예전에 그런트란드라고 불렸기 때문에

(c) 방문객이 많지 않아서

(d) 유럽으로부터 멀리 떨어진 곳에 위치해 있어서

해설 지문을 잘 들어 보면 그린란드는 초록색과 별로 관련이 없다는 것을 알 수 있다. 따라서 이름과 실제 풍경의 불일치로 인해 놀라게 된다는 (a)가 정답이다.

어휘 **frosty** 서리가 내린, 순백의
seemingly 겉보기에, 표면상
incongruent 모순되는, 일치하지 않는
refer to 나타내다, 가리키다
bay (바다, 호수의) 만

정답 (a)

Sample

1 **해석** W: 다음 주 월요일에 영화 보러 갈래, 축구하러 갈래?

M: _____________________

(a) 응, 나는 다음 주 월요일에 한가해.

(b) 영화를 보는 것은 내가 좋아하는 것 중에 하나야.

(c) 영화를 보고 싶어.

(d) 응, 나는 하키를 하고 싶어.

해설 선택의문문에는 Yes나 No로 대답할 수 없으므로 (a)와 (d)는 답에서 제외시킨다. 질문이 양자택일을 원하므로 응답 역시 둘 중에 하나를 택해서 응답하면 된다. 따라서 정답은 (c)이다.

정답 (c)

2 **해석** W: 크리스, 오늘 밤 나랑 저녁 식사 함께 할래?

M: 좋아! 근사한 거 먹자.

W: 쇠고기와 돼지고기 중에 어떤 거 먹을래?

M: _____________________

(a) 왜 그런 것들을 권하는 거지?

(b) 네가 원하는 건 아무거나 괜찮아.

(c) 고마워, 난 생선 먹을래.

(d) 아니, 난 돼지고기 싫어. 지방이 너무 많거든.

해설 선택의문문은 A or B 혹은 A, B, or C의 형태로 등장한다. 답변은 제시된 것들 중 하나를 선택하거나 제3의 선택 또는 선택을 포기하는 응답도 가능하다. 난이도가 높은 문제는 제3의 선택이나 이 문제처럼 선택을 포기하는 선택지가 정답으로 제시되기도 한다. 선택의문문에서는 Yes나 No로 응답할 수 없으므로 (d)는 답에서 제외한다.

어휘 pork 돼지고기

suggest 제안하다, 권하다

정답 (b)

3 **해석** W: 교회로 가는 훨씬 더 빠른 길 없나요?

M: _____________________

(a) 네, 제가 알기론 없습니다.

(b) 아뇨, 두 길 모두 빠르지 않습니다.

(c) 아뇨, 어떤 방향이든 괜찮습니다.

(d) 지하철은 많은 통근자들에게 가장 빠른 교통수단이죠.

해설 교회로 가는 더 빠른 길이 없는지 물었으므로 긍정이나 부정의 대답이 와야 한다. 부정의문에 대한 응답

은 우리말 간섭으로 헷갈리기 쉽다. 우리말 해석과는 상관없이 긍정이면(있으면) Yes, 부정이면(없으면) No로 응답한다는 점에 주의한다. (b)와 (c)는 Yes, Sure 뒤에 이어지는 응답이 적절하지 못해 답이 될 수 없다. (a) not that I know of는 '내가 알기론 아니다'로 '내가 알기론 더 빠른 길이 없다'는 뜻이다.

어휘 not that I know of 내가 알기론 그렇지 않다

commuter 통근자

정답 (a)

4 **해석** M: 너와 헨리가 다시 서로에게 말을 해야 한다고 생각해.

W: 아니, 난 그를 보고 싶지가 않아.

M: 하지만 네가 먼저 그를 만나서 대화를 해봐야 한다고 생각하지 않니?

W: _____________________

(a) 너와 나는 궁합이 안 맞아.

(b) 알았어. 내 부모님을 뵙도록 노력해 볼게.

(c) 힘내, 세상이 끝난 건 아니잖아.

(d) 아니, 그러는 건 시간 낭비일 거야.

해설 남자가 여자에게 먼저 헨리와 만나서 대화를 해보는 것이 좋지 않겠느냐고 의견을 묻고 있으므로 여자는 남자의 의견에 동조하거나 반대하는 응답을 할 수 있다. 남자의 제안에 동의하면 Yes로 시작되는 긍정의 답변을, 동의하지 않으면 No로 시작되는 부정의 답변을 할 수 있다. 따라서 남자의 의견에 반대하고, 반대의 이유를 밝힌 (d)가 가장 적절한 응답이다.

어휘 chemistry 궁합, 공감대

Snap out of it. 힘내. 기운 내.

정답 (d)

Actual Test

1 **해석** W: 제 이름은 린다입니다. 저는 이 회사의 창립자입니다. 처음 뵙겠습니다.

M: _____________________

(a) 오랜만입니다.

(b) 저는 제인입니다. 잘 지냈어요.

(c) 저는 조입니다. 저도 만나 뵙게 되어 반갑습니다.

(d) 린다, 안녕?

해설 How do you do?는 처음 만나는 사람한테 건네는 인사이다. 따라서 (c)만이 정답이 된다. What's up? 같은 표현은 매우 친한 친구들 사이에서 주로 사용된다.

어휘 founder 창립자, 설립자
What's up? 요즘 어때? 잘 지냈어?

정답 (c)

2 해석 M: 사형에 대해 어떻게 생각하니?
W: _________________
(a) 사업을 시작하려면 충분한 자금이 필요해.
(b) 물론 사형은 폐지되어야 해.
(c) 그 건에 대해서는 어떤 것도 단언할 수 없어.
(d) 말보다는 행동이 중요해.

해설 capital punishment는 '사형'이라는 뜻으로 해석된
다. (a)에서 capital은 '자본'이라는 뜻으로 사용되었
으므로 주의해야 한다. 사형 제도에 대해 여자의 의견
을 묻는 질문이므로 대답은 (b)가 적절하다.

어휘 capital punishment 사형
capital 자본, 돈
abolish 철폐하다, 폐지하다
affirm 확언하다, 긍정하다

정답 (b)

3 해석 M: 어떻게 해야 하지? 사라가 아직도 나한테 화나 있어.
W: _________________
(a) 그게 네가 사라한테 해줄 수 있는 최소한의 것이야.
(b) 너 사라를 의사에게 데려갔니?
(c) 진정해. 너희들 곧 화해할 테니.
(d) 부러워. 그녀가 너를 무지 좋아하지, 응?

해설 사라가 화난 것에 대해 걱정하는 남자에게 여자가 할
수 있는 말은 안심하라는 말일 것이다. Take it easy.
로 시작하는 (c)가 정답이다.

어휘 be mad at sb ~에게 화내다, ~에게 화나 있다
make up 화해하다

정답 (c)

4 해석 W: 무슨 비자로 여기에 체류하고 계신가요?
M: F1이요. 학생 비자예요.
W: 비자가 소멸되면 어떻게 할 거예요?
M: _________________
(a) 그 정보에 대해서는 말해 줄 수 없어요.
(b) 새 신용카드를 발급받아야 해요..
(c) 비자를 갱신하러 출국해야 해요.
(d) 어디로 휴가를 떠날 거예요.

해설 expire는 자동사로 '기한이 만료되다, 소멸되다'라는
뜻이다. 비자가 만료되면 갱신해야 하므로 (c)가 정답

이다.

어휘 expire 만료되다
renew 갱신하다
take a vacation 휴가를 가다

정답 (c)

5 해석 W: 좀 저렴한 일본행 여객선 티켓을 구하고 싶은데요.
M: 가장 저렴한 표는 부산-후쿠오카로 운행하는 야간
여객선입니다.
W: 가능하면 오늘 도착했으면 싶은데요.
M: _________________
(a) 물론이죠. 저는 항상 일본에 가고 싶었어요.
(b) 좋아요. 도쿄행 오후 비행기가 있습니다.
(c) 고속 여객선이 있기는 한데, 요금이 좀 더 비쌉니다.
(d) 죄송합니다. 가능한 빨리 하고 있어요.

해설 문맥상 여자가 이용할 수 있는 여객선에 대한 안내가
이어져야 하므로 (c)가 정답이다.

어휘 inexpensive 비싸지 않은
overnight 하룻밤 동안의
ferry 여객선
pricy 비싼, 돈이 드는

정답 (c)

6 해석 W: 도착해서 천만다행이다. 우리 디자인을 보여 줄 차
례가 거의 다 되었어. 어디 갔었니?
M: 오는 길에 차가 고장 났어.
W: 흠, 적어도 택시나 버스를 탔어야지.
M: 문제는 내가 차를 대어 놓을 장소가 전혀 없었다는
거지. 그래서 견인 트럭이 올 때까지 기다려야 했어.
W: 그래, 무사히 와서 다행이다.
M: 고마워. 재수 없는 일들이 이제 다 끝났기를 바라
는 수밖에.
W: 그래. 시작할 시간이야. 네가 만든 슬라이드 쇼 디
스크 좀 줘봐.
M: 이런! 나쁜 소식이 더 있어.
Q. 이 대화로부터 추론할 수 있는 것은 무엇인가?
(a) 남자는 디스크를 가져오지 않았다.
(b) 남자는 보통 운이 좋은 편이다.
(c) 남자는 자신의 일에 대해 만족하지 못하고 있다.
(d) 남자는 또 늦을 것이다.

해설 남자의 맨 마지막 말에서 불운이 아직 끝나지 않았다
는 것은 디스크를 안 가져왔다는 것과 일맥상통한다.
따라서 정답은 (a)이다.

어휘 Thank God! 천만다행이다! 살았다!
break down 고장 나다
tow truck 견인 트럭

정답 (a)

7 해석 서부 시각으로 저녁 10시, 허리케인 루시는 프레이저
군도 남부 약 50마일 부근에서 북쪽으로 시속 20마일
의 속도로 이동하고 있었습니다. 폭풍 중심 부근의 최
고 풍속은 시속 70마일로 증가하였습니다. 루시는 폭
우와 돌발 홍수, 위험도 높은 강한 바람을 동반할 것
으로 예상됩니다. 허리케인 경보가 발효 중이니 주민
여러분께서는 집 안에 머물러 계시기 바랍니다. 그러
나 며칠 후 폭풍은 동부 궤도로 이동함에 따라 세력을
잃을 것으로 예상됩니다.

Q. 기상 예보에 따르면 다음 중 어느 것이 옳지 않은
가?

(a) 주민들은 그 지역에서 대피해야 한다는 얘길 들었다.
(b) 폭우와 강한 바람이 예상된다.
(c) 허리케인 루시는 이틀 후에 약해질 것이다.
(d) 돌발성 홍수가 일부 지역에서 발생할 것이다.

해설 예보에 의하면 주민들은 stay indoors(실내에 머물
다) 해야 한다고 하였으므로 evacuate(대피하다)해서
는 안 된다. 따라서 정답은 (a)이다. 참고로 (d)의
sudden and severe floods와 지문의 flash
floods는 의미상 비슷한 표현이다.

어휘 flash flood 돌발 홍수
issue a warning 경보를 발하다
intensity 강도
evacuate 피난[대피]시키다

정답 (a)

Sample

1 해석 W: 존, 내 생일을 잊어버리다니 어이가 없어.
M: 정말 미안해. 깜박했어.
W: 너한테 실망했어. 이번이 처음이 아니잖아.
M: _______________

(a) 단 좀 내려 주시겠어요?
(b) 네 마음대로 하려고 하지 마.
(c) 맞아. 나 얼음 위에서 미끄러졌어.
(d) 네가 화낼 만도 해.

해설 선택지에 등장한 관용 표현들을 알고 있어야 풀 수 있
는 유형의 문제이다. 여자가 자신의 생일을 잊어버린
남자 친구에게 화를 내고 있으므로 미안해 하거나 상
대의 화난 마음을 가라앉히는 응답이 오는 것이 자연
스럽다. 따라서 화난 상대의 마음을 달래 주는 (d)가
정답이다. You have every right to be angry.를
직역하면 '너는 화낼 모든 권리를 가지고 있다.'인데,
'네가 나한테 화내는 것도 충분히 이해된다.'는 뉘앙
스를 가진 표현이다.

어휘 slip one's mind 잊어버리다
be disappointed in *sb* ~에게 실망하다
let the hem down (천, 옷의) 단을 길게 하다, 단
을 내리다
have it one's way 자기 맘대로 하다
have every right to ~할 충분한 이유가 있다,
~하는 것이 당연하다

정답 (d)

2 해석 M: 오늘 난 몸이 좀 안 좋아.
W: _______________

(a) 내일은 맑을 거야.
(b) 나도 알아. 오늘은 날씨가 좋아 보여.
(c) 뭐가 문제야? 잠을 못 잤니?
(d) 일기예보에 따르면 오늘은 청명한 날씨일 거래.

해설 under the weather(몸이 좋지 않은)라는 관용 표현
을 알고 있어야 풀 수 있는 문제이다. 상대의 몸이 좋
지 않다는 말에 대한 간접 응답은 셀 수 없을 정도로
많지만, 선택지 (c)처럼 이유를 물어보는 것이 가장 보
편적인 응답이다. (a), (b), (d)는 질문지에 등장한 어휘
weather의 '날씨'라는 뜻으로 유도한 오답 선택지들
이다.

어휘 sort of 조금, 약간

under the weather 몸이 좋지 않은

call for 예측[예보]하다

정답 (c)

3 해석 M: 켈리, 어젯밤 소개팅 어땠는지 얘기 좀 듣고 싶어.

W: ________________________

(a) 축하해! 그러겠다고 대답했니?

(b) 그 얘길 들으니 너무 기뻐.

(c) 무슨 말 하는지 알겠어.

(d) 안 나갈 걸 그랬어.

해설 평서문에 대한 응답은 정형화되어 있지 않기 때문에 답변을 예상하기보다는 선택지 하나하나를 정확히 들어 소거법을 적용시키는 것이 바람직하다. 소개팅이 어땠냐는 남자의 질문에 좋았다거나 나빴다는 식의 직접적인 응답도 예상해 볼 수 있지만, 선택지 (d)처럼 소개팅에 나가지 말 걸 그랬다고 과거에 대한 강한 후회와 아쉬움을 표현하는 방법도 충분히 가능한 응답이다. (a) Congratulations! Did you say yes?는 주로 청혼을 받았다는 여자에게 하는 응답이다.

어휘 blind date 소개팅

정답 (d)

4 해석 M: 여보, 점심 준비 다 됐어요? 배고파 죽겠어요.

W: ________________________

(a) 전 질입니다. 저 역시 만나서 반갑습니다.

(b) 거의 다 됐어요. 밥상 좀 차려 줄래요?

(c) 아, 정말? 그럼 먹을게.

(d) 죄송합니다, 손님. 오늘은 영업을 하지 않습니다.

해설 연인이나 부부 사이의 대화이다. 의문문과 평서문이 동시에 나왔을 경우에는 의문문에 중점을 두고 응답을 고르는 것이 바람직하다. 점심 준비가 다 되었느냐고 묻고 있으므로 준비가 됐는지 안 됐는지를 밝히는 응답이 와야 한다. 따라서 준비가 거의 다 됐으니 밥상을 차려 달라는 (b)가 가장 적절한 응답이다.

어휘 set the table 식탁을 차리다, 밥상을 차리다

정답 (b)

Actual Test

1 해석 M: 이 스프를 이렇게 맛나게 만든 비법을 말해 줘.

W: ________________________

(a) 난 한때 모든 종류의 다이어트를 시도해 봤어.

(b) 내가 맛을 보기 전에 아무것도 넣지 마.

(c) 나도 잘 먹었어.

(d) 인스턴트 스프였어.

해설 남자는 맛있는 스프를 만든 방법에 대해 질문하고 있는데, 선택지의 다른 답변들은 질문과 전혀 상관이 없다. 좌절스러운 내용이기는 하지만 결국 인스턴트 믹스를 사용했다는 (d)의 답변이 가장 자연스럽다.

어휘 try out 시도하다, 실험해 보다

instant mix packet 인스턴트 믹스(일회용으로 포장된 커피 믹스나 수프 등의 제품)

정답 (d)

2 해석 W: 제발 사업이 곧 나아져야 할 텐데.

M: ________________________

(a) 일단 여행 시즌이 시작되면 개선될 거예요.

(b) 내 일에 신경 좀 꺼 줘.

(c) 넌 항상 열심이구나.

(d) 넌 가게를 차려야 해.

해설 pick up은 '회복되다'라는 뜻으로 해석된다. 따라서 여행 시즌이 시작되면 사업이 나아질 것이라는 답변을 하고 있는 (a)가 가장 적합하다.

어휘 pick up 나아지다, 좋아지다

stay out of one's business ~의 일에 참견하지 않다

burn the midnight oil 밤늦게까지 공부[일]하다

정답 (a)

3 해석 M: 새로 출시된 영화는 얼마 동안 빌릴 수 있죠?

W: ________________________

(a) 내 친구 잭이 곧 출소할 거야.

(b) 이틀 후에 반납하셔야 합니다.

(c) 돈을 안 내면 비디오를 빌려 가실 수 없어요.

(d) 우린 시간이 그렇게 많지 않아.

해설 new release는 새로 출시된 CD, 비디오, DVD 등을 가리키는데, 여기서는 대여하는 것이므로 '새로 나온 영화'라는 뜻으로 보면 된다. (a)의 release는 '풀어주다, 석방하다'라는 뜻인데 이것에 현혹되어서는 안 된다.

어휘 new release 새로 출시된 영상이나 음반

be released from prison 감옥에서 나오다, 출소하다

정답 (b)

4 **해석** W: 난 설탕 들어간 그 오렌지 주스 안 마실 거야.

M: 왜? 그것도 다양한 영양소가 들어 있고 가격도 저렴한 제품인데.

W: 실은 오늘부터 설탕 들어간 모든 제품을 안 먹으려고 노력 중이거든.

M: _______________________

(a) 글쎄, 난 예전에 설탕이 들어간 제품을 다양하게 먹어 봤어.

(b) 글쎄, 진실을 포장할 필요는 없어.

(c) 글쎄, 어떤 당은 에너지를 얻는 데 필수적이야.

(d) 글쎄, 네가 그렇게 말하니까 배고프다.

해설 문맥상 설탕이 에너지 대사에 필수적이라는 조언을 하는 것이 자연스럽다. 그러므로 정답은 (c). 참고로, sugar coat는 설탕으로 코팅하는 것, 즉 쓴 알약에 설탕으로 코팅한 당의정 등을 말하는 것으로 (b)에서는 진실을 숨기기 위해 사탕발림한다는 의미로 해석하면 된다.

어휘 nutrient 영양소

reasonably priced 저렴한[적당한] 가격의

the thing is ~ 실은, 그 이유는 ~

sugar coat ~을 받아들이기 좋게 꾸미다

now that ~ ~이니까

정답 (c)

5 **해석** M: 왜 화장 안 해?

W: 난 네가 자연스러운 모습을 좋아하는 줄 알았어.

M: 그렇긴 해. 하지만 이따금 좀 특별한 걸 할 수 있잖아.

W: _______________________

(a) 내 생각엔 너도 특별한 거 같아.

(b) 너 나한테서 눈을 뗄 수가 없지, 그렇지?

(c) 내가 너한테 그다지 매력이 없다는 거야?

(d) 화장품이 점점 비싸지고 있어.

해설 가끔은 화장을 좀 했으면 좋겠다는 남자의 말에 화가 난 여자에게서 기대할 수 있는 반응은 (c) 정도가 되겠다. 나머지 선택지는 남자의 말에 대한 반응으로 어색하다.

어휘 once in a while 가끔씩, 때때로

can't take one's eyes off ~로부터 눈을 못 떼다

정답 (c)

6 **해석** W: 그럼 네가 시작했다던 극단에 대해 말해 봐.

M: 기대에 비해 잘되지 않고 있어.

W: 왜?

M: 배우들이 서로 궁합이 잘 안 맞는 거 같아.

W: 사람들이 서로 유대 관계를 형성하도록 게임 같은 걸 해본 적 있어?

M: 아니. 다들 개성이 너무 달라. 별로 친해지고 싶어 하지 않는 것 같아.

W: 그들에게 신뢰를 형성하고 공통점을 발견할 수 있도록 해주는 창조적인 게임을 시도해 봐야 해.

M: 충고 고마워. 어떻게 될지 지켜보자.

Q. 대화로부터 추론할 수 있는 것은 무엇인가?

(a) 좋은 극장은 배우들 사이의 공감대를 필요로 한다.

(b) 공통된 경험을 갖는 것은 사람들을 더 친밀하게 만든다.

(c) 창조적인 게임은 비슷한 성격을 가진 사람들 사이에서만 효과가 있다.

(d) 서로 다른 성격을 가진 사람들은 창조적인 게임에 참여하기를 좋아한다.

해설 (b)의 shared experiences와 대화의 some things in common은 같은 것을 지칭하는 표현이다.

어휘 theater troupe 극단, 연극패

compared to ~에 비해

work out (계획 등이) 잘되어 가다

chemistry 궁합, 공감, 친화력

bond with *sb* 친밀한 관계를 맺다, 유대를 형성하다

engage in 참여하다

정답 (b)

7 **해석** 신생아 에어로빅이 다음에 크게 유행할 운동법인가? 아기를 위한 운동 프로그램이 유행하면서 몇몇 부모들이 그런 프로그램에 가입하고 있는데, 스트리저 박사와 같은 소아과 의사들은 그러한 프로그램이 시간과 돈 낭비에 지나지 않는다고 주장한다. 스트리저 박사는 유아들의 근육 구조는 발달이 아직 안 되어 있어서 그러한 활동을 통해 이득을 얻기 어렵다고 설명한다. 한편, 일부 의사들은 아기들이 어린 나이에 운동 습관을 기르므로써 비만과의 싸움에서 유리한 위치를 점할 수 있다고 주장한다.

Q. 위 이야기를 통해 내릴 수 있는 결론은 무엇인가?

(a) 아기 때 운동을 했던 사람들은 그렇지 않았던 사람들보다 훨씬 더 건강하다.

(b) 비만에 관한 의료계의 논쟁이 여전히 남아 있다.

(c) 신생아에게 운동을 강요하는 것은 아동 학대에 가까운 행위이다.

(d) 신생아 운동의 이점에 관한 찬반양론이 있다.

해설 신생아의 운동을 반대하는 스트리저 박사 같은 의사들과 비만을 방지하기 위해 조기 운동이 필요하다는 의사들의 의견이 대립되고 있음을 알 수 있다. 따라서 정답은 (d)이다.

어휘 fad 일시적인 유행

sign on 서명하다, 계약하다

pediatrician 소아과 의사

little more than 겨우, 단지, ~에 지나지 않는

muscular 근육의

underdeveloped 발달이 불충분한, 미숙한

get a head start on ~에서 유리하다, 유리한 위치에 놓이다

obesity 비만

develop (습관을) 붙이다

border on ~에 가깝다, 마치 ~와 같다

child abuse 아동 학대

pros and cons 찬반양론

정답 (d)

Chapter 06 대의 파악

Sample

1 **해석** M: 저녁 식사 후 산책할래?

W: 조금 피곤해. 영화 한 편 보는 게 더 좋을 거 같아.

M: 하지만 여유롭고 편안한 산책이 소화에 도움이 될 거야.

W: 그렇겠군. 그리고 강아지도 좋아할 거고.

M: 영화는 돌아와서 언제든지 볼 수 있잖아.

W: 좋아. 좋은 생각이야.

Q. 화자들은 무엇에 대해 말하고 있는가?

(a) 저녁 식사 후 계획

(b) 운동의 이점

(c) 그들이 좋아하는 영화

(d) 산책할 장소

해설 남자와 여자는 저녁 식사 후 무엇을 할 것인지에 대해 이야기하고 있다. 남자가 저녁 식사 후에 산책을 제안하자 처음에 여자는 피곤해서 영화 보는 게 낫겠다고 말하지만 산책이 소화에 좋다는 남자의 말에 둘은 산책을 하기로 한다.

어휘 leisurely 느긋한, 여유 있는

stroll 산책

digest 소화되다

정답 (a)

2 **해석** M: 최근에 전 상당한 치통을 겪고 있어요.

W: 그러세요? 치과에는 가보셨나요?

M: 예. 치료받아야 할 충치가 4개나 있더라고요.

W: 지금부터 치아 관리를 잘하셔야겠어요.

M: 걱정하지 마세요. 잘하겠습니다.

W: 치과 치료는 고통스러울 뿐만 아니라 비용도 많이 들잖아요.

Q. 대화의 주제는 무엇인가?

(a) 치아 건강을 위해 해야 할 것

(b) 얼마나 자주 양치질을 해야 하는가

(b) 구강 관리가 중요한 이유

(d) 치아 관리에 드는 비용

해설 dental pain, dentist, cavities, teeth 등의 어휘를 통해 치아 관리에 대한 대화임을 짐작할 수 있으므로 정답은 (c)이다. (a) 치아 건강을 위해 해야 할 일은 구체적으로 나와 있지 않으며, (b) 바람직한 양치질의 횟수와 (d) 치아 관리에 드는 비용 또한 전혀 언급되어 있지 않으므로 답이 될 수 없다.

어휘 dental pain 치통
cavity 충치
oral 입의, 구강의
정답 (c)

3 해석 감기는 200개가 넘는 변종이 있는 바이러스에 의해 발생하며, 사람들이 기침이나 재채기를 할 때 방출되는 자그마한 감염된 침방울을 숨을 쉴 때 들이마시면서 걸립니다. 대부분의 성인들은 적어도 일 년에 두세 번씩 감기에 걸립니다. 추운 날씨와 연관이 있는데 왜냐하면 우리는 겨울 동안 사람이 붐비는 상태에서 안에 있으려고 하는 경향이 있기 때문입니다. 그래서 우리가 흡입하는 공기 내에 존재하는 바이러스에 더 쉽게 감염됩니다.
Q. 이 담화문은 주로 무엇에 관한 것인가?
(a) 감기에 걸리는 빈도
(b) 감기의 지속 기간
(c) 감기에 걸리는 경로
(d) 감염성 세균
해설 감기는 200개가 넘는 변종 바이러스에 의해 발생하는데, 기침이나 재채기를 할 때 방출되는 감염된 침방울과 붐비는 실내의 공기를 흡입함으로써 바이러스에 감염된다는 내용이다. 따라서 감기에 걸리는 경로를 나타내는 (c)가 정답이다.
어휘 variety 변종, 종류
breathe in 숨을 들이쉬다
expel 방출하다
infected 감염된
droplet 작은 물방울
cough 기침하다
sneeze 재채기하다
inhale 들이마시다, 흡입하다
infectious germ 감염성 세균
정답 (c)

Actual Test

1 해석 W: 내가 심부름 다녀오는 동안 설거지 좀 해주면 안 될까?
M: ____________________
(a) 내가 같이 가줄게.
(b) 물론 괜찮지. 기꺼이 할게.
(c) 응, 그거 하기 싫지는 않아.

(d) 뛰지 마. 다칠지도 몰라.
해설 얼핏 들으면 (c)도 정답이 되는 것 같지만 Do you mind ~ ? 의문문에 긍정의 대답을 할 경우에는 No, (I don't mind ~)로, 부정의 대답을 할 경우에는 Yes, (I mind ~)로 대답해야 하는데 (c)는 Yes, I don't mind ~ 라고 했으므로 말 자체가 어색하다. 따라서 정답은 (b)이다.
어휘 run errands 심부름 가다
정답 (b)

2 해석 W: 감독이 앤드류를 캐스팅하기로 한 거 옳은 결정이라고 생각하니?
M: ____________________
(a) 네가 그 제안을 거절했다니 믿을 수 없어.
(b) 앉아서 천천히 고민해 볼 시간이 정말 없었어.
(c) 시간이 지나 봐야 알겠지.
(d) 둘 중에 어느 하나로 결정하는 것은 정말 어려워.
해설 분명하게 Yes, No로 대답하지 않고 앞으로 지켜보자는 식으로 대답한 (c)가 정답이다.
어휘 cast (배우를) 캐스팅하다, ~에게 배역을 맡기다
turn down 거절하다
Only time will tell. 시간만이 말해줄 것이다. 시간이 지나 봐야 알 수 있다.
정답 (c)

3 해석 W: 이 청바지 10호 사이즈로 있는지 궁금하네요.
M: ____________________
(a) 같이 입으니까 오히려 좋아 보이네요. 그렇죠?
(b) 네, 대량으로 구입하시면 절약이 됩니다.
(c) 당장에 알 수는 없지만 기꺼이 찾아보겠습니다.
(d) 그것들은 제가 마음에 두고 있던 바로 그건 아니네요.
해설 offhand는 '즉석에서' 라는 뜻으로 당장은 모르지만 찾아보겠다는 대답이 가장 자연스러우므로 (c)가 정답이다.
어휘 in bulk 대량으로
offhand 즉석에서, 당장
정답 (c)

4 해석 W: 새로 산 차를 끊임없이 자랑하는 직장 동료가 한 명 있어.
M: 꽤 짜증나겠구나.
W: 난 그렇게 물질만능주의적인 사람은 만난 적이 없어.

M: ___________________

(a) 그 남자의 수리공이 누군지 궁금하군.

(b) 그 남자는 네 사생활에 간섭하지 말아야 해.

(c) 그 사람의 자아가 꽤 건전하구나.

(d) 주목받고 싶은 모양이구나.

해설 brag는 '자랑하다'라는 뜻이다. 끊임없이 자랑을 해 대는 사람은 보통 관심을 끌기 위한 행동이라고 여겨지는데, 이런 식의 답변인 (d)가 정답이다.

어휘 brag 자랑하다

materialistic 물질주의적인

stay out of ~에 참견하지 않다

정답 (d)

---

5 **해석** M: 면접 잘 봤니?

W: 정반대야. 망했어.

M: 정말? 뭐가 잘못되었는데?

W: ___________________

(a) 걔가 이 말 들으면 팔짝 뛸걸.

(b) 지나치게 적극적이었나 봐.

(c) 걔가 그 문제를 제대로 인식하지 못한 것 같아서 유감이야.

(d) 난 즉시 채용되었어.

해설 bomb은 미국의 속어로 '망치다, 망하다'라는 뜻이고 come off는 '~한 상태가 되다'라는 뜻으로 해석되는데, come off too desperate이라고 하면 우리말로는 '너무 들이대다' 정도로 풀이할 수 있다. 일자리를 꼭 얻어야 한다는 생각에 당당함을 잃어버리고, 약간은 비굴할 정도로 지나치게 들이대거나 적극적인 경우를 too desperate이라고 보면 된다.

어휘 bomb ~에 실패하다

hit the roof 발끈 화를 내다

come off 결국 ~되다, ~해지다

appreciate 올바르게 인식하다, 통찰하다

정답 (b)

---

6 **해석** M: 안녕, 위니? 무슨 일이니?

W: 코치님, 이번 주말에 열릴 경기에서 제가 투수를 했으면 해서요.

M: 무슨 특별한 이유라도 있니?

W: 저희 가족이 시내에 올 건데 제 경기를 보게 했으면 해서요.

M: 너 팔을 조심해야 하잖아. 더 이상 부상을 당하고 싶지는 않을 거 아냐.

W: 나아지고 있어요. 경기를 하기에 충분한 거 같아요.

M: 음, 1회에 선발 투수로 뛰게 해줄게. 그리고 네가 어떻게 하는지 지켜보겠어.

W: 고맙습니다, 코치님! 잘할게요.

Q. 대화에 따르면 옳은 것은 무엇인가?

(a) 여자는 부상 때문에 의학적 도움이 필요하다.

(b) 여자는 가족 면담의 기회를 요청하고 있다.

(c) 여자는 경기에 출전할 기회를 놓쳤다.

(d) 여자는 이전에 경기 중 부상을 당한 경험이 있다.

해설 대화 중 You don't want to hurt it any further. 에서 여자가 이미 부상을 한 번 입었음을 알 수 있다. 따라서 정답은 (d)이다.

어휘 pitch 공을 던지다, 투구하다, 등판하다

inning (야구의) 회

정답 (d)

---

7 **해석** 많은 사람들이 약초 치료법이 자연적이기 때문에 그에 관련된 위험은 만일 있다 하더라도 거의 미미할 것이라고 생각한다. 이것은 분명히 잘못된 생각이다. 많은 약초 치료법이 처방전 없이 살 수 있는 약에 대한 효과적인 대안책이기는 하지만, 그것들은 여전히 주의를 기울여 사용해야만 한다. 여느 다른 약들과 마찬가지로 많은 약초 치료법들은 몸이 작용하는 방식에 근본적으로 영향을 끼칠 수 있어서 복용량에 대한 지시를 주의해서 따라야 한다. 많은 약초 치료법들이 심각한 부작용을 일으키는 경우가 적은 것은 사실이지만 일부는 부적절하게 사용될 경우 위험하거나 치명적일 수도 있다.

Q. 담화의 주제로 알맞은 것은 무엇인가?

(a) 약초 치료법이 효과가 별로 없는 이유

(b) 처방전 없이 살 수 있는 약을 피해야 하는 이유들

(c) 신체에 미치는 약초의 긍정적인 효과들

(d) 자연 약초 치료법의 위험성

해설 많은 사람들이 약초를 이용한 치료법이 자연적인 것이어서 위험성이 없다고 생각하는데 이것은 잘못된 생각이라고 말하고 있다. 약초 치료법이 효과가 있는 것은 사실이지만 다른 약품처럼 약초를 이용한 치료법도 제대로 사용되지 않을 경우 위험할 수 있고 치명적일 수도 있다고 설명하고 있다. 담화의 내용이 약초 치료법의 효능을 부정하는 것이 아니라 많은 사람들이 그 위험성을 깨닫지 못하고 있다는 점을 강조하고 있으므로 (a)는 담화의 주제로 적절하지 않다. over-the-counter drugs가 언급되긴 했지만 그것을 피해야

한다는 내용은 언급되지 않았으므로 (b)도 정답이 아니다. 약초는 신체의 기능에 근본적인 영향을 끼칠 수 있기 때문에 복용량을 주의해서 따라야 한다고 했으므로 (c) positive effects라고도 할 수 없다.

어휘 herbal 약초의

associated with ~와 관련된

myth 잘못된 생각, 허구

alternative 대용물

over-the-couhter 의사 처방 없이 팔리는

radically 근본적으로

dosage 복용량

side effect 부작용

정답 (d)

Sample

1 **해석** W: 집에 오는 길에 상점에 들를 거예요. 필요한 거 없어요?

M: 네, 있어요. 요구르트 좀 사다 줄래요? 다 떨어졌거든요.

W: 그러죠. 어떤 맛을 원하세요?

M : 복숭아 맛이요.

W: 알았어요. 아이스크림도 필요하나요?

M: 아뇨, 됐어요. 그냥 요구르트만 사다 주세요.

W: 좋아요. 조금 있다가 봐요.

Q. 남자가 자신을 위해 여자에게 사다 달라고 부탁한 것은 무엇인가?

(a) 복숭아

(b) 아무 맛 나지 않는 요구르트

(c) 아이스크림

(d) 복숭아 맛 요구르트

해설 (남자) Could you get some yogurt? → (여자) What flavor do you want? → (남자) Peach, please. 남자는 여자에게 복숭아 맛 요구르트를 사다 달라고 부탁하고 있다. 아이스크림도 필요하냐고 묻자 남자는 No thanks, just the yogurt.라고 답했으므로 (c)는 오답.

어휘 stop by 들르다

flavor 맛

unflavored 아무 맛 나지 않는

정답 (d)

2 **해석** 안녕하십니까, 신사 숙녀 여러분. LA 탐 브래들리 국제공항을 출발하여 캐나다 밴쿠버 국제공항으로 가는 노스웨스트 항공 007기 편에 탑승하신 걸 환영합니다. 저는 비행을 책임지고 있는 기장 캐빈 윌리엄스입니다. 보시다시피 현재 LA의 날씨는 남동풍이 약간 부는 매우 화창한 날씨입니다. 여러분 모두 알고 계시겠지만 비행 소요 시간은 약 7시간 정도가 될 것이며, 저녁 8시경에 밴쿠버에 도착할 것입니다. 밴쿠버 현지 날씨 또한 매우 온화합니다. 도중에 난기류를 만났을 경우 당황하지 마시고 안전벨트를 착용하신 채로 좌석에 그대로 앉아 계시기 바랍니다. 노스웨스트 항공을 이용해 주셔서 감사합니다.

Q. 안내 방송에 따르면 옳은 것은 무엇인가?

(a) 비행기는 현지 시간으로 7시 정각에 도착할 것이다.

(b) 현재 밴쿠버 날씨는 흐리다.

(c) 비행기는 LA에서 오후 1시경에 이륙했다.

(d) 안전벨트 등이 꺼지면 노트북을 사용할 수 있다.

해설 비행기 이륙 시 기내에서 흘러나오는 안내 방송을 듣고 진위를 파악하는 문제이다. 비행 소요 시간이 7시간 정도이고 목적지인 밴쿠버에 도착 시간은 저녁 8시경이므로 이 비행기는 오후 1시경에 이륙했다고 볼 수 있다. 따라서 지문의 내용과 일치하는 것은 (c)이다. (a)는 7시가 아니라 8시이며, (d)는 언급되지 않았다.

어휘 turbulence 난기류

local time 현지 시간

overcast 흐린

정답 (c)

3 **해석** W: 안녕하세요. 오늘은 무엇을 도와 드릴까요?

M: 귀 은행에서 제공하는 텔레뱅킹 서비스에 대한 정보를 알고 싶습니다.

W: 알겠습니다. 저희 은행 계좌를 가지고 계시면 하루 24시간 내내 모든 은행 업무를 전화로 이용하실 수 있습니다.

M: 제 계좌에 어떻게 접근하나요?

W: 은행에 전화를 해서 접근 비밀 번호를 누르시고 이용 가능한 선택 메뉴를 들으세요.

M: 훌륭하네요. 어떤 것들을 할 수 있죠?

W: 고객님 계좌의 잔고를 확인할 수 있고, 공과금을 낼 수 있으며, 거래 내역서를 신청할 수 있고, 다른 계좌로 돈을 이체할 수도 있습니다.

M: 좋군요. 그런데 문제가 발생했을 경우엔 어떻게 하나요?

W: 자동 응답기가 있으며 매일 영업 시간 동안에는 직원과 연락하실 수 있습니다.

Q. 대화로부터 추론 가능한 것은 무엇인가?

(a) 남자는 은행을 한 번도 방문한 적이 없다.

(b) 남자는 은행에서 일한다.

(c) 남자는 텔레뱅킹을 한 번도 이용한 적이 없다.

(d) 여자는 남자의 좋은 친구이다.

해설 대화를 통해 남자는 은행 고객, 여자는 은행 직원임을 알 수 있다. 남자는 I'd like some information on the telephone banking services offered by your bank.라고 말하면서 여자에게 텔레뱅킹 이용 방법을 묻고 있다. 따라서 (c)가 정답임을 알 수 있고, 남자는 이미 자신의 계좌를 가지고 있으므로 (a)는 오답이다.

어휘 account 계좌

banking 은행 업무

access 접근하다

key in 자판으로 ~을 입력하다

access code 접근 비밀 번호

balance 잔고, 잔액

pay a bill 요금을 내다

statement 거래 내역서

transfer money 송금하다, 이체하다

정답 (c)

4 **해석** 중고차를 구입하는 데 필수적인 충고는 항상 "구입자여 조심하라"입니다. 이 충고는 여전히 유효하지만, 지난 몇 년 동안 신차와 경트럭의 가격이 많은 소비자들의 소득을 앞지르고 있어 중고 자동차의 수요가 증가하고 있습니다. 중고 자동차를 구입하는 것은 여전히 불확실성으로 가득하지만 만족스러운 구매를 할 가능성을 높일 수 있는 방법들이 있습니다.

Q. 담화로부터 추론 가능한 것은 무엇인가?

(a) 중고차는 대부분의 구입자에게 골칫거리이다.

(b) 중고차 구입이 더욱 인기를 끌고 있다.

(c) 중고차 구입은 안전하다.

(d) 중고차는 오늘날 가격이 더 저렴해지고 있다.

해설 중고차 구매가 아직은 많은 위험성을 안고 있지만 신차 가격이 터무니없이 비싸서 중고차의 수요가 증가하고 있다고 언급되었으므로 중고차 구입이 더욱 인기를 끌고 있다는 것을 추론할 수 있다. 따라서 정답은 (b)이다. 중고차 구입은 여전히 불확실성을 안고 있기 때문에 안전하다고는 볼 수 없으므로 (c)는 잘못된 추론이다. (a), (d)는 담화에서 언급되지 않았다.

어휘 beware 조심하다

hold true 유효하다, 진실이다

outpace 앞지르다, 추월하다

send up 올리다, 오르게 하다

uncertainty 불확실성

problematic 문제가 있는, 골칫거리의

foolproof 안전한, 위험하지 않은, 바보라도 할 수 있는

정답 (b)

Actual Test

1 **해석** W: 있잖아. 조셉이 프린스턴 대학에 합격했대.

M: _______________________

(a) 나도 알아. 반장 선거 유세를 언제 할 생각이니?

(b) 잘했어. 네가 너무 자랑스러워.

(c) 음, 난 과제를 훑어봤을 뿐이야.

(d) 난 그가 해낼 줄 알았어.

해설 여자가 조셉이 프린스턴 대학에 합격했다는 소식을 남자에게 알리고 있으므로 축하하거나 놀라거나 그럴 줄 알았다는 태연한 반응 등을 예상해 볼 수 있다. 따라서 선택지 중에서는 그럴 줄 알았다는 (d)가 가장 적절한 응답이다. (a)와 (c)는 생뚱맞은 답변이고, (b)는 you가 아니라 him이 되어야 한다.

어휘 Guess what! 있잖아.

get accepted into ~에 합격하다, 입학 허가를 받다

hit the campaign trail 선거 유세를 하다

Well done! 잘했어!

browse through 훑어보다

make it 해내다, 성공하다

정답 (d)

2 해석 M: 윌리엄 교수님, 제 논문 제출 마감 기한을 연장해 주실 수 있으신가요?

W: ___________________

(a) 너무 부정적으로 생각하지 말게. 괜찮아질 거야.

(b) 우리 학교 이사회는 부정행위를 하다 걸린 학생들에게 어떤 예외도 두지 않는다.

(c) 이번 주말 이전에 제출만 한다면.

(d) 응, 지금은 어느 정도의 확장이 필요한 시기야.

해설 남자가 여자 교수를 찾아가서 논문 제출 마감 기한을 연장해 달라고 요청하고 있으므로 요청에 대한 완곡한 거절이나 흔쾌히 승낙하는 직접적인 응답이 오는 것이 보통이며, 간혹 선택지 (c)처럼 특별한 조건을 내세워서 수락하는 응답도 가능하다. 주말 이전에 낸다는 조건에서만 연장을 해주겠다, 즉 주말까지만 연장해 주겠다는 (c)가 가장 적절한 응답이다.

어휘 get an extension 연장을 얻어내다, 연장받다

thesis 논문

turn in 제출하다

정답 (c)

3 해석 M: 제인, 오늘 오후에 우리 프로젝트를 위한 자료 좀 찾아볼 시간 있니?

W: ___________________

(a) 고맙지만 이건 받을 수 없어.

(b) 물론, 지금은 3시 15분 전이야.

(c) 안 될 이유가 없지.

(d) 나도 알아. 그는 너무 물질만능주의적이야.

해설 조동사 do로 시작되는 의문사 없는 의문문에 대한 응답을 고르는 문제이다. 남자가 여자에게 프로젝트에 필요한 자료를 수집할 시간이 있느냐고 완곡하게 물어보고 있지만, 사실상 요청하는 문장이라고 볼 수 있으므로 요청이나 요구를 수락하거나 거절하는 응답이 와야 한다. 따라서 선택지 중에서는 흔쾌히 수락하는 (c)가 가장 적절한 응답이다.

어휘 pick up 수집하다

material 자료

materialistic 물질주의적인

정답 (c)

4 해석 W: 매튜, 오늘 아침에 그린 가든으로 채소 한 상자 배달했나요?

M: 아뇨, 실은 말하려고 했는데요. 우리 다른 곳으로부터 주문을 받는 게 좋겠어요.

W: 왜 그런 말을 하는 거죠?

M : ___________________

(a) 그들은 우리 지역에서 가장 훌륭한 업체들 중 하나예요.

(b) 어젯밤 즐거웠어요. 우리는 정말 서로 죽이 잘 맞는 것 같아요.

(c) 그 사람들 대금을 갚지 않은 지 두 달이 넘었거든요.

(d) 그들은 우리 서비스에 상당히 만족해 하고 있어요.

해설 남자는 그린 가든이라는 업체로부터 오는 주문을 더 이상 받지 말고 다른 업체로부터 주문을 받자고 여자에게 제안하고 있다. 이에 여자가 남자에게 그렇게 말하는 이유를 묻고 있으므로 그 이유로서 타당한 응답을 골라야 한다. 선택지 중에서 거래를 끊어야 할 만한 이유는 (c)밖에 없다.

어휘 hit it off 서로 궁합이 잘 맞다, 죽이 잘 맞다

delinquent 지불 기일이 넘은, (세금, 부채 등이) 체납된

정답 (c)

5 해석 W: 괜찮은 컴퓨터 수리점 아는 데 있니?

M: JPU 브로드밴드가 평판이 좋은 컴퓨터업체지.

W: 그거 잘됐네. 거기서 내 컴퓨터를 고칠 수 있으면 좋겠다.

M: ___________________

(a) 다시 한 번 더 시도해 보는 게 어때?

(b) 실망하지 않을 거야. 저렴하고 믿을 수 있는 곳이야.

(c) 나는 숙련된 수리공이야.

(d) 고치지 못할 거라 생각해. 그렇게 평이 좋지는 않아.

해설 남자가 여자에게 컴퓨터 수리점을 추천했기 때문에 안심을 시키거나 재확신을 시키는 응답이 가장 보편적일 것이다. 따라서 실망하지 않을 거라고 안심시키는 (b)가 선택지 중에서는 가장 자연스럽다.

어휘 reputable 평판이 좋은

That's good to know. 그거 잘됐네.

shot 시도

let down 실망시키다

정답 (b)

6 **해석** W: 지금 차가운 아이스크림 하나 먹으면 더할 나위 없이 좋을 텐데.

M: 길 아래에 살 수 있는 가게가 있어.

W: 그럴 수 있다면 좋겠지만 나한테 유당 알레르기가 있다더라고. 그래서 배가 가끔씩 아파.

M: 우유 조금 먹는다고 죽지는 않아.

W: 아니야. 어제 의사 말로는 이번 주말까지는 내 위를 가지고 모험을 하지 않는 게 좋을 거래.

M: 그럼 콩 디저트를 먹는 건 어때?

W: 아, 그게 더 좋겠다.

Q. 대화로부터 추론 가능한 것은 무엇인가?

(a) 여자는 아이스크림을 조금 먹어 볼 것이다.

(b) 남자는 콩 디저트를 아이스크림만큼 좋아하지는 않는다.

(c) 여자는 일주일 동안 아이스크림을 먹으면 안 된다.

(d) 여자는 고통을 잘 참지 못한다.

해설 여자의 의사가 이번 주말까지는 아이스크림을 먹는 모험을 하지 않는 게 좋다고 말했다는 언급으로 볼 때 여자는 일주일 동안 아이스크림을 먹어서는 안 된다고 짐작해 볼 수 있다. 따라서 정답은 (c)이다. 남자가 아이스크림 조금 먹는 것은 문제없다고 말했지만 여자가 단호하게 거절했으므로 (a)는 적절한 추론이 아니다. (b)는 대화에 전혀 언급되지 않았으므로 올바른 추론이 아니다. (d) 역시 여자가 고통을 잘 참지 못한다는 것은 충분히 가능한 상황이지만 위 대화를 통해서는 추론이 불가능하므로 올바른 추론이라고 할 수 없다.

어휘 hit the spot 정말 딱이다, 더할 나위 없다

lactose intolerant 락토오스(유당)에 알레르기가 있는, 유당을 소화 못 시키는

take a chance 운에 맡기고 해보다, 위험을 무릅쓰다

tolerance 인내, 참을성

정답 (c)

7 **해석** 최근 조류독감의 발병으로 인해서 가금 육류의 구매가 현저하게 떨어졌습니다. 그러나 닭고기와 다른 익힌 고기를 먹어서 그 질병에 걸릴 위험은 거의 없습니다. 비록 독감 바이러스의 매개체인 대다수의 새들이 야생에서 발견되지만 이러한 사육되지 않은 새들은 병의 어떤 증세도 거의 보이지 않습니다. 반대로, 병에 더 쉽게 걸려서 죽을 것처럼 보이는 건 바로 농장이나 집에서 길러진 가금류입니다. 감염되었을 수도 있는 가금류와의 접촉을 피하는 것이야말로 병으로부터 안전한 가장 효과적인 전략입니다.

Q. 보도문에 따르면 맞는 것은 무엇인가?

(a) 닭을 키우는 농부들이 소비자보다 감염될 가능성이 더 크다.

(b) 야생의 새들은 독감 바이러스에 노출되어 있지 않다.

(c) 전문가들은 조류독감의 대량 발발을 예상하고 있다.

(d) 고기를 익힌다고 먹기 안전해지지는 않을 것이다.

해설 조류독감에 대한 보도문을 듣고 진위를 파악하는 문제이다. 마지막 부분에 조류독감에 안 걸리는 가장 효과적인 방법은 가금류와의 접촉을 피하는 것이라고 했기 때문에 일반 소비자보다 가금류와 접촉이 많을 수밖에 없는, 닭을 기르는 농부들이 조류독감에 걸릴 위험이 더 크다고 할 수 있으므로 보도문의 내용과 일치하는 선택지는 (a)이다.

어휘 outbreak (병이나 질병의) 발발, 발생

avian influenza 조류독감

dramatic drop 극적인 감소, 현저한 감소

poultry 가금류

contract (병에) 걸리다

carrier 매개체, 보균자

domesticated 길들여진, 집에서 사육된

susceptible to ~에 걸리기 쉬운, 취약한

potentially infected 감염되었을지도 모르는

정답 (a)

Sample

1 해석 축하합니다! 당신은 키친 에이드에서 가장 질 좋은 식
칼을 구입하셨습니다. 저희 제품의 모든 칼은 평생 보
증됩니다. 만족하지 못하면 언제든지 가져오셔서 전액
환불받으실 수 있습니다. 키친 에이드 식칼은 특별히
신경 쓰시기 바랍니다. 비눗물에 칼을 담가 두지 마세
요. 칼날이 무뎌집니다. 씻은 후에는 항상 바로 칼을
말려서 안전한 곳에 두세요. 키친 에이드 제품을 구입
해 주셔서 감사합니다.

Q. 광고에 의하면 키친 에이드 칼에 대해 옳은 것은
   무엇인가?

(a) 평생 보증된다.

(b) 칼날은 적셔 둬야 한다.

(c) 칼을 씻은 후에 공기 중에 말려야 한다.

(d) 싸고 품질이 떨어진다.

해설 광고는 키친 에이드 식칼을 구매한 소비자에게 감사하
는 내용이다. 모든 칼이 평생 보증된다(All of our
knives are guaranteed for life.)고 언급되었으므
로 정답은 (a)이다. (b), (c)는 물에 담가 두지 말고 씻
은 후 바로 말리라고 했다. 최고 품질의 식칼이라고
했으므로 (d) 역시 오답이다.

어휘 chef's knife 식칼

guarantee 보증하다

for life 평생 동안

full refund 전액 환불

soapy water 비눗물

blade 칼날

dull 무디어지다

air dry 자연 건조시키다

of poor quality 질이 나쁜, 품질이 떨어지는

정답 (a)

2 해석 익스플로어 카드를 오늘 구입하세요. 그러면 내일 절
약됩니다! 익스플로어 카드로 당신은 수많은 소매상에
게서 상당한 절약과 보너스를 받을 것입니다. 당신이
어디서 절약할 수 있는지 알기 위해서 저희 웹사이트
인 www.explorecard.com을 보세요. 각 소매상의
할인 범위는 10~15%이며, 미용실에서 항공사까지 다
포함돼 있습니다. 익스플로어 카드는 단지 49불 99센
트에 당신 것이 될 수 있으며 평생 만기가 없습니다!
다음 장소 중 한 곳에서 하나 구입하세요.

Q. 무엇이 광고되고 있는가?

(a) 사용자에게 보상해 주는 신용카드 프로그램

(b) 만기 날짜가 없는 할인 카드

(c) 자주 여행하는 사람을 위한 마일리지 카드

(d) 소매상에게 현금을 돌려 주는 카드

해설 정답을 (d)로 착각하기 쉬운 문제이므로 선택지를 주
의해서 들어야 하는 문제이다. 소매상들을 위한 카드
가 아니라 소매점에서 물건을 구입하는 소비자들을 위
한 할인 카드이므로 정답은 (b)이다.

어휘 retailer 소매상

substantial 상당한

respective 각각의

expire 말소되다, 만기가 되다

정답 (b)

3 해석 고객 여러분, 주목해 주세요! 지금 모든 고객분들께서
는 쇼핑백 안을 들여다보고 엉뚱한 가방을 가지고 있
지 않은지 확인해 주시기 바랍니다. 반복합니다. 잠시
시간을 내시어 실수로 다른 사람의 가방을 가져가지
않았는지 확인해 보시기 바랍니다. 만일 그렇게 한 것
을 알게 되셨으면 즉시 본관에 있는 고객 서비스 데스
크로 알려 주시길 바랍니다. 주목해 주셔서 감사드리
고 힐사이드 몰에서 쇼핑해 주셔서 감사합니다.

Q. 왜 이 안내 방송을 하고 있는가?

(a) 쇼핑백이 부족하다.

(b) 일부 상품이 도난당했다.

(c) 많은 명품 가방이 분실되었다.

(d) 한 고객이 쇼핑백을 분실하였다.

해설 안내 방송 도입부에 please take a moment to
check that you have not mistakenly taken
someone else's bags를 통해 어떤 고객이 가방을
분실해서 안내 방송을 한 것임을 알 수 있다.

어휘 verify 확인하다

mistakenly 실수로

designer 유명 디자이너의, 고급[고가]의

정답 (d)

4 해석 휴일이 생산성에 끼치는 영향을 최소화하기 위해서 여
러분이 다음 사항을 고려해 주기를 바랍니다. 첫째, 모
든 사람의 휴가 요청을 수용하는 것은 불가능합니다.
둘째, 경영진은 각 직원에게 추수 감사절, 크리스마스,
새해 중에서 두 번의 휴가만을 보장할 것입니다. 셋
째, 우선권은 작년에 선택권을 갖지 못한 직원에게 먼

저 주어질 것입니다.

Q. 공지에 따르면 다음 중 맞는 것은 무엇인가?

(a) 일부 직원은 올해 우선 선택권을 갖게 될 것이다.

(b) 회사는 공휴일에 휴업할 것이다.

(c) 직원들은 휴가에 대해서는 보수를 받지 못할 것이다.

(d) 모든 직원은 세 번의 공휴일을 갖게 될 것이다.

해설 추수 감사절, 크리스마스, 새해 중에서 두 번을 골라 쉴 수 있지만 선택권은 작년에 선택권을 받지 못한 사람에게 먼저 주어질 것이라고 말하고 있다. 그러므로 일부 직원이 우선 선택권을 갖게 될 것임을 추측할 수 있다.

어휘 consideration 고려할 사항
accommodate 편의를 도모하다, (부탁을) 들어주다
day off 비번, 휴일
next to impossible 거의 불가능하다
priority 우선권
preference 우선권, 선취권
pick 선택(권)

정답 (a)

Actual Test

1 해석 M: 루크가 다른 회사에서 더 좋은 제안을 받았대.

W: ＿＿＿＿＿＿＿＿＿＿＿

(a) 요즘은 누구도 믿어서는 안 돼.

(b) 그가 해고되리라고는 예상 못했어.

(c) 그는 월급을 올려 받을 자격이 있어.

(d) 그는 좋은 기회는 절대 놓치지 않지.

해설 평서문을 듣고 적절한 응답을 고르는 문제로, 정형화된 응답보다는 여러 가지 간접 응답을 예상하면서 소거법을 적용해 풀 필요가 있다. 남자가 여자에게 제3자인 루크라는 사람이 다른 회사로부터 지금 근무하고 있는 회사보다 더 좋은 제안을 받았다는 소식을 전하고 있으므로 그 조건을 수락할 것이라고 간접적으로 암시하는 (d)가 선택지 중에서 가장 자연스럽다. 남을 믿어서는 안 된다는 (a)는 전혀 엉뚱한 대답이고, (b)는 루크가 해고된 것은 아니므로 답이 될 수 없으며, (c)는 다른 회사에서 좋은 제안을 받았다는 내용이지 승진된 것은 아니므로 답으로 부적절하다.

어휘 depend on 믿다, 신뢰하다

정답 (d)

2 해석 W: 나는 이 영화보다 더 말도 안 되는 영화는 본 적이

없어!

M: ＿＿＿＿＿＿＿＿＿＿＿

(a) 정말 그래.

(b) 무슨 일이니?

(c) 나도 그래. 다시 보자.

(d) 그럼 가지 마.

해설 여자가 남자에게 함께 본 영화에 대해 실망을 표현하고 있으므로 동조를 하거나 반대 의견을 제시하는 응답이 가장 자연스럽다. 따라서 여자의 의견에 동조를 하고 있는 (a)가 정답이다. (d)는 Me, too.까지는 자연스럽지만 Let's watch it again. 부분이 어색하다.

어휘 absurd 터무니없는, 말도 안 되는
You're telling me. 네 말이 맞아. 그렇고 말고.

정답 (a)

3 해석 W: 네 휴대폰 좀 잠깐 빌려도 되겠니?

M: ＿＿＿＿＿＿＿＿＿＿＿

(a) 나한테 말해.

(b) 좋은 생각이야.

(c) 물론이야.

(d) 유감스럽지만 그래.

해설 여자가 남자에게 남자의 휴대폰을 잠깐 써도 되겠느냐고 허락을 구하고 있으므로 흔쾌히 승낙하거나 부드럽게 거절하는 응답이 나와야 한다. 정답은 흔쾌히 승낙하는 (c)이다. By all means.는 상대방의 요청에 흔쾌히 허락하는 표현으로 Of course, Certainly, Sure. 등의 표현과 같다. (d)는 Unfortunately, no. 가 되어야 한다.

어휘 By all means. 그럼요. 좋다뿐인가

정답 (c)

4 해석 M: 자동차를 팔고 싶어.

W: 벌써? 불과 2달 전에 산 거 아니니?

M: 그래, 하지만 엔진에서 계속 이상한 소리가 나서.

W: ＿＿＿＿＿＿＿＿＿＿＿

(a) 차에 최선을 다해 봐.

(b) 좋은 조건인 거 같아.

(c) 전에는 소리에 문제가 없었거든.

(d) 정비사에게 얘기해 보는 게 어떻겠니?

해설 남자가 불과 2달 전에 산 자동차를 팔고 싶어 하는데, 엔진에서 이상한 소음이 나서라고 이유를 밝히고 있다. 따라서 남자에게 조언이나 충고를 해주는 표현을 예상해 볼 수 있다. 이런 경우 가장 보편적인 응답

은 정비사에게 점검을 한번 받아 보라는 내용이다. 따라서 (d)가 가장 자연스러운 응답이다.

어휘 mechanic 정비사, 수리공

정답 (d)

5 해석 W: 그 프로젝트 제안서에 대해 닉의 생각은 어땠어?

M: 실은, 별로 열정적이지가 않아.

W: 찬성하지 않았다는 뜻이니?

M: ___________________

(a) 아니, 그는 꽤 완강했어.

(b) 응, 거의 찢어 버리려고 했어.

(c) 아니, 완전히 마음에 들어 했어.

(d) 아니, 너를 보고 싶어 했어.

해설 less than enthusiastic이 결정적인 힌트이므로 놓치지 않고 들어 줘야 문제를 풀 수 있다. 닉이 프로젝트 아이디어에 대해 시큰둥했다(less than enthusiastic)는 걸로 보아, 그 프로젝트에 찬성하지 않았다는 걸 유추할 수 있으므로 그 프로젝트 제안서를 거의 찢어 버릴 뻔했다는 내용의 (b)가 가장 자연스러운 응답이다.

어휘 less than 결코 ~않다

agree to 찬성하다

adamant 완강한

tear up 찢다

정답 (b)

6 해석 W: 집들을 둘러보고 나서 후보를 3개로 좁혔어요.

M: 어떤 집이 가장 마음에 드시나요?

W: 해변가 집이 가장 맘에 듭니다만 비싸더군요.

M: 그건 그 집이 마을에서 입지가 가장 좋기 때문입니다. 바다가 보이는 전망이 멋지잖아요.

W: 그건 그렇지만, 비바람에 많이 낡은 것 같더군요. 페인트가 좀 벗겨지고 배관도 녹슬었던데요.

M : 이 집은 가장 잘나가는 집들 중에 하나입니다. 아무래도 고객님이 원하시는 가격대에 맞는 곳을 찾아 드려야겠군요.

Q. 남자의 의도는 무엇인가?

(a) 여자를 위해 그 집을 다시 페인트칠한다.

(b) 여자가 그 집을 사지 못하도록 한다.

(c) 가격에 상관없이 집을 팔려고 한다.

(d) 원래 가격에 집을 팔려고 한다.

해설 여자가 마음에 들어 하는 집이 있지만 가격이 비싸서 여자는 집이 낡았다고 말하며 은근히 할인을 원하고

있다. 하지만 남자는 가장 잘 팔리는 집이라고 말하면서 마지막에 여자가 원하는 가격대로 찾아 주겠다고 말한 걸로 보아 남자는 그 해변가 집을 깎아 줄 생각이 없다. 즉 원래 가격에 파려는 속셈으로 마지막 말을 했다고 볼 수 있다. 따라서 정답은 (d)이다.

어휘 narrow down 범위를 좁히다

pricy 값비싼

gorgeous 멋진, 굉장한

chip 깨지다, 이가 빠지다

rusty 녹슨

plumbing 배관

lot 용지, 부지

정답 (d)

7 해석 오늘 밤 여러분의 대학에서 강연하도록 허락해 주신 것에 감사를 표하고 싶습니다. 여러분도 아시다시피 제 이름은 마가렛 앳우드입니다. 저는 우리나라 최고의 마케팅 회사들 중 몇몇 회사에 컨설팅 일을 해주고 있습니다. 성장하고 있는 세계 시장에 경제가 개방됨에 따라 마케팅을 전공한 사람들을 위한 일자리 기회가 기하급수적으로 증가할 것입니다. 기업 마케팅을 전공한 대다수 졸업생들은 졸업하자마자 대기업에 채용될 것입니다. 게다가 마케팅 공부에 수반되는 광범위한 기술들을 익히게 됨으로써 졸업생들은 다른 많은 관련 분야에서 일할 자격을 갖추게 될 것입니다.

Q. 담화에 따르면 마케팅을 전공한 졸업자들의 취업 전망은 어떠한가?

(a) 몇몇 전문 분야에 국한되어 있다.

(b) 국제화로 인해 불안정할 것이다.

(c) 가까운 미래에 매우 좋지 않다.

(d) 다가오는 몇 년간 아주 밝다.

해설 마케팅 회사에 컨설팅을 해주는 연설자가 마케팅 전공 졸업 예정자들에게 취업 전망을 얘기하고 있다. 경제가 세계화되면서 마케팅을 전공한 졸업자들에 대한 수요가 기하급수적으로 늘 것이고, 졸업과 동시에 대기업에 취직이 가능하다고 언급하고 있으므로 마케팅을 전공한 졸업자들의 취업 전망은 아주 밝다고 볼 수 있다.

어휘 gratitude 감사

open up 개방하다

exponentially 기하급수적으로

graduate 졸업생

recruit 채용하다

broad range of 광범위한

be qualified to ~할 자격을 갖추다

job prospect 취업[직업] 전망

specialized field 전문 분야

fluctuate 불안정하다

slim 희박한, 빈약한

정답 (d)

Sample

1 해석 M: 실례합니다. 저축예금 계좌를 개설하고 싶습니다.

W: ____________________

(a) 네, 여기에서 수표를 현금으로 바꿀 수 있습니다.

(b) 이 수표 이서해 주세요.

(c) 왜 안 되는 거죠? 여기 제 계좌입니다.

(d) 물론이죠. 이 신청서를 작성해 주세요.

해설 open a savings account는 '저축 계좌를 계설하다'라는 뜻이다. 은행에서 계좌 계설을 원할 경우 가장 보편적인 응답은 신청서를 작성해 달라는 응답일 것이다.

어휘 savings account 저축예금 계좌

cash the check 수표를 현금으로 바꾸다

endorse (수표에) 이서하다

fill out 작성하다

application form 신청서

정답 (d)

2 해석 M: 안녕하세요. 아들에게 돈을 좀 보내려고 합니다.

W: 네, 고객님. 저희 은행 계좌 있으세요?

M: 네, 자동이체를 할 수 있나요?

W: ____________________

(a) 물론이죠. 고객님의 사회보장 카드와 계좌 번호가 필요합니다.

(b) 네, 고객님을 댁까지 곧장 모셔다 드릴 수 있습니다.

(c) 실은 고객님의 계좌가 필요합니다.

(d) 그 차 얼마 주고 사셨죠?

해설 direct billing은 우리말로 '자동이체'로 해석할 수 있다. 남자가 여자에게 자동이체로 아들에게 송금이 가능하냐고 묻고 있으므로 가능성 여부를 밝히는 응답이 필요하다. 따라서 가능하다고 밝히고 자동이체에 필요한 사회보장 카드와 계좌 번호를 요구한 (a)가 가장 적절한 응답이다.

어휘 remit (돈을) 보내다, 송금하다

direct billing 자동이체

정답 (a)

3 해석 M: 월러스 코퍼레이션은 합병에 관심이 있는데, 우리에게 많은 도움이 될 수 있어요.

W: 맞아요. 많은 경험과 깊이를 가지고 있는 회사죠.

M: 그들의 제안을 꼭 아주 신중하게 검토해 봐야겠어요.

W: _____________________

(a) 그들은 월러스 코퍼레이션과 똑같은 생각을 가지고 있어요.

(b) 우리 회사가 그들의 회사를 인수해서는 안 된다고 생각해요.

(c) 그 회사의 모든 자산만 있으면 우린 시장에서 최고가 될 수 있어요.

(d) 아뇨, 그들에게 연락해서 만남을 주선해 볼게요.

해설 같은 회사를 다니는 남자와 여자는 월러스 코퍼레이션과의 합병에 대해 긍정적임을 대화를 통해 짐작할 수 있으므로 남자의 마지막 말에 대한 여자의 응답 역시 합병에 대한 기대감을 표현하는 응답이 오는 것이 문맥상 자연스럽다. 따라서 정답은 (c)이다.

어휘 merger 합병
definitely 확실히
resources (보통 pl.) 자원, 재원, 자력(資力)
take over 인수하다
asset 자산

정답 (c)

4 **해석** W: 융자 신청을 거절당하셨죠?
M: 네, 솔직히 정말 놀랐어요.
W: 은행이 신청을 거절한 이유를 아시나요?
M: _____________________

(a) 제가 안정적인 수입이 없어서 그런 거 같아요.

(b) 제 경비가 더 이상 충당되지 않을 겁니다.

(c) 아니요, 단지 총 5만 불을 요청했어요.

(d) 네, 주중에는 10에서 3시까지만 영업합니다.

해설 간접의문문도 의문사나 접속사를 잘 들어 줘야 한다. 여자가 남자에게 남자의 대출 신청이 거절된 이유를 묻고 있으므로 대출 신청 거절의 사유가 될 만한 내용이 응답으로 와야 한다. 따라서 안정적인 수입이 없어서 그런 것 같다는 (a)의 응답이 적절하다.

어휘 turn down 거절하다(= reject)
loan request 대출 신청
expense 지출, 경비, 비용
cover 감당하다

정답 (a)

Actual Test

1 **해석** M: 요즘 들어 눈이 쓰라리고 아파.

W: _____________________

(a) 네가 그렇게 생각하다니 유감이다.

(b) 안과에 가보는 게 어때?

(c) 산부인과에 가보는 게 어떻겠니?

(d) 널 속이려는 게 아니야!

해설 남자가 눈이 쓰라리고 아프다고 했으므로 안과를 방문해 보라는 (b)가 가장 자연스러운 응답이다. pull the wool over one's eyes는 우리말로 '눈 가리고 아옹하다' 라는 말과 일대일 매칭이 되는 표현으로 누군가를 '감쪽같이 속이다' 라는 뜻이다.

어휘 irritated 따끔따끔한
sore 아픈
oculist 안과 의사
What do you say to ~ ? ~하는 것이 어때?
obstetrician 산부인과 의사
pull the wool over one's eyes 속이다, 눈 가리고 아옹하다

정답 (b)

2 **해석** W: 표정이 왜 그래?
M: _____________________

(a) 여기 오는 길에 강도를 당했어.

(b) 빨리 낫길 바랄게.

(c) 내 기분이 어떤지 표현할 수 없어.

(d) 성형수술 받았어.

해설 glum expression은 '무뚝뚝하고 뚱한 표정, 침울한 표정' 이라는 뜻이다. 여자가 남자에게 왜 우울한 표정을 하고 있느냐고 묻고 있으므로 적절한 이유를 말한 (a)가 정답이다. glum expression보다 자주 쓰이는 long face도 함께 알아 둘 필요가 있다.

어휘 glum 뚱한, 침울한
get mugged 강도에게 습격당하다

정답 (a)

3 **해석** M: 너 이번 주말에 한가하면 너랑 함께 놀고 싶어.
W: _____________________

(a) 내 전화를 받지 않은 이유가 분명 있겠지.

(b) 다음으로 미루면 안 될까?

(c) 난 지금 집에 혼자 있어.

(d) 옷을 차려입는 동안 기다려 줘.

해설 do something together는 '함께 놀다' 라는 뜻이다. 남자가 여자에게 주말에 만나서 같이 놀자고 제안하고 있으므로 제안을 승낙하거나 거절하는 응답이 적

절하다. 따라서 다음으로 미룰 수 있느냐고 응답함으로써 이번 주말에는 불가능하다고 정중하게 거절한 (b)가 가장 적절하다. Can I take you up on that some other time?은 '다음 기회에 너의 그 제안을 수락해도 되겠니?'로 직역되는데 다음으로 미루고 싶을 때 쓰는 표현으로 Can I take a rain check on that?과 같은 뜻이다.

어휘 take *sb* up on *sth* ~의 제안을 받아들이다
be all alone 혼자 있다
get dressed 차려입다

정답 (b)

4 해석 M: 고관절 치환 수술을 받았다는 게 사실이니?
W: 맞아. 거의 일주일 동안 병원에 있었어.
M: 안됐다. 보험 적용은 받았니?
W: ______________________
(a) 아니, 그건 좋은 조건이야.
(b) 응, 막대한 비용이 들 거야.
(c) 아니, 재정상에 타격을 입을 거야.
(d) 응, 몸 전체가 매우 아파.

해설 남자가 여자에게 여자가 받은 고관절 수술에 대해 보험 적용을 받았느냐고 묻고 있으므로 보험 적용을 받았다는 응답이나 받지 못했다는 응답을 예상해 볼 수 있다. 정답은 보험 적용을 받지 못해서 큰돈이 들 것이라는 내용의 (c)이다. hurt the pocketbook은 '재정에 타격을 주다' 정도로 해석할 수 있다. (b)는 Yes가 아니라 No가 되어야 한다.

어휘 hip replacement surgery 고관절 치환 수술
cost *sb* an arm and a leg 막대한 비용이 들다, 큰돈이 들다
hurt the pocketbook 재정상의 타격을 주다

정답 (c)

5 해석 W: 포틀랜드 인더스트리즈에 전화 주셔서 감사합니다. 저는 제니스입니다.
M: 안녕하세요. 저는 진 씨와 통화하고 싶습니다.
W: 진 씨는 사업상 회의 때문에 사무실을 비우셨습니다.
M: ______________________
(a) 제가 전화했다고 전해 주시겠어요?
(b) 저희 사무실은 하루 종일 영업합니다.
(c) 그는 오후 1시 30분쯤에 돌아올 것입니다.
(d) 진 씨세요?

해설 전화상의 대화이다. 남자가 여자에게 진 씨를 바꿔 달

라고 요청하자 여자는 진 씨가 부재중이라고 말한다. 전화해서 누군가와 통화를 원했으나 부재중이라는 얘기를 들었을 때 가장 보편적인 응답은 '메시지를 전해 달라', '언제쯤 사무실에 돌아오냐?', '전화해 달라고 전해 달라' 또는 '다시 전화하겠다'는 등의 응답일 것이다. 이 문제의 경우 전화했다고 전해 달라는 내용이 선택지 (a)에 가장 적절한 응답으로 제시되었다.

정답 (a)

6 해석 W: 오늘 밤 뭘 봐야 할지 모르겠어.
M: 지난번 영화처럼 심각한 건 아니었으면 해.
W: 이거 봤니? 이거 꽤 괜찮아 보여.
M: 외화니? 내가 자막을 잘 못 읽는 거 너도 알잖아.
W: 상 받은 영화야. 게다가 아주 낭만적이래.
M: 분명 다른 걸 찾을 수 있을 거야. 시간 내내 자막을 읽는다면 영상을 즐길 수 없거든.
W: 알았어. 네가 한번 골라 보는 게 어때?
M: 좋아. 기분 전환으로 코미디가 좋겠어.
Q. 대화에 따르면 다음 중 맞는 것은 무엇인가?
(a) 남자는 영화 장르에 까다롭지 않다.
(b) 남자는 로맨틱 영화 보는 것을 즐긴다.
(c) 두 사람은 오늘 밤 어떤 영화도 빌리지 않기로 했다.
(d) 남자는 모국어로 된 영화를 보기를 원한다.

해설 비디오를 빌리는 남녀 사이의 대화를 듣고 진위를 파악하는 문제이다. 남자는 자막을 잘 못 읽기 때문에 외화 보는 것을 꺼린다고 나와 있으므로 남자는 모국어로 된 영화를 보고 싶어 한다는 내용의 (d)가 정답이다. (a)는 남자가 영화 장르에 까다로운 걸로 짐작할 수 있으므로 대화의 내용과 일치하지 않으며, 남자가 로맨틱 영화를 좋아한다는 내용은 언급되어 있지 않고 로맨틱 영화를 좋아하는 사람은 여자이므로 (b)도 대화 내용과 일치하지 않는다. 남자의 마지막 말에서 알 수 있듯이 남자가 코미디 영화를 보자고 했으므로 어떤 영화도 빌리지 않기로 했다는 내용의 (c) 역시 오답이다.

어휘 subtitle 자막
change 기분 전환
picky 까다로운

정답 (d)

7 해석 편지를 보내는 것에서부터 음악을 다운로드하기 위해 검색을 하는 것에 이르기까지 인터넷은 점점 더 많은우리의 일상 활동에서 다른 매체들을 대신하고 있습니다.

사람들이 온라인 계약을 이용해서 문서 계약처럼 법적 구속력이 있는 사업적인 거래를 할 수 있도록 새로운 법안이 마련되었습니다. 사람들은 그들의 신원이 진짜임을 인증해 주는 기술 덕분에 수표, 유언장, 집문서에 전자 서명을 할 수 있게 될 것입니다. 비록 편리함이 이 새로운 시스템의 가장 큰 장점이긴 하지만, 많은 보안 관련 업체와 소비자 단체들이 악용 가능성에 대해 우려하고 있습니다.

Q. 이 뉴스 보도의 주제는 무엇인가?
(a) 인터넷 계약을 제한하는 법안
(b) 새로운 정보 보안 기술
(c) 전자 서명을 합법화시키는 법안
(d) 사이버 도둑을 잡는 방법

해설 인터넷상에서 이뤄지는 온라인 거래가 법적 효력을 가질 수 있도록 전자 서명을 합법화하는 법안이 마련되었다는 내용을 알리는 뉴스이므로 이 뉴스의 주제는 (c) 전자 서명을 합법화시키는 법안이다. 인터넷 계약을 제한하는 법안이 아니므로 (a)는 보도 내용과 일치하지 않으며, (b)와 (d)는 보도에 언급되어 있지도 않으며 무관한 내용이다.

어휘 conduct research 검색하다
replace 대신하다
medium 매체
legislation 법안
pave the way for ～의 길을 닦다, ～을 가능하게 하다
business transaction 사업상의 거래
counterpart 상응하는 것
legally binding 법적으로 구속력이 있는
put one's signature 서명하다
will 유언장, 유서
house deed 집문서
authorize 승인하다, 인증하다
identity 신원, 정체
legitimate 진짜인, 합법적인
bill 법안

정답 (c)

Chapter 10 쇼핑과 교통

Sample

1 **해석** W: 모두 합쳐 15달러 46센트입니다.
M: 신용카드로 결제해도 되나요?
W: 죄송하지만 곤란합니다. 이곳은 10개 이하의 상품에 대해서는 현금 결제만 가능한 계산대입니다.
M: 죄송해요. 몰랐습니다. 하지만 이번 한 번만 신용카드로 결제할 수 없을까요?
W: 음, 손님 뒤에 다른 손님이 없기 때문에 이번만 해 드릴게요.
M: 감사합니다.

Q. 대화에 따르면 남자는 무엇을 하겠는가?
(a) 그가 구매한 상품을 현금으로 결제한다.
(b) 다른 계산대로 간다.
(c) 신용카드로 결제한다.
(d) 매니저와 이야기한다.

해설 남자가 계산하려는 카운터는 10개 이하의 상품을 구매한 경우에 현금만 받는 카운터이므로 신용카드로 결제할 수 없지만 남자가 이번 한 번만 신용카드로 결제해 달라고 조르자 여자가 마지못해 이번 한 번만 (just this time)이라는 단서를 달고 신용카드로 결제해 주기로 했으므로 신용카드로 지불한다는 내용의 (c)가 정답이다.

어휘 come to (금액이) ～이 되다
shopping 구입한 물건

정답 (c)

2 **해석** M: 이 바지들을 교환할 수 있을까요? 너무 길어서요.
W: ______________________
(a) 영수증을 갖고 계시면요.
(b) 죄송하지만 저희는 수선을 해 드리지 않습니다.
(c) 음, 돈을 추가로 내셔야 합니다.
(d) 네, 바지가 손님에게 조금 짧아 보이네요.

해설 남자가 여자에게 구입한 바지의 교환이 가능한지 물어보고 있다. 바지가 너무 길다는 것은 교환을 원하는 이유에 해당한다. 상식적으로 물건을 교환해 달라는 요청을 들어주기 위해서는 그 상점에서 샀다는 걸 증명해 주는 영수증이 반드시 있어야 한다. 따라서 가장 적절한 응답은 (a)이다. (b)와 (c)는 수선과 관련된 질문에 대한 대답으로 가능하다.

어휘 tailoring 수선

정답 (a)

3 해석 W: 이 양말 좀 반품할 수 있을까요?

M: 물론이죠. 영수증 좀 보여 주시겠어요?

W: 네, 여기 있습니다. 그리고 여기 양말입니다

M: 부인, 양말이 더럽네요! 착용되지 않은 의복만 반품하실 수 있습니다.

W: 아, 몰랐어요.

Q. 여자는 왜 환불을 받을 수 없었는가?

(a) 양말을 이미 신었기 때문에

(b) 영수증을 갖고 있지 않아서

(c) 양말을 가지고 오지 않아서

(d) 양말을 다른 데서 구입해서

해설 남자의 마지막 말에 단서가 나와 있다. 남자가 양말이 더럽다며 입어 보지 않은 의복에 대해서만 반품해 준다고 말한 걸로 보아 여자가 환불받지 못한 이유는 (a)이다.

어휘 unworn 착용되지 않은, 입지 않은
elsewhere 다른 곳에서

정답 (a)

4 해석 W: 실례합니다만 가장 가까운 우체국이 어딘지 알려 주시겠어요?

M: 혹시 우표가 필요하신 거면 모퉁이 가게에서 살 수 있어요.

W: 아뇨, 일본에 있는 동생을 놀라게 해줄 소포를 보내야 해요.

M: 그러면 시내에 있는 우체국에 가셔야 해요.

W: 어떻게 가는지 알려 주시겠어요?

M: 물론이죠. 이 길로 두 블럭을 곧장 내려가서 노스 가를 찾으세요.

W: 두 블럭을 가면 노스 가란 말이죠. 어느 쪽으로 돌아야 하나요?

M: 노스 가에서 좌회전하세요. 쉽게 찾으실 거예요.

Q. 대화에서 유추할 수 있는 내용은 무엇인가?

(a) 남자는 우체국이 어딘지 모른다.

(b) 여자의 동생은 소포에 대해 모르고 있다.

(c) 남자와 여자 모두 이 도시 출신이 아니다.

(d) 여자는 아마도 모퉁이 가게에 갈 것이다.

해설 여자는 일본에 사는 동생에게 소포를 보내기 위해 우체국을 찾고 있다. 남자는 아마도 이 지역 출신으로 동네 지리를 잘 알고 있다. 여자가 일본에 있는 동생을 깜짝 놀라게 해줄 소포를 보내야 한다고 했으므로 (b)가 정답이다

어휘 direct to sb ~에게 …로 가는 길을 알려 주다

hit (장소에) 도착하다, 이르다

정답 (b)

5 해석 W: 글로브 여행사입니다. 전화를 어디로 돌려 드릴까요?

M: 안녕하세요. 항공편 취소에 대해 문의할 것이 있습니다.

W: 네. 무엇이 알고 싶습니까?

M: 금요일 라스베이거스행 비행 편을 예약했는데요. 취소해야 할 것 같습니다.

W: 적어도 24시간 안에 취소 통보를 하시면 위약금이 없습니다.

M: 그렇다면 제가 하루 미만으로 취소하게 되면요?

W: 출발 하루 전에 하는 취소는 전부 위약금이 발생합니다.

M: 알겠습니다. 알게 되어 다행이네요. 나중에 다시 전화하겠습니다.

Q. 남자는 주로 무엇을 하고 있는가?

(a) 그의 예약을 취소하고 있다.

(b) 라스베이거스행 좌석을 예약하고 있다.

(c) 항공 취소 정책을 조회하고 있다.

(d) 예약 표에 대해 환불을 요청하고 있다.

해설 여행사 직원과 고객의 대화를 듣고 고객이 전화한 이유를 파악하는 문제이다. 남자가 자신이 예약한 비행 편을 이 대화가 끝나고 취소할 수도 있겠지만 이 전화 대화에서는 사실상 취소 관련 정책만 알아보고 취소는 하지 않았으므로 정답을 (a)로 고르지 않도록 유의해야 한다. 따라서 정답은 (c)이다.

어휘 cancellation 취소
penalty 위약금, 벌금
incur 초래하다, (손실을) 입다

정답 (c)

Actual Test

1 해석 M: 데릭 젠슨에게 사회자가 되어 달라고 부탁해야 하지 않을까?

W: ____________________

(a) 나도 알아. 인기는 없을 거야.

(b) 사람들 앞에서 이야기하는 건 무서워.

(c) 아마 참여하는 데 흥미를 느낄 거야.

(d) 지난번에 훌륭한 연설자들이 많았어.

해설 남자가 여자에게 데릭 젠슨에게 사회자가 되어 달라고 부탁하는 것이 어떻겠느냐고 의견을 구하고 있으므로

그러한 요청을 수락할 수도 있다는 의견을 말한 (c)가
가장 적절한 응답이다.

어휘 **master of ceremonies** 사회자, 진행자
terrifying 끔찍한, 무서운

정답 (c)

2 해석 W: 워워, 조심해! 하마터면 자전거 타고 있는 저 사람
을 칠 뻔했잖아.

M: ___________________

(a) 이런, 집중을 안 하고 있었어.

(b) 자전거보다 자동차를 보고 싶어.

(c) 문제없어. 난 보험에 가입되어 있거든.

(d) 나는 자전거보다는 차를 훨씬 잘 운전해.

해설 여자가 남자에게 자전거 타는 사람을 거의 칠 뻔했다
며 조심하라고 경고하는 걸로 보아 남자는 운전 중임
을 알 수 있다. 따라서 주의를 기울이지 않고 있었다
고 변명한 (a)가 가장 자연스러운 응답이다.

어휘 **bicyclist** 자전거 타는 사람
insured 보험에 가입한

정답 (a)

3 해석 M: 차를 몰고 가는 대신 우리 자전거를 타고 가는 게
어때?

W: ___________________

(a) 지금 당장 충분한 현금이 없어.

(b) 난 이런 식의 옷이 마음에 들어.

(c) 바깥이 너무 추워.

(d) 알았어. 여기 버스 정류장이 있다.

해설 남자가 차를 몰고 가는 대신 자전거를 타고 가자고 제
안하고 있으므로 제안을 수락하거나 거절하는 표현이
적당하다. 바깥 날씨가 너무 춥다고 거절한 간접 응답
인 (c)가 정답이다.

어휘 **What do you say ~ ?** ~하는 것이 어때?
way too 너무

정답 (c)

4 해석 M: 여기 교통이 점점 나빠지고 있어.

W: 나도 알아. 밖에 나가는 것조차 건강에 위험해져
버렸어.

M: 뭔가 대책이 있는지 궁금해.

W: ___________________

(a) 기름 값이 더 저렴해지면 도움이 될 텐데.

(b) 회사들이 전기 소비를 줄이면 돼.

(c) 자동차 가격을 올리면 돼.

(d) 대중교통을 이용하는 것이 한 가지 해결책이지.

해설 교통이 점점 나빠져서 밖에 나가는 것만으로도 누군가
의 건강이 위험하게 된 상황을 해결하기 위해 어떤 일
을 해야 하는지 의문을 던지고 있으므로 이러한 교통
문제를 해결하기 위한 가장 적절한 방법을 제시한 선
택지를 고르면 된다. 교통량 증가로 인한 대기 오염의
해결 방안으로 가장 적절한 것은 대중교통을 이용하는
것이라고 볼 수 있으므로 선택지 중 (d)가 가장 적절
하다. 기름 값이 더 저렴해지면 교통량이 증가할 것이
므로 (a)는 적절한 응답이 될 수 없고, (b)와 (c) 역시
교통량 증가를 막기 위한 직접적인 방법이라고는 볼
수 없으므로 답이 될 수 없다.

어휘 **affordable** (가격이) 알맞은, 감당할 수 있는

정답 (d)

5 해석 M: 완다, 너를 여기서 다 만나다니!

W: 에드, 무지 오랜만이야. 엘리자베스는 잘 지내지?

M: 더할 나위 없어. 사실 그녀의 첫 번째 책이 막 출
간됐거든.

W: ___________________

(a) 그래? 축하한다고 전해 줘.

(b) 나는 모든 것들이 좋아지길 바라.

(c) 그 불운이 오래 가진 않을 거야.

(d) 너는 너무 겸손해.

해설 두 사람은 오랜만에 만났다. 여자가 남자에게 엘리자
베스의 안부를 묻자 그녀의 첫 번째 책이 출간되었다
고 전하고 있다. 첫 번째 책을 출판한 일은 축하해 줄
만한 일이므로 축하를 전해 달라고 응답한 (a)가 가장
적절하다.

어휘 **Fancy ~ !** ~하다니!
run into 우연히 만나다
things couldn't be better 더 이상 좋을 수 없다
change for the better 좋아지다
modest 겸손한

정답 (a)

6 해석 M: 자, 이제 우리 가야겠어.

W: 목걸이를 찾는 동안 잠시만 기다려.

M: 왜 항상 이런 일이 생기지? 우리 늦겠어.

W: 몇 분만 더 줘.

M: 벌써 20분째 기다리고 있잖아.

W: 자, 거기 서 있지 말고 찾는 걸 도와줘.

M: 봐. 내내 이 서랍 속에 있었잖아.

W: 그거 아니야. 내가 찾고 있는 건 다이아몬드 박힌 거야.

Q. 대화로부터 추론 가능한 것은 무엇인가?

(a) 두 사람은 파티에 제시간에 도착할 것이다.

(b) 남자는 여자에게 목걸이를 준 걸 후회하고 있다

(c) 여자는 특정한 목걸이를 생각하고 있다.

(d) 여자는 보통 목걸이를 서랍 속에 둔다.

해설 두 사람이 어딘가에 가려는데 여자가 목걸이를 찾느라 늑장을 부리고 있는 상황이다. 여자의 마지막 말(I'm talking about the one with diamonds.)로 보아 여자가 찾고 있는 목걸이는 특정한 목걸이라고 볼 수 있으므로 (c)가 정답이다. (a)는 여자가 늑장을 부리고 있어서 두 사람이 파티에 제시간에 도착할 가능성보다 늦을 가능성이 더 높으므로 적절한 추론이 아니다. (b)와 (d)는 대화를 통해 추론이 불가능하다.

어휘 **get going** 가다, 출발하다

give *sb* **a hand** ~를 도와주다

drawer 서랍, 장롱

정답 (c)

---

7 해석 예비 대학생의 가장 큰 관심사 중에 하나는 자신이 원하는 대학에 진학하는 것입니다. 이런 입학 절차는 나라마다 매우 차이가 있으며, 그 차이들을 이해하는 것이 학생들이 자신들에게 가장 알맞은 상황을 결정하는 데 도움을 줄 수 있습니다. 독일 대학 대 스웨덴 대학 사이의 차이점을 예로 들어 보겠습니다. 독일 대학들은 경쟁적인 입학 기준을 갖고 있으며 때때로 매우 배타적인 반면, 중등 교육을 이수한 사람은 누구나 스웨덴의 대학들에 입학할 수 있습니다.

Q. 다음 중 독일 대학의 시스템과 스웨덴 대학의 시스템의 가장 뚜렷한 차이점은 무엇인가?

(a) 학업 수준

(b) 시민권

(c) 입학 정책

(d) 다양한 옵션

해설 각 나라마다 입학 절차가 다르다는 것을 설명하고 있다. 독일의 대학과 스웨덴의 대학을 예로 드는데 독일은 매우 까다로운 입학 기준을 갖고 있지만 스웨덴은 중등 교육만 마치면 누구나 들어갈 수 있다. 따라서 독일과 스웨덴의 대학 시스템의 확실한 차이는 입학 정책이 다르다는 것이다.

어휘 **college-bound student** 예비 대학생

get accepted into ~에 입학하다

admissions process 입학 절차

versus ~대, ~와 대비[비교]하여

at times 때때로, 가끔

exclusive 배타적인

secondary education 중등 교육

citizenship 시민권

an array of 다양한, 각양각색의

정답 (c)

Sample

1 **해석** M: 안녕하세요. 잠시 얘기 좀 할 수 있을까요?

W: 물론이죠. 무슨 일이죠?

M: IT 부서의 공석에 대해 사장님과 말씀하셨는지 궁금해서요.

W: 아, 이런. 제가 그러겠다고 말만 하고 깜박해 버렸네요.

M: 오늘 해주실 수 있나요?

W: 사실, 저희 사장님이 한 달간 브라질로 출장 가셨어요.

Q. 대화로부터 추론 가능한 것은 무엇인가?

(a) 남자는 일자리에 관심이 있다.

(b) 여자는 남자의 사장이다.

(c) 남자는 은퇴를 생각하고 있다.

(d) 여자는 남자의 말을 듣지 않는다.

해설 남자의 두 번째 대화문(I was wondering if you spoke to your boss about an opening in your IT department.)에서 알 수 있듯이 남자는 여자 회사의 빈 일자리에 관심이 있음을 알 수 있으므로 대화로부터 추론 가능한 것은 (a)이다.

어휘 opening 공석, 일자리

retire 은퇴하다

정답 (a)

2 **해석** W: 전 점심 때 직원회의에서 당신을 보지 못했는데요.

M: ＿＿＿＿＿＿＿＿＿＿＿＿

(a) 알아요. 참석을 못했으니까요.

(b) 직원 부족 문제가 좀 있어요.

(c) 대신 제가 참석할까요?

(d) 네, 점심때 뵐게요.

해설 여자가 점심 때 있었던 직원회의에서 남자를 보지 못했다고 말하고 있으므로 남자의 답변은 그와 관련된 말(이유 등)이 나와야 한다. 회의에서 못 본 이유는 참석을 못했기 때문이라고 밝힌 (a)가 가장 자연스럽다. 선택지 (b)는 질문지에 등장한 단어 sfaff를 이용한 오답 함정임에 주의해야 한다. 따라서 정답은 (a)이다.

어휘 staff meeting 직원회의

concern 문제

정답 (a)

3 **해석** M: 오늘 안색이 별로 좋아 보이지 않는데 괜찮으세요?

W: 네, 그다지 좋지 않습니다.

M: 무슨 일인지 말씀해 주실 수 있으세요?

W: 별로 하고 싶지는 않지만 오늘 아침부터 상사로부터 정산표를 일찍 제출하지 않았다고 꾸중을 들었어요.

M: 그는 언제 그 정산표가 필요하였나요?

W: 어제 저녁이요. 하지만 저는 일이 너무 많아서 마감이 연장되었어야만 했어요.

M: 그래 그 일은 끝났나요, 아니면 여전히 하고 계신가요?

Q. 화자들이 주로 하고 있는 이야기는 무엇인가?

(a) 여자가 사무실에 지각한 이유

(b) 여자가 다른 직장을 찾고 있는 이유

(c) 여자가 힘들어 하는 이유

(d) 상사가 여자에게 화가 난 이유

해설 대화의 주제는 여자가 왜 오늘 기분이 좋지 않은지에 대한 것이므로 (d)보다는 (c)가 주제에 적합하다. 대화의 전체 분위기가 여자를 중심으로 이루어지기 때문이다.

어휘 chew *sb* out 호되게 꾸짖다, 호통치다

spreadsheet 스프레드시트, (펼친) 셈판, 확장 문서

have a rough time 힘들어 하다, 고통스러운 시간을 보내다

정답 (c)

4 **해석** W: 우리 회의를 다음 주로 연기하는 게 가능할까요?

M: 왜요? 무슨 문제라도 있는 건가요?

W: 실은 회의를 위한 자료 준비를 아직 끝내지 못했거든요.

M: ＿＿＿＿＿＿＿＿＿＿＿＿

(a) 거기에 대해 오늘 오후에 부장님과 상의해 볼게요.

(b) 다음 주말까지 끝내겠다고 약속할게요.

(c) 말은 쉽죠.

(d) 상사랑 한바탕했어요.

해설 여자가 회의에 사용할 자료 준비를 끝내지 못해 회의를 연기하고 싶어서 연기가 가능한지 남자에게 물어봤으므로 남자가 회의를 연기할 권한이 있다면 연기 가능성 여부를 직접 응답으로 대답해 줄 수 있지만, 없는 경우는 선택지 (a)처럼 다른 사람과 상의해 보겠다는 제3의 응답도 충분히 가능하다.

어휘 have yet to 아직 ～하지 않았다, 아직 ～해야 한다

easier said than done 말은 쉽다

have words with ～와 말다툼하다, 언쟁하다

정답 (a)

Actual Test

1 **해석** M: 번지점프 하러 갔었다며? 어땠니?

W: ＿＿＿＿＿＿＿＿＿＿＿

(a) 몇 번 해봤어.

(b) 위험하다고 들었어.

(c) 놀랍고 유쾌했어.

(d) 놀라울 거야.

해설 번지점프를 해본 경험이 어땠는지 묻고 있으므로 번지점프를 해본 소감을 응답한 (c)가 정답이다. (d)는 시제가 틀렸다.

어휘 petrifying 놀라운, 무서운, 몸을 굳게 하는

exhilarating 유쾌한, 신나는

incredible 놀라운, 믿기 어려운

정답 (c)

2 **해석** M: 끝내는 데 왜 이리 오래 걸리는 거야?

W: ＿＿＿＿＿＿＿＿＿＿＿

(a) 나는 모든 장비를 집으로 가져갔어.

(b) 필요한 만큼 시간을 가져.

(c) 긴 이야기가 아니야.

(d) 예상했던 것보다 더 어려워.

해설 남자가 여자에게 왜 그렇게 오래 걸리느냐고 묻고 있으므로 예상보다 어려워서 오래 걸리고 있다고 이유를 밝힌 (d)가 가장 자연스러운 응답이다. (a), (b), (c)는 모두 대화에 등장한 단어를 선택지에 다시 등장시킨 오답 함정이다.

어휘 equipment 장비

정답 (d)

3 **해석** M: (재채기) 죄송합니다.

W: ＿＿＿＿＿＿＿＿＿＿＿

(a) 미안합니다.

(b) 다 잘될 거야.

(c) 뭘 원하니?

(d) 신의 가호가!

해설 재채기를 한 사람에게 흔히 Bless you!라고 말한다. 원래 재채기는 전염병의 첫 징후로 여겨졌고, 재채기를 하면 영혼이 순간적으로 육체를 이탈한다고 믿어서 순간적으로 육체를 떠난 영혼이 악마에게 붙잡히지 않도록 옆에 있던 사람들이 God bless you!라고 외친 것에서 유래된 표현이다. Bless you!라고 외치면 영혼이 무사히 육체로 되돌아온다고 믿었다고 한다. Bless you! 라고 말해 준 사람에게는 보통 Thank you.나 Thanks.로 응답한다.

어휘 sneeze 재채기하다

Bless you! 신의 축복이 있기를! 몸조심하세요.

정답 (d)

4 **해석** M: 안녕하세요. 저는 에릭 슈바르츠입니다.

W: 저는 조슬린 그래프입니다. 만나서 반갑습니다.

M: 그래프 씨, 당신을 어떻게 부르면 됩니까?

W: ＿＿＿＿＿＿＿＿＿＿＿

(a) 저는 휴대폰이 없어요.

(b) 오후 4시 이후에 저에게 전화해 주세요.

(c) 그냥 조라고 불러 주세요.

(d) 정말입니다. 만나서 정말 반갑습니다.

해설 남녀가 서로 소개를 하고 있다. How do you like to be addressed?는 '당신을 어떻게 부르면 좋겠습니까?' 라는 질문이다. 남자가 여자에게 앞으로 호칭을 어떻게 불러야 할지 묻고 있으므로 원하는 호칭을 알려 주는 (c)가 가장 자연스러운 응답이다.

어휘 address ~라고 부르다

정답 (c)

5 **해석** M: 너랑 얘기 좀 해야겠어.

W: 지금은 일 때문에 정신이 없거든.

M: 그냥 간단한 질문이야. 약속할게.

W: ＿＿＿＿＿＿＿＿＿＿＿

(a) 좋아. 하지만 요점만 말해.

(b) 어떻게 감히 내 결정에 이의를 제기하니?

(c) 물론. 그것은 결국엔 그만한 가치가 있어.

(d) 알았어. 처음부터 천천히 시작해.

해설 남자가 여자와 잠깐 얘기를 나누고 싶어 하는 상황이다. 하지만 여자가 일 때문에 정신없다고 얘기하자 간단한 질문이라며 종용하고 있다. 보통 이 경우엔 빨리 요점만 간단히 말해 보라는 (a)가 가장 보편적인 응답이다.

어휘 overwhelmed 짓눌린

get to the point 요점만 말하다

worth it 그만한 가치가 있는

정답 (a)

6 **해석** M: 그러니까 필립이 당신 프로젝트 팀에서 일하고 있다는 건가요?

W: 네. 그 사람 어떤가요?

M: 부지런하고 점잖은 사람이죠.

W: 그 말을 들으니 놀랍네요.

M: 정말요? 당신 팀과 잘 어울리지 않나요?

W: 전혀요. 물속의 기름 같아요.

Q. 필립은 그의 프로젝트 팀에서 어떻게 지내고 있는가?

(a) 많이 발전하고 있다.

(b) 근면함에 대해서 칭찬받고 있다.

(c) 상사에게 좋은 인상을 주었다.

(d) 잘 적응하지 못하고 있다.

해설 여자의 마지막 말이 결정적인 힌트이다. like oil in water는 물속의 기름처럼 잘 맞지 않는다는 뜻이므로 필립은 새 프로젝트 팀에서 잘 적응하지 못하고 있다, 잘 어울리지 못하고 있다는 내용의 (d)가 정답이다. a square peg in a round hole은 '둥근 홈에 네모난 쐐기'로 직역되는데 '잘 어울리지 못하는 사람, 부적임자'라는 뜻으로 주로 사용된다.

어휘 hard-working 열심히 일하는, 부지런한

decent 점잖은, 괜찮은

fit in with ~와 잘 맞다, 잘 어울리다

Far from it. 전혀 그렇지 않아요.

diligence 근면, 부지런함

impress 좋은 인상을 주다

a square peg in a round hole 적임이 아닌 사람, 부적격자

정답 (d)

7 **해석** 수사 당국은 5일 전 하와이에서 휴가를 보내다 실종된 10대 소녀를 아직도 찾고 있습니다. 섬 전역에 수색 팀이 동원되었지만, 지금까지 아무런 결과가 없습니다. 수사관들은 범죄의 가능성이 있을 수도 있다고 밝혔지만, 아직 어떤 용의자도 발표하지 않았습니다. 가족들은 그녀의 행방에 대한 어떤 정보라도 가지고 있는 사람은 즉시 경찰에 연락해 줄 것을 당부하고 있습니다. 제보는 023-989-8763으로 전화를 걸어서 익명으로 하실 수 있습니다. 그녀의 마을 주민들은 그녀가 무사하길 바라고 있습니다.

Q. 녹음된 메시지에 따르면 맞는 것은 무엇인가?

(a) 경찰은 소녀 실종의 용의자들을 체포했다.

(b) 실종된 소녀는 하와이 거주자다.

(c) 경찰은 대중으로부터 그녀를 찾는 데 도움을 받기를 희망한다.

(d) 관계 당국은 그들이 곧 이 사건을 곧 해결할 것이라고 확신한다.

해설 실종된 소녀에 대한 안내문을 듣고 진위를 파악하는 문제이다. (a) 경찰은 아직 용의자를 파악하지도 못했다. (b) 하와이에서 휴가를 보내고 있었다고 했으므로 하와이 주민이라고는 볼 수 없다. (c) 지문 마지막 문장에서 알 수 있듯이 수사 당국에서는 일반 시민들의 제보를 기다리고 있는 걸로 보아 일반 대중들로부터 그녀를 찾는 데 도움 받기를 희망하고 있다고 볼 수 있다. (d) 사건이 꼭 해결되리라 확신하고 있다는 내용은 언급되어 있지 않다. 따라서 지문의 내용과 일치하는 것은 (c)이다.

어휘 mobilize 동원하다

foul play 범죄, 살인

suspect 용의자

whereabouts 행방

anonymously 익명으로

wellbeing 안녕, 무사함

apprehend 체포하다

정답 (c)

Sample

1 해석 W: 여보세요. 저는 패트리샤 화이트입니다. 타이어 씨하고 통화하고 싶습니다.

M: _______________________

(a) 당신을 뵙고 싶었어요.

(b) 여기에 서명해 주세요.

(c) 무슨 용건인지 여쭤 봐도 될까요?

(d) 그에게 전화를 해보지 그러세요?

해설 전화상으로 누군가를 찾을 경우에는 바꿔 주겠다거나 부재중이라서 전화를 받을 수 없다고 응답하는 것이 거의 대부분이다. 간혹 본인이 전화 건 사람이 찾는 사람일 경우에는 (This is he/she) Speaking.의 응답이 대부분이고, 선택지 (c)처럼 이 과정을 생략하고 전화한 용건이 뭐냐고 바로 물어보는 경우도 충분히 가능하다.

어휘 sign 서명하다

May I ask what this is regarding? 전화한 용건이 뭔가요?

정답 (c)

2 해석 M: 조스 씨와 통화할 수 있을까요? 다니엘입니다.

W: _____________________

(a) 죄송하지만 그녀는 지금 샤워 중이에요.

(b) 당신이 그녀에게 전화해야 합니다.

(c) 메시지를 남기세요.

(d) 아니요, 다니엘 씨는 여기에 없어요.

해설 전화를 건 사람이 다니엘이므로 (d)는 오답이고 (c)도 아무 설명 없이 바로 메시지를 남기라는 말은 어색하므로 오답이다.

정답 (a)

3 해석 매머드 의료 센터에 전화 주셔서 감사합니다. 모든 간호사가 현재 바쁩니다. 긴급 의료 상황이면 전화를 끊으시고 911로 전화하십시오. 예방접종을 예약하시려면 1번을 눌러 주세요. 건강 문제와 관련하여 간호사와 상담하고 싶으시면 전화를 끊지 말고 대기해 주세요. 가능한 한 빨리 간호사와 연결될 것입니다.

Q. 메시지로부터 추론 가능한 것은 무엇인가?

(a) 사무실이 현재 닫혀 있다.

(b) 이 전화 회선은 응급 상황 전용이다.

(c) 예방접종 예약을 하려면 전화를 끊지 말고 기다려

야 한다.

(d) 간호사들이 현재 다른 환자들을 상대하고 있다.

해설 전화 메시지이다. 현재 간호사들이 바빠서 전화를 받을 수 없다고 했으므로(All of the nurses are currently busy.) (d)가 정답이다. (c) 예방접종은 1번을 누르라고 언급되었다.

어휘 hang up 전화를 끊다

immunization 예방접종

stay on the line 전화를 끊지 않고 기다리다

정답 (d)

4 해석 W: 안녕하세요. 이걸 캐나다에 보내야 해요.

M: 이 운송 라벨을 작성하셨나요?

W: 네, 여기 있어요.

M: 좋습니다. 보통우편으로 보내실 건가요, 아니면 속달우편으로 보내실 건간요?

W: 보통우편도 괜찮아요. 급한 게 아니에요.

M: 액체류나 상하기 쉽거나 깨질 수 있는 물건인가요?

W: 아니요, 하지만 귀중한 물건이 들어 있어요.

M: 그러면 보험에 가입하시라고 권하고 싶네요.

Q. 대화에 따르면 맞는 내용은 무엇인가?

(a) 남자는 소포를 보험에 들 것을 권한다.

(b) 여자는 속달우편으로 보내고 싶어 한다.

(c) 남자는 보통우편을 이용하라고 권한다.

(d) 여자는 운송 라벨을 작성하지 않았다.

해설 우체국에서 벌어지는 대화이다. 여자는 보통우편으로 소포를 캐나다에 보내려고 한다. 남자는 내용물이 귀중한 물건이면 보험에 드는 게 좋다고 권한다.

어휘 fill out 작성하다

perishable 부패하기 쉬운

fragile 깨지기 쉬운

valuables 귀중품

insure 보험에 들다

정답 (a)

Actual Test

1 해석 M: 안녕, 베티. 별일 없니?

W: ___________________

(a) 지금 당장 갈게.

(b) 라면을 좀 끓이고 있어.

(c) 별일 없어. 너는?

(d) 그녀는 몰라.

해설 What's cooking?은 '별일 없니, 뭐 새로운 일 없
      니, 무슨 일이야?' 정도로 해석되는 표현으로 가볍게
      근황을 묻는 질문이다. 비슷한 표현으로 What's
      up?, What's new? What's going on? 등이 있
      다. 주로 이런 표현에 기계적으로 또는 습관적으로 나
      오는 응답으로는 Nothing particular, Nothing
      special, Not much. 등이 있다. 따라서 선택지 중
      가장 자연스러운 응답은 (c)이다.

어휘 What's cooking? 무슨 일이야? 별일 없니?
      Not much. 별일 없어. 별거 아냐.

정답 (c)

2 해석 M: 내가 승진할 가능성이 있을까?
       W: ___________________
       (a) 응, 넌 휴가를 얻을 자격이 충분해.
       (b) 아니, 계약서를 갱신할 필요 없어.
       (c) 아니, 난 도박을 하지 않아.
       (d) 응, 가능할 거라고 봐.

해설 남자가 여자에게 자신이 승진할 가능성이 있겠느냐고
      묻고 있으므로 가능성 여부에 대한 의견을 말한 응답
      이 와야 한다. 따라서 가능성이 있다고 긍정적인 의견
      을 밝힌 (d)가 가장 자연스러운 응답이다.

어휘 chance 가능성, 가망
      well-deserved 당연한
      engage in 참여하다
      gambling 도박
      possibility 있을 수 있는 일, 있음직한 일

정답 (d)

3 해석 M: 아이들로부터 병을 옮았나 봐요.
       W: ___________________
       (a) 그렇게 용감한 아이들을 둬서 자랑스럽지 않으세요?
       (b) 조심하세요. 곤충은 위험할 수 있거든요.
       (c) 어서 집에 가서 하루 푹 쉬세요.
       (d) 전 아이들과 공놀이하는 것도 좋아해요.

해설 catch a bug는 '병에 걸리다'라는 뜻이다. 남자가
      자신의 아이들로부터 병이 옮아서 아픈 것 같다고 말
      하고 있으므로 충고나 조언을 해주는 표현이 적절하
      다. 따라서 집에 가서 휴식을 취하라는 내용의 (c)가
      가장 자연스러운 응답이다. 나머지 선택지들은 대화에
      나온 단어를 선택지에 등장시켜서 혼동을 유도하는 오
      답 선택지들이다.

어휘 bug (병균으로 인한 가벼운) 병

for the day 그날은, 하루
play catch 공놀이하다, 캐치볼을 하다

정답 (c)

4 해석 W: 이제야 도착하다니. 기다리다 지쳐서 그냥 갈 뻔
          했어.
       M: 내 잘못이 아니야. 타이어가 펑크 나서 교체해야
          했거든.
       W: 그런 상황이었으면 적어도 전화라도 해서 알려 줬
          어야지.
       M: ___________________
       (a) 나는 타이어 교환을 그리 잘하진 못하거든.
       (b) 또다시 그런 일이 생기면 그렇게 할게.
       (c) 거기에 대해 난 크게 걱정하지 않아.
       (d) 알았어. 가능한 한 빨리 전화할게.

해설 약속 시간에 늦게 나타난 남자와 그를 기다린 여자 간
      의 대화이다. 자동차 타이어가 펑크 나서 교체하느라
      고 약속 시간에 늦었다고 변명하는 남자의 말에 여자
      가 전화라도 했어야 한다고 꾸짖고 있으므로 그런 일
      이 또 생기면 전화하겠다는 내용의 선택지 (b)가 가장
      적절한 응답이다.

어휘 get a flat tire 타이어가 펑크 나다

정답 (b)

5 해석 M: 가족 간 무료 통화를 제공하는 이동통신사가 있다
          는 얘기 들어 봤니?
       W: 아니, 못 들어 봤어. 나로서는 정말 많은 돈이 절약
          되겠는걸. 전화 요금 대부분이 부모님과 통화 요금
          이거든.
       M: 나는 좀 회의적이야. 그렇게 좋은 조건은 분명 어
          딘가에 함정이 있을 거라 생각해.
       W: ___________________
       (a) 당장 엄마한테 전화할 거야.
       (b) 장거리 전화 요금은 엄청나게 비싸.
       (c) 우리 가족은 그 서비스를 마음에 들어 하지 않을
          거 같아.
       (d) 가입하기 전에 세세한 사항들을 알아봐야 해.

해설 남자가 가족끼리 무료 통화 서비스를 제공하는 통신사
      가 있다고 말하자 여자는 무료 통화 서비스에 무척 관
      심을 가진다. 하지만 남자가 그런 좋은 조건의 서비스
      에는 함정이 있을 거란 의견을 밝히고 있으므로 이 의
      견에 동조하거나 반대하는 응답이 적절하다. 함정을
      피하기 위해 가입하기 전에 세부 사항을 알아보는 것

이 중요하다고 남자의 의견에 동의하는 (d)가 가장 자
연스러운 응답이다.

어휘 chat 잡담

skeptical 회의적인

catch 함정

sign up 가입하다, 신청하다

정답 (d)

6 **해석** W: 존, 이렇게 뜻밖에 만나다니 정말 반갑다!

M: 안녕, 레이첼. 며칠 전 케이티와 얘기했는데, 우리
언제 한번 모여서 술이나 한잔 마시자고 하더라.

W: 좋아. 언제쯤 이야기할까?

M: 이번 주 금요일은 너무 급작스러울까?

W: 아냐, 나는 금요일 괜찮아. 저녁 식사 어때?

M: 케이티가 집에서 맛있는 걸 구워 주겠다고 했어.

W: 재미있겠다. 난 와인을 가져갈게.

M: 좋아. 그럼 이번 주 금요일 케이티네 집이야.

W: 기대가 되는군. 너희들을 본 지 정말 오랜만이잖아.

M: 그래, 너무 오랜만이지. 그럼, 금요일에 보자.

Q. 대화에 따르면 맞는 것은 무엇인가?

(a) 존과 레이첼은 금요일에 데이트 약속을 잡았다.

(b) 케이트는 저녁 식사 예약을 했다.

(c) 레이첼은 와인을 제공할 것이다.

(d) 세 친구는 자주 만난다.

해설 오랜만에 우연히 만난 남녀 사이의 대화이다. (a) 존과
레이첼 둘이 데이트를 하는 게 아니라 케이티까지 세
사람이 만난다. (b) 케이티는 저녁 식사를 식당에 예약
한 것이 아니라 자신의 집에서 손수 저녁 식사를 대접
하기로 했다. (d) 오랜만에 만난 거라고 했으므로 세
친구는 자주 만나지 않는다. (c) 레이첼이 와인을 가져
간다고 말했으므로 와인을 제공하는 사람은 레이첼이
맞다. 따라서 대화의 내용과 일치하는 선택지는 (c)이다.

어휘 What a pleasant surprise! 너무 반갑다!

short notice 갑작스런 통보

정답 (c)

7 **해석** 비원어민 학생들에게 영어를 가장 잘 가르칠 수 있는
방법에 대한 논쟁이 캘리포니아 교사들 사이에서 일고
있습니다. 집중적인 ESL 방식을 지지하는 교사들은
비원어민 학생들의 영어 실력을 빨리 원어민과 같은
교실에서 수업을 들을 수 있을 정도로 끌어올리기 위
해 ESL 방식이 필요하다고 주장하고 있습니다. 그러
나 몇몇 교사들은 2개국어를 사용하는 수업 방식이 아

이들에게 더 도움이 될 것이라고 생각하고 있습니다.
그들의 모국어로 핵심 교과과정을 가르치고 동시에 영
어 교육을 제공함으로써 때론 정신적 충격이 되는 새
문화에 대한 적응이 더 느려지겠지만 보다 원활해질
것이라고 교사들은 생각하고 있습니다.

Q. 지문에 따르면 맞는 것은 무엇인가?

(a) 가장 빠른 방법이기 때문에 교육자들은 집중적인
ELS 교육 방식을 선호한다.

(b) 2개국어를 사용한 방식에서는 영어 학습은 선택사
항이며 강조되지 않는다.

(c) 2개국어를 사용하는 교육 방식은 새로운 문화로의
전환을 수월하게 하기 때문에 더 좋은 방법이다.

(d) 집중적인 ESL 교육 방식은 아이들이 원어민 친구
들과 듣는 수업에 더 빠르게 적응할 수 있도록 고안
되었다.

해설 2가지 영어 교수법에 대한 짧은 담화를 듣고 진위를
파악하는 문제이다. 양론을 단순하게 소개할 뿐 어느
쪽 방법이 더 낫다고 주장하는 것은 아니므로 (c)는 담
화 내용과 일치하지 않는다. 또한 교육자들이 ESL 방
식을 선호한다는 내용은 언급되어 있지 않으므로 (a)
역시 일치하지 않는다. (b) 2개국어를 사용하는 영어
교육 방식에서 영어를 배우는 것은 선택 사항이 아니
라 필수이기 때문에 (c) 또한 일치하지 않는다. 두 번
째 문장에서 언급되어 있듯이 집중적인 ESL 교육 방
식은 원어민 학생들과 함께하는 수업에 적응할 수 있
도록 고안되었다고 언급되었으므로 정답은 (d)이다.

어휘 controversy 논쟁, 논란

brew 일어나고 있다

proponent 지지자

assimilate into 동화되다, 융합되다

bilingual instruction 2개국어를 사용하는 교육

simultaneously 동시에

traumatic 마음 고생이 되는, 정신적 충격이 큰

adjustment 적응

transition 전환, 변화

accelerate 촉진하다, 빠르게 하다

acclimation 새 환경 순응

peer 동료, 친구

정답 (d)

Sample

1 해석 W: 6월에 2인실을 예약하려고요. 저희는 러셀의 결혼
식 들러리들입니다.

M: 알겠습니다. 그분들 예약에는 요금을 할인해 드립
니다.

W: 아, 잘됐네요. 그럼 얼마죠?

M: 금요일에서 일요일까지 계실 건가요?

W: 네, 호텔에서 금요일과 토요일 밤을 보낼 거예요.

M: 그 날짜의 할인된 주말 요금은 345달러입니다.

Q. 대화에서 주로 일어나고 있는 것은 무엇인가?

(a) 남자가 결혼식을 계획하고 있다.

(b) 여자가 예약을 취소하고 있다.

(c) 화자들은 호텔 요금에 대해 이야기하고 있다.

(d) 남자는 여자에게 데이트를 신청하고 있다.

해설 여자는 호텔을 예약하고 있고, 남자는 호텔 요금을 알
려 준다. 선택지에 대화에서 나오는 단어를 이용한 오
답이 나온다. (a)는 wedding을, (b)는 reservation
을 이용한 오답이다. (d)는 남자의 마지막 말 중
those dates에서 dates를 날짜가 아닌 '데이트'라
는 뜻으로 해석하도록 유도한 오답이다.

어휘 ask *sb* out on a date ~에게 데이트 신청하다

정답 (c)

2 해석 M: 이 호텔은 룸서비스 제공하나요?

W: _______________

(a) 제공합니다. 오전 8시부터 5시까지입니다.

(b) 그것은 즉시 거기에 있어야 합니다.

(c) 저희는 종합 체육관이 있습니다.

(d) 아니요, 방이 모두 다 예약되었습니다.

해설 조동사 Does로 시작되는 의문사 없는 의문문이다.
(a) (Yes.) We do(= We offer room service),
from 8 am-5 pm. (c)는 질문의 service를 중복해
서 쓴 오답이다. 질문의 service, hotel 등의 단편적
인 단어만 듣고 (c)나 (d)를 답으로 혼동하지 않도록
주의한다.

어휘 promptly 신속하게, 즉시
full-service gym 종합 체육관

정답 (a)

3 해석 W: 저녁 식사 정말 근사했어요. 정말 고마워요.

M: 천만에요. 그리고 제가 살게요.

W: 아뇨, 각자 내죠.

M: _______________

(a) 아뇨, 반반씩 내요.

(b) 여기 있어요. 거스름돈은 됐어요.

(c) 어떻게 드실래요?

(d) 네, 물론이죠. 특히 암스테르담에 가고 싶어요.

해설 Let's go Dutch.는 비용을 각자 부담하자는 뜻이고,
Let's go fifty-fifty.는 총액에서 반반씩 부담하자는
뜻이다. 두 표현의 차이점을 염두에 두자.

어휘 It's on me. 내가 살게. 내가 쏠게.
change 거스름돈

정답 (a)

4 해석 W: 브래드 자동차 정비소입니다. 오늘 어떻게 도와 드
릴까요?

M: 자동차 수리 예약을 해야 하는데요.

W: 네, 뭐가 필요하신데요?

M: _______________

(a) 트럭을 운전하는 게 더 좋아요.

(b) 내일 두 시 좋습니다.

(c) 오일 교환을 할 때가 됐어요.

(d) 자동차를 가지고 가셔도 돼요.

해설 대화 당사자들이 어떤 관계인지 재빨리 파악해야 질문
을 잘 이해할 수 있는 문제이다. 여자가 정비소(auto
repair shop)에서 근무하고 있음을 파악해서 여자가
남자에게 어떤 종류의 차 수리를 원하는지 묻고 있는
지 빨리 캐치하는 게 관건이다. (b)는 마지막 질문을
제대로 못 들었을 경우, 대화에 나온 단어
appointment 때문에 연상될 수 있는 오답 선택지이
고, (d) 역시 대화에 나온 단어 car가 다시 등장한데
다 화자를 바꾼 오답 선택지이다.

정답 (c)

Actual Test

1 해석 M: 잊어버려. 불량배 몇 명에게 괴롭힘당하는 것은 큰
일 아니야.

W: _______________

(a) 그것은 나쁜 조건이야.

(b) 사람들을 괴롭히면 안 돼.

(c) 거기에 문제 있니?

(d) 아, 그래? 내 입장에서 생각해 봐.

해설 남자가 불량배들에게 괴롭힘을 당하고 있는 여자에게

충고랍시고 불량배들에게 괴롭힘을 당하는 건 대수롭지도 않은 일이라고 일축해 버림으로써 여자의 기분을 오히려 상하게 하고 있다. (d) Try walking in my shoes.는 내 입장에서 생각해 보라는 뜻으로 네가 괴롭힘을 당하면 그렇게 말할 수 있겠느냐고 정색하며 따지는 표현이다.

어휘 get over 잊어버리다

tease 괴롭히다

bully 불량배, 약자를 괴롭히는 사람

pick on 괴롭히다

walk in one's shoes ~의 입장에서 생각하다, ~의 입장이 되어 보다

정답 (d)

2 해석 M: 파라에게 거짓말을 하지 말았어야 했는데.

W: _______________________

(a) 지금 당장 일어나.

(b) 왜 그녀에게 진실을 얘기해 줬니?

(c) 너한테 실망했어.

(d) 너희 둘은 좋은 커플이 될 줄 알았는데.

해설 상당히 고난이도의 문제로, 제대로 들었다고 해도 표현에 대한 이해가 없으면 답을 찾기가 까다로운 문제이다. I wish I hadn't ~ 는 가정법 과거완료로 과거 사실의 반대를 소망하거나 아쉬움을 표현한다. I wish I hadn't lied to Fara.는 파라에게 거짓말을 하지 않았어야 했는데 파라에게 거짓말을 했다는 뜻이다. I thought you were better than that.은 우리말로 해석하기가 쉽지가 않다. 상황에 따라 너무나 다양하게 해석될 수 있기 때문이다. 직역하면 '당신이 그것보다는 나을 줄 알았다.' 또는 '네가 파라에게 거짓말을 할 정도로 어리석지는 않을 줄 알았다.'로 해석되는데 주로 상대에게 실망감을 표현할 때 쓰는 표현이므로 '너한테 실망이다. 네가 겨우 그 정도였니? 네가 그 정도밖에 안 되는 사람일 줄은 몰랐어.'와 같이 다양한 의역이 가능하다.

어휘 I thought you were better than that. 너한테 실망이야.

make a good couple 좋은 커플[연인]이 되다

정답 (c)

3 해석 M: 왜 내가 청첩장을 받지 못한 걸까?

W: _______________________

(a) 왔으면 하는 사람은 누구든지 초대해.

(b) 우린 신혼여행지를 바꿨어.

(c) 아마도 우편 배달 중에 분실됐을 거야.

(d) 네가 와줘서 기뻐.

해설 남자가 청첩장을 받지 못한 이유를 궁금해 하고 있으므로 그 타당한 이유가 될 만한 응답이 이어져야 자연스럽다. 따라서 도중에 분실됐을 것이라고 응답한 (c)가 가장 적절한 대답이다.

어휘 Glad you could make it. 와줘서 기뻐. (주로 파티 등에 참석한 사람에게 하는 말)

정답 (c)

4 해석 M: 요즘 허리가 다시 아파.

W: 의사한테 진찰은 받아 봤어?

M: 응, 비싼 수술을 권하더라고.

W: _______________________

(a) 최근에 수술 기술이 발전했어.

(b) 그런 문제들이 다시 생길 것 같진 않아.

(c) 돈이 문제라면 내가 기꺼이 도와줄게.

(d) 농구하다가 다쳤어.

해설 남자의 마지막 말에서 형용사 expensive가 결정적인 힌트이다. 남자가 허리 통증으로 의사의 진찰을 받아 봤지만 비싼 수술비 때문에 고민하고 있으므로 돈이 문제라면 도와주겠다는 내용의 (c)가 선택지 중에서 가장 자연스러운 응답이다.

어휘 back problem 허리 통증, 요통

concern 근심, 걱정

정답 (c)

5 해석 M: 떠나기로 결심한 건 언제야?

W: 지난달에 결심했어. 오레곤으로 이사 갈 거야.

M: 로스앤젤레스를 떠나는 이유가 뭐니?

W: _______________________

(a) 자연과 더 가까이 살고 싶어서.

(b) 네가 왜 떠나려고 하는지 알겠어.

(c) 방문하고 싶은 가족이 있어서.

(d) 거기로 캠핑 여행을 갈 계획이야.

해설 남자는 여자가 로스앤젤레스를 떠나는 이유를 묻고 있으므로 여자가 떠나는 이유가 포함된 답변이 이어져야 자연스럽다. 따라서 답은 (a) 자연에 더 가까이 살고 싶어서 이사 가는 것이다.

정답 (a)

6 해석 M: 1달러 더 내시고 사탕 1상자를 추가하시겠어요?

W: 아니요, 됐어요. 그냥 영화 두 편만 빌릴게요.

M: 알겠습니다. 전부 21달러 78센트입니다.

W: 말도 안 돼요. 비디오 두 개 빌리는 게 정말 그렇게 비싸요?

M: 영화 두 편 값은 8달러지만 연체료가 10달러 있으시고요. 거기에 세금까지 합친 금액이지요.

W: 아, 예. 그걸 깜박했네요. 여기 자주 오는데 연체료를 감면해 줄 수는 없나요?

M: 가끔 매니저가 단골손님들의 연체료를 없애 주는 경우가 있는데 매니저가 지금 여기 없네요.

W: 그렇다면 그냥 빌려가야겠네요.

Q. 여자가 원하는 것은 무엇인가?

(a) 영화 간식을 싼 가격에 사기

(b) 연체료 감면받기

(c) 영화 대여 회원에 가입하기

(d) 더 낮은 가격에 영화 구입하기

해설 여자는 비디오 대여점에서 영화를 빌리며 연체료를 감면해 줄 수 있는지 묻고 있다. 대부분의 영화 대여점에서는 사탕류나 팝콘 같은 영화관에서 볼 수 있는 간식도 함께 판매하는 경우가 많다. 대화의 첫 부분에 직원이 1달러에 사탕 한 통을 추가하겠느냐고 물었지만 여자는 거절했으므로 (a)는 정답이 아니다. 여자는 자신이 단골이므로 연체료를 감면해 줄 수 없겠냐고 묻고 있다. 보통 매니저가 감면해 주는 경우가 있지만 자리에 없어서 감면을 받지 못한다. 그러므로 여자가 원하는 것은 연체료를 감면받는 것이라는 (b)가 정답으로 가장 적절하다. (c) 여자는 이 비디오 대여점에 단골이라고 했으므로 이미 회원이라는 것을 알 수 있다. 여자는 영화를 구매하려는 것이 아니라 그저 대여하려는 것이므로 (d) 역시 정답이 아니다.

어휘 late fee 연체료

take off (값을) 깎다

erase 삭제하다

regulars 단골손님

정답 (b)

7 해석 당신이 심장병에 걸릴 확률은 당신의 성별에 따라 현격하게 다릅니다. 여성의 경우, 가족 구성원들과의 문제나 인간관계가 육체적인 스트레스에 비해 심장마비를 일으킬 가능성이 더 높은 감정적인 스트레스를 유발할지도 모릅니다. 남성에 대한 연구 조사는 완전히 반대되는 상황을 보여 줍니다. 과학자들의 이론에 따르면 남성과 여성의 신체는 다양한 종류의 스트레스에 다르게 반응한다고 합니다. 여성은 감정적인 자극에 의해 심장 활동이 증가되는 반면, 남성의 심장박동률은 격한 육체적 활동을 하는 동안 가장 크게 증가하는 것으로 드러났습니다.

Q. 지문에 따르면 맞는 내용은 무엇인가?

(a) 여성이 심장마비에 걸릴 가능성이 더 적다.

(b) 여성은 열심히 일할 때 특히 심장병에 걸리기 쉽다.

(c) 남성은 여성보다 육체적 스트레스로 더 나쁜 영향을 받는다.

(d) 감정적인 스트레스에 대한 성별 반응 간에 차이점이 거의 없다.

해설 여성과 남성의 심장병에 걸릴 확률이 차이가 있다는 요지의 글로 여성의 경우는 정서적인 스트레스에 의해서 심장병에 걸릴 확률이 높고, 반면 남성의 경우는 격한 육체 활동으로 심장병에 걸릴 확률이 더 높다고 설명하고 있으므로 담화의 내용과 일치하는 선택지는 (c)이다. (a) 여성이 심장마비에 걸릴 가능성이 더 적다는 내용은 언급되지 않았다. (b) 역시 여성은 인간관계나 가족 관계 같은 정서적인 스트레스로 심장병에 걸릴 확률이 더 높으므로 일치하지 않는다. (d)는 지문의 내용과 반대되는 진술이므로 옳지 않다.

어휘 susceptibility to (병)에 걸리기 쉬움

dramatically 현저하게, 극적으로

depending on ~에 따라

gender 성별

incite 유발하다, 불러일으키다

theorize 이론화하다

respond to ~에 반응하다

trigger 자극

exertion 심한 활동

adverse impact 나쁜 영향

정답 (c)

Sample

1 해석 M: 정말 푹푹 찌는군! 바깥은 펄펄 끓고 있어.

W: 나도 알아. 오늘도 아주 무더울 것 같아.

M: 오늘 비가 좀 내렸으면 해.

W: ______________________

(a) 소나기가 내릴 거란 거 어떻게 알았니?

(b) 실은 오늘 비가 좀 내릴 거라고 들었어.

(c) 오후에는 갤 거야.

(d) 오늘은 날씨가 흐린 것 같아.

해설 평서문에 대한 응답을 고르는 문제로, 정형화된 답이
없으므로 가장 상식적이고 논리적인 대화를 완성시킬
수 있는 선택지를 고르면 된다. 너무 더우니 비라도
좀 내렸으면 좋겠다는 남자의 마지막 말에 실제로 비
가 내릴 거라는 얘기를 들었다는 (b)가 선택지들 중에
서는 가장 자연스러운 응답이다.

어휘 **What a sizzler!** 푹푹 찌는군!

boiling 펄펄 끓는

scorcher 타는 듯이 더운 날

shower 소나기

clear up (날씨가) 개다

overcast 흐린

정답 (b)

2 해석 M: 밖에 날씨 봤니?

W: 아니, 하루 종일 실내에 있었어.

M: 아쉬워할 거 하나도 없어. 우중충하고 비 와.

W: ______________________

(a) 사실 시원한 소나기가 오면 좋지.

(b) 7월은 너무 더워.

(c) 창문 없니?

(d) 거기에 가본 적 없어.

해설 간단해 보이지만 난이도가 있는 문제이다. 밖에 날씨
가 안 좋아서 집에 있는 게 더 낫다는 상대방에게 자
신은 시원한 소나기를 원한다고 우회적으로 말하는
(a)가 가장 적절하다. **You're not missing
anything.**은 밖에 날씨가 안 좋아서 별 볼일 없었기
때문에 하루 종일 실내에 있었어도 아쉬울 게 없다는
의미이다.

어휘 **could use** ~가 있었으면 좋겠다, ~가 필요하다

정답 (a)

3 해석 오늘 일기예보는 아주 강한 토네이도의 강타에 대한
것입니다. 전문가들이 현재 펜실베니아 남해안 앞바다
에서 토네이도를 추적하고 있습니다. 바람은 최고 시
속 75마일에 이를 것으로 추산되며 폭우가 예상됩니
다. 해안 지역 주민은 즉시 내륙으로 이동하시길 강력
히 요구합니다. 토네이도가 아주 빠른 속도로 방향을
바꾸고 있으며, 토네이도가 지나가는 지역에 큰 피해
를 입히고 있습니다. 지방 경찰이 대피를 돕기 위해
출동 중입니다. 경찰 지시에 따라 주시기 바랍니다.

Q. 일기예보에 따르면 다음 중 맞는 것은 무엇인가?

(a) 폭풍우가 방향을 바꿀 것 같지 않다.

(b) 해안 지역의 사람들은 토네이도 때문에 집을 떠날
것이 요구되고 있다.

(c) 경찰은 대피를 도울 자원봉사자들을 간절히 필요로
한다.

(d) 일기예보관은 그 폭풍우를 추적해 봤자 소용이 없
다고 말한다.

해설 선택지 중 글의 내용과 맞는 것이나 틀린 것을 고르는
문제는 글의 세부 내용을 알아야 풀 수 있다. 즉, 글의
전체 내용을 골고루 알고 있어야 한다. 첫 번째 듣기
에서는 전체 흐름과 질문 및 선택지 듣기에 집중한다.
두 번째 듣기에서는 선택지 내용을 확인하며 본문에서
답을 찾아야 한다. 여기서 선택지 중 (b)의 내용이 If
you are a resident of a coastal area, it is
strongly urged that you move inland
immediately로 나와 있다. 지문의 move inland와
evacuation을 leave their hometown으로 바꿔
쓴 것이다. (a)는 this tornado is changing its
position quite quickly라는 내용을 근거로 오답,
(d)는 chasing을 tracking으로 바꿔 썼지만 언급된
내용이 아니다.

어휘 **call for** 예보하다

off ~의 앞바다에서

urge 요구하다, 촉구하다

devastate 파괴하다, 초토화하다

evacuation 대피

there's no point in -ing ~해봤자 소용없다

정답 (b)

4 해석 오늘 파리의 일기예보는 밤새 비가 올 가능성과 함께 다
소 흐린 날씨입니다. 최고 기온은 70도를 조금 웃돌고
최저 기온은 약 53도까지 내려갑니다. 내일은 햇빛을 보
게 될 수 있는 가능성이 가장 높은 날이 될 것입니다.

다음 주 월요일까지 주말 내내 비와 60도 후반이나 70도를 조금 웃도는 낮은 기온이 예상됩니다. 맑은 날씨는 다음 화요일에 되돌아올 것으로 예상되고 그 이후로는 내내 맑은 날씨를 보이겠습니다.

Q. 내일 날씨는 어떻겠는가?

(a) 다소 흐림

(b) 비가 옴

(c) 맑음

(d) 쌀쌀함

해설 일기예보를 듣고 세부 정보를 파악하는 문제이다. 내일 날씨가 언급되는 부분을 집중해서 들으면 쉽게 풀 수 있다. 3번째 문장에서 내일은 햇빛을 볼 수 있는 가능성이 가장 높은 날이 될 것이라고 했으므로 정답은 (c)이다.

어휘 high 최고 기온

dip 내려가다

정답 (c)

Actual Test

1 **해석** W: 너 최근 들어 저녁 식사를 많이 거르는구나.

M: ______________________

(a) 나도 알아. 내 자신이 꽤 자랑스러워.

(b) 알았어. 지금부터 널 귀찮게 하지 않을게.

(c) 그래. 내일부터 다이어트 할 거야.

(d) 미안하지만 속이 좋지 않아서 그래.

해설 비록 평서문의 형태지만 여자가 남자에게 최근에 저녁을 많이 거르는 이유가 뭐냐고 간접적으로 묻고 있으므로 저녁을 거르는 이유를 밝히는 (d)가 가장 자연스럽다. act up은 문맥에 따라 여러 가지 뜻이 있는데 여기서는 '상태가 안 좋아지다' 정도의 뜻으로 쓰였다.

어휘 skip 거르다, 건너뛰다

act up (병이) 재발하다

정답 (d)

2 **해석** M: 방금 저 남자 앞에 새치기하셨죠.

W: ______________________

(a) 괜찮아요. 기다릴 수 있어요.

(b) 지방 섭취를 줄이고 있어요.

(c) 그런 줄 몰랐습니다.

(d) 그가 왜 서두르는 걸까?

해설 남자가 여자에게 새치기를 했다고 지적하고 있다. 이렇게 타인으로부터 좋지 않은 행동이나 실수에 대해 지적받았는데, 고의로 그런 게 아닌 경우에 그런 줄 몰랐다는 식의 (c)와 같은 응답이 가장 자연스럽다. 또는 고의로 그런 게 아니라는 뜻의 I didn't do it on purpose.라는 표현도 자주 쓰인다.

어휘 cut in line 새치기하다

cut down on 줄이다, 삭감하다

be in a rush 서두르다

정답 (c)

3 **해석** M: 요즘 네 영화가 상당한 화제가 되고 있어. 네가 무척 자랑스러워.

W: ______________________

(a) 가까운 극장에서 찾아봐.

(b) 정말이야. 그 책이 훨씬 더 좋아.

(c) 난 오디션을 잘 볼 수 있을 거라 확신해.

(d) 고마워. 하지만 영화가 성공한 건 나 때문이 아니야.

해설 남자가 여자의 영화에 대해 칭찬하고 있으므로 감사 인사를 하고 겸손을 표현하는 (d)가 가장 자연스럽다. 표현 take responsibility for는 '~에 대해 책임을 지다' 라는 뜻인데, for 뒤에 failure 같은 부정어가 오면 쉽게 해석이 되지만 success 같은 긍정적인 내용이 오면 '성공에 대해 책임을 지다' 라는 어색한 해석이 되므로 해석을 달리해야 한다. A take responsibility for B라고 하면 'B는 A 덕분이다, B는 A 때문이다' 라고 해석해야 영어식 사고방식으로 표현을 이해하는 것이다.

어휘 apparently 겉보기에, 분명히

make a buzz 화제가 되다, 화제를 불러일으키다

infinitely 훨씬

go well 잘되다

정답 (d)

4 **해석** W: 전 서커스단에 들어가기로 결심했어요. 제 결정을 받아들여 주셨으면 해요.

M: 너 미쳤니? 서커스는 직업이 될 수 없어.

W: 그래도 전 결심했어요.

M: ______________________

(a) 네가 좋은 결정을 할 줄 알았어!

(b) 나 일찍 죽는 꼴 보려고 작정을 했구나!

(c) 자, 그럼 축하하자!

(d) 부전자전이구나!

해설 서커스단에 입단하기로 결심한 딸과 그 결정에 반대하는

아버지의 대화이다. 아버지의 만류에도 딸이 끝까지 결심을 굽히지 않고 있으므로 부모와 자식 간에 의견 충돌 시 부모가 자식의 완강한 고집에 대해 유감과 아쉬움을 표현할 때 자주 쓰는 표현인 (b)가 선택지 중에서 가장 자연스럽다. '절대로 안 된다'는 뜻을 우회적으로 재미있게 표현한 것이다.

어휘 early grave 젊어서 죽음, 요절
The apple doesn't fall far from the tree!
부전자전!

정답 (b)

5 해석 W: 그렇게 많은 복권을 사는 게 아니었는데.
M: 맞아. 이런 말 하기 좀 그렇지만 넌 도박 중독이야.
W: 못하도록 날 말렸어야지.
M: ___________________
(a) 내가 말했다고 해도 달라졌을 거라곤 생각 안 해.
(b) 어쨌든 네가 돈을 충분히 가지고 있을 거라 생각했어.
(c) 넌 더 이상 복권을 살 필요 없어.
(d) 씀씀이를 조절하기 위해 너 스스로 한계를 정해야 해.

해설 여자가 복권을 너무 많이 산 걸 후회하면서 남자에게 그러지 못하도록 말렸어야 했다고 아쉬움을 토로하고 있다. 여자가 도박 중독 증세가 있다고 남자가 말한 걸로 보아 말렸다고 해도 달라지지 않았을 것이라는 내용의 (a)가 가장 자연스러운 응답이다.

어휘 lottery ticket 복권
gambling issue 도박 문제, 도박 중독

정답 (a)

6 해석 W: 일은 어떻게 잘되어 가니?
M: 좋아. 일이 탄력적인 게 정말 마음에 들어.
W: 그러니까 시간 제약이 없다는 얘기니?
M: 꼭 그런 건 아니야.
W: 응? 무슨 뜻이야?
M: 매달 완수해야 할 할당량이 있어.
W: 내가 원하는 게 그런 조건인데.
Q. 남자의 직업에 대해 대화로부터 추론 가능한 것은 무엇인가?
(a) 할당량을 완수하는 데 시간이 추가로 더 걸린다.
(b) 동료들보다 더 많이 일하지 않는다.
(c) 그의 업무 총량은 월간 기준으로 계산된다.
(d) 그의 할당 업무량은 가용한 시간에 따라 유동적이다.

해설 남자의 마지막 말에서 알 수 있듯이 남자는 매달 완성해야 할 할당 업무량을 부여받는다고 했으므로 총업무량이 월간 기준으로 계산된다는 것을 유추할 수 있다. (a)와 (b)는 대화를 통해 추론이 불가능하다. (d) 역시 그의 할당 업무량은 그의 가용 시간과는 상관없이 일정량이 부여되므로 대화의 내용으로 추론되는 사실이 아니다.

어휘 flexible 탄력적인, 융통성이 있는
time constraint 시간 제약
quota 할당량

정답 (c)

7 해석 두 차례의 대규모 지진이 월요일 밤 일본을 강타해서 카시와자키 시에서만 8명이 사망하고 800명이 부상을 입었습니다. 섬나라 일본은 전 세계에서 가장 지진이 자주 일어나는 지역들 중 한 곳에 있지만, 최근의 지진들은 대부분의 지진보다 더 심해서 잦은 지진을 견디어 내도록 지어진 일본의 건물들을 파괴했습니다. 도로, 주택, 다른 건물들이 붕괴되었습니다. 그러나 가장 심각한 피해는 원자력발전소에서 발생한 화재에 의해 일어났습니다. 다행스럽게도 쓰나미 경보는 잘못된 경보로 밝혀졌습니다.
Q. 기사로부터 추론 가능한 것은 무엇인가?
(a) 일본은 단층선 위에 위치해 있다.
(b) 지진 발생 후에 해일이 발생했다.
(c) 원자력발전소는 영원히 폐쇄될 것이다.
(d) 카시와자키는 일본의 가장 큰 도시들 중 하나이다.

해설 일본은 지진이 가장 쉽게 일어나는 지역들 중 한 곳에 있다고 언급되었으므로 (a) 일본이 단층선 위에 위치해 있음을 추론할 수 있다. 마지막 문장에서 쓰나미 경보는 잘못된 경보로 밝혀졌다고 언급되었으므로 (b) 지진 발생 후에 해일이 발생했다는 내용은 기사의 내용과 일치하지 않는다. (c)와 (d)는 그럴 가능성도 있겠지만 기사로부터 합리적인 추론이 불가능하다.

어휘 rock 뒤흔들다, 요동시키다
earthquake-prone 지진이 자주 일어나는
quake 지진
tremor 진동, 지진
crumble 붕괴되다, 무너지다
troubling 심각한, 심한
fault line 단층선
tidal wave 해일, 쓰나미

정답 (a)

Sample

1 **해석** 이 시점에서 사람들이 다른 사람들과 상호작용하는 방법을 기술이 변화시켰다는 것에는 논란의 여지가 없습니다. 휴대폰, 이메일, 메신저 그리고 페이스북 같은 네트워킹 사이트들 덕분에 사람들이 하루 종일 연락을 취하는 것이 더 쉬워졌습니다. 하지만 기술이 상황을 더 좋은 쪽으로 바꿨는지는 의문입니다. 통신의 용이함과 빈도가 늘어나고 있지만 질적인 측면은 어떻습니까? 사람들은 보다 쉬운 통신 수단에도 불구하고 더욱 더 단절되어 가고 있습니다.

Q. 화자에 따르면 다음 중 맞는 것은 무엇인가?

(a) 기술이 의사소통을 더욱 어렵게 만들어 버렸다.

(b) 통신의 증가가 질적 향상을 의미하지는 않는다.

(c) 사람들은 인터넷이 생기기 이전보다 덜 단절되어 있다.

(d) 기술은 사람들이 상호작용하는 방법에 영향을 미치지 않았다.

해설 중반의 The question, though, is whether technology has changed things for the better. 이후의 내용을 통해 (b)가 지문과 일치함을 알 수 있다. (a), (c), (d)는 지문과 반대되는 내용이다.

어휘 indisputable 논란의 여지가 없는
interact with ~와 상호작용하다

정답 (b)

2 **해석** 어젯밤 수백만 명의 시청자들이 누가 세계에서 최고로 매력적인 애완동물 대상을 받게 될지 가슴을 졸이며 지켜보았습니다. 물론 인간 주인들의 도움으로 전국에서 온 수천 마리의 개, 고양이, 새, 뱀, 그리고 다른 동물들은 누가 결승에 진출하여 백만 불의 상금을 타게 될지 보기 위해 대회에 참가했기 때문에 결승전에 도달하기까지의 길은 분명히 험한 것이었습니다. 시청자들이 매회 방송이 끝나고 나서 전화를 걸어 가장 좋아하는 동물에게 투표하도록 해서 참가자는 셋만 남게 되었습니다. 방송을 놓치신 분들을 위해 2번 채널에서 화요일 저녁 8시에 결승전을 다시 방송할 것이므로 승자가 누구인지 알려 드리지 않겠습니다.

Q. 위 방송의 목적은 무엇인가?

(a) 대회 우승자를 발표하기 위해서

(b) 시청자들에게 재방송에 대해 알려주기 위해서

(c) 시청자들에게 대회에 대해 알리기 위해서

(d) 새로운 TV 프로그램을 광고하기 위해서

해설 어젯밤에 방송된 애완동물 대회에 대해 설명하고 있다. 이 대회는 전국에서 모인 온갖 애완동물들이 출연하는데 매회 방송 후에 시청자들이 전화를 걸어 투표하는 방식으로 진행되었고 세 마리의 애완동물이 결승전에 이르게 되었다. 이미 방송이 끝난 상태이고 승자도 결정된 상태이지만 재방송이 있을 예정이기 때문에 방송을 보지 못한 시청자들을 위해 승자를 알려 주지 않겠다고 하고 있다. 그러므로 우승자를 발표하기 위한 것이라는 (a)는 오답이 된다. 맨 마지막 부분(For those of you who missed it, I won't give away the winner since channel 2 is re-airing the final show at 8 PM on Tuesday.)에 방송의 목적이 잘 나타나 있다. 또한 대회에 대해 알리기 위한 것이라는 (c)와 새로운 TV 프로그램을 광고하기 위한 것이라는 (d)도 옳지 않다.

어휘 be on the edge of one's seat 마음을 졸이다
bumpy 평탄치 않은, 쉽지 않은
companion 동반자
take part in 참가하다
whittle down 줄이다

정답 (b)

3 **해석** 이번 달 들어 두 번째로 브랜든의 한 지역 패스트푸드 체인점이 강도를 당했습니다. 이번에는 보안상의 이유로 저희는 그 상점 카메라에 찍힌 강도 사건의 영상을 보여 드릴 수 없습니다. 저희가 알고 있는 바로는 문을 연 바로 몇 분 후인 오전 6시 34분에 복면을 한 남자가 상점에 들어와 계산대에서 일하고 있었던 여성에게 총을 겨누었습니다. 그 여성이 금고를 여는 동안 나머지 모든 직원들은 아래층 냉장고 안에 감금되었습니다. 그 강도는 늦은 아침까지는 은행 예금이 되지 않는다는 걸 알고 있었음에 틀림없습니다. 그래서 그 전날 밤의 매상액 6천 불이 넘는 돈을 가지고 걸어 나갔습니다.

Q. 뉴스에 따르면 그 강도에 대해 맞게 진술한 것은 무엇인가?

(a) 그는 이번 달 초기에 같은 패스트푸드 체인점을 강도질하였다.

(b) 그는 그 상점 은행 예금 시스템에 대해 잘 알고 있었다.

(c) 그는 마스크를 쓰고 무기 없이 걸어 들어왔다.

(d) 그는 이 특정 상점의 단골이었다.

해설 마지막 문장 The robber must have been aware that the bank deposit would not be made until later in the morning, and walked away with over $6,000 in sales from the night before.를 통해 (b)가 정답임을 알 수 있다.

어휘 footage 영상
hold a gun to ~에게 권총을 들이대다
bank deposit 은행 예금

정답 (b)

4 해석 오늘 밤 주요 뉴스입니다. 비행기 공중 납치범인 제임스 윌슨이 괌에서 체포됐습니다. 그는 괌의 한 관광 나이트클럽에서 체포되었습니다. 그 지역의 한 경찰서에서 조사를 받고 있으며 아마 시카고로 송환될 것입니다. 2001년에 제임스는 시카고 국제공항에서 발생한 비행기 공중 납치 사건에 가담한 죄로 징역 17년형을 선고받은 적이 있습니다. 그는 7월에 일리노이 주립 교도소에서 탈옥한 이후로 지금까지 10개국에서 목격되었습니다.

Q. 위 뉴스에 따르면 다음 중 사실인 것은 무엇인가?
(a) 비행기 공중 납치범은 괌 경찰서로부터 탈출했다.
(b) 비행기 공중 납치범은 시카고에서 체포되었다.
(c) 비행기 공중 납치범은 여러 국가에서 목격되었다.
(d) 비행기 공중 납치범은 공항에서 체포되었다.

해설 납치범은 괌 경찰로부터 탈출한 것이 아니라 미국 교도소를 탈출했으므로 (a)는 답이 될 수 없으며, 체포된 곳은 시카고가 아니라 괌의 한 관광 나이트클럽이므로 (b)와 (d) 역시 답이 될 수 없다. 따라서 정답은 마지막 문장(Since then he has been seen in ten different countries.)에서 알 수 있듯이 (c)이다.

어휘 hijacker 공중 납치범
question 심문하다
sentence 구형하다
penitentiary 교도소

정답 (c)

Actual Test

1 해석 M: 쟤네들 둘은 완전히 똑같이 생겼어.
W: ___________________
(a) 걔들은 같은 날 태어났어.
(b) 사실 쟤들은 항상 함께 붙어 다녀.

(c) 나조차도 누가 누군지 헷갈려.
(d) 아버지를 닮았어.

해설 똑같이 생겼다는 말에 가장 논리적인 응답은 나도 누가 누군지 구분이 안 된다는 내용의 (c)이다. 같은 날에 태어난 쌍둥이도 일란성이 아니면 닮지 않을 수도 있으므로 (a)는 (c)보다는 부적절하며, 함께 붙어 다니는 거랑 똑같이 생긴 것과는 별 상관관계가 없으므로 (b) 역시 부적절한 응답이다. 아버지를 닮은 것과 똑같이 생긴 것도 크게 상관관계가 없으므로 (d) 역시 답이 될 수 없다.

어휘 identical 동일한, 똑같은
tell who's who 누가 누군지 구분하다
take after 닮다

정답 (c)

2 해석 M: 이 호텔에서는 무료 아침식사를 제공해 주나요?
W: ___________________
(a) 먹어 본 것 중 최고의 아침 식사였어.
(b) 약간의 추가 요금을 지불하시면요.
(c) 오전 7시부터 10시까지요.
(d) 저희 식당은 위층에 있어요.

해설 남자가 여자에게 호텔에서 아침 식사를 무료로 제공해 주는지 묻고 있다. (a)는 동문서답형 응답이고, 남자가 궁금한 것은 아침 식사의 제공 여부가 아니라 아침 식사가 유료인지 무료인지 궁금한 것이므로 (b)는 질문의 핵심을 벗어난 응답이다. 식당의 위치를 물어본 것이 아니므로 (d) 역시 적절한 응답이 될 수 없다. 따라서 아침 7시부터 10시까지 무료 아침 식사가 제공된다고 간접적으로 응답한 (c)가 가장 적절하다.

어휘 complimentary 무료의
extra charge 추가 요금

정답 (c)

3 해석 M: 너희 오빠는 원예에 대해서 많이 알고 있지 않니?
W: ___________________
(a) 그는 오늘 오후 늦게 집에 올 거야.
(b) 원예에 재능이 있다고 할 수 있지.
(c) 그는 과일과 채소를 정말 좋아해.
(d) 나는 해충 문제가 있는 것 같아.

해설 관용 표현 green thumb에 대한 이해가 필요한 문제이다. green thumb은 '원예에 대한 재능'이라는 뜻이므로 (b)가 남자의 질문에 대한 가장 자연스러운 응답이다. (c)와 (d)는 질문에 등장한 gardening의 연상

어휘(fruits, vegetables, pests)를 이용한 오답함정
들이다.

어휘 gardening 원예

have a green thumb 원예에 재능이 있다

pest 해충

정답 (b)

4 **해석** W: 이 오디오 얼마죠?

M: 89달러 99센트입니다. 이보다 더 싼 가격은 없습
니다!

W: 마스 뮤직에선 70달러에 살 수 있던데요.

M: ＿＿＿＿＿＿＿＿＿＿＿

(a) 그 얘길 들으니 유감이군요.

(b) 우리의 환불 정책은 2주 동안입니다.

(c) 그게 사실이라면 저희 가격을 깎아 드리겠습니다.

(d) 저희가 싸다고 말씀드렸죠!

해설 오디오 가게에서 벌어지는 고객과 점원사이의 대화이
다. 점원이 여자가 물어본 오디오 가격이 가장 싼 가
격이라고 말하자 여자는 다른 가게에서 더 싼 가격에
팔고 있다고 말한다. 보통 이런 경우 점원은 정색하며
그 가게에서 사라든가 아니면 가격을 깎아 주겠다고
대답하는 것이 보통이므로 정답은 (c)이다.

어휘 stereo 오디오, 전축

cheaper deal 더 싼 조건, 더 싼 거래

buck 달러

money-back policy 환불 정책

if that's the case 그게 사실이라면, 그렇다면

정답 (c)

5 **해석** M: 대학 등록금으로 얼마나 냈어?

W: 딸랑 500달러.

M: 농담이겠지. 어떻게 그렇게 싼 거야?

W: ＿＿＿＿＿＿＿＿＿＿＿

(a) 나머지는 장학금을 받아서 냈어.

(b) 명문 대학이었어.

(c) 나는 마감에 임박해서 등록했어.

(d) 나는 항상 거기에 가고 싶었어.

해설 남자가 여자에게 대학 등록금을 왜 500달러밖에 내지
않았는지 묻고 있으므로 그 이유를 설명한 응답이 와
야 한다. 따라서 장학금을 타서라고 그 이유를 밝힌
(a)가 가장 자연스러운 응답이다.

어휘 tuition 등록금

scholarship 등록금

cover 충당하다

prestigious 일류의, 명성이 있는

at the last minute 막판에, 마감에 임박해서

dream of ～을 꿈꾸다, ～하고 싶어 하다

정답 (a)

6 **해석** M: 여기 자전거 타고 왔니?

W: 아니, 차 갖고 왔어.

M: 라디오에서 들었는데 차가 막혔다며?

W: 끔찍했어. 사람들이 이런 날씨에는 어떻게 운전해
야 하는지 모르더라고. 사실은 여기 오는 길에 접
촉 사고를 당했거든.

M: 뭐? 괜찮니?

W: 응. 피해는 아주 가벼워.

Q. 대화에 따르면 맞는 내용은 무엇인가?

(a) 여자는 다른 사람들의 운전이 서툴다고 생각한다.

(b) 남자는 교통이 너무 막혀서 충격을 받았다.

(c) 여자가 당한 차 사고는 심각하지 않았다.

(d) 날씨 때문에 남자는 직장에 차를 가지고 갔다.

해설 형용사 cosmetic이 교통사고에서 발생된 상해
(damage)를 설명하는 경우에는 '표면적인'의 뜻으
로 해석된다. 결국 사고로 당한 피해가 차량의 표면에
기스가 나거나 살짝 찌그러진 정도의 손상이라는 뜻이
다. 따라서 여자가 당한 차 사고는 심각하지 않았다는
(c)가 대화 내용과 일치한다. 여자는 사람들이 날씨가
나쁜 상황에서 운전하는 방법을 모른다고 생각하는 것
이지, 사람들의 운전이 서툴다고 생각하는 것은 아니
므로 (a)는 대화문의 내용과 일치하지 않는다. 차가 너
무 막혀서 남자가 충격을 받았다는 내용은 언급되어
있지 않으며, 남자가 직장에 차를 가지고 왔는지 여부
도 대화에 나와 있지 않으므로 (b)와 (d) 역시 오답 처
리된다.

어휘 be hit by a car 차에 치이다

cosmetic 표면적인

정답 (c)

7 **해석** 라임병의 발병 사례가 최근 몇 년 동안 더욱더 빈번해
졌습니다. 그 보건 위험(라임병)의 원인은 이 질병의
매개체인 사슴 개체 수의 폭발적인 증가에 있습니다.
1세기 전 사슴은 사냥, 천적, 지금보다 덜 풍부한 먹이
로 억제되었습니다. 주거 지역의 잔디밭에 심어진 다
양한 관목 및 어린 묘목과 더불어 오늘날 사냥 제한
규정이 생태학적인 불균형의 결과를 초래하였습니다.

이 문제를 해결하고 라임병에 사람들의 노출을 줄이기 위해 다양한 전략이 시도되고 있습니다.

Q. 이 강의로부터 추론 가능한 것은 무엇인가?

(a) 개발로 인해 사슴의 라임병 발병률이 더 높아졌다.

(b) 몇몇 전략은 사슴의 수를 줄이는 것을 포함할 수도 있다.

(c) 교외 거주자들은 사슴을 유인하기 위해 식물을 기른다.

(d) 라임병은 사슴의 천적들을 멸종시켰다.

해설 라임병 발병에 관한 짧은 강의를 듣고 추론하는 문제이다. 라임병 발병이 늘어나고 있는 주된 원인이 라임병의 매개체인 사슴의 수가 급격하게 늘어나고 있기 때문이라고 언급되었으므로 라임병 발병률을 낮추기 위한 방법으로 사슴의 수를 줄이는 것도 포함될 가능성이 있다고 짐작할 수 있기 때문에 정답은 (b)이다. 라임병은 사슴이 걸리는 게 아니라 사람이 걸리는 질병이므로 (a)는 답이 될 수 없다. (c) 역시 사슴이 라임병의 매개체인데, 사슴을 유인하기 위해 식물을 기르는 것은 상식적으로 맞지 않기 때문에 올바른 추론이 아니다. 라임병은 사람이 걸리는 질병이므로 라임병 때문에 사슴의 천적들이 멸종하는 것은 불가능하므로 (d) 또한 올바른 추론이 아니다.

어휘 case (질병의) 발병 사례

exploding 폭발적으로 증가하는

population 개체 수

carrier 보균자, 매개체

check 억제하다

natural predator 천적

restriction 제한 규정

shrub 관목

sapling 어린 묘목

residential 거주의, 주거 지역의

ecological 생태학적인

kill off 멸종시키다

정답 (b)

Chapter 01 동사의 활용

Actual Test

1 **해석** A: 잭, 무슨 일이니? 화가 많이 난 것처럼 보여.

B: 오늘 밤따라 모두가 날 못살게 굴고 있어. 이젠 누가 문을 두드리고 있군.

해설 지각동사 hear가 5형식 문형을 취할 때, 목적어와 목적격 보어의 관계가 능동이면 목적격 보어 자리에 현재분사나 원형부정사를 써야 하고, 수동 관계이면 과거분사를 써야 한다. someone은 문을 두드리는 행위(knock)의 주체이므로 목적어와 목적격 보어의 주술 관계가 능동이다. 따라서 빈칸에는 현재분사나 원형부정사가 와야 하므로 정답은 (c) knocking이다.

어휘 annoyed 화가 난, 짜증 난

정답 (c)

2 **해석** A: 스프 맛이 이상해.

B: 정말? 조리법을 정확히 따랐던 거 같은데.

해설 감각동사(look, taste, feel, sound, feel)가 불완전자동사로 2형식을 취할 경우엔 상태 동사로 간주하기 때문에 진행형을 쓸 수 없다. 따라서 빈칸에는 현재형인 (a) tastes가 가장 알맞다. 참고로 감각동사라도 타동사로서 3형식 문형에 쓰인 경우에는 동작 동사로 간주하여 진행형을 쓸 수 있다.

e.g. She is tasting the soup.

정답 (a)

3 **해석** A: 존은 퇴근했습니다. 전할 말씀 있으세요?

B: 네, 전 앤드류 퍼킨스입니다. 존에게 내일 전화 좀 해달라고 전해 주시겠어요?

해설 동사의 유형을 묻는 문제이다. 사역동사(make, let, have)는 5형식 문형을 취할 때, 목적어와 목적격 보어의 주술 관계가 능동일 경우 원형부정사를, 수동일 경우에는 과거분사를 목적격 보어로 취한다. 목적어인 him이 전화를 하는 것이므로, 즉 him과 call의 관계가 능동이므로 원형부정사가 와야 한다. 따라서 정답은 (a)이다.

어휘 have gone for the day 퇴근하고 없다

정답 (a)

4 **해석** A: 제이슨, 전에 다른 직장에서 일해 보신 경험 있으세요?

B: 물론이죠. 한때 스미스소니언 협회에서 일했었죠. 지금은 퇴직해서 대부분의 시간을 여행하고 손자들을 봐주면서 지내고 있습니다.

해설 '~하곤 했었다'는 뜻을 나타내는 used to는 조동사로, 뒤에 동사원형이 와야 하므로 첫 번째 빈칸은 work가 알맞다. 두 번째 빈칸은 주어 I의 현재 상태를 설명하는 형용사 자리인데 '퇴직한, 은퇴한'의 의미를 가진 형용사는 retired이다. 퇴직을 한 상태지 퇴직하고 있는 중이 아니므로 retiring은 의미상 적합하지 않다. 한 가지 주의할 점은 여기서 retired는 '퇴직시키다'라는 의미의 타동사 retire의 과거분사가 아니라 '퇴직해버린'이라는 의미로서 완료적 의미를 가지는 자동사 retire의 과거분사에서 파생된 형용사라는 점이다.

정답 (c)

5 **해석** A: 캐서린, 네 아버지께 편지 안 쓴 지 한참 됐지. 그렇지?

B: 응, 죄송한 마음이야. 실은 편지 안 쓴 지 한 달이 다 됐거든.

해설 동사 owe는 '~를 …의 탯[덕분]으로 돌리다'의 뜻으로 쓰일 경우에는 3형식(owe + 직목 + to 간목)의 어순으로만 써야 하며, '~에게 …를 빚지고 있다'라는 의미로 쓰일 경우에는 4형식 어순인 〈owe + 사람(간목) + 사물(직목)〉 또는 3형식 어순인 〈owe + 사물(직목) + to 사람(간목)〉의 형태를 취한다. 이 문제에서는 후자의 의미로 쓰였으므로 3형식과 4형식 어순 모두가 가능하다. 한 달 동안 아버지에게 편지 한통을 빚진 상태라는 것은 편지를 한 달 동안 한 통도 쓰지 못했다는 의미가 숨어 있다고 볼 수 있다. 따라서 정답은 (c)이다. (a)와 (b)는 태가 틀렸으므로 답에서 제외된다.

어휘 owe *sth* to *sb* ~에게 …를 빚지다, …를 ~탯[덕분]으로 돌리다

e.g. I owe my success to him.
나의 성공은 그의 덕분이다.
I owe a letter to him.
= I owe him a letter.

정답 (c)

6 **해석** A: 따님께서 약을 규칙적으로 복용하도록 하세요.

B: 걱정 마세요. 그럴 겁니다.

해설 준사역동사에 해당하는 동사 get은 5형식 문형에서 목적어와 목적격 보어의 관계가 능동일 경우에 목적격 보어 자리에 원형부정사가 아니라 to부정사를 취해야 하며, 수동 관계일 경우에는 다른 사역동사와 마찬가지로 과거분사를 취한다. 이 문제의 경우 목적어인 딸이 약을 복용하는 것이므로 목적어와 목적격 보어의 주술 관계가 능동이다. 따라서 to부정사 형태인 (b) to take가 정답이다. 참고로 사역동사 get은 목적어와 목적격 보어의 관계가 능동이고 진행의 의미를 강조할 경우 to부정사 대신 현재분사(-ing)를 목적격 보어로 취하기도 한다.

e.g. I couldn't get the car running/going.

어휘 medication 약, 약물치료
regularly 규칙적으로, 정기적으로

정답 (b)

7 **해석** A: 샘, 들었니? 마크가 싸움을 하다가 코뼈가 부러졌대.

B: 가엾어라! 다시는 싸우지 말라고 했건만.

해설 사역동사 have의 목적격 보어의 형태를 묻는 문제이다. 사역동사 have는 목적어와 목적격 보어의 관계를 따져서 능동이면 원형부정사를 취하고, 수동 관계이면 과거분사를 취한다. 코는 '부러지는' 것이므로 수동의 의미를 가지는 과거분사 (b) broken이 정답이다.

어휘 have one's nose broken 코뼈가 부러지다
Poor thing! 가엾어라!

정답 (b)

8 **해석** A: 기말 보고서는 어떻게 잘 제출했니?

B: 잘했어. 어머니께 교정을 좀 봐달라고 부탁을 드렸더니 몇 가지 좋은 조언을 해주시더라고.

해설 알맞은 사역동사를 고르는 문제이다. 사역동사 make, let, have는 목적격 보어 자리에 원형부정사를 취하고, 사역동사 get은 to부정사를 취한다. 목적격 보어 자리에 to부정사(to proofread)가 왔으므로 정답은 (d) got이다.

어휘 final paper 기말 보고서
proofread 교정보다

정답 (d)

9 **해석** A: 매기, 영양사에게 네 식사의 영양 분석을 해달라고 부탁하는 게 좋을 거 같아.

B: 좋아, 그럴게.

해설 ask의 어법을 묻는 문제이다. ask는 5형식 문형에서 목적어와 목적격 보어의 관계가 능동일 때는 to부정사를, 수동 관계일 때는 과거분사를 목적격 보어로 취하는 동사이다. 목적어인 the dietitian이 show라는 행위의 주체이므로 능동 관계이다. 따라서 정답은 (b) to show이다.

어휘 dietitian 영양사, 영양학자

정답 (b)

10 해석 규칙적으로 운동하는 것과 건강한 식사를 하는 것은 심장병을 예방하기 위한 중요한 전략이다.

해설 첫 번째 빈칸은 주어 자리이므로 동사가 아닌 동명사 eating이 알맞고, 두 번째 빈칸은 동사 자리인데 동명사가 2개 이상 and로 연결된 경우는 복수 취급을 하므로 복수 동사 are가 알맞다. 따라서 정답은 (d)이다. 참고로 to부정사는 주어 자리에 2개 이상 and로 연결된 경우일지라도 단수 취급하여 단수 동사를 쓴다.

정답 (d)

11 해석 그 학생들은 졸업 파티를 하기 위해 그 식당에서 친구들을 만났다.

해설 주어인 학생들이 친구들을 만나는 것으로 태가 능동이 되어야 하므로 수동형인 선택지 (c)와 (d)는 답이 될 수 없다. meet는 타동사로서 목적어를 바로 취하므로 선택지 (b)는 전치사 to를 삭제해야 옳다. 따라서 빈칸에 알맞은 정답은 (a) met their friends for이다.

정답 (a)

12 해석 수많은 팬들이 그 영화의 시사회에 참석하는 영화배우들을 보기 위해 위해 모였다.

해설 amass는 '모으다, 수집하다'라는 뜻의 타동사로도 쓰이고, '모이다'라는 뜻의 자동사로도 쓰인다. 문맥상 빈칸에는 후자인 자동사가 들어가야 한다. 참고로 이 문제는 문장 구조만 파악해도 답을 쉽게 구할 수 있는 유형이다. 문장 구조상 빈칸은 동사 자리인데 선택지 중 동사는 (c) amassed밖에 없다. attend를 동사로 착각할 수도 있으나 attend는 to부정사구 내의 지각동사 see의 목적격 보어로 쓰인 것이다. 즉 attend의 주체는 전체 문장의 주어인 팬들이 아니라, 영화배우들이므로 전체 문장의 동사가 될 수 없다. 따라서 빈칸이 전체 문장의 동사 자리인 것이다.

어휘 massive 대규모의
amass 모이다

premiere 시사회, 첫 공연

정답 (c)

13 해석 지금 드시고 계시는 음식에는 저희 옥상 정원에서 기른 채소가 들어가 있습니다.

해설 include의 어법을 물어보는 문제이다. include는 '포함하다, 함유하다'라는 뜻을 가진 상태 동사로 간주하여 진행형을 쓰지 않기 때문에 (d)는 답에서 제외된다. 전체 문장의 주어 meal이 단수 가산명사이므로 주어와 동사의 수 일치 원칙에 따라 (c) 역시 답이 될 수 없다. 그다음, 태를 따져야 하는데 주어인 meal이 채소를 함유하는 것이므로 주술 관계가 능동이다. 따라서 정답은 (a) includes이다. 참고로 include는 타동사로만 쓰이므로 반드시 목적어를 취해야 한다.

어휘 rooftop 옥상의, 옥상에 있는

정답 (a)

14 해석 선생님은 그 학생이 자신의 숙제를 끝내게 만들었다.

해설 동사의 유형을 묻는 문제이다. 사역동사 make는 5형식 문형을 취할 때 목적어와 목적격 보어의 주술 관계가 능동일 경우 원형부정사를, 수동일 경우에는 과거분사를 목적격 보어로 취한다. 목적어인 the student가 끝내는 행위(finish)의 주체이므로, 즉 목적어와 목적격 보어의 주술 관계가 능동이므로 원형부정사인 (c) finish가 정답이다.

정답 (c)

15 해석 어젯밤 5번가를 따라 걷다가 형사가 강도를 추격하고 있는 모습을 봤다.

해설 지각동사 see의 목적격 보어의 형태를 묻는 문제이다. 지각동사(see, watch, hear, feel)는 목적어와 목적격 보어의 관계가 능동이면 목적격 보어 자리에 현재분사 또는 원형부정사를 써야 하고, 수동 관계이면 과거분사를 쓴다. 목적어인 detective가 강도를 '추격하는' 것이므로 목적어와 목적격 보어의 주술 관계가 능동이다. 따라서 정답은 (c) chasing이다.

어휘 detective 형사, 탐정
chase 추격하다, 쫓다
robber 강도

정답 (c)

16 해석 이 특별한 책은 문학 평론가들에 의해 선별된 20개의 이야기로 구성되어 있다.

해설 consist의 동사 지식을 물어보는 문제이다. consist
는 자동사로만 쓰이므로 수동형을 쓸 수 없으며, 형태
는 능동형이지만 '~로 구성되다' 라는 수동적인 의미
로 해석되고 항상 전치사 of를 수반한다. 따라서 정답
은 (c) consists of이다.

어휘 literary 문학의

　　 analyst 분석가

정답 (c)

17 해석 (a) A: 컴퓨터 고쳐 줘서 정말 고마워. 오늘 밤 저녁 살게.

　　 (b) B: 아니야. 네 돈 축내고 싶지 않아. 게다가 난 컴
　　　　　퓨터 만지는 걸 좋아하거든.

　　 (c) A: 음, 네 덕분에 정말 많은 시간이 절약됐어. 내가
　　　　　보답할 수 있게 해줘.

　　 (d) B: 좋아, 정 그렇다면 그렇게 해. 그런데 정말 별
　　　　　일도 아니었어.

해설 5형식 구문의 목적격 보어의 형태를 묻는 문제이다.
사역동사 let은 목적격 보어 자리에 원형부정사를 취
해야 하므로 (a)의 to buy를 buy로 고쳐야 한다.

어휘 make it up to *sb* ~에게 보답하다, 보상하다

　　 big deal 대단한 것[일], 큰일

정답 (a) to buy → buy

18 해석 (a) A: 안녕하십니까. 존 F. 케네디 경영 대학원입니다.

　　 (b) B: 안녕하세요. 다가올 학기에 경영학 석사 과정에
　　　　　지원 방법을 알아보려고 전화드렸습니다.

　　 (c) A: 우선, 접수비와 함께 작성하신 지원서를 제출하
　　　　　셔야 합니다.

　　 (d) B: 알겠습니다. 그리고 장학제도에 대해서도 여쭤
　　　　　보고 싶습니다.

해설 자동사와 타동사의 구분을 묻는 문제이다. reach는
자동사로 오인하기 쉬운 완전타동사이므로 목적어 앞
에 전치사 to를 쓸 수 없다. 따라서 (a)의 reached
to는 reached가 되어야 문법에 맞는 문장이다.

어휘 reach (전화로) 연락하다, 연락을 취하다

　　 business school 경영 대학원

　　 application form 지원서, 신청서

　　 registration fee 등록 수수료, 접수 비용, 신청비

　　 scholarship program 장학제도

정답 (a) reached to → reached

19 해석 (a) A: 윌리엄 교수님, 다음 주 월요일 저녁 식사 하러
　　　　　저희 집에 오셨으면 합니다.

　　 (b) B: 아, 죄송하지만 다음 주 내내 엄청 바쁠 겁니다.

　　 (c) A: 그럼 다음 주 금요일은 어때요?

　　 (d) B: 노력은 하겠지만 약속은 못 드리겠네요.

해설 busy는 동사가 아니라 형용사이다. 따라서 (b)의 조
동사 will 다음에 동사원형인 be가 필요하다.

어휘 terribly 몹시, 대단히

　　 drop by 들르다(= stop by, swing by, come over)

정답 (b) will terribly busy → will be terribly busy

20 해석 (a) 뉴욕 시는 최근에 시내 전역의 모든 술집과 식당에
서 흡연 금지령을 시행했다. (b) 술집과 나이트클럽 주
인들은 이 새로운 법이 그들 영업에 해가 될 거라 걱
정하고 있다. (c) 그 금지령은 건강주의자와 암 예방
단체들의 오랜 캠페인의 결과였다. (d) 사실상 미국 내
에서 해마다 수천 명의 사람들이 폐암으로 사망하고
있다.

해설 태 일치를 물어보는 문제이다. (a)의 implement는
'시행하다' 라는 뜻을 가지고 있으며 타동사로만 쓰이
는 동사이다. 주어인 뉴욕 시가 금지령을 시행하는 것
이므로 주어와 술어의 관계가 능동이 되어야 한다. 따
라서 was implemented를 능동형인 implemented
로 바꿔야 한다.

어휘 implement 시행하다, 이행하다, 실시하다

　　 ban 금지령

　　 metropolis 대도시

　　 health activist 건강주의자

　　 lung cancer 폐암

정답 (a) was implemented → implemented

Actual Test

1 해석 A: 있잖아. 이 교실에서 이상한 냄새가 나.
　　　 B: 맞아. 당장 문을 열어야겠어.
　 해설 2형식을 취하는 look, sound, taste, feel, smell
　　　 등의 감각동사는 상태 동사이므로 진행형을 쓸 수 없
　　　 고, 대화의 순간인 현재에 냄새가 나고 있는 것이므로
　　　 현재형인 (c) smells가 정답이다.
　 어휘 You know what? 있잖아. 이봐.
　　　 weird 이상한, 기이한
　　　 You're telling me. 내 말이 그 말이야.
　 정답 (c)

2 해석 A: 일본 어땠니?
　　　 B: 가볼 만한 재미있는 장소였지만 입맛에 맞는 음식
　　　　 을 찾기가 어렵더군.
　 해설 전체적인 얘기가 대화 시점보다 이전인 과거의 일본
　　　 방문 경험에 대한 것이므로 과거 시제인 (c) was가
　　　 알맞다.
　 어휘 fit ~에 꼭 맞다
　 정답 (c)

3 해석 A: 배터리로 작동되는 차량이 가까운 미래에는 불티나
　　　　 게 팔릴 거야.
　　　 B: 전적으로 동의해
　 해설 sell은 '팔다'라는 의미의 타동사로도 쓰이고, '팔리
　　　 다'라는 뜻으로 해석되는 자동사로도 쓰이지만, 사물
　　　 이 주어로 오고 well, easily, ⟨like + 명사⟩ 등의 양
　　　 태 부사구와 함께 쓰일 경우에는 자동사로 써야 한다.
　　　 따라서 정답은 (c) will sell이다. 이와 같은 용법으로
　　　 쓰이는 동사에는 peel, wash, read, break 등이 있
　　　 다.
　 어휘 sell like hot cakes 불티나게 팔리다
　 정답 (c)

4 해석 A: 이 책은 매우 재미있어. 많은 웃음을 줘.
　　　 B: 지금 무슨 책을 읽고 있어? 나도 좀 봐도 되겠니?
　 해설 at the moment(지금, 현재)는 현재 진행형과 어울리
　　　 는 부사구이므로 정답은 (b)이다. 참고로 상태 동사는
　　　 now나 at the moment 같은 부사와 함께 쓰이더라
　　　 도 현재형으로 써야 한다.
　　　 e.g. I don't have any money at the moment.
　 정답 (b)

5 해석 A: 따님께서는 직업이 있으신가요?
　　　 B: 예. 고교 졸업 이후부터 계속 일하고 있어요.
　 해설 특별한 문맥이 없는 경우 접속사 since는 '특정 과거
　　　 시점 이후로 지금까지'의 의미를 가지고 있으므로 현
　　　 재완료 시제랑 어울린다. 주로 since 뒤에는 과거 시
　　　 점이나 과거 동사가 오고, 주절은 현재완료나 현재완
　　　 료 진행형이 쓰인다. 참고로 동사 work, study, live
　　　 등은 상태 동사로도 보고 동작 동사로도 보기 때문에
　　　 현재완료 진행형으로 쓰든 현재완료형으로 쓰든 의미
　　　 상의 차이가 없다.
　 정답 (d)

6 해석 A: 난 문구점 운영하는 것이 정말 재미있어요.
　　　 B: 언제 시작하셨나요?
　 해설 현재완료는 구체적인 과거 시점(yesterday, last
　　　 night, in 1999, 3 years ago)을 나타내는 부사(구)
　　　 와는 함께 쓸 수 없다. 의문부사 when은 의미의 특
　　　 성상 구체적인 과거 시점을 나타내므로 현재완료 시제
　　　 와는 함께 쓸 수 없으며 단순 과거 시제로 써야 한다.
　 어휘 run 운영하다
　　　 stationery store 문방구
　 정답 (d)

7 해석 A: 숲에 가는 김에 딸기 열매 좀 따다 줘.
　　　 B: 혹시라도 발견하게 되면 가져올게.
　 해설 시간이나 조건을 나타내는 부사절에서는 비록 미래의
　　　 일일지라도 현재 시제가 미래를 대신하므로 (a)가 정
　　　 답이다.
　 어휘 berry 딸기류의 열매
　 정답 (a)

8 해석 A: 너희들이 이 여행을 시작한 지 얼마나 됐니?
　　　 B: 내일이면 5개월 연속으로 여행하는 셈일 거야.
　 해설 부사구 By tomorrow로 기준 시점이 미래임을 알
　　　 수 있다. for five months를 통해서 By tomorrow
　　　 라는 미래의 특정 시점까지 진행 중인 동작의 지속 기
　　　 간을 강조하는 시제는 미래완료 진행 시제(will have
　　　 been V-ing)이다. 참고로 상태를 강조하면 미래완료
　　　 시제(will have p.p.)를 쓴다. 그리고 How long 뒤
　　　 에는 has it been이 생략되어 있다고 보면 된다.
　 어휘 straight 연속으로, 연달아서
　 정답 (d)

9 **해석** A: 한 친절한 사람의 도움으로 가난에서 벗어난 이후로 나는 항상 기쁜 마음으로 다른 가난한 사람들에게 보답해 왔습니다.

B: 당신의 관대함에 감사를 표합니다.

해설 도움을 받은 특정 과거 시점부터 지금까지 지속되는 상태를 표현하는 시제는 현재완료이다. 〈since + 과거 시점/동사〉가 들어 있는 문장의 주절은 주로 현재완료 시제라는 점을 기억해 두면 좋다.

어휘 poverty 가난
return the favor 보답하다, 신세를 갚다
in need 어려움에 처한, 궁핍한
generosity 관대, 아량

정답 (d)

10 **해석** 그가 퇴근해서 집에 도착했을 무렵 게임은 이미 끝나 버렸다.

해설 과거의 두 사건이나 동작 중 먼저 일어난 일을 나타내는 시제는 과거완료이다. 그가 집에 도착한 것보다 게임 끝난 것이 먼저임을 나타내는 시제인데, 특히 시간 접속사 when이나 by the time이 이끄는 부사절에서는 사건 선후를 밝히기 위해 반드시 과거완료 시제를 써줘야 한다. 반면, 시간 접속사 before나 after는 사건 선후를 밝히기 때문에 과거완료를 써도 되고 쓰지 않아도 된다.

e.g. I ate(= had eaten) dinner before I watched TV.

정답 (d)

11 **해석** 미국에서 노예는 거의 200년 전에 해방되었지만, 많은 흑인들이 아직까지 제도화된 인종차별의 잔재로 고통을 받고 있다.

해설 시제와 동사 지식을 동시에 묻는 문제이다. 일단 빈칸은 동사 자리이므로 (c)는 답에서 제외된다. 동사 emancipate는 '해방하다'라는 뜻의 타동사이므로 빈칸에는 수동형이 되어야 하기 때문에 (b) 역시 답이 될 수 없다. two hundred years ago와 같이 과거의 구체적인 시점을 나타내는 부사구와 함께 쓰이는 시제는 단순 과거 시제이므로 정답은 (a) were emancipated이다. 〈기수 + 단위명사 + ago〉는 무조건 과거 시제랑 어울린다고 봐도 무방하다.

어휘 slave 노예
emancipate 해방하다
legacy 유산, 잔재

institutionalized 제도화된
racism 인종적 차별
discrimination 차별, 차별 대우

정답 (a)

12 **해석** 제리가 어제 아침에 차로 출근한 이후로 우리는 그를 전혀 보지 못했다.

해설 시간 접속사 since가 이끄는 부사절이 답을 찾는 단서이다. 과거의 특정 시점 이후로 지금까지 지속되고 있는 상태를 강조하는 시제는 현재완료이므로 (c)가 정답이다. 기준 시점이 현재일 경우 〈since + 과거 시점〉, 〈for + 숫자 + 기간 명사〉와 어울리는 시제는 완료 시제이다.

어휘 sign 흔적

정답 (c)

13 **해석** 바깥으로 나오자마자 땀이 나기 시작했다.

해설 시제와 어순을 묻는 문제이다. scarcely, rarely, seldom, never, no sooner 등의 부정부사가 문두에 오면 주어와 동사의 도치가 일어나서 〈조동사 + 주어〉 형태의 의문문 어순이 되어야 하므로 (b)와 (d)는 답에서 제외된다. 그리고 바깥으로 나온 것이 땀이 나기 시작한 것보다 이전 상황이므로 과거완료 시제인 (a) had I가 정답이다.

어휘 scarcely A when B A하자마자 B하다
take a step 발걸음을 내딛다
sweat 땀이 나다

정답 (a)

14 **해석** 호텔 엘리베이터에 갇힌 이후부터 항상 폐소 공포증을 느껴 왔다.

해설 접속사 since가 답을 찾는 결정적인 단서이다. 〈since + 과거 시점/동사〉의 부사구나 부사절이 쓰인 문장에서 주절 동사는 주로 현재완료 시제로 쓴다. 엘리베이터에 갇혔던 시점 이후로 지금까지 항상 폐소 공포증을 느껴 왔으므로 현재완료가 가장 적절하다.

어휘 claustrophobic 폐소 공포증의

정답 (d)

15 **해석** 1960년대부터 1970년대까지 수많은 한국인 광부와 간호사들이 남한의 실업 문제뿐만 아니라 독일의 노동력 부족을 해결하기 위해 서독에 파견되었다.

해설 1960년대부터 1970년대까지의 시간은 구체적인 과거의

시점이므로 과거 시제가 알맞다.

어휘 **mine worker** 광산 노동자, 광부

　　 workforce 노동력

정답 (b)

16 해석 (a) A: 제리에게 우리 약속에 대해 얘기했니?

　　　 (b) B: 물론, 오늘 오후 일찍 얘기했어.

　　　 (c) A: 올 수 있대?

　　　 (d) B: 오늘 밤에 전화 준대.

해설 this afternoon은 문맥이 없으므로 미래일 수도 있고, 과거일 수도 있고, 현재일 수도 있다. 하지만 A의 물음에 B가 Sure라고 대답했으므로 this afternoon은 구체적인 과거의 시점, 즉 명백한 과거 시점을 나타내는 부사가 되므로 과거 시제를 써야 한다. 따라서 we've spoken을 we spoke로 고쳐야 한다.

어휘 **make it** 오다, 출석하다

　　 give *sb* **a ring** ~에게 전화하다

정답 (b) we've spoken → we spoke

17 해석 (a) A: 제리, 이번 주말에 우리랑 함께 영화 보러 갔으면 해.

　　　 (b) B: 미안, 핀란드에 있는 내 친구를 방문해야 해.

　　　 (c) A: 정말? 재미있겠네. 조심해서 다녀와.

　　　 (d) B: 고마워. 돌아올 때 사진도 몇 장 가져올게.

해설 시간이나 조건의 부사절에서는 비록 미래의 일일지라도 현재 시제가 미래를 대신하므로 (d)의 will come을 come으로 고쳐야 한다.

정답 (d) will come → come

18 해석 (a) A: 엄마, 최근에 허리가 많이 아파요. 특히 걷거나 허리를 굽힐 때 말이에요.

　　　 (b) B: 사실 허리 문제는 우리 가족 내력인 거 같다, 얘야. 병원에 가봤니?

　　　 (c) A: 아직요. 하지만 더 심해지면 선택의 여지가 없겠죠.

　　　 (d) B: 어서 가봐. 이런 종류의 부상은 제대로 치료되지 않으면 영구적일 수 있어.

해설 if가 '~라면'으로 해석되는 조건 부사절에서는 미래의 일일지라도 현재 시제로 미래를 대신하므로 (c)의 will get worse를 gets worse로 수정해야 한다. 참고로 if가 '~인지 아닌지'로 해석되며 타동사의 목적어가 되는 명사절을 이끄는 경우에는 현재 시제가 미래를 대신할 수 없기 때문에 〈will + 동사원형〉 형태를 써야

한다.

어휘 **bend over** 허리를 구부리다

　　 run in one's family 집안 내력이다

정답 (c) will get → gets

19 해석 (a) 제임스는 사람들에게 장난을 치는 나쁜 습관을 가지고 있었다. (b) 3주 전에 그는 경찰에 장난 전화를 걸어서 이웃에 강도가 발생했다고 신고했다. (c) 그가 집에 돌아왔을 때, 그는 자신의 집에 누군가 무단 침입한 걸 알게 되었다. 그 사건 이후 그는 다시는 장난 전화를 하지 않았다.

해설 시제 일치를 물어보는 문제이다. (c)에서 그가 발견한 시점보다는 그의 집이 무단 침입당한 것이 먼저이므로 is를 had been으로 고쳐야 옳다.

어휘 **pull pranks on** *sb* 장난치다, 골려 주다

　　 crank call 장난 전화

　　 make a call to ~에 전화를 걸다

　　 burglary 강도 (사건)

　　 break into 침입하다

　　 incident 일어난 일, 우발적 사건

정답 (c) is → had been

20 해석 (a) 고대로부터 현대에 이르기까지 권력 기관은 권력을 행사하고 유지하기 위한 수단으로 오락을 이용해 왔다. (b) 로마 제국의 악명 높은 카니발 축제는 그들의 제국이 멸망하는 동안 로마 시민의 관심을 축제의 볼거리에 집중시켰다. (c) 올더스 헉슬리는 그의 소설 《멋진 신세계》에서 기존의 사회질서에 기꺼이 순응할 수 있도록 주민들이 쇼에 정신이 팔리고 약물에 취해 버리고 마는 반이상향을 그렸다. (d) 저명한 학자 노암 촘스키는 맹목적인 애국주의적 태도를 주입하고 사람들의 관심을 진정한 사회문제로부터 딴 데로 돌리는 데 있어서 현대의 관람 스포츠가 했던 역할에 대해 언급한 적이 있다.

해설 시제 일치를 물어보는 문제이다. 전체적인 글이 역사적 사실을 기술하고 있다. 사람들이 사회문제에 무관심하도록 만드는 데 있어서 스포츠 경기가 했던 역할에 대해 노암 촘스키가 언급한 것은 과거에 있었던 일이므로 play 역시 과거 시제로 시제 일치가 되어야 한다.

어휘 **modernity** 현대(성)

　　 dominant establishment 권력 기관, 지배층

　　 entertainment 오락

exert authority 권력을 행사하다

notorious 악명 높은

carnival 사육제, 축제

spectacle 구경거리

crumble 무너지다, 붕괴하다

envision 상상하다, 마음속에 그리다

distract 산만하게 하다, 주의를 돌리다

sedate 진정시키다

conform to ~에 순응하다, 따르다

prevailing 널리 퍼진, 지배적인

spectator sport 관람 스포츠, 보는 스포츠 (관람 위주의 스포츠 경기를 뜻함.)

cf. participant sports 직접 하는 스포츠

instill 서서히 주입시키다

jingoistic 맹목적 애국주의의

정답 (d) play → played

Actual Test

1 해석 A: 윌리엄, 지금까지 아내랑 결혼 생활이 어땠나요?

　　　B: 환상적이죠. 우리는 함께 살면서 서로에 대해 정말 많은 것들을 배웠어요.

　　해설 태와 시제를 함께 묻는 문제이다. learn이 타동사로 쓰여, 주어 We가 learn의 대상이 아니라 주체이므로 태는 능동이어야 한다. 따라서 (a)는 답이 될 수 없다. 그리고 시제에 있어서는 A가 과거부터 지금까지의 결혼 생활이 어땠느냐고 물어보고 있으므로 과거완료인 (c)는 답이 될 수 없다. so many things가 답의 단서이다. 횟수(twice, three times, many times, several times)나 수량 정보(many people, many things, 100 movies, 3 cups of coffee)는 진행형이나 완료 진행 시제와는 함께 쓸 수 없다. 결혼하고부터 대화의 시점인 지금까지 총체적 경험을 말하는 것이므로 (d) have learned가 정답이다.

　　정답 (d)

2 해석 A: 총회에서 워렌 버핏이 정부의 예산 문제와 관련해서 뭐라고 말했나요?

　　　B: 부자들이 더 많은 세금을 내도록 해야 한다고 했어요.

　　해설 지각동사나 사역동사가 사용된 5형식 문장의 목적격 보어인 원형부정사(동사원형)는 수동태 문장에서는 반드시 to부정사로 바뀌어야 한다. 문맥상, 주어 the wealthy는 사역동사 make의 의미상 목적어이므로 수동이 되어야 하기 때문에 (c)는 답이 될 수 없다. 그리고 pay는 의미상 주어인 the wealthy가 행위의 주체이므로 능동 부정사를 써서 정답은 (a) be made to pay가 된다. 참고로 해당 절을 능동태로 바꾸면 the government should make the rich pay more taxes이다.

　　어휘 with regard to ~에 관해

　　정답 (a)

3 해석 A: 실례합니다. 오늘 밤 대회에 제 개가 참여해도 되나요?

　　　B: 죄송합니다. 학생만 장기 자랑 대회에 참여할 자격이 있습니다.

　　해설 주어인 학생들이 자격을 부여하는 것이 아니라 자격을 부여받는 것이므로 태는 수동이 되어야 한다. 따라서 (a)와 (b)는 답이 될 수 없다. 동사 qualify는 5형식의

능동 문장에서 목적격 보어로 to부정사를 취한다.
〈qualify + 목적어 + to부정사〉 형태의 5형식 문장을
수동문으로 고치면 〈be + qualified + to부정사〉의
형태가 되므로 (c) are qualified to enter가 가장 알맞
다.

어휘 perform 공연하다
qualified 자격이 있는
talent show 장기 자랑 대회

정답 (c)

4 해석 A: 어제 너희 집에 경찰이 왜 온 거야?
B: 내가 쇼핑하러 나간 동안 집에 강도가 들었어.

해설 구동사의 수동태를 묻는 문제이다. 집은 무단 침입을
하는 것이 아니라 무단 침입 당하는 것이므로 수동태
가 되어야 한다. 따라서 (b)는 답에서 제외되며, 구동
사의 수동태는 전치사를 빠뜨리지 않아야 하므로 (a)
역시 답이 될 수 없다. 마지막으로 a burglar는 행위
자인데, 수동문에서 행위자 앞에는 전치사 by를 써줘
야 한다. 따라서 정답은 (d) was broken into by a
burglar이다.

어휘 break into 무단 침입하다
burglar 강도, 도둑

정답 (d)

5 해석 A: 켄드릭 부인, 따님 소피가 아직 혼자 사나요?
B: 아니요. 약 5년 전에 결혼했어요.

해설 marry는 용법에 주의해야 하는 동사이다. 타동사와
자동사로 모두 쓰이며 목적어를 취하지 않는 자동사일
경우에는 주어가 they나 we 같은 복수 주어가 되어
야 한다. (e.g. They married 3 years ago.) 따라
서 marry가 자동사로 쓰였다고 본다면 주어가 복수
가 아닌 she이므로 (a)와 (b)는 답이 될 수 없다.
marry를 타동사로 간주하더라도 marry의 목적어가
없으므로 역시 답이 될 수 없다. 특정한 대상이 뒤에
나오지 않고 '결혼하다'라는 표현으로는 '결혼한 상태
가 되다'라는 뜻의 동작 수동인 get married를 쓴다.
five months ago가 있으므로 과거 시제이며, 목적
어를 취하지 않았기 때문에 동작 수동형인 (d) got
married가 정답이다.

정답 (d)

6 해석 A: 루크, 집이 상당히 낡아 보여. 재건축이 필요하지
않을까?

B: 음, 사실은 이사를 갈까 생각 중이야.

해설 want, need, require, deserve 등의 타동사는 목
적어로 동명사가 올 때 의미가 수동이어서 수동 동명
사(being + p.p.)를 써야 할 것 같지만 능동 동명사
를 써야 하는 동사들이다. 반면, 목적어로 to부정사를
취할 경우에는 태를 따져서 수동이면 수동 to부정사
to be remodeled 형태로 사용해야 한다.

정답 (c)

7 해석 A: 오늘 내 공연이 어땠는지 네 생각을 듣고 싶어.
B: 마음에 들었어. 감명받았어.

해설 impress는 '~에게 좋은 인상을 주다, 감동시키다'라
는 의미의 타동사이다. 주어 I와 impress의 주술 관
계는 I가 감명을 받는 것이므로 수동 관계이다. 따라서
(d) I'm impressed.가 정답이다. (a)는 It is
impressive.가 되어야 한다.

어휘 performance 공연

정답 (d)

8 해석 A: 주말에 제 애완동물들에게 밥 좀 주시겠어요?
B: 걱정 마세요. 잘 보살펴 드릴게요.

해설 동사구의 수동태를 묻는 문제이다. they는 애완동물
이므로 동사구 take care of의 주체가 아니라 대상이
다. 따라서 수동의 형태가 되어야 하는데 take care
of처럼 〈동사 + 명사 + 전치사〉 형태의 동사구는 수
동태에서도 전치사를 빠뜨리지 않도록 주의해야 한다.
따라서 정답은 (b) be taken care of이다.

정답 (b)

9 해석 A: 이 야생 버섯 먹어도 되나요?
B: 예. 이 버섯 안내 책자에 따르면 수천 년 동안 원주
민들이 먹어 왔다는군요.

해설 태와 시제을 함께 묻는 문제이다. 일단 시제는 과거부
터 현재까지의 기간을 나타내는 for thousands of
years가 있는 걸로 보아 완료 시제가 적절하므로 (a)
와 (b)는 답이 될 수 없으며, they는 동사 eat의 주체
가 아니라 대상이므로 태는 수동태가 되어야 한다. 따
라서 (d) have been eaten이 정답이다.

어휘 edible 먹을 수 있는, 식용에 알맞은
native 원주민

정답 (d)

10 해석 A: 앵글로 · 색슨족이 캐나다의 최초 정착민들이었나요?

B: 아니요. 사실 퀘백 지역은 프랑스 사람들이 최초로 정착했어요.

해설 어떤 장소에 정착한다는 뜻을 가진 동사 settle은 자동사(settle in + 장소)로도 쓰이고, 타동사(settle + 장소)로도 쓰인다. 하지만 주어 the Quebec region은 장소로, settle의 주체가 아니라 대상이므로 수동태가 되어야 한다. 따라서 (b) was first settled by가 정답이다. 참고로 B는 문맥상 역사적 사실에 대해 얘기하고 있으므로 과거 시제가 되어야 한다. 따라서 (a)와 (d)는 태는 맞지만 각각 수 일치와 시제가 맞지 않아서 답이 될 수 없다.

정답 (b)

11 해석 동물학자들은 그 코끼리가 희귀한 유전적 질환으로 죽었다고 추정했다.

해설 동사 유형을 묻는 문제이다. '추측하다'라는 뜻의 타동사 speculate는 〈동사 + 목적어 + to부정사〉 형태의 5형식을 취할 수 없고 that 명사절을 목적어로 취하므로 (d) that the elephant died가 정답이다. 참고로 자동사로 쓰일 경우에는 주로 〈speculate on/about + 명사(구)〉 형태를 취한다.

어휘 zoologist 동물학자
speculate 추측하다
genetic disorder 유전적 질환, 유전병

정답 (d)

12 해석 심문하는 동안 용의자는 강도 사건 뒤의 배후자가 누군지 폭로하도록 설득되었다.

해설 문장 구조상 빈칸은 동사 자리이며, 주어 the suspect는 동사 persuade의 주체가 아니라 대상이므로 수동이 되어야 하는데, 선택지 중 수동태는 (b)밖에 없다. persuade는 '설득하다'라는 뜻으로, 5형식 문형을 취할 때 목적격 보어로 to부정사나 〈into + V-ing〉를 취하는데, 수동태 문장에서도 목적격 보어인 to부정사는 be p.p. 다음에 그대로 써줘야 하기 때문에 정답은 (b) was persuaded to reveal이다.

어휘 interrogation 심문
suspect 용의자
mastermind 배후자, 주모자

정답 (b)

13 해석 최근까지만 해도 많은 사람들이 기술 발전이 인류의 대부분의 문제들을 해결할 거라고 믿었다.

해설 목적어가 that절인 문장의 수동태에 관한 문제이다. 선택지 네 개 모두 it으로 시작하므로, 주어 it과 believe의 주술 관계를 파악해서 태를 구분하면 된다. it은 가주어이고 that 이하의 명사절이 진주어이다. 결국 that 이하를 가리키는 it은 believe의 주체가 아니라 대상이므로 수동 관계임을 알 수 있다. 능동 문장은 Many believed that technological progress would solve most of humanity's problems.로 이 문장을 수동태로 고치면 It was believed by many that technological progress would solve most of humanity's problems.가 된다. 참고로 recently는 현재완료 시제와 함께 쓸 수 있지만 until recently는 무조건 과거 시제로만 써야 한다.

어휘 up until recently 최근까지만 해도

정답 (b)

14 해석 존 윌리암스 총장은 정부 보조금과 다른 형태의 재정적 지원이 한정되어 있기 때문에 학생들이 다가오는 학기에 수업료 내기가 불가능할 것이라고 주장했다.

해설 수동태 문제이면서도 주어와 동사의 적절한 호응 관계를 묻는 문제이다. limit는 '제한하다'라는 뜻을 가진 타동사이므로 수동태가 되어야 하고 주어는 빈칸 바로 앞에 있는 aid가 아니라 grants and other forms이다. 그러므로 빈칸에 들어갈 적절한 서술어 형태는 (d) were limited이다.

어휘 tuition cost 등록금
grant 보조금, 지원금

정답 (d)

15 해석 전 파키스탄 대사가 인질 석방 협상 임무를 맡은 호위대를 이끌도록 선택되었다.

해설 기본적인 태를 묻는 문제이다. '선출하다'라는 뜻의 타동사 select와 ambassador의 문맥상 주술 관계는 수동이고 주어가 3인칭 단수이므로 (c) has been selected가 정답이다.

어휘 ambassador 대사
convoy 호위대
hostage 인질

정답 (c)

16 해석 홍역은 3~4일간 지속되고 심한 통증을 유발하며 죽음에 이르게 할 수 있는 흔한 유형의 전염병이다.

해설 수동이 불가능한, 주의해야 할 자동사를 묻는 문제이
　　 다. '지속되다' 라는 뜻의 last는 자동사이므로 수동으
　　 로 쓸 수 없다. 따라서 (a)와 (d)는 답에서 제외된다.
　　 3~4일간 지속될 수도 있다는 건 가능성(possibility)
　　 이지 능력(ability)이 아니다. be able to는 능력을
　　 뜻하므로 빈칸에 들어가기에는 문맥에 맞지 않는다.
　　 따라서 가능성을 나타내는 (b) can last가 정답이다.

어휘 **measles** 홍역
　　 contagious 전염성의
　　 intense 극심한

정답 (b)

17 해석 (a) A: 마리아, 당신 자신만의 집을 지을 거란 얘기를
　　　　　 들었어요.
　　　 (b) B: 맞아요. 하지만 나를 도와줄 경험이 더 많은 사
　　　　　 람들을 만나고 싶어요.
　　　 (c) A: 내 옛날 반 친구가 집을 잘 짓죠.
　　　 (d) B: 그래요? 언제 한번 그 친구분 좀 소개시켜 주
　　　　　 시겠어요?

해설 문장 (a)에서 태가 틀렸다. 주어 I가 동사 hear의 주
　　 체이고 hear의 목적어는 that절이므로 I've been
　　 heard를 I've heard 또는 I heard로 고쳐야 한다.

어휘 **be great at** ~에 능숙하다

정답 (a) I've been heard → I've heard *or* I heard

18 해석 (a) A: 그럼 하와이로 여행을 가실 건가요?
　　　 (b) B: 아뇨. 제 아내가 더 중요한 걸 위해 돈을 절약
　　　　　 해야 한다고 하더군요.
　　　 (c) A: 그럼 많이 실망스럽겠군요.
　　　 (d) B: 조금요. 하지만 그녀 말이 맞는 것 같아요.

해설 기본적인 태를 물어보는 문제이다. (b)에서 주어인
　　 My wife와 동사 said가 능동 관계, 즉 문맥상 말한
　　 다는 행위의 대상이 아니라 주체이므로 was said를
　　 said로 고쳐야 한다.

정답 (b) was said → said

19 해석 (a) 노벨상은 스웨덴 실업가 알프레드 노벨에 의해 제
　　　　 정되었다. (b) 그는 자신의 가장 유명한 발명품 중 하
　　　　 나인 다이너마이트로 부자가 되었다. (c) 다이너마이트
　　　　 가 파괴적인 용도로 사용되는 걸 보고 그는 자신의 유
　　　　 산이 죽음의 유산이 될 것 같아 걱정하게 되었다. (d)
　　　　 그는 자신의 유언장에서 그의 재산을 과학, 문학, 그리
　　　　 고 평화를 장려하는 데 기증했다.

해설 found는 '제정하다, 설립하다' 라는 의미의 타동사이
　　 다. 문장 (a)에서 주어인 노벨상(The Nobel Prizes)
　　 은 '제정되는' 것이므로 수동태가 되어야 하는데
　　 founded 앞에 be동사가 없어서 틀린 문장이다. 따
　　 라서 founded를 were founded로 고쳐야 한다.

어휘 **legacy** 유산

정답 (a) founded → were founded

20 해석 세상이 성별이 아니라 능력에 근거하여 작가를 받아들
　　　 이고 판단하도록 만드는 데는 많은 용감하고 재능 있
　　　 는 여성들의 노력이 있었다. 너무 오랫동안 여성들은
　　　 사회의 기준에 의해 적절하다고 여겨진 주제들에 대해
　　　 서만 글을 쓸 수 있었고, 최고의 여성 작가들조차도
　　　 남성 작가와 동등하게 여겨지지 않았다. 요즘 저명한
　　　 여성 작가가 자신이 선택한 주제에 대해 글을 쓰는 것
　　　 은 전혀 드문 일이 아니다. 물론 대부분의 여성 작가
　　　 들은 성공한 작가라 할지라도 그들의 직업에 좀 더 평
　　　 등을 가져오기 위해서는 아직 할 일이 많이 남아 있다
　　　 고 말할 것이다.

해설 태를 묻는 문제이다. For too long, women
　　 expected to write only about subjects that
　　 were considered proper by society's
　　 standards, and even the best female writers
　　 were never considered equal to a male
　　 writer.에서 여성들은 오랜 기간 동안 사회의 기준에
　　 의해 적절하다고 여겨진 주제에 대해서만 글을 쓰도록
　　 기대되었다는 의미가 되어야 하므로 expected는
　　 were expected 같은 수동태가 되어야 한다. 능동태
　　 는 행위를 하는 사람에, 수동태는 행위의 영향을 받는
　　 사람에 초점을 맞출때 사용한다. 이 문장에서는 행위
　　 자를 나타내지 않고 있지만 문맥상 사회, 일반인들이
　　 라는 것을 알 수 있다.

어휘 **celebrated** 저명한
　　 rarity 드문 것[일]

정답 (b) expected → were expected

Actual Test

1 해석 A: 많은 경주에서 우승한 말은 흰색 털에 검은 반점이 있어.

B: 저 말은 처음 보는 말이야.

해설 주어와 동사의 수 일치를 묻는 문제이다. that won many races는 주어를 수식하는 형용사절이고 문장의 주어는 The horse이므로 단수 동사가 빈칸에 들어가야 한다. 〈말 = 흰 털〉일 수는 없으므로 be동사는 곤란하고 '가지고 있다'는 의미의 (a) has가 정답이다.

정답 (a)

2 해석 A: 전쟁에 찬성투표를 했던 국회의원들이 이제는 반전 운동을 하고 있어.

B: 그 얘길 들으니까 그들의 잘못된 결정에 대해 왜 아무도 책임을 지지 않는지 궁금해지는군.

해설 빈칸은 의문사 why가 이끄는 명사절의 동사 자리이다. 주어인 nobody는 항상 3인칭 단수 취급하므로 단수 동사를 써야 한다.

어휘 congressman 국회의원

vote for 찬성투표하다

hold *sb* accountable for *sth* ~에 대해 …에게 책임을 지게 하다

정답 (d)

3 해석 A: 연극은 어떻게 잘되어 가니?

B: 별로. 두 학생 모두 대본을 지난주에 암기했어야 했는데.

해설 대명사 일치를 물어보는 문제이다. 부정대명사 both나 부정형용사 〈both + 명사〉는 항상 복수 취급하므로 대명사도 격에 따라 복수 대명사인 they, them, their로 받아야 한다.

어휘 theater scene 연극

progress 진행되다, 진척되다

정답 (c)

4 해석 A: 크로커다일과 앨리게이터의 가장 큰 차이점이 뭐야?

B: 구조적으로 크로커다일은 앨리게이터처럼 넓고 강력한 턱을 가지고 있지 않지.

해설 문맥상 빈칸에는 가지고 있지 않다는 부정의 의미가 들어가야 자연스럽다. 〈the + 단수 명사〉로 종족 대표를 나타내는 경우 동사는 단수 동사를 써야 하므로 정답은 (c) doesn't possess이다.

어휘 crocodile 악어

alligator 악어

jaw 턱

정답 (c)

5 해석 A: 제 실수에 대해 진심으로 사과합니다. 일을 그만두는 게 좋겠어요.

B: 너무 심각하게 생각하지 마세요. 당신도, 나도, 그 누구도 그 일에 대해 잘못이 없어요.

해설 B as well as A와 both A and B를 제외한 대부분의 상관접속사는 동사와 가장 가까운 주어에 일치를 시킨다. 상관접속사 neither A nor B, either A or B, not only A but also B 등은 동사에 가까운 B에 수를 일치시킨다. 여기서는 마지막의 anyone else에 일치를 시키면 되는데 anyone else는 3인칭 단수이므로 (c) is가 정답이다.

정답 (c)

6 해석 A: 소방관들이 도착했을 무렵 그 집엔 아무것도 남아 있지 않았어요.

B: 정말 안됐군요!

해설 주어와 동사의 수 일치와 시제를 묻는 문제이다. 소방관들이 화재 현장에 도착했을 무렵의 과거의 상태를 나타내고 있으므로 과거 시제가 되어야 하고 주어인 nothing은 항상 단수 취급하므로 정답은 (b) was이다.

어휘 That's a shame! 안됐네요! 그거 유감이네요!

정답 (b)

7 해석 A: 아빠, 용돈 좀 더 받을 수 있을까요?

B: 얘야, 이미 많이 줬잖니. 200달러는 아빠가 어렸을 땐 큰돈이었단다.

해설 과거의 구체적인 시점(when I was young)이 나와 있으므로 과거 시제가 알맞고 시간(two hours), 거리(ten miles), 금액(three dollars), 무게(ten pounds) 등의 단위 표현은 형태는 복수일지라도 하나의 덩어리로 간주하여 단수 취급하므로 정답은 (c) was이다.

어휘 allowance 용돈

정답 (c)

8 해석 A: 그 학생을 정학시키는 건 좀 가혹한 처벌로 보이지 않나요?

B: 전혀요. 선생님들께서 학교에서 흡연은 용인되지 않을 거라고 수차례 경고했거든요.

해설 repeatedly는 과거부터 현재까지 누적된 경험을 표현하므로 현재완료 시제가 적절하며, 주어가 The teachers로 복수이므로 복수 동사인 (d) have warned가 가장 알맞다.

어휘 suspend 정학시키다

harsh 가혹한

tolerate 용인하다, 너그럽게 보아주다

정답 (d)

9 해석 당신이 불만에 찬 고객들을 상대했던 방식은 아주 프로다웠습니다.

해설 주어와 동사의 수 일치를 물어보는 문제이다. 주어는 단수인 The way이므로 단수 동사를 써야 하고, 시제는 주어를 수식하는 형용사절의 동사 시제가 과거(handled)이므로 주절 동사 역시 과거 시제가 알맞다.

어휘 disgruntled 불만에 찬

정답 (c)

10 해석 스튜어트 부인을 대리하도록 선택된 변호사들은 그 분야에서 최고이다.

해설 chosen to represent Mrs. Stewart는 주어를 수식해 주는 형용사구이고 전체 문장의 주어는 The lawyers로 복수이다. 따라서 복수 동사인 (d) are가 정답이다. 참고로 상태 동사인 be동사는 진행형이 불가능하므로 (b) were being은 답이 될 수 없다.

정답 (d)

11 해석 제조된 모든 상품은 안전성과 내구성에 대한 엄격한 검사를 받아야 했다.

해설 made는 product를 후치 수식하는 과거분사이고 빈칸은 동사 자리이다. 〈every + 단수 명사〉는 항상 단수 취급하므로 단수 동사인 (c) has가 빈칸에 가장 알맞다.

어휘 be subject to + 명사 ~을 받아야 한다, ~을 조건으로 한다

rigid 엄격한

durability 내구성

정답 (c)

12 해석 당국에 의해 발표된 실업에 관한 통계 자료는 정말 헷갈린다.

해설 statistics는 학문명인 '통계학'의 의미로 쓰일 때는 항상 단수 동사를 쓰지만 '통계 수치, 통계 자료'의 의미일 때는 복수 취급해서 복수 동사를 써야 한다. 이 문제에서는 후자로 쓰였으므로 복수 동사를 써야 하며, be동사는 상태 동사이므로 진행형을 쓸 수 없다. 따라서 정답은 (b) are이다.

정답 (b)

13 해석 이사들과 함께 그 최고 경영자는 다음에 어떤 조치를 취하는 것이 최선인지 곰곰이 생각했다.

해설 〈S + along with / together with / in addition to / besides / coupled with / combined with / plus / as well as + V〉 구조에서 주어는 동사에 일치시켜야 한다. 등위접속사 and와 비슷하다고 착각하여 무조건 복수 동사를 고르도록 착각하게 만드는 수식어구들이므로 수 일치에 유의해야 한다. 주어가 The CEO이므로 단수 동사인 (d) has contemplated가 정답이다.

어휘 board of directors 이사회

contemplate 심사숙고하다

정답 (d)

14 해석 앉아서 생활하는 것과 건강한 식사가 부족한 것이 현재 비만 질환의 주요인이다.

해설 동명사 주어는 단수 취급하여 단수 동사를 쓰는 것이 원칙이지만 동명사구 2개 이상이 and로 연결된 경우에는 복수 취급하여 복수 동사를 써야 한다. 따라서 정답은 (c) lacking a healthy diet are가 정답이다. 참고로 (a)는 병치가 되지 않으므로 답이 될 수 없다.

어휘 sedentary 앉아 있는, 앉아서 일하는

obesity epidemic 비만 질환

정답 (c)

15 해석 한국 야구 위원회는 오늘 WBC 대회에 참가할 선수 24명을 최종적으로 발표했는데, 그 24명은 처음의 50명의 후보들 중에서 뽑혔다.

해설 choose는 타동사이기 때문에 구조적으로 항상 목적어를 취해야 한다. 빈칸 뒤에 목적어 없이 전치사 from이 이어지고 있기 때문에 choose의 형태는 수동태가 되어야 한다. 의미적으로도 who는 players를 가리키고, players는 choose의 주체가 아니라

대상이므로, 즉 뽑히는 것이므로 수동이 되어야 한다.

정답 (a)

16 해석 그의 학생들뿐만 아니라 앤더슨 교수도 새로운 인터넷 시스템 사용법을 배우고 있다.

해설 상관접속사의 수 일치를 묻는 문제이다. 대부분의 상관접속사(not only A but also B, either A or B, neither A nor B)는 동사와 가까운 B에 동사를 일치시키지만 A as well as B는 정반대로 동사와 거리가 먼 A에 일치를 시켜야 한다. 따라서 정답은 (b) is learning이다.

정답 (b)

17 해석 다른 사람들을 돕고 세상을 개선하는 데 자신의 삶을 바치는 사람들은 영화배우나 스포츠 스타만큼 찬사를 받을 자격이 있다.

해설 주어와 동사의 수 일치를 물어보는 문제로 형용사구나 절처럼 주어를 꾸며 주는 수식어를 걸러 낼 수 있다면 쉽게 풀 수 있다. 주어 People은 복수 명사이므로 복수 동사를 써야 하며, deserve는 to부정사를 목적어로 취하는 동사이므로 (b) deserve to가 정답이다.

정답 (b)

18 해석 (a) A: 여자 친구와 그녀의 가족이 이번 주말에 우리 마을에 와.

(b) B: 그녀가 〈USA 투데이〉 기자라는 사람이니?

(c) A: 맞아. 와서 그녀를 만나 보는 게 어때?

(d) B: 미안하지만 곤란해. 이번 주말에 선약이 있거든.

해설 주격 관계대명사절 내의 동사는 선행사와 수가 일치해야 한다. 선행사가 the one이므로 write를 단수형 writes로 고쳐야 한다.

정답 (b) write → writes

19 해석 (a) A: 작년 여름에 미국에 갔다 오셨다는 소문이 있던데요.

(b) B: 예, 그랬어요. 집중 어학연수를 받았어요.

(c) A: 어땠나요? 굉장히 어려웠나요?

(d) B: 아뇨, 괜찮았어요. 전 세계에서 온 사람들과 친구가 됐어요.

해설 (c)의 복수 대명사 they가 가리킬 만한 복수 명사가 앞에서 전혀 언급되지 않았으므로 Were they를 Was it으로 고쳐야 한다. language program에서 공부하는 것이 어렵지 않았느냐고 물어보았다고 보는

것이 자연스럽다.

어휘 The rumor has it that S + V ~라는 소문이 있다, 소문에 따르면 ~이다
intensive 집중적인

정답 (c) Were they → Was it

20 해석 외양간을 탈출했던 소 한 마리가 살 수 있는 자유를 얻었다. (b) 그 소는 자물쇠를 풀고 외양간 문을 여는 데 성공했다. (c) 그러고 나서 울타리를 뛰어넘어 헤엄쳐서 강을 건넜다. (d) 그 소의 집요함에 감명받은 농부는 그 소를 도살하지 않기로 결심했다.

해설 주어와 동사의 수 일치를 물어보는 문제이다. (a)에서 주어가 A cow이므로 복수 동사 were를 was로 고쳐야 한다.

어휘 barn 헛간, 외양간
tenacity 집요, 끈기
slaughter 도살하다, 죽이다

정답 (a) were → was

Actual Test

1 **해석** A: 레이첼, 네 생일 파티에 날 데려가겠다고 약속한
거 잊지 마.
B: 걱정 마. 전화할게.

해설 동사 promise는 목적어로 to부정사를 취하므로 (a)
와 (b)는 답이 될 수 없으며, 〈동사 + 부사〉 형태의 타
동사구가 대명사를 목적어로 취할 경우엔 목적어인 대
명사는 반드시 동사와 부사 사이에 위치해야 하므로
정답은 (c) to take me out이다.

정답 (c)

2 **해석** A: 제리, 난 지금 비행기를 타야겠어. 작별할 시간이야.
B: 잘 가, 캐시. 여행 잘 하고 잊지 말고 부모님께 내
안부 전해 줘.

해설 동사 forget은 to부정사와 동명사 둘 다 목적어로 취
할 수 있으나 뜻이 달라진다. '해야 할 일을 잊어버리
다' 라는 의미로는 to부정사를 써야 한다. 과거에 '했
던 일을 잊어버리다' 라는 뜻으로는 동명사를 쓴다. 이
문제에서는 앞으로 해야 할 일을 잊지 말라고 주지시
키고 있으므로 to부정사를 쓰는 것이 알맞다.

정답 (b)

3 **해석** A: 일 끝나고 영화 보러 가는 게 어때?
B: 그러고 싶지만 오늘 밤 선약이 있어.

해설 대부정사를 물어보는 문제이다. would like와 would
love는 동사 want와 같은 뜻을 가지고 있으며 to부
정사만을 목적어로 취한다. B의 말을 완전한 문장으로
쓴다면 I would love to go to the movies after
work, but ~ 으로, 앞에서 A가 말한 내용 중 반복되
는 going to the movies after work를 한 단어 to
를 써서 대신할 수 있는데, 이를 대부정사라고 하며
이 경우 to는 절대 생략할 수 없다. 따라서 정답은 (d)
이다.

정답 (d)

4 **해석** A: 내가 아파서 집에 있는 동안 찰스가 매일 병문안을
왔어.
B: 정말? 참 친절도 해라.

해설 to부정사의 의미상 주어를 묻는 문제이다. 〈It is 형용
사 ~ to부정사〉 형태의 가주어 구문에서 사람의 성격
이나 성품을 나타내는 형용사가 올 경우, to부정사의

의미상 주어 앞에 for 대신 of를 써야 한다.
thoughtful은 사람의 성품을 나타내는 형용사이고
사려 깊은 행동을 한 사람은 제3자인 Charles이므로
(c) thoughtful of him이 가장 적절하다.

어휘 thoughtful 사려 깊은, 친절한

정답 (c)

5 **해석** A: 여러 가지 옷을 입어 보고 있구나. 오늘 밤 차려입
으려고?
B: 저녁 식사에 뭘 입고 가야 할지 고민이야.

해설 어순을 묻는 문제이다. to부정사의 의미상 목적어가
의문사인 경우에 의문사의 위치를 묻고 있다. 의문사
는 항상 to부정사 앞에 위치하므로 (c) what to
wear가 정답이다. 의문사와 to부정사가 함께 쓰일 경
우에는 항상 〈의문사 + to부정사〉 어순을 취한다.

어휘 try on (시험 삼아) 입어 보다
dress up 쫙 빼입다, 차려입다
have trouble -ing ~하는 데 어려움을 겪다
figure out 생각해 내다

정답 (c)

6 **해석** A: 논문 제출 마감일이 바로 다음 주야. 하지만 별로
한 게 없어.
B: 장담하는데 기간 연장을 요청하는 것 말고 별다른
방법이 없어.

해설 '~할 수 밖에 없다' 라는 의미의 〈have no choice
but + to부정사〉 구문을 묻는 문제이다. but은
except처럼 '~을 제외한' 의 뜻을 가진 전치사로 쓰
였다. 정답은 (c) to ask for an extension이다.

어휘 dissertation 학술[학위] 논문
have no choice but to V ~할 수밖에 달리 도
리가 없다

정답 (c)

7 **해석** A: 〈반지의 제왕〉을 보시겠어요, 아니면 〈나니아 연대
기〉를 보시겠어요?
B: 어떤 걸 선택해야 할지 결정을 못하겠어요.

해설 타동사 decide의 목적어인 명사구를 완성하는 문제
이다. to부정사(to choose)의 의미상 목적어가 의문
사(which)인 경우에 의문사는 항상 to부정사 앞에 위
치해야 하므로 (c) which to choose가 정답이다

어휘 chronicle 연대기

정답 (c)

8 해석 A: 어떻게 킴을 알고 계신 거죠?

B: 작년에 우리 텝스반 수업에 있었던 게 기억나.

해설 remember는 목적어로 동명사와 to부정사 둘 다 취할 수 있지만 의미 차이가 난다. 동명사를 취할 경우 remember보다 이전 시점의 일, 즉 과거에 지나간 일을 기억한다는 의미이며, to부정사를 취할 경우에는 remember보다 이후 시점, 즉 앞으로 해야 할 일을 기억한다는 뜻이 된다. 여기서는 last year가 단서이다. 문맥상 작년에 수업을 함께 들었던 것이 기억난다는 의미가 적절하므로 동명사인 (a) being이 빈칸에 알맞다.

정답 (a)

9 해석 내 여동생 제인은 지난주에 있었던 네 결혼식에 초대되지 않은 것에 대해 아직도 화가 나 있어.

해설 주로 '싫어하다'(resent, mind, abhor, dislike), '피하다'(avoid, help)류의 동사는 목적어로 동명사만을 취한다. 따라서 정답은 (c) having been이다. 참고로 분노하는 것은 현재이고, 초대가 되지 않은 것은 지난주로 과거이다. 이처럼 동명사의 시제가 주절 동사보다 한 시제 앞섰음을 강조하기 위해서 완료 동명사를 쓴다. 하지만 remember, forget, regret 등의 동사 뒤에는 완료 동명사나 단순 동명사나 의미 차이가 없으므로 굳이 완료 동명사를 쓸 필요는 없다.

어휘 resent 분개하다, 괘씸하게 생각하다

정답 (c)

10 해석 실례합니다. 이 카푸치노가 별로 따뜻하지가 않습니다. 데워야 해요.

해설 want, need, require, deserve 등의 동사는 주어가 사물일 때 비록 수동의 의미를 가지고 있을지라도 수동 동명사(being heated)를 쓰지 않고 능동 동명사(heating)를 써야 하는 동사들이다. 반면, to부정사를 취할 경우엔 태를 따져서 수동이면 수동 to부정사(to be heated) 형태로 사용해야 한다.

정답 (c)

11 해석 사소한 것들에 대해 걱정하면 좌절감만 더 느끼게 될 것이다.

해설 obsess는 타동사와 자동사로 모두 쓰이는 동사이다. 타동사일 경우에는 거의 수동형인 be obsessed with/by 형태로 쓰여 '~에 사로잡히다, ~에 강박관념을 가지다'라는 뜻이고, 자동사일 경우에는 뒤에 전치사 about이나 over가 이어지고 '~대해 걱정하다'라는 의미를 가진다. 빈칸은 전체 문장의 주어 자리이므로 동명사나 to부정사가 적절하다. 여기서는 빈칸 뒤에 전치사 over가 있으므로 자동사 obsess의 동명사(Obsessing)나 to부정사(To obsess)가 들어갈 수 있다. 따라서 정답은 (a) Obsessing이다.

어휘 obsess 끙끙거리며 걱정하다

frustrated 좌절한, 실망한

정답 (a)

12 해석 내 친구 제임스는 반 친구들 앞에서 놀림당하는 것을 매우 창피해 했다.

해설 동명사의 태를 묻는 문제이다. 주어인 James는 조롱을 당하는 것이므로 수동 동명사가 빈칸에 들어가야 한다. make fun of처럼 〈동사 + 명사 + 전치사〉형태의 타동사구의 수동태는 〈 be + p.p. + 명사 + 전치사〉의 어순을 그대로 취한다. 따라서 정답은 (b) being made fun of이다.

정답 (b)

13 해석 아주 멋진 공연이었어. 축하해. 지난 학기에 피아노 연습을 정말 열심히 한 모양이구나.

해설 to부정사의 시제를 묻는 문제이다. seem은 보어로 to부정사를 취하므로 (a)와 (b) 중에서 정답을 예상해 볼 수 있다. 본동사 seem은 현재이고 피아노 연습을 한 것은 지난 학기로 seem보다 이전 시점이므로 단순 부정사보다는 완료 부정사 형태의 (a) to have practiced가 빈칸에 가장 알맞다. 참고로 드문 경우지만 seem 뒤에 (d)처럼 as if가 이어지기도 하는데, as if 다음에는 〈주어 + 동사〉 형태의 절이나 to부정사가 이어져야 한다. 따라서 (d)가 답이 되려면 as if practicing이 아니라 as if to have practiced가 되어야 한다.

정답 (a)

14 해석 은행을 턴 남자가 돈을 가지고 막 도망가려던 순간에 경찰에게 체포되었다.

해설 전치사 뒤에는 동명사가 원칙이지만 '막 ~하려는 참이다'라는 뜻의 관용구에서는 전치사 about 뒤에 to부정사가 올 수 있다. 참고로 〈be + anxious/ready/afraid + to부정사〉 구문처럼 〈be about + to부정사〉에서 about을 형용사로 보기도 한다.

어휘 apprehend 체포하다

carry away 가져가 버리다

정답 (b)

15 해석 (a) A: 차를 살까 생각 중이야.

(b) B: 왜? 직장이 아주 가깝잖아.

(c) A: 하지만 언젠가 필요할지도 몰라.

(d) B: 정말 필요하지 않으면 차를 가지고 있을 이유가 없어.

해설 동명사의 관용구문을 물어보는 문제이다. '~할 이유가 없다'는 의미의 관용 표현으로 There is no point (in) -ing를 쓴다. 따라서 (d)의 to have를 (in) having으로 고쳐야 한다.

어휘 contemplate 생각하다, 심사숙고하다
There is no point (in) -ing ~할 이유가 없다

정답 (d) to have → (in) having

16 해석 (a) A: 오늘 어떻게 출근할 거야?

(b) B: 자전거를 타고 갈까 생각 중이었어.

(c) A: 그러기엔 바깥 날씨가 좀 춥지 않니?

(d) B: 음, 날씨가 좀 추운 건 상관없어.

해설 전치사 뒤에는 동사를 동명사 형태로 써야 한다. 따라서 (b)의 take를 taking으로 고쳐야 한다.

정답 (b) take → taking

17 해석 (a) A: 여동생이랑 나, 너와 함께 연극 보러 가지 못할 거 같아.

(b) B: 정말? 무슨 일이라도 생긴 거니?

(c) A: 응, 여동생이 아파서 병원에 데려가려고.

(d) B: 아, 이런! 더 건강해진 그녀 모습을 보길 바라.

해설 hope는 to부정사를 목적어로 취하는 타동사이므로 (d)의 seeing을 to see로 바꿔야 한다.

어휘 It turns out that ~ ~인 것으로 밝혀지다[드러나다]

정답 (d) seeing → to see

18 해석 (a) A: 오늘 오후에 특별한 계획 있어?

(b) B: 영화 보러 나갈까 생각 중이었어.

(c) A: 나 돈에 좀 쪼들리거든. 대신 영화나 한 편 빌려 보면 안 될까?

(d) B: 그것도 재밌겠네.

해설 '꺼리다, 싫어하다'라는 뜻을 가진 mind는 동명사만을 목적어로 취하는 동사이므로 (c)의 rent를 renting으로 고쳐야 한다.

어휘 be low on ~이 부족하다, 조금 남아 있다

정답 (c) rent → renting

19 해석 (a) 그 사고 후에 자니는 긴 재활 과정을 시작했다. (b) 그는 물리치료사와 함께 매일 운동했다. (c) 그 당시엔 비록 걸을 수도 없었지만 그는 에베레스트 산을 등반하겠다고 얘기했다. (d) 결국 자니는 완전히 회복 해서 그의 꿈을 이루었다.

해설 전치사 뒤에는 보통 명사 상당 어구가 이어져야 한다. (c)에서 전치사 about 뒤에 동사 hike를 동명사인 hiking으로 고쳐야 한다.

어휘 rehabilitation 재활
physical therapist 물리치료사

정답 (c) hike → hiking

20 해석 (a) 사람들이 채식주의자가 되기로 결심하는 다양한 이유가 있다. (b) 어떤 사람들은 동물을 죽이는 것이 근원적으로 잘못된 거라 생각한다. (c) 다른 사람들은 공장형 농장에서 동물들이 사는 열악한 조건을 반대한다. (d) 또 어떤 사람들은 그들이 생각하기에 가장 건강하다고 믿는 식단을 따를 뿐이다.

해설 모든 문장에는 주어와 동사가 있어야 한다. 문장 (c)에서 objecting to 부분은 동사 자리이므로 현재분사인 objecting을 동사 object로 고쳐야 한다.

어휘 inherently 근본적으로
object to 반대하다

정답 (c) objecting → object

Actual Test

1 **해석** A: 왜 이렇게 늦었어? 네가 그녀를 데려다만 주고 바로 집으로 올 줄 알았는데.

B: 응, 그러려고 했는데 그녀가 모두 남아서 저녁을 먹고 가야 한다고 고집을 부려서.

해설 insist, suggest, propose, demand, order, desire, wish, request 등의 동사 다음에 나오는 that절 내에는 should가 관용적으로 쓰인다. 하지만 미국식 영어에서는 should를 생략하고 동사원형을 쓰는 경우가 더 많다. 참고로 insist 뒤에 that절 대신 명사가 올 때는 insist on이나 insist upon을 쓴다.

정답 (a)

2 **해석** A: 셸리로부터 최근에 소식 들은 거 있니?

B: 사실 어제 도서관에서 그녀를 봤어.

해설 과거의 특정 시점인 yesterday가 있으므로 단순 과거 시제인 (c) did see가 가장 알맞다.

정답 (c)

3 **해석** A: 말만 해놓고 잔디를 깎지 않았구나.

B: 이런! 깜박 잊어버렸나 봐요.

해설 문맥상 빈칸에는 추측을 나타내는 조동사가 필요하다. 과거의 강한 추측을 나타내는 영어 표현은 (a) must 이다. 참고로 (d) should는 과거에 대한 유감을 나타내는 표현으로 과거에 했어야 했지만 하지 못한 일을 나타낼 때 써야 하므로 문맥에 어울리지 않는다. (b) will은 미래완료 시제이고 (d) do는 문법적으로 불가능하다.

어휘 mow the lawn 잔디를 깎다

정답 (a)

4 **해석** A: 스펜서는 자기가 장기 자랑 대회에서 우승할 거라 확신하더군.

B: 그가 우승한다면 나는 깜짝 놀랄 거야. 다른 참가자들이 개인기가 상당히 뛰어나던데.

해설 조동사 did와 가정법 문제이다. 주절의 동사가 〈would + 동사원형〉으로 if절 역시 가정법 과거 시제가 되어야 하므로 정답은 (a) did이다. 여기서 did는 won the talent show를 대신하는 대동사의 성격을 가지고 있으며, B는 가정법 과거 시제로 대답한 것으로 보아 스펜서가 우승하는 일은 거의 불가능하다고

생각하고 있다고 볼 수 있다.

어휘 be convinced that ~ ~을 확신하다

정답 (a)

5 **해석** A: 어떻게 배웠길래 러시아 말을 그렇게 잘하는 거니?

B: 실은 많은 러시아 사람들과 가게에서 한때 일했던 적이 있는데 그 사람들이 많이 가르쳐 줬어요.

해설 A가 과거 시제로 질문하고 있다는 점이 답을 찾는 결정적인 단서이다. 과거에 어떤 경로로 러시아 어를 배웠느냐고 물어봤으므로 과거 시제로 대답하는 것이 가장 알맞다. 따라서 한때는 함께 일했지만 지금은 아니라는 뜻의 (d) used to work가 빈칸에 가장 알맞다.

정답 (d)

6 **해석** A: 오늘은 별로 요리하고 싶은 기분이 아니야.

B: 걱정 마. 내가 요리할게.

해설 문맥에 맞는 적절한 조동사를 고르는 문제이다. (b) have와 (c) am은 문법적으로 불가능하므로 일단 답에서 제외된다. (d)는 문법적으로는 가능하지만 시제도 틀렸고 바로 앞의 문장 Don't worry about it.과도 내용상 모순이 생긴다. 따라서 빈칸에는 즉석 결심, 즉 주어의 의지를 나타내는 조동사 (a) will이 가장 알맞다.

정답 (a)

7 **해석** A: 그는 전처의 결혼식에 참석할 필요가 없어.

B: 그건 좋지 않은 생각이야!

해설 조동사 need에 대한 문제이다. 조동사 need는 긍정문에 쓰일 수 없으며 부정문과 의문문에서만 사용된다. 부정문의 형태는 〈need not + 동사원형〉의 형태를 취한다. 반면 일반동사 need는 뒤에 to부정사가 이어지며 긍정문에서도 사용될 수 있고 부정형은 〈don't/doesn't need to + 동사원형〉의 형태를 취한다. 또한 일반동사로 쓰인 경우에는 시제나 인칭의 영향을 받기 때문에 주어가 3인칭 단수이고 시제가 현재일 경우 need에 -s 어미를 붙여서 〈needs to + 동사원형〉의 형태가 되어야 한다. 따라서 위의 조건을 충족시키는 선택지는 (c) need not밖에 없다. 선택지 (a)의 need to는 주어 He가 3인칭 단수이므로 needs to가 되어야 한다. 일반동사 need의 부정은 need 앞에 don't/doesn't를 붙여서 만들어야 하므로 (b) needs not to는 doesn't need to가 되어야 한다.

어휘 **make an appearance** (모임에) 잠깐 얼굴을 내밀다
ex-wife 전처

정답 (c)

---

8 해석 A: 토마스가 오늘 또 나를 험담하고 있더라고.

B: 너희들 그만 싸우고 화해하는 게 좋겠어.

해설 해석을 해보지 않으면 선택지 (b) making up을 답으로 고르기 쉬운 문제이다. make up은 〈자동사 + 부사〉 형태의 자동사구로 '화해하다'라는 뜻이다. 빈칸을 타동사 stop의 목적어 자리로 본다면 (b) making up이 가능하겠지만 싸우는 것과 화해하는 것을 그만 둬야 한다는 뜻이 되기 때문에 문장의 의미가 어색해진다. 따라서 빈칸은 조동사 should 다음의 동사원형인 stop과 병치 구조에 있는 동사원형 자리라고 보는 것이 의미적으로 자연스럽다. 따라서 정답은 (d) make up이다. 조동사 다음에는 원형부정사가 이어져야 하므로 (a)와 (c)는 문법적으로 불가능하다.

어휘 **say bad things about** *sb* ~에 대해 험담하다
make up 화해하다

정답 (d)

---

9 해석 A: 직장에 또 지각해서 오늘 기분이 우울해.

B: 아침에 좀 더 일찍 일어나는 게 좋겠어. 그렇지 않으면 해고될 거야.

해설 조동사의 기초 용법을 물어보는 문제이다. had better는 두 단어로 된 조동사이다. 조동사 뒤에는 반드시 동사원형이 와야 하므로 정답은 (d) get up이다. 참고로 조동사 had better의 부정형은 had better not이다.

어휘 **sack** 해고하다

정답 (d)

---

10 해석 A: 마이크가 나에게 항상 너무 차갑게 굴지 않으면 좋을 텐데.

B: 그에 대해 그런 험담을 하지 말았어야지.

해설 〈조동사 + have p.p.〉의 의미를 묻는 문제이다. 문법적으로만 따지면 네 개의 선택지 모두 가능하기 때문에 반드시 정확한 해석을 통해 문맥을 파악해야 한다. A는 마이크가 항상 자신에게 차갑게 구는 것에 대해 아쉬움을 토로하며 그 이유를 궁금해 하고 있고, 여기에 대해 B가 응답하는 상황이다. B는 A가 마이크에 대해 험담을 했기 때문에 마이크가 A에게 차갑게 대한다고 귀띔을 해주는 것으로 볼 수 있다. 따라서 때

늦은 충고로, 그런 험담을 하지 말았어야 했다는 뜻으로 문장의 의미를 완성하는 것이 가장 자연스럽다고 볼 수 있으므로 (c) shouldn't가 정답이다. should have p.p.는 '~했어야 했다'라는 뜻으로 과거 행위에 대한 후회나 유감을 나타낼 때 쓰인다. must have p.p.는 과거에 대한 강한 추측으로 '~했었음에 틀림없다'라는 뜻이고, will have p.p.는 과거가 아니라 미래완료 시제이다.

정답 (c)

---

11 해석 당신 미래에 대해 좀 더 진지하게 생각하고, 모든 시간을 친구들이랑 놀면서 보내는 걸 그만두어야 합니다.

해설 조동사 뒤에는 원형부정사가 와야 한다는 조동사의 기초 지식을 묻는 문제이다. 빈칸 뒤에 to부정사가 왔으므로 조동사로만 쓰이는 (a), (b), (c)는 답이 될 수 없다. need는 일반동사로도 사용이 가능한데 일반동사로 쓰일 경우에는 목적어로 to부정사를 취할 수 있다. 참고로 need는 조동사로 긍정문에서는 사용될 수 없다. *e.g.* You need go there. (×)

정답 (d)

---

12 해석 비록 우리는 경쟁자이지만 그녀의 인내심과 직업 정신에 대해 그녀를 존경하지 않을 수 없다.

해설 조동사의 관용 표현 cannot help -ing를 물어보는 문제이다. 빈칸 뒤가 -ing 형태이므로 뒤에 동사원형이 이어져야 하는 (a) have to와 (c) can only는 답에서 제외된다. 동사 avoid와 help는 둘 다 동명사를 목적어로 취하므로 문법적으로는 (b)와 (d) 둘 모두 가능하지만, 앞에 양보의 접속사 even though가 이끄는 부사절의 내용 때문에 (b) must avoid는 의미적으로 어색하여 답이 될 수 없다. 따라서 정답은 (d) cannot help이다.

어휘 **perseverance** 인내
professionalism 전문가 기질, 프로 근성

정답 (d)

---

13 해석 어린 시절 동안 나는 아빠랑 사냥을 하곤 했었는데 야생에 대해서 많이 알게 되었다.

해설 지금은 존재하지 않는 과거의 습관이나 상태를 나타내는 조동사 used to를 묻는 문제이다. 문두의 During my childhood는 명백한 과거 시간 표시 부사구이므로 문맥상 어린 시절의 습관적인 동작을 나타내는 used to가 가장 자연스럽다. 나머지 선택지들은 일단

시제가 맞지 않아 답이 될 수 없다. 〈be used to +
(동)명사〉와 〈used to + 동사원형〉은 혼동하기 쉬우므
로 잘 정리해 둘 필요가 있다. 전자는 '~에 익숙하다'
이고 후자는 '~하곤 했었다'는 뜻으로 해석된다. 참고
로 〈be used to + 동사원형〉의 형태도 가능한데, 이
경우 used는 일반동사 use(사용하다)의 과거분사로
쓰인 경우로서 '~하는 데 사용되다'로 해석한다.

정답 (b)

14 해석 고위 공직에 있는 사람들이 그들의 모든 사업상 인맥
관계를 대중에게 공개할 필요가 있다.

해설 〈It is + 이성 판단의 형용사(necessary/
important/imperative/essential/vital/natural)
+ that 명사절〉 구문에서 that 명사절이 '~해야 한
다'는 내용의 당위절일 경우, that 명사절 안의 동사
형태는 〈(should) + 동사원형〉이다. 따라서 정답은
(d) should이다. 참고로 미국 영어에서는 이 경우 보
통 should를 생략한다.

정답 (d)

15 해석 우리 대다수는 누군가와 심각하게 싸우게 되면 숨어
있는 감정을 드러낼 수밖에 없다.

해설 조동사의 관용 표현을 묻는 문제이다. '~하지 않을 수
없다'는 뜻의 조동사 관용 표현은 cannot help -ing
또는 〈cannot but + 동사원형〉의 형태로 써야 하므
로 정답은 (d) cannot help showing이다.

정답 (d)

16 해석 (a) A: 있잖아. 이번 주에 시험이 세 개 있고, 학기말
보고서를 2개 제출해야 해.

(b) B: 엄청난 작업량인걸. 감당해 낼 수 있겠니?

(c) A: 모르겠어. 이번엔 너무 욕심을 부렸나 봐.

(d) B: 그러게 너무 많은 수업을 듣느라 무리하지 말
라고 내가 말했잖아.

해설 조동사 뒤에는 동사원형이 와야 하므로 (d)의 to
overload를 overload로 고쳐야 한다. 참고로 bite
off more than one can chew는 직역하면 '한입에
다 씹지도 못할 정도로 많은 양을 베어 물다'라는 말로
의욕만 앞서서 무리하게 일을 벌린다는 뜻이다.

어휘 bite off more than one can chew 과욕을
부리다, 무리하다
overload *sb* with *sth* ~가 …로 무리하다

정답 (d) to overload → overload

17 해석 (a) A: 기름이 부족한 거니?

(b) B: 아니. 하지만 피곤해. 여기서 커피 좀 마시고 싶어.

(c) A: 피곤하면 나한테 잠시 운전을 맡겨.

(d) B: 좋은 생각이야. 고마워.

해설 조동사의 적절한 쓰임을 묻는 문제이다. (c)에서 A는
B에게 피곤하면 운전을 자신에게 맡기라고 제안하고
있는데, 조동사 would에는 제안의 뜻이 없다. 따라서
조동사 would를 제안의 뜻을 가지는 조동사 could
나 should로 수정해야 한다. should는 '~해야 한
다, ~하는 게 좋다'는 뜻으로 충고에 가까운 제안이
며, could는 '~하면 돼'의 뜻으로 가벼운 제안을 할
때 사용된다.

어휘 be low on *sth* ~이 부족하다

정답 (c) would → could *or* should

18 해석 (a) A: 오, 하느님! 생물학에서 F 학점을 받다니. 이럴
수가!

(b) B: 그거 참 안됐구나. 그럼 그 수업을 재수강해야
한다는 얘기니?

(c) A: 불행히도 그래. 엄마가 날 죽이려 드실 거야.

(d) B: 기말시험 공부 좀 하라고 했을 때 내 말을 들었
어야 했어.

해설 must have p.p.는 '~했었음에 틀림없다'라는 뜻이
다. 상대방에게 때늦은 충고를 하는 상황이므로 여기
서는 내 말을 들었어야 했는데 듣지 않아서 이렇게 됐
다는 뜻의 should have listened가 되어야 문맥이
자연스러워진다. 따라서 must를 should로 고쳐야
한다.

어휘 biology 생물학

정답 (d) must → should

19 해석 (a) 저희는 머틀 비치에서 근무하실, 자격을 갖춘 사회
복지사를 구합니다. (b) 청소년들을 상대로 일한 경험
이 반드시 있어야 하고, 관리 경력이 있으면 우대합니
다. (c) 주된 업무는 담당하는 청소년들을 관리하는 것
입니다. 다른 업무로는 국가 기준에 부합하는 보고서
작성이 포함될 것입니다. (d) 지원하시는 분들께서는
그 일자리의 최소 근무 기간이 5년이 될 수도 있다는
걸 알아 두시기 바랍니다.

해설 can은 능력, 허락, 가능성, 추측 등 다양한 의미를 지
니고 있다. can을 be able to로 바꾸어 쓸 수 있는
경우는 능력(ability)의 의미로 쓰인 경우에 한해서이
다. (d)의 근무 기간이 5년이 될 수도 있다는 것은 능

력이 아니라 단순한 가능성을 나타내는 것이므로 is able to는 부적절하다. 따라서 문장 (d)의 is able to 를 can으로 고쳐야 한다.

어휘 qualified 자격 있는, 자격을 갖춘
social worker 사회복지사
caseload 담당 건수

정답 (d) is able to → can

20 해석 (a) 많은 청중 앞에서 구두로 발표할 때 긴장되는 것은 아주 자연스러운 것입니다. (b) 따라서 긴장 때문에 사람들 앞에서 말하는 것을 피할 필요는 없습니다. (c) 경험이 많아질수록 여러분은 긴장되는 것에 대해 덜 불안해 하는 자신을 발견하게 될 것입니다. (d) 그러면 사람들 앞에서 발표해 달라는 요청을 받게 되었을 때 여러분은 자연스럽고 유창하게 발표할 수 있을 것입니다.

해설 조동사 need의 쓰임을 묻는 문제이다. '~할 필요가 없다' 는 뜻을 표현하는 방법은 두 가지가 있다. 조동사 need를 써서 〈need not + 동사원형〉의 형태로 쓰든지, 아니면 일반동사 need를 써서 〈don't /doesn't need + to부정사〉 형태로 쓴다. 따라서 (b) need to not avoid는 need not avoid로 수정하거나 don't need to avoid로 바꿔야 한다.

어휘 apprehensive 불안한, 염려하는

정답 (b) need to not → need not or don't need to

Actual Test

1 해석 A: 아빠, 어제 낚시 가셨어요?
B: 물론이지. 물고기를 일곱 마리 잡았어.

해설 명사의 복수형을 묻는 문제이다. '물고기'를 의미하는 fish는 가산명사로 단수와 복수형이 동일한 명사이다. 따라서 정답은 (b)이다. 참고로 fish가 음식인 '생선' 이라는 뜻일 경우에는 불가산명사가 된다. '나는 생선을 많이 먹지 않는다.' 는 표현은 I don't eat many fish.가 아니라 I don't eat much fish.

정답 (b)

2 해석 A: 제임스, 아드님의 소송건은 어떻게 되어 가고 있나요?
B: 음, 주장을 뒷받침해 줄 증거가 많지 않아서 승산이 별로 없습니다.

해설 evidence는 절대 불가산명사로, 복수형으로 쓸 수 없으며 many의 수식도 받을 수 없으므로 (c)와 (d)는 문법적으로 답에서 제외된다. 문맥상 이길 가능성이 없다고 했으므로 '증거가 많지 않기 때문' 이라고 문장을 완성하는 것이 훨씬 자연스럽다. (b) there is not much evidence가 정답이다.

어휘 lawsuit 소송
back up 지지하다, 뒷받침하다

정답 (b)

3 해석 A: 어젯밤 시립 도서관에서 왜 그렇게 오래 있었니?
B: 논문에 필요한 자료를 구해야 했거든.

해설 명사 지식을 묻는 문제이다. some 뒤에는 불가산명사, 가산명사 모두 올 수 있다. (a), (c), (d)는 불가산명사인데 복수형 어미 -s가 붙어 있으므로 답이 될 수 없다. 따라서 복수형을 쓸 수 있는 가산명사 (b) facts 가 정답이다.

어휘 how come 왜(= why)
dissertation 학술[학위] 논문

정답 (b)

4 해석 A: 얼마 전 밤에 열린 브리트니의 콘서트는 성공적이지 못했던 거 같아.
B: 음, 나는 그렇게 생각하지 않는데. 관객이 많았었잖아.

해설 명사 audience는 한 그룹의 사람들을 가리키는 family형의 집합명사로 단수형(audience)과 복수형

(audiences)이 가능한 집합명사이다. 집합의 구성원
이 많다는 의미로는 many를 쓰지 않고 large나 big
을 써야 한다. 예를 들어, '나는 가족이 많다.'는 우리
말을 영어로 표현할 때 I have many families.로
쓰면 안 되고 I have a large family.로 표현해야 하
는 것과 마찬가지로, '청중이 많았다'는 얘기는 청중
이라는 집합을 구성하는 '구성원들이 많았다'는 뜻이
므로 (a) There was a large audience.가 되어야
한다. 참고로 There were many audiences.는 문
법적으로는 가능하지만 '청중 집합들이 여러 개 있었
다.'는 뜻이 되어 문맥에 어울리지 않는다. I have
many families.가 '식구가 많다.'는 뜻이 아니라 '가
족이라는 집합을 여러 개 거느리고 있다.' 즉 '여러 집
살림을 하다.'라는 이상한 뜻이 되는 것과 마찬가지로
이해하면 된다.

정답 (a)

5 **해석** A: 우리 할머니네 집 어땠어?

　　　B: 멋지던걸. 그렇게 많은 옛날 가구들은 처음 봤어.

해설 명사 지식을 묻는 문제이다. furniture는 집합적 물질
명사로, 절대 불가산명사이므로 복수형을 쓸 수 없고
항상 단수 취급하여 단수 동사를 써야 한다. 또한 불
가산명사이므로 수량형용사는 many가 아니라
much의 수식을 받아야 한다. 따라서 정답은 (d)
much antique furniture이다.

정답 (d)

6 **해석** A: 배관공이 되려면 뭐가 필요하죠?

　　　B: 우선, 많은 장비를 갖추고 있어야 하며 적절한 훈련
　　　을 받아야 합니다.

해설 equipment는 집합적 물질명사이다. 집합적 물질명
사는 절대 불가산명사로 복수형으로 쓸 수 없고 단수
취급하여 항상 단수 동사를 써야 한다. 따라서 정답은
(b) a lot of equipment이다. 나머지 선택지들은
equipment의 형태부터 틀렸다.

어휘 plumber 배관공

정답 (b)

7 **해석** A: 요즘 왜 그렇게 바빠 보이는 거야?

　　　B: 가난한 사람들의 법적 변호를 돕고 있어.

해설 빈칸은 helping의 목적어 자리이므로 명사가 와야 한
다. 형용사가 the와 함께 쓰이면 '~한 사람들'이란
뜻의 복수 명사가 된다. 따라서 정답은 복수 보통명사

취급하는 〈the + 형용사〉 형태의 (a) the poor이다.
참고로 poor는 형용사이므로 복수형 어미 -s를 붙일
수 없고 앞에 부정관사를 붙일 수도 없으므로 선택지
(b), (c), (d)는 poor의 품사만 정확히 알아도 답에서
제외할 수 있다.

어휘 defense 변호, 변호인단

정답 (a)

8 **해석** A: 왜 우리랑 함께 놀이 공원에 안 가는 거야?

　　　B: 놀이 기구 타기 위해 오랫동안 줄서서 기다리는 게
　　　싫어서.

해설 추상명사의 보통명사화를 물어보는 문제이다. 명사
time은 일반적인 의미의 추상적 개념인 '시간'의 뜻
으로 쓰일 경우엔 불가산명사이다. 하지만 time에 형
용사가 붙으면 보통명사화되는데, 여기서는 long이라
는 형용사가 time을 수식하고 있기 때문에 부정관사
a를 붙여 주는 것이 맞다. 따라서 정답은 (d) a long
time이다.

어휘 ride 타는 놀이 기구

정답 (d)

9 **해석** A: 오늘 아침 식사를 위해 특별한 것을 준비했어.

　　　B: 빨리 먹고 싶다.

해설 명사 지식을 묻는 문제이다. 일반적이고 넓은 의미의
식사명인 breakfast, lunch, dinner, supper는 보
통은 a나 the를 붙이지 않고 무관사 용법으로 쓴다.
따라서 정답은 (d)의 for breakfast이다. 하지만 식
사명이 형용사의 수식을 받는 경우엔 보통명사화되어
부정관사 a/an을 붙일 수 있다.
e.g. I had a delicious breakfast.

정답 (d)

10 **해석** A: 내가 직장에서 집으로 가져온 서류를 찾고 있어.

　　　B: 나도 열심히 찾아볼게.

해설 빈칸 뒤의 명사가 복수형 documents이므로 단수
명사 앞에 오는 (a), (b), (d) 모두 빈칸에 들어갈 수 없
다. 의미상으로도 that절의 한정을 받는 특정한
documents를 찾고 있는 것이므로 정답은 (c) the
이다.

어휘 keep an eye out 유심히 살피다, 찾아보다

정답 (c)

11 **해석** A: 실례합니다. 가구 완비된 원룸 나온 거 있나요?

B: 물론입니다, 손님. 실은 당장 들어갈 수 있는 것이
　　하나 있지요.
해설 A가 찾고 있는 원룸은 특정한 원룸이 아니라 가구가
　　딸려 있는 원룸 중에 아무거나 하나이므로 특정한 것
　　을 가리킬 때 명사 앞에 붙는 (d) the는 정답에서 제
　　외된다. 모음 발음으로 시작하는 명사 앞에 쓰는 (b)
　　an도 빈칸 뒤의 단어가 fully-furnished이므로 답이
　　아니다. (c) one을 정답으로 생각할 수도 있으나 one
　　은 '하나'라는 것을 굳이 강조할 때 사용하는 것이 일
　　반적이다. 따라서 빈칸에 들어갈 가장 자연스러운 관
　　사는 (a) a이다.
어휘 fully-furnished 가구[시설]가 다 갖추어진
　　studio 원룸
정답 (a)

12 해석 A: 로날드가 우리 아이들을 하루 저녁 봐줄 수 있을
　　　까?
　　B: 물론이지! 정말 다정다감한 사람이거든. 너희 아이
　　　들도 분명히 그를 좋아할 거야.
해설 관사의 위치를 묻는 문제이다. 주로 such, what,
　　quite, rather 뒤에는 〈a/an + 형용사 + 명사〉의 어
　　순이 뒤따르고 so, too, as 뒤에는 〈형용사 + a/an
　　+ 명사〉의 어순이 뒤따른다. 따라서 정답은 (d) such
　　a sweet individual이다.
어휘 babysit (남의) 아이를 봐주다
　　individual 〈형용사와 함께〉 사람, 인간
정답 (d)

13 해석 A: 손님, 이 여행자 수표들을 어떻게 해드릴까요?
　　B: 50달러짜리 지폐로 바꿔 주세요.
해설 〈숫자 + 단위명사〉가 다른 명사 앞에서 그 명사를 수
　　식하는 형용사 역할을 할 경우에 그 단위명사는 항상
　　단수 형태로 써야 하고 bill은 가산명사이므로 정답은
　　(a) fifty-dollar bills이다.
정답 (a)

14 해석 A: 네 남자 친구 무슨 일 해?
　　B: 권투 선수 겸 음악가야.
해설 주어가 He로 단수이므로 보어 자리인 빈칸 역시 단수
　　가 되어야 한다. '권투 선수 겸 음악가'와 같이 동일인
　　을 표현할 때는 관사를 첫 번째 명사 앞에 한 번만 써
　　야 하므로 정답은 (a) a boxer and musician이다.
　　(d)는 정관사 the가 틀렸다. 직업을 묻고 답할 경우에

는 정관사를 쓰지 않고 부정관사를 쓰기 때문이다.
정답 (a)

15 해석 A: 프랭크가 우리 집들이에 오고 싶어 해요. 하지만
　　　이미 20명을 초대한데다 집이 너무 좁아요.
　　B: 걱정 말아요, 여보. 한 명 자리를 더 만들 수 있을
　　　거예요.
해설 명사 지식을 묻는 문제이다. 명사 room은 가산명사
　　로도 쓰이고 불가산명사로도 쓰일 수 있는데, '방'이
　　라는 뜻으로 쓰일 경우에는 가산명사 취급하고 사람,
　　물건 따위가 차지하는 '공간, 장소, 자리'의 뜻이나 '여
　　지, 여유, 가능성'의 뜻으로 쓰일 경우에는 불가산명사
　　이다. 여기서는 '방'의 의미가 아니라 추가된 한 사람
　　을 위한 '공간, 자리'를 뜻하므로 (b) room이 가장
　　알맞다.
어휘 housewarming party 집들이
정답 (b)

16 해석 오늘 직장 동료에게 돈을 좀 빌려 줬어.
해설 money는 물질적 집합명사로 절대 불가산명사이다.
　　따라서 셀 수 있는 명사만 수식할 수 있는 부정형용사
　　many와 several은 빈칸에 들어갈 수 없으며, 부정
　　관사 a 역시 불가산명사 앞에 쓸 수 없기 때문에 정답
　　은 (c) some이다. 참고로 some 뒤에는 가산명사와
　　불가산명사 모두 쓸 수 있다.
정답 (c)

17 해석 보통예금 계좌와 당좌예금 계좌를 개설하기 전에 은행
　　약관을 살펴보셔야 합니다.
해설 〈명사 + 명사〉 형태에서 첫 번째 명사가 형용사 역할
　　을 하는 경우 첫 번째 명사는 단수형을 써야 하는 것
　　이 원칙이지만, savings처럼 단수형(절약)일 때와 복
　　수형(저축)일 때 의미가 달라지는 경우에는 예외적으
　　로 복수 형태로 써야 한다. (e.g. customs
　　declaration) 그리고 account는 가산명사이고 하나
　　의 계좌가 아니라 보통예금 계좌 하나와 당좌예금 계
　　좌 하나를 각각 가리키므로 부정관사를 두 군데 다 써
　　야 한다. 따라서 정답은 (a) a savings account
　　and a checking account이다.
어휘 bank policy 은행 약관
　　savings account 보통예금 계좌
　　checking account 당좌예금 계좌
정답 (a)

18 해석 그의 식당은 음식이 너무나 맛있어서 나는 모든 친구들에게 그곳을 추천합니다.

해설 명사 지식과 such와 so의 구분을 동시에 물어보는 문제이다. such 뒤에는 〈부정관사 + 형용사 + 명사〉의 어순이 이어지며, so 뒤에는 〈형용사 + 부정관사 + 명사〉의 어순이 뒤따른다. 한 가지 주의할 점은 명사가 불가산명사이거나 복수 명사일 경우에는 so를 쓰지 않고 무조건 such를 써야 한다. 이 문제에서 food는 물질적 집합명사인 불가산명사로 쓰였으므로 so가 아니라 such를 써야 하고 부정관사 a 역시 쓸 수 없으므로 정답은 (c) such delicious food이다.

참고 • so great a book (O)
→ 가산명사 단수형이므로 올바르다.
• so great books (X)
→ 명사가 복수형일 경우에는 such great books로 표현해야 한다.
• so nice a weather (X)
→ weather는 불가산명사이므로 부정관사 a를 지우고 so를 such로 바꿔야 한다.
• so nice weather (X)
→ weather는 불가산명사이다. 명사가 불가산명사일 경우에는 반드시 such를 써서 such nice weather로 표현해 줘야 한다.

정답 (c)

19 해석 (a) A: 나한테 이달치 집세 냈지, 그렇지?
(b) B: 내 몫은 냈어. 우리 돈이 부족한 거니?
(c) A: 집세의 4분의 3 정도밖에 거둬지지 않았어.
(d) B: 좋아. 나머지 집세 충당에 대해 다른 세입자들에게 얘기해 볼게.

해설 〈분수/백분율 + of + 명사〉의 수는 of 뒤에 오는 명사의 종류에 따라 수가 결정된다. 단수 명사나 불가산명사가 올 경우에는 단수 취급하여 단수 동사를 써야 하고, 복수 명사가 올 경우에는 복수 취급하여 복수 동사를 쓴다. 따라서 (c)의 the rent는 불가산명사이므로 are를 is로 고쳐야 한다.

어휘 be accounted for 확보되다
housemate 한집에 사는 사람, 동거인

정답 (c) are → is

20 해석 (a) 분광기는 19세기 후반에 인기 있는 오락의 한 형태였다. (b) 다른 각도에서 찍혀진 두 장의 사진을 배열하여 분광기는 3차원의 환영을 만들어냈다. (c) 빅토리아 여왕은 영국에서 입체 영상 관람이라는 취미를 대중화시키는 데 공헌했다. (d) 가장 흔하게 만들어진 슬라이드는 멀리 떨어진 이국적인 풍경들을 보여 주는 관광 영화로 만든 것들이었다.

해설 주어와 동사의 수 일치를 물어보는 문제이다. (a)에서 the spectroscope는 '분광기'라는 뜻으로 분광기 전체를 대표하는 명사의 성격으로 쓰였는데 단수 취급하므로 were를 was로 고쳐야 한다.

어휘 spectroscope 분광기
three dimensions 3차원
stereo 입체적인
travelogue 관광 영화, (슬라이드를 이용하는) 여행담
for-off 멀리 떨어진
exotic 이국적인

정답 (a) were → was

Actual Test

1 **해석** A: 기자시죠, 맞죠? 보통 어떤 분을 인터뷰하시나요?

B: 글쎄요, 유명한 사람은 아무나요. 예를 들면 정치가, 스포츠 스타, 배우 등이요.

해설 -thing, -body 등의 어미로 끝나는 부정대명사를 수식하는 형용사는 부정대명사 뒤에 위치하므로 정답은 (b) Anybody famous이다.

어휘 statesman 정치가

to name but a few 몇 가지만 예를 들면

정답 (b)

2 **해석** A: 미술 전시회 어땠어?

B: 충분히 흥미로웠지만 특별한 건 하나도 없었어.

해설 형용사와 부사의 어순을 묻는 문제이다. 형용사나 부사를 수식하는 enough는 뒤에서 수식하며, -thing이나 -body 등의 어미로 끝나는 부정대명사를 수식하는 형용사는 그 부정대명사 뒤에서 수식하므로 (c) interesting enough but nothing special이 정답이다.

정답 (c)

3 **해석** A: 자녀들이 저 기계를 만지지 못하도록 하세요. 안전해 보이지 않아서요.

B: 걱정해 주셔서 고마워요. 막 치우려던 참이었어요.

해설 형용사 자리와 부사 자리를 구분하는 문제이다. 감각 동사(look, smell, sound, taste, feel)와 유지 동사(remain, stay, keep), 상태 변화 동사(get, go, grow, turn, become) 등의 연결 동사가 2형식을 취할 경우, 주격 보어 자리에는 부사가 올 수 없고 반드시 형용사를 써야 하므로 (b) safe가 정답이다.

어휘 concern 걱정, 관심

put away 치우다

정답 (b)

4 **해석** A: 다시 젊어지고 힘이 넘치게 된다면 멋지지 않을까요?

B: 물론이죠. 하지만 그 나이 때는 신경 쓰지 않았죠. 젊은 사람들은 자신이 가진 것의 가치를 알아보지 못하죠.

해설 빈칸은 문장의 주어 자리이므로 명사 상당 어구가 들어가야 한다. (a)의 Young은 형용사이므로 문법적으로 불가능하고, (b)의 Youth는 명사이긴 하지만 가산명사이므로 복수형 어미 -s를 붙여야 한다. (d)는 형용

사 앞에는 부정관사 a를 붙이지 않으므로 역시 답이 될 수 없다. 〈the + 형용사〉는 복수 보통명사 취급하고 복수 동사를 쓰므로 (c) The young do가 정답이다.

어휘 appreciate ~의 진가를 알다

정답 (c)

5 **해석** A: 프레드릭 교수님 어디 계시니?

B: 음, 실은 오늘 아침에 시내에 가실 거라고 말씀하셨어.

해설 downtown은 '시내'라는 명사로도 쓰이고 '시내에'라는 부사로도 쓰인다. 부사로 쓰이는 경우에는 전치사나 관사 없이 go downtown과 같이 써야 한다. 이처럼 명사뿐만 아니라 부사적 기능도 있어서 앞에 전치사를 쓰지 않도록 주의해야 하는 부사로는 aborad, home, overseas, upstairs, downstairs 등이 있다.

정답 (a)

6 **해석** 일부 회원들은 벽을 허물어야 한다는 데 찬성했고 또 다른 회원들은 그대로 두어야 한다는 것에 찬성했기 때문에 위원회는 그 문제에 대해 의견 일치를 보지 못했다.

해설 some은 복수 명사나 불가산명사와 함께 쓰여 '약간의'라는 뜻으로 쓰인다. any는 부정문, 의문문, 조건문에서 쓰이는 반면, some은 긍정문과 긍정의 대답이 기대되는 의문문에서 쓰인다. 또한 단수 명사와 함께 쓰여 알 수 없는 어떤 것을 가리킬 때 사용할 수 있고 others와 함께 쓰여 '어떤 ~, 또 어떤 …'의 구조로도 사용된다. 여기서는 '일부 회원들은 ~했고 또 다른 회원들은 …했다'라는 some ~ others … 로 쓰였다.

어휘 consensus 의견 일치, 합의

tear down 허물다

정답 (c)

7 **해석** 네 엄마는 그게 좋은 생각이 아니라고 생각하시고 나도 마찬가지야.

해설 '~역시'라는 의미로 긍정문에서는 too, also, as well 등을 쓰며, 부정문에서는 either를 쓴다. 제시된 문제의 예문은 부정문이므로 (b) either가 정답이다. neither는 not과 either가 결합한 형태이기 때문에 don't와 함께 쓸 수 없다.

정답 (b)

8 해석 그녀의 할아버지는 수년 전에 돌아가셨다.

해설 문장의 동사가 과거완료(had passed)라는 것이 답을 찾는 단서이다. '~전에'의 뜻으로는 ago와 before를 쓸 수 있지만, ago는 과거 동사와 같이 쓰이며 기준 시점이 지금이므로 many years ago는 '지금부터 수년 전'이라는 뜻이고, before는 주로 과거완료형과 함께 쓰는데, many years before는 '과거의 특정 시점을 기준으로 수년 전'이라는 뜻이 숨어 있다. 따라서 정답은 (a) many years before이다.

어휘 pass away 죽다

정답 (a)

9 해석 화재가 순식간에 건물 전체로 퍼짐에 따라 극장 관객들을 대피시킬 계획을 세울 시간이 거의 없었다.

해설 양이나 정도를 나타내는 much는 셀 수 없는 불가산 명사와 함께 쓸 수 있지만 양이 약간 있을 때는 a little, 양이 거의 없을 때는 little을 사용한다. 셀 수 있는 명사의 경우 조금 있을 때는 a few, 거의 없을 때는 few를 사용한다. 정리하면 수량형용사 many, a few, few는 셀 수 있는 명사와, much, a little, little은 셀 수 없는 명사와 쓰인다. 여기서는 time이 셀 수 없는 명사이고 시간이 거의 없었다는 의미가 되어야 하므로 (a) little이 가장 적절하다.

어휘 form (계획을) 세우다
evacuate 대피시키다
theatergoer 극장 관객

정답 (a)

10 해석 세금이 너무 올라서 사람들이 화가 났다.

해설 우리말 간섭으로, 잘못 쓰기 쉬운 형용사 구분 문제이다. 우리말은 가격, 세금 등이 '비싸다'고 하지만, 영어에서 가격이나 세금은 '높다, 낮다'로 표현한다. 물건이 비싸다거나 싸다고 할 때는 expensive, cheap을 쓰지만 월급(wage, salary, pay), 가격(price), 세금(tax), 관세(tariff) 등의 돈과 관련된 명사는 '비싸다, 싸다'는 의미로 expensive, cheap, dear 등의 형용사를 쓰지 않고 high나 low 같은 형용사를 사용해야 한다. 따라서 빈칸은 상태의 변화를 나타내는 동사 get의 주격 보어 자리이므로 형용사를 써야 하며, 주어가 taxes이므로 expensive가 아니라 (d) high가 정답이다.

정답 (d)

11 해석 백 세 남성 존슨은 그리운 마음으로 유년 시절의 추억을 회상했다.

해설 〈수사-단위명사〉는 하나의 합성형용사로서 뒤의 명사를 수식할 경우 단위명사(year, week, minute, story, day, dollar, etc.)를 복수 형태로 쓰지 않는다. 예를 들어 '5살짜리 소년'을 영어로 표현한다면 a boy who is 4 years old나 합성형용사를 써서 a 4-year-old boy로 표현할 수 있다. 이처럼 〈숫자-단위명사〉가 다른 명사 앞에서 그 명사를 수식하는 형용사 역할을 할 경우에 그 단위명사는 항상 단수 형태로 써야 하므로 정답은 (d) hundred-year-old man이다.

어휘 fondly 다정하게, 사랑스럽게, 그리운 마음으로

정답 (d)

12 해석 이제 하원은 공화당이 다수 의석을 점하고 있기 때문에 공화당 의원들이 예전에 통과시킬 수 없었던 법안들이 새로 채택될 것이다.

해설 형용사와 부사의 구분 문제이다. 주격 보어인 형용사 unable이 이미 있으므로 빈칸은 문장 구조상 부사 자리이다. 따라서 (a)와 (c)는 답이 될 수 없다. 문맥상 과거에 통과시킬 수 없었던 법안이라는 의미이므로 '이전에'의 뜻을 가진 부사 (b) previously가 알맞다.

어휘 the House of Representatives 미국 하원
dominate 지배하다, 우위를 차지하다
the Republicans 공화당
legislation 법안, 입법
preliminary 예비의
presently 현재

정답 (b)

13 해석 새로 지어진 우리 학교 건물은 화려한 소용돌이 모양들로 멋지게 장식되었는데, 수년 전에 헐린 예전 학교 건물과 매우 똑같았다.

해설 빈칸 뒤에 명사구가 왔으므로 빈칸에는 전치사 like가 들어가야 하기 때문에 (c)와 (d)는 답이 될 수 없다. 그리고 〈like + 명사(구)〉처럼 비슷함을 의미하는 어구를 수식하는 부사는 much이므로 (b) much like가 정답이다.

어휘 flamboyant 화려한, 불꽃 모양의
scrollwork 소용돌이 장식, 당초 무늬
tear down (건물을) 헐다

정답 (b)

14 **해석** 국경 없는 의사회에는 현재 아프리카에서 자원봉사하고 있는 400명의 의료진이 있다.

해설 정확한 수(two, five)와 함께 hundred, thousand 등이 다른 명사 앞에서 그 명사를 수식하는 형용사 역할을 할 경우 hundred, thousand에는 절대 복수형 어미 -s를 붙이지 않는다. 따라서 (c)와 (d)는 답에서 제외된다. '직원들'이라는 의미의 집합명사 staff는 집단에 속한 개인이 아니라 집단 전체를 나타내는 명사이기 때문에 복수의 개념이 들어 있다. 즉, 단수 형태로 복수를 나타내므로 정답은 (a) four hundred medical staff이다. 참고로 집합명사인 staff는 두 명 이상의 사람을 한꺼번에 가리키므로 새로운 직원 한 사람을 a new staff라고 말할 수는 없다. staff를 구성하는 개인을 가리킬 때는 member를 붙여서 staff member라고 말하고 이때는 부정관사 a/an을 함께 쓸 수 있다. staff처럼 집합 내의 개인을 가리킬 때 member를 붙이는 집합명사로는 family, class, faculty, audience, team 등이 있다. 이들 집합 속의 개인을 나타낼 때는 family member, faculty member, team member, audience member, class member 등으로 표현한다.

어휘 Doctors Without Borders 국경 없는 의사회
medical staff 의료진

정답 (a)

15 **해석** 부모들은 그들의 자녀에게 모험을 하고 실험해 보라고 좀처럼 부추기지 않는다.

해설 부정부사가 문두에 위치할 경우에 일어나는 도치를 물어보는 문제이다. seldom은 '좀처럼 ~않게'라는 부정부사인데, 부정부사가 문장 처음에 위치하면 주어와 동사가 도치되어 항상 의문문의 어순 〈조동사 + 주어 + 동사원형〉, 〈be동사 + 주어〉를 취해야 한다. 따라서 정답은 (b) Seldom do parents이다.

어휘 seldom 좀처럼 ~않다
take a risk 위험을 무릅쓰다, 모험을 하다
experiment 실험하다

정답 (b)

16 **해석** 너 상당히 인상적인 우표 수집품들을 소장하고 있더구나.

해설 형용사와 부사의 어순을 묻는 문제이다. 대부분 〈관사 + 부사 + 형용사 + 명사〉(*e.g.* a very beautiful girl)의 어순을 취하는 것이 일반적이지만 부사 such, quite, rather 뒤에는 〈부정관사 + 형용사 + 명사〉의 어순을 취하므로 (b)가 정답이다.

정답 (b)

17 **해석** A: 역사 선생님이 누구셨니?
B: 소머즈 선생님. 그 수업 정말 싫었는데.
A: 정말? 왜 그랬는데?
B: 선생님이 무자비하셨어. 특별한 이유도 없이 자기 기분에 따라 우리를 혼내시곤 했지.

해설 기본적인 품사 구분 문제이다. 동사를 수식하는 품사는 부사이다. 문맥상 (d)의 indiscriminate는 동사 punish를 수식해야 하므로 부사 형태인 indiscriminately로 바꿔야 옳다.

어휘 indiscriminately 무자비하게, 마구잡이로

정답 (d) indiscriminate → indiscriminately

18 **해석** (a) A: 떠날 시간이군요. 프레이저 양, 편지 타이핑은 끝났나요?
(b) B: 아직요. 오늘 오후까지는 끝낼 수 있을 겁니다.
(c) A: 음, 내일 비행기 예약은 했나요?
(d) B: 물론입니다. 이미 비행 편 예약을 했습니다.

해설 부사의 올바른 쓰임을 묻는 문제이다. '이미, 벌써'의 뜻으로 부정문과 의문문에서는 부사 yet을 쓰고, 긍정문에서는 already를 쓴다. 따라서 (d)의 I've made your flight reservation yet.은 긍정문이므로 yet을 already로 고쳐야 한다.

어휘 flight reservation 비행편 예약

정답 (d) yet → already

19 **해석** (a) 지진은 최근까지만 해도 신들의 불가사의한 행위였다. (b) 판구조론의 발견으로 지진의 원인을 알게 되었다. (c) 이제는 지진 공학 덕분에 다가올 지진을 감지할 수 있다. (d) 이것이 생명을 구하는 데 도움이 되었지만 절대적으로 안전한 것은 아니다.

해설 기초적인 품사의 형태를 구분하는 문제이다. 명사를 수식하는 품사는 형용사이다. 따라서 (a)의 부사 mysteriously를 형용사 mysterious로 고쳐야 올바른 문장이다.

어휘 plate tectonics 판구조론
seismic 지진의
oncoming 다가오는, 접근하는
tremor 진동, 미진
foolproof 안전한

정답 (a) mysteriously → mysterious

20 해석 (a) 미구엘 로페즈는 생애의 대부분을 남동생에 대해 알지 못한 채 지냈다. (b) 그는 자신이 외동이라고 생각하며 자랐다. (c) 그의 아버지가 돌아가시고 나서야 어떤 낯선 사람이 그에게 연락해 왔다. (d) 그 낯선 사람은 그의 남동생으로 밝혀졌고, 그들은 그 이후로 가깝게 지내 왔다.

해설 closely는 '가깝게, 자세히'라는 뜻의 부사이다. remain은 주로 2형식을 취하는 동사이므로 뒤에 형용사 보어가 와야 한다. 따라서 (d)의 closely는 close여야 한다.

정답 (d) closely → close

Actual Test

1 해석 A: 너희 집에 불이 났을 때 화나지 않았니?

　　 B: 실수였기 때문에 탓할 만한 사람이 없었어.

해설 주절의 주어와 부사절의 주어가 다른 독립분사구문 문제이다. 분사구문을 만들 때 부사절의 주어가 주절의 주어와 다른 경우, 부사절의 주어를 그대로 두고 분사구문으로 고친 경우를 독립분사구문이라고 한다. Since it was a mistake, there was nobody to blame.에서 접속사를 생략하고 부사절의 주어가 주절의 주어와 다르므로 그대로 둔 채 부사절의 시제와 주절의 시제가 같으므로 단순 분사구문 형태로 바꾸면 It being a mistake, there was no body to blame.이 된다. (c)의 완료 분사구문은 부사절의 시제가 주절의 동사 시제보다 앞선 경우에 써야 하는데, 위 문맥은 부사절이 주절보다 하나 앞선 시제라고 볼 수 없으므로 답이 될 수 없다.

어휘 catch on fire 불이 붙다

정답 (a)

2 해석 A: 발표를 제때 할 수 있도록 사무실을 정리해 주실 수 있나요?

　　 B: 힘들겠지만 할 수 있다고 생각합니다.

해설 준사역동사 get의 동사 활용을 묻고 있다. get은 5형식 문장에서 목적어와 목적격 보어의 관계가 능동이면 to부정사를, 수동 관계일 때는 과거분사를 목적격 보어로 취한다. 이 문제 같은 경우 목적어 the office와 목적격 보어 organize의 관계가 수동이므로 (c) organized가 정답이다.

어휘 organize 조직화하다, 준비하다, 정리하다
　　 confident 확신하는, 굳게 믿는

정답 (c)

3 해석 A: 학생들이 머리 기르는 게 허용되나요?

　　 B: 전통적으로 학교에서는 머리 기르는 것을 별로 안 좋아하죠.

해설 frown은 '눈살을 찌푸리다'라는 뜻으로 frown upon sth은 '~에 대해 싫은 내색을 하다, 언짢은 표정을 하다'라는 뜻이다. 빈칸 앞의 주어 long hair는 동사 frown upon의 주체가 아니라 대상이므로 수동 형태가 되어야 한다.

어휘 frown upon 눈살을 찌푸리다, 난색을 표하다

정답 (d)

4 **해석** A: 그다음에 무슨 일이 있었는지 말해 봐.

B: 좋아. 코치가 경기장으로 걸어 들어가서는 심판하고 말다툼을 했어.

해설 분사구문의 형태와 시제를 묻는 문제이다. 시간적으로 감독이 경기장에 들어간 것이 심판에게 항의를 한 것보다 먼저 발생한 동작이지만, 일정 시간의 간격 차이가 거의 없이 연속적으로 일어나는 동작에는 완료 분사구문을 쓰지 않고 단순 분사구문을 쓸 수 있다. 감독이 경기장에 들어간 것과 심판과 말다툼을 한 것은 연속 동작이므로 정답은 (a) Walking onto이다.

어휘 argue 말다툼하다

referee (운동 경기의) 심판

정답 (a)

5 **해석** A: 사라는 지금 뭐 해?

B: 방 청소를 하고 나서 친구들과 놀러 나갔어.

해설 분사구문의 태와 시제를 묻는 문제로 아주 쉽게 풀 수 있는 문제이다. '청소하다'의 의미상 주어는 사람인 '그녀'가 되어야 한다. 따라서 (c)와 (d)는 답에서 제외된다. 방은 청소하는 행위의 주체가 될 수 없기 때문이다. 그녀가 clean의 주체이므로 현재분사로 시작하는 능동 분사구문이어야 하며, 그녀가 외출한 것보다 청소가 앞선 행위이므로 완료 분사구문의 형태여야 한다. 따라서 정답은 (a) Having cleaned her room이다.

정답 (a)

6 **해석** A: 그 자선 단체와 일하는 데 있어서 가장 의미 있는 일은 뭔가요?

B: 동료들과 함께 일하며 학대당한 동물들을 돕는 일이겠죠.

해설 병치와 분사의 태를 물어보는 문제이다. 일단 문맥상 빈칸은 접속사 and를 기준으로 would be에 연결되어 collaborating with my co-workers와 병치를 이루고 있으므로 빈칸 역시 동명사 형태가 되어야 한다. 그리고 동물을 학대하는 것을 돕는 것이 아니라 학대당하는 동물을 돕는 것이다. '학대당하는 동물들'은 abused animals이다. 이 조건을 충족하는 선택지는 (b) assisting abused이다.

어휘 charity 자선 단체

appreciate 가치를 알다

collaborate 공동으로 일하다, 협력하다

정답 (b)

7 **해석** A: 이 사람이 역대 최고의 대통령이라는 말 진심이었어?

B: 아니. 비꼰 거였어.

해설 〈be동사 + 형용사 보어〉에서 be동사는 상태를 나타내는 동사이므로 진행형을 쓸 수 없다. 하지만 일시적인 상태를 나타낼 경우에는 진행형인 〈be + being + 형용사〉 형태를 쓸 수 있다. 즉 I am/was ironic.은 나의 성격이 비꼬는 성격, 즉 항상 비꼬는 사람이라는 뜻이다. 하지만 평상시에는 비꼬는 성격이 아닌데, 일시적으로 비꼬는 것임을 강조할 경우에는 I am/was being ironic.이라고 쓸 수 있다. 문맥상 이 사람이 역대 최고의 대통령이라고 말하면서 일시적으로 비꼰 거라고 봐야 하므로 진행형인 (b) was being이 정답이다.

어휘 serious 진지한, 진심인

ironic 반어적인, 비꼬는

정답 (b)

8 **해석** A: 디자인이 멋지다. 다음은 뭐야?

B: 서둘러서 저 샘플들을 처리해.

해설 준사역동사 get의 동사 활용과 태를 물어보는 문제이다. get은 목적어와 목적격 보어의 주술 관계가 능동이면 주로 to부정사를, 수동이면 과거분사를 목적격 보어로 취하는 동사이다. 주어진 문제에서 samples는 process라는 행위의 주체가 아니라 대상이므로 과거분사인 (b) processed가 빈칸에 가장 알맞다.

정답 (b)

9 **해석** A: 먹고살기 위해 무술을 하는 것은 고단할 게 분명해.

B: 일단 숙달이 되면 몸이 그 노고에 적응되지.

해설 선택지를 보면 빈칸에 알맞은 분사를 골라 넣으라는 문제임을 쉽게 알 수 있다. 분사구문의 의미상 주어는 별도로 표기되어 있지 않으면 주절의 주어와 동일하다. 따라서 빈칸에 들어갈 분사의 의미상 주어는 your body일 수밖에 없고, your body와 train의 주술 관계는 수동이므로 수동 분사구문이 들어가야 한다. 수동 분사구문은 과거분사로 시작되므로 정답은 (a) trained이다.

어휘 martial arts 무술

exhausting 힘드는, 진을 빼는

정답 (a)

10 **해석** 단 한 명의 상원 의원만이 반대함으로써 그 법안은 62 대 1로 통과되었다.

해설 동사와 태에 관한 지식을 이용해서 빈칸을 완성하는 문제이다. defeat는 타동사로만 쓰이고, pass는 자동사(통과되다, 가결되다)나 타동사(가결시키다, 통과시키다) 모두로 쓰인다는 사실을 알고 있어야 혼동하지 않고 풀 수 있는 문제이다. 따라서 defeat는 반드시 목적어를 취해야 하며 (c)처럼 목적어를 취하지 않을 경우에는 수동이 되어야 하는데, 수동형이 아니므로 (c)는 문법적으로 정답이 될 수 없다. 또한 그 법안을 반대하는 사람이 오직 1명이고, 찬성하는 사람이 62명인데, 62-1로 부결된다는 것은 말이 되지 않으므로 문맥상으로도 답이 되지 못한다. (a)는 pass를 자동사로 본다면 얼핏 정답이 될 수 있어 보이지만 시제가 틀렸다. 법안이 통과되는 것과 같은 동사는 긴 동작으로 볼 수 없는 단발적이고 찰나적인 동작이므로 진행형을 쓸 수 없다. 따라서 자동사 pass를 단순 과거로 쓴 (d) the bill passed 62-1이 정답이다.

어휘 senator 상원 의원
vote against ~에 대해 반대 투표를 하다

정답 (d)

11 해석 캐나다의 대러시아 무역수지 적자는 지난 10년에 비교해 볼 때 400퍼센트가 증가했다.

해설 분사구문의 태와 시제를 묻는 문제이다. 분사구문의 태를 판단할 때는 일부 독립분사구문(Generally speaking, Judging from, Considering, Admitting 등)을 제외하곤 분사구문의 의미상 주어는 주절의 주어와 무조건 일치해야 하기 때문에 반드시 주절의 주어와 주술 관계를 따져서 태를 판단해야 한다. 주절의 주어 Canada's trade deficit는 동사 compare하는 주체가 아니라 compare되는 대상이므로 수동 분사구문이 되어야 하며, 분사구문의 시제가 주절의 시제보다 한 시제 앞섰다고 볼 수 없으므로 완료 분사구문인 (d) having been compared는 답이 될 수 없다. (a) comparing이 가능하려면 위 문장을 다음과 같이 고쳐야 한다. I can safely say that Canada's trade deficit with Russia increased by four hundred percent, comparing it to the previous decade. 주절의 주어 I와 comparing의 의미상 주어 I가 일치하기 때문에 문법에 맞는 문장이 된다. 주절의 주어와 분사구문의 의미상 주어가 일치하지 않는 분사구문을 현수분사구문(dangling participle)이라고 하는데 비문법적인 문장이다.

어휘 trade deficit 무역수지 적자
increase by ~만큼 증가하다

정답 (b)

12 해석 그 건설 노동자는 하루 종일 고된 노동으로 몸이 쑤셔서 소파에 털썩 주저앉아 TV를 켰다.

해설 동사 지식과 분사구문에 대한 이해를 동시에 물어보는 문제이다. ache는 자동사로만 쓰이는 동사로 '아프다, 몸이 쑤시다'라는 뜻이다. 자동사는 수동태가 없으므로 수동 분사구문 형태인 (b)와 (c)는 답에서 제외된다. 그다음, 분사구문의 시제를 결정해야 하는데 그가 소파에 주저앉았던(collapsed) 이유나 배경이 하루 종일 힘든 노동으로 몸이 쑤시고 있었기(was aching from) 때문이므로 주절과 종속절의 시제가 둘 다 과거로 같다. 즉 (d) having been aching처럼 하나 앞선 시제를 나타내는 완료 진행 분사구문을 쓸 이유가 없다. 따라서 (a) aching이 정답이다.

어휘 ache 몸이 쑤시다, 아프다
collapse 주저앉다

정답 (a)

13 해석 일전에 자신의 의상에 대해 언론의 비판을 받은 그 여배우는 다가올 시상식을 위한 의상 조언을 구했다.

해설 분사구문의 시제를 묻는 문제이다. 분사구문의 시제가 주절의 시제보다 하나 앞선다면 having p.p. 형태의 완료 분사구문을 쓴다. 여배우가 의상 조언을 구했던 것보다 의상 때문에 언론의 비판을 받은 것이 먼저이다. 게다가 before가 하나 앞선 상황임을 확인해 주고 있다. 그리고 '비난을 당한' 것이므로 태는 수동이 되어야 한다. 따라서 완료 수동 분사구문의 형태인 (c) Having been criticized가 정답이다.

어휘 the press 언론
outfit 의상, 옷
awards ceremony 시상식

정답 (c)

14 해석 그는 방금 들었던 것에 대해 생각하면서 잠시 동안 문가에 서 있었다.

해설 동사 지식과 부대상황 분사구문을 동시에 묻는 문제이다. 문장 구조를 살펴보면 접속사 없이 〈주어 + 동사〉가 1개 이미 나와 있으므로 빈칸은 동사 자리가 아니라 분사 자리이다. 빈칸에 들어갈 분사의 의미상 주어는 주절의 주어인 He이며, 주어 He는 동사 think의 주체이므로 능동 분사구문 형태인 thinking이 되어야 한다. 그리고 think가 명사절을 목적어로 취하는 타동사로 쓰이는 경우도 있지만, 그 경우엔 주로 의식적인 사고 활동이 아니라 의견(opinion)을 나타내는 경우(*e.g.* I think that she is American.)이다. 주어진 문장에서 자신이 들은 것에 대해 곰곰이 생각하는 것은 의식적인 사고 활동이므로 빈칸에는 〈자동사 + 전치사〉 형태인 (a) thinking about이 적절하다.

어휘 doorway 출입구

정답 (a)

15 **해석** 오늘날 어린이들이 직면한 많은 중요한 문제들 중에서 환경적 건강이 그들의 삶의 질에 가장 지대한 영향을 미칠 것이다.

해설 confront는 타동사로만 쓰이며 '직면하다, 마주하다, 대면하다' 라는 뜻을 가지고 있는데, 수동 형태 be confronted with와 혼동하지 않도록 머릿속에 잘 정리해야 한다. 예를 들어, 능동 문장 Many problems confront children.을 수동태로 고치면 Children are confronted with many problems.가 된다. 이 두 문장의 상관관계를 잘 이해해야 헷갈리지 않고 문제를 풀 수 있다. 문장 구조상 빈칸은 problems를 수식해 주는 분사 자리이다. 현재분사인지 과거분사인지는 problems와 confront의 주술 관계를 따져 봐야 한다. 위 예문에서도 살펴봤듯이 problems는 confront의 주체라고 볼 수 있다. 따라서 능동을 의미하는 현재분사 confronting이 빈칸에 알맞다. 참고로 빈칸 뒤에 전치사 with가 보이는 경우는 수식받는 명사와 confront의 관계가 수동이므로 무조건 과거분사를 고르면 된다. Children _______ with many problems are usually vulnerable to crimes. 에서 빈칸에 들어갈 confront의 알맞은 분사 형태는 confronted이다. 복잡하게 따질 필요 없다. 빈칸 뒤에 with가 보이면 무조건 과거분사(confronted)가, with가 없으면 현재분사(confronting)가 오는 걸로 기억하면 된다. confront와 의미와 용법이 완전히 똑같은 동사 face 역시 같은 방법을 적용해서 분사구문 문제를 풀 수 있다.

어휘 confront 마주하다, 직면하다

정답 (d)

16 **해석** 그 대화에서 영감을 받은 그녀는 자신의 생각을 재빨리 공책에 써두었다.

해설 분사구문의 태를 묻는 문제이다. 분사구문의 의미상 주어는 특별한 경우를 제외하면 주절의 주어와 일치한다. 따라서 inspired가 맞는지 inspiring이 맞는지는 주절의 주어 she와 주술 관계를 따져 봐야 한다. inspire는 '~에게 영감을 주다' 라는 뜻이다. 그녀가 자신의 생각을 공책에 재빨리 적었다는 것은 영감을 받은 것이지 준 것이 아니므로 수동 분사구문이 되어야 하며, the conversation에 의해 영감을 받은 것이므로 the conversation 앞에 행위자를 나타내는 전치사 by를 붙여 줘야 한다. 따라서 정답은 (d) Inspired by the conversation이다.

어휘 inspire 영감을 주다
write down 써두다, 기록하다

정답 (d)

17 **해석** 빠져나갈 방법이 없었기 때문에 그 남자는 경찰에 자수했다.

해설 문장 구조상 접속사가 없으므로 빈칸은 동사 자리가 아니라 분사 자리이다. 선택지 중 분사는 (c) being밖에 없고 나머지는 모두 본동사로 쓰일 수 있는 형태들이다. 접속사 없이 쉼표만으로 두 문장을 하나의 문장으로 연결할 수는 없다. 또 다른 방법으로 이 문제를 푸는 방법이 있다. 분사구문을 절로 복원해 보는 방법이다. 분사구문을 부사절로 복원해 보면 이 문장은 As there was no means of escape, the man surrendered to the police. 였다고 볼 수 있다. 이 문장을 분사구문 만드는 공식에 따라 만들어 보면 There being no means of escape, ~ 가 되므로 빈칸에는 (c) being이 들어감을 알 수 있다.

어휘 surrender to ~에게 항복하다[자수하다]

정답 (c)

18 **해석** A: 최근에 카페에 문제가 좀 있었어.
B: 정말? 어떤 문제?
A: 종업원 두 명이 음료를 무료로 제공하는 것을 지배인이 붙잡았어.
B: 그런 식의 행동은 눈감아 주면 안 될 것 같아.

해설 현수분사구문 구분 문제이다. 현수분사구문이란, 분사구문의 의미상 주어와 주절의 주어가 일치하지 않아 분사구문이 주절의 주어와 문법적으로 연결되지 못하고 따로 노는 분사구문을 뜻한다. 현수분사구문은 비문법적인 문장으로 간주된다. (c)에서 Giving away

free drinks의 의미상 주어는 the manager가 아니
라 two employees이다. 따라서 이 문장을 올바른
문장으로 고치려면 주절의 주어를 분사구문의 의미상
주어와 일치하도록 바꿔 주는 방법이 있는데, 바로
two employees를 주절의 주어로 해서 수동태 문장
(two employees were caught by the
manager)으로 만들어 주는 방법이다. 또 다른 방법
은 the manager를 주어로 그대로 두는 것인데, 이
방법은 주절 앞에 나와 있는 분사구문 Giving away
free drinks를 two employees의 목적격 보어 자
리로 옮기는 것이다. The manager caught two
employees giving away free drinks.

어휘 give away 거저 주다, 주다
　　 tolerate 용인하다, 용서하다

정답 (c) → Giving away free drinks, two employees
　　　　 were caught by the manager.
　　　 or The manager caught two employees
　　　　 giving away free drinks.

19 해석 (a) 바네사는 쇼를 준비하느라 몇 주 동안 바빴다. (b)
그녀는 일주일 내내 매일 하루에 3시간씩 리허설을 했
다. (c) 그녀는 춤을 추다 지치면 노래 연습을 하곤 했
다. (d) 오로지 쇼에만 집중하다 보니 친구들과 가족을
소홀히 했다.

해설 문장 구조 지식을 물어보는 문제이다. 영어에서 문장
의 구성 요건은 적어도 하나 이상의 주어와 동사이다.
주어와 동사가 없으면 아무리 단어들을 길게 나열해도
하나의 문장을 구성할 수 없다. (d)는 두 개의 분사구
문을 쉼표로 나란히 연결했는데 문장이 성립되지 않는
다. 따라서 둘 중에 하나를 주어와 동사를 갖춘 절로
만들어 줘야 한다. 따라서 neglecting을 she
neglected로 수정하거나 Focusing을 She
focused로 수정해 주면 된다.

어휘 prepare for ~에 대해 준비하다
　　 rehearse 예행연습을 하다
　　 exclusively 오로지 ~만
　　 neglect 경시하다, 소홀히 하다

정답 (d) neglecting → she neglected
　　 or Focusing → She focused

20 해석 (a) 며칠 전에 근린 주민 조직에서 각자 음식을 가져와
먹는 회식을 주최했다. (b) 모임의 목적은 지역 사람들
간의 유대 형성을 돕고 지역의 문제들을 토론하는 것

이었다. (c) 토론된 몇 가지 문제들 속에는 범죄, 임대
료 인상, 그리고 교육 체계 등이 포함되어 있었다. (d)
회식이 매우 성공적이었기 때문에 참석자들은 가까운
시일에 다시 한 번 모이기로 약속했다.

해설 분사 관련 문장 구조 지식을 묻는 문제이다. (c)에서
전체 문장의 동사는 included이므로 included 앞부
분은 자연스럽게 주부가 된다. 전체 문장의 주어는
Some이고 of the issues는 Some을 수식하는 형
용사구이며, had discussed는 바로 앞의 명사를 후
치 수식하는 분사가 되어야 한다. had discussed를
그대로 두면 had discussed는 과거완료이므로 동
사의 형태로 볼 수 있는데, 한 문장에서 접속사 없이
동사가 2개인 꼴(included와 had discussed)이
되므로 비문법적인 문장이 된다. 따라서 had
discussed를 후치 수식하는 분사구로 바꿔 주어야
한다. issues와 discuss의 관계는 수동이므로 과거
분사 discussed로 수정해 주면 된다.

어휘 potluck 각자 음식을 가져와서 먹는 회식
　　 bonds 유대
　　 attendee 참석자

정답 (c) had discussed → discussed

Actual Test

1 **해석** A: 여기 음식이 생각했던 것만큼 괜찮니?

B: 훌륭해! 내가 원했던 음식이야.

해설 적절한 관계사를 고르는 문제이다. 문장 구조상 빈칸은 접속사 자리인 동시에 빈칸 뒤에 불완전한 절이 이어지고 있으므로 관계대명사 자리인데, 빈칸 앞에 선행사가 없으므로 선행사를 포함한 관계대명사가 가장 알맞다. 선택지 중 선행사를 포함한 관계대명사는 (c) what이다.

어휘 be in the mood for ~할 기분이다, ~하고 싶다

정답 (c)

2 **해석** A: 지난 수년 동안 이 동네에서 어떤 변화들이 있었습니까?

B: 지난 십 년에 걸쳐 이 동네에는 외국인의 수가 상당히 증가했는데, 대부분이 생산적인 사회 구성원들입니다.

해설 의미로만 따지면 빈칸에는 of them(= of the foreigners)이 들어가야 한다. 하지만 쉼표만으로는 두 개의 문장을 연결할 수 없으므로 빈칸에는 단순한 대명사가 아니라 접속사가 필요하다는 걸 알 수 있고, 빈칸 뒤의 문장이 불완전하므로 접속사의 역할과 대명사의 역할을 하는 관계대명사가 알맞다고 볼 수 있다. 선행사가 foreigners로 사람이므로 정답은 (a) of whom이다. 참고로 B의 문장을 두 문장으로 분리하면 다음과 같다. The neighborhood has seen a substantial increase in the number of foreigners. + Most of them are productive members of society. 이 두 문장을 관계대명사를 이용해서 합친 문장이 문제의 예문이 되고, 접속사를 이용해서 합치면 다음과 같다. The neighborhood has seen a substantial increase in the number of foreigners, and most of them are productive members of society.

정답 (a)

3 **해석** A: 너 뭔가 신나 보여. 무슨 일 있니?

B: 응, 내가 최고의 추상 미술가 중에 한 명으로 꼽는 제임스 캐머론이 다음 주에 온대.

해설 계속적 용법의 관계대명사를 고르는 문제이다. 빈칸 뒤에 문장이 불완전하기 때문에 빈칸은 관계대명사 자리이다. I believe는 삽입절일 뿐이므로 I believe 뒤부터 문장이 완전한지 불완전한지 따져 봐야 한다. I believe 뒤에 동사 is가 바로 이어져서 주어가 빠진 불완전한 문장이므로 빈칸은 주격 관계대명사 자리이다. 선행사인 James Cameron은 사람을 가리키는 고유명사이므로 (c) who가 답이 된다. 참고로 관계대명사 뒤에 오는 〈주어 + think/believe/suppose〉 형태는 대부분 삽입절이므로 이런 삽입절이 포함된 관계대명사절에서는 관계대명사 격을 구분할 때 이러한 삽입절 뒤부터 살펴보아야 한다.

어휘 abstract artist 추상 미술가

정답 (c)

4 **해석** A: 동부에서 온 정착민들은 어디로 갔나요?

B: 최종적으로 캘리포니아 북서부에 정착했는데, 그곳의 비옥한 땅이 수세대에 걸쳐 풍부한 식량을 제공했지.

해설 문장 구조상 빈칸은 접속사 자리인데, 빈칸 뒤가 주어가 빠진 불완전한 절이므로 관계대명사가 알맞다. (a)와 (d)는 답에서 제외된다. 빈칸에는 have provided의 주어 역할과 접속사의 역할을 동시에 수행할 수 있는 어구가 들어가야 한다. 문맥상 California's fertile fields라는 의미가 적절하므로 (b) whose fertile fields가 가장 알맞다. whose 대신에 of which를 써도 되는데 (c)가 정답이 되려면 of which the fertile fields가 되어야 한다.

어휘 settler 정착민

make one's home 정착하다

abundant 풍부한

for generations 수세대에 걸쳐

정답 (b)

5 **해석** A: 여긴 좀 낯익은 장소 같아.

B: 기억 안 나? 이곳은 자기가 나한테 처음으로 청혼한 곳이잖아.

해설 문장 구조상 빈칸은 접속사 자리인데, 빈칸 뒤에 완전한 절이 왔으므로 관계대명사보다는 관계부사가 알맞다. (c)를 제외한 나머지 선택지가 모두 관계부사로 쓰일 수 있으므로 문맥을 따져 봐야 한다. 문맥상 This가 가리키는 것은 장소(This place)이므로 빈칸은 장소를 나타내는 관계부사 (a) where이 가장 알맞다. 참고로 관계부사 앞에 선행사가 일반적 의미의 선행사인 the place, the time, the reason 등일 경우엔

선행사를 생략할 수 있다.

어휘 familiar 친숙한

somehow 어쩐지, 아무래도

propose to ~에게 청혼하다

정답 (a)

6 해석 A: 몇몇 사람들은 그 테러리스트들을 의사(義士)로 묘사하곤 했어.

B: 뭐라고 부르고 싶든 그자들은 반드시 처벌받아야 해.

해설 문장 구조상 빈칸은 부사절 접속사 자리이다. 문맥상 B의 call은 '전화하다'의 뜻인 3형식 동사로 쓰인 것이 아니라 '~를 …로 부르다'라는 뜻의 5형식 동사로 쓰였음을 알 수 있다. 따라서 빈칸 뒤는 목적격 보어가 없는 불완전한 절이므로 빈칸에는 관계대명사가 들어가야 한다. 하지만 빈칸 앞에 선행사가 없으므로 선행사를 포함한 관계대명사가 들어가야 하는데 선택지 중 선행사를 포함하고 양보 부사절을 이끌 수 있는 접속사는 복합관계대명사 (d) Whatever밖에 없다. 참고로 복합관계대명사는 명사절을 이끌 수도 있다. *e.g.* I will give you whatever you want.

어휘 freedom fighter 자유의 투사, 반체제운동가

정답 (d)

7 해석 그 영업 사원은 자신의 여행을 줄이기로 결심했는데, 이는 그녀와 더 많은 시간을 보내고 싶어 했던 그녀의 아이들에게는 좋은 소식이었다.

해설 빈칸 뒤가 불완전한 문장이므로 빈칸에는 관계대명사가 들어가야 한다. 관계대명사 앞에 쉼표가 있으므로 관계대명사의 계속적 용법이라고 볼 수 있는데, 계속적 용법에서는 that이나 what을 쓰지 않는다. 앞 문장 전체를 받아 주는 계속적 용법의 관계대명사는 which만을 써야 한다. 관계대명사 앞에 쉼표가 있는 경우는 대부분 which나 that의 구분 문제일 확률이 높다.

정답 (b)

8 해석 우린 할머니가 20년째 살고 계시는 루마니아에서 여름을 보낼 계획이다.

해설 빈칸은 접속사 자리인데, 빈칸 뒤의 문장이 완전한 절이므로 빈칸은 관계대명사보다는 관계부사가 들어갈 자리이다. 선행사 Romania는 장소를 나타내는 고유명사이므로 관계부사 (c) where가 정답이다.

정답 (c)

9 해석 여러분이 먹는 음식은 체중, 근육량, 피부 상태를 포함해 당신의 외모와 관련하여 많은 것을 결정한다.

해설 알맞은 관계사를 고르는 문제이다. 전체 문장의 동사는 determines이고, 빈칸은 '우리가 먹는 것'의 의미가 되어야 한다. 빈칸 앞에 선행사가 없으므로 선행사를 포함한 관계대명사가 필요한데 선택지 중 선행사를 포함하는 관계대명사는 (a) What밖에 없다.

어휘 determine 결정하다

appearance 외모

muscle 근육

mass 부피, 양

정답 (a)

10 해석 저희 웹사이트를 방문하셔서 여러분이 생각하기에 올해의 예술가가 될 자격이 있는 사람이 누구건 그 사람을 선택해 주세요.

해설 관계대명사 뒤에 오는 〈주어 + think/believe〉 형태는 삽입절이므로 관계대명사 격을 구분할 때는 이 삽입절이 없다 생각하고 격을 구분해 줄 필요가 있다. 삽입절 you think 뒤에 동사 deserves가 바로 나와서 주어가 빠져 있으므로 주격 복합관계대명사가 들어가야 하며, 주격 보어가 artist인 걸로 보아 주어는 사람을 가리키는 복합관계대명사이어야 하므로 (d) whoever가 정답이다.

정답 (d)

11 해석 과학자들은 생약을 만드는 데 유용한 다양한 식물들을 발견했다.

해설 빈칸은 생략을 해도 되는 어구가 들어갈 자리이므로 접속사 중 생략이 가능한 경우의 수를 떠올릴 필요가 있다. 일단 명사절 that이 생략 가능하고, 관계대명사에서는 목적격 관계대명사, 〈주격 관계대명사 + be동사〉가 생략이 가능하다. 따라서 선택지 중 이 경우에 해당되는 것은 (a)와 (c)이다. 관계사절의 동사는 선행사(plants)에 일치시키므로 정답은 (a) which are이다. 참고로 접속사 없이 한 문장에 동사를 2개 쓰는 것은 불가능하므로 (b)와 (d)는 문장 구조상 답이 될 수 없으니 답에서 제외하고 문제를 푸는 것이 정답률을 높일 수 있다.

어휘 natural medicine 생약, 천연 약

정답 (a)

12 해석 기분이 처질 때마다 기운을 북돋기 위해 즐겨 하는 것

이 하나 있다.

해설 문장 구조상 빈칸은 접속사 자리인데 빈칸 뒤가 to do의 의미상 목적어가 없는 불완전한 절이므로 관계대명사가 들어가야 한다. 선행사 one thing은 사물이므로 which가 가장 알맞은데, 선택지 중에 which가 없으므로 which 대신에 쓸 수 있는 (d) that이 정답이 된다.

정답 (d)

13 해석 학교 당국은 기숙사의 3분의 1을 식중독을 앓게 만들었던 오염된 음식의 출처를 밝히려고 여전히 노력하고 있었다.

해설 빈칸 뒤에 바로 동사가 이어지고 선행사가 contaminated food이므로 빈칸에는 관계대명사 which나 that이 알맞다.

어휘 contaminated food 상한 음식, 오염된 음식
dormitory 기숙사
food poisoning 식중독

정답 (d)

14 해석 정치인이 됨으로써 권력과 명성을 얻는 사람은 교활하고 계산적인 사람이다.

해설 〈It is/was + 강조어구 + that ~ 〉형태의 강조구문을 물어보는 문제이다. 빈칸 뒤의 문장이 주어가 빠진 불완전한 문장이므로 빈칸은 관계대명사 자리라고 볼 수 있다. 따라서 (a)와 (d)는 답에서 제외된다. 빈칸 앞에 강조되는 어구 person이 사람이므로 주격 관계대명사 who 또는 It ~ that 강조구문의 that이 빈칸에 들어갈 수 있다. 따라서 정답은 (b) who이다. 참고로 It ~ that 강조구문에서 that은 상황에 따라 관계대명사(who, whom, which)나 관계부사(when, where, why, how)로 바꿔 쓸 수 있다.

어휘 cunning 교활한
calculating 계산적인
prestige 명성

정답 (b)

15 해석 태양 에너지의 사용을 권장하는 사람 중에는 정치인, 음악가, 그리고 저명한 사업가들이 있다.

해설 선택지를 보면 뭘 물어보는 문제인지 알 수 있다. 빈칸에 관계대명사와 적절한 선행사를 넣는 문제이다. 빈칸 뒤에 바로 동사가 이어지고 있으므로 주격 관계대명사가 필요하며, 동사가 복수형 are이므로 선행사

도 복수 형태이어야 한다. 이 조건을 충족시키는 선택지는 (c) the ones who밖에 없다.

어휘 prominent 저명한
promote 촉진하다, 장려하다, 권장하다

정답 (c)

16 해석 프리다 카스트로는 내 생각에 이 위원회의 회장이 될 자격이 가장 충분한 후보이다.

해설 알맞은 접속사를 골라 넣는 문제이다. 일단 빈칸 뒤에 I believe가 삽입절인지 아닌지를 먼저 구분해야 한다. 보통 〈주어 + believe/think〉 뒤에 주어가 없거나 목적어가 빠진 불완전한 문장이 이어지면 삽입절로 판단해서 빈칸은 관계대명사 자리라고 판단하면 되는데, 삽입절 다음에 이어지는 문장에서 주어가 빠져 있으면 주격, 목적어가 빠져 있으면 목적격 관계대명사를 고르면 된다. 동사 is의 주어가 빠진 불완전한 절이므로 빈칸은 주격 관계대명사 자리이며, 선행사 (candidate)가 사람이므로 (d) who가 가장 알맞다. 참고로 삽입절이 들어간 관계대명사절에서는 주격 관계대명사라도 단독으로 생략이 가능하며 who, whom, which 대신 that으로 바꿔 쓸 수도 있다.

어휘 candidate 후보
head ~의 장이 되다, 이끌다
committee 위원회

정답 (d)

17 해석 집에 페인트칠 하는 일자리를 구했는데, 잔디 깎는 일보다 보수가 훨씬 더 좋아.

해설 문장 구조상 빈칸은 접속사 자리인데 빈칸 뒤의 문장이 동사로 시작되고 주어가 빠져 있어 불완전하므로 빈칸에는 주격 관계대명사가 들어가야 한다. 문맥상 선행사가 a job이므로 (b) which가 정답이다. 참고로 관계사 앞에 콤마가 있는 계속적 용법에서 that과 what은 쓸 수 없다.

어휘 mow the lawn 잔디를 깎다

정답 (b)

18 해석 (a) A: 우리가 벌써 졸업을 한다니 안 믿겨져. 세월 참 빠르다.
(b) B: 정말 그래. 졸업 후에 뭐 할지 결정했니?
(c) A: 응. 법률 컨설팅 회사에서 사회에 첫발을 내디딜 거야.
(d) B: 잘됐다. 직장에서 행운이 있길 빌게.

해설 의문대명사 which와 what을 구분하는 문제이다. 문법적으로는 틀린 곳이 없지만, 문맥상 선택의 범위가 주어지지 않았으므로 (b)의 의문대명사 which를 what으로 고쳐야 한다. 문맥상 선택의 범위가 주어진 경우에는 which를, 주어지지 않은 경우는 what을 쓴다.

정답 (b) which → what

19 해석 (a) A: 여행할 때 내가 겪는 어려움 중 하나는 매운 음식을 먹는 거야.

(b) B: 엄청 매운 걸 먹을 땐 어떻게 해?

(c) A: 매운 맛을 가시게 하려고 최대한 물을 많이 마셔.

(d) B: 의외로, 물을 마시면 훨씬 더 매워져. 매운 성분을 흡수하도록 빵이나 밥을 먹는 것이 더 효과적이야.

해설 문장 구조 지식을 묻는 문제이다. (a)에서 전체 문장의 주어는 One problem이고, 동사는 is이며 that I have I travel은 주어인 problem을 수식하는 형용사절이다. 관계대명사 that 이하의 문장 구조를 살펴보면 접속사 없이 두 개의 문장이 합쳐져 있으므로 문맥에 맞게 I travel 앞에 시간을 나타내는 부사절 접속사 when을 넣어 줘야 한다.

어휘 spicy 매운

relieve 완화하다, 덜다

absorb 흡수하다

element 성분

정답 (a) I travel → when I travel

20 해석 (a) 뎅기열이 세계 일주 여행객들 사이에서 더 빈번하게 발생하고 있습니다. (b) 뎅기열은 열대와 아열대 지방에 사는 모기에게 물림으로써 전염됩니다. (c) 증상은 1주 동안 지속될 수도 있고, 고통스럽긴 하지만 치명적이지는 않습니다. (d) 열대 지방으로 여행을 가실 때는 이 병에 걸리지 않도록 적절한 옷과 모기 퇴치제, 모기장을 꼭 사용하세요.

해설 적절한 관계대명사의 쓰임을 묻는 문제이다. 문장 (b)에서 선행사 mosquitoes는 사람이 아니므로 who를 which나 that으로 수정해야 한다.

어휘 frequency 빈도

subtropic 아열대

repellent 방충제, 퇴치제

정답 (b) who → which or that

Chapter 11 어순과 도치, 강조, 삽입

Actual Test

1 해석 A: 그 영화 좀 실망스럽던데.

B: 나도 그랬어.

해설 반복을 피하기 위한 도치구문으로, 상대방의 말에 맞장구칠 때 긍정문에서는 so를, 부정문에서는 neither나 nor를 쓰는데, 이때 〈조동사 + 주어〉의 어순으로 반드시 도치가 되어야 한다. B가 맞장구치는 말은 일반동사 과거형의 긍정문이므로 so와 조동사 did를 쓴 (a) So did I.가 정답이다.

어휘 underwhelming 실망스러운

정답 (a)

2 해석 A: 머리 좀 잘라 주시겠어요?

B: 물론이죠. 얼마나 짧게 잘라 드릴까요?

해설 어순을 묻는 문제이다. 일반적으로 〈관사 + 부사 + 형용사 + 명사〉의 어순을 취하지만 how, so, as, too 등의 부사는 형용사를 관사 앞으로 데리고 나와서 〈how/so/as/too + 형용사 + 관사 + 명사〉의 어순을 취한다. 따라서 (a) short a trim do you want가 빈칸에 가장 알맞다.

어휘 trim (살짝 다듬는) 이발

정답 (a)

3 해석 A: 텔레비전에서 그렇게 재밌는 쇼는 처음 봤어!

B: 빨리 봤으면 좋겠다.

해설 hardly, seldom, never, rarely 등의 부정부사가 문두로 나와서 강조될 경우 주절은 〈조동사 + 주어〉형태의 의문문 어순으로 도치되어야 한다. 현재완료 형태 have p.p.에서 have는 조동사로 간주한다. 따라서 정답은 (c) Never have I seen이다.

정답 (c)

4 해석 A: 이번 달에 돈 좀 빌려 줄 수 있겠니?

B: 미안하지만 집세 낼 돈도 충분하지 않네.

해설 어순을 묻는 문제이다. 부정부사 hardly는 일반동사 have 앞에 써야 하므로 (b)와 (c)는 답에서 제외된다. have의 목적어는 money이고, 명사를 수식하는 enough는 명사 앞에 위치해야 하는데다가 명사를 수식하는 형용사적 용법의 to부정사(to afford)는 수식하는 명사 뒤에 써야 하므로 정답은 (d) hardly have enough money to afford이다.

어휘 **afford the rent** 집세를 내다

정답 (d)

---

5 해석 A: 부모님께서는 내가 형처럼 서커스단에 들어가길 원 하셔.

B: 정말 특이한 가족이네!

해설 What 감탄문의 어순을 묻는 문제이다. How로 시작 되는 감탄문은 〈How + 형용사 (+ 관사) (+ 명사)〉의 어순이고, What으로 시작되는 감탄문은 〈What (+ 관사) (+ 형용사) + 명사〉의 어순을 취한다. 따라서 정 답은 (d) What a unique family이다.

어휘 **unique** 독특한, 특이한

정답 (d)

---

6 해석 A: 야, 노란 재킷 입은 저 남자 보이지? 소개 좀 시켜 줄래?

B: 그러고 싶지만 나도 모르는 사람이야.

해설 간접의문문의 어순과 부사에 관한 문제이다. 간접의문 문의 어순은 〈의문사 + 주어 + 동사〉이므로 (b)와 (d) 는 답에서 제외된다. '~또한, 역시'라는 의미로 긍정 문에서는 too나 as well을 쓰고, 부정문에서는 either를 쓴다. B가 말하는 문장은 부정문이므로 (c) who he is, either가 정답이다. 참고로 neither는 not과 either가 결합한 형태이기 때문에 부정어 not 과 함께 쓸 수 없다.

정답] (c)

---

7 해석 A: 사고가 난 건 전적으로 제 잘못입니다. 진심으로 사과드립니다.

B: 의외로 정직하시군요. 사람들은 실수했을 때 좀처 럼 인정을 하지 않거든요.

해설 도치 어순을 물어보는 문제이다. 정치 문장이라면 부 정부사 seldom의 위치는 일반동사 앞이므로 People seldom admit의 어순이 되는데, 부정부사 seldom을 문두에 써서 강조할 경우엔 〈조동사 + 주 어 + 동사원형/be동사 + 주어〉 형태의 의문문 어순으 로 도치가 된다. 따라서 정답은 (c) Seldom do people admit이다.

어휘 **take responsibility** 잘못이 있다, 책임을 지다

refreshing 신선한, 참신한

정답 (c)

---

8 해석 A: 시체를 검사한 후, 검시관들이 희생자의 사망 시각

을 알아냈어.

B: 희생자는 언제 죽었대?

해설 간접의문문의 어순을 묻는 문제이다. 의문사가 있는 의문문의 간접의문문은 보통 〈의문사 + 주어 + 동사〉 의 어순을 취하지만, 주절 동사가 think, believe, guess, suppose 등의 생각 동사일 경우에는 의문 사를 문두에 써야 한다. 일반적인 간접의문문의 어순 인 Do they believe when he died?에서 의문사 when이 문두로 나간 (a) When do they believe he died?가 정답이다.

어휘 **examine** 검사하다, 조사하다

body 시체, 사체

coroner 검시관

determine 결정하다, 측정하다

정답 (a)

---

9 해석 A: 마틸다가 새로운 직장에서 봉급 인상을 받게 될지 궁금해.

B: 그건 그녀가 회사에 가져다줄 이익의 잠재성을 그 녀의 상사가 알아보느냐 여부에 달려 있지.

해설 어순과 함께 문장의 의미를 바르게 해석해야 해결할 수 있는 문제이다. 마틸다의 상사가 그녀의 잠재성을 알아보느냐 여부에 달려 있다고 해야 의미가 가장 적 절하므로 〈whether or not + 주어 + 동사〉로 쓰인 (d)가 정답으로 가장 적절하다. 접속사 whether는 명 사절의 종속접속사로 주어, 목적어, 보어로 쓰이는 명 사절을 이끌 수 있다. if와 whether는 둘 다 의문사 가 없는 간접의문문을 이끌 수도 있다. 많은 경우에 있어 if와 whether는 서로 바꾸어 쓸 수 있지만 항상 if 대신 whether를 써야 하는 경우들이 있다. 첫 번 째는 to부정사 앞인 경우로 I don't know whether to stay or go.(나는 머물러야 할지 가야 할지 모르 겠다.)라고 할 때, 두 번째는 전치사 뒤에 쓰이는 경우, 세 번째는 or not 바로 앞에 쓰는 경우이다.

어휘 **get a raise** 월급을 올려 받다

potential 잠재성, 잠재력

benefit 이익을 주다

정답 (d)

---

10 해석 내가 바닥 청소를 끝내자마자 주스가 부엌 바닥에 온 통 엎질러졌다.

해설 never, little, hardly, scarcely, rarely, seldom, under no circumstances, not only, no

sooner, neither 같은 부정부사를 문두에 쓸 경우에
는 주절 동사와 주어가 반드시 의문문의 어순(조동사
+ 주어 + 동사원형)으로 도치되어야 한다. 따라서 정
답은 (d) No sooner had I finished mopping이
다. 참고로 정치 문장에서 부정부사 no sooner의 위
치는 조동사 · be동사 뒤, 일반동사 앞이므로 (c)는 I
had no sooner finished mopping의 어순이 되
어야 한다.

어휘   mop 대걸레로 닦다, 청소하다
      spill 엎지르다

정답   (d)

11 해석   그는 내 컴퓨터를 고쳐 줬을 뿐만 아니라 백신 프로그
램도 무료로 설치해 줬다.

해설   상관접속사 not only A but also B 구문에서 A와
B가 각각 주어와 동사를 갖춘 절일 경우, A에 해당되
는 절은 도치되어야 한다. 부정부사가 문두에 위치할
경우랑 똑같이 의문문 어순으로 도치가 된다. 따라서
(b) Not only did he fix my computer가 정답이
다.

어휘   install 설치하다
      virus protection software 컴퓨터 바이러스
      보호 프로그램, 백신 프로그램

정답   (b)

12 해석   그녀는 비록 머리가 좋았지만 선생님이 낸 수수께끼를
풀지 못했다.

해설   양보 부사절에서의 도치를 물어보는 문제이다. 정치
문장에서는 〈Though/Although + S + V〉의 어순
이지만, 형용사나 부사를 문두로 도치할 경우에는 접
속사가 though가 아니라 as를 써야 한다. 〈형용사/
부사/무관사 명사 + as + 주어 + 동사〉의 양보 구문
으로 암기해 두는 편이 좋다. 따라서 정답은 (a)
Smart as she was이다.

어휘   riddle 수수께끼

정답   (a)

13 해석   놀랍게도 민권운동에서 그가 얼마나 중요한 인물이었
는지 알아보는 역사학자는 거의 없다.

해설   어순을 묻는 문제이다. 부사 how, so, as, too 뒤에
는 〈형용사 + 관사 + 명사〉의 어순이 되는데, figure
는 가산명사이므로 관사가 필요하다. 따라서 (c) how
important a figure가 정답이다.

어휘   historian 역사학자
      civil rights movement 민권운동

정답   (c)

14 해석   주민들의 생활을 개선시키는 데 그렇게 많은 개인적인
시간과 에너지를 투자했던 시장은 없었다.

해설   부정부사 never, rarely, seldom, hardly 등이 문
두에 위치하는 경우에는 조동사 도치(의문문 도치)가
되므로 빈칸에는 (b) has a mayor spent가 가장 알
맞다.

어휘   mayor 시장
      livelihood 생계, 살림살이

정답   (b)

15 해석   제임스 피네커는 학교를 단 하루도 다니지 않았고, 자
신의 아이들을 자신이 정부 시설이라고 여기는 곳에
보낼 의향도 없다.

해설   반복을 피하기 위한 도치구문을 물어보는 문제이다.
앞 문장이 부정문이고, 뒤에 이어지는 문장도 부정의
의미를 표현할 경우에는 등위접속사 and와 부정부사
not의 의미가 합쳐진 등위접속사 nor를 써서 문장을
연결하므로 (c) nor does he intend가 정답이다. 참
고로 neither는 부사이고, nor는 〈접속사 + 부사〉의
역할을 한다. 즉 〈and neither = nor〉의 관계이다.
따라서 위 문제는 and neither does he intend가
정답 선택지로 주어질 수도 있다.

정답   (c)

16 해석   종이 울리자마자 학생들은 교실 문 쪽으로 달려갔다.

해설   부정어 도치구문을 묻는 문제이다. 'A하자마자 B하
다' 라는 뜻의 no sooner A than B 구문에서 부정
부사 no sooner가 문두로 나오면 〈조동사 + 주어〉
또는 〈be동사 + 주어〉 형태의 의문문 어순으로 도치
가 되어야 한다. 따라서 (a) had the bell rung이 정
답이다. 참고로 no sooner절에는 과거완료 시제를,
than절에는 과거 시제를 쓴다.

어휘   no sooner A than B A하자마자 B하다
      race 달려가다, 돌진하다

정답   (a)

17 해석   (a) A: 넌 재능이 많은 사람인 거 같아.
      (b) B: 음, 글쓰기와 댄스 실력으로 수많은 상을 받았지.
      (c) A: 이봐, 우린 오늘 밤 내내 거의 완전히 네 얘기

만 했어. 다른 얘기 좀 하면 안 될까?

(d) B: 좋아. 너에 관해 얘기하자. 나 머리 잘랐는데 어때?

해설 부사 앞에는 전치사를 쓸 수 없다. (c)의 almost는 completely를 수식하는 부사이고, completely 역시 동사 have been talking을 수식하는 부사이므로 almost 앞의 전치사 for는 불필요하다. 따라서 for를 삭제해야 한다.

정답 (c) for almost completely

→ almost completely

18 해석 (a) A: 시험공부를 충분히 못했어.

(b) B: 나도 그래. 도서관에서 밤새자.

(b) A: 난 좀 쉬지 않으면 시험을 완전히 망칠 거야.

(d) B: 커피 사줄게. 잠들지 않게 서로 도와주자고.

해설 반복을 피하기 위한 도치구문으로 상대방의 말에 맞장구칠 때는 긍정문에서는 so로, 부정문에서는 neither나 nor로 시작되는 구문을 쓴다. 이때 〈조동사 + 주어〉의 어순으로 반드시 도치가 되어야 한다. B가 맞장구치는 말은 현재완료 부정문(I haven't been able to prepare enough for this test.)이므로 조동사 have를 써서 Neither have I.의 어순이 되어야 한다.

정답 (b) Neither I have. → Neither have I.

19 해석 (a) 지렁이는 모든 정원사들에게 아주 귀중한 도구이다. (b) 이는 지렁이들이 파는 굴에 의한 통풍 때문이다. (c) 그러면 산소가 식물의 뿌리까지 닿을 수 있기 때문에 식물을 더 건강하게 만든다. (d) 지렁이는 산소뿐만 아니라 죽은 잎과 같은 유기물질을 흙 속으로 순환시킴으로써 영양분도를 공급해 준다.

해설 상관접속사 not only A but also B 구문에서 not only가 문두에 올 경우, not only절은 의문문 어순〈조동사 + 주어〉, 〈be동사 + 주어〉로 도치되어야 하므로 (d)의 not only they do add를 Not only do they add로 고쳐야 한다.

어휘 earthworm 지렁이

invaluable 매우 귀중한

aeration 통기, 통풍

dig out 파내다, 파 뚫다

circulate 순환시키다

정답 (d) Not only they do add

→ Not only do they add

20 해석 (a) 점점 더 많은 사람들이 유해한 수준의 수은에 노출되고 있다. (b) 이런 노출의 가장 큰 원인은 해산물을 먹는 것이다. (c) 아이들과 태아가 과다한 수은으로 인한 신경 질환에 걸릴 위험이 가장 크다. (d) 수은 중독의 증상에는 언어, 청각, 보행 장애, 근육 약화 등이 있다.

해설 (d)에서 문맥상 '수은 중독'의 의미가 되어야 하므로 poisoning mercury를 mercury poisoning으로 수정해야 한다. poisoning은 동명사가 아니라 '중독'의 뜻을 가진 명사로 쓰였고, mercury는 의미상 poisoning을 수식하기 때문에 수식받는 명사 앞에 써야 한다.

어휘 mercury 수은

consumption 소비, 소모

fetus 태아

neurological 신경(학)의

disorder 기능 장애, 질환

impairment 장애, 손상

정답 (d) poisoning mercury → mercury poisoning

Actual Test

1 해석 A: 개가 새보다 더 고등동물이라는 건 분명한 사실 아
　　　　닌가요?

　　　　B: 차이가 있겠지만 전 어떤 종도 다른 종보다 열등하
　　　　거나 하지 않다고 생각해요.

　　해설 비교급 관련 전치사를 묻는 문제이다. inferior,
　　　　superior, prior 등의 라틴어 비교급 형용사 뒤에는
　　　　'~보다' 라는 의미의 전치사로 than 대신 to를 쓴다.

　　어휘 advanced 진보된, 고등의

　　정답 (c)

2 해석 A: 일요일에 비가 내릴지 궁금해.

　　　　B: 비 온다는 뉴스는 못 들었어.

　　해설 요일 앞에 쓰는 전치사는 (a) on이다. 참고로 전치사
　　　　on은 날짜(on May 1st), 요일(on Monday), 주말
　　　　(on weekends, on the weekend), 특정일(on
　　　　Chuseok), 특정일의 오전·오후·밤(on the
　　　　morning of Christmas, on Sunday evening)
　　　　등에 사용된다.

　　어휘 be supposed to ~하기로 되어 있다, ~할 예정
　　　　이다

　　정답 (a)

3 해석 A: 언제쯤 피자가 도착하나요?

　　　　B: 30분 내에 배달되지 않으면 피자를 공짜로 드리겠
　　　　습니다.

　　해설 '~후에, ~지나서, ~이내에'의 뜻으로, 현재를 기준으
　　　　로 미래의 시간 경과를 나타낼 때 쓰는 전치사는 (d)
　　　　in이다. 참고로 이 문제에서 in 대신 within을 써도
　　　　의미의 변화는 거의 없다.

　　정답 (d)

4 해석 A: 팀에게 여자 친구가 없다는 게 안 믿겨져. 굉장히
　　　　잘생겼는데 말이야.

　　　　B: 잘생겼을지는 모르지만 자기표현에 항상 서툴거든.

　　해설 '~에 뛰어나다', '~에 서투르다', '~에 우수하다'는
　　　　의미의 표현인 be good/excellent/poor 뒤에 쓰는
　　　　전치사는 at이다.

　　정답 (c)

5 해석 A: 나는 이번 주에 미국으로 떠나.

　　　　B: 정말로 네가 보고 싶을 거야.

　　해설 leave가 '~로 떠나다, ~를 향해 떠나다' 라는 뜻으로
　　　　쓰일 경우에는 leave 뒤에 전치사 for를 쓴다. 이때
　　　　leave는 자동사로 쓰였다. 참고로 leave 뒤에 장소를
　　　　나타내는 명사가 바로 쓰이면 '~를 떠나다' 라는 뜻의
　　　　타동사로 쓰인 것이다.

　　　　e.g. I leave Seoul tomorrow.

　　정답 (b)

6 해석 A: 왜 집에 가지 않는 거니?

　　　　B: 이 일을 끝낼 생각이야. 최소 한 시간 더 머물러야 해.

　　해설 문맥상 빈칸에는 '~동안'의 의미를 가진 전치사 for
　　　　가 알맞다. 참고로 기간이나 시간을 나타내는 명사 앞
　　　　에서 전치사 for는 생략될 수 있는데 이런 경우를 명
　　　　사의 부사적 대격이라고 한다.

　　　　e.g. I waited (for) two hours.

　　어휘 stick around 머물다, 가지 않다

　　정답 (a)

7 해석 A: 자전거를 타고 박물관에 가고 싶어.

　　　　B: 그러지 않는 게 좋을 거야. 오늘 날씨가 좋지 않거든.

　　해설 교통수단을 나타내는 전치사와 관사의 용법을 동시에
　　　　묻는 문제이다. 교통수단을 나타내는 방법은 두 가지
　　　　가 있다. 전치사 by를 쓸 경우엔 무관사 교통수단(by
　　　　bike)이고, 전치사 in이나 on을 쓸 경우엔 교통수단
　　　　앞에 관사를 반드시 써줘야 하므로(on a bike) 정답
　　　　은 (d) by bike이다.

　　정답 (d)

8 해석 A: 올해 우리 회사의 인원을 30퍼센트 감축해야 할
　　　　겁니다.

　　　　B: 해고되는 사람들 중에 한 명이 되긴 싫군요.

　　해설 수나 양, 백분율 등의 증가, 감소 추이의 변동 폭을 나
　　　　타내는 전치사는 by이다. 전치사 by는 차이나 판단의
　　　　기준을 나타낼 때 사용되기도 한다.

　　　　e.g. Don't judge a person by its appearance.
　　　　　　We won the game by 3 points.

　　어휘 workforce 노동력, 직원 수

　　정답 (c)

9 해석 A: 여기 다시 돌아와 가족이랑 함께 살게 되어서 너무
　　　　감사하단다.

　　　　B: 저도요, 할아버지. 할아버지께서 퇴원하신 날 여기

오지 못해서 죄송할 따름이에요.

해설 특정한 날이나 요일 앞에 쓰는 전치사는 on이다. 참고로 날짜나 요일 외에 주말(on weekends, on the weekend), 특정일(on Chuseok), 특정일의 오전·오후·밤(on Sunday evening, on the night of September 1) 등에도 전치사 on을 사용한다.

어휘 grateful 감사하는
get out of the hospital 퇴원하다

정답 (a)

10 해석 A: 존, 네 삼촌 제임스가 영원히 이사를 간 날이 언젠지 말해줄 수 있겠니?
B: 물론이죠, 선생님. 2005년 9월 20일 아침이었던 거 같습니다.

해설 일반적으로 '아침에', '점심에', '저녁에'의 뜻을 가진 부사구 표현은 전치사 in을 써서 in the morning, in the afternoon, in the evening과 같이 나타내지만 특정 요일, 특정일의 오전·오후·밤(on Sunday evening, on the night of September 1)에는 전치사 on을 써야 한다.

어휘 move out 이사하다
for good 영원히

정답 (c)

11 해석 네 어머니에게 그런 식으로 말하는 것은 공손하지 못한 행동이라고 생각해.

해설 사람의 성질이나 성품을 나타내는 kind, polite, nice, generous, smart, foolish 등의 형용사가 〈It ~ to부정사〉 형태의 가주어 구문에서 사용될 경우 to 부정사의 의미상 주어 앞에 쓰는 전치사는 of이다.

정답 (c)

12 해석 그녀의 친구들 사이에서 인기는 없었지만 캐시는 그 밴드를 정열적으로 좋아했다.

해설 접속사와 전치사의 구분을 묻는 문제이다. 문맥상 빈칸에는 양보의 뜻을 나타내는 연결어가 들어가야 한다. 양보의 뜻을 나타내는 연결어구로는 접속사 although, though, even though 등과 전치사로는 despite과 in spite of가 있는데, 접속사 뒤에는 주어와 동사를 갖춘 절이 와야 하며, 전치사 뒤에는 명사 상당 어구가 와야 한다. 문제에서 빈칸 뒤의 their lack of popularity among her friends는 절이 아니라 구이므로 빈칸에는 전치사 (d) despite

가 들어가야 한다.

어휘 passionately 정열적으로, 열렬히
popularity 인기

정답 (d)

13 해석 하루 종일 누구도 아무것도 사지 않았다.

해설 시간 표시 어구 앞에 this, that, last, every, each, next, all 등의 형용사가 붙는 경우에는 전치사를 쓰지 않는다. 예를 들면 in all afternoon이 아니라 all afternoon으로, in this evening이 아니라 this evening, at last night가 아니라 last night, on every Saturday가 아니라 every Saturday로 표현해야 한다. 따라서 정답은 (a) all day이다.

정답 (a)

14 해석 루터 엘드리지는 애틀랜타에서 1931년 3월 15일 자정에 숨졌다.

해설 시간과 장소의 전치사를 묻는 문제이다. 도시 이름 앞에는 in, 날짜 앞에는 on, 시각 앞에는 at을 써야 한다. 따라서 정답은 (c) in – on – at이다.

정답 (c)

15 해석 제작에 투입된 많은 스타들과 상당한 제작비에도 불구하고 〈워터 월드〉는 흥행에 있어서 대실패작이었다.

해설 접속사와 전시사의 구분을 묻는 문제이다. 문맥상 쉼표 앞부분과 뒷부분이 대조되기 때문에 빈칸에는 양보나 대조의 뜻을 갖는 연결어가 들어가야 한다. 양보의 뜻을 나타내는 연결어에는 접속사로는 although, though, even though 등이 있으며, 전치사로는 despite와 in spite of가 있다. 이 문제의 경우 빈칸 뒤가 절이 아니라 구이므로 빈칸은 전치사 자리이다. 따라서 정답은 (d) Despite이다. (a) Despite of는 틀린 표현으로 of를 삭제해야 한다.

어휘 flop 실패작
box office 흥행 수익

정답 (d)

16 해석 당신의 집념 덕분에 획기적인 매체를 만들고자 하는 우리의 꿈이 실현되었습니다.

해설 전치사의 의미를 물어보는 문제이다. 문맥상 이유나 원인을 나타내는 전치사구인 (d) Thanks to가 가장 알맞다.

어휘 persistence 끈기, 인내, 고집

revolutionary 혁명적인, 획기적인

thanks to ~덕분에

according to ~에 따르면

but for ~이 없다면

정답 (d)

17 해석 (a) A: 샘, 이번 주말에 우리랑 함께할 수 있겠니?

(b) B: 응. 하지만 써야 할 글이 좀 밀렸어.

(c) A: 그냥 잠깐 커피 한잔 하고 싶어서 그래.

(d) B: 좋아. 기분 전환 겸 집을 벗어나는 것도 좋을 거 같군.

해설 this, that, last, every, next, all 등의 형용사가 시간 표시 어구 앞에 붙은 경우에는 전치사를 쓸 수 없으므로 (a)의 at this weekend에서 at을 삭제해야 한다.

어휘 catch up on (일, 공부, 잠 따위의 밀린 것을) 만회하다, 따라잡다

real quick 얼른, 잠깐

for a change 기분 전환으로

정답 (a) at this weekend → this weekend

18 해석 (a) A: 그 보고서 작성은 얼마나 오래 걸려?

(b) B: 모르겠어. 하루 종일 걸릴 수도 있을 거 같아.

(c) A: 파티에 갈 수 있도록 서둘러서 끝내.

(d) B: 최대한 빨리 하고 있어. 하지만 끝낼 수 있을 거 같지가 않아.

해설 '작성하다, 작업하다'라는 의미의 동사구 표현은 work in이 아니라 work on이므로 (a)의 working in을 working on으로 수정해야 한다.

어휘 make it 제대로 수행하다, 성공하다

정답 (a) working in → working on

19 해석 (a) 타미의 어머니는 맛있는 과자를 만드는 것으로 유명하다. (b) 타미 친구들의 부모님들은 정기적으로 조리법을 알려달라고 부탁했다. (c) "집안의 비밀이에요"라고 타미의 어머니는 말하곤 했다. (d) 그러나 비밀은 사실 길 아래의 빵집이었다.

해설 〈be known as + 명사〉는 '(별명, 이름)으로 알려지다'라는 뜻이고 '~로 유명하다, ~으로 알려지다'의 의미로는 〈be famous/known for + 명사(구)〉를 써야 한다. 따라서 (a)는 문맥상 후자에 해당되므로 as를 for로 바꿔야 한다.

정답 (a) famous as → famous for

20 해석 (a) 크리스토퍼 리브는 승마 사고로 몸이 마비되었다. (b) 그는 팔과 다리 둘 다 움직일 수 없었다. (c) 그때 이후로 그는 척수 부상 연구에 투자해야 한다고 강력하게 주장하게 되었다. (d) 그러나 그의 용감한 노력들도 2004년 그가 죽는 것을 막지는 못했다.

해설 '~동안'의 의미를 가진 접속사와 전치사를 구분하는 문제이다. while은 접속사이므로 뒤에 주어와 동사가 들어간 절이 이어져야 하는데 (a)의 a horse-riding accident는 명사 상당 어구이므로 접속사 while을 전치사 during으로 바꾸어야 한다.

어휘 paralyze 마비시키다

advocate 옹호자, 지지자

spinal cord 척수

valiant 용감한, 영웅적인

pass away 죽다

정답 (a) while → during

Actual Test

1 **해석** A: 여자 친구에게 줄 특별한 걸 찾고 있어요.

B: 이 목걸이들 중 하나 어떤가요? 각각의 목걸이가 모두 수제품이라서 목걸이마다 독특한 모양과 느낌을 가지고 있습니다.

해설 빈칸은 주어 자리이므로 (대)명사가 들어가야 한다. (c) Every는 형용사로만 사용되므로 답에서 제외되며, of 뒤에 them이 복수 명사이므로 (a) all과 (d) both는 복수 동사를 써야 하는데 동사가 was이므로 답이 될 수 없다. 따라서 대명사로도 쓸 수 있고 단수 동사를 쓰는 (b) Each가 빈칸에 가장 알맞다.

어휘 craft 만들다

정답 (b)

2 **해석** A: 인상적인 정원을 가지고 계시는군요.

B: 대부분의 채소가 잘 자라고 있지만, 이 채소들은 무슨 이유인지 시들시들하네요.

해설 부정대명사 one의 용법을 묻는 문제이다. 앞에 언급된 명사와 동일한 종류의 명사를 가리키면 one을 쓰고, 특정 명사를 가리키면 대명사 it을 쓴다. 부정대명사 one은 it과 달리 항상 가산명사만을 받는데 복수 명사일 경우에는 ones로 받는다. 이 문제의 경우 앞 문장의 복수 명사 vegetables를 받는 부정대명사이므로 복수형인 (a) ones가 가장 알맞다. 참고로 these 뒤에는 복수 명사만 올 수 있다.

어휘 for some reason 무슨 이유인지
struggling 몸부림치는, 고군분투하는

정답 (a)

3 **해석** A: 피자 한 조각만 건네주세요.

B: 남은 게 하나도 없어서 안 되겠네요.

해설 문맥과 문법에 맞는 부정대명사를 고르는 문제이다. B가 I can't로 거절한 걸로 보아 because 이하에는 피자가 한 조각도 남아 있지 않다는 의미가 되어야 하므로 (a)와 (d)는 답에서 제외된다. no one은 사람만을 받고 none은 사람, 사물 둘 다 받을 수 있는 부정대명사인데 피자는 사물이므로 (c) none이 가장 알맞다.

정답 (c)

4 **해석** A: 이 집 맘에 드시나요?

B: 이전 집보다 더 맘에 든다고 인정할 수밖에 없군요.

해설 빈칸 뒤에 명사가 one이기 때문에 비교 대상이 둘임을 간파하는 것이 답을 찾는 결정적인 열쇠이다. 대상이 둘일 때, 둘 중의 하나 this one을 제외한 나머지 다른 하나는 the other one으로 나타내므로 정답은 (d) the other이다. 참고로 other 뒤에는 복수 명사 ones가 와야 하며, others는 대명사이므로 뒤에 one을 쓸 수 없기 때문에로 (b)와 (c)는 답이 될 수 없다. another는 대상이 셋 이상일 때, 하나를 제외한 또 다른 막연한 하나를 가리키므로 비교의 대상이 될 수 없다.

정답 (d)

5 **해석** A: 사람들이 배가 고파지고 있어. 우리 다 같이 먹으러 나가는 게 어때?

B: 다른 사람들은 여기서 계속 일을 하고 너랑 나는 음식을 좀 사가지고 오는 게 어떨까?

해설 전체 집합 People에서 you와 I를 제외한 나머지 다른 사람 전부를 가리키므로 (c) the others가 정답이다. 빈칸 뒤가 복수 동사이므로 (b) another는 답이 될 수 없으며, other는 단독으로는 절대 명사로 쓰일 수 없으므로 (a) other 역시 답이 될 수 없다. (d) few는 부정어이므로 문맥상 빈칸에 알맞지 않다.

정답 (c)

6 **해석** A: 캐나다에 사시겠어요, 미국에 사시겠어요?

B: 음, 캐나다의 의료보험제도가 미국보다 더 광범위하죠.

해설 비교의 대상은 동일해야 한다. 문맥상 캐나다의 healthcare system과 미국의 healthcare system이 비교되고 있다. 비교급에서 반복되는 명사를 대신하는 대명사는 that과 those가 있는데, 반복되는 명사가 단수이면 that을 쓰고, 복수이면 those를 쓴다. 이 문제에서는 단수 명사 healthcare system을 받고 있으므로 (d) that of the US가 정답이다.

어휘 healthcare system 의료보험제도, 건강보험
comprehensive 광범위한, 포괄적인

정답 (d)

7 **해석** A: 제게 하실 말씀 있었나요?

B: 예, 피터. 이런 말 하고 싶진 않지만 당신은 해고되었습니다.

해설 지시대명사 this와 that의 구분 문제이다. 앞에 한 말이 아니라 앞으로 하게 될 말을 가리킬 때 쓰는 대명사는 this이다. 빈칸에 들어갈 대명사가 뒤에 하게 될 말(you're fired)를 가리켜야 하므로 빈칸에는 that 보다는 this가 알맞다.

정답 (c)

8 해석 A: 누군가가 아빠 햄버거를 먹어 버린 것 같아요.

B: 아무도 내 걸 먹지 않았더라면 좋았을 텐데. 배가 너무 고파 죽겠구나.

해설 A의 dad's burger를 받을 수 있는 대명사가 빈칸에 가장 알맞다. 문맥상 B는 A의 아빠이므로 B의 빈칸에는 my burger를 받는 소유대명사 mine이 가장 알맞다.

어휘 I could eat a horse. 말이라도 먹겠다. 배가 몹시 고프다.

had better not have p.p. ~하지 않았더라면 좋았는데

정답 (b)

9 해석 A: 내가 개발한 이 과일 스무디 좀 먹어 봐.

B: 물론이지. 무슨 맛인데?

해설 의문대명사와 의문부사의 구분을 물어보는 문제이다. what은 의문대명사이고, how는 의문부사이다. 문장이 전치사 like로 끝난 경우, like 뒤에는 구조상 목적어가 필요하므로 의문대명사 what을 써야 하고, 전치사 like가 없는 경우에는 문장이 완전하므로 의문부사 how로 시작되는 의문문(How does it taste?)이 되어야 한다. 따라서 정답은 (a) What does it taste like?이다.

정답 (a)

10 해석 A: 베트남 음식을 더 먹고 싶으세요, 캄보디아 음식을 더 먹고 싶으세요?

B: 어떤 것이 더 싼가에 따라 달라질 수 있을 거 같아요.

해설 의문대명사 which와 what의 구분을 묻는 문제이다. 문맥상 선택의 범위가 주어진 경우에는 which를, 주어지지 않은 경우에는 what을 쓴다. 베트남과 캄보디아 음식으로 선택의 범위가 주어졌으므로 (c) which가 알맞다.

정답 (c)

11 해석 A: 안녕, 에릭. 네 휴대폰을 찾았다는 걸 알려 주기 위해 전화했어.

B: 잘됐다! 이번 주 쯤에 우리 집에 갖다줄 수 있겠니?

해설 대명사의 수와 어순을 묻는 문제이다. 〈타동사 + 부사〉 형태의 동사구의 목적어가 대명사일 경우에는 반드시 〈동사 + 대명사 + 부사〉의 어순을 써야 하므로 (a)와 (c)는 일단 답에서 제외되며, 단수 명사 cell phone을 받는 대명사이므로 목적어는 it이 알맞다. 따라서 정답은 (d) drop it off 이다.

어휘 drop off (사람, 물건 등을) ~에 내려놓다, 갖다 놓다

정답 (d)

12 해석 홍역은 대부분의 아이들이 일생을 살면서 한 번은 걸리는 흔한 질병이다.

해설 부정대명사 it과 one을 구분하는 문제이다. 일단 measles는 병명으로 복수형 어미로 끝났지만 단수 취급하는 명사이므로 (a) those와 (b) them은 답이 될 수 없다. 문맥상 빈칸에는 measles를 가리키는 대명사가 들어가야 하는데, 부정대명사 one은 단수 가산명사만을 받으므로 불가산명사인 measles를 받을 수 없다. 반면 대명사 it은 단수 가산명사와 불가산명사 모두 받을 수 있다. 따라서 정답은 (c) it이다.

어휘 measles 홍역

정답 (c)

13 해석 우리가 아무리 개인주의적이라고 생각할지라도 우리가 다른 사람들과 가지는 상호 의존성을 부정할 수는 없다.

해설 문법과 문맥에 맞는 적절한 부정대명사를 고르는 문제이다. 문맥상 빈칸에는 '다른 사람들'의 뜻을 가진 부정대명사가 들어가야 하므로 (a) others가 알맞다.

어휘 individualistic 개인주의적인

deny 부정하다, 부인하다

interdependence 상호 의존성

정답 (a)

14 해석 나는 그녀의 추론에 전혀 문제가 없다고 생각한다.

해설 부정대명사 anything과 something의 구분을 묻는 문제이다. something은 주로 긍정문에 쓰이고, 부정문과 의문문에서는 주로 anything을 쓴다. 제시된 문장이 부정문이므로 anything을 쓰는 것이 자연스럽다.

어휘 anything the matter with ~에 문제가 되는 어떤 것

line of reasoning 추론

정답 (b)

15 **해석** 당신의 문제와 관련하여 조언을 좀 해 드리고 싶지만 드릴 만한 조언이 하나도 없습니다.

해설 접속사 but은 내용상의 직접적인 대조를 나타내므로 but 이하의 문장의 의미는 '충고를 하나도 가지고 있지 않다'는 내용이 되어야 한다. 빈칸 앞의 동사 have는 현재완료의 조동사 have가 아니라 '가지고 있다'는 의미의 일반동사이므로 빈칸에는 목적어로 쓰일 수 있는 명사가 들어가야 한다. 따라서 부사인 (a)와 (c)는 문법적으로 답이 될 수 없다. (b) any는 부정대명사로서 have의 목적어로 쓰일 수 있지만 any가 답이 되려면 빈칸 앞이 I don't have가 되어야 한다. 따라서 not과 any를 합친 부정대명사 none이 빈칸에 가장 알맞다. 참고로 none은 불가산명사와 가산명사 모두 받을 수 있는데, 제시된 예문에서는 불가산명사 advice를 받고 있다.

정답 (d)

16 **해석** 이곳의 복숭아가 시장의 복숭아보다 훨씬 더 좋다.

해설 비교급 문장에서 비교 대상은 동일해야 하므로 (c)와 (d)는 답이 될 수 없다. 비교 대상은 '이곳의 복숭아들'과 '시장의 복숭아들'이다. 앞에서 언급된 명사의 반복을 피하기 위해 단수 명사는 that으로 대신 받고 복수 명사는 those로 받는다. 제시된 문제에서는 복수 명사 peaches를 대신하므로 (b) those at the market이 빈칸에 가장 알맞다.

어휘 peach 복숭아

정답 (b)

17 **해석** (a) A: 음식 맛이 어때?

(b) B: 훌륭해. 네가 이렇게 요리를 잘할 줄은 몰랐어.

(c) A: 요리하는 걸 좋아해. 하지만 내가 할 수 있는 거라곤 즉흥적으로 만드는 것뿐이야.

(d) B: 비법을 나에게 알려 줘야 할 거야.

해설 의문대명사와 의문부사의 구분을 물어보는 문제이다. '~은 어때?'라는 표현은 What 의문문과 How 의문문 둘 다 가능한데, 의문대명사 what은 문장 성분으로 쓰이므로 what 뒤에는 문장이 불완전해야 하고, 의문부사 how 뒤에는 완전한 문장이 이어져야 한다. 따라서 (a)는 How로 시작된 의문문인데, 전치사 like의 목적어가 없는 불완전한 문장이 왔으므로 틀린 문장이다. like를 삭제하거나 like의 목적어인 what을 how 대신에 써주면 된다.

어휘 improvise 즉흥적인, 즉석에서 하는

정답 (a) How → What or like 삭제

18 **해석** (a) A: 줄리, 《목적이 이끄는 삶》 다 읽었니?

(b) B: 아직. 돌려줄까?

(c) A: 지금 당장은 아니야. 다 읽으면 알려 줘.

(d) B: 물론, 그렇게.

해설 〈타동사 + 부사〉 형태의 타동사구의 목적어가 대명사일 경우에는 반드시 〈동사 + 대명사 + 부사〉의 어순을 써야 한다. 따라서 (b)의 give back it을 give it back으로 수정해야 한다. 참고로 명사일 경우에는 목적어의 위치가 자유롭다.

e.g. give the book back (○)

give back the book (○)

어휘 Sure thing. 물론이죠. 그럼요.

정답 (b) give back it → give it back

19 **해석** (a) 산을 트레킹하다가 부상을 당하면 여러분이라면 어떻게 하시겠습니까? (b) 22살의 파커가 바로 그 상황에 처해 있었습니다. (c) 절벽에 고립된 그녀는 가까스로 옷을 밧줄 하나에 묶을 수 있었는데, 그 밧줄이 구조대원들에게 그녀의 위치를 알려 줬습니다. (d) 그녀의 기발함이 그녀의 목숨을 구했던 것입니다.

해설 재귀대명사는 주어, 목적어를 강조하는 강조 용법과 타동사나 전치사의 목적어로 쓰이는 재귀적 용법으로 구분할 수 있다. 재귀대명사는 주어를 강조할 수는 있어도 주어로 쓸 수는 없다. 따라서 (a)의 yourself를 you were로 고쳐야 한다. 주절이 〈조동사 과거 + 동사원형〉 형태의 가정법 과거 시제이므로 if절도 과거동사를 써 you are가 아니라 you were가 되어야 한다. 참고로 (a)에서 그냥 yourself를 삭제해도 부사절 축약 구문이 되어 올바른 문장이 될 수 있다.

어휘 trek (천천히 또는 고생하며) 여행하다, 전진하다

be trapped 꼼짝 못하게 되다

ingenuity 재간, 발명의 재주

정답 (a) yourself → you were

20 **해석** (a) 페인트 속에 납 성분을 함유한 것으로 밝혀진 장난감들의 대량 리콜 사태가 업계 전반에 걸쳐 논란을 불러일으켰다. (b) 장난감 수입업자와 소매업자들은 그들의 상품들 중에 아이들의 건강에 위험한 상품이 혹시 있는지 알아보기 위해 재고 상품들을 정밀 검사하고 있다. (c) 성탄절 쇼핑 시즌이 임박함에 따라 부모들은 자녀들이 갖고 노는 장난감의 안전에 대해 유난히 걱

정하게 되었다. (d) 중국이 특히 비난의 표적이 되었는데, 중국은 그 문제의 장난감들을 가장 많이 생산하는 나라이기 때문이다.

해설 관계대명사는 접속사와 대명사의 역할을 동시에 하는 접속사이다. (b)의 any of 뒤에 쓰인 소유격 관계대명사 whose는 앞에 선행사도 없고, 문장과 문장을 연결하는 역할을 하고 있는 것도 아니므로 쓰임이 잘못되었다. 따라서 whose를 importers와 retailers를 받는 일반 소유격 대명사 their로 고쳐야 한다.

어휘 massive 대규모의
recall (불량 제품의) 회수, 리콜
spark a controversy 논란을 야기하다
importer 수입업자
retailer 소매업자, 소매상인
scrutinize 면밀히 조사하다, 검사하다
inventory 재고
determine 알아보다
pose a risk to ~를 위험하게 하다
loom (불안, 근심 등이) 다가오다

정답 (b) whose → their

Chapter 14 비교

Actual Test

1 **해석** A: 이 사과 사지 말자. 돈을 조금만 더 주면 유기농 사과를 살 수 있어.

B: 왜? 유기농 사과가 화학비료와 농약으로 기른 사과보다 더 영양가가 있는 거야?

해설 비교구문에서 비교 대상은 동일해야 하고, 반복되는 명사를 대신하는 대명사는 that과 those이다. apples가 반복되므로 apples를 대신하는 복수 명사 those를 써야 한다. 형용사구나 절의 한정을 받는 대명사에는 them을 쓸 수 없고 those를 써야 하므로 (a)와 (b)는 답이 될 수 없다. (c)는 문법적으로는 전혀 문제가 없지만 문맥에 맞지 않아 답이 될 수 없다. 따라서 정답은 (d) more nutritious than those가 정답이다.

어휘 organic 유기농의
nutritious 영양분이 있는
chemicals 화학약품

정답 (d)

2 **해석** A: 이 심리 연구에 따르면 여성이 남성보다 얘기를 3배 더 많이 하는 걸로 밝혀졌어.

B: 그걸 알아보려고 과학 연구까지 했단 말이야?

해설 배수사가 포함된 비교구문의 어순을 묻는 문제이다. 배수사가 포함된 비교구문에서 배수사는 비교급과 원급보다 항상 먼저 써야 하므로 (b) three times as much가 정답이다.

어휘 psychological study 심리 연구
determine 측정하다, 알아보다

정답 (b)

3 **해석** A: 금연 방법으로 니코틴 패치가 괜찮을까요?

B: 저에게는 금연 껌을 씹는 것이 패치를 사용하는 것보다 더 효과적이었어요.

해설 원급과 비교급의 기본 형태를 묻는 문제이다. 원급 비교는 〈as + 원급 + as〉 형태이고, 비교급 비교는 〈비교급 + than〉 형태이다. 따라서 정답은 (a) more effective than이다.

정답 (a)

4 **해석** A: 내 개그 공연 어땠니?

B: 지금껏 본 어느 코미디언 못지않게 재능이 있다는

생각이 들었어.

해설 '어느 ~ 못지않게 …한'의 뜻을 가진 원급 관련 관용 표현을 묻는 문제이다. 형용사 talented 뒤에 as any를 눈여겨본다면 쉽게 답을 구할 수 있다.

어휘 standup comedy 관객 앞에 서서 말로 하는 코미디, 개그

정답 (a)

5 해석 A: 마이클 W. 스미스는 현대 기독교 음악 부문에서 베스트셀러이자 가장 영향력 있는 음악가들 중 한 명이라고 생각해.
B: 맞아. 주류 음악 분야에서도 상당한 성공을 거뒀지.

해설 '가장 ~한 중에 하나'의 뜻을 가진 〈one of the + 최상급 + 복수 명사〉 구문과 최상급 뒤에 오는 전치사에 관련된 문제이다. of 뒤에는 동일 대상이 와야 하며 in 뒤에는 장소나 범위, 분야에 해당되는 명사가 와야 한다. comtemporary Christian music은 artist와 동일 대상이 아니라 범위나 분야에 해당되므로 전치사 in이 적절하다. 따라서 정답은 (d)이다.

어휘 influential 영향력 있는
contemporary 현대의, 동시대의
mainstream 주류의

정답 (d)

6 해석 A: 르로이와 샤나를 오늘 밤 우리랑 함께 가자고 초대해야 할까?
B: 물론. 많으면 많을수록 재미있으니까.

해설 '~하면 할수록 더욱더 …하다'라는 뜻의 〈the + 비교급 (+ S + V), the + 비교급 (+ S + V)〉 구문을 물어보는 문제이다. 형용사 merry의 비교급 형태는 merrier이므로 정답은 (b) The more, the merrier.이다.

정답 (b)

7 해석 A: 누가 게임 쇼에서 가장 일등할 것 같니?
B: 단연코 진이야. 다른 어떤 참가자보다 더 많은 재능이 있어.

해설 비교급으로 최상급을 나타내는 최상급 구문으로는 〈비교급 + than + any other + 단수 명사〉 또는 〈비교급 + than + all the other + 복수 명사〉의 형태를 쓰므로 (a) any other contestant가 정답이다. 그 밖의 최상급의 의미를 나타내는 구문도 알아 둘 필요가 있다.

e.g. No other contestant has more talent than she. = No other contestant has as much talent as she.

어휘 contestant (대회) 참가자, 출전자

정답 (a)

8 해석 A: 새로 나온 음악 편집 소프트웨어 프로그램 어땠니?
B: 사용자 편의성 측면에서 볼 때 새로 나온 버전이 처음 나온 버전에 비해 떨어져.

해설 형용사 inferior는 라틴계 비교급 형용사이다. 라틴계 비교급 형용사 뒤에는 '~보다'라는 의미의 전치사로 than 대신 to를 써야 하므로 (b) to가 정답이다.

어휘 user-friendliness 사용자 편의성

정답 (b)

9 해석 A: 베이커 씨가 심장병에 걸렸다는 소문에 대해 한 말씀 해주시겠습니까?
B: 걱정할 게 없습니다. 베이커 씨는 변함없이 건강합니다.

해설 문맥상 여느 때만큼이나 건강하다는 의미가 빈칸에 들어가야 하는데, 빈칸 뒤에 원급 표현을 나타내는 as가 있으므로 원급을 나타내는 (a) as healthy가 빈칸에 가장 알맞다. 참고로 〈as + 원급 + as ever〉는 '매우 ~하다'라는 뜻의 원급 관련 관용구문이다.

어휘 comment on ~에 대해 의견을 말하다
speculation 추측
heart condition 심장 질환, 심장병

정답 (a)

10 해석 비록 속편으로 나온 두 작품 모두 재미있었지만 첫 번째 영화가 전체 3부작 중에서 가장 인상적이다.

해설 trilogy는 '3부작'이라는 뜻이다. 비교 대상이 둘일 경우(of the two movies) 둘 중에서 더 인상적인 작품은 the more impressed로 표현하지만, 비교 대상이 셋 이상일 경우에는 최상급을 써야 한다. 따라서 빈칸에는 (c) the most impressive가 가장 알맞다.

어휘 sequel 속편
entertaining 재미있는
trilogy 3부작, 3부극

정답 (c)

11 해석 언어를 더 많이 연습하면 할수록 더욱더 이해하기 쉬워진다.

해설 '〜하면 할수록 더욱더 …하다' 라는 뜻으로 해석되는 〈the + 비교급 + S + V, the + 비교급 + S + V〉 구문을 물어보는 문제이다. 따라서 빈칸에는 〈the + 비교급〉의 형태인 (c) the easier가 가장 알맞다. 참고로 주어 it은 the language를 가리키고, becomes는 연결 동사, the easier는 주격 보어에 해당된다.

정답 (c)

12 해석 처방전 알약들은 광고에서 묘사하는 것만큼 효과가 없다.

해설 원급 비교의 기초적인 형태와 부정부사 rarely의 위치를 물어보는 문제이다. 부정부사 rarely는 부정어 not의 위치와 동일하므로 동사 are 바로 다음에 써야 한다. 원급 비교는 〈as + 형용사/부사의 원급 + as〉의 형태를 취한다. 따라서 빈칸에는 (b) rarely as effective가 가장 적절하다.

어휘 **prescription pill** 처방전이 필요한 알약, 전문 의약품
portray 묘사하다, 그리다

정답 (b)

13 해석 그녀의 정원에 있는 채소들이 내 정원의 채소들보다 두 배 빨리 자랐다.

해설 배수사가 포함된 비교급 구문에 관한 어순 문제이다. 비교급에 배수 표현을 함께 나타낼 때는 〈배수사 + 비교급 구문〉의 어순이 되어야 한다. 따라서 (a) twice as fast as가 빈칸에 가장 적절하다. 참고로 twice나 half의 경우에는 보통 그 뒤에 〈as + 원급 + as〉가 이어지지만 three times와 ten times 등의 배수사는 〈as + 원급 + as〉뿐 아니라 〈비교급 + than〉을 사용할 수도 있고, 원급과 비교급 사이에 의미 차이가 없다.

e.g. The vegetables in her garden grew three times faster than the ones in mine.

정답 (a)

14 해석 직접 연구하는 것이 간접적인 참고 문헌에 의존하는 것보다 더 효과적이다.

해설 비교구문에서의 병렬 구조를 묻는 문제이다. 비교구문에서도 비교 대상은 대등하고 동일한 문법 구조를 가지고 있어야 한다. 앞부분에 **more effective**가 있으므로 **than**이 있어야 하고, to부정사인 **to conduct**와 병렬 구조가 되어야 하므로 빈칸에는 (b) **than to rely**가 가장 적절하다.

어휘 **conduct** (일, 연구 따위를) 실시하다
directly 직접적으로
rely on 의존하다
second-hand 간접적인
reference 참고 문헌

정답 (b)

15 해석 마가렛은 우리 반에서 다른 어떤 학생보다 더 열심히 공부한다.

해설 비교급으로 최상급을 나타내는 비교구문을 묻는 문제이다. 비교급으로 최상급을 표현하는 최상급 구문으로는 〈주어 + 비교급 + than + any other + 단수 명사〉와 〈주어 + 비교급 + than + all the other + 복수 명사〉 형태가 대표적이다. 따라서 (c) any other student가 정답이다. 참고로 〈부정 주어 + 비교급〉 형태로 최상급을 표현하는 방법도 있다. *e.g.* No (other) student in my class studies harder than Magarette.

정답 (c)

16 해석 (a) A: 방문해서 저희 가족들을 보셔서 너무 기쁩니다.
(b) B: 자녀분들이 모두 아주 귀엽군요.
(c) A: 애나는 아주 영리한 아이죠, 그렇지 않나요?
(d) B: 맞아요. 아이들 중에 가장 영리한 것 같아요.

해설 (d)에서 smartest가 of the bunch의 한정을 받고 있으므로 smartest 뒤에 명사 one이나 girl이 생략되어 있다고 볼 수 있다. 명사를 수식하는 형용사의 최상급 앞에는 반드시 the를 붙여야 하는데, the를 쓰지 않는 경우는 소유격이 붙은 경우밖에 없다. (*e.g.* my best friend) 따라서 최상급 형용사 smartest 앞에 the를 붙여야 한다. 참고로 부사의 최상급 앞에는 the를 쓰지 않아도 된다.

어휘 **adorable** 사랑스런, 귀여운
bunch 무리, 떼

정답 (d) smartest → the smartest

17 해석 (a) A: 폴에 대해 어떻게 생각하니?
(b) B: 좋은 사람이지만 목수로서 돈을 많이 벌진 못할 거야.
(c) A: 솔직히 나에게 있어서 돈은 다른 사람들보다는 덜 중요해.
(d) B: 음, 네가 행복하기만 하다면야 돈은 문제가 되지 않는다고 생각해.

해설 기초적인 비교급 형태를 묻는 문제이다. 열등 비교를
나타낼 때 '~보다 덜'의 뜻으로 〈less + 형용사/부사
의 원급 + than〉 형태를 쓴다. 따라서 '덜 중요하다'
고 할 때는 less important로 표현해야 하므로 (c)의
lesser를 less로 고쳐야 한다.

어휘 carpenter 목수
frankly 솔직히
suppose 추측하다, 생각하다

정답 (c) lesser → less

18 해석 (a) A: 고속도로에서 차가 막혔어.
(b) B: 그것 때문에 운전이 어려웠니?
(c) A: 되돌아오는 데 시간이 두 배나 걸렸어!
(d) B: 운전이 지루했겠구나.

해설 비교급 구문에서 배수사의 위치에 관한 문제이다. 비
교급에 배수 표현(twice, three times)을 함께 나타
낼 때는 〈배수사 + as + 형용사/부사 + as〉 또는 〈배
수사 + 비교급 + than〉의 어순이 되어야 한다. 따라
서 (c)의 as twice long은 twice as long으로 수정
되어야 한다. 참고로 〈as + 원급 + as〉 구문에서 문
맥상 무엇과 비교하는지 명확할 경우에는 두 번째 as
를 생략하기도 한다. 위 문장에서는 as usual이 생략
되어 있다고 볼 수 있다.
e.g. It took us twice as long (as usual) to get
back.

정답 (c) as twice long → twice as long

19 해석 (a) 인사는 아랍어를 쓰는 나라들의 가장 중요한 사회
적 측면들 중 하나이다. (b) 모로코에서 사람들은 서로
의 건강, 가족, 자녀에 대한 일련의 질문들로 인사를
시작한다. (c) 누군가와 만나거나 헤어질 때는 악수도
해야 한다. (d) 악수를 하고 나서는 존중의 표시로 오
른손을 가슴에 대는 것이 관례이다.

해설 최상급 구문의 형태를 묻는 문제이다. '가장 ~한 중에
하나'의 뜻으로 해석되는 비교구문은 〈one of the +
최상급 + 복수 명사〉의 형태를 취하므로 (a)의 one
of most significant social aspect를 one of
the most significant social aspects로 고쳐야
옳다.

어휘 greeting 인사
significant 중요한
shake hands 악수하다
depart 헤어지다, 작별하다

common 일반적인, 통례의, 흔한

정답 (a) most significant social aspect
→ the most significant social aspects

20 해석 구멍가게가 대형 매장에 의해 급속도로 사라지고 있
다. (b) 이러한 거대 매장들은 무한한 상품의 진열을
자랑한다. (c) 규모의 경제 덕분에 대형 매장은 또한
영세 상점보다 더 싼 가격을 제공할 수 있다. (c) 그럼
에도 불구하고 일부 사람들은 구멍가게가 지역에 가져
왔던 공동체가 사라지는 것을 슬퍼한다.

해설 비교급의 올바른 형태를 물어보는 문제이다. 비교급
비교에서 '~보다'의 뜻을 가진 than 앞에는 원급이
아니라 비교급이 와야 하므로 (c)에서 low를 lower
로 고쳐야 한다.

어휘 mom-and-pop shop 구멍가게, 자영 소매점
eclipse 가리다, 무색케 하다
superstore 대형 슈퍼마켓
megastore 거대 상점
boast 자랑하다, 뽐내다
array 진열
economy of scale 규모의 경제
bemoan 슬퍼하다, 개탄하다

정답 (c) low → lower

Actual Test

1 **해석** A: 뭘 해야 할지 모르겠어.

B: 그런 여가 시간이 있다면 난 어딘가로 여행을 갈 거야.

해설 주절의 동사 형태가 가정법 과거(would take)이므로 if절 역시 가정법 과거 시제에 맞게 과거 동사를 써서 정답은 (c) had이다.

정답 (c)

2 **해석** A: 신입 직원이 문제를 일으키고 있다고 말씀하셨죠?

B: 맞아요. 이렇게 행동할 줄 알았더라면 고용하지 않았을 거예요.

해설 주절의 동사 형태가 과거 사실의 반대를 가정하는 가정법 과거완료 형태인 wouldn't have hired이므로 if절의 동사 형태 역시 had p.p.가 들어간 가정법 과거완료가 되어야 한다. 따라서 정답은 if를 생략하고 어순을 도치한 (c) Had I known이다.

정답 (c)

3 **해석** A: 존이 프랜신의 결혼식에서 바보짓을 했어.

B: 그런 행동을 했다니 안 믿겨져. 내가 거기에 있었더라면 조용히 하라고 말했을 거야.

해설 가정법 과거완료와 도치를 물어보는 문제이다. 가정법에서 if를 생략하면 if절이 의문문 어순으로 도치되어야 하므로 (a)와 (b)는 일단 답에서 제외된다. 주절의 동사가 가정법 과거완료(would have told)이므로 if절 역시 가정법 과거완료 시제의 had p.p.가 들어간 (c) Had I been이 빈칸에 가장 알맞다.

어휘 **make a fool of oneself** 바보짓을 해서 웃음거리가 되다

정답 (c)

4 **해석** A: 마침내 빚을 청산했다니 잘됐구나.

B: 네 현명한 충고가 없었더라면 희망을 포기했을지도 몰라.

해설 현재 사실의 반대인 '～가 없다면'은 가정법 과거 형태인 〈If it were not for + 명사(구), 주어 + would + 동사원형〉으로 표현하고, 과거에 '～가 없었더라면'은 가정법 과거완료 형태인 〈If it had not been for + 명사(구), 주어 + would/could + have + p.p.〉 형태로 표현한다. 제시된 문제에서는 주절의 동사가

〈조동사 과거 + have + p.p.〉(might have given up)로 가정법 과거 형태이므로 if 종속절 역시 가정법 과거완료인 If it had not been for 형태여야 한다. if를 생략하면 도치가 되므로 정답은 (b) had it not been for your wise advice이다.

어휘 **get out of debt** 빚을 청산한다, 빚을 갚다

정답 (b)

5 **해석** A: 그들이 위급 상황에 좀 더 준비되어 있었더라면 많은 희생자들이 구출될 수 있었을 텐데.

B: 나도 알아. 참으로 부끄러운 일이야, 그치?

해설 가정법 과거완료의 형태를 묻는 문제이다. 〈If + 주어 + had p.p., 주어 + 조동사의 과거형 + have p.p.〉로 if절의 동사는 had p.p.의 과거완료형을, 주절은 〈조동사의 과거형 + have p.p.〉를 쓴다. 그러므로 빈칸에 알맞은 could have p.p.가 되어야 한다. 희생자들(victims)이 다른 사람들에 의해 '구출되는' 것이므로 수동 형태가 되어 (d)가 정답이다.

참고 가정법 과거: 현재 사실의 반대 상황이나 미래의 가능성이 희박한 상황을 가정

〈If + 주어 + 과거 동사/were, 주어 + would/could + 동사원형〉

가정법 과거완료: 과거 사실의 반대 상황을 가정

〈If + 주어 + had p.p., 주어 + would/could + have p.p.〉

정답 (d)

6 **해석** A: 여자 친구에게 전화해야 하는데. 저 전화 좀 써도 되겠니?

B: 그러지 마. 고장 났어. 이걸 사용해.

해설 would rather 뒤에 that 명사절이 올 때는 반드시 가정법 과거 시제로 써야 하므로 (b) didn't가 정답이다. I'd rather you didn't.는 요청이나 허락을 구하는 상대에게 거절하는 표현이다. 참고로 would rather 뒤에 절이 아닌 경우에는 동사원형을 써야 한다.

어휘 **out of service** 고장 난

정답 (b)

7 **해석** A: 내가 부자라면 더 인기가 있을까?

B: 아마도. 하지만 대부분의 친구 관계가 깊이가 없을 거야.

해설 if절의 주절이 〈조동사 과거 + 동사원형〉으로 현재 사

실의 반대 상황을 가정하는 가정법 과거 시제이므로 if
절 역시 가정법 과거 동사를 써야 한다. 따라서 정답
은 (d) were이다.

어휘 friendship 우정, 친구 관계
superficial 피상적인, 깊이가 없는, 수박 겉 핥기
식의

정답 (d)

8 **해석** A: 내가 지도를 챙겨 왔어야 했는데.
B: 그랬더라면 좋았을 텐데. 그럼 지금 길을 잃어버리
지는 않았을 거야.

해설 I wish 뒤에 that 명사절은 항상 가정법 시제만을 써
야 한다. 현재 사실의 반대 상황을 소망하면 과거 동
사를 쓰고, 과거에 있었던 반대 상황을 가정하면 과거
완료를 쓴다. 지도를 가져오지 않은 것은 과거 사실이
므로 과거 사실의 반대를 가정하는 가정법 과거완료
시제가 적절하다. 따라서 빈칸에는 had brought
the map with us를 받는 대동사 (a) had가 가장
적절하다.

정답 (a)

9 **해석** 제 비서가 더 자세한 정보가 필요하면 당신에게 연락
할 것입니다.

해설 미래의 불확실한 상황을 가정하는 조건문에서 if절의
동사 시제를 물어보는 문제이다. 미래의 불확실한 상
황을 가정할 경우 주절이 〈조동사 + 동사원형〉(will
contact)이면 if절은 동사 현재형이나 가정법 미래
시제인 〈should + 동사원형〉 둘 중 하나의 형태가 가
능하다. 시간이나 조건의 부사절에서는 미래의 뜻이더
라도 현재 시제를 써야 하므로 (c) will need는 답이
될 수 없음에 유의한다. 따라서 정답은 (b) needs이
다.

어휘 secretary 비서
contact 연락하다

정답 (b)

10 **해석** 정부는 일본에 거주하고 있는 모든 뉴질랜드 국민들에
게 그들 대사관에 등록하라고 부탁했다.

해설 요구(demand), 주장(insist), 제안(suggest,
recommend, propose) 등의 동사 다음의 명사절
(that절)이 '~해야 한다'는 내용의 당위절일 경우
that절의 동사는 〈(should +) 동사원형〉을 써야 하므
로 (c) register가 가장 알맞다.

어휘 register with ~에 등록하다
embassy 대사관

정답 (c)

11 **해석** 네가 작업하고 있는 프로젝트의 마감이 연기되어서 오
늘 끝낼 필요가 없어.

해설 〈It is + 형용사(necessary, important, imperative,
essential, vital, natural) + that 명사절〉 형태의
가주어 진주어 구문에서 that 명사절이 '~해야 한다'
는 내용의 당위절일 경우 that절의 동사는 〈(should +)
동사원형〉을 쓰므로 정답은 (a) finish이다.

어휘 work on 작업하다, 작성하다

정답 (a)

12 **해석** 만약 내가 차 사고를 당하지 않았더라면 병원에서 네
어머니를 절대로 만나지 못했을 것이다.

해설 주절이 〈조동사 과거 + have + p.p.〉(would have
never met) 형태인 것으로 보아 과거에 있었던 상황
의 반대를 가정하는 가정법 과거완료임을 알 수 있다.
가정법 과거완료 시제에서 if절은 동사가 과거완료
(had + p.p.) 형태이므로 (a) hadn't been이 가장
알맞다.

정답 (a)

13 **해석** 당신이 보고서의 오류를 제게 지적해 주시지 않았더라
면 그런 당황스런 오류가 실린 채 보고서가 출간되었
을 거예요.

해설 가정법 과거완료와 도치에 관한 문제이다. 주절이
would have been published로 과거 사실의 반대
를 가정하는 가정법 과거완료 시제이므로 if 종속절의
동사 형태 역시 과거 사실의 반대를 가정하는 〈had +
p.p.〉가 되어야 한다. 빈칸 뒤에 〈주어 + p.p.〉가 이
어지고 있으므로 접속사 if가 생략된 형태라고 볼 수
있다. if 가정법에서 접속사 if가 생략될 경우에는 도치
가 되어야 하므로 (d) Had가 정답이다.

어휘 alert ~에게 주의를 주다, 주의를 환기하다
flaw 결함, 오류

정답 (d)

14 **해석** 네가 새로운 일을 하느라 바쁘다는 건 알지만 적어도
가끔씩은 나랑 함께 커피 한잔 정도는 마시도록 하자.

해설 제안 동사 suggest 다음에 이어지는 that 명사절의
내용이 '~해야 한다'는 의미의 당위절일 경우에 that

절의 동사는 《(should +) 동사원형》을 써야 하므로
정답은 (c) have이다.

정답 (c)

15 해석 내가 그 비행기를 탔더라면 나는 지금 죽어 있을 거야.

해설 혼합가정법과 도치를 물어보는 문제이다. 화자는 그
비행기를 과거에 타지 않았기 때문에 지금 살아 있다
는 사실에서 반대의 상황을 가정하고 있다. 즉 if절은
과거 사실의 반대를, 주절은 현재 사실의 반대를 가정
하고 있는 혼합가정법이므로 (a) Had I boarded가
정답이다. 원래의 if절은 If I had boarded that
plane이었는데 if를 생략하면 도치가 되어야 한다. 참
고로 혼합가정법은 주절에 now, today, like this
등의 부사 어구가 나와 있는 경우가 일반적이다.

어휘 board 탑승하다

정답 (a)

16 해석 그 집값이 그렇게 많이 올라갈 줄 알았더라면 우리는
그 집을 팔지 않았을 것이다.

해설 가정법의 시제와 if 생략에 따른 도치를 묻는 문제이
다. 일단 주절의 동사 형태가 과거 사실의 반대를 가
정하는 가정법 과거완료이므로 if절 역시 과거 사실의
반대를 가정하는 가정법 과거완료형(had known)이
와야 하며, if를 생략하면 도치가 되므로 정답은 (c)
Had we known이다.

정답 (c)

17 해석 (a) A: 마이크와 난 카누를 타러 가 강변에서 피크닉
을 했어.

(b) B: 아주 낭만적이네.

(c) A: 그리고 나서 야외 음악 콘서트에 갔는데 환상적
이었어.

(d) B: 우와. 내 남편도 그런 것들을 하면 정말 좋을
텐데.

해설 I wish 뒤에 절이 올 경우에는 무조건 가정법 시제만
와야 한다. 현재 사실의 반대를 소망하면 과거 동사를
쓰고, 과거 사실의 반대를 소망하면 과거완료형을 쓴
다. B의 남편은 A의 남편인 마이크처럼 카누를 타러
가고, 야외 콘서트를 가는 등 그런 여가 활동을 하지
않기 때문에 B가 그 반대의 상황, 현재 사실의 반대
상황을 소망하고 있으므로 do를 did로 고쳐야 한다.

정답 (d) do → did

18 해석 (a) A: 내일 큰 시험이 있는데 공부하고 있어야 하지
않니?

(b) B: 응, 하지만 운동을 하고 나면 정말 공부가 더
잘되거든.

(c) A: 음, 꾸물대고 있는 것이 아니길 바라.

(c) B: 내가 너라면 다른 사람의 일에 상관하지 않을
거야.

해설 if 가정법에서 현재 사실의 반대나 미래의 실현 가능성
이 아주 희박한 상황을 가정할 때, if절은 과거 동사를
쓰고 주절은 《조동사 과거형 + 동사원형》의 형태를 써
야 한다. (d)에서 if절이 현재 사실의 반대를 가정하는
가정법 과거 시제이므로 주절 역시 《조동사 과거형 +
동사원형》의 형태가 되어야 한다. 따라서 will을
would로 고쳐야 한다.

어휘 workout 운동

procrastinate 꾸물거리다, 늦장 부리다

stay out of one's business ～의 일에 상관하
지 않다

정답 (d) will → would

19 해석 (a) 지금보다 운전을 줄여야 할 많은 큰 이유들이 있
다. (b) 그중 한 가지 이유는 도로에 차가 줄어들면 사
고가 줄어들 것이기 때문이다. (c) 비록 일시적이지만
운전을 삼가면 (대기) 오염 수치에 상당한 영향을 미칠
것이다. (d) 이렇게 함으로써 우리의 폐는 좋아지고 우
리는 기름 값을 절약하게 된다.

해설 (c)의 Should we abstain from driving은 《If + S
+ should + 동사원형》 형태의 가정법 미래의 if 조건
문에서 if를 생략하고 조동사와 주어가 도치된 문장 형
태이다. if절에 should가 들어간 가정법 미래의 주절
은 《조동사 과거형 + 동사원형》(would/could have)
이나 《조동사 + 동사원형》(will have) 둘 다 가능하
다. 참고로 조동사 없이 명령문의 형태도 아주 자주
쓰인다. 따라서 (c)에서 would have had를 will
have나 would have로 고쳐야 옳은 문장이 된다.

어휘 abstain from ～을 삼가다

temporarily 일시적으로

have a significant impact on ～에 상당한
영향을 미치다

benefit 이득을 보다, 이로움을 얻다

정답 (c) would have had

→ will have *or* would have

20 해석 (a) 여러분 자녀의 대학 학비를 위해 언제쯤 저축을 시작하는 게 좋을까요? (b) 많은 부모님들이 심지어 아이들이 태어나기도 전에 등록금을 위해 돈을 저축하기 시작했습니다. (a) 부모의 모든 의무들 중에 자녀에게 좋은 교육을 받을 수 있도록 해주는 것은 가장 중요한 것들 중 하나입니다. (d) 만약 여러분이 자녀를 갖고 싶다면 이 중요한 투자금을 어떻게 마련할지에 대해 신중하게 생각해 볼 필요가 있습니다.

해설 가정법은 현재나 과거 사실의 반대 상황을 가정할 때 써야 한다. (d)에서 아이를 갖기를 원하는 것은 현재 사실의 반대를 가정하는 것으로 볼 수 없으므로 가정법 과거 시제 대신 직설 조건문(단순 조건문)으로 써야 한다. 따라서 wanted를 want로 고쳐야 한다.

어휘 expense 경비, ~비
　　 tuition 등록금
　　 parental 부모로서의
　　 access 접근, 이용 권리

정답 (d) wanted → want

Chapter 16 접속사

Actual Test

1 해석 A: 날씨가 나빠도 여전히 호수에 가고 싶으신가요?
　　 B: 좋은 질문이군요.

해설 문맥상 빈칸에는 '비록 ~일지라도' 라는 양보의 의미를 가진 접속사가 필요하므로 (b) if가 정답이다. if는 가정의 뜻인 '~라면' 의 뜻뿐만 아니라 문맥에 따라 '만약 ~일지라도' 라는 양보적 의미의 접속사로도 쓰일 수 있다. 참고로 if 대신에 even if를 쓸 수도 있다.

정답 (b)

2 해석 A: 그람시의 새로 나온 책 어땠어?
　　 B: 너무나 흥미로운 읽을거리여서 두 번 읽었어.

해설 내용과 문법에 맞는 적절한 접속사를 고르는 문제이다. 문맥상 '너무 ~해서 …하다' 는 의미가 적절하므로 결과 부사절 접속사 that이 가장 알맞다. 결과 부사절을 나타내는 방법에는 〈such (+ 관사) (+ 형용사) + 명사 + that + S + V〉 형태와 〈so + 형용사/부사 + that + S + V〉 형태가 있다.

어휘 publication 출판(물), 간행(물)
　　 read 읽을거리

정답 (d)

3 해석 A: 남편분의 이상한 습관들에 대해 미리 알고 계셨나요?
　　 B: 아뇨. 함께 살게 되고 나서야 남편의 문제점들을 알게 되었어요.

해설 It ~ that 강조구문 안에 강조된 부사절을 완성하는 문제이다. 빈칸 앞에 부정어 wasn't를 놓치지 않는 것이 문제 해결의 결정적인 열쇠이다. 문맥상 '남편의 문제점들을 함께 살기 시작하기 전까지는 깨닫지 못했다.' 또는 '남편의 문제점들을 깨닫게 된 것은 동거를 하기 전까지는 아니었다.' 는 의미가 되어야 한다. 위 문장을 강조구문이 아니라 보통의 문장으로 풀어 쓰면 I did not grow aware of his problems until we moved in together.가 되고, 여기서 부정어 not과 until 이하의 부사절을 하나로 묶어 It ~ that 강조구문의 it과 that 사이에 넣어서 강조한 문장이 B가 말한 문장으로 제시된 것이다(It was not until we moved in together that I grew aware of his problems). 따라서 정답은 (a) until이다. '~하고 나서야 비로소 …하다' 의 뜻을 가진 〈It was not until ~ that S V〉 구문으로 암기하고 있어도 쉽게 풀 수 있다.

어휘 beforehand 미리

move in together 함께 살기 시작하다

정답 (a)

4 해석 A: 카일은 이번 여름에 디즈니랜드에 간다는 사실에
들떠 있는 게 분명해.

B: 많이는 아니야. 그의 아이디어이긴 했지만 별로 열
성적인 것 같지는 않아 보여.

해설 문장 구조상 빈칸은 부사절 접속사가 들어가야 하는
자리인데, 부사절의 내용(자신의 아이디어였다)이 주절
의 내용(별로 열성이 없어 보인다)과 대조를 이루고 있
으므로 양보적 의미의 접속사 (a) Even though가
빈칸에 가장 알맞다.

정답 (a)

5 해석 A: 댁의 아드님이 오늘 모욕적인 농담을 해서 반 친구
들을 화나게 했습니다.

B: 또요? 더 이상 나쁜 말을 하지 않도록 얘기를 해봐
야겠군요.

해설 B가 아들과 얘기해 보려고 하는 목적은 아들이 나쁜
말을 계속하지 않게 하기 위한 것이므로 빈칸에는
'~하기 위하여'라는 목적의 의미를 갖는 부사절 접속
사 (d) so that이 가장 알맞다. (c) in that은 '~라는
점에 있어서'라는 뜻으로 because와 같은 의미를
가지고 있다.

어휘 insulting 모욕적인, 무례한

mean 비열한, 상스러운

정답 (d)

6 해석 A: 저 그림들 인상적이야. 자레드는 상당한 재능을 가
지고 있어.

B: 그는 자신이 보고 있는 사물을 정교하게 그릴 수
있는 능력이 있어.

해설 문장 구조상 빈칸은 접속사 자리인데, 빈칸 뒤의 문장
이 불완전하므로 관계대명사 자리이다. 선행사가 없으
므로 선행사를 포함한 관계대명사 (d) what이 가장
알맞다. 참고로 detail은 with detail이라는 부사구를
형성하므로 빈칸 이하의 관계사절의 수식을 받는 선행
사가 아님에 주의해야 한다. what he is looking at
은 draw의 목적어로 쓰인 명사절이다.

어휘 with precise detail 정교하게, 정확하고 치밀하게

정답 (d)

7 해석 A: 셀라는 공부를 열심히 하지 않음에도 불구하고 전
과목 A학점을 받아.

B: 나도 알아. 그녀의 비결을 알고 싶어.

해설 빈칸은 문장 구조상 접속사 자리이다. 공부를 열심히
하지 않는 것과 전 과목에서 A학점을 받는다는 것은
대조적인 내용이므로 (b) even though가 문맥상 가
장 자연스럽다. 참고로 (d) as if는 '마치 ~인양'의 뜻
을 가진 접속사이고, (a) even은 접속사가 아니라 부
사이다.

어휘 straight A's 전 과목 A학점

정답 (b)

8 해석 A: 나는 그가 그 자리에 뽑히지 않았다는 사실에 정말
놀랐어.

B: 몇몇 사람들은 너랑 의견이 다른 것 같던데.

해설 문장 구조상 빈칸은 명사절을 이끄는 접속사가 들어가
야 할 자리이다. 빈칸 뒤의 문장이 완전한 절이므로
(b) Which와 (c) What은 답이 될 수 없으며, 문장의
내용상 (a) That이 가장 자연스럽다. 사람이 놀라는
것은 어떤 사실에 놀라는 것이지 이유에 놀라는 것은
아니므로 (d)는 의미상 답이 될 수 없다.

정답 (a)

9 해석 A: 데이브는 정원에서 일하는 걸 별로 좋아하지 않을
거야.

B: 좋든 싫든 하게 될 거야. 그건 그의 직업인걸.

해설 빈칸에 알맞은 접속사를 고르는 문제이다. that, if,
whether는 명사절의 종속접속사로 주어, 목적어, 보
어로 쓰이는 명사절을 이끌 수 있다. 또한 if와
whether는 둘 다 의문사가 없는 간접의문문을 이끌
수도 있다. 예를 들어 직접의문문 He asked her,
"Are you tired?"를 간접의문문으로 바꾼 He
asked her if/whether she was tired.에서는 if와
whether가 모두 가능하다. 하지만 if가 아니라 반드
시 whether를 써야 하는 경우들이 있다. 첫째는 부
정사 앞에서이다. I don't know whether to laugh
or cry.(웃어야 할지 울어야 할지 모르겠다.)라고 할
때는 if 대신 whether를 쓴다. 둘째, 전치사 뒤에서도
if 대신 whether를 쓰는데, 예를 들어 I have my
doubts about whether he's telling me the
truth.(나는 그가 나에게 진실을 말하는지 의심이 간
다.)라고 할 때 whether는 if로 대체할 수 없다.

정답 (a)

10 해석 나는 그 영화를 볼 생각이 없으며 내 아이들이 나가서
그 영화를 보는 것도 원하지 않는다.

해설 문장 구조상 빈칸은 접속사 자리이므로 부사인 (c)
neither와 (d) never는 답에서 제외된다. 빈칸 뒤가
의문문의 어순으로 도치되어 있다는 점과 문맥상 and
와 not이 합쳐진 부정의 의미를 가진 접속사가 필요
하므로 (b) nor가 가장 알맞다. 참고로 nor는 and
neither로 바꿔 쓸 수 있으므로 (c)가 and neither
라면 답이 될 수 있다.

정답 (b)

11 해석 그가 우리에게 자신의 계획에 대해서 통보조차 하지
않았다는 사실이 매우 실망스럽다.

해설 전체 문장의 동사가 was이므로 빈칸부터 plans까지
는 전체 문장의 주어에 해당된다고 볼 수 있다. 빈칸
에 접속사와 주어를 넣어서 명사절이 되어야 한다. 일
단 (d)는 접속사가 없고, (c)의 because는 부사절 접
속사이므로 답에서 제외된다. (a)의 what과 (b)의
that 모두 명사절을 이끌 수 있지만, what은 의문대
명사가 되든 관계대명사가 되든 뒤에는 항상 불완전한
절이 이어져야 하므로 답이 될 수 없다. 따라서 정답
은 (b) That he이다.

어휘 notify 통지하다, 알리다

정답 (b)

12 해석 많은 문제들에 대한 그녀의 의견과 통찰력을 존중하지
만, 나는 그녀가 유독 이 문제 하나에 대해서는 잘못
된 분석을 하고 있다는 생각이 들었다.

해설 문장 구조상 빈칸은 부사절 접속사가 들어갈 자리이
다. 선택지 네 개 모두 부사절 접속사이므로 부사절과
주절이 어떤 관계인지 파악해서 문맥에 맞는 접속사를
골라 넣어야 하는데, 부사절의 내용과 주절의 내용이
서로 대조를 이루고 있으므로 (d) While이 가장 알맞
다.

어휘 insight into ~에 대한 통찰력
issue 문제
flawed 잘못된, 결함 있는

정답 (d)

13 해석 내 생각에 UFO에 대해서 그 농담을 한 사람은 바로
빌 힉스였다.

해설 It ~ that 강조구문에서 that은 상황에 따라 관계대명
사나 관계부사로 바꾸어 쓸 수 있다. 선택지 네 개 모

두 관계대명사 who 또는 whom으로 시작되기 때문
에 먼저 격을 구분해야 하는데, 삽입절 I believe는
관계대명사 바로 뒤에 쓰며, 격을 구분할 때는 I
believe 뒤부터 따져야 한다. had told의 주체는 I가
아니라 Bill Hiks이므로 I believe 뒤에 연결되어야
내용상 자연스럽다. 정답은 (b) who I believe had
told that joke이다. 참고로 삽입절이 까다롭게 느껴
지면 삽입절이 없다고 생각하고 격 구분과 어순을 배
열하고 나서 관계대명사 바로 뒤에 I believe를 삽입
하는 방법도 있다.

정답 (b)

14 해석 마감일 전에 학기말 보고서를 제출하세요. 그렇지 않
으면 성적이 10점 감점될 것입니다.

해설 명령문 뒤에 and는 '~해라, 그러면'의 뜻이고, or는
'~해라, 그렇지 않으면'의 뜻이다. 빈칸 뒤의 내용이
앞 문장의 반대 급부를 제시하고 있으므로 '그렇지 않
으면'의 뜻인 (c) or가 빈칸에 가장 알맞다.

어휘 hand in 제출하다
final paper 학기말 보고서

정답 (c)

15 해석 내가 비록 로만 폴란스키의 열성팬이긴 하지만 오늘
영화 보고 싶은 기분이 아니다.

해설 누구의 열성팬이라는 것과 영화를 보고 싶지 않은 것
은 서로 상반되는 대조 관계이므로 양보의 의미를 가
진 접속사 (a) Although가 빈칸에 가장 자연스럽다.

어휘 feel like -ing ~하고 싶은 기분이 들다
provided ~라면(= if)

정답 (a)

16 해석 다른 사람들과 함께 음식을 먹는 동안 트림하는 것은
무례한 것으로 여겨진다.

해설 문맥에 알맞은 접속사를 고르는 문제이다. eating은
현재분사이고, 문맥상 명백한 의미상 주어 you와 진
행의 be동사인 are가 생략된 분사구문이라고 볼 수
있으므로 빈칸은 분사구문의 뜻을 명확하게 해주는 접
속사가 들어갈 자리이다. 의미상 트림하는 것은 비교
적 짧은 동작이고, 음식을 먹는 행위는 비교적 긴 동
작이다. 영어에서는 동시에 발생하는 2개의 행위를 묘
사할 때, 배경이 되는 긴 동작은 진행형으로 표현하는
데, 이때 진행형이 쓰인 절에 주로 '~하는 동안'의 의
미를 가진 접속사 while을 쓴다. 따라서 정답은 (d)

while이다.

어휘 burp 트림하다

정답 (d)

17 해석 (a) A: 시간이 많이 늦었어. 빨리 텐트를 쳐야 해.

(b) B: 응, 맞아, 풀이 없는 평평한 장소를 찾아봐.

(c) A: 오늘 밤 동물들이 우리를 성가시게 할까?

(d) B: 텐트 바깥에 음식을 두지만 않으면 괜찮을 거야.

해설 접속사 what과 that을 구분하는 문제이다. 둘 다 명사절을 이끌 수 있지만, what은 의문사이건 관계대명사이건 뒤에 불완전한 절이 이어진다. 반면 명사절 접속사 that 뒤에는 주어, 목적어, 보어가 빠지지 않은 완전한 절이 이어진다. (c)는 what 뒤에 완전한 문장이 왔으므로 what을 that으로 고쳐야 옳은 문장이 된다.

어휘 set up 설치하다

flat 평평한

clear of ~이 없는

vegetation 식물

정답 (c) what → that

18 해석 (a) A: 우리가 아는 사람 중에 누가 스페인어를 할 줄 알지?

(b) B: 음, 탐과 제프 둘 다 스페인어를 할 수 있을 거 같은데.

(c) A: 정말? 걔네들이 내가 이 보고서 작성하는 걸 도와줄 수 있을까?

(d) B: 둘 중 한 명은 분명히 도와줄 수 있을 거야.

해설 상관접속사를 물어보는 문제이다. both는 and와 연결되어 both A and B 구조로 쓰이므로 (b)의 or를 and로 고쳐야 한다.

정답 (b) or → and

19 해석 (a) 심하게 스트레스를 받으면 "투쟁 또는 도피" 반응이라 불리는 신체 반응이 일어난다. (b) 이 반응은 우리의 두뇌에 박혀 있으며, 우리를 위험으로부터 보호하기 위해 고안된 생물학적 반사 작용이다. (c) 본질적으로, 투쟁 또는 도피 반응은 우리를 "공격" 모드로 이끌면서 우리의 이성적인 마음보다 우선한다. (d) 우리의 공포는 과장되고, 우리의 생각은 왜곡되어서 결국 우리는 위험이 되지 않는 상황에 과잉 반응하게 된다.

해설 접속사와 전치사의 구분을 묻는 문제이다. 전치사 뒤에는 명사 상당 어구가 와야 하며, 접속사 뒤에는 주어와 동사가 있는 절이 오거나 주어와 동사가 축약된 분사구문이 이어질 수 있다. (c)에서 moving us into "attack mode"는 분사구문이므로 during을 접속사 while로 고쳐야 한다. while it is moving us into "attack" mode에서 it is를 축약한 형태이다.

어휘 bodily reaction 신체 반응

trigger 유발하다, 일으키다

hard-wired 굳어진, 고유한, 내장된

biological 생물학적인

reflex 반사 작용, 반사 행동

by its very nature 본질적으로

override ~에 우선하다, 앞서다

exaggerate 과장하다

distort 왜곡하다

overreact 과잉 반응하다

정답 (c) during → while

20 해석 (a) 프레더릭 더글라스는 노예 신분에서 저명한 작가이자 연설가, 운동가가 되었다. (b) 어린 시절 동안, 그는 주인에 의해 노예에게 행해지는 수많은 잔혹 행위들을 목격하였다. (c) 일단 노예 신분을 벗어나자 그는 노예제 철폐를 주장하는 신문을 출간했다. (d) 1863년에 노예제도가 폐지되었을 때 마침내 더글라스의 꿈은 이루어졌다.

해설 접속사의 올바른 쓰임을 묻는 문제이다. what 뒤에는 항상 불완전한 절이 이어져야 하는데, (d)에서 what 뒤에 완전한 절이 이어지고 있으므로 (d)는 접속사 what이 틀린 문장이다. 문맥상 what은 '~할 때'의 뜻을 가진 부사절 접속사 when이나 이유를 나타내는 because 정도로 수정되는 것이 의미상 자연스럽다.

어휘 salve 노예

renowned 저명한

activist 운동가

witness 목격하다

numerous 수많은

atrocity 만행, 잔학 행위

master 주인

slavery 노예제도

abolition 철폐, 폐지

fulfill 성취하다, 달성하다

abolish 철폐하다, 폐지하다

정답 (d) what → when *or* because

Actual Test

1 **해석** A: 이 문제 푸는 것 좀 도와줄 수 있겠니?

B: 도와주고 싶지만 약속 시간이 거의 다 되어서. 실은 정말로 가봐야 해.

해설 get은 다음에 동사원형을 취할 수 없으므로 (b) go는 정답이 될 수 없다. 상태의 변화를 나타내는 동사 get 뒤에 형용사가 와야 하므로 (a)와 (b)는 답에서 제외된다. '시작하다, 출발하다'라는 의미로 get 뒤에 going을 쓴다. 참고로 '~을 진행시키다'라는 의미로 〈get + 목적어 + going〉 형태를 쓰기도 한다.

e.g. I got the game going.

어휘 give *sb* a hand ~를 도와주다

get going 떠나다, 출발하다

정답 (c)

2 **해석** A: 날씬한 몸매를 유지하기 위해 뭘 하시나요?

B: 모르겠어요. 아마 좋은 유전자? 가족 내력인 거 같아요.

해설 '~은 가족 내력이다, 유전이다'라는 뜻의 영어 표현은 run in the family라고 하므로 (b) run in이 정답이다.

어휘 trim figure 날씬한 몸매

run in the family 가족 내력이다, 집안 유전이다

정답 (b)

3 **해석** A: 맛있는 저녁 식사 값을 내는 데 돈을 좀 보태고 싶어요.

B: 안 돼요. 저희가 당신을 초대한 겁니다. 이건 저희가 살게요.

해설 밥값을 보태겠다는 A의 제안에 B의 빈칸 뒤의 응답으로 초대한 건 우리이기 때문에 우리가 산다는 내용이 이어지고 있으므로 빈칸에는 부정의 응답이 문맥에 자연스럽다. 즉 빈칸 뒤의 내용으로 보아 B는 A의 제안을 거절했을 가능성이 크므로 거절의 표현인 (c) Certainly not.이 가장 알맞다.

어휘 This is our treat. 우리가 살게요.

정답 (c)

4 **해석** A: 마이클이 올해의 선수로 뽑혔어!

B: 설마!

해설 청해 파트 1에도 자주 등장하는 표현으로 믿기지 않거

나 놀라운 소식을 들었을 때 '설마!'의 뜻으로 쓰이는 관용 표현은 You don't say!이다.

어휘 You don't say! 설마!

정답 (d)

5 **해석** A: 차 좀 얻어 탈 수 있을까요?

B: 어디로 가시느냐에 달려 있죠.

해설 where 이하가 전치사 on의 명사절로 빈칸에는 〈주어 + 동사〉의 간접의문문 어순이 와야 하므로 (b)와 (d)는 답이 될 수 없다. 직접의문문에서 어디로 가느냐고 물어볼 때는 Where are you headed? 또는 Where are you heading?이라고 말하므로 정답은 (c) you are headed이다. (a) you were heading은 과거 진행형으로 시제가 틀렸다. you are heading이 되어야 답이 될 수 있다.

어휘 get a lift 차를 얻어 타다

정답 (c)

6 **해석** A: 제레미와 잠깐 얘기를 해야 해요.

B: 잠시 나갔는데 금방 돌아올 거예요.

해설 '돌아오다'라는 표현은 be back으로 쓰고 '곧, 금방'이라는 표현은 시간의 경과를 나타내는 전치사 in을 써서 in no time으로 쓰므로 정답은 (c) back in no time이다.

어휘 have a word with ~와 잠깐 얘기를 나누다

step outside 나가다

in no time 즉시, 곧

정답 (c)

7 **해석** A: 왜 나한테 전화하지 않았니?

B: 배터리가 나갔거든. 그래서 대신에 만나러 왔잖아.

해설 빈칸은 이유를 묻는 의문사가 들어갈 자리이다. 직접의문문에서 Why 뒤에는 〈동사 + 주어〉 형태의 일반적인 의문문 어순이 와야 하고, How come 뒤에는 의문문이지만 〈주어 + 동사〉순의 평서문 어순이 온다. 빈칸 뒤의 어순이 평서문 어순이므로 정답은 (a) How come이다.

어휘 come over 찾아오다, 건너오다

정답 (a)

8 **해석** A: 수염 깎았는데 나 어때?

B: 엄청 달라 보여!

해설 What 감탄문의 어순을 묻는 문제이다. How로 시작

되는 감탄문은 〈How + 형용사 (+ 관사) (+ 명사)〉의
어순이고, What으로 시작되는 감탄문은 〈What (+
관사) (+ 형용사) + 명사〉의 어순을 취한다.
difference는 원래는 추상명사지만 감탄문에서는 보
통명사화되어 가산명사로 쓰이므로 부정관사 a가 필
요하다. 따라서 정답은 (d) What a이다. 참고로
How 뒤에는 반드시 형용사나 부사가 이어져야 한다.
형용사나 부사 없이 명사만 이어질 경우에는 반드시
What 감탄문만 써야 한다.

어휘 beard 턱수염

정답 (d)

9 **해석** A: 이번 주말에 도니의 결혼식이 있어.

B: 결혼식 얘기가 나온 김에 하는 말인데, 난 못 갈 거
같아.

해설 대화 중에 상대방의 말에서 특정 어구나 명사를 관계
대명사 which로 받아서 Speaking of which로 표
현하곤 하는데 우리말로는 '얘기가 나와서 하는 말인
데, 말 나온 김에 하는 말인데' 정도로 해석하면 된다.

어휘 speaking of which 얘기가 나와서 하는 말인데
make it 출석하다, 참석하다

정답 (d)

10 **해석** A: 있잖아! 하와이행 공짜 티켓 두 장이 생겼어.

B: 이봐 그만 좀 해. 나 놀리는 거지!

해설 상대방이 한 말이 도저히 믿겨지지 않을 때 '설마 농
담이겠지! 놀리는 거지?' 라는 표현은 현재 진행형의
형태인 You're pulling my leg!로 표현한다. 현재
속이고 있는 상황이라 현재 진행형을 쓰는 것으로 이
해해도 된다.

어휘 Give me a break! 그만 좀 해!
pull one's leg ~를 놀리다, 속이다

정답 (d)

11 **해석** A: 레오가 5월에 여기로 온대.

B: 알아. 빨리 그를 보고 싶어 죽겠어.

해설 '몹시 ~하고 싶다, ~하는 것이 몹시 기다려지다' 라는
뜻으로 〈I can't wait to + 동사원형〉을 관용적으로
쓴다.

어휘 come into town 방문하다, 이리로 오다

정답 (b)

12 **해석** 아침 식사로 차와 주스 같은 것을 마셔 봤지만 뜨거운
커피 한 잔만큼 아침 일찍 나를 움직이게 만드는 것은
정말 없어.

해설 〈get + 사람 + to부정사〉라고 판단해서 (c)를 답으로
고르기 쉬운 문제이다. '(사람)을 ~하도록 자극하다,
움직이게 만들다, ~을 계속 움직이게 하다' 라는 뜻으
로는 관용적으로 〈get + 사람 + going〉의 형태를 쓴
다. 여기서 going은 '활동 중인, 진행 중인' 의 뜻을
가진 하나의 형용사로 간주하면 된다.

어휘 get *sb* going ~를 움직이도록 자극하다

정답 (d)

13 **해석** 내가 보이 스카우트 캠프에서 돌아온 후, 아버지는 몇
가지 기술들을 가르쳐 달라고 부탁을 하셨는데, 소위
나의 제자가 된 셈이었다.

해설 문맥에 알맞은 적절한 삽입구를 물어보는 문제이다.
문장 중간이나 끝에 쓰여 우리말로 '소위, 이른바, 말
하자면' 의 뜻을 가진 삽입구는 as it were이다.

어휘 apprentice 견습생, 제자

정답 (c)

14 **해석** 나는 어학 강좌 하나를 등록했다. 하지만 좀 지루하다.

해설 '종류' 라는 뜻으로 쓰일 경우에는 kind가 가산명사이
므로 앞에 관사(a, the)나 지시형용사(this, that), 부
정형용사(every, each, all) 등이 반드시 붙어야 한
다. 하지만 형용사 앞에서 '조금, 약간' 의 뜻으로 형용
사를 수식할 경우에는 한정사 없이 항상 kind of 형태
로만 써야 한다. boring은 형용사이므로 (b) kind of
가 정답이다.

어휘 sign up for 등록하다, 신청하다

정답 (b)

15 **해석** 정원이 어때 보여요? 가꾸는 데 많은 시간이 걸렸어요.

해설 상대방의 의견이나 느낌을 물을 때 자주 쓰이는 표현
How do you like ~ ?를 묻는 문제이다. 정답은 (c)
How do you like the way이다. 여기서 How는 의
문부사이다. 참고로 관계부사 용법 중에서 선행사 the
way와 관계부사 how는 나란히 함께 쓸 수 없으므로
(a)는 답이 될 수 없다. how나 the way 둘 중에 하
나를 생략하면 (a)도 답이 될 수 있다.

어휘 tend 돌보다, 가꾸다

정답 (c)

16 해석 (a) A: 기분이 안 좋아 보이네. 무슨 문제라도 있는 거
니?

(b) B: 어제 또 이반한테 바람맞았어.

(c) A: 뭐? 사과는 했니?

(d) B: 아니, 나 지금 정말 화났거든. 그에게 복수할
거야.

해설 〈타동사 + 부사〉 구조의 동사구 지식을 물어보는 문제
이다. '바람맞히다, 만날 약속을 어기다'는 stand up
이므로 (b)의 stood를 stood up으로 고쳐야 한다.

어휘 under the weather 좀 기분이 나쁜, 몸이 안 좋은
stand *sb* up ~를 바람맞히다
make *sb* pay for ~에게 대가를 치르게 하다, ~
에게 복수하다

정답 (b) stood → stood up

17 해석 (a) A: 전 이 집이 정말 맘에 드는군요.

(b) B: 그러시다니 기쁘네요.

(c) A: 둘러봐도 되겠습니까?

(d) B: 얼마든지요.

해설 〈타동사 + 부사〉 구조의 동사구를 물어보는 문제이다.
(c)에서 문맥상 집을 '둘러보다, 살펴보다'라는 뜻이므
로 check it up을 check it out으로 수정해야 한다.

어휘 check out 확인하다, 살펴보다
Be my guest. 맘대로 하세요.

정답 (c) check it up → check it out

18 해석 (a) A: 송 씨와 통화하려고 전화했습니다.

(b) B: 전데요.

(c) A: 안녕하세요. 전 노라 라자르입니다. 저 기억나
세요?

(d) B: 예, 물론이죠. 전화 주시다니 정말 뜻밖인걸요!

해설 전화 영어 표현을 물어보는 문제이다. 전화상으로 '전
데요.'라고 말할 때는 This is he/me (speaking).
또는 Speaking.이라고 하지 Spoken.이라고 하지
는 않는다. 따라서 (b)의 Spoken.을 Speaking.으
로 고쳐야 한다.

어휘 hear from ~로부터 전화 연락을 받다

정답 (b) Spoken. → Speaking.

19 해석 (a) A: 이 차는 시중에 나와 있는 가장 비싼 차들 중
하나잖아.

(b) B: 나도 알아.

(c) A: 그럼 그 차를 어떻게 살 거야?

(d) B: 믿기지 않겠지만 나 지난주에 복권에 당첨됐거든.

해설 혼동하기 쉬운 동사의 쓰임을 묻는 문제이다. I see
와 I know는 전혀 다른 뜻이다. I see는 상대방의 말
이나 설명을 듣고 이해가 됐다, 이제 알겠다는 뜻이다.
반면 I know는 상대방의 말이나 설명을 듣기 전부터
어떤 사실을 이미 알고 있다는 의미로 쓰인다. 위 대
화의 문맥에서는 already가 있으므로 I see보다는 I
know가 자연스럽다. I see를 I know로 고쳐야 한
다.

어휘 can afford to ~할 여유가 되다
win the lottery 복권에 당첨되다

정답 (b) see → know

20 해석 (a) 초영웅들은 단지 순수 오락일 뿐일까요, 아니면 어
린아이들에게 영향을 미칠 수 있는 역할 모델을 대표
하는 걸까요? (b) 몇몇 사람들은 긍정적인 역할의 여
성과 유색인 초영웅이 없다는 점을 크게 우려합니다.
(c) 또 다른 사람들은 초영웅들이 아이들에게 폭력과
공격성을 미화한다고 생각합니다. (d) 여러분은 인기
있는 초영웅들이 자라나는 아이들에게 어떤 부정적인
영향을 미친다고 생각하십니까?

해설 주어와 동사의 수 일치를 묻는 문제이다. 문장 (b)에서
주어는 The lack이고, of positive female and
non-white superheroes는 주어 The lack을 수
식하는 형용사구일 뿐이므로 주어와 동사의 수 일치에
영향을 미치지 않는다. 따라서 동사 are를 단수 동사
is로 바꿔야 한다.

어휘 superhero 초영웅, 초인
innocent 무해한, 순수한
non-white 비백인의, 유색인종의
concern 근심, 걱정
glorify 미화하다
aggressiveness 공격성
developing 성장기의, 자라나는

정답 (b) are → is

Chapter 01 동사구 이디엄
Actual Test

1 **해석** A: 너 왜 그렇게 나에게 무례하니?
B: 사돈 남 말 하시네. 너야말로 배려가 없어!
해설 say와 tell은 타동사로 목적어를 필요로 하므로 일단 답이 될 수 없다. speak는 순수하게 말하는 행위 그 자체에 초점을 두고, talk는 말의 내용에 초점을 둔다는 정도의 미묘한 차이가 있다. 위 대화에서 B가 A에게 시비조로 따지는 것은 대화의 내용이지 언어 행위가 아니므로 talking이 자연스럽다.
어휘 rude 무례한
Look who's talking. 사돈 남 말 하시네
inconsiderate 배려가 없는
정답 (d)

2 **해석** A: 야, 잊지 않고 개를 수의사에게 데려갔니?
B: 이런. 그러려고 했는데. 까먹은 거 같아.
해설 B가 Oops.라고 말한 걸로 보아 빈칸에는 깜박 잊어버렸다는 내용이 알맞다. B의 대명사 it은 '개를 수의사에게 데려가는 것'인데, 마음을 미끄러져 빠져나갔다는 의미가 깜박 잊어버린다는 뜻과 가장 일맥상통하므로 (a) slipped가 정답이다. 참고로 slip에는 '(기억에서) 사라지다'라는 뜻이 있지만, slide에는 그런 뜻이 없다. slide는 타동사로 쓰일 경우 '~을 미끄러지게 하다'라는 뜻이므로 mind를 목적어로 취하면 뜻이 통하지 않는다.
어휘 vet 수의사
slip one's mind 잊어버리다
spill 엎지르다
slide 미끄러지다
shift 이동하다
정답 (a)

3 **해석** A: 제이비어가 준결승을 통과했니?
B: 응, 사실 결승까지 진출했어.
해설 대명사 it을 목적어로 취해서 '성공하다, 해내다'라는 뜻을 지니는 동사를 고르는 문제이다. it과 어울려 이러한 뜻을 지니게 되는 동사는 make이다. 참고로 make it은 '성공하다'라는 뜻 외에 '(약속 장소에) 가다, 만나다, 시간 내에 도착하다'라는 뜻으로도 자주 쓰인다.
어휘 make it 성공하다, 해내다
정답 (c)

4 **해석** A: 왜 내 농담에 웃지 않니?
B: 솔직히 이해를 못하겠어.
해설 문맥상 빈칸에는 '이해하다'라는 의미를 가진 동사가 들어가야 한다. 선택지 중에서는 (d) get이 '받아들이다, 이해하다'라는 뜻을 지니고 있다. 따라서 정답은 (d) get이다.
어휘 get it 이해하다
정답 (d)

5 **해석** A: 너 아직도 세탁기 작동 방법을 모른다는 얘기니?
B: 방법을 익히는 데 시간이 좀 걸리고 있어.
해설 명사 hang에도 '사용법, 요령, 방법'의 뜻이 있다. '~의 방법을 익히다'라는 뜻으로는 way를 쓰지 않고 주로 hang을 쓴다. 관용 표현으로 get the hang of를 암기하면 쉽게 풀 수 있다. 참고로 hang 대신에 knack을 쓰기도 하고, know the ropes도 같은 뜻의 관용 표현이다.
어휘 get the hang of ~의 요령[방법]을 알다
정답 (d)

6 **해석** A: 네 인생에서 힘들 때 가장 큰 힘이 되어 준 사람이 누구였니?
B: 전적으로 부모님으로부터 도움을 받았어요.
해설 문맥상 빈칸은 '빚을 진, 신세를 진, 은혜를 입은, 도움을 받은'의 뜻을 지닌 형용사가 들어가야 한다. 빈칸 뒤의 전치사 to가 단서이다. (a) dependent는 on이나 upon이 이어져야 하고, (b) helped는 by가 뒤따라야 의미가 통하며, (d) owned는 의미적으로 가능하지 않다. 선택지 중 전치사 to랑 연결되어 '~에게 신세를 지다'의 뜻을 가지는 형용사는 (c) indebted 뿐이다. B의 말은 직역하면 '힘들 때 나를 도와준 것에 대해 부모님께 완전히 빚졌다.'로 '부모님으로부터 힘들 때 많은 도움을 받았다.' 정도로 의역된다.
어휘 trial 시련
be indebted to *sb* for *sth* ~에게 … 의 빚을 지다, …한 것은 ~덕택이다
stick by one's side ~를 도와주다, ~에게 큰 힘이 되다
정답 (c)

7 **해석** A: 왜 쿠퍼 씨가 우리에게 주먹을 흔들고 있지?

B: 아직도 나한테 화가 나 있나 봐.

해설 화가 난 모습을 가장 잘 나타내는 행동은 주먹을 흔드는 동작일 것이므로 (c) fist가 정답이다. 동사는 wave보다 shake를 더 많이 쓴다.

어휘 wave/shake one's fist (분노의 표시로) 주먹을 흔들다

정답 (c)

8 **해석** 거길 간 적이 있는지는 기억나지 않지만 이름은 들어본 거 같아요.

해설 '벨을 울리다'로 직역되는데 '뭔가 생각나는 게 있다, 뭔가를 떠올리게 한다'는 의미를 가진 표현은 ring a bell이다. The name rings a bell.이라고 하면 우리말로는 '이름이 귀에 익다.' '이름을 어디에선가 들어본 거 같다.'라는 표현과 아주 유사하다. 참고로 chime a bell도 가능한 표현이지만 ring a bell처럼 은유적으로 쓰이지는 않는다.

어휘 ring a bell (뭔가를) 생각나게 하다, 귀에 익다

chime (차임) 벨을 울리다

ding 땡땡 울리게 하다

정답 (a)

9 **해석** 이 회의에서 무슨 일이 일어날지 모르기 때문에 나는 그때그때 상황에 따라 행동할 것이다.

해설 '준비 없이 즉흥적으로 하다'라는 뜻의 관용 표현 play it by ear를 묻고 있다. 문자 그대로 음악을 귀로 듣고 바로 연주한다는 뜻으로 음악에서 유래된 표현이다. '어떤 일을 즉흥적으로 하다, 임기응변으로 하다, 상황에 따라 되는대로 행동하다'의 뜻이 파생되어 나온 것으로 이해하면 된다.

어휘 play it by ear 임기응변으로 처리하다

정답 (c)

10 **해석** 의사가 처방해 준 약이 효과가 없으면 대체 요법을 한번 고려해 보세요.

해설 대체 요법을 권하고 있으므로 if 종속절은 '의사가 처방해 준 약이 듣지 않으면'의 뜻이 되어야 자연스럽다. '약이 잘 듣다, 효과가 있다'는 표현은 do the trick이다.

어휘 do the trick (약이) 효능 또는 효과가 있다

정답 (a)

Actual Test

1 **해석** A: 나 몸을 좀 만들어야겠어.

B: 그럼, 언제 나랑 체육관에 가자.

해설 체육관에 가는 주된 목적은 체력을 단련하고 몸을 가꾸기 위해서이므로 (d) shape가 정답이다. shape는 '형체, 모양, 모습'이라는 뜻인데, 운동을 하지 않으면 몸이 망가지고 운동을 하면 몸이 원래의 모습으로 돌아온다는 의미에서 몸을 가꾸고 단련하는 것을 get into shape라고 한다. 몸이나 건강 상태가 좋은 것은 in shape라고 하고, 그 반대는 out of shape라고 한다. 단순히 몸매가 좋은 것을 in shape라고 하지 않는다는 점을 주의해야 한다. 몸매보다는 건강 상태, 체력이 좋은 상태를 뜻한다.

어휘 get into shape 몸을 단련하다

정답 (d)

2 **해석** A: 이번 주말쯤에 한번 만나자.

B: 안 되겠는데. 이번 주 내내 출장이야.

해설 문맥상 빈칸에는 '집, 도시를 떠나 있다'는 표현이 적절하다. 출장, 여행 등으로 거주 지역에 없다는 뜻의 영어 표현은 be out of town을 쓴다. No can do.는 '(나로서는) 불가능하다, 할 수 없다, 못한다'는 뜻의 관용 표현이다.

어휘 No can do. (나로선) 불가능해. 그럴 수 없어.

be out of town (집, 도시를) 떠나 있다

정답 (a)

3 **해석** A: 조금 있다가 한잔할래?

B: 좋아, 하지만 지금은 해야 할 일이 많아서 정신없이 바쁘거든.

해설 up to one's eyeballs/ears는 물에 눈까지 잠긴 것처럼 일에 파묻혀 꼼짝도 못할 정도로 바쁜 경우를 은유적으로 나타내는 관용 표현이다.

어휘 in a little bit 조금 있다가, 조만간, 곧

grab a drink 가볍게[잠깐] 한잔하다

keep one's chin up 용기를 잃지 않다

a screw loose 결함, 고장

up to one's eyeballs ~때문에 정신없는

I've had it up to here with you. 너에게 질렸어.

정답 (d)

4 **해석** A: 브라이언은 아직도 너희 집에 사니?

B: 아니, 마침내 취직해서 지금은 독립해서 혼자 살고 있어.

해설 취직했으므로 더 이상 얹혀살지 않고 독립해서 혼자 힘으로 살고 있다는 내용이 문맥상 빈칸에 적절하다. 남의 도움 없이 '혼자 힘으로, 독립적으로'의 뜻을 가진 표현은 on one's own이다. 참고로 on one's own은 by oneself(홀로)와 for oneself(혼자 힘으로)의 뜻을 동시에 지니고 있으므로 두 표현 대신에 바꿔 쓸 수 있다.

어휘 on one's own 혼자서, 독립하여
on one's behalf ~를 대신하여

정답 (a)

5 **해석** A: 나 라오스로 여행 가기 전에 예방 접종 받아야 해.

B: 꼭 그렇게 해야 해. 내 말은, 너의 건강이 걸려 있다는 뜻이야.

해설 B는 A에게 예방 접종을 꼭 받아야 하는 이유를 설명하고 있다. 예방 접종 여부에 따라 건강이 걸려 있다는 뜻이 문맥에 자연스러우므로 (b) stake가 정답이다. at stake는 목숨, 명예, 건강, 행복 따위가 '걸려 있는, 달려 있는, 위기에 처해 있는'의 의미를 가지고 있다.

어휘 get vaccinated 예방 접종을 받다
well-being 건강
at stake 걸려 있는, 달려 있는

정답 (b)

6 **해석** A: 프랜, 너랑 피터는 귀여운 커플이 될 거야. 어떻게 생각해?

B: 너 미쳤구나. 난 그 남자한테 관심 없거든.

해설 피터랑 좋은 커플이 될 거라는 A의 말에 B가 정색하며 그에게 관심 없다고 말하고 있으므로 '정신이 나간, 미친'의 뜻이 되도록 빈칸에는 (d) mind가 가장 알맞다.

어휘 out of order 고장 난
out of shape (몸이) 망가진
sanity 제정신, 온전
out of one's mind 정신이 나간

정답 (d)

7 **해석** A: 그 약을 받기 위해 처방전이 필요한가요?

B: 그렇지 않아요. 처방전 없이 받으실 수 있습니다.

해설 문맥상 빈칸에는 A의 get a prescription의 의미와 상반된 내용이 들어감을 유추해 볼 수 있다. 따라서 빈칸에 적절한 전치사를 넣어서 '처방전 없이'라는 뜻의 부사구를 만들면 되는데, '처방전 없이'라는 뜻의 영어 표현은 over the counter이다.

어휘 get a prescription 처방전을 받다
medication 약
over the counter 처방전 없이(= OTC)
under the counter (거래 따위를) 불법으로

정답 (c)

8 **해석** 엄마는 다가오는 니나의 결혼식 준비를 어떻게 해야 할지 막막해 하신다.

해설 wit's 뒤에 어울리는 명사를 고르면 된다. 어찌할 바를 모르는 상태가 되도록 빈칸을 완성해야 하는데, '어찌할 바를 몰라'의 관용 표현은 at one's wit's end이다. 문자 그대로 재치가 끝난 상태라는 뜻과 '어찌할 바를 모른다'는 뜻이 일맥상통한다.

어휘 at one's wit's end 어찌할 바를 몰라 하는, 막막해 하는

정답 (b)

9 **해석** 클라이드는 그의 자동차로 나무를 정면으로 들이받고 그 자리에서 즉사했다고 발표됐다.

해설 문맥상 나무를 들이받아 즉사했다는 뜻이 가장 자연스러우므로 '현장에서, 그 자리에서'의 뜻을 가진 부사구가 되도록 빈칸에는 (d) spot가 정답이다. spot에는 '장소, 지점, 자리'의 뜻이 있다.

어휘 pronounce 선고하다
on the spot 현장에서, 즉석에서

정답 (d)

10 **해석** 나는 오히려 평화롭고 조용한 곳에 있고 싶은 기분입니다.

해설 '~하고 싶은 기분이다'라는 뜻을 가진 표현은 〈be in the mood to + 동사〉이다. 〈be in the mood for + 명사〉로 쓰기도 한다.

어휘 urge 충동, 욕구
be in the mood to + 동사 ~하고 싶은 기분이 들다

정답 (c)

Actual Test

1 **해석** A: 베로니카, 얼굴 표정이 왜 그래?

B: 별거 아니야. 연중 이맘때면 가끔씩 좀 우울해져.

해설 B가 가끔씩 우울해진다고 했으므로 A는 B에게 표정이 왜 그러느냐고 물어봤을 것이다. 우울하거나 슬픈 표정을 long face라고 한다. What's with the long face?는 상대방의 기분이나 안색이 좋지 않아 보일 때 안부를 묻는 말로 쓸 수 있다.

어휘 What's with long face? 왜 그리 울상이야?

odd 이상한

oval 타원형(의)

get dow 침울해지다

정답 (b)

2 **해석** A: 오늘 무대에 올라갈 자신 있니?

B: 아니, 너무 긴장돼서 속이 울렁거려.

해설 중요한 일을 앞두고 너무 초조하고 긴장되어서 속이 메스껍고 울렁거리는 상태를 표현할 때 have/get butterflies in one's stomach라는 관용 표현을 자주 쓴다. butterflies에는 '불안감, 두려움, 초조함'이라는 뜻이 있다.

어휘 have butterflies in one's stomach (어떤 일을 하기도 전에) 극도로 긴장하다, 안절부절 못하다

nerve 배짱, 용기

insect 곤충

정답 (a)

3 **해석** A: 그는 지난밤 술집에서 술을 많이 마셨어.

B: 맞아. 그는 정말 술고래야.

해설 술을 지나치게 많이 마신다는 표현을 우리말로는 술고래라고 하는데, 영어에서는 물고기처럼 술을 마신다고 표현한다. 따라서 빈칸에 들어갈 말은 (b) a fish이다.

어휘 drink like a fish 술을 많이 마시다

정답 (b)

4 **해석** A: 좋습니다. 잡담하느라 시간을 많이 허비했네요.

B: 맞아요. 본론으로 들어갈 시간입니다.

해설 '본론으로 들어가다'는 get down to business라는 관용 표현을 쓴다. 원래는 '본격적으로 일에 착수하다'라는 뜻에서 2차적 의미가 파생된 것이다. 따라서 정답은 (c) business이다.

어휘 chitchat 잡담, 수다

get down to the business 본론으로 들어가다

정답 (c)

5 **해석** A: 점보 사이즈의 핫 소스 한 병 주세요.

B: 사실, 지금 당장은 재고가 없습니다.

해설 문맥상 A가 사려고 하는 상품의 재고가 없다는 뜻이므로 빈칸에는 (d) stock이 가장 알맞다. 재고(stock)란 판매하기 위해 선반이나 창고에 준비해 두는 상품을 가리킨다. 재고가 없다는 표현은 We are out of stock in that.으로 쓰기도 한다.

어휘 jumbo-sized 특대형의

in stock 재고가 있는

정답 (d)

6 **해석** A: 케이크 믹스 샀니?

B: 아니. 완전 처음부터 만들고 싶었거든.

해설 B가 케이크 믹스를 사지 않은 이유는 케이크 믹스조차도 손수 만들고 싶었기 때문이다. scratch는 카드 놀이에서 0점 상태를 가리키는 말인데 여기서 '아무것도 없는 상태에서, 완전 무에서부터, 처음부터'라는 의미가 파생되었다.

어휘 from scratch 처음부터, 아무것도 없는 상태에서

정답 (c)

7 **해석** A: 내 차를 세차하는 데 30달러를 달라더라고.

B: 완전 바가지군! 네가 직접 하는 게 훨씬 싸겠다.

해설 빈칸 뒤의 B의 말로 미루어 보아 B는 A가 지불한 30달러의 세차 비용이 지나치게 비싸다고 생각하고 있음을 유추해 볼 수 있다. 그러므로 완전 바가지를 썼다는 (c) rip-off가 빈칸에 가장 적절하다.

어휘 deal 거래, 계약

rip-off 바가지, 폭리

play-off (무승부, 동점일 때의) 결정전

put-off 발뺌, 변명

정답 (c)

8 **해석** A: 숙제 도와줘서 고마워.

B: 천만에.

해설 감사에 대한 응답 Don't mention it.을 물어보는 문제이다. '감사하다는 말씀 마세요.'로 직역이 되는데, 우리말로는 '별말씀을 다 하시네요.' 정도의 겸양 표현과 일맥상통한다. 감사에 대한 응답은 Don't mention it. 외에 You're welcome. No problem. Never mind. My pleasure. 등이 있다.

어휘 Don't mention it. 천만에요.

정답 (a)

9 해석 A: 내일 저녁 식사에 사람들을 몇 명 초대하려고요.
B: 정말요? 무슨 날이에요?

해설 멋지게 차려입은 사람이나 한턱 쏘겠다는 사람에게 '무슨 날이라도 되냐?, 무슨 행사라도 있나?' 라고 말할 때 What's the occasion?이라는 표현을 쓴다. 이 경우 occasion은 '특별한 행사' 라는 의미로 쓰인다.

어휘 What's the occasion? 무슨 날이에요?

정답 (b)

10 해석 A: 다리를 지나고 나서 우회전하셔서 도로가 끝날 때까지 계속 가세요.
B: 이런. 마지막 부분을 못 알아들었어요. 어디에서 또 돌아야 한다고 하셨죠?

해설 이름, 숫자, 설명 등을 '놓치지 않고 알아듣다' 라는 뜻으로 catch를 쓴다. see는 어떤 설명을 듣고 '몰랐던 사실을 새로 깨닫다' 라는 의미이므로 상황에 맞지 않는다. (a)는 시제가 맞지 않아 답이 될 수 없다.

어휘 catch 알아듣다

정답 (c)

11 해석 A: 난 이번 주 아무 때나 시간이 돼.
B: 나로서는 수요일이 가장 좋은 시간이야.

해설 글을 쓰거나 말을 할 때, 화두를 던질 때 '~에 관한 한' 의 뜻으로 〈as far as + 주어 + be동사 + concerned〉 형태를 쓴다. When it comes to, As for 등의 표현을 쓰기도 한다.

어휘 〈as far as + 주어 + be동사 + concerned〉 ~에 관한 한

정답 (c)

12 해석 A: 직장에 별일 없지?
B: 으응, 지난주에 새로운 상사가 왔어.

해설 가벼운 근황을 물을 때 What's up?과 같은 의미로 What's new?라는 표현을 자주 쓴다. '뭐 새로운 거 있니?' 라는 직역이 우리말의 '별일 없니?' 와 아주 잘 매칭되는 표현이다.

어휘 What's new? 별일 없지?
neat 깔끔한, 단정한

정답 (c)

13 해석 A: 조니 있나요?
B: 전화하신 분은 누구시죠?

해설 전화 대화이다. 전화상으로 전화한 사람이 누구냐고 물어볼 때는 calling 또는 speaking을 써서 May I ask who is calling/speaking?으로 표현한다. 따라서 정답은 (c) calling이다.

어휘 Who's calling?(전화 대화에서) 누구세요?

정답 (b)

14 해석 A: 언제 낚시하러 갈래?
B: 물론이지! 멋진 장소를 몇 군데 알고 있어.

해설 문맥상 빈칸에는 B가 A의 제의를 흔쾌히 수락하는 표현이 들어가야 한다. You bet!은 돈을 걸어도 될 만큼 확실하다는 의미로 자주 쓰인다. 위 문맥에서는 내가 낚시를 가고 싶어 한다는 것은 돈을 걸어도 좋을 만큼 확실하다는 의미로 이해하면 된다.

어휘 You bet! 물론이지!

정답 (c)

15 해석 A: 왜 이렇게 늦게 왔니? 음식이 벌써 차가워.
B: 어쩔 수 없었어. 오늘 차가 정말 많이 막혔어.

해설 싫은 것을 피하는 경우는 help를 쓰고, 좋아하는 것을 거부하거나 삼간다는 의미로는 resist를 쓴다. 문맥상 늦는 것을 피할 수 없었다는 뜻이므로 help가 더 알맞다.

어휘 can't help it 어쩔 수 없다
resist 저항하다, 거부하다

정답 (c)

Actual Test

1 **해석** A: 나랑 아침 식사 약속에 왜 나오지 않았니?

　　　 B: 자명종이 울리지 않았어.

　　해설 자명종이 '울리다' 라는 뜻의 동사구 표현 go off를 물어보는 문제이다. go off는 '폭탄이 폭발하다' 라는 뜻으로 많이 쓰이고, 소리 따위가 갑자기 크게 울리는 경우에도 go off를 쓴다.

　　어휘 sound off (기상, 소등) 신호 나팔을 불다

　　　　break up 분쇄하다, 해체하다

　　　　run up (가격이) 올라가다

　　정답 (d)

2 **해석** A: 제가 식당에 예약해야 하나요?

　　　 B: 아니요, 그냥 오시기만 하면 바로 음식이 준비됩니다.

　　해설 A가 예약이 필요하냐고 물어보니 B가 그럴 필요 없다고 했으므로 빈칸에는 '나타나다, 오다' 라는 뜻을 가진 표현을 골라 넣으면 된다. 따라서 정답은 (d) show up이다.

　　어휘 come through 성공하다, 해내다

　　　　see through 꿰뚫어 보다, 간파하다

　　정답 (d)

3 **해석** A: 이 보고서가 기말 성적에 얼마나 반영되나요?

　　　 B: 점수의 4분의 1을 차지해요.

　　해설 A가 보고서를 제출하면서 기말 성적에 얼마나 반영되는지 묻고 있는 걸로 보아 B는 성적의 4분의 1을 '차지한다' 고 말했음을 유추할 수 있다. '~에 해당되다, ~의 비율을 차지하다' 라는 뜻을 가진 영어 표현은 account for이다. 참고로 account for에는 '설명하다' 라는 뜻도 있다는 걸 알아 둘 필요가 있다

　　어휘 count 세다, 셈에 넣다

　　정답 (b)

4 **해석** A: 같은 문제에 대해 밤새 얘기했네요.

　　　 B: 맞아요. 이만 접어 두고 끝냅시다.

　　해설 문맥상 토론을 '마무리하다' 라는 의미가 빈칸에 적절하다. 선택지 중 '마무리하다' 라는 뜻을 가진 구동사 표현은 (b) wrap이다. wrap up은 원래 포장해버린다는 뜻인데, 다 끝난 일을 포장해서 치워 둔다는 어감에서 일을 마무리 짓는다는 의미가 파생되었다고 볼 수 있다. 문장 끝에 call it a day 역시 wrap it up과

비슷한 의미를 가진 관용 표현이다.

　　어휘 wrap up (일을) 마치다, 끝내다

　　　　call it a day (그날 하루 일을) 끝내다, 마감하다

　　　　draw up 정렬시키다, (문서, 계획 따위를) 작성하다

　　　　call up ~에게 전화하다

　　정답 (b)

5 **해석** A: 어젯밤에 하기로 되어 있던 축구 경기는 어떻게 된 거야?

　　　 B: 비 때문에 경기가 취소됐어.

　　해설 '취소하다' 의 의미를 가진 구동사 표현 call off를 물어보는 문제이다. due to rain이 단서이다. 비가 내리면 경기가 대개 취소되기 때문에 빈칸에는 '취소되었다' 는 의미가 되게 (c) called off가 적절하다.

　　어휘 cut off 베어내다, 중단하다

　　　　put down 기록하다, 작성하다

　　　　call off 취소하다

　　　　keep down 가라앉히다, 진압하다

　　정답 (c)

6 **해석** A: 당신이 하겠다고 말했던 것을 했다면 좋았을 텐데.

　　　 B: 실망시켜서 죄송합니다.

　　해설 문맥상 빈칸은 '실망시키다' 라는 뜻의 구동사 표현이 적절하다. 선택지 중에서 down과 함께 쓰여 상대방을 실망시킨다는 뜻을 가지는 동사는 (c) let이다. turn down은 '거절하다' 이고, calm down은 '진정시키다' 라는 뜻이다. mark down은 '가격을 내리다, 할인하다' 라는 뜻으로 사람을 목적어로 취할 수 없으므로 답이 될 수 없다.

　　어휘 turn down 거절하다

　　　　mark down 가격을 할인하다, 적어두다

　　　　calm down 진정시키다, 가라앉히다

　　정답 (c)

7 **해석** A: 진정해. 결국 다 잘될 거야.

　　　 B: 그러면 좋겠어.

　　해설 일이나 상황이 '잘 풀리다, 잘 해결되다' 라는 의미의 구동사 표현 work out을 물어보는 문제이다. work out은 자동사로는 '운동하다', 타동사로는 문제를 '해결하다' 라는 뜻도 있다.

　　어휘 get over 극복하다, 이겨내다

　　　　make out 작성하다, 이해하다

　　정답 (a)

8 해석 A: 스티브가 왜 그런 식으로 행동하려는지 모르겠어.

B: 나도 가끔씩 이해가 안 가.

해설 figure out은 구어체에서 굉장히 자주 쓰이는 표현으로 '찾아내다, 알아내다' 라는 뜻과 어떤 사람(의 행동)을 '이해하다' 라는 뜻으로 주로 사용된다. take away는 '제거하다, 죽이다' 이고, sort through와 follow down은 없는 표현이다.

어휘 sort 분류하다

take away 제거하다

follow 뒤따르다

정답 (b)

9 해석 A: 며칠 전에 캠퍼스에서 네 동생을 만났어.

B: 어, 그래? 나는 한동안 통 못 봤는데.

해설 문맥상 '우연히 만났다' 는 뜻을 가진 (b) ran into가 빈칸에 알맞다. 참고로 run across와 bump into 역시 '우연히 만나다' 라는 뜻으로 자주 쓰이는 표현이다.

어휘 get along with ~랑 사이좋게 잘 지내다

come over (건너)오다, 들르다

try out 시험해 보다

정답 (b)

10 해석 A: 예약 했니?

B: 아니. 극장에 전화를 해봤는데 통화가 안 됐어.

해설 여러 번 전화를 했다는 내용이 앞에 나오고, 그 뒤에 but이 나왔으므로 통화를 할 수 없었다는 내용이 자연스러울 것이다. 빈칸에는 '통화가 되다' 라는 뜻의 get through가 가장 적절하다. 선택지 (b)와 (d)는 모두 목적어를 필요로 하는 구동사들로, 빈칸 뒤에 목적어가 없기 때문에 답이 될 수 없다.

어휘 keep track (of) 놓치지 않고 따라가다, 추적하다

get hold of 붙잡다, 연락하다, 이해하다

keep up with 따라잡다

정답 (c)

11 해석 A: 너희들 운동 프로그램 시작했니?

B: 시작은 의욕에 차서 했는데 모두가 끝까지 갈 수 있을지 의문이에요.

해설 역접, 대조의 접속사 but이 있으므로 빈칸에는 started off diligently와 상반되는 의미가 들어가야 한다. 운동은 처음에는 의욕에 차서 시작하지만 끝까지 지속하는 것이 어렵다. 따라서 빈칸에는 '끝까지 해내다' 라는 의미의 stick with가 가장 적절하다.

어휘 start off 출발하다, 시작하다

diligently 부지런히, 열심히

take over 떠맡다, 인수하다

run over (차가 사람을) 치다

sniff at 킁킁거리며 냄새를 맡다

정답 (b)

12 해석 A: 이네즈가 그 영화의 배역을 못 따서 속상해 하고 있어.

B: 곧 극복할 거라 생각해.

해설 get over는 어떤 고민이나 걱정 따위로부터 벗어나거나 극복하거나 잊어버리는 것을 의미한다. 배역을 따지 못해서 속상해 하지만 조만간 그 사실을 언제 그랬느냐는 듯이 잊어버릴 거라는 뉘앙스로 볼 수 있다.

어휘 break down 붕괴하다, 분해하다

fall behind 뒤처지다

turn into ~로 바뀌다, 변신하다

정답 (b)

13 해석 네가 이 논문을 훑어보고 어떻게 생각하는지 나에게 말해 주면 좋겠어.

해설 문맥상 빈칸은 '훑어보다' 라는 뜻을 가진 동사구 표현이 들어갈 자리이다. 선택지 중 '훑어보다' 라는 뜻을 가진 표현은 (d) skim through이다.

어휘 see through 간파하다, 꿰뚫어 보다

cut through 헤치고 나아가다, 끼어들다

skim through 대충 훑어보다

정답 (d)

14 해석 강의에 대해 그렇게 걱정하지 말고 읽기 과제에 집중해 봐.

해설 전치사 on에 주목할 필요가 있다. 빈칸에는 '집중하다' 라는 뜻을 가진 표현이 필요한데, 전치사 on과 함께 쓸 수 있는 단어는 (a) focus밖에 없다. (d) attend는 on이랑 쓸 수도 있지만 '시중들다, 돌보다' 라는 전혀 다른 뜻이 된다. attend가 '주목하다, 주의하다' 라는 뜻일 때는 전치사 to랑 함께 써야 하므로 답이 될 수 없다. accompany는 완전타동사로 전치사 없이 바로 목적어를 취해야 하므로 의미를 떠나 문법적으로도 들어갈 수 없다.

어휘 accompany ~와 동행하다, 동반하다

venture 모험하다

assignment 과제, 숙제

정답 (a)

15 해석 자크는 몸이 안 좋아서 그 쇼를 전부 다 볼 수는 없었다.

해설 문맥상 빈칸에는 쇼를 '처음부터 끝까지 보다'라는 뜻
을 가진 구동사 표현 sit through가 적절하다. 원래
sit through는 재미없는 영화나 쇼가 끝날 때까지 자
리를 뜨지 않고 가만히 있는다는 의미이다. sit은 '앉
아 있다'는 뜻이고, through는 '처음부터 끝날 때까
지'를 의미한다. 정답은 (b) sit through이다. lay
through는 없는 표현이다.

어휘 lay up 따로 비축하다, (문제 따위를) 보류하다
sit up 자지 않고 깨어 있다

정답 (b)

Actual Test

1 해석 A: 네가 그 정도 부자는 아닌 걸 알아. 그렇게 큰 집을
어떻게 살 수 있었니?

B: 지난달에 은행에서 꽤 큰돈을 대출받았어.

해설 의미를 혼동하기 쉬운 유의어 구분 문제이다. B가 큰
집을 살 수 있었던 건 은행으로부터 거금을 대출받았
기 때문이다. 은행 등으로부터 받는 대출금은 loan이
라고 한다. lease는 '임대차 계약'을 뜻한다.

어휘 investment 투자(금)
loan 대부금, 대출
lease 장기 임대

정답 (c)

2 해석 A: 그거 알아? 배리가 장기 자랑 대회에서 일등을 했어.

B: 우왜! 나가서 축하해 주자.

해설 우리말로는 모두 답이 될 수 있어 보이는 유형의 문제
이다. (a), (c) (d)는 모두 목적어를 필요로 하는 타동
사란 사실을 알아야 풀 수 있다. 일등을 기념하는 축
하 파티를 하자는 뉘앙스이므로 (b) celebrate가 정
답이다.

어휘 You know what? 있잖아. 그거 알아?
congratulate 축하하다
celebrate 축하하다, 축하 행사를 하다
commend 칭찬하다, 찬양하다
compliment 칭찬하다

정답 (b)

3 해석 A: 정말 멋진 우표다! 진기해 보여.

B: 어떻게 알았어? 우표 수집하니?

해설 유의어 구분 문제이다. gather와 collect 둘 다 '모
으다'라는 뜻으로 문법상 크게 문제 없고 의미 전달에
도 문제가 없지만, 수금을 한다거나 우표나 동전 등을
수집한다는 뉘앙스로는 collect를 쓰는 게 일반적이
다. gather는 사람이든 사물이든 한 곳으로 모은다는
뉘앙스로 collect보다는 광의의 어휘이다.

어휘 pick 고르다, 가려내다
choose 고르다, 선택하다

정답 (d)

4 해석 A: 창가 쪽 자리 부탁합니다.

B: 죄송합니다. 창가 쪽 자리는 다 찼네요.

해설 A가 창가 쪽 자리를 부탁하자, 창가 쪽 자리는 다 차서 더 이상 '이용이 불가능한' 상태라고 말하는 뉘앙스이므로 (b) available이 빈칸에 적절하다. possible은 '있을 수 있는, 가능한'의 뜻을 가지고 있어서 우리말로는 답이 될 수 있어 보이지만 호텔 방이나 비행기 좌석, 극장표 등이 예약이나 이용 가능하다는 의미로는 쓰이지 않기 때문에 답이 될 수 없다. accessible은 장소, 사람 등이 '접근하기 쉬운, 접근 가능한'의 뜻이므로 문맥상 적절하지 않다.

어휘 accessible 접근이 용이한
available (이용, 예약 등이) 가능한
possible 있을 법한, 가능한
preferable 선호할 만한, 바람직한

정답 (b)

5 해석 A: 오래 전에 컴퓨터 주식에 투자했더라면 좋았을걸.
B: 그랬다면 지금쯤 엄청 부자가 됐을 텐데.

해설 문맥상 A는 주식 투자를 의미하고 있다고 볼 수 있다. '~에 (시간이나 돈)을 투자하다'라는 뜻의 동사는 invest이다. preserve는 '보존하다, 보관하다'이며 전치사 in과 어울리지 않는다. participate는 '참여하다'라는 뜻이고, '포함하다, 연루시키다'의 뜻을 가진 involve는 타동사로만 쓰이므로 의미를 떠나 문법적으로 빈칸에 들어갈 수 없다.

어휘 involve 포함하다, 연루시키다
preserve 보존하다, 보관하다

정답 (d)

6 해석 A: 남편과 문제가 좀 있다고 들었는데.
B: 집안의 모든 돈 관리를 자기 혼자서 하려고 하거든.

해설 유의어 구분 문제이다. 문맥상 빈칸에는 일 따위를 '취급하다, 다루다, 처리하다'라는 의미를 가진 handle이 가장 적절하다. treat는 예를 들어 어린애 취급하다라는 말에서처럼 '대접하다, 대우하다, 간주하다'라는 뉘앙스이므로 뜻 구분에 유의해야 한다.

어휘 grasp 꽉 쥐다, 이해하다
shift 옮기다, 이동시키다

정답 (c)

7 해석 A: 고양이들이 새 집이 싫은가 봐.
B: 환경이 바뀐 것을 감지했을 거야.

해설 문맥상 빈칸에는 '눈치채다, 감지하다'라는 뜻의 동사가 알맞다. 문제 해결의 단서는 빈칸 뒤에 나온 that

명사절이다. smell 역시 '눈치채다, 낌새를 채다'라는 뜻이 있지만 that절을 목적어로 취할 수는 없으므로 that절을 취할 수 있는 (c) sense가 더 적절하다.

어휘 reach 도달하다, 다다르다

정답 (c)

8 해석 A: 이 숲에는 얼마나 많은 곰이 살고 있나요?
B: 확실히는 알 수 없어요. 하지만 어림잡아 200마리 정도가 공원 내에 서식하고 있습니다.

해설 다소 고난도의 유의어 구분 문제이다. 어떤 한 지역을 구분해 주는 '경계선'의 의미로는 boundary가 가장 적절하다. 공원 내에 서식한다는 말은 공원 지역임을 나타내는 공원 구분 경계선 내에 서식한다는 의미로 볼 수 있다. 자칫 (d) territories를 답으로 고를 수도 있겠지만, territory는 '영토'라는 뜻으로 park 자체에 territory의 의미가 들어 있어서 의미가 중복되므로 차라리 within the park로만 표현하는 것이 낫다. barrier는 '방벽, 장애물'이라는 뜻이므로 문맥에 맞지 않으며, margin은 어떤 지역의 '가장자리, 변두리, 변방'의 뜻이 강하다.

어휘 boundary 경계선(= border)
margin 가장자리, 변두리
barrier 장벽

정답 (a)

9 해석 A: 스티븐스는 이름인가요, 성인가요?
B: 성이에요. 밥 스티븐스죠.

해설 기초적인 생활 영어 어휘를 물어보는 문제이다. '이름'은 first name이라고 하고, '성'은 last name이라고 한다. Christian name은 '세례명'이라는 뜻이며, given name은 first name과 같은 의미이다.

어휘 family name 성씨(= last name)

정답 (c)

10 해석 A: 지난번 감독을 해고하지 말았어야 했어.
B: 동감이야. 새 감독이 훨씬 더 안 좋아.

해설 B가 A의 말에 동의하면서 새로 부임한 감독이 훨씬 안 좋다고 말한 걸로 보아 A는 지난번 코치를 해고하지 말았어야 했다는 얘기를 했을 거라 유추할 수 있다. 따라서 빈칸에는 '해고하다'라는 의미의 (b) dismissed가 가장 알맞다. (a) retired는 문법적으로도 의미적으로도 가능해 보이지만, B가 두 감독을 비교하면서 유감을 표한 걸로 볼 때 은퇴보다는 해고

했다고 보는 것이 더 자연스럽다.

어휘 **retire** 은퇴하다, 은퇴시키다

recruit (신병, 신입 직원을) 모집하다

dispatch 파견하다

정답 (b)

11 해석 A: 댄은 정말 웃겨.

B: 놀랄 일도 아니야. 개네 아빠도 완전 똑같았어.

해설 빈칸 앞에 정관사 the가 문제를 풀기 위한 결정적인 열쇠이다. 선택지 중에서 앞에 the가 붙어 똑같다는 의미를 가지는 선택지는 (c) same밖에 없다. (b) equal은 just the equal 형태로 쓰지 않으며 '균등한, 동등한'의 의미이므로 문맥적으로 맞지 않는다. (a) like는 전치사이기 때문에 뒤에 반드시 목적어를 취해야 하고, 전치사 like 앞에는 the를 붙이지 않는다. and the like나 or the like처럼 형용사 like 앞에 the를 붙이는 경우는 있는데, 그 경우엔 뜻이 '기타 등등'의 의미이므로 문맥상 부자연스럽다. 오히려 like를 써서 표현한다면 His father was just like him.처럼 표현하는 것이 옳다. (d) similar 역시 just the similar 형태로 쓰지 않으며 He and his father are just similar (alike). 또는 His father is just similar to him.처럼 쓰는 것이 문법에 맞을 것이다.

어휘 **just the same** 마찬가지인, 똑같은

정답 (c)

12 해석 A: 35번 고속도로가 공사 때문에 임시 폐쇄되었어.

B: 우리가 갈 수 있는 우회 도로가 분명 있을 거야.

해설 고속도로가 공사 때문에 막힌 경우라면 우회 도로를 찾는 것이 상식일 것이다. 따라서 빈칸에는 동사 take와 자연스럽게 연결되면서 '우회 도로'의 뜻을 가진 (c) detour가 가장 알맞다. (a) curb는 인도와 차도를 구분하는 도로의 '연석'을 뜻하며, (b) circuit 역시 '우회로'라는 의미가 있긴 하지만 동사 take와는 잘 쓰이지 않는다. make a circuit 형태로 주로 쓰이는데 '순회하다'라는 뜻이다. (d) driveway는 도로에서 집 차고까지 연결된 '진입로'를 말한다.

어휘 **detour** 우회(로)

circuit 순회, 우회로

driveway (차로에서 집 차고까지 연결된) 진입로

curb (도로의) 연석

정답 (c)

13 해석 그 지원자는 자신이 성별 때문에 차별을 받았다고 생각했다.

해설 어구 because of her gender로 판단해 볼 때, 지원자가 성차별을 받았다고 생각했음을 유추할 수 있다. 인종이나 성 때문에 사람을 '차별하다'라는 부정적인 의미를 함축하고 있는 동사는 discriminate이다. distinguish는 단순하게 '구별하다, 구분하다'라는 의미로 부정적인 의미는 내포되어 있지 않다.

어휘 **gender** (생물학적, 사회적, 문화적) 성(性)

classify 분류하다, 등급을 매기다

recognize 분간하다, 인식하다, 인정하다

정답 (a)

14 해석 비타민 C가 풍부한 식품이 임산부에게 도움이 될 수 있다는 것을 예비 연구 조사들이 보여 주고 있지만 보다 많은 연구가 요구되고 있다.

해설 보다 많은 연구가 필요하다는 주절의 내용을 감안해 볼 때 비타민 C가 풍부한 음식이 임산부에게 좋다는 사실을 밝힌 연구 조사는 최종적이고 공식적인 연구가 아니라 사전 예비 연구 조사임을 유추할 수 있다. 나머지 선택지들은 문맥상 부자연스럽다.

어휘 **superficial** 피상적인

haphazard 되는 대로의, 무계획의

compulsive 강제적인, 충동적인

preliminary 예비의, 임시의

정답 (a)

15 해석 주말에는 대체로 맑은 하늘과 시원한 기온이 예상됩니다.

해설 하늘이 깨끗하고 맑다고 할 때는 형용사 clear를 쓴다. clean skies는 문법적으로도 맞고 의미적으로도 통하지만, 하늘이 맑다는 뉘앙스가 아니라 오염되지 않은 '깨끗한 하늘'이라는 뉘앙스이므로 문맥에 맞지 않는다.

어휘 **fresh** 새로운, 신선한

정답 (a)

Actual Test

1 **해석** A: 저녁 감사합니다. 정말 맛있었습니다.

B: 함께해 주셔서 감사합니다. 또 오세요.

해설 문맥상 빈칸에는 '함께 있어줌, 동석, 동반' 의 뜻을 지니는 (d) company가 가장 알맞다. association은 '교제, 사귐' 이라는 뜻으로 문맥에 맞지 않아 답이 될 수 없다. (a) accompaniment는 '부속물, 딸린 것' 의 뜻이다.

어휘 accompaniment 부속물, 반주

company 함께 있어줌, 동석

정답 (d)

2 **해석** A: 아야! 발에 가시가 박혀 있어.

B: 가시를 뺄 핀셋을 찾아볼게요.

해설 tweezers(핀셋)는 손가락이나 발에 박힌 가시를 빼는 기구인데, 이 기구를 찾는 이유가 될 만한 내용이 A의 빈칸에 알맞을 것이므로 빈칸에는 '가시' 라는 뜻을 지닌 (c) splinter가 정답이다.

어휘 tweezers 핀셋, 족집게

splice 이어 맞춘 것, 접목

split 쪼개다; 쪼개진[갈라진] 금[틈]

splinter 쪼개진 조각, (나무, 대나무 등의) 가시

sprint 전력 질주, 단거리 경주

정답 (c)

3 **해석** A: 휴가 계획이 뭐니?

B: 가을 단풍을 즐기러 숲속에 갈 거야.

해설 형태가 비슷해서 혼동하기 쉬운 어휘를 구분하는 문제이다. autumn의 수식을 받을 수 있는 단어는 (b) foliage이다. (a)의 falling은 '붕괴, 하락' 의 뜻이며, (c) florin은 화폐의 종류이고 (d) flotage는 '부양(력), 표류물' 의 뜻이므로 모두 문맥과 동떨어져 답이 될 수 없다.

어휘 falling 낙하, 붕괴

foliage (한 그루 초목의) 잎 (전부), 무성한 잎

florin 플로린 은화

flotage 부양, 부력

정답 (b)

4 **해석** A: 보고서를 제시간에 끝내지 못하면 어쩌죠?

B: 마감 기한 연장을 해달라고 부탁하는 것 외에 방법 이 없어.

해설 접두어 ex-로 시작되는 형태 중 혼동하기 쉬운 어휘를 구분하는 문제이다. 보고서나 과제물 등의 마감 기한을 연장해 주는 것은 (a) extension이다. extension은 길이나 기간, 날짜를 연장하는 것이고, expansion은 사방으로 팽창, 확장되는 것을 뜻한다.

어휘 extension (기간, 길이의) 연장

expansion 확장, 팽창

extinction 소멸, 멸종

expiration 만료, 만기

정답 (a)

5 **해석** 그처럼 대형 프로젝트를 떠맡으려고 하는 사람은 어느 누구나 그게 결코 쉬운 일이 아니라는 사실을 금방 알게 될 것이다.

해설 문맥상 such a big project라는 어구로 보아 빈칸에는 '업적, 공적' 의 뜻을 가진 단어가 들어가는 것이 가장 자연스럽다. '공적, 위업, 업적' 등의 의미를 가진 어휘는 (b) feat이다.

어휘 take responsibility for ~을 떠맡다, 책임지다

small feat 쉬운 일, 간단한 일

flea 벼룩

feud 불화, 앙숙

정답 (b)

6 **해석** 우리가 매일 노출되는 많은 광고들 중에서 우리의 의식적인 관심을 끌 수 있는 광고는 극소수에 불과할 것이다.

해설 동사와 명사의 어울림을 묻는 〈동사 + 명사〉 형태의 연어 문제이다. 선택지 중에서 명사 attention과 연어를 이룰 수 있는 동사는 (c) command밖에 없다. command sb's attention은 '~의 관심[주목]을 끌다' 라는 뜻이다.

어휘 commercial 광고 방송

precious few 극소수(의)

contend 주장하다

convert 변화시키다, 변환하다

command 불러일으키다, (동정, 존경 등을) 모으다

convene 모으다, 소집하다

정답 (c)

7 **해석** 다이애나가 왕실 유명 인사에서 세계적인 우상이 될 수 있었던 것은 그녀의 패션 감각 때문이 아니라 오히

려 수수께끼 같은 그녀의 성격 때문이었다.

해설 다이애나를 세계적인 우상이 되게 만들 만한 성격은
(a) 시샘하는 성격도 아니고, (d) 백과사전적인 성격도
아니다. (c) 수수께끼 같은 성격이었다고 보는 것이 문
맥에 가장 자연스럽다. 따라서 정답은 (c) enigmatic
이다.

어휘 equestrian 기수의, 승마의
enigmatic 수수께끼 같은, 불가사의한
encyclopedic 백과사전적인, 박식한

정답 (c)

8 해석 많은 현대 언어학 연구에 의하면 인터넷이 언어 변화
의 온상임이 밝혀지고 있다.

해설 형태를 혼동하기 쉬운 어휘를 구분하는 문제이다. 문
맥상 인터넷이 언어 변화의 '온상'이라는 뜻이 되어야
한다. 선택지 중 '온상'의 뜻을 가진 어휘는 (d)
hotbed이다.

어휘 linguistic 언어학의
mutation 변화, 변형
hotfoot 모욕, 자극
hot line 직통전화
hot seat 궁지, 곤란한 차지
hotbed 온상, 소굴

정답 (d)

9 해석 직장에서 긴 하루를 끝내고 집에 돌아온 호프만 씨는
소파 위에 풀썩 주저앉았다.

해설 문맥상 호프만 씨가 피곤한 몸을 이끌고 집에 와서 소
파 위에 풀썩 쓰러졌다는 의미가 빈칸에 적절하다. 선
택지 중 그런 뜻으로 사용될 수 있는 단어는 (c) crashed
이다.

어휘 crash 붕괴하다, 와르르 무너지다
crush 으스러지다, 구겨지다
crack 금이 가다
creak 삐걱거리다

정답 (c)

10 해석 강한 목소리와 큰 키는 그가 할리우드 영화에서 주연
배역을 따내는 데 도움이 됐다.

해설 빈칸 앞의 tall은 키를 설명하는 형용사이므로 빈칸에
는 '신장, 키'를 뜻하는 명사가 들어가야 한다. '신장'
은 영어로 stature라고 하므로 정답은 (b)이다. (c)
status는 '사회적인 지위'를, (d) statute는 '법령,

법규'를 뜻한다.

어휘 leading role 주연, 주역
stature 신장, 키
status 지위
statute 법령, 법규

정답 (b)

11 해석 하와이 산호초는 수많은 수중 생물의 서식지이다.

해설 산호초가 바닷속에 있다는 것을 생각하면 간단하게 풀
수 있는 문제. 산호초가 '수중 생물'의 집이므로 빈칸
에 들어갈 단어는 (b) aquatic이다.

어휘 coral reef 산호초
an abundance of 많은, 풍부한
arctic 북극의
aquatic 물속에 사는, 물의
continental 대륙의
terrestrial 육지의, 육상의

정답 (b)

12 해석 직장을 그만둘 생각이라면 2주 미리 통보해서 원활한
업무 인수인계를 위해 고용주가 새로운 사람을 찾을
시간을 주도록 하세요.

해설 직장을 관둘 때 2주 전에 미리 통보해서 고용주에게
새 후임 직원을 뽑을 시간을 주는 이유는 원활한 업무
인수인계를 위함이라고 보는 것이 자연스럽다. 따라서
빈칸에는 '인수인계'를 뜻하는 (b) transition이 가장
알맞다.

어휘 thereby 그로 인해, 그 때문에
transition 이행, 전환
transit 통행, 운송
transmission 전달, 전송
transformation 변형

정답 (b)

13 해석 강 건너편에 다다르기 위해서는 약 800미터를 더 가
세요. 그러면 걸어서 건널 수 있을 만큼 수심이 얕은
곳이 나옵니다.

해설 강을 걸어서 건널 수 있으려면 수심이 얕아야 할 것이
다. 강이나 개울의 수심이 얕다는 뜻의 어휘는 (d)
shallow이다. 참고로 (b) sheer는 한정적 용법으로
만 쓰이는 형용사이므로 의미를 떠나 문법적으로 성립
될 수 없다.

어휘 thin (두께가) 얇은

sheer 완전한, 순전한

narrow (폭 또는 넓이가) 좁은

shallow 얕은

정답 (d)

14 해석 교수가 주제에서 벗어나면 주제로 되돌아올 것을 요구
하는 것은 부적절한 것이 아니다.

해설 주절에 주제로 되돌아올 것을 요구한다는 내용이 언급
된 것으로 보아 빈칸에는 주제에서 '벗어나다' 라는 뜻
의 동사 (d) digresses가 가장 알맞다.

어휘 leap 도약하다, 뛰어오르다

digress 빗나가다, (주제에서) 벗어나다

distract (주의, 마음 따위를) 딴 데로 돌리다

정답 (d)

15 해석 한방 백과사전은 전 세계 전문가들에 의해 편찬되었다.

해설 백과사전은 전문가들에 의해 편찬되는 것이므로 빈칸
에는 '편찬하다' 의 뜻을 가진 (b) compiled가 들어
가야 한다.

어휘 herbal medicine 한방, 약초요법

conjoin 연합하다, 결합하다

correlate 서로 관련시키다

compile (자료를) 하나로 모으다, 편찬하다

combine 결합하다, 연합하다

정답 (b)

Actual Test

1 해석 A: 오늘 밤 묵을 방 있습니까?

　　B: 죄송합니다. 빈방이 없습니다.

해설 호텔 직원과 고객의 대화이다. A가 하룻밤 묵을 방이
있는지 물어보았으므로 문맥상 빈칸에는 '빈방' 의 뜻
을 가진 단어가 필요하다. 보통 vacancy는 '공석, 비
어 있음' 의 뜻이지만 호텔이나 여관의 '빈방' 을 가리
키기도 한다.

어휘 vacancy 빈방

정답 (a)

2 해석 A: 내일 얘기하러 잠깐 들러도 되겠습니까?

　　B: 물론이에요. 오후 내내 한가할 거예요.

해설 내일 들러도 되겠느냐는 A의 질문에 B가 Sure로 흔
쾌히 승낙했으므로 오후 내내 '한가하다' 는 뜻의 형용
사 (b) free가 문맥에 가장 자연스럽다.

어휘 drop by 잠깐 들르다

chat 잡담

정답 (b)

3 해석 A: 내 빨간 티 봤니?

　　B: 모자 달린 거? 어제 세탁실에 있었어.

해설 의미를 혼동하기 쉬운 어휘를 구분하는 문제이다. 문
맥상 스웨터에 달린 모자를 가리키므로 (c) hood가
적절하다.

어휘 sweatshirt 천이 도톰한 티셔츠

laundry 세탁실

lid 뚜껑, 모자

hat 테가 있는 모자

hood 두건, 두건 모양의 모자

정답 (c)

4 해석 A: 잠깐 얘기 좀 할 수 있을까?

　　B: 응, 하지만 잠깐만이야. 나 시간에 쫓기고 있거든.

해설 문맥상 시간에 대해 '압박을 받다, 쫓기다' 라는 뜻의
어휘가 빈칸에 적절하다. (a) busy 역시 가능할 것 같
지만 부사구 for time과 연결이 되지 않는다. 타동사
press는 경제적, 시간적으로 '압박하다, 쪼들리게 하
다' 라는 뜻이다. 보통 수동형 be pressed for
time/money는 '시간[돈]에 쪼들리다' 라는 뜻이다.

어휘 be pressed for ~에 쫓기다, 쪼들리다

정답 (d)

5 **해석** A: 왜 독서 클럽이 없는거죠? 끝났나요?

B: 예, 몇 주 일찍 해산됐어요.

해설 접두어 dis-로 시작되고 형태를 혼동하기 쉬운 어휘를 구분하는 문제이다. 문맥상 it은 독서 클럽을 가리키고, 독서 클럽이 '해산되었다' 는 뜻이 자연스러우므로 빈칸에는 '해산되다' 라는 뜻의 (b) dissolved가 가장 알맞다.

어휘 dissolve 해산하다, 용해하다

dissolute 무절제한, 방탕한

dissonant 불협화음의, 귀에 거슬리는

dissident 의견을 달리하는, 반체제의

정답 (b)

6 **해석** A: 심사 위원이 무작위로 선출된 이유를 아니?

B: 심사 위원과 참가자 사이의 결탁을 막기 위한 방편인 것 같아요.

해설 심사 위원을 무작위로 선출한 이유가 될 만한 내용이 빈칸에 적절하다. 참가자와 심사 위원이 서로 '결탁' 하는 것을 막기 위함이었다고 보는 것이 가장 자연스러우므로 (c) collusion이 정답이다. 참고로 prevent 의 대상이 될 만한 어휘는 (c) collusion밖에 없다.

어휘 randomly 무작위로, 임의로

contestant (대회) 출전자, 참가자

collision 충돌

conclusion 결론

collusion 결탁, 공모

correlation 상관관계, 상호 관련

정답 (c)

7 **해석** A: 이 돈이 가짜일 수도 있을까?

B: 내 눈엔 진짜로 보여. 왜 진짜가 아니라고 생각해?

해설 접두어 counter-로 시작되고 형태를 혼동하기 쉬운 어휘를 묻는 문제이다. B가 A에게 돈이 왜 진짜가 아니라고 생각하는지 묻고 있는 것으로 보아 A는 돈이 가짜일 수도 있다고 의문을 제기했다고 볼 수 있으므로 빈칸에는 '가짜의, 위조의' 라는 뜻을 가진 (d) counterfeit가 문맥상 가장 자연스럽다.

어휘 genuine 진짜의

counterpart 한 쌍의 한쪽, 등가물

counterstep 대책

countenance 용모, 표정

counterfeit 위조의, 가짜의; 모조품, 위폐

정답 (d)

8 **해석** 뜨거운 팬에 물을 부으면 그것은 수증기로 변할 것이다.

해설 문맥상 빈칸에는 뜨거운 팬 위에 물을 '붓다' 라는 표현이 가장 자연스럽다. 물을 '붓다, 따르다' 는 (b) pour를 쓴다. 나머지 선택지들은 의미적으로 어색하여 water를 목적어로 취할 수 없다.

어휘 turn into ~으로 변하다

cover 덮다

pour 붓다, 따르다

sink 가라앉(히)다

roll 말다, 굴리다

정답 (b)

9 **해석** 모든 거미가 먹이를 잡기 위해 거미줄을 치는 것은 아니다.

해설 문맥상 빈칸에는 '먹이' 의 뜻을 가진 단어가 들어가는 것이 가장 자연스럽다. 선택지 중 '먹이' 라는 뜻을 가진 단어는 (d) prey이다.

어휘 cub (동물의) 새끼

breed 품종; 기르다

정답 (d)

10 **해석** 사람들은 보통 편지를 서명으로 마무리한다.

해설 우리말 간섭으로 혼동하기 쉬운 어휘를 묻는 문제이다. 유명인 등에게 '싸인' 을 받는다고 할 때 autograph를 쓰고, 주로 편지나 서류 등에 하는 서명은 signature라고 한다. 따라서 문맥상 빈칸에는 (b) signature가 가장 알맞다.

어휘 autograph (유명인의) 친필 싸인

signature (편지, 서류 등에 하는) 서명

manuscript 원고, 필사본

autobiography 자서전

정답 (b)

11 **해석** 일부 암 환자들은 병원 치료의 고통스러운 부작용을 극복하기 위해 전통 요법이나 대체 요법을 찾는다.

해설 빈칸에는 traditional과 비슷한 의미의 단어가 들어가야 한다. 선택지 중에서 명사 therapy를 앞에서 수식할 수 있는 형용사는 (c) alternative밖에 없다. 참고로 traditional therapy와 alternative therapy는 사실상 같은 의미로 통하는 용어이다.

어휘 alterative 점진적으로 체질을 바꾸는[개선하는]

altercate 언쟁하다, 말다툼하다

alternative 대안의, 대체의

alliterate ~에 두운을 쓰다

정답 (c)

12 해석 더 심하게 부어오를 수도 있기 때문에 벌에 쏘인 곳에 연고를 바르지 마세요.

해설 문맥상 벌이 쏘인 곳에 연고를 바르면 붓는 증상을 악화시킬 수도 있다는 내용이 자연스러우므로 '악화시키다, 가중시키다'라는 의미를 가진 (c) aggravate가 정답이다.

어휘 ointment 연고
bee sting 벌에 쏘인 상처
swelling 부어오름, 부기
aggress 공격하다
ingrate 은혜를 모르는 사람
aggravate 악화시키다
gratify 만족시키다, 기쁘게 하다

정답 (c)

13 해석 대학을 졸업하고 서커스단에 들어갔을 때 나는 내 소지품을 몽땅 처분했다.

해설 문맥상 '처분하다'라는 의미가 적절하고, 문법적으로도 빈칸 뒤에 전치사 of가 있기 때문에 (c) disposed가 정답이다. 나머지 선택지들은 전치사 of랑 함께 쓰지 않는 동사들이다.

어휘 depart 출발하다
deposit 예금하다, 맡기다
dispose of 처분하다
disburse (돈, 경비를) 지불하다, 쓰다

정답 (c)

14 해석 야당의 목적은 선거의 가장 유력한 후보를 비방하고 공격하는 것이었다.

해설 문맥상 attack과 병치관계에 있는 어휘가 빈칸에 적절하다. 상대의 유력한 후보를 공격하는 것은 곧 비방한다는 것과 일맥상통하므로 빈칸에는 (a) defame이 가장 알맞다.

어휘 opposition party 야당
front-runner 선두 주자
defame 비방[중상]하다
inflame 불을 붙이다, 자극하다
deform 불구로 만들다, ~의 모양을 훼손하다
inflate 부풀리다

정답 (a)

15 해석 설사 발생한다고 해도 우연적인 사건들은 실생활에서 좀처럼 발생하지 않지만 주류 영화 속에서는 자주 인위적으로 꾸며진다.

해설 실생활에서는 좀처럼 발생하지 않는 우연적인 사건들이 영화 속에는 자주 등장하는데, 그 이유는 인위적으로 꾸며낸 것이기 때문이라는 것은 상식이다. 따라서 빈칸에는 '~을 인위적으로 꾸며내다'라는 뜻을 가진 동사 contrive의 과거분사 (a) contrived가 가장 알맞다.

어휘 serendipitous 우연히 발견하는, 우연히 운 좋은
contrive 꾸며내다, 꾀하다
contingent ~에 의존하는, ~에 달려 있는
contrite 회개하는, 죄를 깊이 뉘우치는
contrastive 대조적인

정답 (a)

Actual Test

1　해석　A: 다음 주에 이탈리아로 휴가를 갈 예정이야.

　　　　B: 요즘이 가장 성수기인데. 호텔 방은 예약했니?

　　해설　〈동사 + 명사〉 형태의 연어(collocation)를 묻는 문제이다. 비행편이나 호텔 방 등을 '예약하다' 라는 의미의 동사는 book이다. 문맥상 선택지 중 명사 hotel room과 가장 어울리고 자주 쓰이는 동사는 (b) booked이다.

　　어휘　book 예약하다

　　정답　(b)

2　해석　A: 오늘 아침에 뭐 할 거야?

　　　　B: 시내에 심부름 갈 건데, 내가 뭐 좀 사다 줄까?

　　해설　〈동사 + 명사〉 형태의 연어(collocation)을 묻는 문제이다. 빈칸 앞에 나온 동사 run이 답을 찾는 결정적인 단서이다. 선택지 중 동사 run과 함께 쓰는 명사는 (b) errands이다. 나머지 선택지에 등장한 tasks, jobs, chores 등은 run과 함께 쓰지 않는다.

　　어휘　pick up 사다

　　　　errand 심부름

　　　　chores 집안일

　　　　task 일, 임무

　　정답　(b)

3　해석　A: 좋아요. 총비용은 44달러 58센트입니다.

　　　　B: 그럼, 누구 앞으로 이 수표를 쓸까요?

　　해설　〈동사 + 명사〉 형태의 연어 문제이다. 일반적으로 '수표를 쓰다, 발행하다' 라는 표현은 write/issue a check 또는 make out a check 등을 쓴다. 따라서 정답은 (a) make이다.

　　어휘　make out a check to ~앞으로 수표를 발행하다, 작성하다

　　정답　(a)

4　해석　A: 판매를 증대시킬 방법을 찾아야 해.

　　　　B: 잡지에 광고를 내보는 게 어때?

　　해설　잡지에 광고를 내는 목적은 판매를 '증대시키기' 위함이다. sales는 동사 extend와 persuade의 대상이 될 수 없다. sales와 어울리는 동사는 (c) boost밖에 없다. 게다가 extend는 길이, 기간을 연장한다는 뜻이므로 sales를 목적어로 취할 수 없다.

　　어휘　alleviate 완화시키다

　　　　persuade 설득하다

　　　　boost 증대하다, 올리다

　　　　extend (거리, 기간, 기간 따위를) 연장하다, 늘리다

　　정답　(c)

5　해석　A: 흐린 날에도 보습제와 자외선 차단제를 발라야 한다고 들었어.

　　　　B: 맞아. 자외선이 구름을 뚫고 피부와 계속 접촉하니까.

　　해설　〈동사 + 명사〉 형태의 연어를 물어보는 문제이다. 화장품이나 연고를 바른다고 할 때는 동사 apply를 쓴다.

　　어휘　moisturizer 보습제

　　　　sunblock 자외선 차단제

　　　　apply (약 따위를) 바르다

　　정답　(a)

6　해석　A: 그런데, 믹서는 환불받았니?

　　　　B: 아니, 환불을 원한다고 말하자마자 판매담당자가 화를 냈어.

　　해설　문맥상 판매원이 화를 냈다는 내용이 되어야 자연스럽다. 문법적으로는 nasty가 형용사이므로 빈칸에는 상태의 변화를 나타내는 연결 동사가 필요하므로 (c) turned가 가장 알맞다.

　　어휘　take back 환불하다, 취소하다

　　　　blender 믹서

　　　　refund 환불

　　　　turn nasty 화내다, 난폭하게 굴다

　　정답　(c)

7　해석　오마하법은 어떤 형태든 불필요한 수술을 시술하는 의사에게 형사처벌을 부과한다.

　　해설　〈동사 + 명사〉 형태의 연어 문제이다. 선택지 중 의미적으로 punishment를 목적어로 취할 수 있는 동사는 (b) imposes밖에 없다. impose A on B는 주로 벌금, 세금, 형벌 등을 '~에게 부과하다' 라는 뜻이고, expose는 전치사 to를 써야 한다.

　　어휘　penal punishment 형사처벌

　　　　depose 면직하다, 해고하다

　　　　impose ~ on (세금, 형벌, 의무 등을) 부과하다

　　　　expose 노출시키다, 드러내다

　　　　repose 쉬다, 휴식하다

　　정답　(b)

8 **해석** 교육부 장관은 중학생 교복 착용 의무화의 장점을 알아보기 위해 위원회를 소집할 것이다.

해설 uniforms 뒤의 전치사 on을 눈여겨봐야 답을 고를 수 있는 문제이다. 간접목적어 앞에 전치사 on을 쓰는 동사는 impose밖에 없으므로 정답은 (b) imposing이다. on 이하가 없다면 모두 uniforms를 목적어로 취할 수 있는 동사들이므로 답을 고르기가 쉽지 않다. suggest와 recommend는 on 대신에 전치사 to를 써야 한다.

어휘 convene 소집하다
impose (의무 등을) 지우다, 강요하다

정답 (b)

9 **해석** 법원은 뜻밖에도 고소를 모두 기각하고 피소된 스파이를 석방했다.

해설 〈동사 + 명사〉 형태의 연어(collocation)를 물어보는 문제이다. charge는 '고소'라는 뜻으로 쓰였다. 선택지 중에서 charge를 목적어로 취할 수 있는 동사, 즉 charge와 어울리는 동사는 '기각하다'라는 뜻의 (a) dismissed밖에 없다. 목적어가 all charges이므로 선택지의 다른 동사들과는 어울리지 않는다.

어휘 surprisingly 뜻밖에도, 의외로
dismiss 기각하다, 해산시키다
tolerate 참다, 용인하다
punish 벌주다, 처벌하다
admire 찬양하다

정답 (a)

10 **해석** 관광부에서는 우리나라에 외국인 관광객을 유치하기 위해 열심히 노력하고 있다.

해설 foreign visitors와 가장 많이 쓰이고 잘 어울리는 동사를 고르는 문제이다. 문맥상 관광객을 유치하기 위해 노력한다는 뜻이 되는 것이 자연스럽고, 관광객을 '유치하다'라고 할 때는 동사 draw나 attract를 사용하므로 정답은 (a) draw이다.

어휘 draw (손님을) 끌다, 유인하다

정답 (a)

11 **해석** 연설이 끝난 후에, 관객들은 패널들에게 질문할 수 있는 기회를 갖게 될 것이다.

해설 문맥상 빈칸에는 질문에 '답변하다'라는 뜻보다 '질문을 하다'라는 뜻이 더 적절하다. '질문을 하다, 문제를 제기하다'라고 할 때 명사 question과 어울리는 동사

는 (b) raise이다.

어휘 raise (문제, 의문, 질문 등을) 제기하다

정답 (b)

12 **해석** 고심 씨가 상당히 좋은 지적을 하셨는데, 좀 더 검토해볼 필요가 있다.

해설 '제기하다'라는 뜻의 동사 raise와 어울릴 수 있는 명사를 고르는 문제이다. raise와 어울리는 명사는 question, issue, problem 등이 있는데, 문맥상 '좋은 지적을 하다'라는 의미가 되어야 하므로 빈칸에는 (c) point가 가장 알맞다. 나머지 선택지들은 raise의 목적어로 쓰일 경우 문맥에 전혀 어울리지 않는 명사들이다.

어휘 consideration 검토, 고려
raise a good point 좋은 지적을 하다

정답 (c)

13 **해석** 운동가들은 정치적 부패에 대한 인식을 높이기 위해 시위를 했다.

해설 명사 demonstration과 어울리는 동사를 고르는 연어 문제이다. 문맥상 시위를 한다는 뜻이 적절하며, 이 경우 demonstration 앞에 주로 쓰는 동사는 stage와 hold이다. 나머지 선택지의 동사들은 demonstration과 함께 쓰면 어울리지 않는 동사들이다.

어휘 raise awareness 인식을 높이다
corruption 부패, 부정행위
hold/stage a demonstration 시위를 하다

정답 (c)

14 **해석** 이 〈뉴요커〉 전집은 유명한 정치 풍자가들의 삽화를 담고 있다.

해설 문맥에 알맞은 동사를 고르는 문제이다. 〈뉴요커〉에서 발췌한 전집이 삽화들을 포함하고 있거나 담고 있다고 문장을 완성하는 것이 가장 자연스러우므로 (b) contains가 정답이다.

어휘 political satirist 정치 풍자가

정답 (b)

15 **해석** 이 나라의 대부분의 사람들은 자신들이 차에 넣은 기름이 실제로 어디에서 생산된 건지 모른다.

해설 빈칸 앞의 the gas와 어울리는 동사를 고르는 〈동사 + 명사〉 형태의 연어 문제이다. '차에 기름을 넣다' 또

는 '주유하다'라고 말할 때 the gas 앞에 쓰는 동사
는 (d) pump이다. 나머지 선택지의 동사들은 the
gas랑 어울리지 않는 동사들이다.

어휘 pump (the) gas (차에) 기름을 넣다

정답 (d)

Actual Test

1 해석 A: 오늘 아침 그 비행기에 무슨 일이 생긴 거죠?

　　　B: 조종사가 시계 제로인 상황에서 비상 착륙을 시도
　　　　했어요.

　　해설 〈명사 + 명사〉 형태의 연어(collocation)를 묻는 문
　　　　제이다. 빈칸에는 문맥상 '완전 무'를 뜻하는 단어가
　　　　들어가야 한다. 선택지 모두 아무것도 없음을 뜻하는
　　　　단어들이지만 visibility와 함께 물리적으로 측정 가능
　　　　한 정도에 있어 zero를 쓴다. 부정대명사 none과
　　　　nothing은 형용사로 쓰일 수 없으므로 visibility를
　　　　수식할 수 없다. (c) void는 속이 텅 비었다는 뜻으로
　　　　visibility와는 어울리지 않는다.

　　어휘 emergency landing 비상 착륙

　　　　void 텅 빈, 헛된

　　　　zero visibility 앞이 전혀 보이지 않음

　　정답 (b)

2 해석 A: 누군가가 계속해서 나한테 장난 전화를 걸고 있어.

　　　B: 그런 식으로 널 괴롭히는 이유가 뭘까?

　　해설 B의 응답으로 보아 사람을 괴롭히는 전화라고 볼 수
　　　　있으므로 '장난 전화'라는 뜻이 문맥상 적절하다고 볼
　　　　수 있다. '장난 전화'는 crank call로 표현한다.

　　어휘 a crank call 장난 전화

　　　　trick 속임수

　　　　joke 농담

　　　　fake 가짜(의)

　　정답 (a)

3 해석 A: 손님께서 요청하셨던 MP3 플레이어 기종은 더 이
　　　　상 생산되지 않습니다.

　　　B: 혹시 그거랑 비슷한 기종 있나요?

　　해설 고객과 점원의 대화이다. 고객 입장에서는 전자 제품
　　　　을 구입할 때 찾는 물건이 단종되었다는 얘기를 듣게
　　　　되는 경우, 그와 비슷한 동급 모델을 구입하는 것이
　　　　일반적일 것이다. (b) equivalent와 (d) equal은 둘
　　　　다 '동등한'의 의미가 있지만 전자 제품의 '동급' 기
　　　　종이라는 뜻으로는 equivalent를 쓰므로 정답은 (b)
　　　　equivalent이다. 참고로 the same model은 완전
　　　　히 동일한 기종을 말하는 것이고, equivalent
　　　　model은 분명 다른 기종이지만 동등한 기능과 특징
　　　　을 가진 비슷한 기종이라는 뜻이다.

어휘 default 태만, 불이행
　　　delegate 대표, 대리
　　　equivalent 동등한, 맞먹는
　　　equal (수량, 거리, 가치 등이) 같은, 동등한
정답 (b)

4　해석 A: 나 머리가 많이 빠지는 거 같아. 대머리가 되는 게
　　　　　 아니었으면 해.
　　　　 B: 절대로 아니야. 넌 아직 머리숱이 많아.
　　해설 단어의 어울림(collocation)을 묻는 문제이다. 대화의
　　　　 문맥상 '머리숱이 많다'는 내용이 되도록 문장을 완성
　　　　 해야 한다. '머리숱이 많다'고 할 때 hair 앞에 쓰는
　　　　 형용사는 thick이다. 반면 '머리숱이 적다'는 형용사
　　　　 thin을 쓴다. 따라서 정답은 (c) thick이다. 참고로 액
　　　　 체가 끈적끈적하다거나 묽다고 말할 때도 형용사
　　　　 thick과 thin을 쓴다.
　　어휘 thick hair 숱이 많은 머리
　　　　 glossy 광택 있는, 반들반들한
　　정답 (c)

5　해석 A: 밥의 결혼식 1주 전에 총각 파티가 있을 거야. 같이
　　　　　 갈래?
　　　　 B: 물론이지. 갈 거야.
　　해설 문맥상 '총각 파티'라는 의미가 되도록 빈칸을 완성해
　　　　 야 한다. 결혼식 전에 신랑과 신랑 친구들이 벌이는
　　　　 파티를 '총각 파티'라고 하는데 영어로는 bachelor
　　　　 party로 표현한다. 참고로 (b) reception은 party와
　　　　 함께 쓰지 않고 단독으로 써야 하므로 의미를 떠나 답
　　　　 이 될 수 없다.
　　어휘 farewell party 송별회
　　　　 bachelor party 총각 파티(= stag party)
　　　　 reception 피로연
　　　　 housewarming party 집들이
　　정답 (a)

6　해석 A: 제 가방 중에 하나가 없어졌어요!
　　　　 B: 진정하세요. 저희가 처리해 드릴게요. 수화물 표 아
　　　　　 직 갖고 계신가요?
　　해설 공항에서 짐을 찾기 위해서는 수화물 표가 필요한데,
　　　　 이 '수화물 표'를 영어로는 baggage claim ticket
　　　　 이라고 한다. 참고로 동사 claim에는 '자기 물건임을
　　　　 주장하다, 소유권을 주장하다, 물건을 회수하다'라는
　　　　 뜻이 있다.

어휘 baggage claim ticket 수화물(수취) 표
　　　declaration 신고, 선언
　　　customs declaration 세관 신고(서)
　　　security 보안
정답 (b)

7　해석 A: 뭐가 문젠가요, 경관님?
　　　　 B: 제한 속도를 초과하여 주행하셨습니다. 운전면허증
　　　　　 과 차량 등록증 좀 주시겠습니까?
　　해설 일상 생활 어휘를 묻는 문제이다. 과속 등의 교통법규
　　　　 위반으로 경찰관에게 걸렸을 경우, 운전면허증과 자동
　　　　 차 등록증을 제시하라고 요구받는데, 대화의 문맥상
　　　　 빈칸은 '등록증'의 뜻을 갖는 어휘가 들어갈 자리이
　　　　 다. '차량 등록증'은 vehicle registration으로 표현
　　　　 하므로 정답은 (d) registration이다.
　　어휘 legislation 입법(화)
　　　　 ticket (교통 위반) 딱지
　　　　 vehicle registration 차량 등록(증)
　　정답 (d)

8　해석 A: 이 소포를 푸에르토리코에 보내고 싶습니다.
　　　　 B: 항공우편으로요? 아니면 보통우편으로요?
　　해설 양자택일을 뜻하는 접속사 or로 보아 빈칸은 airmail
　　　　 과 상반되는 단어가 들어가야 한다. 항공우편과 상반
　　　　 되는 우편은 해로나 육로를 이용한 '보통우편'인데 지
　　　　 면과 해면을 이용한다고 해서 surface mail로 표현
　　　　 한다. 지면과 해면의 표면을 달려 우편을 운반한다는
　　　　 의미일 것이다.
　　어휘 airmail 항공우편
　　　　 surface mail (항공 우편을 제외한) 보통우편
　　정답 (c)

9　해석 A: 나는 높은 실업률이 낮아지리라 기대하고 있어.
　　　　 B: 나도 그런 낙관적인 전망을 하고 싶지만 경제 현실
　　　　　 은 그쪽 방향을 가리키지 않아.
　　해설 실업률이 낮아질 거란 A의 전망에 B는 찬성하지 않고
　　　　 있음을 but 이하의 문장을 통해 알 수 있다. 상식적으
　　　　 로 실업률이 떨어질 것이라고 기대하는 것은 긍정적이
　　　　 고 낙관적인 전망이라고 볼 수 있다. 우리말에도 낙관
　　　　 적인 전망을 장밋빛 전망이라고 하듯이 영어에서도
　　　　 '낙관적인 전망'을 rosy view로 표현한다.
　　어휘 have hope that~ ~이라는 기대를 품다
　　　　 pink 분홍색(의), 흥분한, 화난

rosy view 낙관적인 전망

point in that direction 그 방향을 가리키다

정답 (b)

10 해석 A: 가지고 오신 식물이나 과일, 동물이 있습니까?

B: 아니요, 없습니다. 이건 제 세관 신고서입니다.

해설 수화물 중에 식물이나 과일, 동물이 있느냐고 물어보는 것으로 보아 공항에서 벌어지는 대화이고, 문맥상 여자가 제시한 것은 '세관 신고서'임을 유추할 수 있다. 동식물은 세관 신고서에 반드시 신고해야 하는데, 이 '세관 신고서'를 영어로는 customs declaration 이라고 한다.

어휘 customs declaration 세관 신고(서)

proposition 제안, 제의

announcement 알림, 공고

testimony (법정에서) 선서 증언

정답 (a)

11 해석 A: 저 여자가 정말 메리 맞아? 10년은 더 젊어 보여.

B: 나도 알아. 최근에 몇 차례 주름 제거 수술을 받은 게 분명해.

해설 대화의 문맥상 Mary라는 여자가 10년은 더 젊어 보인다고 한 걸로 보아 안면 성형수술을 받은 것으로 유추할 수 있다. '안면 성형수술'은 '주름 제거 수술'이라고도 하는데 영어로는 facelift라고 한다. 참고로 facelift는 자동차 용어로도 아주 많이 쓰이는데, 새로 나온 신차가 구형 모델에서 디자인과 외관만 살짝 수정하여 나온 경우를 가리킨다.

어휘 C-section 제왕 절개 수술

jackpot 누적된 상금

facelift 안면 성형

pink slip 해고 통지서

정답 (c)

12 해석 군법을 위반하면 군법회의에 회부될 수 있다.

해설 court-martial이라는 어휘를 알면 너무 쉬운 문제이고, 모르면 답을 찾기가 쉽지 않은 문제이다. court-martial은 '군법회의'라는 뜻이므로 이와 가장 관련이 있는 (d) military가 정답이다. 이처럼 어휘는 많이 알면 알수록 고득점에 유리하다.

어휘 military code 군법

court-martial 군법회의

정답 (d)

13 해석 그녀는 그녀의 최신 음반 판매로부터 나오는 모든 수익금을 국제 자선단체에 기부함으로써 자신보다 불운한 사람들을 돕기로 결심했다.

해설 자신보다 불운한 사람들을 돕기 위해 돈을 기부할 곳은 결국 자선단체일 것이므로 빈칸에는 '자선단체'란 뜻을 가진 어휘가 가장 알맞다. '자선단체'는 영어로 charity라고 하므로 정답은 (d)이다.

어휘 charity 자선단체

proceeds 수익금

contribution 공헌, 기부(금)

chastity 순결, 정조

corpus (문서, 법전 등의) 집성, 전집

정답 (d)

14 해석 점점 더 많은 가수들이 인기를 유지하기 위해 성형수술을 받고 있다.

해설 가수들이 인기를 유지하기 위해 받는 수술은 심장 수술이 아니라 성형수술이다. '성형수술'은 영어로 plastic surgery라고 한다. 참고로 plastic에는 '신용카드'라는 뜻과 '비닐'이란 뜻도 있다는 점에 유의한다.

어휘 plastic surgery 성형수술

aesthetic 미학의, 심미적인

artistic 예술적인

정답 (b)

15 해석 영양에 관한 새로운 의학 연구가 평균 수명을 연장하는 데 도움을 줄 것으로 기대된다.

해설 평균 수명은 길이에 해당되므로 늘리거나(prolong, lengthen) 연장하거나(extend) 줄인다(shorten)고 표현한다. 문맥상 예상 수명을 '연장하다'라는 의미가 적절하므로 정답은 (a) prolong이다.

어휘 prolong 연장하다, 늘리다

life expectancy 평균[예상] 수명

attach 붙이다, 첨부하다

정답 (a)

Actual Test

1 **해석** A: 사장이 정말 까다로워.

B: 맞아. 직원들에게 매우 높은 기준을 적용해.

해설 사장이 직원들에게 매우 높은 기준을 적용한다고 한 것으로 보아 사장이 매우 '까다로운' 사람임을 추론할 수 있으므로 정답은 (b) picky이다. picky 외에 성미가 까다롭다는 뜻의 형용사에는 finicky, choosy, demanding, fastidious, fussy 등이 있다.

어휘 picky 까다로운

lenient 인자한, 관대한

humdrum 평범한, 단조로운

정답] (b)

2 **해석** A: 파가니니가 누구였는지 아니?

B: 물론! 유명한 바이올린의 대가였지.

해설 문맥상 파가니니는 바이올린을 아주 잘 연주한 '명연주가', 다시 말해 바이올린의 '대가'였다고 문장을 완성하는 것이 가장 자연스러워 보이므로 (d) virtuoso가 정답이다. 나머지 선택지에 등장한 단어들은 모두 사람을 가리키는 단어가 아니므로 답이 될 수 없다.

어휘 virtuoso (예술의) 대가, 거장

fiasco 대실패

relic 유적, 폐허

artifact 가공품, 인공물

정답 (d)

3 **해석** A: 나는 잠들기 바로 직전에 커피 한 잔과 담배 한 대를 즐겨.

B: 정말? 그런 자극제들을 섭취하면 난 잠이 오지 않던데.

해설 단어의 뜻만 알면 쉽게 풀 수 있는 유형이다. 커피와 담배는 의약품(medications), 마약(narcotics), 무기물(minerals)이 아니라 사람을 흥분시키는 '자극제'이므로 정답은 (a) Stimulants이다.

어휘 stimulant 자극제

narcotics 마취제

medication 약물

mineral 무기물, 광물

정답 (a)

4. **해석** A: 너희 팀이 지다니 너무 안됐어. 승리를 기대했던

걸로 알고 있는데.

B: 결과가 믿겨지지 않아. 나는 완전히 충격 먹었어!

해설 B는 승리하리라 기대했던 경기에서 졌기 때문에 망연자실하거나 충격을 받았다(devastated)고 보는 것이 적절할 것이다. 너무나 충격을 받아서 정신적으로 '맛이 간' 상태를 가장 잘 표현하는 단어가 (a) devastated일 것이다.

어휘 devastate 망연자실하게 하다

hypnotize 최면을 걸다

repress 억제하다

placate 달래다, 진정시키다

정답 (a)

5 **해석** 이러한 어구들은 의미에 있어서 똑같아 보이지만 가지고 있는 함축적 의미는 미묘하게 다르다.

해설 난이도가 상당히 높은 문제이다. 얼핏 보면 의미상 차이가 없어 보이지만 숨어 있는 뜻, 즉 함축된 의미가 다른 경우가 있는데, 이처럼 어떤 단어나 어구의 표면적으로 드러난 의미 외에 그 이면에 숨어 있는 의미를 영어로는 connotation이라고 한다. 예를 들어 값이 싸다는 표현에 cheap이 있는데, cheap에는 '싸구려, 천한' 등의 부정적인 의미가 내포되어 있다. 이런 경우에 cheap에는 negative connotation이 들어 있다고 말한다.

어휘 connotation 함축적 의미

conjunction 연결, 결합

conjecture 짐작, 추측

configuration 배열, (컴퓨터) 시스템의 설정

정답 (d)

6 **해석** 몇몇 사람들은 미국 정부가 2개국어 상용 정책을 촉진하기 시작함으로써 영어가 미국 내의 많은 경쟁 언어들 중에서 단지 하나에 불과한 언어가 되는 시나리오를 만들어내지는 않을까 염려하고 있다.

해설 영어가 미국 내의 수많은 언어들 중에 단지 한 언어에 불과해질 가능성이 있는 이유는 미국 정부가 2개국어 상용 정책을 방해하기(hamper) 시작해서가 아니라, 적극 추진하기 시작해서라고 문장을 완성하는 것이 문맥에 알맞다. 따라서 빈칸에는 '추진하다, 촉진하다'라는 뜻을 지니는 동사 (b) foster가 가장 알맞다.

어휘 foster 촉진하다, 추진하다

hamper 방해하다

emulate 경쟁하다

mesmerize 최면술을 걸다

정답 (b)

7 **해석** 갑작스러운 심한 서리 때문에 일 년간의 수확물을 잃은 것은 우리를 매우 맥 빠지게 했다.

해설 한 해 동안 고생해서 가꾼 농작물을 갑작스런 서리로 잃어버리는 것은 매우 '낙담시키는' 일이고 '맥 빠지게 하는' 일이라고 문장을 완성하는 것이 자연스러우므로 (d) unnerving이 정답이다.

어휘 fussy 야단법석인
endearing 사랑스런
unnerving 맥 빠지게 하는, 낙담시키는

정답 (d)

8 **해석** 당신의 주장을 설득력 있게 뒷받침하기 위해 확고한 정보는 필수 불가결이다.

해설 어떤 주장을 설득력 있게 뒷받침하기 위해서 증거로 제시하는 정보는 구체적이고 믿을 만해야 할 것이다. 이렇게 '믿을 만하고 구체적인 정보'를 solid information 이라고 한다. (c)의 credulous는 사람에게만 쓰는 형용사로 '남의 말을 쉽사리 믿는, 잘 속는'의 뜻이다.

어휘 convincingly 설득력 있게
back up 입증하다, 뒷받침하다
solid 확고한, 구체적이고 믿을 만한
credulous 잘 속는, 쉽게 믿는
crafty 교활한, 솜씨 있는

정답 (a)

9 **해석** 숲에서 독초를 먹은 후에 칼은 해독제로 치료를 받아야 했다.

해설 독초(poison plant)를 먹었다고 했으므로 빈칸에는 '해독제'라는 뜻의 단어가 들어가는 것이 적절하므로 정답은 (c) antidote이다.

어휘 antidote 해독제
anecdote 일화, 비화
antithesis 대조, 대립
anaesthetic 마취제

정답 (c)

10 **해석** 전쟁 상황에 대해 훨씬 더 불길한 소식이 도착했고, 사람들 머리 위에 절망적인 구름을 드리웠다.

해설 사람들에게 절망감을 가져다주었다는 내용이 뒤에 이어지므로 밝고(bright) 장래성 있는(promising) 소식이 아니라 어두운 소식이 도착했다는 내용으로 문장을 완성하는 것이 자연스럽다. 따라서 정답은 (a) grim이다.

어휘 grim 어두운

정답 (a)

11 **해석** 그 아이는 일주일 내내 반복된 이상한 꿈을 그의 엄마에게 얘기했다.

해설 일주일 내내(throughout the week)라는 부사어구가 단서이다. 일주일 내내 잠을 자면서 꾼 이상한 꿈이 아니라 일주일간 잠을 잘 때마다 반복적으로 꾼 이상한 꿈이므로 반복해서 되풀이된다는 뜻의 (a) recurred가 정답이다.

어휘 relate 이야기하다, 말하다
recur 반복되다, 되풀이되다
incur 초래하다
reverberate 울려퍼지다, 반사하다
vaporize 증발하다

정답 (a)

12 **해석** 저희 회사는 인종, 국적, 신념 또는 성별에 기초한 그 어떤 종류의 차별도 막기 위해 강력한 조치들을 취해 왔습니다.

해설 선택지 중 인종, 국적, 신념, 성별 등과 가장 관련이 있는 단어는 '차별'의 뜻을 가진 (c) discrimination이다. 사람들은 인종, 국적, 신념, 성별에 근거해서 차별을 한다.

어휘 discrimination 차별 (대우), 구별
harassment 괴롭히기, 희롱
enforcement (법률의) 시행, 집행
distinction 구별, 차이

정답 (c)

13 **해석** 진료소를 운영하는 것 외에도 래리는 가난한 아이들을 가르치는 것과 같은 자선 활동을 하면서 여가 시간을 보내는 걸 좋아했다.

해설 형용사 underprivileged(혜택받지 못한, 가난한, 소외 계층의)의 뜻을 모르면 다소 까다로운 문제이다. 가난한 아이들을 가르치면서 여가 시간을 보내는 것은 금전적인 대가가 목적(financial cause)인 활동이 아니라 자선 그 자체가 목적(philanthropic cause)인 활동의 하나이므로 정답은 (d) philanthropic이다.

philanthropic은 '인류를 좋아하는, 박애주의적인' 의 뜻에서 '자선의, 자선 사업의' 라는 뜻이 파생되어 나왔다고 볼 수 있다. 민간이 하는 모든 봉사 활동은 philanthropic cause(자선 목적)를 가지고 있다고 이해하면 된다.

어휘 underprivileged 혜택받지 못한, 가난한
philanthropic 자선의, 박애(주의)의
cause 동기, 목적, 대의
phonetic 음성(학)의
pharmaceutical 제약의
phenomenal 경이적인, 놀랄 만한

정답 (d)

14 해석 텁수룩한 쌍둥이 형과는 달리 앤디는 맞춤 양복을 입고 깔끔하게 보이려고 애를 썼다.

해설 전치사 unlike가 있으므로 형용사 disheveled와 상반된 의미의 형용사를 고르면 된다. disheveled는 '텁수룩한, 단정치 못한, 지저분한' 의 뜻이므로 빈칸에는 '깔끔한, 말쑥한' 의 뜻을 가진 형용사가 들어가는 것이 가장 자연스럽다. 선택지 중에서는 (a) impeccable이 가장 근접한 뜻을 가지고 있다. impeccable은 '나무랄 데 없는, 흠잡을 데 없는' 의 뜻인데, 옷차림이 흠잡을 데 없다는 것은 깔끔하다는 말과 일맥상통한다.

어휘 disheveled (머리가) 헝클어진, 단정치 못한
take pains 수고하다, 애쓰다
tailor-maid 몸에 꼭 맞는, 맞춤(양복)의
impeccable 깔끔한, 나무랄 데 없는
disconsolate 절망적인, 불행한
gullible 속기 쉬운, 잘 속는

정답 (a)

15 해석 그 영화는 전혀 예측할 수 없는 줄거리로 여러분의 시선을 화면에 고정시킬 것이다.

해설 영화가 화면에서 눈을 뗄 수 없게 만든다고 했으므로 스토리가 전혀 '예측 불가능한' 영화라고 문장을 완성하는 것이 가장 자연스럽다. (c) unprecedented 는 얼핏 답이 될 수 있다고 생각할 수도 있지만 영화가 '전례 없는, 전에는 없었던 새로운' 스토리를 가지고 있다고 반드시 관객들의 시선을 화면에 고정시키는 것은 아니므로 답으로 부적절하고, (a) impenetrable은 '이해하기 어려운' 스토리로 관객의 시선을 고정시킨다는 뜻이 되므로 내용상 모순이 생겨 부자연스럽다.

어휘 rivet 고정시키다
unpredictable 예측할 수 없는
impenetrable 이해할 수 없는
unprecedented 전례 없는, 새로운
unpronounceable 발음하기 어려운

정답 (b)

Chapter 01 빈칸 위치가 상단

Sample

해석 많은 과학자들은 나이와 관련된 시력 상실을 노화 단계(과정) 외의 요인으로 돌린다. 실제로 중년이 넘어서도 완벽한 시력을 유지하는 사람은 드물다. 시력 상실은 피할 수 없는 것은 아니며, 인간의 눈이 여든 살 넘어서까지 좋은 시력을 유지하지 못할 이유는 전혀 없다. 그러나 자외선, 오염, 영양 부족 같은 요인이 눈을 해친다.

(a) 장수의 비밀
(b) 행복의 한 단계
(c) 나이에 따른 시력 상실
(d) 선천성 실명

해설 빈칸이 지문 상단에 위치한 유형으로 주제문의 완성을 요구하는 문제이다. 사람이 나이가 들면 시력이 저하되는데 자연스러운 노화 과정으로 인해 시력이 나빠지는 것이 아니라 노화 과정 외의 자외선 같은 외부 요인이 시력 저하의 원인이기 때문에 시력 저하는 충분히 피할 수 있다는 요지의 글이므로 빈칸에는 '시력 상실'이라는 내용이 들어가야 한다. 이런 유형의 문제를 풀기 위해서는 주제문을 뒷받침하는 문장들을 통해 글쓴이가 도대체 무엇을 얘기하려는지 의중을 파악하려는 시도가 선행되어야 한다. 특히 일반인의 통념을 뒤집는 Loss of vision is not inevitable 부분을 주목하고, However 이하의 주제문을 뒷받침하는 내용에 유의한다면 쉽게 답을 구할 수 있는 문제이다.

정답 (c)

Actual Test

1 **해석** 알츠하이머병에 걸린 사람은 결국 자신이 누구인지 잊어버리게 된다. 한 의학 관련 회사의 연구진은 이 심각한 질병의 원인이 되는 효소 물질을 발견했다고 믿고 있다. 당장 치료약이 나오는 것은 아니지만 이는 세상의 가장 치명적인 질병들 중 하나를 퇴치하는 데 있어서 중요한 발걸음이 됨을 의미할 수도 있다.

(a) 동급의
(b) 필요한
(c) 궁극적인
(d) 당장의

해설 한 회사의 연구자들이 알츠하이머병의 원인이 되는 효소를 발견했다는 내용의 글이다. 빈칸이 위치한 문장에 접속사 while이 있으므로 while절은 주절 문장과 대조되는 내용이 와야 한다. 이 발견이 알츠하이머병을 치료하는 데 아주 중요할 거라는 내용이 주절에 나왔으므로 그 앞의 while절은 치료약이 당장 이용 가능한 것은 아니라는 내용이 와야 대조가 이루어진다. 따라서 '당장의, 즉각적인'의 의미를 가진 (d) immediate가 정답이다.

어휘 be inflicted with ~로 괴로움을 당하다
ultimately 결국
enzyme 효소
equivalent 동등한, 동급의
forthcoming 가까워오는, 닥쳐오는
signify 의미하다, 나타내다
devastating 무서운, 지독한
eventual 궁극적인, 최종적인
immediate 즉각적인, 당장의

정답 (d)

2 **해석** 단백질이 강화된 앳킨스 다이어트는 체중 관리에 신경 쓰는 여성들이 성공적으로 아기를 낳을 수 있는 가능성을 떨어뜨릴 수도 있다. 앳킨스 다이어트에서는 주로 고기, 생선, 그리고 계란의 섭취는 권장하는 반면 빵, 밥, 파스타, 그리고 전분이 들어 있는 채소 같은 탄수화물의 섭취는 제한한다. 연구 결과에 따르면 주로 단백질을 섭취한 설치류의 배아들은 자궁 착상에 실패했다. 이러한 연구 결과는 아기를 낳고 싶어 하는 여성들에게는 심각한 걱정거리가 될 수 있다.

(a) 체중을 걱정하는
(b) 아기를 낳고 싶어 하는
(c) 고기를 너무 많이 먹는
(d) 다이어트를 할 수 없는

해설 빈칸이 하단에 위치한 유형으로 주제문을 재진술하는 유형이다. 단백질 위주의 앳킨스 다이어트가 여성의 임신 가능성을 떨어뜨릴 수도 있다는 내용의 글로 단백질을 주로 섭취한 쥐의 배아가 착상에 실패했다는 연구 결과를 증거로 대고 있다. 따라서 연구 결과에 대해 어떤 종류의 여성들이 크게 걱정할지 생각해 보면 답을 쉽게 찾을 수 있다.

어휘 protein-intensive 단백질이 강화된
weight-watching 체중 관리에 신경 쓰는
carbohydrate 탄수화물
starchy 전분이 든, 녹말질의

embryo 태아

rodent 설치 동물(쥐, 다람쥐)

ingest 섭취하다

womb 자궁

implantation (수정란의) 착상

findings 연구[조사] 결과

interpret 해석하다

정답 (b)

3　**해석**　어디에나 있는 물질인 술은 우리 사회의 안정에 점점 더 해롭게 되었다. 술은 인간관계에 매우 해롭다. 술은 가정을 파괴하고 전통적인 가치를 서서히 파괴할 수 있다. 나는 술 취한 남편들에 의해 여성들이 끔찍하게 학대받는 것을 목격했다. 이런 현실에도 불구하고 나는 술을 금지하려는 사람들의 의견에 동의하지 않는다. 술이 금지되면 술을 만드는 노동자들이 고통받을 것이다. 술 유통에 종사하는 사람은 누구나 실직하게 될 것이다. 게다가 술을 금지하는 것은 불법적으로 술을 밀수할 방법을 찾으려는 범죄 조직만 다시 들끓게 만들 것이다.

(a) 밀수하다

(b) 끊다

(c) 마시다

(d) 조직하다

해설　술을 금지하는 데 반대하는 사람이 쓴 글이다. 빈칸에 들어갈 내용이 지문에 직접적으로 언급되어 있지 않으므로 글 전체의 대의를 파악하고 세부 정보를 추론해서 빈칸에 넣어야 하는 유형의 문제이다. 글쓴이는 술을 금지하게 될 경우 생길 수 있는 여러 가지 문제점을 언급하며 특히 술 제조와 유통을 금지하면 범죄 조직이 다시 활개 치게 될 것이라고 경고하고 있다. 따라서 빈칸에는 술 판매 금지와 더불어 범죄 조직이 할 만한 행위를 선택지 중에서 고르면 된다. 아무래도 술 제조와 판매가 금지되면 술을 밀수하려는 사람이 증가한다고 볼 수 있으므로 (a)가 가장 알맞다.

어휘　ubiquitous 도처에 존재하는

erode 부식시키다, 서서히 파괴하다

time-honored value 전통적인 가치관

awful 끔찍한

intoxicated 취한, 중독된

outlaw 금지하다

brewery 양조장

reinvigorate 다시 활기를 불어넣다

smuggle 밀수하다

abstain from 삼가다

정답 (a)

4　**해석**　이제 현대의 우리 삶에 침투하는 기술이 이로운 것으로 여겨질 수 있겠지만 그 기술에는 일부 못 미더운 측면들 또한 존재한다. 예를 들어, 쌍방향 통신 기술이 궁극적으로 사람들의 마음을 조정하고, 사생활을 침해하고, 사람들이 가족의 의무와 인간관계를 저버리게끔 영향을 미칠 것인가? 유전자 조작된 식품이 우리의 건강에 장기적으로 어떤 영향을 끼칠 것인가? 첨단 의학을 이용한 질병 치료가 사람들의 수명을 늘릴 수 있다. 하지만 사람들을 전반적으로 더 행복하고 만족하게 만들 수 있을까? 두고 봐야 할 일이다.

Q. 이 글의 가장 알맞은 제목은 무엇인가?

(a) 쌍방향 미디어와 현대의 딜레마

(b) 인간의 건강과 기술

(c) 기술 발전의 필연적인 힘

(d) 기술 발전의 장점과 단점

해설　기술 발전에 긍정적인 측면이 있음을 인정하면서도 기술 발전의 부정적인 측면들을 넌지시 비추면서 회의적인 반응을 보이며 의심하고 있다. 따라서 기술 발전의 장점과 단점, 또는 찬반양론(Pros and Cons)을 가장 적절한 제목으로 볼 수 있다.

어휘　permeate 침투하다, 스며들다

questionable 의심할 만한, 못 미더운

interactive 상호적인, 쌍방향의

manipulate 조작하다, 조정하다

eliminate 고려하지 않다, 무시하다

genetically modified food 유전자 조작 식품

sophisticated 첨단의, 정교한

contentment 만족

wait and see 두고 보다, 지켜보다

the pros and cons of ~에 대한 찬반양론,
~의 장단점

정답 (d)

5　**해석**　오늘날 서구 사회에서 부모는 그들의 아이들에게 기초 윤리를 가르쳐야 하고 정규 교육을 제공해야 한다. 그러나 이와는 별도로 어떤 한 개인의 성장은 대체로 유전인자나 무작위 우연성에 달려 있다고 여겨지고 있다. 이러한 견해와는 반대로, 그들의 자녀가 사회의 행복하고 성공적인 구성원이 될 수 있도록 부모가 훨씬

더 많은 부문에서 기여할 수 있다는 것을 암시하는 지
난 십 년간의 많은 연구 자료들이 있다.

Q. 다음 중 이 글의 가장 알맞은 제목은 무엇인가?

(a) 왜 부모들이 보다 많이 해야 하는가

(b) 자녀를 기르는 알맞은 방법

(c) 부모 자식 관계

(d) 개성의 유전적 근원

해설 오늘날 서구 사회에서 부모의 역할에 대해 설명한 글
을 읽고 적절한 제목을 고르는 문제이다. 부모가 자녀
들에게 할 수 있는 일이 단순하게 기본 윤리를 가르치
고 학교에 보내 정규 교육을 받게 하는 것에 국한되지
않고, 자녀의 행복과 성공을 위해 훨씬 더 많은 부분
에서 아이들을 도와줄 수 있다는 요지의 글이므로 (a)
Why Parents Should Do More가 제목으로 가장
알맞다.

어휘 instruct 교육하다, 가르치다
formal education 정규[학교] 교육
apart from ~외에, ~와는 별도로
genetic factor 유전인자
random coincidence 무작위 우연성
a growing body of 많은 양의

정답 (a)

6. **해석** 면학을 최우선으로 하는 것은 중요하다. 하지만 자신이
좋아하고 마음을 편안하게 해주는 활동을 하기 위해
시간을 보내는 것 또한 중요하다. 신중한 학생들은 종
종 자신들이 숙제와 학교에 관련된 활동들 외에는 어
떤 것도 할 시간이 없다고 주장한다. 그들은 취미가 공
부 시간을 빼앗아 갈 수 있다고 생각한다. 하지만 그들
이 깨닫지 못하고 있는 것은 중요한 책임들로부터 잠
시나마 휴식을 취하도록 해주는 활동이 학교 성적을
높여 줄 수도 있다는 사실이다. 시간을 내어 휴식을 취
하고 취미를 즐기는 것은 스트레스를 감소시켜 주고
공부를 해야 할 시간에 집중하는 것을 더 쉽게 해준다.

Q. 위 글의 내용을 가장 잘 요약하고 있는 것은 무엇
인가?

(a) 학교 외의 활동을 하는 것이 학업 성적에 도움이
된다.

(b) 오늘날 많은 학생들은 할 일이 너무 많다.

(c) 취미를 즐기기 위한 시간을 찾는 것은 종종 힘든 일
이다.

(d) 여가 시간에 무얼 하는가가 성적에 영향을 끼칠 수
있다.

해설 흔히 학생들은 공부 외에 다른 것을 할 시간이 없다고
생각하지만 해야 하는 일들을 잠시 잊고 자신이 하고
싶은 일을 하는 것이 오히려 나중에 공부를 해야 할
때 집중력을 높여 줘서 성적에 도움이 된다는 내용이
므로 정답은 (a)이다.

어휘 academic pursuit 면학
priority 우선순위, 우위
maintain 주장하다
performance 성적

정답 (a)

7 **해석** 왜 부유한 유명 인사들만 화려한 결혼식을 올릴 기회
를 가져야 합니까? (a) 누구나 큰돈을 쓰지 않고 멋진
결혼식을 올릴 수 있어야 합니다. (b) 유명인들의 결혼
식에서 아이디어를 얻어 혁신과 저비용 고효율에 중점
을 두면서 유명인들의 결혼식을 비슷하게 흉내 내어
보실 것을 제안합니다. (c) 유명한 사람들은 국제적으
로 잘 알려진 디자이너를 고용해서 결혼 예복을 만들
게 할 만큼 많은 돈을 가지고 있습니다. (d) 제 말을
믿으세요. 파산하지 않고 멋진 영화배우 스타일의 결
혼식을 모방할 수 있는 수많은 방법이 있습니다.

해설 누구나 큰돈 들이지 않고 유명 인사들처럼 멋지고 화
려한 결혼식을 올릴 수 있다는 요지의 글이다. 그 방
법은 돈을 최대한 적게 쓰면서 유명 인사의 결혼식 스
타일을 모방하는 것이라는 내용이다. 그런데 선택지
(c)는 유명 인사들은 자신들의 결혼 예복을 제작할 디
자이너를 고용할 만큼 돈이 많다는 내용이므로 글 전
체의 흐름과는 맞지 않는다.

어휘 celebrity 유명 인사
lavish 호화로운, 사치스러운
tie the knot 결혼하다, 결혼식을 하다
in style 화려하게
spend a fortune 큰돈을 쓰다
carry out 실행하다
innovation 혁신
cost efficiency 저비용 고효율
buck 돈, 달러
Take it from me! 내 말 믿으세요! 정말이에요!
infinite 무한한, 수많은
glamorous 매혹적인, 황홀하게 하는

정답 (c)

Sample

해석 학교에서 남학생이 선호된다는 오랜 믿음은 사실이 아니다. 실제로는 그 반대가 사실일지도 모른다. 학교에서 행해지는 대부분의 시험에서 여학생은 남학생보다 좋은 성적을 보인다. 평균적으로 남학생은 읽기 성적에서 여학생보다 일 년 반 정도 뒤떨어져 있다. 여학생은 난이도가 좀 더 높은 수업을 선택하고 학생회와 우등생 클럽에 더 많이 참가한다. 또한 남학생은 퇴학을 당하는 경우가 더 잦고 그래서 대학에 갈 확률이 떨어진다.

(a) 읽기 성적에서 여학생보다 일 년 반 정도 뒤떨어진다.

(b) 보통은 과학과 수학을 여학생보다 잘한다.

(c) 일반적으로 교사의 관심을 여학생보다 못 받는다.

(d) 학교에서 문제를 일으키는 경향이 여학생보다 많다.

해설 학교가 여학생보다 남학생을 선호한다는 일반적인 통념과는 달리 여학생을 더 선호할지도 모른다는 요지의 글을 읽고 글의 흐름에 맞게 빈칸에 세부 사항을 골라 넣는 문제이다. 여학생이 선호될 수도 있다는 주장을 뒷받침하는 이유를 나열해서 설명하고 있는데, 빈칸의 위치는 여학생이 남학생보다 시험 성적이 더 좋다는 첫 번째 이유를 뒷받침해 줄 수 있는 구체적인 근거가 들어가야 할 자리이다. 이것만 재빨리 파악하면 아주 짧은 시간에 정답을 고를 수 있는 유형의 문제이다.

정답 (a)

Actual Test

1 **해석** 인구 과잉은 아마도 우리의 생태학적 위기의 가장 중요한 요인일지도 모른다. 과학과 현대 농업 기술 덕분에 많은 사람들이 유년기를 무사히 지나 성인이 되고, 아이를 낳고, 예전보다 더 오래 살 수 있게 되었다. 동시에 우리는 우리의 선조보다 지구의 제한된 자원을 더 많이 뽑아 쓰고 있다. 몇몇 선진국에서 인구 성장률이 감소하고 있으나 여전히 전 세계적인 출산률은 증가하고 많은 사람들이 충분한 음식을 공급받는 데 어려움을 겪고 있다. 우리가 진정으로 이 난국을 막고자 한다면 우리는 인구 증가를 억제하는 데 중점을 둬야 한다.

(a) 더 많은 자원을 개발하는 것

(b) 인구 증가를 억제하는 것

(c) 석유 소비를 줄이는 것

(d) 태양 에너지 기술을 마스터하는 것

해설 인류에게 가장 중요한 위협이 인구 과잉일 수도 있다는 요지의 글이다. 옛날에 비해 좋아진 환경 때문에 전 세계적으로 인구 증가율이 계속 높아지면서 음식을 충분히 섭취하지 못하고 있는 사람들이 늘고 있어 문제라는 내용이다. 마지막 문장에서 이런 문제점을 해결하기 위한 해결책을 제시하고 있는데, 해결책이 되는 부분에 빈칸이 위치하고 있다. 글 전체가 인구 과잉 문제의 심각성을 다루고 있으므로 문제 해결 방법으로 인구 증가를 억제해야 한다고 주장했을 가능성이 가장 높다고 볼 수 있기 때문에 정답은 (b)이다.

어휘 overpopulation 인구 과잉

ecological 생태학적인

simultaneously 동시에

extract 추출해내다, 개발하다

predecessor 선조, 조상

dilemma 딜레마, 난국

exploit 개발하다, 착취하다

curb 억제하다

정답 (b)

2 **해석** 초콜릿 하면 달콤한 초콜릿바와 시럽이 뿌려진 밀크셰이크를 떠올릴지도 모르지만 최초의 초콜릿은 완전히 다른 혼합물이었다. 중미와 멕시코에서 적어도 3천 년 동안 즐겨 왔던 초콜릿은 원래는 아즈텍 인이나 마야 인에 의해 쓴맛을 지닌 음료로 사용되었다. 널리 대중화된 단맛이 나는 밀크 초콜릿이 대체로 몸에 좋지 않다고 여겨지는 반면, 다크 초콜릿은 의사들에 의해 혈압을 낮춰 주는 것으로 밝혀졌다.

(a) 이와 비교해 볼 때

(b) 결국

(c) ~에 관해서

(d) 결과적으로

해설 초콜릿에 관한 글을 읽고 빈칸에 연결어를 넣는 문제이다. 문장 구조상 빈칸은 있어도 그만, 없어도 크게 문제가 없는 접속부사 자리이다. 힌트는 접속사 while 이다. while은 대조를 나타내는 접속사이다. while 부사절에서는 밀크 초콜릿이 몸에 좋지 않다는 내용이고, 그 뒤의 주절에서는 다크 초콜릿은 혈압을 낮춰 주는 효과를 가지고 있다는 내용이 서로 대조 또는 비교되고 있다고 볼 수 있으므로 (a) by comparison 이 가장 알맞다.

어휘 conjure up 상기시키다, 떠올리다

candy bar 초콜릿바

dramatically 현저하게, 크게

concoction 혼합물

cultivate 탐닉하다

millennium 천 년

bitter-tasting 쓴맛이 나는

blood pressure 혈압

정답 (a)

3 해석 내가 거주하고 있는 지역은 끊임없이 폭력이 악순환되고 있는 지역으로 두 그룹의 사람들이 상대를 증오하고 있다. 삶은 스트레스와 위험으로 가득 차 있다. 나는 내가 우리 고국에서 살 수 있어야 한다고 생각한다. 그러나 모두가 그렇게 생각하는 것은 아니므로 어떤 사람들은 우리가 우리의 고향에 되돌아오는 것을 격렬하게 저지하고 있다. 일주일 전에 나의 가까운 친구 몇 명이 살해되었다. 그들이 집에서 잠을 자고 있을 때 미사일이 그들의 집에 떨어졌던 것이다. 또 다른 친구 한 명은 국경을 건너려다 총에 맞았다. 나는 이런 잔혹한 일들이 내 주변 사람들에게 발생하는 것을 보고 종종 낙심하게 된다. 다른 한편으로는 가까운 미래에 분쟁 해결이 이루어질 것 같은 몇 가지 징후들을 보고 희망을 느낀다.

(a) 다른 한편으로는

(b) 결론적으로

(c) 게다가

(d) 게다가

해설 빈칸 앞부분은 분쟁 지역에 거주하면서 주변 사람들의 비극을 목격하며 절망감을 느꼈다는 내용이 나왔고, 빈칸 뒤에서는 이런 분쟁이 가까운 장래에 해결될 것 같은 징조들이 보여 희망을 품는다는 내용이 이어졌으므로 빈칸에는 대조의 접속부사구인 (a) On the other hand가 가장 알맞다.

어휘 reside 살다, 거주하다

resent 증오하다, 분개하다

existence 생활, 삶

homeland 모국, 고국

vehemently 격렬하게

disheartened 낙심한, 의기소침한

atrocity 잔학 행위

inflict (타격, 고통, 따위를) 가하다, 주다

indication 징후, 징조, 조짐

resolution 해결책, 해답

정답 (a)

4 해석 익살스런 시를 써서 작가로서의 경력을 시작한 마크 트웨인은 인간의 허영, 위선, 살인 행위를 기록한 검은 연대기들을 쓴 작가로 성장했다. 그가 《허클베리 핀》을 썼을 때까지만 해도 그의 문체는 풍부한 유머, 탄탄한 구성, 사회 비판을 각각 겸비하고 있었다. 트웨인은 구어를 사용하는 데 재능이 있었고, 미국 상징주의와 언어에 기반을 둔 독특한 미국 문학을 대중화하는 데 성공했다. 트웨인의 대다수 작품들은 그 시절 내내 많은 이유로 탄압받았다. 구체적으로 말해 《허클베리 핀의 모험》은 종종 미국 학교에서 금지되었는데, 특히 그 책이 쓰였던 당시에 널리 쓰였던 비속어의 빈번한 사용 때문이었다.

(a) 그러나

(b) 구체적으로 말하자면

(c) 게다가

(d) 이에 불구하고

해설 마크 트웨인의 작품의 특징을 설명한 글을 읽고 연결어를 넣는 문제이다. 빈칸 앞부분에서 마크 트웨인의 작품들이 많은 이유로 탄압받았다는 내용이 나오고 빈칸 뒤에서는 탄압받은 구체적인 작품명과 이유가 나왔으므로 정답은 (b) Specifically이다.

어휘 comical 익살스런, 웃기는

verse 운문, 시

chronicle 연대기

vanity 허영, 공허

hypocrisy 위선

murderous act 살인 행위

combine 겸하다, 겸비하다

be gifted with ~의 재능을 타고나다

colloquial speech 구어

suppress 탄압하다, 억압하다

restrict 제한하다, 금지하다

not least 특히

vulgar language 비속어

in use 쓰이고 있는, 일반적으로 행해지고 있는

prevalent 유행하는, 널리 퍼진

정답 (b)

5 해석 해외에서 몰입식 교육을 통해 영어를 배우고자 하는 학생들은 영어권 국가에는 단순히 언어 그 이상의 것

이 있다는 사실을 알아야 한다. 《영어 학습자를 위한 문화 가이드》는 학생들에게 단순히 문법을 설명해 주는 것을 넘어서서 그들이 공부하는 나라에 대해 통찰력을 주기 위해 특별히 고안된 책이다. 미국, 남아프리카, 호주, 아일랜드 모두 영어를 말하는 나라들이지만 그 나라들은 매우 다른 역사적, 문화적 상황 안에서 영어를 쓰고 있다. 이 책은 영어를 공부하는 학생들이 오직 한 영어권 문화만을 접했을 때 발생하는 문제를 해결하기 위해 고안되었다. 한 영어권 문화만을 접했을 경우엔 실제 상황에서 학생들의 준비가 불충분하게 된다.

Q. 누가 이 책을 주로 이용하겠는가?

(a) 외국의 영어 교사

(b) 영어를 배우는 교환 학생

(c) 문화 관광 중인 여행자

(d) 시험을 준비하는 학생

해설 영어 학습자를 위한 책을 소개하는 글을 읽고 누구를 대상으로 하는 책인지 세부 정보를 추론해야 하는 문제이다. 첫 번째 줄 immersing themselves abroad 부분이 단서이다. 선택지 중에서 (b) 영어를 배우는 교환 학생들만이 해외에서 몰입식으로 영어를 배우는 사람들의 범주에 속한다고 볼 수 있다. 따라서 정답은 (b)이다.

어휘 immerse oneself 몰두[몰입]하다
insight into ~에 대한 통찰력
break down 분석하다
context 상황, 정황, 배경
ill-equipped 준비가 제대로 안 된

정답 (b)

6 **해석** 파리지옥은 기르기 힘든 식물일 수 있습니다. 파리지옥은 기후 환경에 민감하기 때문에 유리 온실을 사용해서 그 안에 재배해야 합니다. 염소는 파리지옥에게 해롭기 때문에 절대 수돗물을 주지 마세요. 대신에 생수나 빗물을 사용하세요. 화분용 혼합물로는 60%의 물이끼와 40%의 소독된 모래를 써보세요. 파리지옥은 잘만 기르면 7년 이상까지 살 수 있습니다.

Q. 지문의 내용과 일치하는 것은 무엇인가?

(a) 빗물은 파리지옥에 해롭다.

(b) 파리지옥은 실외에서 자라야 한다.

(c) 파리지옥은 신중하게 조절된 환경이 필요하다.

(d) 파리지옥은 초보 식물 재배자들이 기르기 좋은 식물이다.

해설 파리지옥 재배 요령을 설명한 글을 읽고 진위를 파악하는 문제이다. 파리지옥은 유리 온실 안에서 재배해야 하며 수돗물을 주지 말아야 한다는 등 재배하기 까다로운 식물이라고 언급되었으므로 파리지옥은 신중하게 조절된 환경을 필요로 한다고 볼 수 있다. 따라서 정답은 (c)이다. (a)는 빗물이 해로운 것이 아니라 수돗물이고, (b) 역시 야외가 아니라 실내에서 재배되어야 하므로 오답이다. 파리지옥은 재배하기 힘든 식물로 초보자가 기르기에 좋은 식물이라고 볼 수 없으므로 (d) 역시 답이 될 수 없다.

어휘 Venus Flytrap 〈식물〉 끈끈이주걱, 파리지옥
challenging 힘드는, 도전적인
terrarium 유리 온실
tap water 수돗물
chlorine 〈화학〉 염소
bottled water 생수
potting mixture 화분용 혼합물
peat moss 물이끼
sterilized 소독된

정답 (c)

7 **해석** 역사를 통틀어 정부에 맞선 사람들이나 단체들은 종종 큰 탄압을 받았다. (a) 철학자 버트란드 러셀은 제1차 세계대전에 참가한 것에 대해 영국과 적국을 함께 비판한 후 그러한 탄압을 받았다. (b) 그는 사회에 의해 억압된 사람들을 돕기 위해 끊임없이 노력했다. (c) 그는 벌금형을 받았고, 나중에 투옥되었으며, 결과적으로 캠브리지 대학으로부터 해고되었다. (d) 러셀은 감옥에서 매우 열악한 환경에 부딪혔지만 감옥에 있는 그 시기에도 책을 집필했다.

해설 역사적으로 정부를 비판한 사람들이 탄압을 받았다는 내용의 첫 문장이 주제문이고, 버트란드 러셀의 예를 들어 주제문을 뒷받침하고 있는 형식의 글이다. (a) (c), (d)는 러셀이 영국 정부를 비판해서 당한 고초를 설명한 글이지만, (b)는 러셀에 관한 글이긴 하지만 정부를 비판했다가 받은 탄압과는 무관한 문장이므로 흐름상 맞지 않는 문장이다.

어휘 throughout history 역사를 통틀어
stand up to ~에 맞서다, 저항하다
persecution 박해, 탄압
foe 적
oppress 탄압하다
imprison 투옥하다

subsequently 그 결과로서

encounter (위험, 곤란 등에) 부닥치다

adverse 불리한, 나쁜, 열악한

author a book 책을 쓰다

정답 (b)

Sample

1 **해석** 존 듀이는 상호 작용이 학습에 있어서 필수라고 믿었던 미국의 이론가였다. 듀이는 새로운 정보를 이해하기 위해서는 새로운 경험을 옛 경험에 연결시켜야 한다는 철학의 초기 옹호자였다. 그는 공립 학교의 급진적인 개혁과 경험의 연속성을 옹호했다. 학습은 개인의 경험에서만 나오는 것이며 새로운 지식이 의미를 갖기 위해서는 이 개인의 경험이 과거의 경험 위에 축적되어야 한다.

(a) 과거의 경험 위에 축척되다.

(b) 미래의 목표와 관련이 있다.

(c) 정신의 중요성을 포함하다.

(d) 동료들에 의해 공공연히 논의되다.

해석 존 듀이의 교육 철학을 짧게 설명하는 글로서 주제를 파악하면 쉽게 빈칸을 넣을 수 있는 문제이다. 지문의 첫 번째 문장이 주제문이고, 두 번째 문장이 주제문을 부연 설명하는 형식의 글이다. 두 번째 문장을 빈칸이 있는 마지막 문장이 다시 한 번 paraphrase(다른 말로 풀어서 설명)하고 있으므로 빈칸은 결국 주제를 고르라는 문제와 같다고 볼 수 있다.

정답 (a)

Actual Test

1 **해석** 미국의 발명가이자 사업가인 토마스 알바 에디슨은 축음기와 오래가는 전구를 포함하여 전 세계 사람들에게 깊은 영향을 준 많은 장치들을 개발한 장본인이었다. 그는 대량 생산의 원리를 발명 과정에 도입한 최초의 발명가 중 한 사람이었다. 그래서 그는 종종 최초의 산업 연구 실험실을 설립한 사람으로 여겨진다. 가장 왕성한 발명가들 중 한 사람으로 여겨지는 에디슨은 본인 이름으로 1,093개의 미국 발명 특허를 받았다.

(a) 유감스럽게도

(b) 그래서

(c) 그럼에도 불구하고

(d) 그러나

해설 미국의 발명가 에디슨에 관한 이야기이다. 그가 대량 생산의 원리를 발명에 도입한 최초의 발명가 중 한 사람이라는 빈칸 앞의 내용과 최초의 산업 연구 실험실을 설립한 사람으로 여겨진다는 빈칸 뒤의 문장이 인과 관계라고 볼 수 있으므로 빈칸에 알맞은 말은 (b)

Thus이다.

어휘 profound 심오한, 깊은

phonograph 축음기

light bulb 백열전구

mass production 대량 생산

be credited with ~한 공로를 인정받다

prolific 다작의, 왕성한

patent 특허

regrettably 유감스럽게도

정답 (b)

2 해석 워커 씨께,

제 개인적인 친구인 제임스 맥도걸의 이력서를 보냅니다. 그는 라디오 방송 분야에 경험이 많습니다. 수년 동안 그는 제 회사에 대해 귀중한 미디어 관련 조언을 자주 해주었습니다. 제임스가 잠재 고객 추천을 부탁해 왔고, 이것이 그가 제공한 지난 서비스에 대한 보상으로서 제가 할 수 있는 최소한이라는 생각이 들어서 이렇게 연락을 드립니다. 제임스와 같은 기술을 가진 사람의 덕을 볼 수도 있는 기업체를 혹시 알고 계신다면 주저 마시고 제임스를 그들에게 소개시켜 주십시오. 그의 전문 지식이 필요할 경우를 대비해서 그의 이력서를 잠시 보관해 두시고 그의 라디오 방송 경험을 염두에 두셨으면 합니다.

그럼,

에릭 A. 슈미트

(a) 그런 기술을 가진 사람의 덕을 볼 수 있는

(b) 우리 제품에 관심이 있는

(c) 자기 회사를 시작할 계획이 있는

(d) 파산 신청을 고려하고 있는

해설 슈미트는 자신에게 미디어 관련 자문을 해준 개인적인 친구인 제임스 맥도걸의 이력서를 동봉하면서 취업을 청탁하고 있는 상황이므로 슈미트는 워커 씨에게 제임스와 같은 능력을 가진 사람의 덕을 볼지도 모를 잠재적 고용주에게 그를 소개시켜 줄 것을 부탁하고 있다. 따라서 정답은 (a)이다.

어휘 experienced 경험이 많은

reference 추천

in return for ~에 대한 보상으로

hang on to 꼭 붙잡고 있다, ~에 귀 기울이다

of use 유용한, 쓸모 있는

benefit from ~로부터 혜택[이득]을 보다

정답 (a)

3 해석 책을 믿을 수 없을 만큼 빠르게 읽고 싶었던 적이 있습니까? 전문적인 속독 과정은 학생들에게 집중을 더 잘할 수 있는 많은 쉬운 기술을 제공합니다. 움직임은 자연스럽게 눈의 주의를 끕니다. 속독 기술을 통해 그 움직임은 책을 읽는 데 사용됩니다. 똑바로 앉아서 왼손에 책을 쥐고, 오른손은 읽는 속도에 맞춰서 글자들을 따라갑니다. 어휘와 문법에 대한 완벽한 이해가 없다면 속독은 도움이 되지 않을 것입니다. 그러므로 이런 방법들을 배우려는 사람은 이미 독서 능력을 갖춘 사람이어야 합니다.

(a) 적합한 자리에 있다.

(b) 가능한 많은 책을 읽는

(c) 이미 독서 능력을 갖추고 있다.

(d) 기술을 실제로 활용해 보는

해설 속독은 어휘와 문법에 대해 완벽히 이해한 사람에게나 도움이 되는 읽기 방법임을 설명하는 글이다. 빈칸 바로 앞 문장에서 어휘와 문법 실력이 탄탄하지 않으면 별 도움이 되지 않는다고 했으므로 속독 기술을 익히기 전에 우선은 어느 정도 문법과 어휘 실력을 갖추어야 한다는 내용이 논리적으로 빈칸에 적절하다. 문법과 어휘 실력을 완벽하게 갖추고 있다는 것은 독서 능력을 갖춘 사람이라고 볼 수 있으므로 정답은 (c)이다.

어휘 upright 똑바로, 직립하여

trace 따라가다, 쫓다

pace 속도

have a firm grasp of 확실히 이해하고 있다

정답 (c)

4 해석 사람들은 산업적으로 생산된 우유는 화학물질로 가득 차 있고, 동물을 학대하며, 위장이 안 좋은 사람에게 해롭다고 지적해 왔다. 이런 사실에도 불구하고 대부분의 사람들은 단점보다 장점이 더 크다고 생각한다. 일례로 우유는 저렴하고 쉽게 칼슘을 섭취할 수 있는 방법이다. 누구나 건강한 뼈를 형성하기 위해 칼슘을 섭취해야 한다. 게다가 우유에는 아이들에게 바람직한 다른 영양소들이 풍부하다. 유제품을 포함한 균형 잡힌 식단이 심장병의 위험을 줄이는 데 도움이 된다는 사실이 기록에 의해 충분히 증명되었다. 뿐만 아니라 몇몇 과학자들에 따르면 우유가 특정 유형의 암을 예방하는 요인이 될 수도 있다고 한다.

(a) 비타민은 일일 칼슘 필요량을 제공한다.

(b) 우유는 그들이 알고 있는 유일한 음료수이다.

(c) 우유를 마시는 것은 가능하면 피해야 할 것이다.

(d) 장점이 어떤 단점보다 더 크다고 여겨진다.

해설 Despite this가 단서이다. 즉 앞 문장과 대조적인 내
용이 빈칸에 들어가야 한다. 빈칸 앞 문장에서 우유의
부정적인 측면을 언급했고, 빈칸 뒤의 문장들에서 우
유가 가진 건강상 이점들을 구체적으로 나열하고 있으
므로 빈칸은 빈칸 뒤의 내용을 포괄하는 내용이 되어
야 한다. 우유의 장점이 어떤 단점보다 더 크게 여겨
진다는 내용의 (d)가 가장 알맞다.

어휘 point out 지적하다

be packed with ~로 가득차다

animal abuse 동물 학대

be enriched with ~가 풍부하게 들어 있다

well-documented 기록에 의해 충분히 입증된

정답 (d)

5 **해석** 자각몽은 사람이 꿈을 꾸고 있는 순간에 자신이 꿈을
꾸고 있다는 것을 자각할 때 발생한다. 대부분의 꿈에
서와는 달리 자각몽을 꾸고 있는 사람은 꿈속 환경에
적극적으로 참여하고 영향을 미칠 수 있다. 꿈속에서
자각의 정도에 따라 자각몽은 상당히 사실적일 수도
있다. 자각몽은 두 가지 방법으로 발생한다고 여겨지
고 있다. DILD, 즉 꿈에서 시작된 자각몽은 꿈을 꾸
는 사람이 자신이 꿈속에 있다는 걸 깨닫고 있다는 사
실을 제외하면 보통의 꿈처럼 시작된다. WILD, 즉 깨
어 있는 상태에서 시작된 자각몽은 꿈꾸는 사람이 깨
어 있는 상태로부터 엄밀히 말해 수면 상태로 가지 않
고 꿈꾸는 상태로 바로 전환할 때 발생한다.

Q. 이 글의 주된 내용은 무엇인가?

(a) 비정상적인 꿈 경험

(b) DILD와 WILD의 장점과 단점

(c) 자각몽을 꾸는 기술

(d) 자각몽에 대한 설명

해설 자각몽을 DILD와 WILD, 두 종류로 나누어 설명하는
글이다. (a) 자각몽을 비정상적인 꿈의 경험이라고 하
기엔 범위가 너무 크고, (b) DILD와 WILD의 장점과
단점에 대해 언급한 내용이 없으며, (c) 자각몽을 꾸는
기술에 대한 언급도 없다. 이 글은 자각몽이 무엇인지
대략적으로 설명하는 글이므로 정답은 (d)이다.

어휘 lucid dream 자각몽

self-awareness 자각

transition 전환하다

abnormal 비정상적인

정답 (d)

6 **해석** 포도 재배자들을 위한 희소식이 있다. 적당량의 포도
주를 마시는 것이 심장병 발병 확률을 낮춘다는 유명
한 이론이 새로운 연구에서 사실로 입증됐다. 과학자
들의 결론에 따르면 포도주를 마시지 않는 사람들과
비교해 봤을 때 포도주를 약간 마시는 사람들이 질병
으로 사망할 확률이 3분의 1 정도 더 적다고 한다. 일
반적으로 포도주를 마시는 사람들은 심장마비에 걸릴
확률이 훨씬 적었다. 사실, 연구에 따르면 술을 마시는
것이 어느 정도 좋은 점이 있다고 밝혀졌다. 그러나
가장 뚜렷한 결과는 포도주를 주로 마신 사람들에게서
나타났다.

Q. 지문의 주된 내용은 무엇인가?

(a) 포도주의 건강상 이점

(b) 심장병 예방

(c) 알콜 섭취의 결과

(d) 포도주가 인기 있는 이유

해설 포도주에 관한 글을 읽고 글의 대의를 파악하는 문제
이다. 적당량의 포도주를 마시는 것이 심장병 발병 확
률을 낮추고, 포도주를 조금 마시는 사람들이 마시지
않는 사람들과 비교해 봤을 때 질병으로 사망할 가능
성이 더 낮다는 내용이 언급되고 있으므로 이 글의 주
제는 (a) 포도주의 건강상 이점임을 알 수 있다.

어휘 validate 증명하다

moderate 적당한

lower chances of ~의 가능성을 낮추다

contrast 대조하다, 비교하다

be less likely to ~할 가능성이 더 낮다

occurrence 발생

consumption 섭취, 소비

at all 적어도, 조금이나마

dramatic 뚜렷한, 두드러진

primarily 주로

정답 (a)

7 **해석** 좋든 싫든 익스트림 스포츠는 널리 보급되어 있다. (a)
더 젊은 세대일수록 스노우보드, 스케이트보드 혹은
카이트 서핑의 스릴을 즐기기 위해 자신들의 생계를
위험에 빠뜨리고 싶어 더욱더 안달이 난 것처럼 보인
다. (b) 농구 역시 전 세계적으로 엄청나게 인기를 얻
었는데, 각 나라 고유의 스포츠 게임을 제치고 젊은이
들에게 가장 인기 있는 오락으로 자리매김하고 있다.
(c) 가장 위험한 신종 스포츠 중 하나는 스카이 서핑인
데, 비행기에서 뛰어내려서 보드를 이용해 자신들의

낙하를 조절하는 운동이다. (d) 이 익스트림 스포츠는
아드레날린을 분출시키는 흥분을 가져오는 데 있어서
스카이다이빙과 번지점프에 버금간다.

해설 글 전체가 익스트림 스포츠에 대한 내용인데 반해 (b)
는 농구가 전 세계적으로 젊은이들에게 엄청난 인기를
얻게 되었다는 내용으로 익스트림 스포츠와는 무관한
문장이다.

어휘 like it or not 좋든 싫든
be here to stay 널리 보급되어 있다
livelihood 생계
indigenous 고유의, 토착의
number one pastime 가장 인기 있는 오락
manipulate 조정하다
descent 하강, 낙하
delivery 방출
adrenaline rush excitement 아드레날린을
분출시키는 흥분

정답 (b)

Chapter 04 연결사 넣기

Sample

해석 국제 경제에서 자국 아이들에게 우위를 제공하기 위한
바람으로 많은 국가들이 조기 교육 프로그램을 보조하
기 시작했다. 조기 교육을 받은 아이들은 결국에는 좀
더 짧은 시간에 더 많은 것을 배우게 될 것이라고 기
대된다. 하지만 비평가들은 그에 반대되는 증거를 언
급한다. 스웨덴은 어리게는 한 살까지의 영아들을 위
한 국가 보조 취학 전 프로그램을 실시하고 있는 나라
중 하나이다. 인구학적으로 유사한 이웃 나라 핀란드
와 비교해 스웨덴 아이들은 국제 기준 시험에서 높은
성적을 얻을 것이라고 기대된다. (핀란드 아이들은 일
곱 살에 학교를 다니기 시작한다.) 그러나 핀란드 아이
들은 지속적으로 스웨덴 아이들보다 높은 성적을 보인
다.
(a) 그러나
(b) 예를 들면
(c) 따라서
(d) 대체로

해설 조기 교육이 예상과는 달리 역효과를 불러올 수 있다
는 요지의 글이다. 연결사를 넣는 문제는 빈칸의 앞뒤
문장만 정독해도 정답을 고를 수 있는 경우가 대부분
이다. 이 문제 역시 빈칸이 위치한 문장 critics cite
evidence to the contrary에서 contrary라는 단
어에만 주목해도 답을 아주 쉽게 찾을 수 있다. 이 부
분을 놓쳤다고 해도 빈칸을 기점으로 빈칸 앞부분은
조기 교육이 아이들의 학습에 긍정적인 효과를 미칠
것이라는 일반적인 통념을 소개하고, 빈칸 뒷부분은
스웨덴과 핀란드 아이들의 실례를 들어 이러한 통념을
완전히 뒤집는 근거를 제시하고 있으므로 글의 구조상
역접의 의미를 가진 연결사가 들어가야 한다는 것을
쉽게 알 수 있다.

정답 (a)

Actual Test

1 **해석** 방화벽은 네트워크 정보 거래량을 감시하고 일련의 규
칙에 근거해 접근을 규제하는 컴퓨터 장치이다. 방화
벽은 적합하게 설정되어 있지 않으면 거의 무용지물이
될 수도 있다. 방화벽이 어떻게 작동하는지 이해하지
못하는 많은 사람들이 설치하는 동안에 잘못하여 '기
본 값'을 선택함으로써 시스템과 네트워크 문제가 발

생할 가능성이 훨씬 높아지게 된다.

(a) 스팸 메일 발생을 만든다.

(b) 전체 네트워크를 보호한다.

(c) 시스템과 네트워크 문제가 생긴다.

(d) 값비싼 장비를 구입하게 한다.

해설 빈칸 앞부분에 나온 mistakenly라는 부사가 결정적인 단서이다. 방화벽 설치 시 기본 값을 선택하는 것은 잘못이라고 했으므로 시스템과 네트워크에 문제가 발생할 가능성이 높아진다고 문장을 완성하는 것이 가장 자연스럽다.

어휘 firewall (컴퓨터) 방화벽

device 장치

monitor 감시하다

regulate 규제하다

default 기본 값, 초기 설정

setup 설치, 설정

significantly 크게, 상당히

probable 가능성 있는

정답 (c)

2 해석 학생들은 그들이 받는 교육이 실제 세상과 관련이 없어 보일 때 교육에 대해 쉽게 실망할 수 있다. 학습이 추상적으로 되면 많은 학생들은 공부할 동기를 상실한다. 그래서 학생들의 흥미를 충족시키는 교육 과정을 실행하는 것이 학습을 단순히 지식을 받아들이는 활동에서 활발하게 참여하는 활동으로 전환시킬 수 있다. 다양한 연구에 따르면 학생들은 자신들을 단순히 수동적인 관객으로 만드는 수업보다는 학습 관련 결정을 내릴 권한을 제공하는 수업에서 학업을 더 잘 수행한다고 한다.

(a) 그들이 숙제를 다 하도록 강요하는

(b) 비효율적이고 시대에 뒤떨어진 교과서에 의존하는

(c) 창의력을 강조하는

(d) 그들을 단순히 수동적인 관객으로 만드는

해설 교육의 두 가지 방식을 비교한 글이다. 현실과 동떨어진 교육과 학생들의 흥미를 충족시키는 수업이 대조되고 있고, 단순한 지식을 습득하는 학습 방법과 활발하게 참여하는 학습이 대조되고 있다는 점을 간파하는 것이 문제 해결의 열쇠이다. 학습 관련 결정을 내릴 권한을 부여받는 수업이란 학생들이 적극적으로 참여하는 수업을 뜻하므로 빈칸에는 학생들이 적극 참여하는 수업과 대조되는 형태의 수업 형태라고 볼 수 있는 (d)가 가장 자연스럽다.

어휘 disillusioned 환멸을 느낀, 실망한

relevant 관련이 있는, 적절한

abstraction 추상

motivation 동기

curriculum 교과과정

cater to ~를 충족시키다

dynamic 동적인, 역동적인, 활력 있는

engagement 참여

outdated 낡은

put an emphasis on ~를 강조하다

spectator 관객

정답 (d)

3 해석 나에게 있어 인생에서 내 목표를 달성했다는 생각이 나에게 커다란 기쁨을 준다는 것을 나는 기꺼이 인정하겠다. 굉장히 노력했지만 삶의 대부분을 무명으로 지냈던 작가라면 명성과 부를 기쁘게 환영할 것이라는 것에 당신은 동의하지 않는가? 어떤 사람들은 돈으로 행복을 살 수 있다고 단언한다. 어느 정도는, 이 말은 피할 수 없는 사실이다. 그러나 나는 야망을 달성하는 것이 우리가 성취감을 찾아 나서게 하는 많은 요인들 중 하나에 지나지 않는다고 믿는다. 만약 그것이 누군가의 삶에서 추구하는 유일한 목표라면 그는 비참해질 것이 거의 확실하다.

(a) 현재로서는

(b) 특정한 시점이 지난 후에

(c) 어느 정도까지는

(d) 더욱더

해설 빈칸 전후의 한두 문장을 눈여겨볼 필요가 있다. 돈으로 행복을 살 수 있다는 일부 사람들의 의견을 소개하고 나서, 빈칸 뒤에 이 의견은 엄연한 사실이라는 문장이 연결되고 있다. 하지만 However 뒤에서 글쓴이는 야망의 실현인 돈과 성공은 우리 인생에서 우리가 성취감을 맛보기 위해 찾아 나서는 하나의 요소일 뿐이라고 주장을 폈기 때문에 글쓴이는 돈으로 행복을 살 수 있다는 생각에 전적으로 동의하는 것이 아니라 부분적으로 동의하는 것으로 추론할 수 있으므로 빈칸에는 '어느 정도까지는'의 뜻을 가진 (c)가 가장 자연스럽다.

어휘 readily 기꺼이

accomplish 달성하다, 성취하다

fame 명성

fortune 돈

with certainty 확신을 가지고
inevitably 불가피하게, 필연적으로
realization 실현
quest 탐험, 탐구, 추구
fulfillment 성취감
sole 유일한, 하나뿐인
miserable 비참한

정답 (c)

4 해석 어떤 의사라도 당신이 심장병에 걸릴 위험에 처해 있
다면 운동하고 건강하게 먹는 것이 중요하다고 당신에
게 말할 것이다. 과체중이고 가족력에 심장병이 있는
사람들은 고위험군에 있는 사람에 속한다. 이것은
전 세계적으로 심각한 건강 문제이고, 적극적인 예방
조치가 없다면 문제는 장래에 더 심각해질 것이다.
(a) 신체 활동을 제한한다.
(b) 근심 없는 생활을 한다.
(c) 운동하고 건강하게 먹는다.
(d) 실험적인 치료를 고려한다.

해설 상식적인 차원에서 접근해도 답을 풀 수 있는 유형의
문제이다. 심장병에 걸릴 위험이 있는 사람에게 의사
가 충고해 줄 만한 내용으로 적절한 것은 선택지 중에
서 운동하고 건강하게 먹으라는 (c)이다.

어휘 be at risk of -ing ~할 위험에 놓여 있다
family history 가족력
high risk category 고위험군
aggressive 적극적인
down the road 장래에, 앞으로

정답 (c)

5 해석 자기실현적인 예언은 예언된 결과를 일으키는 예언이
다. 다시 말해서 충분히 많은 사람들에게 영향을 미칠
수 있는 거짓 예언이 그 사람들로 하여금 실제로는 틀
렸던 예언을 결국엔 실현시켜 버리는 방식으로 반응하
게끔 할 수 있다는 것이다. 흔하게 일컬어지는 예는
재정적으로 안정된 한 은행의 고객들이 그 은행이 곧
파산할 거라는 얘기를 듣게 되는 경우이다. 그 소문이
사실이라고 믿는 고객들은 돈을 찾으러 달려가서 결국
엔 지불 능력이 있는 그 은행을 파산시키게 된다.
Q. 지문의 가장 적절한 제목은 무엇인가?
(a) 예언이 현실이 되는 과정
(b) 실현된 미래에 대한 예언
(c) 은행에 미치는 소문의 위험성

(d) 사람들의 행동에 영향을 미치는 방법

해설 자기실현적인 예언이 무엇인지 설명하고 있다. 예언이
어떠한 방식으로 실현되는지에 대해 은행 파산 과정을
예로 설명한 글이므로 이 글의 가장 적절한 제목은 (a)
예언이 현실이 되는 과정이다.

어휘 self-fulfilling 자기실현적인
prophecy 예언
financially sound 재정적으로 튼튼한
bankrupt 파산시키다
solvent 지급 능력이 있는, 채무 능력이 있는

정답 (a)

6 해석 내 친구들과 나는 지난여름에 멕시코로 가장 멋진 여
행을 했다. 우리는 멕시코의 매운 음식, 고대의 유적,
그리고 멋진 해변 등 모든 것이 맘에 들었다. 그러나
가장 기억에 남을 부분은 카리브 해에서 스쿠버다이빙
을 한 것이었다. 그렇게 자유롭게 움직여 보고, 이상하
고 아름다운 바다 생물들을 발견하는 짜릿함을 느껴
본 것은 난생처음이었다. 나는 심지어는 그물로 바다
가재를 잡아서 저녁 식사로 요리했다. 그 경험은 이
지구 하나에 얼마나 많은 다양한 세상이 존재하는지를
알게 해주었다.
Q. 다음 중 글의 내용과 일치하는 것은 무엇인가?
(a) 글쓴이는 아무도 동행하지 않고 여행을 갔다.
(b) 글쓴이는 그 지역의 요리를 즐겼다.
(c) 글쓴이는 저녁으로 먹을 바다가재를 샀다.
(d) 글쓴이는 스쿠버 다이빙을 자주 한다.

해설 글 도입부에서 멕시코의 매운 음식을 맘에 들어 했다
는 내용이 언급되었으므로 글의 내용과 일치하는 것은
(b)이다. 혼자 여행을 간 것이 아니라 친구들과 여행을
같이 갔고, 바다가재는 산 것이 아니라 잡은 것이므로
(a)와 (c)는 지문의 내용과 일치하지 않는다. 스쿠버
다이빙을 한 이후에 그러한 짜릿함을 느껴 본 것은 난
생처음이라고 했으므로 (d) 스쿠버 다이빙을 자주 하
지는 않는다.

어휘 ancient ruins 고대 유적
gorgeous 멋진, 아름다운
lobster 바다가재
local cuisine 현지 요리

정답 (b)

7 해석 1870년대에 봄까지 기다리라는 경고를 받은 후, 앨퍼
드 패커는 5명의 다른 남자들과 함께 로키 산맥 횡단

을 시도했다. (a) 길을 잃고 보급품이 다 떨어져서 패커는 사람을 먹게 되었다. (b) 인류학자들은 일반적으로 식인 행위가 그 행위를 하는 사람에게는 특별한 의미를 갖는다고 믿고 있다. (c) 앨퍼드 패커는 결국 그 여행에서 유일한 생존자가 되었고, 근처의 캠프에 도착했다. (d) 그는 정당방위였다고 주장했지만 그의 말을 믿는 사람은 거의 없었고, 그는 살인으로 기소되어 수감됐다.

해설 앨퍼드 패커라는 사람이 로키 산맥을 횡단하면서 길을 잃고 굶주림에 사람을 잡아먹은 후 유일한 생존자가 되었지만 살인죄로 기소되어 투옥된 사건을 설명한 글이다. 하지만 (b)는 식인 행위에 대한 인류학자들의 의견을 소개한 문장이다. 따라서 글의 흐름과 상관 없는 문장은 (b)이다.

어휘 resort to ~에 의지하다, 호소하다
cannibalism 식인
hold ~라고 생각하다, 여기다
anthropologist 인류학자
self-defense 정당방위
be accused of ~로 고소당하다, 기소되다

정답 (b)

Chapter 05 대의 파악

Sample

1 **해석** 1940년대 후반, 텔레비전이 막 등장했을 때 라디오 광고는 이미 안정된 산업이었다. 라디오 산업의 성공적인 형태를 기본으로 하여 텔레비전은 광고 매체로서 계획적으로 개발되었으며 그 이후로 가장 효율적이고, 그래서 가장 인기 있는 상품 판매 수단이 되었다. 현대 텔레비전 방송국이 존재하는 주된 이유는 광고로 중단되는 당신이 가장 좋아하는 쇼가 아니라 정규 광고 시간이다. 프로그램 편성은 시청자들의 주의를 끌어서 그들을 광고 시간 동안 텔레비전 앞에 앉아 있도록 만들기 위한 수단에 불과하다. 만일 시청자가 채널을 바꾸면 광고를 보지 않게 되므로 프로그램은 시청자들이 기대를 갖고 텔레비전 앞에 붙어 있도록 만들 필요가 있다.

Q. 주로 무엇에 관한 내용인가?
(a) 텔레비전 프로그램의 발전
(b) TV에서 방송된 최고의 광고
(c) 광고 수단으로서의 텔레비전
(d) 텔레비전 방송망의 역사

해설 텔레비전 광고에 관한 설명글을 읽고 대의를 파악하는 문제로 주제문이 지문 중간에 위치한 경우이다. 글의 흐름이 비교적 짜임새 있게 전개되기 때문에 대의 파악이 쉬운 문제에 해당된다. 글의 요지는 텔레비전은 프로그램이 아니라 광고가 주목적이라는 내용으로 The regular commercial breaks, not your favorite shows that they interrupt, are the main reason any modern-day television networks exist.가 주제 문장이다.

정답 (c)

Actual Test

1 **해석** 현대의 경영 간부들 대부분은 MBA, 즉 경영학 석사 학위를 취득한다. 이 프로그램은 20세기 초에 대기업을 경영하게 될 사람들에게 리더십 기술을 함양시키기 위한 한 방편으로 만들어졌다. 처음 고안되었을 당시, MBA는 학생들이 경영 기초 지식에 정통해지는 2년간의 교육 과정으로 구성되었다. 그러나 오늘날에는 학교들이 그 교육 과정을 이수하기 위한 보다 다양한 방법을 수용하기 위해 교육 과정 형태를 변형시켰다. 이런 융통성을 제공함에 따라 훨씬 더 많은 수의 학생

들이 MBA 프로그램에 몰두하게 되었다.

(a) 이 학교의 건설

(b) 아주 많은 강사들을 고용하는 것

(c) 이런 융통성을 제공하는 것

(d) 최근의 이런 자금 출처

해설 MBA가 처음엔 경영 기초 지식에 정통해지는 2년간의 교육 과정으로 구성되었다가 오늘날엔 MBA 과정을 이수할 수 있는 다양한 방법을 수용하도록 교육 과정을 변형시켰다는 앞 문장의 내용을 요약한 선택지를 골라야 한다. 교육 과정을 변형시킨다는 것은 융통성을 제공한다는 뜻과 일맥상통하므로 (c)가 가장 자연스럽다.

어휘 take the reigns of ~를 경영하다

devise 고안하다

versed in ~에 정통한

alter 변경하다, 변형하다

accommodate 수용하다, 받아들이다

flexibility 유연성, 융통성

정답 (c)

2 **해석** 중국 문헌들에 따르면 에페드라 시니카로도 알려져 있는 마황을 약초용으로 사용한 것은 기원전 2700년까지 거슬러 올라간다. 이 식물은 현대의 약물 에페드린의 출처인데, 이 약물은 그 식물의 대략 2% 정도를 차지한다. 이 중국 약초와 후에 추출된 그 의약품은 천식, 알레르기성 비염, 상기도 감염과 감기를 포함한 많은 질병 치료에 사용되었다. 흥분제로도 사용되어 때때로 남용되기도 했다. 화학 물질 에페드린은 상당한 흥분효과를 지니고 있어서 때때로 마약처럼 사용되었으며, 심장 발작과 중독을 일으킨다는 비난을 받았다. 이런 부작용들 때문에 미 식약청은 의약품이나 건강 보조제로서 에페드린의 사용을 금지시켰다.

(a) 효과가 없는 의약품이라고

(b) 사람들이 체중을 감소시키는 데 도움이 된다고

(c) 심장 발작과 중독을 유발한다고

(d) 아이들에게 사용 가능하다고

해설 빈칸 뒤의 these negative effects에 해당하는 내용이 빈칸에 적절하다. 에페드린이라는 물질을 미 식약청에서 금지 약물로 규정할 정도의 부정적인 효과는 선택지 중에서 (c)밖에 없다. 나머지 선택지들은 negative effects와는 전혀 무관한 내용이다.

어휘 herbal 약초의

account for 차지하다, 해당되다

ailment 질병

asthma 천식

allergic rhinitis 알레르기성 비염

upper respiratory infection 상기도 감염

stimulant 흥분제

recreationally (마약이) 기분 전환용으로

heart attack 심장 발작, 심장마비

ban 금지하다

supplement 건강 보조제, 식품 보조제

정답 (c)

3 **해석** 너무 많은 근심은 건망증을 유발할 수 있다는 사실을 알고 계셨습니까? 심한 스트레스를 겪는 동안 코티졸이라고 알려진 물질이 뇌에서 분비됩니다. 많은 양의 이 물질(코티졸)이 분비되면 기본적인 기억의 기능을 다루는 뇌 부분을 손상시키는 것 같습니다. 이런 해마상 융기 세포들이 손상되면 주소와 이름을 기억하는 데 어려움을 겪는 것과 같은 기억 장애를 경험하게 됩니다.

(a) 우리를 아프게 한다.

(b) 건망증을 유발한다.

(c) 우리의 결정을 약화시킨다.

(d) 우리가 일에 집중하지 못하게 한다.

해설 마지막 문장에서 주소와 이름을 기억하는 데 어려움을 겪는 것과 같은 기억 장애를 초래한다고 한 것으로 보아 정답은 (b)이다.

어휘 excrete 분비하다

impairment 손상

hippocampus (뇌의) 해마상 융기

memory problem 기억 장애

sap (서서히) 약화시키다

distract 산만하게 하다, (마음, 주의)를 딴 데로 돌리다

정답 (b)

4 **해석** 인류 역사상 가장 극적인 혁명 중 하나는 10,000년 전에 발생했다. 신석기 혁명이 아마도 사회 구조의 계급 조직화를 발생시킨 중요한 촉매제였을 것이다. 부랑하던 유목민들은 농업을 발견했고, 정착되고 안정된 사회를 형성했다. 영토 소유권의 분할이 점차 중요해졌고, 교역에 근거한 경제는 토지를 가진 사람들과 그렇지 못한 사람들 사이에 불평등을 야기했다. 일반적으로 곡물과 채소를 먹게 됨에 따라 인구가 크게 팽창하게 되었다. 인구 밀도가 높아질수록 사회는 질병과

기근에 더욱더 취약해져 갔다.

(a) 세계화된 농업 경제를 형성하는 것

(b) 발전하는 기술로 자연을 지배하는 것

(c) 사회 구조의 계급 조직

(d) 이웃 유목 부족을 박해하는 것

해설 신석기 혁명의 역사적 의의를 설명한 글이다. 빈칸 뒤에 나온 내용에서 신석기 혁명으로부터 어떻게 사회 구조의 계급 조직이 발생되었는지 설명하고 있으므로 빈칸에는 이런 내용을 요약하는 (c)가 가장 자연스럽다.

어휘 Neolithic 신석기 시대의

catalyst 촉매제

nomadic tribe 유목 민족[부족]

agriculture 농업

inequality 불평등

population density 인구 밀도

vulnerable 취약한, 약한

famine 기아

hierarchical organization 계급 조직

oppress 탄압하다, 억압하다

정답 (c)

5 **해석** 많은 사장들은 직원들의 의견을 수용하는 것을 중시한다. 직원이 회사에 영향을 주는 어떤 문제에 대해 논의하고 싶어 한다면 사장은 귀를 기울여야 한다는 것이다. 그러나 회사 리더십의 개념은 변화하기 시작했고, 어떤 직원들은 때때로 만날 수 있는 사장 그 이상을 원한다. 그들은 그들의 직장에 영향을 미치는 중요한 결정에 참여하고 싶어 한다. 그들은 회사 운영에 관여하고 싶어 하고 그들의 기여가 어떻게 실현되고 평가되는지 경험하고 싶어 한다.

Q. 노사 관계에 대한 새로운 태도를 어떻게 특징지을 수 있겠는가?

(a) 착취적인

(b) 수평적인

(c) 긍정적인

(d) 협력적인

해설 노사 관계의 변화에 대해 설명하는 글이다. 지문의 마지막 문장에서 드러난 노사 관계의 성격을 가장 잘 요약하는 선택지를 고르면 된다. 직원들이 예전과 달리 회사의 중요한 의사 결정에 참여하고 회사 경영에 관여하고 싶어 한다고 했으므로 노사 관계가 일방적인 관계가 아니라 서로 협력적인 관계로 변화했다고 보는

것이 가장 적절하다. 따라서 정답은 (d)이다.

어휘 make a point of -ing ~하는 것을 중시하다

receptive to ~을 잘 받아들이는, 수용하는

feedback 의견

be all ears 귀 기울이다, 경청하다

have a stake in ~에 이해관계를 가지다, ~에 참여하다

influential 영향력 있는, 중요한

workplace 직장

정답 (d)

6 **해석** 상반되는 수많은 증거와 경험에도 불구하고 미국이 전 세계의 부지런한 사람들이 자신들의 꿈을 실현할 수 있는 곳이라는 믿음은 수세기 동안 살아남아 있다. 가난한 집안 출신 사람들이 열심히 노력해서 경제적 또는 정치적 성공을 이룬 특수한 사례들이 그런 꿈의 증거로 요란스럽게 선전되는 반면에, 미국을 그들의 조국이라고 부르는 대다수의 이민자들, 소수 민족들, 그리고 가난한 사람들의 이야기들은 대체로 그저 무시될 뿐이다.

Q. 지문의 주제는 무엇인가?

(a) 미국은 더 이상 과거에 그랬던 기회의 땅이 아니다.

(b) 비범한 사람들은 확실히 미국에서 성공할 것이다.

(c) 놀랍게도 대부분의 사람들은 미국에서 성공하는 데에 다른 곳에서보다 고생을 한다.

(d) 미국이 기회의 땅이라는 생각은 그릇된 통념에 불과하다.

해설 미국이 꿈의 나라로 불리지만 그건 열심히 노력해서 성공을 달성한 사람들의 특수한 사례일 뿐이며 성공하지 못한 대다수의 이민자들과 소수 민족들, 가난한 사람들의 이야기들이 부각되지 않고 무시되기 때문에 미국이 기회의 땅이라는 믿음이 유지되고 있다는 내용의 글이므로 미국이 기회의 땅이라고 하는 생각은 허구에 불과하다는 내용의 (d)가 이 글의 주제이다.

어휘 a mountain of 수많은

to the contrary 반대되는, 상반되는

exceptional 예외적인

work one's way (up) to success

열심히 노력해서 성공을 이루다, 자수성가하다

tout 선전하다

immigrant 이민자

minority 소수민족

impoverished 가난한, 빈곤에 허덕이는

for the most part 대부분

myth 잘못된 통념, 허구

정답 (d)

7 해석 어느 중국 전설에 따르면 황후 누조가 누에고치가 그녀의 찻잔 속에 떨어졌을 때 비단을 발견했다고 한다. (a) 중국인들은 최초로 비단을 재배했고, 그 재배법을 철저하게 비밀로 했다. (b) 바닷길이 점점 일반화되면서 중세 시대 동안 비단길의 이용은 쇠퇴했다. (c) 중국 황제는 비단의 비밀을 누설하는 사람은 어느 누구든 죽이겠다고 위협했다. (d) 전하는 이야기에 따르면 누에를 속이 빈 막대기 안에 넣어서 유럽으로 밀수했던 사람은 바로 중국 승려였다고 한다.

해설 전체적으로 비단의 역사에 대한 글이지만 (b)는 비단길에 대한 내용이므로 전체적인 흐름과 상관없는 문장이다.

어휘 silkworm cocoon 누에고치

cultivate 경작하다

threaten with death 죽이겠다고 협박하다

reveal 폭로하다

monk 중, 승려, 수도승

smuggle 밀수하다

정답 (b)

Chapter 06 글의 목적, 제목 찾기

Sample

해석 인간은 의식과 잠재의식에 따라 생각하고 행동하며 이 두 가지는 똑같이 중요하다. 심리학자 칼 융은 이 이론을 그의 모든 후속 이론의 토대로 삼았다. 우리는 주로 의식 세계에서 활동하기 때문에 개인적인 문제와 사회적인 문제를 해결할 때 똑같은 행동 패턴을 사용하려고 하는 것이 당연하다. 그러나 융은 의식적인 문제를 해결하기 위해서는 잠재의식의 영역에 초점을 맞추어야 한다고 전제한다. 우리가 잠재의식의 세계를 인정하지 않으면 우리의 존재와 사회의 중요한 부분을 부인하는 것이다.

Q. 이 글의 제목으로 알맞은 것은 무엇인가?

(a) 사회적 행동의 습득

(b) 사고의 심리학

(c) 무의식의 중요성

(d) 잠재의식을 통한 문제점의 인정

해설 융의 심리학 이론에 관한 짧은 글을 읽고 제목을 찾는 문제이다. 이 글 역시 의식 세계만큼 무의식의 세계도 중요하다는 주장이 담긴 첫 번째 문장이 주제문이고 그 이후 문장들은 그 이유를 뒷받침한다고 볼 수 있는 두괄식 구조를 취하고 있다. 제목 찾기 문제 역시 문제를 접근하는 방법은 주제를 찾는 방법과 크게 다르지 않다. main topic, main idea, best title, mainly about, tone, attitude, purpose 등은 결국 주제 파악 능력을 요구하는 문제로 보아도 무방하므로 TEPS 독해에서 주제 파악은 아무리 강조해도 지나치지 않다. 다만 제목 찾기를 할 때 지문에 언급은 되었지만 제목으로 잡기에는 너무 광범위한 것이나 지문에 언급된 일부분에만 해당되는 너무 좁은 선택지는 오답 함정 선택지이므로 주의해야 하겠다.

정답 (c)

Actual Test

1 해석 어디서 하건 결혼식은 신비로운 순간이 될 수 있다. 그럼에도 불구하고 적절한 장소를 고르기란 어렵고도 중요한 일이다. 그러한 결정을 내리기 전에 여러분은 어떤 종류의 공간이 여러분의 경제적 형편에 가장 잘 부합하는지 파악해야 한다. 형편이 빠듯한 가정에게는 호텔 웨딩홀을 빌리는 것조차 달갑지 않은 짐이 될 수 있다. 만약 예비 신랑 신부가 같은 종교를 믿는다면

교회는 격식 있고 저렴한 예식장이 될 것이다. 야외 결혼식은 무료는 아니지만 보통 비용이 적게 드는 편이며, 여러분의 특별한 추억을 위한 멋진 배경을 제공해 줄 수 있다.

(a) 여러분의 시간적 제약
(b) 여러분의 경제적 형편
(c) 여러분 가족의 준비
(d) 여러분 마음의 평정에 대한 필요성

해설 지문에서 말하고자 하는 목적을 빨리 파악해야 풀 수 있는 문제로 글에서 자주 등장하는 중심 어휘를 파악하는 능력을 갖추어야 쉽게 풀 문제이다. 빈칸 뒤에 이어지는 문장들을 살펴보면 형편(budget issues)이 빠듯한 가정이라든지, 저렴한(inexpensive) 예식장이라든지 비용에 관련된 어휘가 자주 목격된다. 즉 빈칸에 들어가야 할 것은 경제적 형편(financial circumstances)이라는 것을 비교적 쉽게 찾아낼 수 있다. 따라서 정답은 (b)이다.

어휘 venue (행사) 장소
budget issue 예산 문제, 돈 문제
unwelcome 환영받지 못하는, 달갑지 않은
burden 부담, 짐
compatibility (공존, 조화)의 가능성, 양립 가능성
time constraint 시간적 제약

정답 (b)

2 해석 자외선 차단제가 피부암 발생에 대한 절대 안전한 대비책이라고 기대해서는 안 된다. 많은 의사들은 자외선차단제가 태양 광선을 완벽히 방어하지 못하며, 그렇게 강한 확신을 가지고 그것에 의존하지 말아야 한다는 주장을 펴고 있다. 이들은 머리와 피부를 가리기 위해 천을 사용할 것을 추천한다. "소량의 자외선 차단제를 바름으로써 햇볕으로부터 안전하다는 것은 그릇된 상식이다"라고 브리너 박사는 말한다. 결과적으로 보다 현명한 방법은 전체적인 노출을 제한하면서 자외선 차단제를 겸용하는 방법일 것이다.

(a) 상관없이
(b) 게다가
(c) 결과적으로
(d) 마찬가지로

해설 문장과 문장을 연결하는 적절한 접속사를 찾는 문제이다. 빈칸의 앞 문장들을 살펴보면 자외선 차단제에 의존하지 말고 천을 사용하여 피부 노출을 줄이라는 내용이 있다. 빈칸 뒤의 문장은 앞에서 나온 내용을 정

리하면서 결과를 알려주는 것이므로 (c) As a result가 가장 적절한 답이다.

어휘 sunblock 자외선 차단제, 선크림
foolproof 절대 위험하지 않은, 안전한
barrier 방책, 방벽
rely on 의지하다, 믿다
shield 보호하다, 감싸다
common misbelief 그릇된 통념, 그릇된 상식
a dab of 소량의
solar radiation 태양 복사열

정답 (c)

3 해석 과학자들에게 있어서 칼로리 섭취의 제한이 장수를 촉진시킨다는 사실은 비밀 이야기가 아니다. 새롭게 발견된 사실은 만족스러울 만큼 음식을 잔뜩 먹더라도 이와 유사한 결과를 보인다는 것이다. 적포도주, 콩류, 및 다른 야채류는 최근에 칼로리 제한과 동일한 노화 방지 특성을 보인다고 밝혀진 분자를 함유하고 있다. 이 소식은 노화 방지 약품 및 그와 관련된 질병의 치료법을 개발하고 있는 연구자들에게 도움을 줄 것으로 기대된다.

(a) 칼로리 섭취의 제한이 장수를 촉진시킨다.
(b) 건강한 식이요법이 스테미너를 증대시킬 수 있다.
(c) 유전공학이 많은 문제를 초래할 수 있다.
(d) 맛 좋은 음료에는 약효 특성이 존재한다.

해설 지문의 주제문은 빈칸 바로 뒤에 이어지는 문장이다. 음식을 많이 먹어도 앞 문장과 유사한 결과를 보인다고 하였고, 이어지는 문장에서는 '노화 방지 특성(age-combating properties)'이라는 말이 나온다. 두 번째 문장이 '새롭게 발견된 사실은'으로 시작했기 때문에 빈칸이 포함된 문장은 두 번째 문장과 반대되는 내용이 들어가야 한다. 즉 '적게 먹는 것'과 '노화'라는 의미가 들어 있는 선택지가 있는지 살펴보면 된다. 따라서 두 가지 모두 포함된 (a) limiting caloric intake facilitates longevity가 가장 적절하다.

어휘 facilitate 촉진하다, 용이하게 하다
longevity 장수
pleasurable 유쾌한, 기분 좋은
indulgence 포식
legume 콩류
age-combating 노화 방지의
property 특성, 속성
identical 동일한

restriction 제한

aid 돕다

anti-aging 노화 방지의

stamina 정력, 체력

medicinal 약용의, 약효 있는, 치유력이 있는

정답 (a)

4 **해석** 어린이들이 성인과 유사한 저지방 식사를 해야 한다는 믿음은 설령 그것이 위험하지는 않다고 하더라도 잘못된 조언이다. 아주 어린 아이들은 에너지를 내기 위해 지방을 필요로 하고, 중요한 성장기에 필요한 기타 비타민류의 섭취가 필요하다. 설탕과 소금이 다량 함유된 건강 유해 식품은 부적합하지만 어린이들의 먹거리는 종류 면에 있어서 풍성하며 칼로리가 충분해야만 한다. 일단 어린이들이 조금 더 나이가 들게 되고 신체가 더 발달하게 된 시점에서 부모는 성인의 식단, 즉 지방 함량이 낮은 식단으로 조정하는 것을 생각해 보아도 될 것이다.

(a) 지방 함량이 낮은

(b) 양분이 훨씬 더 풍부한

(c) 보다 균형 있는

(d) 철분을 함유한

해설 글의 전체적인 내용을 잘 파악해야만 풀 수 있는 문제이다. 지문 첫째 문장을 잘 해석해 보면 성인의 경우 저지방 식사가 필요하다고 전제하고 있다. 그러나 이어지는 문장들에서는 어린이의 경우 충분한 지방 공급이 필요하다고 했다. 두 가지를 모두 염두에 두고 빈칸이 포함된 맨 마지막 문장을 읽어 보면 나이가 들게 되면 결국 '저지방 식단'으로 조정할 필요성이 생기게 될 것임을 유추할 수 있다. 따라서 (a) has less fat content가 정답이다.

어휘 low-fat diet 저지방 식사

akin to ~와 비슷한

misguided 잘못된, 잘못 안

growth stage 성장기

inappropriate 부적절한

nutritious 영양가 있는, 영양소가 풍부한

more balanced 보다 균형 있는

contain 함유하다

정답 (a)

5 **해석** 학계에 몸담고 있는 동안 저는 확신을 가지고 가능한 한 많은 학과에 관여해 왔습니다. 제가 학제 간 담론

을 성사시키기 위해 학과 내에 새로운 장을 창출해왔던 것은 제 자긍심의 원천이 되었습니다. 제 가장 큰 희망과 포부가 바로 이 대학교에 있습니다. 다 같이 독창적이고 역동적인 환경, 혁신, 활동, 그리고 학과 간의 경계를 넘어선 토론을 창출해낼 수 있다고 저는 믿고 있습니다. 동시에 우리는 실용주의적으로 사고해야 하며 사회와 연대해야 합니다. 제가 이곳 학부에서 일할 수 있게 된 것을 특권으로 생각하며, 본교가 미래로 나아가는 여정을 인도하는 직책을 맡게 된 것을 영광으로 생각합니다.

Q. 이 글은 주로 무엇에 대한 것인가?

(a) 어떤 사람의 과거 경력에 대한 평가

(b) 학교 안내 소책자

(c) 기금 마련 프레젠테이션

(d) 새로 임명된 사람의 연설

해설 글의 목적을 파악하고 있는지 묻는 문제이다. 이 글은 지문의 첫 문장의 어조만 살펴보아도 쉽게 답을 구할 수 있는 문제이다. 연설문의 형식을 띠고 있는 지문의 맨 마지막 문장을 보면 I consider it a privilege to work(일하게 된 것을 특권이라고 생각한다)와 같은 표현을 보면 새로 부임한 직장에서 취임사를 하고 있다는 것을 눈치챌 수 있다. 따라서 정답은 (d)이다.

어휘 academia 학계

discipline 학과, 학문의 분야

interdisciplinary discourse 학제 간 담론

innovation 혁신

pragmatic 실용주의적인

privilege 특권

faculty 학부, 교직원, 교수단

assessment 평가

brochure 소책자

fundraising 기금 마련

정답 (d)

6 **해석** 예전에 에이즈 전염이 국제적인 주목을 끌어 대대적인 대책 동원을 촉구하였던 때 이후로, 이 문제는 점차적으로 주요 매체에 의한 대중의 주목으로부터 멀어졌다. 정부 역시 이따금 입에 발린 말을 하는 것 말고는 치료나 예방에 실질적인 투자를 집중하지 못하고 있다. 개발도상국에서는 구명 약품을 간절히 필요로 하는 970만 명 중에서 기껏해야 31% 정도만이 사실상 약품을 공급받고 있다. 이제 단순히 아프리카에서뿐만 아니라 전 세계적으로 에이즈는 어떤 인구학적인 예외

도 없이 놀라운 속도로 확산되고 있다.

Q. 지문의 전체적인 어조는 다음 중 어느 것인가?

(a) 중립적인

(b) 경각심을 일깨우는

(c) 야심찬

(d) 통렬한

해설 지문의 내용을 파악하여 어떠한 어조로 이야기하는지를 묻는 문제이다. 세 번째 문장부터 살펴보면 에이즈 감염자들의 약품 수급률이 낮음을 지적하고 있으며, 맨 마지막 문장에서는 에이즈가 빠른 속도로 확산됨을 경고하고 있다. 따라서 (b) Cautionary(경각심을 일깨우는) 어조라고 볼 수 있다.

어휘 epidemic 전염병, 유행병
draw attention 주목을 끌다
massive 대규모의, 대대적인
mobilization 동원
resource (대처하는) 수단, 방편, 방책
spotlight 세인의 주목, 스포트라이트
mainstream 주류의
lip service 입에 발린 말
rally 모으다, 규합하다
substantive 실질적인
life-saving drug 구명 약품
be in desperate need for ~을 절박하게 필요로 하다
at alarming rates 놀라운 속도로
scathing 냉혹한, 통렬한
spare 면하게 하다, 당하지 않게 하다

정답 (b)

7 해석 애팔래치아 농촌의 이주민들에 대한 빈번한 공격이 그 지역 이주자 공동체에 공포를 조장하였다. (a) 한 멕시코 이주민은 한 고등학생 깡패로부터 구타를 당하여 의식을 잃었는데, 당시 인종적 비방을 폭언하고 친구에게 그들의 마을에서 꺼지라 했다고 한다. (b) 다수의 부모들은 그들 자녀의 여가 시간을 차지할 적절한 방과 후 활동이 결여되어 있다고 불평하고 있다. (c) 인권 단체들은 관용과 다양성을 가르치기 위한 다문화 교육뿐 아니라 법적 조치의 필요성에 대해 거침없이 주장해왔다. (d) 이러한 인종 차별적 폭력은 스페인어를 사용하는 이주자가 일자리를 찾아 새로운 지역으로 이주함에 따라 계속 증가해 왔다.

해설 글을 읽고 주제와 관련 없는 문장을 고르는 문제이다.

지문은 애팔래치아 이주민들의 인종 차별에 대해 다루고 있다. (a)는 인종 차별의 사례, (c)는 인종 차별 문제를 해결하기 위한 인권 단체들의 활동, (d)는 인종 차별 행태의 근황에 대해 이야기하고 있는 반면, (b)는 전혀 관련 없는 방과 후 활동에 대해 말하고 있으므로 이것이 정답이다.

어휘 a rash of 계속 일어나는, 빈번한
rural 시골의
migrant 이주민, 이주자
unconscious 의식이 없는, 의식 불명의
acial slur 인종 모독적인 욕설, 비방
after-school activity 방과 후 활동
legal action 법적 조치
multi-cultural education 다문화 교육
tolerance 관용, 인내
diversity 다양성
in search of ~을 찾아서

정답 (b)

Sample

1 **해석** 사우스윅 어린이 병원의 어린 환자들은 더 많은 편안함과 편리함, 사생활을 보호받을 자격이 있습니다. 그들의 개인 병실에 필요한 치료 기구들을 모두 들여 놓기는 어렵습니다. 예를 들어 휠체어를 놓을 만한 충분한 공간도 없습니다. 환자의 부모들은 아이들과 함께 병원에 있고 싶어 하지만 병원에는 침대가 없습니다. 대신 그들은 병실에 머무르고 싶으면 의자에서 잠을 자야 하고 가방을 놓을 만한 공간도 없습니다. 우리 병원 직원들은 병실이 편안하고 보기 좋도록 꾸미기 위해 열심히 노력하지만 개선이 절실히 필요합니다. 이러한 이유들을 참고하셔서 여러분들이 환자들과 가족들, 우리 직원들을 위한 시설들의 개선을 위해 저희의 재개발 제안을 고려해 주시길 바랍니다.

Q. 위 보고서의 내용과 일치하는 것은 무엇인가?

(a) 시설을 개선할 자금이 없다.

(b) 병원은 개조가 필요하다.

(c) 부모들은 병실에서 잘 수 없다.

(d) 어린이들을 위해 새 부속 건물이 지어질 것이다.

해설 공간 부족으로 환자와 그 보호자들이 불편을 겪고 있는 아동 병원의 직원들이 병원의 재개발을 요청하는 제안서 형식의 글이다. 지문의 진위 여부를 물어보는 이런 유형의 문제는 철저하게 지문 자체의 내용에만 의존해야 하며 지문을 통한 추측이나 견해 등은 답이 될 수 없다. 따라서 지문에 구체적인 언급이 없는 (a)나 (d)는 먼저 답에서 제외되어야 하고, (c)의 경우 환자의 부모가 원하는 경우 recliner(등받이가 뒤로 젖혀지는 의자)에서 잠을 자야 한다는 지문의 내용과 일치하지 않는다.

정답 (b)

Actual Test

1 **해석** 두 일류 대학에 의해 발표된 한 건강 연구가 많은 도시 계획자들이 이미 제안한 녹지대가 건강을 증진시킨다는 내용을 확인시켜 주었다. 복잡한 지역 중심가에 자리한 비록 작은 공원이라도 주민들에게 큰 건강상의 효과가 있는 것으로 보인다. 지역을 좀 더 미적으로 만족스럽게 해주는 것 외에도 공원이 도시 거주자들 사이에서 운동을 증가시키고 스트레스의 전반적인 감소를 초래한다는 것을 연구 결과는 보여 준다. 또한 이

연구에 관련된 연구자들은 저소득 지역에서 녹지대의 수를 늘리는 것이 부유한 주민들과 가난한 주민들 사이에 존재하는 건강상의 불평등을 해결하는 것을 도와줄 수 있다고 지적했다. 초록의 나무들이 많은 지역에 사는 부유한 사람들이 녹지대가 거의 없고 인구 밀도가 더 높은 지역에 사는 경향이 있는 가난한 사람들에 비해 특정 질병에 걸릴 위험이 더 적은 것으로 보인다.

(a) 녹지대가 건강을 증진시킨다.

(b) 도시 거주자들은 종종 아프다.

(c) 더 적은 수의 공원들이 건설되고 있다.

(d) 공원은 부동산 가격을 상승시킨다.

해설 빈칸 바로 뒤에 나오는 문장을 살펴보면 도시에 있는 공원은 그 규모가 작더라도 주민들의 건강에 큰 영향을 끼친다고 했으므로 도시 계획과 건강에 관련된 내용이라는 것을 알 수 있으므로 건강에 관련된 내용인 (a)와 (b)로 정답의 범위를 좁힐 수 있다. 하지만 도시의 녹지대가 미적으로 효과가 있을 뿐만 아니라 주민들이 더 많이 운동하도록 만들고 스트레스를 감소시켜 준다고 했으므로 (a)가 정답으로 가장 적절하다고 할 수 있다.

어휘 leading 일류의, 선두의
profound 심오한, 깊은
aesthetically 미적으로
point out 지적하다, 가리키다
prevalent 만연한
adress (어려운 문제 등을) 다루다, 처리하다
greenery 푸른 잎[나무]
at risk 위험에 처한
densely populated 인구 밀도가 높은

정답 (a)

2 **해석** 전통적인 의학이 실패하거나 제한적인 정도의 효과만을 제공할 때 많은 환자들은 대체 의학에 희망을 건다. 그러나 의학 전문가들은 일반적으로 그들이 선전하는 효과에 미치지 못하는 검증되지 않은 치료법을 주의하라고 환자들에게 경고한다. 대체 의약품 회사들은 그들을 막을 법이 거의 존재하지 않는 인터넷상에서 주로 광고되는데 약효를 간절하게 바라는 환자들이 기꺼이 시도해 보고 싶어 할 만한 믿기 힘든 주장을 한다. 이러한 웹사이트들은 종종 의사들이 치유 불능이라고 생각해 온 질병들에 대한 치료법을 확실한 과학적 사실과 믿을 만한 임상 실험이 아닌 개인 성공 사례들을 들어 광고한다. 일부 대체 치료법들은 효과

가 없더라도 환자에게 몇 달러가 들 뿐이지만 어떤 치료법들은 수천 달러가 드는데다 실제로 증상을 악화시킬 수도 있다. 많은 전문가들이 좀 더 강력한 규제를 요구하는 것이 놀랄 일은 아니다.

(a) 이 새로운 치료법을 실험해 보고자 한다.

(b) 이러한 치료법들이 인기 있는 이유를 발견한다.

(c) 대체 의학을 환자들에게 권한다.

(d) 좀 더 강력한 규제를 요구한다.

해설 대체 치료법들이 규제가 별로 없는 인터넷상에서 광고를 하는데다가 경우에 따라서는 환자들의 증세를 악화시킬 수도 있다고 했으므로 전문가들이 좀 더 강력한 규제를 요구한다는 것이 정답으로 가장 적절하다. 지문 후반부의 Some alternative remedies, while ineffective, may only set the patient back a few dollars, while others may cost thousands of dollars and may actually worsen a condition.이라는 내용이 문제 해결을 도와주는 결정적 단서이다.

어휘 look to ~에 기대를 걸다

be wary of ~을 조심[경계]하다

live up to (기대에) 부응하다

alternative medicine 대체 의학[의료]

incredible 믿을 수 없는, 놀라운

desperate for ~을 간절히 원하는

be eager to 간절히 ~하고 싶어 하는

deem 여기다, 간주하다

incurable 불치의

clinical trial 임상 실험

ineffective 효과가 없는

set sb back ~에게 비용이 (얼마) 들다

push for 요구하다

정답 (d)

3 해석 처음 나왔을 때 비평가들의 혹평을 받고 영화관에서 상영되는 동안 관객들에 의해 무시된 많은 영화들이 수 년이 지난 후에 인기 있는 대여 비디오가 되는 데는 이유가 있다. 일부 영화들은 "길티 플레져"로 알려지게 되었다. 많은 영화들이 의도하지 않은 웃음을 일으키는 순간들이 있지만, 길티 플레져 영화들은 너무 형편없이 제작되고 연기도 너무 형편없어서 귀여울 정도로 유머스러운 데가 있다. 최고 최악의 영화는 영화광들이 보통 편하게 집에 앉아 즐거운 아이러니를 느끼며 영화를 보는 것을 즐기게 됨에 따라 종종 열광적

인 팬 집단을 형성한다.

(a) 수년이 지난 후에 인기 대여 비디오가 된다.

(b) 많은 감독들이 새로운 극본을 꺼리도록 만들었다.

(c) 영화 관객의 수를 증가시켰다.

(d) 일부 배우들이 일자리를 잃도록 만들었다.

해설 개봉 당시에는 인기가 없었던 영화가 수년이 지난 후 비디오 대여점에서 인기를 얻게 되는 현상을 설명하고 있으므로 정답은 (a)이다. guilty pleasure는 흔히 자신에게 좋지 않다는 것을 알지만 여전히 즐겨 하는 일이나, 자신은 좋아하지만 다른 사람들이 이상하게 여기는 경향이 있기 때문에 좋아한다는 사실을 숨기게 되는 행동들을 가리킨다. 여기서는 많은 사람들이 형편없다고 생각하지만 자신은 어떤 이유에서든 재미있다고 생각하는 영화를 가리키는 말로 사용되었다.

어휘 pan 혹평하다

critic 비평가

neglect 무시하다

inspire 영감을 주다

endearingly 사랑스럽게

cult following 숭배자 집단

gleeful 즐거운

정답 (a)

4 해석 전 세계에서 가장 인구가 밀집한 지역들 중 한 곳에 살고 있는 사람들에게 도시 생활은 심각한 피해를 줄 수 있다. 사람들로 붐비는 대도시는 관광객들에게는 쇼핑을 하고 식사를 하고 문화 행사들을 경험할 수 있는 신나는 장소로 여겨지는데 반해서 그곳에 거주하는 사람들은 종종 도시 생활이 불쾌하다고 생각한다. 작은 마을에 사는 사람들은 자신들이 지역 사회의 일원으로 강한 소속감을 느낀다고 자주 말하지만, 도시 거주자들은 수백만 명의 사람들 곁에서 자신이 하찮고 외롭다고 느낄 수도 있다. 도시에서의 활동이 전혀 속도를 늦추지 않는 것처럼 보이고 주민들이 서둘러 움직이는 군중의 무리에 휩싸이게 됨에 따라 도시 생활의 속도는 또한 스트레스를 줄 수도 있다.

(a) 심각한 피해를 준다.

(b) 단조롭고 반복적이다.

(c) 독립심을 길러 준다.

(d) 활력을 주는 경험이다.

해설 관광객들에게 대도시는 번화하고 활기찬 곳으로 보이지만 그곳에 거주하는 사람들은 많은 사람들 사이에서 상대적인 고립감을 느끼게 된다고 한다. 그러므로 도시

거주민들에게 도시 생활은 심각한 피해를 줄 수도 있다는 (a)가 글의 흐름상 가장 적절하다. 참고로 unpleasant, feel insignificant and lonely, stressful 같은 표현들로 도시 생활을 묘사하고 있는 것으로 볼 때 도시 생활의 부정적인 면이 빈칸에 알맞은 내용이라는 것을 쉽게 짐작할 수 있다.

어휘 teeming 붐비는

metropolis 대도시

insignificant 하찮은

pace 속도

rush 분주한 활동, 혼잡

take a toll 피해를 주다, 손해를 끼치다

정답 (a)

5 해석 대부분의 범죄자들에게 감옥은 책임감 있는 시민으로서 사회로의 성공적인 통합을 막는 형벌이다. 감옥 체계는 범죄자들을 회복시키기보다는 그들을 더 악화시키는데, 비폭력 전과자들의 경우에는 특히 그러하다. 폭력이 지배하고 하루하루가 철저하게 조직화된 세계에서 석방된 후, 수감자는 생산적인 인생을 설계하도록 요구된다. 이것은 투옥 기간 동안에 범죄 행위를 막는 방법들을 연구하고 제공하는 일종의 중재가 없이는 불가능하다. 대다수의 사람들은 갱생 프로그램이 교도소 체제 내에 존재해야 한다고 믿는다. 많은 갱생 프로그램들이 수감자들이 다시 사회로 돌아가고 또 다른 처벌을 피하는 데 필요한 감정적, 직업적, 때로는 영적인 도구들을 제공한다.

Q. 위 글의 내용과 일치하는 것은 무엇인가?

(a) 갱생은 비폭력 전과자에게만 효과가 있다.

(b) 갱생 훈련은 투옥 기간 동안 행해진다.

(c) 많은 사람들이 갱생 훈련으로 수감을 대체해야 한다고 믿는다.

(d) 범죄자들은 종종 필요한 것 이상으로 가혹한 형을 받는다.

해설 감옥이 형을 마치고 난 범죄자들이 다시 사회로 복귀할 수 있도록 도움을 주어야 한다는 내용의 글로, 글쓴이는 투옥 기간 중 갱생 프로그램을 통해 범죄자들이 사회의 일원으로 복귀할 수 있도록 해야 한다고 주장하고 있으므로 (b)가 정답이다.

어휘 stifle 억제하다

integration 통합

redeem 회복하다, 구원하다

inmate 수감자

regiment 조직화하다

intervention 중재, 관여

incarceration 투옥

counter 거스르다, 맞서다

rehabilitation 갱생, 사회 복귀

spiritual 영적인

sentence 형, 선고

정답 (b)

6 해석 깨끗한 물은 모든 사람들의 생존에 필요하지만 많은 지역에서 깨끗한 물의 공급은 구하기 힘든 사치다. 그러나 과학자들은 정화 능력이 있는 것으로 보이는 흔한 사막 식물의 특성들을 연구하고 있다. 가시많은배모양선인장의 점액을 이용하는 관습은 남미에서 수백 년 동안 전해 내려왔다. 이 끈적끈적한 물질은 선인장이 수분을 저장하도록 도와주는데 이것을 끓인 후에 그 결과로 생긴 액체를 오염된 마실 물에 붓는다. 물 위로 뜨는 조각들이 바닥으로 가라앉으면 깨끗한 물이 위로 떠오른다. 과학자들은 또한 이 점액이 72시간 만에 비소를 정화할 수 있다는 것을 발견했다.

Q. 위 글의 내용과 일치하는 것은 무엇인가?

(a) 남미의 마실 물에서는 비소가 종종 발견된다.

(b) 선인장 물은 남미 시장에서 매우 인기 있다.

(c) 점액의 화학 물질이 해로운 입자를 용해시킨다.

(d) 점액을 이용하여 정수하는 것은 고대 풍습이다.

해설 선인장을 이용하여 물을 정화하는 것은 남미에서 수백 년 동안 행해진 관습(The practice of using the mucilage from prickly pear cactuses has been around in Latin America for many hundreds of years.)이라고 했으므로 (d)가 정답으로 가장 적절하다. 마지막 문장에서 선인장의 점액이 72시간 만에 독이 든 비소를 정화시킬 수 있다고 언급한 것은 그것의 뛰어난 정화 능력을 제시하기 위한 예이므로 남미의 마실 물에서 비소가 종종 발견된다는 (a)는 일치하지 않는다. 선인장을 이용해 정화한 물이 판매되고 있다는 것은 언급되어 있지 않으며, 선인장의 점액을 이용한 정화의 원리는 해로운 물질들을 가라앉게 만들고 깨끗한 물이 위로 떠오르도록 하는 것이지 실제 해로운 물질들을 용해시키는 것은 아니므로 (b)와 (c) 역시 지문의 내용과 일치하지 않는다.

어휘 properties 특성, 속성

filtration 정화

mucilage 점액

prickly 가시투성이의

cactus 선인장

gooey 끈끈한

resultant 결과로 얻어진

contaminated 오염된

clear away 없애다, 제거하다

arsenic 비소

정답 (d)

7 해석 많은 구직자들은 깨끗하게 다려진 양복과 이력서만을 손에 든 채 면접에 가는 경우가 많다. (a) 하지만 전문가들은 성공적인 면접을 위해서는 면접을 받는 사람의 입장에서 준비가 필요하다고 주장한다. (b) 먼저 구직자들은 자신이 일하고자 하는 회사에 대해 최대한 많은 정보를 익히는 것이 중요한데 이것이 면접관에게 좋은 인상을 남기기 때문이다. (c) 많은 구직자들이 자신이 일에 적격인 것처럼 보이기 위해 자신의 경력을 꾸며대는 실수를 저지른다. (d) 도움이 될 만한 또 하나의 조언은 면접 전에 흔한 질문에 대한 답변이 적절한지를 확인하기 위해 연습을 하는 것이다.

해설 면접에 임하는 사람이 해야 할 일에 대한 글이다. 깨끗한 복장과 이력서만 들고 면접에 임하는 경우가 많은데 미리 준비해야 할 두 가지 사항을 이 글에서는 소개하고 있다. 하지만 (c)는 면접 시 해야 할 일이 아니라 하지 말아야 일이므로 여기서는 글의 흐름에 벗어난다고 할 수 있다.

어휘 interview 면접, 인터뷰

press 다림질하다

insist 주장하다, 조르다

preparation 준비

interviewee 면접을 받는 사람

embellish 꾸미다

accomplishment 성취, 업적

qualified 자격을 갖춘

rehearse 예행연습하다

정답 (c)

Chapter 08 추론 문제

Sample

해석 제1형 진성 당뇨병(DM-I)으로 알려진 병이 최근 몇십년 사이에 증가하고 있다. 이것은 질병의 원인에 관한 연구자들의 이해가 바뀌게 했다. 전 세계적으로 매년 2.8%씩 증가하고 있는 이 질병의 발생은 영국에서만 연간 4%의 증가를 보였다. 호주는 매년 3%의 증가를 보고하고 있다. 역사적으로 DM-I은 유전적인 것으로 여겨졌지만 발병이 갑자기 증가한 것으로 보아 전문가들은 환경적인 요인도 원인에 포함시켜야 한다고 말한다.

Q. 위 글에서 추론할 수 있는 내용은 무엇인가?

(a) 제1형 당뇨병의 발생은 성인에 있어서는 감소하고 있다.

(b) 영국에서 DM-I의 사망률을 낮추기 위해 좀 더 많은 노력이 필요하다.

(c) 호주인들은 필요한 당뇨 치료를 받지 못하고 있다.

(d) 제형 당뇨병 발생의 인과 관계는 재평가되어야 한다.

해설 최근 제1형 진성 당뇨병(DM-I) 발병의 증가 추이를 설명한 글을 읽고 추론하는 문제이다. 그동안은 DM-I 발병 원인이 유전이라고 믿어져 왔지만 발병률이 증가함에 따라 환경적 요인과 같은 다른 요인이 있을지도 모른다는 요지의 글이다. 따라서 (d)가 정답이다. 추론 문제 역시 세부 사항과 관련된 내용을 추론해야 하는 문제도 출제되지만 글의 대의를 파악하고 그 대의를 바탕으로 결론을 추론해야 하는 유형이 훨씬 더 많이 출제되므로 주제를 먼저 파악하고 문제 풀이에 접근하는 게 유리하다. 선택지가 헷갈리는 경우에는 좀 더 주제와 관련 있는 선택지를 고르는 게 정답률을 높이는 방법이다.

정답 (d)

Actual Test

1 해석 근로자들이 그들의 작업 시간을 필요에 맞게 조정하도록 해줌으로써 재택근무는 더욱더 인기 있는 대안이 되고 있다. 그들은 틈이 날 때 일을 시작할 수 있다. 그들은 밤에 일하고 낮 동안 자유 시간을 만끽할 수 있다. 그들은 통근하느라 많은 시간을 낭비할 필요가 없다. 사무실에 갇혀 있는 직장 동료들과는 달리 그들은 멋진 하루를 직접 경험할 수 있다. 더욱이 재택근무는 부모가 그들의 사랑하는 자녀들과 함께 보낼

시간을 제공해 준다.

(a) 동료를 더 잘 알게 되도록

(b) 집에서 더 생산적으로 일하도록

(c) 업무 시간을 필요에 맞게 조정하도록

(d) 업무를 완수하는 데 필요한 시간을 넉넉하게 쓰도록

해설 첫 문장에서 핵심어는 telecommuting(재택근무)이다. 재택근무를 하면서 얻게 되는 혜택 중 강조하는 것은 시간을 자유롭게 활용할 수 있다는 점을 이어지는 문장들에서 설명하고 있다. 재택근무를 하면 동료와는 자주 볼 수 없게 되므로 (a)는 상식적으로 말이 안 되며, (b)와 (d)는 본문에서 언급된 바가 없다. 따라서 빈칸에 들어갈 말은 (c) '업무 시간을 필요에 맞게 조정하도록'이 가장 적절하다.

어휘 telecommuting 재택근무

alternative 대안

at one's leisure 시간이 될 때

boxed-in 사무실에 갇혀 있는

on top of ~에 더하여, ~외에

정답 (c)

2 **해석** 미국에서 역대 가장 인기가 많았던 텔레비전 프로그램 중 하나인 〈심슨 가족〉은 전 세계적으로 알려진 최고 프로그램이다. 그러나 그 프로그램에서 다루는 복잡하고 이따금 성인용인 토픽들은 심심치 않게 논란거리가 되고 있으며, 심지어 일부 시청자들에게는 불쾌한 프로그램으로 여겨질 수도 있다. 〈심슨 가족〉이 청소년층에게 영향을 미쳤다는 사실에는 의심의 여지가 거의 없다.

(a) 그러므로

(b) 그러나

(c) 따라서

(d) 그 결과

해설 빈칸 앞의 문장에서는 〈심슨 가족〉 프로그램이 인기가 많다는 이야기를 하고 있고, 뒤에서는 논란의 여지가 되고 있다는 이야기를 하고 있다. 즉 빈칸 앞뒤 문장이 서로 역접 관계에 놓여 있다. 따라서 역접 접속사인 (b) However를 빈칸에 넣어야 자연스럽게 문장이 이어진다.

어휘 all-time 역대의

top-rated 일류의, 최고의

mature 성인용의

deal with 다루다

controversial 논란의 소지가 있는, 논란거리의

offensive 불쾌한, 거슬리는

have an influence on ~에 영향을 미치다

정답 (b)

3 **해석** 포유동물이 되기 위해 필요한 습성인 공격성은 인간들에게 있어서도 근본적인 동기 부여 요소가 된다. 공격 행동은 목표물을 해치거나 적에게 겁을 주어 달아나게 할 의도를 지닌 동물의 행위로 묘사될 수 있다. 제럴드 M. 조스는 공격성을 해침과 살육을 의도한 모든 육체적 또는 언어적 행동으로 특징짓는다. 공격 행동은 명백한 의도를 가진 물리적인 행위부터 애매한 동기에 의한 비물리적인 행위에 이르기까지 매우 다양하다. 예를 들어 공격 행동은 치명적이거나 유익할 수 있고, 의도되지 않거나 명백히 의도적일 수 있으며, 폭력적이거나 또는 심리적인 것일 수도 있다.

(a) 예를 들어

(b) 첫째로

(c) 오히려

(d) 여하튼

해설 빈칸의 앞 문장에서 공격 행동이 다양하다는 것을 이야기했고, 이어지는 문장에서 그것들의 구체적인 예시가 나열되어 있으므로 (a) For example이 가장 적절하다.

어휘 mammal 포유동물

aggression 공격(성)

primal 주요한, 근본적인

motivating factor 동기 부여 요인

scare away 겁주어 쫓아버리다

characterize 특징짓다

verbal 언어적인, 구두의

vary 다양하다

agenda 계획, 행동 지침

overt 명백한, 공공연한

정답 (a)

4 **해석** 1900년대 초기 미국의 건축 디자인은 대부분 19세기 후반의 화려한 역사적 테마 양식을 따랐다. 그 시기에 건축된 초고층 빌딩들은 정교하게 기교를 넣은 고딕 또는 로마 양식을 종종 남기기도 하였다. 이러한 복잡한 장식의 시대에 일부 진보적인 예술가들은 자연스럽고 통합된 양식을 사용하자는 방향으로 움직이려는 운동을 전개하기 시작하였다.

(a) 복잡한 장식

(b) 유기적인 형식

(c) 깔끔하고 단순한 디자인

(d) 미래 지향적 테마

해설 빈칸의 앞 문장들을 살펴보면 fancy(화려한), finely crafted(정교하게 제작된) 등의 수식어구로 1900년대 건축물의 특징을 요약할 수 있음을 알 수 있다. 따라서 이와 동일한 흐름을 유지하는 (a) intricate ornamentation(복잡한 장식)이 빈칸에 들어갈 수 있다.

어휘 architectural design 건축 디자인

for the most part 대체로, 대부분은

fancy 화려한, 장식적인

motif 주제, 모티프

skyscraper 초고층 빌딩, 마천루

entail 수반하다

finely 정교하게, 아름답게

craft 정성들여 만들다

intricate 복잡한

ornamentation 장식(품)

maverick 독자적인 노선을 취하는

united 통합된

organic 유기적인

futuristic 미래 지향적인

정답 (a)

5 **해석** 사실은 어떠한 과학자도 4개월에서 4세 사이의 임의의 어린이가 지닌 호기심의 절반도 지니고 있지 못하다는 것이다. 어른들은 자주 모든 사물에 대한 이러한 높은 호기심을 주의력 부족으로 잘못 해석한다. 어린이들은 태어난 시점부터 학습 과정을 시작해 유치원을 시작하면서 이미 놀라울 정도의 정보량을 쌓는데 이것은 이후 그들이 나이가 들면서 배우게 될 것보다 훨씬 더 많은 양일지도 모른다. 어른들은 어린이들의 호기심을 인정하는 동시에 자극하면서 이들의 강력한 학습 과정을 지원해 주어야 할 것이다.

Q. 지문에 따르면 다음 중 어느 것이 옳은가?

(a) 어린이들의 천부적인 호기심은 과학 조사의 한 형태이다.

(b) 어린이들은 더 어린 나이에 학교에 들어가야 한다.

(c) 어린이들의 집중 부족은 과도한 양의 호기심으로부터 종종 규명될 수 있다.

(d) 어린이들이 강력한 호기심을 탐구할 수 있도록 하는 것이 학습을 도와줄 것이다.

해설 지문은 어린이들의 호기심이 굉장한 것이며, 학습에 지대한 영향을 미친다는 내용을 담고 있다. (a), (b), (c)는 본문에서 언급된 바가 없다. 따라서 정답은 (d)이다.

어휘 possess 소유하다

misinterpret 잘못 해석하다

heighten 높이다, 높게 하다

amass 모으다, 축적하다

subsequently 그 후에

simultaneously 동시에

정답 (d)

6 **해석** 엄청난 양의 자기소개서들 가운데서 눈에 띄는 일은 위압적인 도전이다. 만약 여러분이 기본적인 요령을 배우면 주목받을 확률을 높일 수 있을 것이다. 우선 여러분은 이력서에 특별한 내용을 넣어야 한다. 적절히 문학적인 인용문을 사용하는 것도 유용할 수 있다. 여러분이 고용되고자 하는 곳과의 개인적인 연고를 보여주는 것도 유리하게 작용할 수 있다. 그렇지 않으면 아마도 강력한 시각적 효과를 포함하는 독특한 양식을 이용하는 것이 가장 효과적일 수 있다.

Q. 지문에 가장 적합한 제목은 다음 중 어느 것인가?

(a) 주목을 끄는 이력서 쓰기

(b) 왜 이력서가 필요한가?

(c) 지원 과정 선점하기

(d) 디자인 양식에 대한 추천

해설 지문 첫머리에서 Standing out(눈에 띄는), getting noticed(주목받는) 등의 표현이 힌트가 될 수 있고, 글 전체적으로 독특하고 효과적인 이력서 쓰기에 대한 이야기를 하고 있다. (c)가 함정이 될 수 있는데, 이것은 다소 광범위한 제목이라서 그보다는 범위를 좁힌 (a) 주목을 끄는 이력서 쓰기 정도가 가장 적당하다고 할 수 있겠다. 만약 (a)가 없었더라면 (c)가 정답이 될 수도 있다. 따라서 선택지 가운데에서는 (a)가 가장 적절한 제목이라고 볼 수 있다.

어휘 stand out 두드러지다, 눈에 띄다

cover letter 자기소개서

daunting 위압적인, 기를 죽이는

fundamental 기본적인

for starters 우선

quote 인용문

tactfully 재치 있게

work in one's favor 유리하게 작용하다

utilize 이용하다

visual impact 시각적 효과

ace ~에 대한 준비를 완벽하게 하다

정답 (a)

7 해석 잘 알려지지는 않았지만 중요한 새 교육 정책 규정은 학생들의 이름, 주소, 전화번호를 신병 징병관에게 제공함으로써 군대를 지원하도록 학교측에 강요할 것이다. (a) 미 국방부는 이러한 정보가 나라를 위해 싸울 미래의 군인들을 검색하는 데 도움을 준다고 말하고 있다. (b) 그러나 부모와 학교 직원들 및 다른 시민들은 걱정을 하고 있으며 그러한 모병 전략이 잘 모르는 젊은이들을 착취하는 위험한 것으로 보고 있다. (c) 신병 징병관들은 미 국방부의 사령부와 직접적으로 연결되어 있다. (d) 이 정책에 협조하기를 거부하는 학교 제도는 예산 지원 삭감의 위험에 놓여 있다.

해설 본문은 새로운 모병 제도에 따른 학교, 국방부, 부모들의 입장에 대한 내용을 다루고 있다. 이 중 (c)는 신병 징병관들이 미 국방부 사령부와 직접 연관이 되어 있든 안 되어 있든 제도에 영향을 준다거나 학교의 대응에 영향을 주는 것이 아닐 뿐더러 본문과 상관없으므로 빼야 한다.

어휘 provision 규정, 조항

military recruiter 신병 징병관

potential soldier 미래의 군인, 잠재적인 군인

tactic 전략

exploitation 착취, 이용해 먹기

uninformed 뭔가를 잘 모르는, 충분한 지식이 없는

headquarters 본부, (군대의) 사령부

risk -ing ~할 위험을 무릅쓰다

정답 (c)

Chapter 09 기타 유형

Sample

해석 지난 백 년 동안 지구의 평균 기온은 약 화씨 1도가 증가했다. 지구 온난화의 정확한 원인에 대해서는 아직도 논의가 계속되고 있지만 그 영향은 예상이 가능하다. 기후 변화는 강수량 패턴과 해수면의 변화를 가져오게 될 것이며 이것은 인간과 야생 동물에게 다양한 영향을 끼치게 될지도 모른다. 다행히도 지구 온난화의 속도를 늦추기 위해 여러분이 할 수 있는 일이 몇 가지 있다.

Q. 다음에 바로 이어질 내용으로 알맞은 것은 무엇이겠는가?

(a) 온실가스를 줄이기 위한 전 세계적인 노력

(b) 지구 온난화의 가능한 이유들

(c) 기온이 오르는 것을 줄이기 위해 취할 수 있는 대책들

(d) 지구 온난화의 영향을 변화시키는 방법

해설 지구 온난화에 대한 짧은 글을 읽고 다음에 이어질 내용을 묻는 문제 유형이다. 대개 글의 마지막 한두 문장이 다음 단락에 어떤 내용이 나올지에 대한 실마리가 된다. 이런 유형의 문제는 시간 관리상 지문 전체를 정독하기보다는 skimming을 통해 글의 대의 정도만 재빨리 파악하고 마지막 한두 문장을 정독하는 게 바람직하다. 이 문제 역시 글의 마지막 문장에 단서가 명확히 제시되어 있다. 글의 맨 마지막에서 there are several things you can do to help slow the rate of global warming이라고 했으므로 지구 온난화에 대해 구체적으로 어떤 조치를 취할 수 있는지에 대한 예가 나올 것으로 예상해 볼 수 있다.

정답 (c)

Actual Test

1 해석 재능 있는 미국인 사무엘 모스는 대부분의 사람들이 일생에 해낼 수 있는 것 이상을 성취하였다. 즉, 그는 서로 동떨어진 두 개의 분야에서 명성을 얻었다. 젊었을 때 그는 예일 대학에서 예술을 전공하였다. 이후 그는 런던으로 가서 그의 창작품에 대한 호평을 받았다. 런던에서 그는 헤라클레스 조각품으로 아델피 미술 협회로부터 금메달을 받았고, 영국 왕립 미술원에서 그의 미술 작품 두 점을 골라 전시했다. 이러한 예술적 업적과는 별개로 모스는 주로 전신기와 그의 이

름을 딴 통신 부호로 알려져 있다. 1844년 5월 24일, 그는 워싱턴 DC에서 볼티모어까지 전신선을 연결하고 점과 긴 선으로 이루어진 모스 부호로 된 메시지를 전달하였다.

(a) 그의 예술 작품을 새로운 발견으로 변형시켰다.
(b) 여러 나라에 살면서 예술과 과학을 공부하였다.
(c) 서로 동떨어진 두 개의 분야에서 명성을 얻었다.
(d) 예술에서의 기술을 실험하였다.

해설 지문의 전체적인 내용을 잘 파악해야 추론할 수 있는 문제이다. 힌트는 첫 문장에서 '대부분의 사람들이 일생에 해낼 수 있는 것 이상'의 업적이라고 했으니 여러 가지 업적을 성취했다고 생각할 수 있다. 뒤에 이어서 미술에서 두각을 나타냈다는 것과 전신기의 모스 부호를 창안했다는 두 가지 업적에 대해 나열하였는데, 이 두 가지 분야는 서로 동떨어진 분야라고 볼 수 있으므로 빈칸에는 자연스럽게 (c) 서로 동떨어진 두 개의 분야에서 명성을 얻었다고 이어지는 것이 옳다.

어휘 gifted 재능 있는
fulfill 달성하다, 성취하다
warm reception 호평
apart from ~외에, ~와는 별개로
primarily 주로
telegraph 전신기
communication code 통신 부호
dot 점
dash (문장부호) 긴 선, 장부호
renown 명성
distant 먼, 동떨어진
sphere 영역, 분야

정답 (c)

2 해석 도로시 파커는 다재다능한 작가로 20세기 초 미국에서 사회에 대한 재치 있고 풍자적인 해석으로 명성을 얻었다. 그녀는 1916년에 여성 잡지사에서 일을 시작하면서 작가로서 최초로 돈을 벌게 되었다. 9년 후에 그녀는 〈뉴요커〉지에 정기적으로 서평을 투고하였다. 뉴요커에서 일하는 것 외에도 그녀는 다수의 시를 지었으며 삶에 대한 냉소적인 견해가 주류를 이루는 단편 작가였다.

(a) ~외에도
(b) ~에 대하여
(c) 그러나
(d) ~라기보다는

해설 맨 첫 문장에서 도로시 파커는 다재다능한 작가였다는 점에 힌트가 있다. 즉 여러 재능을 가지고 서평뿐만 아니라 시, 단편 등도 많이 썼음을 암시하고 있다. 따라서 가장 적절한 접속사는 (a) Besides가 되겠다.

어휘 multi-talented 다재다능한
rise to fame 유명해지다, 명성을 얻다
satiric 풍자적인
take 견해, 해석
land one's job 일자리를 얻다
book review 서평
on a rgular basis 정기적으로
prolific 다작의
cynical 냉소적인
outlook 견해
ever-present 늘 존재하는, 항상 등장하는

정답 (a)

3 해석 미국의 결혼 관련 법은 연방 정부 수준이 아니라 주 정부 차원에서 다루어진다. 그래서 결혼 규정이 종종 서로 간에 차이를 보인다. 이런 일관성의 부재는 주마다 동성애 결혼의 허가에서 분명하게 드러난다. 대부분의 주에서는 오로지 남성과 여성만이 부부로서의 혜택을 받을 수 있다. 그러나 캘리포니아와 버몬트 주에서는 동성 커플이 다른 이들과 마찬가지로 부부로서 권리를 갖는다.

(a) 종종 서로 간에 차이를 보인다.
(b) 최고 법원 수준에서 결정되도록 내버려 두는 것이 낫다.
(c) 사람들의 실제 관계에 거의 영향을 미치지 않는다.
(d) 너무 복잡해서 적절히 시행되기 어렵다.

해설 첫 번째 문장에서 각 주마다 결혼 관련 법을 따로 제정한다고 했고, 세 번째 문장에서도 주마다 동성애 결혼의 허가가 다르다고 하였으니 빈칸에는 다름, 차이점에 대한 언급이 있어야 자연스럽다. (b)는 본문의 내용으로 유추하기 어렵고 (c), (d) 역시 본문에서 언급된 바 없다. 따라서 정답은 (a)가 된다.

어휘 uniformity 통일성, 일관성
recognition 허가, 승인
be at odds with ~와 조화하지 못하는, 일치하지 않는
complicated 복잡한
enforce (법을) 집행하다, 시행하다

정답 (a)

4 **해석** 소셜필 센터의 목표는 일반 학교에서 전형적으로 다루지 않는 웅변 능력을 길러 주는 것이다. 참여 학생들은 자신감, 발음 도구, 조직력 및 잘 작성된 연설문을 교실 환경과 야외에서 전달할 수 있는 능력을 습득하게 될 것이다. 간단히 말해서, 센터는 다른 학생들이 의사소통 훈련 경험이 없는 상태에 있을 때, 교육생들이 중요한 우위를 차지하도록 노력하고 있다.

(a) 공립 학교의 요구 사항에 대한 교과 과정을 설계하는 동안

(b) 일반 학교에서 전형적으로 다루지 않는

(c) 끊임없는 반복과 말하기 훈련을 통하여

(d) 학생들을 사회적 상호 작용 시나리오에 빠져들게 함으로써

해설 이 문제는 단순히 지문을 해석한다고 해서 답을 구하기가 쉽지 않은 문제이다. 즉 지문의 내용을 바탕으로 잘 유추해야만 답을 찾을 수 있다. 빈칸 뒤에 오는 문장에서는 소셜필 센터에서 제공하는 프로그램을 통해 얻게 되는 능력에 대해 나열하고 있고, 맨 마지막 문장에서는 보통의 학생들은 의사소통 훈련 경험이 없어서 웅변 능력을 계발시키기 어렵다는 말을 하고 있다. 바꾸어 말하면 보통의 학생들이 다니는 학교에서는 그러한 프로그램을 다루지 않는다는 것이다. (a), (c), (d)는 본문의 내용만으로는 유추해내기 어려운 내용을 비약적으로 설명하고 있다. 따라서 정답은 (b)이다.

어휘 nurture 양성하다, (재능을) 길러주다

self-assuredness 자신감

organization 구성

capacity 능력

in short 간단히 말해서

endeavor 노력하다

edge 우위

address 다루다, 처리하다

정답 (b)

5 **해석** 테러에 대한 두려움은 국제 관광업에 커다란 영향을 주었다. 구체적인 통계 자료는 아직 분명하지 않지만, 침체 경향은 부인할 수 없다. 사람들은 비행기로 여행하기보다는 자동차를 이용하거나 전혀 여행을 하지 않으려 하고 있다. 이것이 초래한 경기 침체는 관광업 관련 직장의 실업률에 반영되어 있다. 이러한 종류의 나쁜 소식은 당분간 반등하기 어려울 것으로 보인다.

Q. 지문은 무엇에 대한 글인가?

(a) 정치 폭력의 근원

(b) 고용 기회의 부족

(c) 세계 여행의 둔화와 그 영향

(d) 관광업에서의 실업률

해설 지문을 해석하기만 했다면 정답은 비교적 고르기 쉬운 문제이다. (a)는 지문과 전혀 관련이 없고 (b), (d)는 테러에 대한 두려움이 빚어낸 결과들 중 일부에 해당하는 것이므로 지문이 이러한 것을 다룬다고 보기에는 너무 비약적이다. 따라서 보다 포괄적인 (c) 세계 여행의 둔화와 그 영향이 가장 적합하다.

어휘 impact 영향을 미치다

downward turn 침체 경향, 하강 국면

undeniable 부인할 수 없는

devastation 황폐, 파괴

reverse 역으로 되다, 반대가 되다

for the foreseeable future 가까운 장래에, 당분간

정답 (c)

6 **해석** 오늘밤 9시까지 글로체스터와 해리엇 카운티에 폭풍 주의보가 발효될 것입니다. 이 지역에는 강한 번개가 치고 있으며, 지금까지 스프링필드 지역의 집 한 채가 낙뢰 폭풍에 의해 피해를 입어 두 명의 부상자가 발생하였습니다. 폭우는 회오리바람을 따라 동쪽으로 계속 이동하고 있습니다. 지금까지 수백여 채의 가정에 정전 사태가 빚어지고 있으며, 회오리바람의 피해가 그칠 때까지 더 많은 정전 사태가 예상됩니다. 이 지역에 계신 주민 여러분께서는 폭풍우가 지속되는 동안 집 안에 머물러 계시기를 당부드립니다.

Q. 지문에 따르면 다음 진술 중 어느 것이 옳은가?

(a) 수천 채의 가정에 정전이 발생했다.

(b) 밤 9시경에 해리엇 카운티에 폭풍이 불 것으로 예상된다.

(c) 두 명이 낙뢰에 의해 사망하였다.

(d) 회오리바람은 동쪽으로 향하고 있다.

해설 (a)는 지문 마지막에서 두 번째 문장에서 수천이 아니라 수백여 채의 가정이라고 했으므로 틀렸고, (b)는 9시경(by 9 pm)이 아니라 9시까지(until 9 pm)라고 했으므로 답이 아니다. (c)는 두 명이 사망한 것이 아니라 injured(부상)이다. 따라서 지문과 일치하는 (d)가 정답이다.

어휘 twister 회오리바람, 트위스터

watch 주의보

in effect 유효한, 실시 중인

apply to ~에 적용되다

lightening blast 낙뢰 폭풍

torrential downpour 폭우

eastward 동쪽으로

reportedly 보도에 따르면

duration 지속 (기간)

정답 (d)

7 해석 인간이 처음으로 바다에 갔던 이후로 거대하고 푸른 깊은 바다는 경외심과 두려움의 전설을 만들도록 영감을 주었다. (a) 바다에 관한 인기 있는 이야기는 해저 세계의 성질이 못된 통치자였던 데비 존스를 다루고 있다. (b) 전설에 따르면 바닷속으로 떨어져 바닥에 이르는 모든 물체는 데비 존스의 함에 도달하게 된다고 한다. (c) 이 함을 힐긋이라도 보고 싶어 하는 선원은 단 한 명도 없다. (d) 과학자들은 구약에 나오는 인물 중에 고래 안에 갇혔던 인물인 "요나"의 이름이 "존스"와 연관이 있다고 추측해 왔다.

해설 본문은 바다와 관련된 전설에 대해 이야기하고 있다. 그런데 (d)에서는 갑자기 밑도 끝도 없이 구약 성서에 나오는 인물의 이름과 데비 존스라는 이름의 연관성에 대해 이야기하고 있다. 따라서 이 문장이 본문의 흐름을 방해한다.

어휘 take to ~에 가다, 나아가다

depths 심해

inspire 영감을 주다

awe 경외심

ill-tempered 성질이 못된

chest 상자, 궤

hard-pressed 곤란한

keen on -ing ~을 열망하는, 몹시 바라는

get a glimpse of ~을 힐긋 보다

speculate 추측하다

the Old Testament 구약 성서

정답 (d)

Chapter 10 흐름 찾기

Sample

해석 계절성 정서 장애, SAD는 전 세계 인구의 6%에게 영향을 끼치고 있는 정서 장애이다. (a) 적도에서 멀리 떨어져 있는 국가들은 20% 높은 비율을 보이고 있는데, 이것은 햇빛이 감정적인 안정도와 직접적으로 관련되어 있다는 가설을 정립했다. (b) 태양은 혈액 내에 비타민 D를 증가시키는 데에도 중요한 역할을 한다. (c) 겨울 우울증이라고도 알려진 SAD는 계절적으로 햇빛이 감소된 시기 동안에 경험되는 일반적인 우울증적 증세들을 가리킨다. (d) 이 증세들로는 피로, 식욕 감퇴, 신경질적인 반응을 포함한다.

해설 흐름에 맞지 않는 문장을 고르는 문제로 계절성 정서 장애(SAD)라는 질병이 햇빛과 관련이 있으며 일조량이 적은 시기에 경험하게 되는 우울증이라고 설명하는 글이다. 이런 유형의 문제는 글의 전체적인 흐름을 파악해서 글의 통일성(coherence)을 해치는 문장을 고르라는 문제가 대부분이다. 영어는 하나의 문단엔 하나의 아이디어만 제시되어야 한다는 사실을 명심하고 문제에 접근하면 쉽게 풀 수 있는 유형이다. 항상 첫 문장에 제시된 토픽과 관련이 없거나 거리가 먼 내용이 답이 된다는 점을 명심하자.

정답 (b)

Actual Test

1 해석 오늘날의 지폐와 유사한 황금은 역사적으로 다른 통화와 비교하여 확실한 이점을 가지고 있었다. 특히, 그것은 확실한 시장 시세를 유지한다. 교통수단이 극히 제한적이었던 고대부터 황금이 광범위하게 수용되었다는 것은 다른 지역과 문화의 사람들 사이에서 그것을 녹여 원거리 무역의 통화로 사용했음을 의미한다. 오늘날에는 지폐가 우세하기는 하지만 황금은 세계 모든 나라에서 가치를 인정받는다. 사람들은 그것에 무언가 가치가 있다고 생각하기 때문에 황금은 여전히 훌륭한 화폐로서 인정받고 있다.

(a) 그것은 여행을 활성화시키기에 유용하다

(b) 그것은 확실한 시장 시세를 유지한다.

(c) 그것은 쉽게 재가공되고 표준화될 수 있다.

(d) 그것은 비할 데 없는 아름다움으로 높이 평가된다.

해설 빈칸 다음에 이어지는 문장을 읽어 보면 황금의 광범위한 수용, 모든 나라에서 가치를 인정받음 등의 내용으로 요약된다. (c) 쉽게 재가공되는 것은 맞는 말이지만 표준화되지는 않았다. 표준화된 것은 맨 마지막 문장에 의하면 오히려 지폐가 될 것이다. (a) 여행 활성화, (d) 비길 데 없는 아름다움 같은 것은 언급된 바도 없고 유추하기도 어렵다. 결국 황금이 널리 통용됨으로써 확실한 시세를 유지한다는 선택지가 문맥의 흐름상 가장 적합하다고 할 수 있다. 그러므로 정답은 (b)이다.

어휘 paper money 지폐
currency 통화, 화폐
specifically 구체적으로, 특히
disparate 본질적으로 다른
valid (가치가) 유효한
predominance 우세, 우월, 지배
facilitate 촉진하다, 활성화하다, 용이하게 하다
market rate 시장 시세
standardize 표준화하다

정답 (b)

2 **해석** 오존층의 오염을 전적으로 초래하는 유일한 원인이라는 것은 존재하지 않지만 거대한 산불은 지구촌 일부 지역에서 문제를 악화시켰다. 브라질의 농부들은 그들의 토지에 불을 놓도록 정부로부터 장려금을 받았다. 1997년의 극심한 가뭄으로 가난이 널리 퍼졌다. 대출을 받으려고 필사적이었던 농부들이 점점 늘어나 그러한 불놓기 행각이 행해졌다. 대규모 불은 대기 중으로 유독한 연기를 방출하였고, 생성된 연기 구름이 그 주위와 인근 지역을 위협하였다. 많은 주민들이 연기로 인한 호흡기 질환에 걸리게 되는 결과를 빚었다.

(a) 거대한 산불은 문제를 악화시켰다.
(b) 인간이 유력한 용의자로 지목되고 있다.
(c) 자동차 배기가스로부터의 오염이 기여하는 것으로 알려져 있다.
(d) 선진국의 과소비가 주요 원인이었다.

해설 빈칸 뒤의 문장들에서는 불 놓기와 관련하여 유발되는 문제에 대해 이야기하고 있다. 그리고 (b), (c), (d)는 위에서 언급된 바가 없다. 따라서 이와 관련된 (a)가 정답이 된다.

어휘 monetary incentive 장려금
set fire 불을 지르다
devastating 극심한
drought 가뭄
poverty 가난
loan 대출(금)

carry out 행하다
endanger 위태롭게 하다, 위험에 빠뜨리다
end up sick 결국 병에 걸리다
respiratory ailment 호흡기 질환
exacerbate 악화시키다

정답 (a)

3 **해석** 연구에 의해 밝혀진 결과에 의하면 의사소통은 다른 어떠한 사회적 활동보다도 더 많은 시간을 요구한다고 한다. 그럼에도 불구하고 의사소통은 사람들이 그것에 대해 논하거나 정의하기 어려울 수 있는 개념이다. 이 용어는 비인간적인 활동을 포함시킬 수 있다. 어떤 사람은 동물들이 의사소통의 형태로 서로 상호 작용하는 방식을 표현해낼 수 있다. 마찬가지로 전자 장치들은 보통 의사소통 수단으로 불린다. 그러나 의사소통은 보통 인간의 상호 작용을 의미한다. 그러므로 어떤 측면에서는 의사소통이란 상호 간에 감정이나 개념이 교환되는 방법이다.

(a) 물론
(b) 단순히
(c) 그러나
(d) 오히려

해설 빈칸 앞의 내용에서는 의사소통의 범주를 정의하기 어려우며 동물, 장치 등과의 관련성을 포함하는 의미라고 하였으나, 빈칸 뒤에서는 일반적으로 의사소통은 인간의 상호 작용을 의미한다 하였으므로 내용적으로 역접이 된다. 따라서 여기서는 (c) However가 가장 적합하다.

어휘 prove 증명하다
take up 차지하다, 요구하다
define 정의하다
encompass 포함하다
interact with 상호 작용하다
signify 의미하다
interaction 상호 작용
in a sense 어떤 의미에서는

정답 (c)

4 **해석** 옥스퍼드 대학교는 부유한 미국 경쟁자들을 따라잡기 위하여 유럽 역사상 최대 규모의 기금 마련 캠페인이라고 불리는 사업을 시작하였다. 학교는 세계 정상의 교수를 유치하기 위해 현재 야심차게 25억 달러를 쏟아붓고 있다. 2만 명 이상의 기증자들이 이미 거의 10

억 달러를 기탁하기로 약정하였다. 옥스퍼드는 스스로
를 세계 수준의 교육 기관으로 보고 있으나 아이비리
그 학교들의 자금력과 경쟁하기에는 역부족이었다.
(a) 새로운 세계적인 연구소를 여는 것
(b) 최상급의 선수들로 팀을 개선하는 것
(c) 부유한 미국 경쟁자들을 따라잡는 것
(d) 재정난에서 벗어나는 것

해설 맨 마지막 문장에서 옥스퍼드는 스스로를 세계 수준의
교육 기관으로 보고 있다고 했지 새로운 연구소를 연
다는 말은 없었으므로 (a)는 틀렸다. (b)의 경우 최상
급의 선수가 아니라 교수진이다. (d)에 나오는 재정난
은 언급된 바 없다. 맨 마지막 문장 뒷부분에서 아이
비리그 학교들의 자금력과 경쟁한다는 말이 나오는데,
이것이 바로 (c)와 일맥상통하는 내용이 되겠다. 따라
서 정답은 (c)이다.

어휘 with the aim of -ing ~할 목적을 가지고, ~하
기 위해서
attract 유치하다
shoot for 가진 돈을 몽땅 걸다
academic 교수
donor 기증자
pledge 약속하다
monetary strength 자금력
match ~에 필적하다, ~와 대등하다

정답 (c)

5 **해석** 파리에서 예술을 감상하든, 태국에서 최고의 일품요리
를 시식하든, 코스타리카에서 파도타기를 하든 여러분
이 그랜트 호텔 및 여관을 지금부터 2009년 10월 30
일까지 특별한 가격에 이용할 수 있는 이 기회를 놓칠
이유는 되지 않을 것입니다. 이 할인가 외에도 일부
지역에서는 룸 업그레이드, 무료 저녁 식사, 관광 및
환영 음료를 포함한 특별한 혜택을 제공합니다. 이 캠
페인에 참여하는 호텔 목록을 얻거나 여러분의 여행
계획을 시작하시려면 여행사를 통해 알아보십시오.
Q. 지문은 주로 무엇을 광고하고 있는가?
(a) 세계 여행 패키지 상품의 세부 내역
(b) 그랜트 호텔 및 여관에서 제공하는 한정 특별 혜택
(c) 그랜트 호텔에서 편안하게 여행하는 유용 정보
(d) 태국을 여행하는 저렴한 방법

해설 위 글은 전체적으로 그랜트 호텔과 여관에서 제공하는
special rate(특가) 및 special benefits(특별 혜택)
에 대한 광고문이다. 선택지의 나머지 내용들은 본문

에서 언급되지 않았다. 따라서 정답은 (b)이다.

어휘 contemplate 감상하다
sample 시식하다
exquisite 훌륭한
special rate (호텔 등의) 특별 요금
cuisine 요리
get in touch with 연락하다

정답 (b)

6 **해석** 기차가 발명된 이래로 기차는 수많은 이야기, 신화, 영
화를 낳으면서 사람들의 가슴속에 특별한 공간을 차지
했다. 어떤 낭만적인 마력이 기차를 좀 더 흔한 다른
여행 방법과는 다른 것으로 만들었고 그 환경적 친화
성은 이제 진가를 인정받고 있다. 기차는 오염시키지
않으며 궂은 날씨에 거의 영향을 받지 않고 시차 피로
를 초래하지 않는다. 비행기는 훨씬 더 비싸고, 버스는
다소 불편한데, 기차는 천천히 지나가는 광경을 선사
하면서 마음을 편안하게 만들어 준다. 버스가 사라진
다 해도 그것을 그리워할 사람은 거의 없을 것이다.
공항은 감상적인 낭만의 장면을 거의 보여 주지 않는
다. 그러나 대부분의 사람들은 기차가 지나갈 때 멈춰
서서 그것을 쳐다보며 감탄할 것이다.
Q. 지문에 의하면 다음 중 어느 것이 맞는 말인가?
(a) 기차는 다양한 창조 매체에 영감을 주었다.
(b) 비행기는 기차 여행에 비해 위험하다.
(c) 비행기 여행은 낭만적인 여행 방법이다.
(d) 버스 여행은 저렴한 가격으로 최상의 경치를 제공
한다.

해설 첫 번째 문장에서 기차가 이야기, 신화, 영화에 영향을
주었다고 했으니 (a)가 맞는 말이다. (b)는 언급된 바
가 없고, (c)는 비행기가 아니라 기차 여행이 낭만적인
여행법이라고 했다. (d)는 버스가 아니라 기차가 좋은
광경을 선사한다고 하였다. 따라서 정답은 (a)이다.

어휘 evoke 환기시키다, 불러일으키다
benignity 다정함
jet lag 시차로 인한 피로
tranquil 평온한, 고요한
scene 경치
sentimental 감상적인
admire 감탄하다, 찬양하다
at cheap rates 저렴한 가격에

정답 (a)

7 **해석** 나한테 북경을 가장 흥미롭게 만들어 주는 것은 전통
과 현대의 병치에 있다. (a) 북경에서는 각국의 음식을
빠짐없이 찾아볼 수 있지만, 전통 요리는 일부 방문객
들에게는 소화시키기 어려울지도 모른다. (b) 마오쩌둥
의 빛나는 얼굴이 주식 거래자들이 국제 무역 변동과
싸우고 있는 모습을 내려다보고 있는 것을 볼 수도 있
다. (c) 오늘날의 기술이 중국에 스며들었지만 정부를
비판하는 웹사이트는 차단되어 있다. (d) 북경은 이러
한 모순들을 축약하고 포용하고 있으며 태연하게 빠른
속도로 앞으로 나아가고 있다.

해설 얼핏 보면 (a)가 전통과 현대의 병치와 관련 있을 것처
럼 생각할 수 있겠지만, 자세히 살펴보면 이것이 잘못
된 것이다. (b), (c), (d)는 모두 개방의 영향에도 불구
하고 여전히 닫혀 있는 중국의 체제에 대하여 풍자적
으로 비판하고 있는 한편, (a)에서는 일부 여행객들이
전통 요리를 소화시키지 못할 수도 있다는 생뚱맞은
이야기를 꺼내고 있다. (a)에서 international이라든
지 traditional cuisine이라는 단어에 현혹되어 이것
을 전통과 현대의 병치와 관련지으려 한다면 함정에
빠지는 것이다. 따라서 정답은 (a)이다.

어휘 juxtaposition 병렬, 병치
stomach 소화하다
overlook 내려다보다
fluctuation 변동, 파동
permeate 침투하다, 스며들다
be critical of ～에 대해 비판적이다
epitomize 요약하다, ～의 전형이다
embrace 받아들이다, 포용하다
contradiction 모순
unabashedly 태연하게
at a rapid pace 빠른 속력으로

정답 (a)

특별함이 있는 학습자를 위한 공간
Special Space for Students
www.saramin.com
사람in 홈페이지에 오시면 더욱 유용한 자료들을 만날 수 있습니다.
항상 여러분의 목소리에 귀를 기울여서 같이 만들어가는 공간으로 활용하고자 합니다.